INTERNATIONAL LAW STUDIES

Volume 85

The War in Afghanistan: A Legal Analysis

Michael N. Schmitt
Editor

Naval War College
Newport, Rhode Island
2009

EDITORIAL OFFICE
International Law Studies
International Law Department
Naval War College (36)
686 Cushing Road
Newport, RI 02841-1207
Telephone: +1-401-841-4949
Fax: +1-401-841-3989
DSN: 948-4949
E-mail: ILD@usnwc.edu

The International Law Studies ("Blue Book") series was initiated by the Naval War College in 1901 to publish essays, treatises and articles that contribute to the broader understanding of international law. OPNAVINST 5450.207 (series) formally tasks the Naval War College with publishing the "Blue Book" series. The thoughts and opinions expressed in this publication are those of the authors and are not necessarily those of the US government, the US Department of the Navy or the Naval War College.

Proper Citation

The International Law Studies should be cited according to the following examples:

– For citing a Blue Book with an editor: Title (editor, year) (Vol. __, US Naval War College International Law Studies);

– For citing a Blue Book with an author: Author, Title (year) (Vol. __, US Naval War College International Law Studies);

– For citing a chapter: Author, Title of Chapter, pages, finish citation with one of the two previous samples, as appropriate.

INTERNATIONAL LAW STUDIES

Volume 85

IN MEMORIAM

This book is dedicated to the memory of Professor Howard S. Levie—soldier, scholar, patriot and dear friend.

Table of Contents

The War in Afghanistan: A Legal Analysis

BLUE BOOKS
International Law
Studies/Documents/Situations/Decisions/Topics/Discussions

VOL 84

INTERNATIONAL LAW AND MILITARY OPERATIONS (Michael D. Carsten ed., 2008) (Vol. 84, US Naval War College International Law Studies).

VOL 83

GLOBAL LEGAL CHALLENGES: COMMAND OF THE COMMONS, STRATEGIC COMMUNICATIONS AND NATURAL DISASTERS (Michael D. Carsten ed., 2007) (Vol. 83, US Naval War College International Law Studies).

VOL 82

THE LAW OF WAR IN THE 21ST CENTURY: WEAPONS AND THE USE OF FORCE (Anthony M. Helm ed., 2006) (Vol. 82, US Naval War College International Law Studies).

VOL 81

INTERNATIONAL LAW CHALLENGES: HOMELAND SECURITY AND COMBATING TERRORISM (Thomas McK. Sparks & Glenn M. Sulmasy eds., 2006) (Vol. 81, US Naval War College International Law Studies).

VOL 80

ISSUES IN INTERNATIONAL LAW AND MILITARY OPERATIONS (Richard B. Jaques ed., 2006) (Vol. 80, US Naval War College International Law Studies).

VOL 79

INTERNATIONAL LAW AND THE WAR ON TERROR (Fred L. Borch & Paul S. Wilson eds., 2003) (Vol. 79, US Naval War College International Law Studies).

VOL 78

LEGAL AND ETHICAL LESSONS OF NATO'S KOSOVO CAMPAIGN (Andru E. Wall ed., 2002) (Vol. 78, US Naval War College International Law Studies).

VOL 77

LILLICH ON THE FORCIBLE PROTECTION OF NATIONALS ABROAD (Thomas C. Wingfield & James E. Meyen eds., 2002) (Vol. 77, US Naval War College International Law Studies).

VOL 76

COMPUTER NETWORK ATTACK AND INTERNATIONAL LAW (Michael N. Schmitt & Brian T. O'Donnell eds., 2002) (Vol. 76, US Naval War College International Law Studies).

VOL 75

INTERNATIONAL LAW ACROSS THE SPECTRUM OF CONFLICT: ESSAYS IN HONOUR OF PROFESSOR L.C. GREEN ON THE OCCASION OF HIS EIGHTIETH BIRTHDAY (Michael N. Schmitt ed., 2000) (Vol. 75, US Naval War College International Law Studies).

VOL 74

GEORGE K. WALKER, THE TANKER WAR, 1980–88: LAW AND POLICY (2000) (Vol. 74, US Naval War College International Law Studies).

VOL 73

ANNOTATED SUPPLEMENT TO THE COMMANDER'S HANDBOOK ON THE LAW OF NAVAL OPERATIONS (A.R. Thomas & James C. Duncan eds., 1999) (Vol. 73, US Naval War College International Law Studies).

VOL 72

THE LAW OF MILITARY OPERATIONS: LIBER AMICORUM PROFESSOR JACK GRUNAWALT (Michael N. Schmitt ed., 1998) (Vol. 72, US Naval War College International Law Studies).

VOL 71

THE LAW OF ARMED CONFLICT: INTO THE NEXT MILLENNIUM (Michael N. Schmitt & Leslie C. Green eds., 1998) (Vol. 71, US Naval War College International Law Studies).

VOL 70

LEVIE ON THE LAW OF WAR (Michael N. Schmitt & Leslie C. Green eds., 1998) (Vol. 70, US Naval War College International Law Studies).

VOL 69

PROTECTION OF THE ENVIRONMENT DURING ARMED CONFLICT (Richard J. Grunawalt, John E. King & Ronald S. McClain eds., 1996) (Vol. 69, US Naval War College International Law Studies).

VOL 68

READINGS ON INTERNATIONAL LAW FROM THE NAVAL WAR COLLEGE REVIEW 1978–1994 (John Norton Moore & Robert F. Turner eds., 1995) (Vol. 68, US Naval War College International Law Studies).

VOL 67

LEGAL AND MORAL CONSTRAINTS ON LOW-INTENSITY CONFLICT (Alberto R. Coll, James S. Ord & Stephen A. Rose eds., 1995) (Vol. 67, US Naval War College International Law Studies).

VOL 66

J. ASHLEY ROACH & ROBERT W. SMITH, EXCESSIVE MARITIME CLAIMS (1994) (Vol. 66, US Naval War College International Law Studies).

VOL 65

TARGETING ENEMY MERCHANT SHIPPING (Richard J. Grunawalt ed., 1993) (Vol. 65, US Naval War College International Law Studies).

VOL 64

THE LAW OF NAVAL OPERATIONS (Horace B. Robertson ed., 1991) (Vol. 64, US Naval War College International Law Studies).

VOL 63

ALFRED P. RUBIN, THE LAW OF PIRACY (1988) (Vol. 63, US Naval War College International Law Studies).

VOL 62

READINGS IN INTERNATIONAL LAW FROM THE NAVAL WAR COLLEGE REVIEW 1947–1977, II *The Use of Force, Human Rights and General International Legal Issues* (Richard B. Lillich & John Norton Moore eds., 1980) (Vol. 62, US Naval War College International Law Studies).

VOL 61

READINGS IN INTERNATIONAL LAW FROM THE NAVAL WAR COLLEGE REVIEW 1947–1977, I *Role of International Law and an Evolving Ocean Law* (Richard B. Lillich & John Norton Moore eds., 1980) (Vol. 61, US Naval War College International Law Studies).

VOL 60

DOCUMENTS ON PRISONERS OF WAR (Howard S. Levie ed., 1979) (Vol. 60, US Naval War College International Law Studies).

VOL 59

HOWARD S. LEVIE, PRISONERS OF WAR IN INTERNATIONAL ARMED CONFLICT (1977) (Vol. 59, US Naval War College International Law Studies).

VOL 58

WILLIAM T. MALLISON JR., STUDIES IN THE LAW OF NAVAL WARFARE: SUBMARINES IN GENERAL AND LIMITED WARS (1966) (Vol. 58, US Naval War College International Law Studies).

VOL 57

(Not Published)

VOL 56

NEILL H. ALFORD JR., MODERN ECONOMIC WARFARE: LAW AND THE NAVAL PARTICIPANT (1963) (Vol. 56, US Naval War College International Law Studies).

VOL 55

CARL Q. CHRISTOL, THE INTERNATIONAL LAW OF OUTER SPACE (1962) (Vol. 55, US Naval War College International Law Studies).

VOL 54

NATO AGREEMENTS ON STATUS: TRAVAUX PRÉPARATOIRES (Joseph M. Snee ed., 1961) (Vol. 54, US Naval War College International Law Studies).

VOL 53

CARL M. FRANKLIN, THE LAW OF THE SEA: SOME RECENT DEVELOPMENTS (WITH PARTICULAR REFERENCE TO THE UNITED NATIONS CONFERENCE OF 1958) (1959–60) (Vol. 53, US Naval War College International Law Studies).

VOL 52

ROLAND J. STANGER, CRIMINAL JURISDICTION OVER VISITING ARMED FORCES (1957–58) (Vol. 52, US Naval War College International Law Studies).

VOL 51

BRUNSON MACCHESNEY, SITUATION, DOCUMENTS AND COMMENTARY ON RECENT DEVELOPMENTS IN THE INTERNATIONAL LAW OF THE SEA (1956) (Vol. 51, US Naval War College International Law Situation and Documents).

VOL 50

ROBERT W. TUCKER, THE LAW OF WAR AND NEUTRALITY AT SEA (1955) (Vol. 50, US Naval War College International Law Studies).

VOL 49

HANS KELSEN, COLLECTIVE SECURITY UNDER INTERNATIONAL LAW (1954) (Vol. 49, US Naval War College International Law Studies).

VOL 48

INTERNATIONAL LAW DOCUMENTS 1952–53: *Peace Treaties; Defense Agreements; European Unions* (Manley O. Hudson ed., 1954) (Vol. 48, US Naval War College International Law Documents).

VOL 47

INTERNATIONAL LAW DOCUMENTS 1950–51: *The Protection of Victims of War* (*Part I: Conventions before 1949; Part II: Geneva Conventions of 1949*) (Manley O. Hudson ed., 1952) (Vol. 47, US Naval War College International Law Documents).

VOL 46

INTERNATIONAL LAW DOCUMENTS 1948–49: *International Organization; Trials of War Criminals; Rights Claimed by Littoral States in Adjacent Seas; et al.* (Manley O. Hudson ed., 1950) (Vol. 46, US Naval War College International Law Documents).

VOL 45

INTERNATIONAL LAW DOCUMENTS 1946–47: *The Treaties of Peace of 1947; Instrument of Japanese Surrender; et al.* (Manley O. Hudson ed., 1948) (Vol. 45, US Naval War College International Law Documents).

VOL 44

INTERNATIONAL LAW DOCUMENTS 1944–45: *Contraband of War; The Crimea Conference; Act of Chapultepec; et al.* (Payson S. Wild Jr. ed., 1946) (Vol. 44, US Naval War College International Law Documents).

VOL 43

INTERNATIONAL LAW DOCUMENTS 1943: *Visit and Search; Destruction of Prizes; War Zones; Defense Zones; et al.* (Payson S. Wild Jr. ed., 1945) (Vol. 43, US Naval War College International Law Documents).

VOL 42

INTERNATIONAL LAW DOCUMENTS 1942: *Orders to American Military Forces in India; Crimes against Civilian Populations in Occupied Countries; et al.* (Payson S. Wild Jr. ed., 1943) (Vol. 42, US Naval War College International Law Documents).

VOL 41

INTERNATIONAL LAW DOCUMENTS 1941: *Freezing of Japanese and Chinese Assets in the United States; The Atlantic Charter; et al.* (Payson S. Wild Jr. ed., 1943) (Vol. 41, US Naval War College International Law Documents).

VOL 40

INTERNATIONAL LAW DOCUMENTS 1940: *Proclamations and Regulations Concerning Neutrality of the United States in the War between Germany and Norway; et al.* (Payson S. Wild Jr. ed., 1942) (Vol. 40, US Naval War College International Law Documents).

VOL 39

INTERNATIONAL LAW SITUATIONS 1939: *Neutral Duties and State Control of Enterprise; Neutrality Problems; Contiguous Zones; et al.* (Payson S. Wild Jr. ed., 1940) (Vol. 39, US Naval War College International Law Situations).

VOL 38

INTERNATIONAL LAW SITUATIONS 1938: *Belligerent and Neutral Rights in Regard to Aircraft; Force Short of War; et al.* (Payson S. Wild Jr. ed., 1940) (Vol. 38, US Naval War College International Law Situations).

VOL 37

INTERNATIONAL LAW SITUATIONS 1937: *Protection by Vessels of War; Naval Protection during Strained Relations; et al.* (George G. Wilson ed., 1939) (Vol. 37, US Naval War College International Law Situations).

VOL 36

INTERNATIONAL LAW SITUATIONS 1936: *Insurrection, Belligerency, Statehood; Visit by and Internment of Aircraft; et al.* (George G. Wilson ed., 1937) (Vol. 36, US Naval War College International Law Situations).

VOL 35

INTERNATIONAL LAW SITUATIONS 1935: *Vessels and Neutral Ports; Action during Civil Strife; et al.* (George G. Wilson ed., 1936) (Vol. 35, US Naval War College International Law Situations).

VOL 34

INTERNATIONAL LAW SITUATIONS 1934: *Transfer and Capture; Interference with Ships; et al.* (George G. Wilson ed., 1936) (Vol. 34, US Naval War College International Law Situations).

VOL 33

INTERNATIONAL LAW SITUATIONS 1933: *Contraband and Blockade; Independent Philippine Islands; et al.* (George G. Wilson ed., 1934) (Vol. 33, US Naval War College International Law Situations).

VOL 32

INTERNATIONAL LAW SITUATIONS 1932: *Belligerents in Neutral Waters; Artificial Structures and Maritime Jurisdiction; et al.* (George G. Wilson ed., 1934) (Vol. 32, US Naval War College International Law Situations).

VOL 31

INTERNATIONAL LAW SITUATIONS 1931: *Neutrality and Aircraft; Neutrality and Territorial Waters; Belligerency and Maritime Jurisdiction* (George G. Wilson ed., 1932) (Vol. 31, US Naval War College International Law Situations).

VOL 30

INTERNATIONAL LAW SITUATIONS 1930: *London Naval Treaty; Absence of Local Authority; Belligerent Aircraft; et al.* (George G. Wilson ed., 1931) (Vol. 30, US Naval War College International Law Situations).

VOL 29

INTERNATIONAL LAW SITUATIONS 1929: *Neutrality and Vessels; Status of Islands in Pacific Ocean; Neutral Obligations* (George G. Wilson ed., 1931) (Vol. 29, US Naval War College International Law Situations).

VOL 28

INTERNATIONAL LAW SITUATIONS 1928: *Maritime Jurisdiction; Carriage of Mail in Time of War; Enemy Persons on Neutral Vessels* (George G. Wilson ed., 1929) (Vol. 28, US Naval War College International Law Situations).

VOL 27

INTERNATIONAL LAW SITUATIONS 1927: *Goods on Neutral Merchant Vessels; Visit and Search; Armed Merchant Vessels* (George G. Wilson ed., 1929) (Vol. 27, US Naval War College International Law Situations).

VOL 26

INTERNATIONAL LAW SITUATIONS 1926: *Continuous Voyage; Submarines; Angary; Aircraft in Neutral Ports* (George G. Wilson ed., 1928) (Vol. 26, US Naval War College International Law Situations).

VOL 25

INTERNATIONAL LAW DOCUMENTS 1925: REGULATION OF MARITIME WARFARE (George G. Wilson ed., 1926) (Vol. 25, US Naval War College International Law Documents).

VOL 24

INTERNATIONAL LAW DOCUMENTS 1924: INTERNATIONAL AGREEMENTS (*Five Power Limitation of Naval Armament; Nicaraguan Canal Route; Danish West Indies; et al.*) (George G. Wilson ed., 1926) (Vol. 24, US Naval War College International Law Documents).

VOL 23

INTERNATIONAL LAW DECISIONS 1923: *Vessels (The Haelen, etc.); Armed Vessels (Submarine E14, etc.); Search in Port (The Bernisse, etc.); et al.* (George G. Wilson ed., 1925) (Vol. 23, US Naval War College International Law Decisions).

VOL 22

INTERNATIONAL LAW DECISIONS 1922: *The Berlin; The Miramichi; The Maria; et al.* (George G. Wilson ed., 1924) (Vol. 22, US Naval War College International Law Decisions).

VOL 21

INTERNATIONAL LAW DOCUMENTS 1921: CONFERENCE ON THE LIMITATION OF ARMAMENT (George G. Wilson ed., 1923) (Vol. 21, US Naval War College International Law Documents).

VOL 20

INTERNATIONAL LAW DOCUMENTS 1920: THE TREATIES OF PEACE WITH AUSTRIA AND WITH HUNGARY AND PROTOCOLS AND DECLARATIONS ANNEXED THERETO (George G. Wilson ed., 1922) (Vol. 20, US Naval War College International Law Documents).

VOL 19

INTERNATIONAL LAW DOCUMENTS 1919: THE TREATY OF PEACE WITH GERMANY (George G. Wilson ed., 1920) (Vol. 19, US Naval War College International Law Documents).

VOL 18

INTERNATIONAL LAW DOCUMENTS 1918: NEUTRALITY, CONDUCT AND CONCLUSION OF HOSTILITIES (George G. Wilson ed., 1919) (Vol. 18, US Naval War College International Law Documents).

VOL 17

INTERNATIONAL LAW DOCUMENTS 1917: NEUTRALITY; BREAKING OF DIPLOMATIC RELATIONS; WAR (George G. Wilson ed., 1918) (Vol. 17, US Naval War College International Law Documents).

VOL 16

INTERNATIONAL LAW TOPICS 1916: NEUTRALITY PROCLAMATIONS AND REGULATIONS (George G. Wilson ed., 1917) (Vol. 16, US Naval War College International Law Topics).

VOL 15

INTERNATIONAL LAW TOPICS 1915: DOCUMENTS ON NEUTRALITY AND WAR (George G. Wilson ed., 1916) (Vol. 15, US Naval War College International Law Topics).

VOL 14

INTERNATIONAL LAW TOPICS AND DISCUSSIONS 1914: *Classification of Public Vessels; Regulations Relating to Foreign Ships of War in Waters under the Jurisdiction of the United States; et al.* (George G. Wilson ed., 1915) (Vol. 14, US Naval War College International Law Topics and Discussions).

VOL 13

INTERNATIONAL LAW TOPICS AND DISCUSSIONS 1913: *Marginal Sea and Other Waters; Commencement of Hostilities; Limitation of Armaments; et al.* (George G. Wilson ed., 1914) (Vol. 13, US Naval War College International Law Topics and Discussions).

VOL 12

INTERNATIONAL LAW SITUATIONS 1912: *Merchant Vessels and Insurgents; Air Craft in War; Cuba Neutral; et al.* (George G. Wilson ed., 1912) (Vol. 12, US Naval War College International Law Situations).

VOL 11

INTERNATIONAL LAW SITUATIONS 1911: *Asylum in Neutral Port; Protection to Neutral Vessels; Destruction of Neutral Vessels; et al.* (George G. Wilson ed., 1911) (Vol. 11, US Naval War College International Law Situations).

VOL 10

INTERNATIONAL LAW SITUATIONS 1910: *Coaling within Neutral Jurisdiction; Declaration of War; Days of Grace; et al.* (George G. Wilson ed., 1911) (Vol. 10, US Naval War College International Law Situations).

VOL 9

INTERNATIONAL LAW TOPICS 1909: THE DECLARATION OF LONDON OF FEBRUARY 26, 1909 (George G. Wilson ed., 1910) (Vol. 9, US Naval War College International Law Topics).

VOL 8

INTERNATIONAL LAW SITUATIONS 1908: *Termination of Liability for Breach of Blockade; The Twenty-Four Hour Rule; Sequestration of Prize; et al.* (George G. Wilson ed., 1909) (Vol. 8, US Naval War College International Law Situations).

VOL 7

INTERNATIONAL LAW SITUATIONS 1907: *Fugitive from Cuban Justice at Guantanamo; Status of United States Auxiliary Collier in Foreign Harbor; et al.* (George G. Wilson ed., 1908) (Vol. 7, US Naval War College International Law Situations).

VOL 6

INTERNATIONAL LAW TOPICS AND DISCUSSIONS 1906: *Use of False Colors; Transfer of Flag of Merchant Vessels during or in Anticipation of War; et al.* (George G. Wilson ed., 1907) (Vol. 6, US Naval War College International Law Topics and Discussions).

VOL 5

INTERNATIONAL LAW TOPICS AND DISCUSSIONS 1905: *Inviolability of Private Property at Sea; Contraband of War; Restriction of Visit and Search; et al.* (George G. Wilson ed., 1906) (Vol. 5, US Naval War College International Law Topics and Discussions).

VOL 4

INTERNATIONAL LAW SITUATIONS 1904: *Merchant Vessels Adapted for Conversion into Auxiliary Cruisers; Rights of Foreigner under Martial Law; Asylum for Insurgent Troops on War Vessel; et al.* (George G. Wilson ed., 1905) (Vol. 4, US Naval War College International Law Situations).

VOL 3

INTERNATIONAL LAW DISCUSSIONS 1903: THE UNITED STATES NAVAL WAR CODE OF 1900 (George G. Wilson ed., 1904) (Vol. 3, US Naval War College International Law Discussions).

VOL 2

INTERNATIONAL LAW SITUATIONS 1902: *Submarine Telegraphic Cables in Time of War; Asylum on Ships of War; Waters of Leased Territory; et al.* (George G. Wilson ed., 1903) (Vol. 2, US Naval War College International Law Situations).

VOL 1

INTERNATIONAL LAW SITUATIONS 1901: *Coast Warfare; Contraband; Transportation of Military Persons; et al.* (John B. Moore ed., 1901) (Vol. 1, US Naval War College International Law Situations).

Foreword

From June 25 to 27, 2008, the Naval War College had the honor to convene an International Law Expert's Workshop, "The War in Afghanistan – A Legal Analysis." This volume captures the legal lessons of the war in Afghanistan as reported, studied and debated by a rare gathering of eminent scholars and practitioners of international law.

The workshop's mission was to provide a comprehensive legal examination of the Afghan conflict—from the decision to use force, to the manner with which force was employed, to the legal construct for the evolution of military operations transitioning away from the use of force. Renowned international academics and legal advisers, both military and civilian, representing military, diplomatic, nongovernmental and academic institutions from throughout the world contributed to the workshop and this volume.

The historic International Law Studies "Blue Book" series was initiated by the Naval War College in 1901 to publish essays, treatises and articles that contribute to the broader understanding of international law. Dedicated to the memory of professor, US Army colonel and esteemed friend of the College Howard S. Levie, this eighty-fifth entry in the series stands as a proud exemplar of that tradition. Readers and researchers will find herein a meticulous study of the Afghanistan conflict, as well as its profound implications for the future of international law and military operations.

The workshop and this "Blue Book" were made possible with generous support from the Naval War College Foundation and the *Israel Yearbook on Human Rights.* The International Law Department of the Center for Naval Warfare Studies, Naval War College, hosted the workshop.

On behalf of the Secretary of the Navy, the Chief of Naval Operations and the Commandant of the Marine Corps, I extend our thanks and gratitude to all the participants, contributing authors and supporters. Your invaluable contributions to this project and to the better understanding of the complex legal issues involved have prepared us to better meet and respond to future global operational challenges.

JAMES P. WISECUP
Rear Admiral, U.S. Navy
President, Naval War College

Introduction

On October 7, 2001 the United States commenced Operation Enduring Freedom, striking terrorist training camps and infrastructure in Afghanistan to dismantle the threat posed by Al Qaeda and its supporters. Over the ensuing seven years, the United States, NATO allies and coalition partners saw the evolution of the Afghan conflict reveal not only an entirely new paradigm of warfare, but a test of the very structure and ability of international law to regulate armed conflicts in the new millennium.

Since its founding in 1884, the US Naval War College has pioneered the study and teaching of the law impacting military operations. For three days in June 2008 the College convened a unique colloquium of experts to take another leap forward in the development and understanding of international law. The workshop, "The War in Afghanistan—A Legal Analysis," drew together fifty of the world's most distinguished academics and elite practitioners of international law to provide a comprehensive debate and explication of the conflict. Panelists and participants engaged in thorough discussions germane to both the Afghan war and future military operations involving the legal basis for the conflict, the law governing the conduct of hostilities and the emerging legal framework to transition from hostilities to a stable peace.

This edition of the Naval War College's internationally acclaimed International Law Studies ("Blue Book") series captures the insights and lessons shared by the workshop participants. Employing the Naval War College's Decision Support Center resources, panelists were able to access participant notes from their presentations, augmenting and strengthening their own written work. The fruits of these discussions are contained in the eminent scholarship found in this volume.

The workshop was organized by Major Michael D. Carsten, US Marine Corps, of the International Law Department, assisted by Ms. Heidi Eldridge and Mrs. Jayne Van Petten. The workshop was made possible through the support of the Naval War College Foundation and the *Israel Yearbook on Human Rights*. Without the dedicated efforts and support of these individuals and organizations, the workshop would not have taken place.

I give thanks to Marshall Center Dean Michael N. Schmitt, the 2008–09 Stockton Professor of International Law, for serving as the editor of this volume, and to Jack Grunawalt and Captain Ralph Thomas, JAGC, US Navy (Ret.), who undertook the lion's share of the editing process with the assistance of Captain

Robert Huard, JAGC, US Navy Reserve (Ret.), and the staff of the College's Desktop Publishing Department. I also extend thanks to Captain Charles T. Passaglia, JAGC, US Navy Reserve, Commanding Officer, NR Naval War College (Law)—the reserve unit assigned to the International Law Department. His willingness to assist, often at a moment's notice, made this publication possible. Although I am grateful to all the officers of the reserve unit, a special note of thanks goes to Commander Eric M. Hurt, JAGC, US Navy Reserve, for his work in preparing the index. This publication is a testament to their tireless efforts and devotion to the Naval War College and to the International Law Studies series.

Special thanks go to Rear Admirals Jacob Shuford and Philip Wisecup, past and current Presidents of the Naval War College, and Professor Barney Rubel, Dean of the Center for Naval Warfare Studies, for their leadership and support in the planning and conduct of the workshop, and the publication of this volume.

The International Law Studies series is published by the Naval War College and distributed worldwide to US and international military organizations, academic institutions and libraries. This year we have added a catalog of all previous "Blue Books" right after the table of contents to facilitate research. Volumes 59–85 of the International Law Studies series are available electronically at http://www.usnwc.edu/cnws/ild/ild.aspx. This "Blue Book," like its predecessors, exhibits the Naval War College's long-standing dedication to the scholarly discourse and understanding of legal issues at the strategic, operational and tactical levels.

Finally, and most importantly, we once again thank our friend and mentor Professor Howard Levie, to whom this volume is dedicated, for his many enduring contributions to the Naval War College.

DENNIS L. MANDSAGER
Professor of Law & Chairman
International Law Department

Preface

It has become fashionable in law of armed conflict (LOAC) circles to claim that whatever "war" one is considering, it is a new form of conflict, one that challenges existing LOAC norms, uncovers lacunae in the law or reveals where extant norms have fallen into desuetude. Hybrid warfare, three-block war, postmodern war, asymmetrical war, the global war on terrorism—all have their proponents and detractors, the latter claiming, often accurately, that the packaging of the conflict as this or that form of warfare is nothing more than old wine in new bottles. The discovery of new forms of warfare has become a cottage industry, one that is equally fascinating . . . and distracting.

Such is the case with the war in Afghanistan and its attendant relationship with transnational terrorism, thrust into the global spotlight by the al Qaeda attacks of September 11, 2001 against the United States. Indeed, the conflict does exhibit seemingly new features. Among these, the nexus with transnational counter-terrorism is perhaps most prominent. The nexus has perplexed international law practitioners and scholars considering such matters as the juridical character of the conflict, the status of its participants and the existence (or the lack thereof) of belligerent occupation. Other unique normative issues are raised by the complex matrix of forces found in Afghanistan—the Taliban, armed opposition groups such as the Northern Alliance, transnational terrorists, the US-led coalition comprising Operation Enduring Freedom, Pakistani security forces operating in the tribal areas and NATO, participating as the UN-sanctioned International Security Assistance Force (ISAF). Further, the conflict has generated vibrant doctrinal debates over, *inter alia*, counterinsurgency, counterterrorism and stability operations, which have thus far been somewhat starved for serious analysis by the broader international legal community.

This book attempts to begin painting the normative backdrop to the conflict. To do so, the Naval War College's International Law Department brought together a select group of international scholars and practitioners who have either particular expertise in the issues it raises or experience in providing legal advice to those responsible for conducting operations. This combination created a particularly fertile environment in which to deconstruct and analyze the events of the past seven years from both a practical and scholarly perspective. The chapters that follow are the product of that sophisticated dialogue.

Part I sketches the conflict and its legal issues in the broad sense. Professor Sir Adam Roberts explores Afghanistan in the context of international security. In particular, he addresses challenges posed by fitting Western military doctrines, practices and institutions to Afghan realities. Professor Roberts concludes with a discussion of actual and possible future effects of the war on international security, including that on the United Nations and NATO, and offers a summary of potential responsive policy choices.

Professor Yoram Dinstein addresses terrorism in the context of the conflict. He distinguishes terrorism that is purely internal from that launched from a foreign country and perhaps warranting action in or against that foreign country. Of particular note, he deals with the issue of attacks by non-State actors and the question, seemingly settled in the aftermath of the attacks of 9/11 but thrust into controversy by the International Court of Justice's *Wall* Advisory Opinion, of whether they constitute "armed attacks" under Article 51 of the UN Charter. Professor Dinstein focuses on action against terrorists within a foreign country. He deals with action taken with the consent of that State, with action taken against the State itself and with the timely issue of "extraterritorial law enforcement." Also of particular note is his conclusion that the inter-State war that began on October 7, 2001 continues unabated.

Part I concludes with a contribution by Professor Michael Reisman which considers the relationship between the missions assigned by the political branches of government and international law. He suggests that the feasibility of such missions and the costs to the nation in terms of life and treasure will be affected by the degree of their compliance with the requirements of international law. Thus, Professor Reisman argues, international law is directly relevant to the design of such missions, suggesting that a "less-is-more" approach may be merited when international expectations of lawfulness appear unlikely to support broader missions.

Part II addresses the legal basis for the military operations that have been conducted. Professor John Murphy argues that many of the issues raised with regard to Afghanistan constitute major challenges to international law and international institutions. They will require the United States and other members of the world community to make hard choices that will alter the future of international law. In support of his thesis, he examines the *jus ad bellum*, *jus in bello*, governance, the roles of the United Nations and NATO, problems created by the use of the tribal areas in Pakistan as a safe haven by the Taliban and al Qaeda, and the impact of Afghanistan on the current unstable political situation in Pakistan.

An examination of the international legality of US cross-border operations from Afghanistan into Pakistan by Professor Sean Murphy follows. He assesses their consistency with the *jus ad bellum* norms enshrined in Articles 2(4) and 51 of the UN Charter, an issue of relevance not only to events in that region, but to analogous operations elsewhere, for instance the Turkish operations in northern Iraq and Colombia's forays into Ecuador. According to Professor Murphy, self-defense provides a basis for those operations that respond to raids by militants from Pakistan into Afghanistan, so long as the US operations remain necessary and proportionate and the Afghan government consents to the presence of US forces. However, a broader right of self-defense against al Qaeda targets in Pakistan based on the attacks of 9/11 is, for Professor Murphy, far more problematic.

Part II concludes with a discussion by Commander Alan Cole of the Royal Navy as to the legal issues surrounding the formation of the ad hoc coalition established to conduct operations in Afghanistan. He distinguishes the coalition created for Operation Enduring Freedom from the NATO-led ISAF. Commander Cole concludes that operating two separate missions at two different tempos in the same country in an attempt to suppress the same enemy is a recipe for a conflict of laws. Nevertheless, he also concludes that the countries that contribute to the missions have accommodated their legal differences in pursuit of mission success.

In Part III, attention turns to *jus in bello* conduct of hostilities issues. Professor Charles Garraway begins by analyzing the character of the conflict, asking whether the situation in Afghanistan, considered in the wider context of the war on terror, constituted a new paradigm which removed it from the extant law of war or whether it was a mutation of an existing normative structure capable of accommodation within the current legal framework. He discusses the positions of the various US agencies in their attempts to fashion a coherent policy for the United States, pointing out that adoption of the State Department approach might have narrowed discussion to combatancy, thereby avoiding much of the controversy that ensued on the characterization issue.

Professor Geoffrey Corn also tackles the characterization of conflict issue, noting that characterization is an essential first step in determining the norms that govern a conflict. He notes the difficulty of applying the traditional categories of either international or non-international armed conflict. Professor Corn considers and develops a possible third category to address the situation of extraterritorial military operations conducted by States against non-State actors, one he labels "transnational armed conflicts."

Three pieces addressing traditional law of war issues follow. Professor Gary Solis surveys various LOAC issues encountered during US ground combat in Afghanistan. He focuses on those that recurrently surfaced during the conference—status of the conflict, status of actors, detention, targeted killings, Guantanamo and war crimes prosecution.

Mr. W. Hays Parks of the Office of the General Counsel at the US Department of Defense takes on the issue of combatants, surely one of the most controversial emanating from the conflict. He analyzes the Taliban's status as a government and the combatant status of Taliban and al Qaeda fighters, explores the US administration's legal rationale for denial of prisoner of war status to captured al Qaeda and Taliban personnel, and considers the law of war issue of special operations forces' wear of indigenous attire. Mr. Parks concludes with an evaluation of the administration's findings on these issues.

Professor Michael Schmitt's contribution identifies and analyzes targeting issues during the conflict. He examines practices, with particular emphasis on counterinsurgency doctrine, concluding that the policy restrictions necessary to conduct such operations effectively greatly exceed those required by the law of armed conflict.

Part IV looks at detention operations during the conflict. Professor Matthew Waxman dissects three issues—the minimum baseline treatment standards required as a matter of international law, the adjudicative processes international law requires for determining who may be detained and how foreign military forces operating in a counterinsurgency transition detention operations to effective civilian institutions. He also thoughtfully presents reflective observations regarding the convergence of law and strategy.

Mr. Stephane Ojeda of the International Committee of the Red Cross surveys the law applicable to detention during armed conflict before turning to the specific issue of the detention of Taliban fighters. He distinguishes detention during the period before the establishment of the Afghan transitional government in June 2002 from that occurring thereafter. His analysis is premised on the existence of an international armed conflict before June 2002 and a non-international armed conflict thereafter. Mr. Ojeda concludes by suggesting that international humanitarian law, properly implemented, adequately addresses the various situations present during the conflict vis-à-vis detention.

Professor Ryan Goodman next delves into the rationales suggested for detention during the conflict, focusing on security threats and intelligence value. He begins by affirming the applicability of the law of armed conflict to non-international armed conflicts. Professor Goodman then turns to two central questions: (1) is it lawful to detain civilians who have not directly participated in hostilities and (2) is it lawful to detain individuals for a long or indefinite period for the purpose of gathering intelligence? As to the first, he notes that the law of armed conflict allows such detentions in appropriate circumstances, but cautions that US law may impose additional requirements. Regarding the second, he rejects the premise that individuals may be detained for long or indefinite periods solely for the purpose of gathering intelligence.

The final operational practice examined during the conference, stability operations, is addressed in Part V. Mr. David Turns of the UK Defence Academy opens by surveying the place of stability operations within international law, specifically the *jus ad bellum* and the *jus in bello*, and, within the latter, the law applicable in international and non-international armed conflicts. He discusses application of the law of armed conflict to stability operations, including such issues as the status, treatment and targeting of insurgents. Mr. Turns pays particular attention to UK practices and policies.

Brigadier General Kenneth Watkin of the Canadian Forces offers a second coalition perspective, although his contribution is widely applicable to any forces engaged in such operations. He starts by outlining the definition, scope and purpose of stability operations, asking whether such operations are "new" or simply a catch-all category for a variety of missions that have already challenged doctrine writers and lawyers. General Watkin next tackles operations at the lower end of the spectrum of conflict in an effort to ascertain the degree to which international law has adapted to them. He continues by considering stability operations in the context of a coalition environment. General Watkin concludes by reflecting on the American doctrinal approach to "war amongst the people."

Professor Marco Sassòli offers a comprehensive analysis of the international legal framework for stability operations, specifically addressing the issue of when international forces can conduct attacks or detain individuals in these operations. He usefully addresses these matters in the context of both the LOAC and international human rights law, examining which prevails in the event they lead to different results. For Professor Sassòli, the answer to the question is tied to the specific circumstances attendant to a particular situation in which these laws apply.

Finally, the focus on stability operations narrows as Lieutenant Colonel Eric Jensen of the US Army and Ms. Amy Pomeroy describe and discuss US Army rule of law operations. They highlight three lessons learned: (1) the need to integrate rule of law operations into all phases and aspects of military operations; (2) the need to coordinate and synchronize the rule of law efforts of various actors, including the host nation; and (3) the need for rule of law operations to be effects-based.

The book concludes in Part VI by focusing on a topic of particular importance in operations such as those conducted in Afghanistan—human rights law. Professor Hampson begins consideration of the topic by asking whether human rights law is of any relevance to operations in Afghanistan. She analyzes five key issues:

(1) whether human rights law remains applicable when the law of armed conflict applies, (2) whether human rights law obligations apply extraterritorially, (3) the impact of the territorial State's human rights obligations for other States assisting it, (4) the effect of a Security Council mandate on legal obligations that would otherwise be applicable, and (5) whether human rights notions offer useful guidance to armed forces, whether or not human rights law is applicable de jure.

The final chapter of the book, by Mr. Stephen Pomper of the US State Department, examines the US government's approach to human rights obligations during the conflict in Afghanistan, pointing to issues with which the new administration will have to grapple. The Bush administration took the view that the law of war did not provide an adequate framework for addressing those legal issues that arise during a conflict with a non-State group, but argued that legal and policy considerations weighed against filling the lacunae by resort to human rights law. He explores the topic by looking to, *inter alia*, the argumentation of the Bush administration, including that bearing on International Court of Justice opinions and other case law, as well as Canadian litigation. Mr. Pomper suggests that the Obama administration would be well served by considering this history in fashioning its own approach to the subject.

As the book was being finalized, the international law community was saddened to learn that one of its giants, Professor Howard Levie, had passed away at the age of 101. Professor Levie had a long and distinguished service as a judge advocate in the US Army, including acting as a key drafter of the Korean War Armistice Agreement, before becoming a renowned academic at Saint Louis University. He served as the Charles H. Stockton Professor at the Naval War College in 1971–72 and remained active as a frequent lecturer at the College following his retirement as Professor Emeritus from Saint Louis and his move to Newport, Rhode Island. Over the decades, Professor Levie mentored many young judge advocates and scholars; it was my honor to be among them.

In 1998, the Naval War College published *Levie on the Law of War* to honor Professor Levie and to recognize the enormous impact of his writings on the law applicable during armed conflict. In the book's Foreword, Professor Emeritus Richard J. Grunawalt, the current Stockton Professor and former head of the Oceans Law and Policy Department at the Naval War College, observed:

> Once in a great while, someone comes along who makes a significant and lasting contribution to his or her chosen profession, a contribution that comes to define the paradigm of that calling. With respect to the development and articulation of the law of war, Professor Howard Levie is just such an individual.

This book is dedicated to the memory of Professor Howard S. Levie—soldier, scholar and patriot. We shall all miss him deeply.

MICHAEL N. SCHMITT
2008–09 Charles H. Stockton
Professor of International Law
United States Naval War College

PART I

THE WAR IN AFGHANISTAN IN CONTEXT

I

Afghanistan and International Security

Adam Roberts*

Today there are remarkably few international wars. This does not mean the end of war, which still continues, but it does mean that the type of war emblematic of the contemporary era is not classic international war, but rather a kind of civil war familiar to students of colonial history: a conflict that may begin largely within a society, but becomes internationalized, involving foreign forces on one or both sides. Very often such wars begin, and continue, because the structure of the State is weak: this fact enables insurgents to operate, and it also results in outside governments getting involved in various ways, not least in the attempt to bolster the State's credibility and performance. Where there is more than one weak State in a region and a porous border area between, the opportunities for insurgents are magnified. In all these respects the ongoing conflict in Afghanistan is typical of wars of the twenty-first century. Yet it is also unique, not only because it has distinctive attributes, but also because, as will be indicated below, it has had extraordinary effects on international relations.

The central question that is explored here is: what are the implications of wars in Afghanistan for international security, not only in the region, but also more generally? In exploring this question there is much to draw upon, not just from Western involvement in Afghanistan since 2001, but also from the past two centuries of

* Senior Research Fellow of the Centre for International Studies, Department of Politics and International Relations, University of Oxford, and President-elect of the British Academy. A shortened version of this paper is *Doctrine and Reality in Afghanistan*, 51 SURVIVAL 29 (2009).

Afghan history. However, we cannot foresee exactly how the present war will conclude. Events that may determine how it ends are by nature unknowable: for example, the accuracy or otherwise of an assassin's bullet, another major scandal in the treatment of prisoners, bombings from the air resulting in massive civilian deaths, an al-Qaeda attack that alienates more than it mobilizes or the emergence elsewhere of a new conflict which distracts attention from Afghanistan.

Despite these uncertainties, the central question can be approached by looking first into four related questions about wars in Afghanistan and their influence on international security.

- What have been the effects of previous wars in Afghanistan, particularly in the nineteenth century and in the Soviet period 1979–89, on regional and international security?
- How should the almost continuous wars in Afghanistan since 1989 be characterized, and what have been the effects of their Pakistani dimension?
- What have been the roles of the United Nations in the long-running Afghan crisis, including its post-2001 post-conflict peace-building role and in assisting the return of refugees?
- In the war since 2001, what problems have there been in fitting Western military doctrines, practices and institutions to Afghan realities? What has been the role of airpower? How has NATO performed in this unanticipated commitment? Are counterinsurgency (COIN) doctrines fit for the purpose for which they are being used in Afghanistan? And how can progress be judged?

The exploration of the fourth question, which forms the main part of this survey, leads to the concluding discussion of the actual and possible future effects of the war on international security, including on two major institutions, the United Nations and NATO. Some policy choices are briefly summarized.

I. Lessons from Afghan Wars up to 1989

Much is often made of how warfare in general has, or has not, been transformed. Perhaps because several of us have had training in history, in Oxford University's research program "The Changing Character of War" we attempt to draw a sharp distinction between what is new and what merely appears to be new. That attempt is certainly necessary when considering the war in Afghanistan. It is often said that modern wars constitute a "new paradigm." This proposition depends, to a greater or lesser degree, on the implicit assumption that past international wars were a straightforward matter of so-called "conventional" forces fighting each other. They were not. In considering what is unique about the ongoing war in

Afghanistan, it may be useful to bear in mind two parts of the country's historical legacy: nineteenth-century wars and the experience of the Soviet war.

The Nineteenth Century and After

Many modern wars, including that in Afghanistan, fit quite well the general description of colonial conflicts offered by Major C.E. Callwell of the Royal Artillery in 1899 in his justly famous manual *Small Wars.* Callwell himself had served during the closing stages of the Second Anglo-Afghan War, when he marched through the Khyber Pass to join the Kabul field force.[1] It was on the basis of experience that he wrote two decades later:

> Small wars are a heritage of extended empire, a certain epilogue to encroachments into lands beyond the confines of existing civilization, and this has been so from early ages to the present time. Conquerors of old penetrating into the unknown encountered races with strange and unconventional military methods and trod them down, seizing their territory; revolts and insurrections followed, disputes and quarrels with tribes on the borders of the districts overcome supervened, out of the original campaign of conquest sprang further wars, and all were vexatious, desultory, and harassing. And the history of those small wars repeats itself in the small wars of to-day.[2]

In the nineteenth century the British Army was involved in two major campaigns in Afghanistan, in 1839–42 and 1878–80. The first, fought ostensibly to assist a weak ruler and to provide a friendly buffer State on India's northwest border, was a hubristic enterprise that was marked by disaster—the wiping out of a reduced garrison as it struggled back to the Khyber Pass.[3] The second war, which was fought to counterbalance Russian influence in Afghanistan, provided evidence that apparent success in Afghanistan can be quickly followed by uprisings and setbacks. The British, having defeated the Afghan State, had no political solution except to appoint a suitable "warlord" as head of State. What did Callwell have to say specifically about the type of war that had been encountered in Afghanistan and elsewhere in the late nineteenth century? His words are as pertinent today as when they were penned over a century ago:

> With the capture of the capital any approach to organized resistance, under the direct control of the head of the State, will almost always cease; but it does not by any means follow that the conflict is at an end. . . . [T]he French experiences in Algeria, and the British experiences in Afghanistan, show that these irregular, protracted, indefinite operations offer often far greater difficulties to the regular armies than the attainment of their original military objective.[4]

The wars in Afghanistan in the nineteenth century have been the foundation for a view of the country and its peoples—especially the latter—as unusually resistant to any kind of foreign influence or control, actual or perceived. David Loyn, the veteran BBC reporter on Afghanistan who has charted these previous conflicts, argues that mistakes are being repeated today because of a neglect of the study of history. He charges that the United States and Britain have failed to understand the extent of resistance in Afghanistan to anything that looks like foreign control. It follows, states Loyn, that it is necessary for outsiders to accept a very limited role, and to negotiate with the Taliban.[5] This is one important perspective on wars in Afghanistan. However, it should not be taken to imply that there is uniform hostility to all foreign influence. Both between and within Afghanistan's distinct ethnic groups there is a long tradition of bitter contestation, and in all Afghanistan's wars some groups have had arrangements of one kind or another with outside patrons and powers.

Much of the country's history exposes the fragility of the idea of the Afghan State. Twentieth-century Afghanistan was characterized not only by wars against foreigners, such as the Third Anglo-Afghan War, of May 1919, but also by civil wars, assassinations and coups, as in the conflict of 1928–31 and the seizures of power by Daud Khan in 1953 and 1973. Throughout the twentieth century, there was a continuous interplay between the development of constitutional government and the continuation of political violence. The role of the Pashtun peoples in Afghanistan was one of many bones of contention. The political culture of Afghanistan was characterized by State weakness and general instability.

The Soviet War in Afghanistan, 1979–89

The war in 1979–89 between the Soviet-backed government of Afghanistan and its *mujahidin* adversaries had major effects on international politics. In particular, the war had a vast impact in the Soviet Union. It accentuated the Soviet Union's sense of imperial overstretch, contributed to a decline of faith in the use of force to maintain the empire and accentuated doubts about a central purpose of Soviet foreign policy—the maintenance of a network of dependent, demanding and hardly popular socialist regimes in an assortment of countries around the world. It formed part of the background to the role of civil resistance movements in central and Eastern Europe pursuing their struggles by non-violent means to a successful outcome in 1989. In short, the Afghan war contributed to the collapse of the Soviet empire. This very fact is not only proof of the fateful consequences that may flow from war in Afghanistan, but is also one driver of the present war. Osama Bin Laden has made no secret of his belief that, having helped to destroy the Soviet Union, he aims to do the same for the United States. One down, one to go! This was not the only case of post–Cold War hubris—there were also many variants of this condition elsewhere, including in the British and American governments—but it was a notably severe one. Bin Laden's interpretation of events led him to 9/11 and engulfed Afghanistan in continuing war.

There were other ways in which the Soviet-Afghan war led to subsequent wars. The channeling of much international aid to *mujahidin* groups through Pakistan reinforced the fateful link between events in Pakistan and those in Afghanistan. The power of non-State groups and regional military chiefs, and their tendency to rely on threats and uses of force not controlled by any State, became more deeply engrained than before in both Afghanistan and the frontier areas of Pakistan. The religious element in Afghan politics—which was particularly prominent in the struggle against Soviet influence, and was encouraged by the outside powers that provided much-needed finance and weapons for the *mujahidin*—did not disappear with the departure of Soviet forces in 1989. Indeed, within a few years religious warriors trained in the hard school of combat against Soviet forces in Afghanistan were to turn up in a wide range of other locations, including in the former Yugoslavia.

These legacies of the war against Soviet control remain most important in Afghanistan itself. The problems of non-State violence, regional rivalries and the religious element in politics are not new to Afghanistan, but they were reinforced. Long-held suspicions toward certain types of foreign presence remained prominent.

II. The Wars in Afghanistan since 1989

The current multifaceted and complex situation in Afghanistan is best understood as the continuation of a protracted war over the country's future which began many years before 2001. Understanding its character is important not only for developing military and political policy in the country, but also for understanding its likely impact on international security generally. There are fundamental differences of understanding about its nature.

Whether viewed as a war or a stabilization mission, there is a tendency to present the situation as a conflict between an essentially progressive cause represented by the Karzai government in Kabul on the one side, and two reactionary Islamist forces on the other: the Taliban and al-Qaeda. This view may be too simple in its views both of the Afghan government and of its opponents. Most strikingly, it tends to overstate the effectiveness of the Afghan government. It also understates the importance of ethnic/linguistic divisions within Afghanistan, where the largest ethnic group, the Pashtuns, constitutes over 40 percent of the population.

Elements of Afghan and Pashtun nationalism play a significant part in the resistance to the Afghan government and its foreign backers. A review of the twenty years' crisis in Afghanistan since the Soviet withdrawal, and of the place of Pakistan in that crisis, is necessary for an understanding of the nature of this war.

The Crisis since 1989

Following the withdrawal of the last Soviet forces from Afghanistan in January 1989, an internal crisis and war erupted. Indeed, the war within Afghanistan, always involving patrons around the region to sustain the war efforts of the parties, can be traced back further, and can be said to have begun in about 1978.[6] It has never really ended. Throughout the two decades since 1989 there have been continuing regional rivalries and ongoing conflict between modernizers and Islamists. There have been two moments when the conflict was viewed by some as having ended—after the Taliban victory in September 1996 and after the Northern Alliance victory in December 2001.[7] However, on both occasions the conflict continued in new forms.

This first phase of Afghanistan's long-running war following the departure of Soviet forces was only partially concluded on September 26, 1996 when Kabul fell to the Taliban, which established a theocratic style of government throughout the areas under their control and in 1997 renamed the country "Islamic Emirate of Afghanistan." Then and thereafter the Northern Alliance continued to control an area of northern Afghanistan and to challenge Taliban rule.

From October 7, 2001 onward, following the al-Qaeda attacks in the United States on September 11, direct US and coalition military intervention in Afghanistan changed the character of this continuing war. Of course it did not transform the situation completely: resistant to change as ever, rival warlords sought to maintain their fiefdoms against intervention unless it could offer more by extending the chance of collaboration. However, there was now an undeniably international war inside Afghanistan. There was not much doubt that this was, for a few months, an international war in the sense of a war between sovereign States—the US-led coalition versus the Taliban government of Afghanistan. In November–December 2001 the US-led intervention, and the military campaign of the Northern Alliance, toppled the Taliban regime, which had been supported by al-Qaeda. This military action was widely, though not universally, viewed as a justifiable response to the Taliban for having allowed Afghan territory to be used for preparing attacks on the United States, and additionally had the effect of freeing Afghanistan from an unpopular regime. Initially there was much popular support in Kabul and elsewhere for the incoming forces of the International Security Assistance Force (ISAF), but this situation was to change.

The international war of October–December 2001 had been superimposed on two other more enduring conflicts: the non-international armed conflict of the Taliban versus Northern Alliance, and the US-led struggle against al-Qaeda terrorists. Both of these "other conflicts" continued. The war against al-Qaeda and related terrorists, who were now based in Pakistan as well as Afghanistan, carried on without interruption. In addition, there was growing resistance in southern Afghanistan to the new regime. This insurgency began relatively slowly, so that its seriousness was not recognized for some time.

How should this resistance be characterized? It is commonly labeled as the Taliban insurgency, a description which may conceal the possibilities that the sources of support for the insurgency have been more numerous than the label "Taliban" suggests, or that the ideology of the Taliban may have evolved. The insurgent movement has drawn on elements of both Afghan and Pashtun nationalism, it has operated alongside traditional forms of social organization and systems of justice, its recruiting has been facilitated by Afghanistan's high levels of unemployment and by the fact that it is able to pay its soldiers, and its willingness to support poppy cultivation not only increases its acceptance in certain provinces but also exposes the incoherence of the policies of the various NATO countries on this issue.[8] None of this is to suggest that all those forces labeled Taliban should be seen simply as heroic patriots or as Pashtun traditionalists. Ahmed Rashid has written:

> The United States and NATO have failed to understand that the Taliban belong to neither Afghanistan or Pakistan, but are a lumpen population, the product of refugee camps, militarised madrassas, and the lack of opportunities in the borderland of Pakistan and Afghanistan. They have neither been true citizens of either country nor experienced traditional Pashtun tribal society. The longer the war goes on, the more deeply rooted and widespread the Taliban and their transnational milieu will become.[9]

Into this ongoing conflict a new element was added from 2005 onward: the involvement in combat activities of contingents of the NATO-led ISAF. The original authorization of ISAF in 2001 had been "to assist the Afghan Interim Authority in the maintenance of security in Kabul and its surrounding areas, so that the Afghan Interim Authority as well as the personnel of the United Nations can operate in a secure environment."[10] Initially, in January 2002, the United Kingdom took the lead in organizing ISAF, followed at six-month intervals by other "lead States" until NATO as such took over in August 2003. ISAF's remit gradually extended across Afghanistan and in some provinces came to involve direct combat.[11] By 2006 ISAF comprised troops from thirty-two countries. Those deployed in the southern provinces of Afghanistan became increasingly geared to a counterinsurgency campaign. This campaign had not been part of ISAF's original role: the transition to it, involving a gradual stretching of the initial mandate, resulted in some unavoidably uneven burden-sharing between NATO member States. Thus NATO had put itself in the unenviable position of staking its impressive reputation on the outcome of a distant and little-understood war in a country well known to be a graveyard for foreign military adventures.

The problem is exacerbated by the limited nature of the involvement of outsiders—military and civilian—in Afghan society. In the years since 2001, both soldiers and civilians have generally had short-term tours of duty. Few of them have learned the relevant languages, and there is remarkably limited institutional memory, especially as regards knowledge of local communities and political traditions. Indeed, on the civilian side there has been a conscious break from the experience of colonial administration, which has meant, unfortunately, a break from understanding the society's structure and the tangled history of its links with outsiders.

One special feature of the ongoing war in Afghanistan that distinguishes it from certain other post–Cold War US involvements has been that the US-led forces had at the start significant allies within the country: originally the Northern Alliance, then the government of Afghanistan. This made the Afghan involvement different from some of the other conflicts in which the United States has been involved, including Iraq in the first years of the US-led presence and Somalia over a much longer period, in neither of which were there strong local forces in place with which to work.

However, this apparently favorable situation had inherent limitations and was vulnerable to change. Even after its capture of Kabul in December 2001, the Northern Alliance, which at the best of times was an unstable coalition, never controlled all of Afghanistan. The Afghan authorities conspicuously lacked the bureaucratic backup that provides the essential underpinning of most governments around the world. The Pashtuns generally resented the Northern Alliance's US-assisted victory; and when, around 2003–04, the Pashtuns came back strongly in the government (thanks to the new constitution and law on political parties), Afghan opinion critical of the United States found a voice. Indeed, the boot was now on the other foot, with minorities complaining of Pashtun nationalism and structural exclusion. In short, the social foundations of the foreign presence in Afghanistan proved to be weaker than they had first seemed in 2001–02.

In legal terms, there has been a tendency to focus attention on the question of whether particular aspects and phases of the ongoing war in Afghanistan should be characterized as "international," "non-international" or something else. The main problem with debates on this topic is that the passion for pigeonholing risks obstructing understanding of a complex reality. Actually the wars in Afghanistan have been all of these things. If one were forced to apply a single label to all their aspects, it would probably be "internationalized civil war," an under-explored but important category of wars. Yet whichever of these terms is adopted has only limited relevance to, or effect on, policy making. Although technically it is true that more rules apply to international war than to non-international armed conflict, in this case most of the powers involved in the war do at some level recognize the need for restraint in the conduct of the war, a matter discussed further below.

The Pakistani Factor

Afghanistan's neighbors—including China, Iran, Tajikistan, Turkmenistan and Uzbekistan—all have legitimate interests in the country and its long-running conflicts. Many other States, including India and Russia, also have legitimate interests in whether Afghanistan can manage to stay together, make progress in development and attract refugees back. Of all the relationships with other States, that with Pakistan is the most complex, and has contributed most to Afghanistan's ongoing divisions.

All borders are artificial constructs created in peoples' minds. Thus in itself it is hardly a remarkable statement to say that the border between Afghanistan and Pakistan—the Durand Line imposed by the British on a reluctant Afghan government in 1893—is artificial. What is significant about this border is that Pashtuns on either side of the line view it as artificial. This does not mean that they are committed to a definite idea of a new state of "Pashtunistan" separate from both Pakistan and Afghanistan. Rather it means that conflicts on either side of the line immediately acquire a cross-border and therefore an international dimension. What creates an issue, both for governments and peoples, is its chronic porousness, the existence of linked conflicts on both sides of it, the strength of the bonds of common identity and experience that link Pashtuns in Afghanistan and Pakistan, and the inherent weakness of both of these States. It is too simple to say that the frontier areas of both States are ungovernable: they have their own systems of authority, which leave little room for control by the State.

Pakistan's Federally Administered Tribal Areas (FATA), which run along the border with Afghanistan, remain almost completely outside the control of the Pakistani government, and have provided fertile ground for the exercise of dominance by the Taliban and al-Qaeda. They are a legacy of empire. The British had also practiced containment, occasional chastisement and periodic negotiation; and resistance meant that a final occupation was simply too expensive to justify in imperial terms. One remarkable feature of this situation is that successive Pakistani governments have had no counterinsurgency policy in these areas. Occasional sweeps and demonstrations of firepower are in no way substitutes for a serious policy aimed at gaining a degree of consent from the population or the powerbrokers.

The United States has not used the power that ought to come with its generous support for Pakistan to persuade it to adopt a strategy in these areas. The FATA constitutes a haven for terrorists that is in some respects comparable to the one that existed in Afghanistan before 2001.

Overlapping with all this, and compounding the problem of relations between the two countries, is the fact that opinion in Pakistan generally on matters relating to the use of force has never favored the US vision of the "War on Terror." A BBC World Service Poll in twenty-three countries, published in September 2008, when asking respondents to indicate their feelings regarding al-Qaeda, found high levels of support for it in Pakistan. This was combined with a mere 17 percent of Pakistanis stating that they had negative views of al-Qaeda, the lowest proportion of respondents in any of the countries polled.[12] However, this may reflect more a desire to take an anti-US position than an acceptance of terrorist bombings. Indeed, in four weeks in the autumn of 2008 an anti-terror petition in Pakistan—"This is Not Us"—attracted almost sixty-three million signatures in what is possibly the biggest such lobbying effort anywhere in the world.[13] The responses to terrorist bombings in Pakistan in early 2009 do not suggest general support for the acts of terrorists.

The Pakistani connection has deeply affected events in Afghanistan in all the wars there since the Soviet intervention in 1979. Throughout, Pakistan's Inter-Services Intelligence has had a major, and not always controlled, role. In the 1980s Pakistan, with massive Western support, provided crucial assistance for the anti-Soviet rebels in Afghanistan. Then from 1994 onward there was extensive Pakistani official support for the Taliban movement in Afghanistan.[14]

In the ongoing war in Afghanistan a number of consequences in the security field have flowed from the Pakistani connection. The first is that, since Pashtuns on either side of the border are more likely than most others to view the Western military presence in Afghanistan as illegitimate, there is inevitably a transborder hinterland for the insurgency. Second, since Pashtuns play a large part in the Pakistan Army—and in the Frontier Corps, which comes under the Ministry of Interior—there are built-in difficulties in Pakistani government attempts to impose the capital's rule by force on the various Pashtun-inhabited areas.[15] As a consequence of these two factors, the insurgency in southern Afghanistan is likely for the foreseeable future to have safe base areas inside Pakistan. In sum, like so many border regions in the world, the Pakistan-Afghanistan border presents excellent opportunities for the organization and continuation of insurgency. The fluidity of the situation on both sides of the border suggests that there are not two wars in the region, but one.

This creates the third consequence of the Pakistani connection: the strong pressure on US military leaders to take the war unilaterally into the territory of Pakistan. US policy toward Pakistan notoriously lacks strategic coherence.[16] The fact that the United States considers the Pakistani authorities unreliable, with certain elements willing to pass on intelligence to US enemies, means that the US military role on the territory of Pakistan cannot be based on close military cooperation. As a result, US military action in Pakistan is bound to be perceived as an infringement of Pakistan's sovereignty. The US killings of Pakistani soldiers in several such incidents, and the strong reactions to this in Pakistan, confirmed the chaotic and inflammatory character of the situation.[17] George Bush's presidential order of July 2008, authorizing US strikes in Pakistan without seeking the approval of the Pakistani government, while an understandable reaction to a troubling situation on the border, risks further destabilizing a country that is a crucial if deeply flawed ally.[18] It is sobering to reflect that the Soviet Union, in the course of its counterinsurgency operations in the 1990s, engaged in hundreds of cross-border strikes in Pakistan, getting few if any results from them.[19]

III. The Many Roles of the United Nations in Afghanistan since 1979

The United Nations has a long history of involvement in the conflicts in Afghanistan and such a continuing commitment there that failure would impact on the UN's already tarnished reputation. There have been three main phases of UN involvement: during the Soviet war from 1979 to 1989, in the largely civil war of 1990–2001 and in the war since 2001 that continues today.

UN Roles during the Soviet War in Afghanistan (1979–89)

During the Soviet war the main action was not in the Security Council: there the Soviet Union could veto any direct UN involvement in the conflict, so the Council referred the matter to the General Assembly under the UN's "Uniting for Peace" procedure.[20] From then on the conflict was mainly handled in the General Assembly and in the office of the Secretary-General. In January 1980 the General Assembly called for "the immediate, unconditional and total withdrawal of the foreign troops from Afghanistan."[21] Subsequently, under the auspices of the Secretary-General, the UN initiated a "good offices" function to assist negotiations involving the Afghan and Soviet governments on the one hand, and Pakistan on the other. This led eventually to the April 1988 Geneva Accords on Afghanistan, which were a crucial landmark in the ending of the Cold War.[22] Later in 1988 the UN Good Offices Mission in Afghanistan and Pakistan (UNGOMAP) was established.[23] This was the first UN peacekeeping mission since the establishment of United Nations Interim Force in Lebanon in March 1978, evidence of the key part played by Afghan events in the post–Cold War re-emergence of the UN.

At the same time, the process of ending the Soviet involvement posed a classic dilemma for the United Nations. The internal conflict presented the delicate question of the extent to which the United Nations, as an organization of governments, could be seen to negotiate with rebel forces that were battling it out throughout the country. As Secretary-General Javier Pérez de Cuéllar put it in 1988, it would be "against our philosophy to be in touch with the enemies of governments."[24] Yet that is exactly what the United Nations started to do in the following year, in the attempt to facilitate a comprehensive political settlement and to set up a broad-based government. In presenting the United Nations with this dilemma, the war in Afghanistan was truly characteristic of the post–Cold War era. The UN's limited success in persuading the parties to a largely internal conflict to agree to a peace settlement would also be a harbinger of things to come.

UN Roles in the Continuing Civil War (1990–2001)

The continuing civil war following the Soviet departure presented a difficult challenge for the United Nations. By March 1990 UNGOMAP, having completed its key mission of observing the Soviet withdrawal, was wound up. Yet there was a chaotic situation on which the Security Council, the General Assembly and the Special Representative of the Secretary-General had remarkably little capacity to influence events. The General Assembly established the UN Special Mission to Afghanistan (UNSMA) in 1993, in the distant hope of facilitating national rapprochement and reconstruction.[25] The post of Special Representative for Afghanistan, who headed the mission, was held successively by two of the ablest and most experienced UN troubleshooters, Lakhdar Brahimi and Francesc Vendrell. However, they could achieve little in UNSMA's lifetime, which ended in 2001–02.

At the same time the Security Council gradually became more actively involved with Afghanistan. One month after the Taliban came to power in September 1996 the Council passed a resolution which staked out a number of critically important positions. As well as stating its unsurprising conviction that "the United Nations, as a universally recognized and impartial intermediary, must continue to play the central role in international efforts towards a peaceful resolution of the Afghan conflict," it called for an immediate end to all hostilities, denounced the discrimination against girls and women, and called for an end to the practices that had made the country a fertile ground for drug trafficking and terrorism.[26] Then in August 1998, following an upsurge in the fighting between the Taliban and the Northern Alliance, the Security Council passed a further resolution, again setting out some useful principles. It noted that there was "a serious and growing threat to regional and international peace and security, as well as extensive human suffering, further destruction, refugee flow and other forcible displacement of large numbers of people"; it expressed concern at "the increasing ethnic nature of the conflict"; it deplored the fact that, despite numerous UN pleas, there was continuing foreign interference; condemned the attacks on UN personnel in the Taliban-held areas; condemned the Taliban's capture of the Iranian Consulate-General in Mazar-e-Sharif; reaffirmed that "all parties to the conflict are bound to comply with their obligations under international humanitarian law"; and demanded the Afghan factions "to refrain from harboring and training terrorists and their organizations and to halt illegal drug activities."[27] In October 1999, it imposed sanctions on the Taliban regime in Afghanistan:[28] arguably this decision undermined whatever was left of the UN's good-offices mission. The Council may have been ineffective in the 1990s civil war in Afghanistan, but it was certainly not asleep. Some of the positions that it had staked out would be important for the future, in that they provided a basis for subsequent tough action against the Taliban and for serious efforts to rebuild the Afghan State.

UN Roles in the War since September 2001

The attacks on the United States on September 11, 2001 were a clear indication of the connection between Afghanistan and international security. In 1996 and 1998 the Council had warned of the terrorist danger in Afghanistan. Now it was to have a more prominent role, giving implicit authorization to the US-led use of force, and becoming deeply involved in the subsequent reconstruction of Afghanistan.

The most significant acts of the Council after 9/11 took the form of two resolutions which had profound implications for the management of international security issues. The first—Resolution 1368, passed the day after the attacks—by recognizing "the inherent right of individual or collective self-defence in accordance with the Charter" implicitly accepted the proposition that it could be lawful for a State to take action against another State if the latter failed to stop terrorist attacks being launched from its territory. The same resolution called on all States to bring the perpetrators to justice, and to cooperate to prevent and suppress terrorist acts.[29]

In this Resolution the Council accepted that a right of self-defense could apply to a State when it was attacked by a non-State entity. To those who believe that action against terrorists should be confined to police methods, this was controversial. However, the Resolution was passed in the specific and hopefully unique circumstances of 9/11, when the Taliban regime was refusing to take any action against the terrorists in their midst. The Resolution does not mean that there is or should be general Council approval of responding to terrorist attacks by cross-border military actions, or that such action should generally be viewed as lawful. The history of such responses is dismal, as evidenced for example by the Hapsburg attempt to wipe out the terrorist "hornets' nest" in Serbia in 1914, and the various Israeli counterterrorist operations in Lebanon in the past thirty years. The initial effectiveness of the military campaign in Afghanistan in late 2001 appears to be an exception to the proposition that it is unwise to attack States from which terror originates, but in the aftermath the proposition has recovered some credibility. Yet the resulting caution about military intervention is bound to face severe challenges if State-sponsored or State-tolerated terrorism continues to be a major feature of international politics.

The second key resolution passed by the Council in September 2001, Resolution 1373, recognized "the need for States to complement international cooperation by taking additional measures to prevent and suppress, in their territories through all lawful means, the financing and preparation of any acts of terrorism." It then indicated the remarkable extent of such measures, and the key role of the Council in overseeing them. It used strong language—the Council "decides that all states shall" take action, rather than merely calling on them to do so.[30] The General Assembly—often wary of any increase in the Security Council's powers—was duly nervous but did not go against the Council's approach.[31] It remains possible that in the long run the greatest effect of Afghanistan on international security will be that it compelled the Council to take on a more intrusive role in relation to States than had ever previously been contemplated.

Yet the actual role of the Council in the events following the 9/11 attack was limited. True, its resolutions and other actions were important for the international legitimacy of the US-led military action in Afghanistan and for the attempts to build up a post-Taliban system of government there.[32] However, there was no way in which the Council could have been centrally involved in mustering and commanding the military coalition that resulted in the closing of the al-Qaeda bases in Afghanistan and the removal of the Taliban from power in Kabul. The most striking feature of the Council's role in the hostilities of late 2001 is its limited character.

Following the installation of the Karzai government in Kabul on December 22, 2001, the two main tasks facing the new government and its outside backers were perceived to be reconstruction and the provision of security. The United Nations was widely seen—even by the US administration—as being pivotal in tackling these tasks. The key statement of this period, which did much to define the role not just of the United Nations but of the international community generally, was made by Lakhdar Brahimi, Special Representative of the Secretary-General for Afghanistan. In discussing the planned UN Assistance Mission in Afghanistan (UNAMA), he famously said: "It will be an integrated mission that will operate with a 'light footprint,' keeping the international United Nations presence to the minimum required, while our Afghan colleagues are given as much of a role as possible."[33]

This immediately raises the question of whether a light footprint is indeed possible in a country with such a limited—and distrusted—State structure as that of Afghanistan. The concept was inevitably buffeted by events and modified to the point where some did not recognize it. Within a year or two a reviving insurgency, and major military operations on Afghan territory by the United States and NATO, created the dual risks that the footprint would be perceived as heavy and that UNAMA would be seen as powerless to implement important parts of its mandate. It was not the only part of the UN system that faced the problem of appearing to be partial, or powerless, or both. As Gilles Dorronsoro has pointed out in a critical survey of the Security Council's roles in Afghanistan up to the end of 2006, "the direct involvement by Permanent Members of the Security Council in a counterinsurgency war has resulted in the Council being silent on specific violations of international humanitarian law."[34]

In the years since 2002 in which it has operated in Afghanistan, UNAMA has sought to assist political and economic transition and the rule of law. The report of its activities up to March 2008 presented a sobering picture:

> [T]he political transition continues to face serious challenges. The Taliban and related armed groups and the drug economy represent fundamental threats to still-fragile political, economic and social institutions. Despite tactical successes by national and international military forces, the anti-Government elements are far from defeated. Thirty-six out of 376 districts, including most districts in the east, south-east and south, remain largely inaccessible to Afghan officials and aid workers. . . . Meanwhile, poor governance and limited development efforts, particularly at the provincial and district levels, continue to result in political alienation that both directly and indirectly sustains anti-Government elements.[35]

IV. Fitting Military Doctrine and Practice to Afghan Realities

The limitations of military doctrines and practice are often exposed, not by arguments, but by events. Thus it was mainly events in Iraq and Afghanistan that exposed the inadequacies of the so-called "revolution in military affairs," an idea that was popular in the United States from the mid-1990s until at least 2003.[36] Afghanistan was always likely to be a difficult theater of operations for outside military forces. Seeing this (and perhaps also because he did not want an ongoing distraction from the future invasion of Iraq, for which he was already lobbying) Paul Wolfowitz said in November 2001, "In fact, one of the lessons of Afghanistan's history, which we've tried to apply in this campaign, is if you're a foreigner, try not to go in. If you go in, don't stay too long, because they don't tend to like any foreigners who stay too long."[37]

Many problems have been encountered in implementing and adapting military doctrine and practice in face of Afghan realities. Three issues considered here are the role of airpower, the complexities of operating in an alliance framework, and the appropriateness or otherwise of COIN doctrine. The first two are touched on here briefly: more attention is paid to the third. Many key developments, of considerable relevance to containing the insurgency, cannot be covered: they include particularly the key role of the Afghan National Police.

Airpower in Afghanistan

Ever since October 2001 airpower (which mainly means US airpower) has played an important part in military operations in Afghanistan. The apparent success of the use of airpower in October–December 2001 was deceptive: a major factor in the Taliban's defeat was the advance of ground forces—those of the Northern Alliance. Since then, the role of airpower in the Afghan conflict has been a subject of contestation, principally between the Army and Marines on the one hand, and the US Air Force on the other. A key issue has been whether airpower is a major instrument in its own right, or is mainly useful in supporting ground forces. Self-evidently, the US and NATO ground forces in Afghanistan, widely dispersed and few in number, frequently need airpower in support of their ground operations. Indeed, tactical air support has been vital to any success they have had, and has often saved the small numbers of ISAF forces from being overwhelmed. In military terms, a "light footprint" on the ground inevitably means a heavy air presence.

Those planning coalition military operations in Afghanistan have shown awareness of the dangers of reliance on airpower, especially of the adverse consequences of killing civilians. On occasion they have even claimed to have set an aim of no civilian casualties.[38] While this aim actually goes further than the strict requirements of existing law applicable in an international armed conflict, in practice it has not been achieved. Part of the difficulty is that the very definition of civilian is problematic in a war such as that in Afghanistan. In addition, many other factors have prevented realization of the aim of no civilian casualties: shortage of ground forces, different approaches of individual commanders, poor intelligence, the heat of battle, weapons malfunction, the co-location of military targets and civilians, and the frayed relationship between ground and air forces operating in Afghanistan.[39] A Human Rights Watch report in September 2008 summarized the situation thus:

> In the past three years, the armed conflict in Afghanistan has intensified, with daily fighting between the Taliban and other anti-government insurgents against Afghan government forces and its international military supporters. The US, which operates in Afghanistan through its counter-insurgency forces in Operation Enduring Freedom (OEF) and as part of the NATO-led International Security Assistance Force (ISAF), has increasingly relied on airpower in counter-insurgency and counter-terrorism operations. The combination of light ground forces and overwhelming airpower has become the dominant doctrine of war for the US in Afghanistan. The result has been large numbers of civilian casualties, controversy over the continued use of airpower in Afghanistan, and intense criticism of US and NATO forces by Afghan political leaders and the general public.
>
> As a result of OEF and ISAF airstrikes in 2006, 116 Afghan civilians were killed in 13 bombings. In 2007, Afghan civilian deaths were nearly three times higher: 321 Afghan civilians were killed in 22 bombings, while hundreds more were injured. In 2007, more Afghan civilians were killed by airstrikes than by US and NATO ground fire. In the first seven months of 2008, the latest period for which data is available, at least 119 Afghan civilians were killed in 12 airstrikes.[40]

That last figure needed to be increased when it was revealed in October 2008 that thirty-three civilians had been killed in a single US airstrike on August 22. Such incidents do serious damage to the coalition cause. Largely as a result of the long history of such incidents, there has been a strong anti-coalition reaction. Already in 2006 the Afghan parliament had demonstrated its concern about coalition military actions, and such expressions of concern have subsequently become more frequent. Meanwhile, President Hamid Karzai, whose authority has been diminishing, has made a number of criticisms of the coalition forces, calling for an end to civilian casualties, and even stating that he wanted US forces to stop arresting suspected Taliban members and their supporters.[41]

The NATO Framework

From 2001 onward the United States has operated in Afghanistan with coalition partners and, especially since August 2003, with the formal involvement of NATO. Indeed, in Afghanistan NATO is involved in ground combat operations for the first time in its history—far from its normal area of responsibility and against a threat very different from the one it had been created to face. The NATO involvement in Afghanistan is widely, but perhaps not wisely, viewed as "a test of the alliance's political will and military capabilities."[42] It is an exceptionally hard test. Indeed, the implication that the future of the alliance hangs on this test is reminiscent of earlier views that US credibility was on the line in Vietnam.

NATO's involvement in Afghanistan is in sharp contrast to its conduct during the Cold War. In that period it repeatedly and studiously avoided involvement in colonial conflicts—the French wars in Indochina and Algeria, the Portuguese wars in Africa, the British in Malaya, the Dutch in Indonesia and so on. Its individual members were involved in these, but the alliance was not. NATO also avoided involvement in postcolonial conflicts or, as in Cyprus, limited itself to an essentially diplomatic role. Now in Afghanistan, which has all the hallmark features of postcolonial States undergoing conflict—especially the lack of legitimacy of the constitutional system, government and frontiers—NATO became engaged, all with little public debate.

The NATO role in Afghanistan began in a problematic way, and so it has continued. On September 12, 2001, the day after the 9/11 attacks, the NATO Council stated:

> If it is determined that this attack was directed from abroad against the United States, it shall be regarded as an action covered by Article 5 of the Washington Treaty, which states that an armed attack against one or more of the Allies in Europe or North America shall be considered an attack against them all.[43]

When the United States gave this offer the brush-off, preferring to have a "coalition à la carte" in which there would be no institutional challenge to its leadership, there was disappointment and irritation in Europe. The war in Afghanistan in October–December 2001, while it was effectively conducted under US leadership, was also one chapter in the story of the declining size of US-led wartime coalitions.

However, NATO rapidly came back into the picture, not least because the United States came to recognize the need for long-term assistance in managing societies that had been freed from oppressive regimes by US uses of force. NATO has been directly involved in Afghanistan at least since August 9, 2003, when it took formal control of the International Security Assistance Force, which had originally been established under UK leadership in January 2002. It was in the autumn of 2003 that an upsurge of violence began as part of a deteriorating security situation.[44] Since 2006 ISAF has undertaken an expanded range of responsibilities in Afghanistan, involving combat as well as peacekeeping, in an expanded area that includes provinces in which conflict is ongoing.

ISAF's notably broad UN Security Council mandate involves it in a wide range of activities, including military and police training. Many of its activities are carried out through Provincial Reconstruction Teams (PRTs)—civilian-military units of varying sizes designed to extend the authority of the central government, provide security and undertake infrastructure projects. There are twenty-six PRTs in twenty-six of the country's thirty-four provinces. Operating under different lead States, with twelve of the twenty-six led by the United States, the PRTs' resources and tasks have varied greatly.

Not surprisingly, there have been controversies about numerous aspects of the overall ISAF mission. Four key problems concern the coherence or otherwise of the policies of the different members of ISAF, the problematic command and control arrangements, differences over detainee treatment, and the difficulty of raising forces.

The lack of coherence of the approaches taken by different foreign forces in ISAF and their governments at home is evident. Different contributing States have different visions of ISAF's role. The most obvious difference is that the United States, United Kingdom and Canada tend to see it, albeit with some variations within each of these countries, as a stability operation, encompassing counterinsurgency actions, while Germany and some others see it more through the lens of a peacekeeping or peacebuilding mission. These positions are not polar opposites, and each may have validity in different provinces of Afghanistan, but the clash of perspective on this issue does not assist cooperation of forces in difficult operations. Daniel Marston has gone so far as to conclude: "As of 2007, the main problem impeding coalition forces' successful application of counterinsurgency was decentralization of responsibility."[45]

The complexity of the command and control arrangements in Afghanistan is greater than that in past counterinsurgency campaigns. Debates about this have inevitably reflected the US desire that more contingents in ISAF should become directly involved in combat operations, and the concern of some contributors that this should not happen. Although ISAF is now under a US commander, and the continuous rotation of senior posts is ceasing, the arrangements for coordinating the work of these distinct forces continue to pose problems.[46]

The important, and scandal-ridden, matter of treatment of detainees is another issue on which there are differences of approach. Anxious not to be associated with shocking US statements and practices in this matter, and insufficiently staffed and equipped to hold on to the prisoners they capture, other NATO members have drawn up separate agreements with the Afghan authorities embodying a variety of different approaches to how they should be treated once in Afghan hands. There are serious concerns that some detainees handed over to the Afghan authorities on this basis have been maltreated.[47]

The provision of forces in the numbers required for ISAF has been a highly contentious matter within NATO States. The coalition of forces acting in support of the Afghan government consists of three basic elements. The first is the Afghan National Army which has been largely re-created in this decade with the help of the United States and other NATO countries. With a manpower level of over seventy thousand, its relatively modest size has led to US accusations that the Afghan government has been slow in building up its army. The second is ISAF, which now comprises some 51,350 troops from forty NATO and non-NATO countries. Much the largest contingents are those of the United States, with 19,950 troops, and the United Kingdom, with 8,745. The third basic element is the force of well over ten thousand troops (almost all of them American) who are part of the US Operation Enduring Freedom, which focuses particularly on the counterterrorist mission in Afghanistan.[48] Granted the scale of the problems in Afghanistan, all these numbers are widely seen as low, yet in many NATO member States there is a reluctance to increase the commitment. Opinion polls in five NATO member States with a high level of involvement in Afghanistan show the public to be highly skeptical about it.[49] An increase in such numbers risks running into opposition in many NATO States, and also further antagonizing Afghan opinion. If counterinsurgency theory is a guide, and the whole country was seen as a theater of war, a massive increase in such numbers would seem to be called for.

So how reliable a guide is the writing on counterinsurgency?

Counterinsurgency Doctrines and Practice

Contrary to myth, counterinsurgency campaigns can sometimes be effective. Doctrines and practices of counterinsurgency—the best of which draw on a wide and varied range of practice—have a long history.[50] The revival of COIN doctrine in the past few years has been driven primarily by events in Iraq, but also, if to a lesser degree, by the development of the insurgency in Afghanistan. This revival of COIN doctrine is hardly surprising. The response of adversaries to the extraordinary pattern of US dominance on the battlefield was always going to be one of unconventional warfare, including the methods of the guerrilla and the terrorist; and, in turn, the natural US counter-response was to revive the most obviously appropriate available body of military doctrine.

The key document of the US revival of COIN doctrine is the US Army Field Manual 3-24 (FM 3-24).[51] It is very much an Army and Marine Corps manual: the Air Force refused to collaborate in the exercise. Improbably for a military-doctrinal document, it has been in demand in the United States. It has been heavily accessed and downloaded on the web, is also available as a published book from a major university press[52] and was the first army publication to receive a review in the *New York Times*.[53] Although it has some flaws, explored further below, it is a significant contribution to COIN literature.

By contrast, the United Kingdom has not yet produced a major new manual. This is partly because, much more than their US counterparts, the British had extant doctrine.[54] It is also because there was some opposition to COIN doctrine on the grounds that it would result in the same hammer being used on every problem. As a result there has not yet been a UK equivalent of FM 3-24. The Ministry of Defence's short (23 pages) Joint Discussion Note of January 2006, *The Comprehensive Approach,* is a more general survey intended to be relevant to a wide range of operations: the word "counterinsurgency" does not appear in it.[55] It was followed in 2007 by a paper entitled *Countering Irregular Activity.*[56] This document, which has not gone into general public circulation and has not been greeted with enthusiasm in the army, "seeks to instruct military personnel about counterinsurgency as a whole and about associated threats, and emphasizes the need for military activity to be part of a comprehensive approach involving all instruments of power."[57] This summary, by Sir John Kiszely, until 2008 Director of the Defence Academy of the United Kingdom, is immediately followed by a down-to-earth reminder that "every insurgency is *sui generis,* making generalizations problematic."[58] This important point has been emphasized by military professionals on both sides of the Atlantic.

The "comprehensive approach," which is central to both the US and UK doctrines, essentially means the application of all aspects of the power of the State within the territory where the insurgency is being fought. The apparent assumption that there is a State with real power is the key weakness of the approach, especially as it applies to Afghanistan. Before exploring this in more detail, it may be useful to glance at the problematic nature of assumptions about the political realm in the counterinsurgency doctrines inherited from past eras.

The US manual revives and updates doctrines that were developed in the Cold War years in response to anti-colonial insurrections (some of them involving leadership by local communist parties). It relies especially heavily on two sources from that era.[59] The first is David Galula's *Counterinsurgency Warfare,* one of the better writings of the French thinkers on *guerre révolutionnaire.*[60] The second is Sir Robert Thompson's *Defeating Communist Insurgency.*[61] Both works had placed emphasis on protecting populations as distinct from killing adversaries—a crucial distinction which implies a need for high force levels.

According to the introduction, FM 3-24 aspires to "help prepare Army and Marine Corps leaders to conduct COIN operations anywhere in the world."[62] This might seem to imply a universalist approach, but the authors emphasize that each insurgency is different. The foreword by Generals Petraeus and Amos is emphatic on this point: "You cannot fight former Saddamists and Islamic extremists the same way you would have fought the Viet Cong, Moros or Tupamaros; the application of principles and fundamentals to deal with each varies considerably."[63] FM 3-24 is also emphatic on the importance of constantly learning and adapting in response to the intricate environment of COIN operations, a point which strongly reflects British experience.[64]

Past exponents of COIN doctrine have generally placed heavy emphasis on achieving force ratios of about twenty to twenty-five counterinsurgents for every one thousand residents in an area of operations. Noting this, the manual states: "Twenty counterinsurgents per 1000 residents is often considered the minimum troop density required for effective COIN operations; however as with any fixed ratio, such calculations remain very dependent upon the situation."[65] This emphasis on force ratios is controversial. In any case, in Afghanistan there appears little chance of achieving such numbers. If the entire country with its thirty-two million inhabitants were to be viewed as the area of operations, a staggering eight hundred thousand counterinsurgents could be needed.[66] Even if the area of operations is defined narrowly, and even allowing for the fact that not all have to be NATO troops, the prospects of getting close to the force ratio indicated must be low.

A flaw in some, but not all, past counterinsurgency doctrine has been a lack of sensitivity to context and, in some cases, an ahistorical character. Some specialists in counterinsurgency have seen their subject more as a struggle of light versus darkness than as a recurrent theme of history or an outgrowth of the problems of a society. Examples of such an ahistorical approach to the subject can be found in the French group of theorists writing in the 1950s and early 1960s about *guerre révolutionnaire*. Some of these theorists denied the complexities—especially the mixture of material, moral and ideological factors—that are keys to understanding why and how guerrilla and terrorist movements come into existence. Colonel Lacheroy, a leading figure in this group and head of the French Army's *Service d'Action Psychologique*, famously stated: "In the beginning there is nothing."[67] Terrorism was seen as having been introduced deliberately into a peaceful society by an omnipresent outside force—namely international communism. It is a demonological vision of a cosmic struggle in which the actual history of particular countries and ways of thinking has little or no place.

A related fault in some counterinsurgency writing was the tendency to distil general rules of counterinsurgency from particular struggles and then seek to apply them in radically different circumstances. The campaign in Malaya in the 1950s, because it was successful in ending a communist-led insurgency, was often upheld as a model, and is described favorably in the US Field Manual.[68] Certain lessons drawn partly from Malaya were subsequently applied by the British in Borneo and Oman with some effect. However, successes such as that in Malaya can be great deceivers. Attempts were made to apply the lessons of Malaya in South Vietnam in the 1960s.[69] These largely failed. The main reason for failure in South Vietnam was that conditions in Vietnam were utterly different from those in Malaya. In Malaya the insurgency had mainly involved the ethnic Chinese minority and had never managed to present itself convincingly as representing the totality of the inhabitants of Malaya. The insurgency was weakened by the facts that the Chinese minority was distinguishable from other segments of society; Malaya had no common frontier with a communist State, so infiltration was difficult; and the British granting of independence to Malaya undermined the anti-colonial credentials of the insurgents. In South Vietnam, by contrast, the communist insurgents had strong nationalist credentials, having fought for independence rather than merely having power handed to them by a departing colonial power.[70] At the heart of the US tragedy in Vietnam was a failure to recognize the unique circumstance of the case, that in Vietnam, more than any other country in Southeast Asia, communism and nationalism were inextricably intertwined.

One lesson that could have been drawn from the Malayan case is that it is sometimes necessary to withdraw to win. FM 3-24 places much emphasis on the fact that the United States withdrew from Vietnam in 1973 only to see Saigon fall to North Vietnamese forces in 1975.[71] It does not note a contrary case: it was the UK promise to withdraw completely—a promise that was followed by the Federation of Malaya's independence in 1957—that contributed to the defeat of the insurgency in Malaya.[72] The value of such promises needs to be taken into account in contemporary COIN efforts and indeed COIN theory. This is especially so, as the idea that the United States intended to stay indefinitely in Iraq and Afghanistan, as evidenced by the networks of bases built there, had a corrosive effect in both countries and more generally. The decision of the Iraqi cabinet on November 16, 2008 that all US forces will withdraw from Iraq by 2011 is evidence that a guarantee of withdrawal is seen as a necessary condition (and not simply a natural consequence) of ending an acute phase of insurgency.

One weakness in the US manual, likely to be remedied in any future revisions, is the lack of serious coverage of systems of justice, especially those employed by the insurgents themselves. The references to judicial systems in FM 3-24 are brief and anodyne, almost entirely ignoring the challenge posed by insurgents in this area.[73] Insurgencies commonly use their own judicial procedures to reinforce their claims to be able to preserve an existing social order or create a better one. The Taliban have always placed emphasis on provision of a system of Islamic justice.[74] In the current conflict, taking advantage of the fact that the governmental legal system is weak and corrupt, they have done this effectively in parts of Afghanistan.

This leads to a more general criticism. In addressing the problem of undermining and weakening insurgencies, both traditional COIN theory and its revived versions in the twenty-first century place emphasis on, but do not discuss in detail, the role of State institutions: political structures, the administrative bureaucracy, the police, the courts and the armed forces. The institutions are often taken for granted, and assumed to be strong. Indeed, the current British COIN doctrine stemmed from a project started in 1995 to capture the lessons and doctrine from Northern Ireland. A common criticism of much COIN practice is that it was enthusiastically pursued by over-powerful and thuggish States, especially in Latin America.[75]

Today, COIN theories risk being out of touch with the realities of assisting the so-called "failed States" and "transitional administrations" of the twenty-first century. These problems are not new; one of the problems that undermined US COIN efforts in Vietnam was the artificiality and weakness of the coup-prone State of South Vietnam. Yet the central fact must be faced that in the two test-beds of the new COIN doctrines of recent years, Iraq and Afghanistan, State institutions have been notoriously weak—in Iraq temporarily, and in Afghanistan chronically. Indeed, in postcolonial States generally, where insurgencies are by no means uncommon, indigenous State systems tend to be fragile and/or contested. The role of the State in people's lives, and in their consciousness, may be thoroughly peripheral or even negative.[76] So when the US manual speaks of "a comprehensive strategy employing all instruments of national power" and stresses that all efforts focus on "supporting the local populace and HN [host nation] government,"[77] it is necessary to remind ourselves that support for government is not exactly a natural default position for inhabitants of countries with such tragic histories as Iraq and Afghanistan. On the other hand, General Petraeus worked on the manual after completing two tours of duty in Iraq, with an eye to applying it there, and then did so to some effect when he was commander of Multinational Force–Iraq. In 2008 the Iraqi government is looking stronger than in the first years after the invasion. The fact that a government is weak in the face of an insurgency does not mean that it is necessarily fated to remain so.

Of the many critiques of the US revival of COIN doctrine, one of the most searching is an American Political Science Association review symposium published in June 2008.[78] Stephen Biddle of the US Council on Foreign Relations queried the manual's fundamental assumption when he stated that

> it is far from clear that the manual's central prescription of drying up an insurgent's support base by persuading an uncommitted population to side with the government makes much sense in an identity war where the government's ethnic or sectarian identification means that it will be seen as an existential threat to the security of rival internal groups, and where there may be little or no supracommunal, national identity to counterpose to the subnational identities over which the war is waged by the time the United States becomes involved.[79]

Biddle also pointed out that the US manual has little to say about the comparative merits of waging COIN with large conventional forces as against small commando detachments, on the relative utility of airpower in COIN, and on the willingness of democracies to support COIN over a long period. Further, the manual does not fit particularly well the realities of Iraq, where the insurgencies are far more regional and localized in character, and more fickle in their loyalties, than were many of the communist and anti-colonial insurgencies of earlier eras. As Biddle points out, the negotiation of local ceasefires between insurgents and US commanders has been of key importance in Iraq.[80] Such webs of local ceasefires, valuable despite their fragility, do not come from counterinsurgency doctrine. These criticisms are another way of saying what General Petraeus knows: that all doctrine is interim, and some parts are more interim than others.

The need to adapt doctrine, so evident in Iraq, applies even more strongly to Afghanistan, a subject about which the US manual says remarkably little.[81] The key issue is whether the revival of counterinsurgency doctrine really offers a useful guide in a situation where there are some distinct elements in the insurgencies, where negotiation with some of the insurgents may have a role and where the State does not command the same loyalty or obedience that more local forces may enjoy.

After a difficult year in 2008, the US and Afghan governments began to place increased emphasis on local social structures. The US ambassador to Afghanistan said at the end of the year that there was agreement to move forward with two programs: first, the community outreach program, "designed to create community shuras" (local councils); and second, the community guard program, which is "meant to strengthen local communities and local tribes in their ability to protect what they consider to be their traditional homes."[82] While neither program was well defined, the move in this direction was evidence of willingness to rely on a less State-based approach than hitherto.

Judging Progress in the War in Afghanistan

Judging progress in counterinsurgency wars is by nature a contentious task, and involves difficult questions about the appropriate methodologies. Sometimes unorthodox methods of analysis yield the most valuable answers. The war in French Indochina from 1946 to 1954 provided a classic case. When a French doctoral student, Bernard Fall (1926–67), went to Vietnam in 1953, the French authorities claimed that the war was going well, and showed maps and statistics indicating that they controlled a large proportion of the territory. But he soon realized that French claims about the amount of territory they controlled were exaggerated, or at least lacked real meaning as far as the conduct of government was concerned. He reached this conclusion both by visiting Vietminh-held areas, and by inspecting tax records in supposedly government-held areas: these latter showed a dramatic collapse in the payment of taxes, and thus indicated a lack of actual government control.[83] In Afghanistan, the long-standing lack of a tax collection system continues today. As Astri Suhrke has shown, taxation constitutes a uniquely small proportion—in 2005 it was only 8 percent—of all estimated income in the national budget.[84]

By one key measure serious progress may appear to be being made in the Afghan war. The numbers of refugee returns to Afghanistan since the fall of the Taliban regime at the end of 2001 are one possible indicator of a degree of progress. According to the Office of the UN High Commissioner for Refugees (UNHCR), which played a key part in the process, between January 1, 2002 and December 31, 2007 a total of 4,997,455 refugees returned to Afghanistan, as follows:

2002	2003	2004	2005	2006	2007
1,957,958	645,864	879,780	752,084	387,917	373,852

This is the largest refugee return in the world in a generation. It is striking that even in 2006, 2007 and 2008, years of considerable conflict in parts of Afghanistan, the returns continued, if at a reduced rate. In the whole period 2002–07, the overwhelming majority of refugees have been in two countries: Iran, from which 1.6 million returned, and Pakistan, from which 3.3 million returned.[85] Impressive as the figures of this return are, four major qualifications have to be made:

- First, they have to be understood against the backdrop of the sheer numbers of Afghan refugees: at the end of 2007 Afghanistan was still the leading country of origin of refugees worldwide, with 3.1 million remaining outside the country. Thus in 2008, even after these returns, Afghan refugees constitute 27 percent of the entire global refugee population.

- Second, not all returns were fully voluntary. Within the countries of asylum there have been heavy pressures on these refugees to return, including the closing of some camps.

- Third, the experience of many returning refugees has included lack of employment opportunities in Afghanistan, and in some cases involvement in property disputes. There has been mismanagement and corruption in the Afghan Ministry of Refugees and Returnees. Some returnees live in dire conditions in makeshift settlements. All this has created much disappointment, bitterness and anti-government feeling.

- Fourth, displacement continues. In the past two years unknown numbers of returnees have left the country again. Also the number of internally displaced persons (IDPs) within Afghanistan has increased, especially due to the fighting in the south of the country, and now stands at about 235,000. Some returnees have seamlessly become IDPs.[86]

Other developments confirm this sobering picture. The Afghan army remains relatively small, and highly dependent on outside support. As for the insurgent forces, they appear to have no shortage of recruits. Large numbers of fighters are able to cross into Afghanistan, mainly from Pakistan; and the Taliban can also employ many locals, especially in seasons when other work is in short supply. The fact that the estimated unemployment rate is 40 percent means that insurgents continue to have opportunities for recruitment. In Kabul and other cities, terrorist attacks, once rare, have become common. Serious observers reported an atmosphere of disappointment and bitterness in Afghanistan in 2008.[87]

The UN Secretary-General's report of September 2008 summarizes the situation thus:

> The overall situation in Afghanistan has become more challenging since my previous report. Despite the enhanced capabilities of both the Afghan National Army and the international forces, the security situation has deteriorated markedly. The influence of the insurgency has expanded beyond traditionally volatile areas and has increased in provinces neighboring Kabul. Incidents stemming from cross-border activities from Pakistan have increased significantly in terms of numbers and sophistication. The insurgency's dependence on asymmetric tactics has also led to a sharp rise in the number of civilian casualties. Civilians are also being killed as a result of military operations carried out by Afghan and international security forces, in particular in situations in which insurgents conceal themselves in populated areas. Another worrying development is the fact that attacks on aid-related targets and non-governmental organizations have become more frequent and more deadly.[88]

The Secretary-General's report states bluntly that the number of security incidents rose to 983 in August 2008, the highest since the fall of the Taliban in 2001, and "represents a 44 percent increase compared with the same month in 2007." It also states: "While the main focus of the insurgency remains the southern and eastern parts of the country, where it has historically been strong, insurgent influence has intensified in areas that were previously relatively calm, including in the provinces closest to Kabul."[89] Overall the report is far from negative. It reports some successes in the campaign against poppy cultivation, and it strongly endorses the Afghanistan National Development Strategy, adopted at the Paris Conference in Support of Afghanistan, held on June 12, 2008. However, as an account of the state of progress in the war against the Taliban, it confirms the picture which has also been depicted by other sources. The latter include the sober report of General David McKiernan, the top US commander in Afghanistan, who, at the same time as he was seeking specific troop increases, rejected simple notions, indeed the terminology, of a military "surge";[90] and the US National Intelligence Estimate on Afghanistan, a draft version of which was leaked in October 2008, which stated that the situation there was in a "downward spiral."[91] One grim statistic of the downward spiral is the casualty rate of ISAF and Operation Enduring Freedom forces in Afghanistan. Fatalities have increased each year from 57 in 2003 to 296 in 2008.[92]

As so often in counterinsurgency wars, the most useful assessments may be those of independent witnesses who, just as Bernard Fall did in French Indochina, have deep knowledge of a society and a healthy open-mindedness about the contribution that outside forces can make to security. Rory Stewart, who walked across Afghanistan in 2002, and later retired from the UK diplomatic service to run a charitable foundation in Kabul, has argued that "we need less investment—but a greater focus on what we know how to do." He is specifically critical of increases in forces:

> A troop increase is likely to inflame Afghan nationalism because Afghans are more anti-foreign than we acknowledge and the support for our presence in the insurgency areas is declining. The Taliban, which was a largely discredited and backward movement, gains support by portraying itself as fighting for Islam and Afghanistan against a foreign military occupation."[93]

V. Conclusions

Four kinds of conclusions follow. First, about the implications of Afghanistan for the UN; second, on the role of NATO; third, on international security generally; and finally, on the debate about policy choices that is emerging from the difficult experience of attempting to transform Afghanistan. These conclusions are based on the presumption that the present campaign in Afghanistan is unlikely to result in a clear victory for the Kabul government and its outside partners, because the sources of division within and around Afghanistan are just too deep, and the tendency to react against the presence of foreign forces too ingrained. The war could yet be lost, or, perhaps more likely, it could produce a stalemate or a long war of attrition with no clear outcome. The dissolution of Afghanistan into regional fiefdoms—already an accustomed part of life—could continue and even accelerate.

To some it may appear remarkable that Afghanistan has not reverted more completely to type as a society that rejects outside intrusion. Part of the explanation may be that this is not the only natural "default position" for Afghans: there have also been countless episodes in which Afghan leaders have sought, and profited from, alliances with outsiders. A second factor is the "light footprint" advocated by Brahimi: for all the limitations of this approach, and the many departures from it since it was enunciated in 2002 with specific reference to UNAMA, no one has convincingly suggested a better one. A third factor is that—notwithstanding the disastrous killings of civilians as a result of using airpower—there has been a degree of restraint in the use of armed force: this has been important in at least slowing the pace of the process whereby the US and other outside forces come to be perceived as alien bodies in Afghanistan. The interesting phenomenon of application of certain parts of the law of armed conflict—namely the rules of targeting—as if this was an international war is part of this process.

The United Nations

A few conclusions on the UN's various roles in Afghanistan flow from this brief survey. First, the United Nations has some remarkable achievements to its credit in Afghanistan. It helped to negotiate the Soviet withdrawal from Afghanistan that was completed in 1989; ever since then it has remained engaged on the ground in Afghanistan; it gave a degree of authorization to the US-led effort to remove the Taliban regime in 2001; it has authorized ISAF and has provided a legitimate basis for its expanded roles throughout the country; it has been involved in the many subsequent efforts to help develop Afghanistan, not least by assisting in the various elections held there since 2001; and it has assisted the largest refugee return to any country since the 1970s.

Second, despite these achievements, the UN's roles have been more limited than those of the United States and its various partners, especially in matters relating to security. The fact that the UN's role in this crisis has been modest is not especially shocking. Neither the terms of the UN Charter nor the record of the Security Council justifies the excessively high expectations that many have had in respect to the Council's roles. It was always a mistake to view the United Nations as aiming to provide a complete system of collective security even in the best of circumstances, and circumstances in and around Afghanistan are far from being favorable for international involvement.

Third, international legitimacy is never a substitute for local legitimacy. The Council's acceptance of regime change in Afghanistan was justified once the Taliban had refused to remove al-Qaeda, and did much to legitimize the aim of regime replacement, which could otherwise have seemed a narrowly neo-colonial US action. Yet there is a danger that such international conferrals of legitimacy can contribute to a failure to address the no-less-important question of securing legitimacy in the eyes of the audience that matters most: in this case, the peoples of Afghanistan and neighboring countries.

NATO

The involvement of the NATO alliance in this distant, difficult and divisive conflict could have fateful consequences for the alliance. It is truly remarkable that the reputation of the longest-lived military alliance in the world, comprised of States with fundamentally stable political systems, should have made itself vulnerable to the outcome of a war in the unpromising surroundings of Afghanistan. There is much nervousness about this among NATO's European members, and this may explain the reluctance of European leaders to make the kind of ringing statements that often accompany war. Knowing that the outcome of any adventure in Afghanistan is bound to be uncertain, they have wisely kept the level of rhetoric low.

There may be another reason for the reluctance of many leaders of European member States to make strong endorsements of their participation in the war in Afghanistan. Many of the claims that can be made in favor of the Afghan cause are also implicitly criticisms of the involvement in Iraq. From the start in 2001, the US-led involvement in Afghanistan and the subsequent involvement of ISAF have both had a strong basis of international legitimacy that was reflected in Security Council resolutions. In Afghanistan there was a real political and military force to support, in the shape of the Northern Alliance. In Afghanistan and Pakistan there were real havens for terrorists. In Afghanistan, up to five million refugees have returned since 2001. To speak about these matters too loudly might be to undermine the US position in Iraq, where the origins and course of the outside involvement have been different, and where the flow of refugees has been outward. NATO leaders, anxious to put the recriminations of 2003 over Iraq behind them, may be nervous about highlighting the differences between Afghanistan and Iraq.

A major question, heavy with implications for international security, is: how are the setbacks experienced in Afghanistan to be explained, especially within NATO member States? The United Nations may be accustomed to failure, but NATO is not. So far, the tendency has been to blame Pakistan, the messy NATO command, the poor attention span of consecutive US governments, the unwillingness of NATO allies to contribute, the weakness of Karzai, the corruption of his government, the shortage of foreign money and troops; in other words, to blame almost everything except the nature of the project.

The various reasons that have been given cannot be lightly dismissed. For example, the lack of NATO unity in certain operational matters has been striking: the inability of member States to agree on a straightforward and defensible common set of standards for treating prisoners in the Afghan operations is symptomatic of deep divisions within the alliance. Political divisions have never been far from the surface and will no doubt be projected into future explanations of what went wrong. Continental Europeans can convincingly blame the Americans and the British for having taken their eye off the ball in Afghanistan in 2002–03, foolishly thinking that the war there was virtually won and that they could afford to rush into a second adventure in Iraq. Americans can blame the Europeans for putting relatively few troops into ISAF, and being slow to back them up when the going got rough in 2006–08. A less blame-centered explanation might be that the reconstruction of Afghanistan, and the pursuit of counterinsurgency there, was always going to be an extremely difficult task; that there are limits to what outsiders should expect to achieve in the transformation of distant societies with cultures significantly different from our own; and that it never made sense to invest such effort in counterinsurgency in Afghanistan without having even the beginnings of a strategy for the neighboring regions of Pakistan.

Impact on International Security

The problem of Afghanistan—including the complex interplay of international actors who have pursued their interests there—has had an impressive and multifaceted impact on international security issues in the past generation. It contributed to the end of the Cold War and indeed of the Soviet Union itself. It assisted, and continues to assist, the rise and proliferation of Islamic militants around the globe. The Taliban regime's failure to control al-Qaeda activities launched the United States into the huge and seemingly endless "War on Terror," led to the United States acquiring unprecedented access to Central Asia, and also resulted in the Security Council claiming unprecedented powers to affect activities within States. The Afghan war has embroiled NATO in a largely civil war thousands of miles from its North Atlantic heartlands. It also threatens to destabilize Pakistan. Even worse, by feeding the mutual suspicion between India and Pakistan, and opening up another front in their long-standing rivalry, it makes war between these two nuclear powers a distinct possibility.

One impact of Afghanistan on international security may turn out to be highly paradoxical. It is obvious that Afghanistan, along with Iraq, has called into question the idea that the United States, in its supposed "unipolar moment," could change even the most difficult and divided societies by its confident use of armed force. But it is not only the ideas of the neo-conservatives and their camp-followers that are in trouble. In many ways the involvement of NATO in Afghanistan was textbook liberal multilateralism: implicitly approved by the UN Security Council, involving troops from forty democracies, cooperating with the UN assistance mission, and pursuing admirable aims to assist the development and modernization of

Afghanistan. The very ideas of rebuilding the world in our image, and of major Western States having an obligation to achieve these tasks in distant lands—whether by unilateral or multilateral approaches—may come to be viewed as optimistic. Or, to put it differently, and somewhat cryptically, Afghanistan may not have quite such a drastic effect on the American *imperium* as it had on the Soviet one in the years up to 1991; but it may nevertheless come to be seen as one important stage on the path in which international order became, certainly not unipolar, and perhaps not even multipolar, but based more on prudent interest than on illusions that Western ideas control the world. Afghanistan, like Somalia, may contribute to greater caution before engaging in interventionist projects aimed at reconstructing divided societies. Whether this is a cause for celebration or regret may be debated: in 1994 Tutsis in Rwanda had good reason to rue the US caution that resulted from the Somalia debacle.

Despite all the difficulties encountered in Afghanistan since the fall of the Taliban in 2001, in the US presidential election campaign in 2008 both Barack Obama and John McCain promised to increase the US commitment to Afghanistan in 2009. There was little prospect either that the insurgency would subside or that the United States would tiptoe out of the war. Furthermore, both candidates advocated continuing and even extending the practice of using US force against Taliban and al-Qaeda targets in Pakistan. The war's international dimension, and its significance for international security more generally, was set to continue.

The Debate on Policy Choices

The Obama administration's policy planning for Afghanistan is based on the sound presumption that the Afghan problem cannot be addressed in isolation. Although many countries have a potentially important role in any settlement in Afghanistan—especially Iran, with its large numbers of Afghan refugees and its major drug problem—Pakistan is at the core of this approach. Granted the indissoluble connection between Afghanistan and Pakistan, any policy in respect to the one has to be framed in light of its effects on the other. At times it may even be necessary to prioritize between these two countries. The simple truth is that Pakistan is a far larger, more powerful and generally more important country than Afghanistan. If the price of saving Afghanistan were to be the destabilization of Pakistan, it would not be worth paying. A principal aim of the United States in the region should have been, and indeed may have been, to avoid creating a situation in which that particular price has to be paid: yet at least once before, in the Soviet-Afghan war in the 1980s, something very like it happened.

The main conclusion of any consideration of the Pakistani factor in the ongoing conflict in Afghanistan has to be that the policy of the United States and allies—to strengthen central government in both countries—has been operating in extremely difficult circumstances, has been pursued erratically and has been largely unsuccessful. While it is not obvious what the alternatives might be—open acceptance of regional autonomy in both societies would have some merits—the general approach of backing non-Pashtuns in Pakistan and Afghanistan risks exacerbating the Pashtun problem in both countries. Three distinct causes—Pashtun, Taliban and al-Qaeda—have become dangerously conflated. It should be a first aim of Western policy to reverse this dangerous trend.

Because of the grim prospects of a stalemate, a war of attrition or worse in Afghanistan, and also because of the advent of new governments in Pakistan in 2008 and the United States in 2009, there has been at least the beginning of consideration of alternative policies. Two stand out: each in its way addresses directly the growth of the insurgency and each is based on a recognition that the Pakistani dimension of the problem has to be considered alongside the Afghan one. Both options take into account the central requirement of any approach—that it be geared to ensuring that neither Afghanistan nor Pakistan offers the kind of haven for organizing international terrorist actions that Afghanistan did under Taliban rule.

The first option centers on negotiation with Taliban and other Pashtun groups. The first question to be faced is whether, on either side of the border, there are sufficiently clear hierarchical organizational structures with which to negotiate. The second question is whether Afghan Taliban/Pashtun goals are framed more in terms of control of the Afghan State along the completely uncompromising lines followed by the Taliban in the years up to 2001, or in more limited terms. Whatever the answers, negotiation in some form with some of the insurgent groups and factions is inevitable. Indeed, in an informal manner some is already happening. Combining fighting with talking is quite common in insurgencies, not least because of their tendency to result in stalemate. Yet it is never easy, and is likely to be particularly difficult for those on both sides who have chosen to see the war in Afghanistan as a war of good against evil. It is also likely to be difficult if, as at present, the Taliban believe they are in a position of strength. A critical question to be explored in any talks is whether, as some evidence suggests, Taliban leaders have learned enough from their disasters since seizing Kabul in 1996, and in particular from their near-death experience in 2001, to be willing to operate in a different manner in today's Afghanistan.[94] The continuing commitment of the Taliban in Pakistan to destroying government schools, and its opposition to education for girls, does not inspire confidence. The scope and content of any agreement are matters of huge difficulty. Some agreements concluded by the Pakistani government in the past few years are widely seen as having given Taliban leaders a license to continue supporting the insurgency in Afghanistan. This serves as a warning of the hazards of partial negotiation. Yet the pressures for negotiation are very strong, and a refusal to consider this course could have adverse effects in both countries.

In October 2008, after a two-week debate that was not always well attended, the Pakistani Parliament passed unanimously a resolution widely interpreted as suggesting above all a shift to negotiation. Actually it was a complex package, in which the Parliament united to condemn terrorism and at the same time was seen as "taking ownership" of policy to tackle it. The Resolution said that regions on the Afghan border where militants flourish should be developed, and force used as a last resort. It opposed the cross-border strikes by US forces in Pakistan, but at the same time indicated a degree of support for US policy. It called for dialogue with extremist groups operating in the country, and hinted at a fundamental change in Pakistan's approach to the problem: "We need an urgent review of our national security strategy and revisiting the methodology of combating terrorism in order to restore peace and stability."[95] At the very least it provides one basis for the Obama administration to recalibrate the United States's largely burnt-out policies toward Pakistan.

The second option under discussion involves a fundamental rethinking of security strategy in both Afghanistan and Pakistan. On the Afghan side of the border it would call for some increase in ISAF or other outside forces, especially to speed up the pace of expansion of the Afghan army, and thereby to provide backup so that certain areas from which the Taliban have been expelled can thereafter be protected. It would also call for cooperation in security matters with local forces and councils, with all the hazards involved. One informed and persuasive critique of the approach to counterinsurgency used in Afghanistan since 2003 suggests that its emphasis on extending the reach of central government is precisely the wrong strategy: its authors, specialists in the region, argue instead for a rural security presence that has been largely lacking.[96] A security strategy based on local forces and councils would also call for expansion of aid and development programs, especially in urgent matters such as food aid in areas threatened by famine, and for a serious effort to address the widespread corruption which makes a continuous mockery of Western attempts to bring reform and progress to Afghanistan. On the Pakistani side it would involve a protracted effort to develop a long-term policy—hitherto non-existent—for establishing some kind of government influence in the FATA, and for a joined-up policy for addressing the Taliban and al-Qaeda presence. On both sides of the border it would necessitate reining in the use of airpower to reduce its inflammation of local opinion.

For reasons indicated in this article, it is highly improbable that either of these options on its own could provide a substantial amelioration of a tangled and tragic situation. However, a combination of the two policies—both negotiating, and rethinking the security strategy—might just achieve some results. Such a dual approach has been supported in 2009 by John Nagl, one of the architects of the new US counterinsurgency doctrine. Advocating the adaptation of this doctrine in the special circumstances of Afghanistan, he has stated: "At the time, the doctrine the manual laid out was enormously controversial, both inside and outside the Pentagon. It remains so today. Its key tenets are simple, but radical: Focus on protecting civilians over killing the enemy. Assume greater risk. Use minimum, not maximum force." His advocacy of these principles is accompanied by emphasis on the importance of dealing with local forces as well as national governments both in Afghanistan and in Pakistan.[97]

An approach along such lines would need to include other elements as well, including a strong and credible commitment to leave as soon as a modicum of stability is achieved. Such a combination would need to be pursued in both Afghanistan and Pakistan. It could only work if a new US administration rejected the worst aspects of previous policies, and pursued the matter with more consistent attention than in the past. It would be likely to result in some unsatisfactory compromises, and might build on, rather than fundamentally change, the pattern of local loyalty and regional warlordism that is so rooted in Afghanistan. Yet if the war in Afghanistan is not to have even more fateful consequences for international order than those seen in the past three decades, it may be the direction in which events have to move.

Notes

1. T.R. Moreman, *Callwell, Sir Charles Edward (1859–1928), in* OXFORD DICTIONARY OF NATIONAL BIOGRAPHY (H.C.G. Matthew & Brian Harrison eds., 2004).

2. C.E. CALLWELL, SMALL WARS: THEIR PRINCIPLES AND PRACTICE 5 (rev. ed., 1899).

3. For an account of the retreat from Kabul in January 1842, see SAUL DAVID, VICTORIA'S WARS: THE RISE OF EMPIRE 55–67 (2006).

4. CALLWELL, *supra* note 2, at 16.

5. DAVID LOYN, BUTCHER & BOLT: TWO HUNDRED YEARS OF FOREIGN ENGAGEMENT IN AFGHANISTAN (2008).

6. ROB JOHNSON, A REGION IN TURMOIL: SOUTH ASIAN CONFLICTS SINCE 1947, at 166 (2005).

7. The Northern Alliance, more correctly called the United Islamic Front for the Salvation of Afghanistan, is a loose association of regional groups founded in 1996 to fight against Taliban control of Afghanistan.

8. On the Taliban's history of supporting opium production, which became the mainstay of their war economy in the late 1990S, see AHMED RASHID, TALIBAN: THE STORY OF THE AFGHAN WARLORDS 117–24 (2001).

9. AHMED RASHID, DESCENT INTO CHAOS: HOW THE WAR AGAINST ISLAMIC EXTREMISM IS BEING LOST IN PAKISTAN, AFGHANISTAN AND CENTRAL ASIA 401 (2008).

10. S.C. Res. 1386, operative paragraph 1, U.N. Doc. S/RES/1386 (Dec. 20, 2001). Five months later the Security Council addressed ISAF's entitlement to use force more explicitly,

authorizing "the Member States participating in the International Security Assistance Force to take all necessary measures to fulfill the mandate of the International Security Assistance Force." S.C. Res. 1413, operative paragraph 2, U.N. Doc. S/RES/1413 (May 23, 2002).

11. S.C. Res. 1510, U.N. Doc. S/RES/1510 (Oct. 13, 2003), expanded ISAF's sphere of operations to other parts of Afghanistan. By the end of 2006, now operating under NATO, it had responsibilities in virtually all of Afghanistan.

12. Al-Qaeda Not Weakening – BBC Poll, BBC NEWS, http://news.bbc.co.uk/2/hi/americas/7638566.stm (last visited Mar. 9, 2009) (survey conducted July 8–September 12, 2008).

13. Saeed Shah, *Pakistanis Unite to Fight Extremism*, GUARDIAN (London), Oct. 10, 2008, at 25.

14. RASHID, *supra* note 8, at 26–29, 45, 90–94, 137–38.

15. On the extent of Pakistani help to the Taliban, see RASHID, *supra* note 9; SETH JONES, COUNTERINSURGENCY IN AFGHANISTAN (2008), *available at* http://www.rand.org/pubs/monographs/2008/RAND_MG595.pdf.

16. For an indictment predicated on the assumption that a serious policy could be devised, see US GOVERNMENT ACCOUNTABILITY OFFICE, COMBATING TERRORISM: THE UNITED STATES LACKS COMPREHENSIVE PLAN TO DESTROY THE TERRORIST THREAT AND CLOSE THE SAFE HAVEN IN PAKISTAN'S FEDERALLY ADMINISTERED TRIBAL AREAS (2008), *available at* http://www.gao.gov/new.items/d08622.pdf.

17. For a report on US killings of Pakistani forces in an incident on June 10, 2008, and on a visit to an area of Pakistan held by Taliban warlords, see Dexter Filkins, *Right at the Edge*, NEW YORK TIMES, Sept. 7, 2008 (Magazine), at 52.

18. Eric Schmitt & Mark Mazzetti, *Bush Said to Give Orders Allowing Raids in Pakistan*, NEW YORK TIMES, Sept. 10, 2008, at A1.

19. See especially the archive-based material on the Soviet war in Afghanistan in ARNE WESTAD, THE GLOBAL COLD WAR: THIRD WORLD INTERVENTIONS AND THE MAKING OF OUR TIMES (2005).

20. S.C. Res. 462, U.N. Doc. S/RES/462 (Jan. 9, 1980).

21. G.A. Res. ES-6/2, U.N. GAOR, 6th Emer. Spec. Sess., Supp. No. 1, at 2, U.N. Doc. A/ES-6/2 (Jan. 14, 1980).

22. On the "good offices" negotiations over Afghanistan, see Thomas M. Franck & Georg Nolte, *The Good Offices Function of the UN Secretary-General, in* UNITED NATIONS, DIVIDED WORLD: THE UN'S ROLES IN INTERNATIONAL RELATIONS 149–51, 180 (Adam Roberts & Benedict Kingsbury eds., 2d ed. 1993).

23. UNGOMAP was mandated to support implementation of the 1988 Geneva Accords on Afghanistan. The Secretary-General's proposal to dispatch military personnel in UNGOMAP was confirmed in S.C. Res. 622, U.N. Doc. S/RES/622 (Oct. 31, 1988) and G.A. Res. 43/20, U.N. Doc. A/RES/43/20 (Nov. 3, 1988).

24. UN Press Release SG/SM/4127, at 6 (Apr. 27, 1988), *cited by* Franck & Nolte, *supra* note 22, at 150.

25. UNSMA was established by G.A. Res. 48/208, U.N. Doc. A/RES/48/208 (Dec. 21, 1993). It was replaced by UN Assistance Mission in Afghanistan (UNAMA) after the December 2001 Bonn Agreement. Agreement on Provisional Arrangements in Afghanistan Pending the Reestablishment of Permanent Government Institutions, attached to Letter from the Secretary-General addressed to the President of the Security Council, U.N. Doc. S/2001/1154 (Dec. 5, 2001).

26. S.C. Res. 1076, U.N. Doc. S/RES/1076 (Oct. 22, 1996).

27. S.C. Res. 1193, U.N. Doc. S/RES/1193 (Aug. 28, 1998).

28. S.C. Res. 1267, U.N. Doc. S/RES/1267 (Oct. 15, 1999). In the ongoing war against the Taliban insurgency, this Resolution has sometimes been seen as a possible obstacle to negotiations with the Taliban.

29. S.C. Res. 1368, U.N. Doc. S/RES/1368 (Sept. 12, 2001).

30. S.C. Res. 1373, U.N. Doc. S/RES/1373 (Sept. 28, 2001).

31. See the General Assembly's notably strong commitments in respect to combating terrorism contained in the World Summit Outcome document, G.A. Res. 60/1, ¶¶ 81–91, U.N. Doc. A/RES/60/1 (Sept. 16, 2005).

32. On these matters relating to the role of the Security Council in Afghanistan since the late 1990s, I agree with Michael Reisman's conclusions in his address "The Influence of the Conflict in Afghanistan on International Law" on June 25, 2008, the first day of the US Naval War College workshop. *See* W. Michael Reisman, *International Legal Dynamics and the Design of Feasible Missions: The Case of Afghanistan*, which is Chapter III in this volume, at 59.

33. U.N. SCOR, 57th Sess., 4469th mtg, U.N. Doc. S/PV.4469 (Feb. 6, 2002).

34. Gilles Dorronsoro, *The Security Council and the Afghan Conflict*, *in* THE UNITED NATIONS SECURITY COUNCIL AND WAR: THE EVOLUTION OF THOUGHT AND PRACTICE SINCE 1945, at 464 (Vaughan Lowe, Adam Roberts, Jennifer Welsh & Dominik Zaum eds., 2008).

35. The Secretary-General, *Report of the Secretary-General on the Situation in Afghanistan and Its Implications for International Peace and Security*, ¶ 2, U.N. Doc. A/62/722, S/2008/159 (Mar. 6, 2008). See also the Secretary-General's report of September 2008 cited *infra* note 88.

36. On the revolution in military affairs and related doctrines, and how their weaknesses became evident, see LAWRENCE FREEDMAN, THE TRANSFORMATION OF STRATEGIC AFFAIRS (2006).

37. Interview of Paul Wolfowitz, US Deputy Secretary of Defense, on *Face the Nation* (Nov. 18, 2001), transcript *available at* http://usembassy-israel.org.il/publish/peace/archives/2001/november/111804.html.

38. Information provided at a conference attended by the author at Allied Rapid Reaction Corps headquarters, Rheindahlen Military Complex–Mönchengladbach, Germany (June 27, 2007).

39. US Army officers have been particularly vocal in expressing their concerns about the performance of the US Air Force regarding such matters as bombing missions gone wrong and insufficient priority to the provision of surveillance aircraft. *See* Thom Shanker, *Edging Away from Air Force, Army Adds Its Own Aviation Unit*, NEW YORK TIMES, June 22, 2008, at A6.

40. HUMAN RIGHTS WATCH, TROOPS IN CONTACT: AIRSTRIKES AND CIVILIAN DEATHS IN AFGHANISTAN 2 (2008), *available at* http://hrw.org/reports/2008/afghanistan0908/index.htm.

41. Carlotta Gall, *Afghan Leader Criticizes U.S., Calling Arrests and Casualties Too High*, NEW YORK TIMES, Apr. 26, 2008, at A6.

42. *See* Paul Gallis & Vincent Morelli, Congressional Research Service, *NATO in Afghanistan: A Test of the Atlantic Alliance* 1, No. 33267 (July 18, 2008).

43. Press Release, North Atlantic Treaty Organization, Statement by the North Atlantic Council (Sept. 12, 2001), *available at* http://www.nato.int/docu/pr/2001/p01-124e.htm.

44. For a particularly well informed account of the evolution of the roles of the United States and NATO since 2001, see Astri Suhrke, *A Contradictory Mission? NATO from Stabilization to Combat in Afghanistan*, 15 INTERNATIONAL PEACEKEEPING 214 (2008), *available at* http://www.cmi.no/publications/file/?3038=a-contradictory-mission.

45. Daniel Marston, *Lessons in 21st-Century Counterinsurgency: Afghanistan 2001–07*, *in* COUNTERINSURGENCY IN MODERN WARFARE 240 (Daniel Marston & Carter Malkasian eds., 2008).

46. *See, e.g.*, Donna Mills, Gates: Afghanistan Command Restructuring Worthy of Consideration (May 2, 2008), http://www.defenselink.mil/news/newsarticle.aspx?id=49769 (Secretary of Defense Robert Gates's expression of concern about dual command and control in remarks at Texarkana, Texas).

47. *See* Adam Roberts, *Torture and Incompetence in the 'War on Terror,'* SURVIVAL, Spring 2007, at 199; AMNESTY INTERNATIONAL, AFGHANISTAN – DETAINEES TRANSFERRED TO TORTURE: ISAF COMPLICITY? 20–30 (2007).

48. Information on ISAF troop numbers and areas of operation from various documents, including ISAF Placemat current as of 1 December 2008, http://www.nato.int/isaf/docu/epub/pdf/placemat_archive/isaf_placemat_081201.pdf (last visited Jan. 11, 2009).

49. *See, e.g.*, Gallis & Morelli, *supra* note 42, at 13.

50. For an excellent overview from the late nineteenth century to the ongoing war in Afghanistan, see COUNTERINSURGENCY IN MODERN WARFARE, *supra* note 45. Marston's chapter at 220 is notably critical of the failure of the United States and its allies to train and equip soldiers for counterinsurgency.

51. Headquarters, Department of the Army & Headquarters, Marine Corps Combat Development Command, FM 3-24/MCWP 3-33.5, Counterinsurgency (2006), *available at* http://www.fas.org/irp/doddir/army/fm3-24.pdf [hereinafter US Army Field Manual 3-24]. This publication has a short foreword by then–Lieutenant General David H. Petraeus (who played a key part in its preparation) and Lieutenant General James F. Amos.

52. HEADQUARTERS, DEPARTMENT OF THE ARMY & HEADQUARTERS, MARINE CORPS COMBAT DEVELOPMENT COMMAND, FM 3-24/MCWP 3-33.5, THE US ARMY/MARINE CORPS COUNTERINSURGENCY FIELD MANUAL (University of Chicago Press 2007). This edition has a new foreword by Lieutenant Colonel John A. Nagl and a new introduction by Sarah Sewall.

53. *See* Samantha Power, *Our War on Terror*, NEW YORK TIMES, July 29, 2007, § 7, at 1.

54. Chief of the General Staff, UK Army Field Manual, Vol. 1 Combined Arms Operations, Part 10 Counter-Insurgency Operations (Strategic and Operational Guidelines) (July 2001). The approach it laid out and its principles are still regarded as being valid. Its biggest problem was the context in which it was set. It makes no mention of coalition operations, or the problems of operating in other people's countries, the religious and cultural dimensions, and the effects of information proliferation and information operations. The task of updating it started in late 2005. It is still in development.

55. UK Joint Doctrine & Concepts Centre, The Comprehensive Approach: Joint Discussion Note 4/05 (2006), *available at* http://www.mod.uk/DefenceInternet/MicroSite/DCDC/OurPublications/JDNP/ (then JDN 4/05 pdf hyperlink).

56. UK Ministry of Defence Joint Doctrine Note 2/07, Countering Irregular Activity Within a Comprehensive Approach (UK Ministry of Defence, March 2007).

57. JOHN KISZELY, POST-MODERN CHALLENGES FOR MODERN WARRIORS 13–14 (2007), *available at* http://www.comw.org/rma/fulltext/0712kiszely.pdf.

58. *Id.* at 14.

59. US Army Field Manual 3-24, *supra* note 51, at viii. Three sources, all cited at length in the text, are listed at this point. (The third, not discussed here, was an article in the *New Yorker* in January 2005.) See also the Annotated Bibliography, *id.* at Annotated Bibliography 1–4, which cites a wider range of sources. It omits key critical writings on the subject, most notably PETER PARET, FRENCH REVOLUTIONARY WARFARE FROM INDOCHINA TO ALGERIA: THE ANALYSIS OF A POLITICAL AND MILITARY DOCTRINE (1964). The omission of this title reflected a view that it is hard to get Americans to take on board French doctrines on COIN.

60. DAVID GALULA, COUNTERINSURGENCY WARFARE: THEORY AND PRACTICE (1964). Galula died in 1968. His work was belatedly published in France as CONTRE-INSURRECTION: THÉORIE ET PRATIQUE (2008).

61. ROBERT THOMPSON, DEFEATING COMMUNIST INSURGENCY: EXPERIENCES FROM MALAYA AND VIETNAM (1966).

62. US Army Field Manual 3-24, *supra* note 51, at ix.

63. *Id.*, Foreword. The Moros, perhaps the least known of the insurgents cited, have been involved in an armed insurrection in the Philippines.

64. *Id.* at 5-31.

65. *Id.* at 1-13.

66. There has not been a census in Afghanistan for well over twenty years. The estimated population was over 32.5 million as of July 2008. *See* Central Intelligence Agency, The World Factbook (2008), https://www.cia.gov/library/publications/the-world-factbook/print/af.html.

67. Colonel Charles Lacheroy, Talk, *La Guerre Révolutionnaire* (July 2, 1957), *reprinted in* LOUIS TROTABA, LA DÉFENSE NATIONALE 322 (1958), *cited in* PARET, *supra* note 59, at 15. Paret comments that "nothing," in this case, means "the secure existence of the *status quo*."

68. US Army Field Manual 3-24, *supra* note 51, at 6-21 & 6-22.

69. See especially THOMPSON, *supra* note 61, at 17–20.

70. The geographical, sociological, political and ethnic differences between Malaya and South Vietnam were evident to knowledgeable observers even while the Vietnam War was still ongoing. *See* BERNARD B. FALL, THE TWO VIET-NAMS: A POLITICAL AND MILITARY ANALYSIS 339–40, 372–76 (1963).

71. US Army Field Manual 3-24, *supra* note 51, at 1-8, 2-13.

72. *See e.g.*, Obituary of Sir Donald MacGillivray, the last British High Commissioner for Malaya, TIMES (London), Dec. 28, 1966.

73. US Army Field Manual 3-24, *supra* note 51, at 5-15, 3-25, 6-21, 8-16.

74. RASHID, *supra* note 8, at 102–03.

75. *See, e.g.*, George Monbiot, *Backyard Terrorism*, GUARDIAN (London), Oct. 30, 2001, at 17 (an ebullient attack on how US counterinsurgency training was implicated in the work of death squads in Latin America over many decades).

76. For a useful account of this general problem (though it does not address the case of Afghanistan), see JOEL S. MIGDAL, STRONG SOCIETIES AND WEAK STATES: STATE-SOCIETY RELATIONS AND STATE CAPABILITIES IN THE THIRD WORLD (1988).

77. US Army Field Manual 3-24, *supra* note 51, at 2-1.

78. Jeffrey C. Isaac, *Review Symposium: The New U.S. Army/Marine Corps Counterinsurgency Field Manual as Political Science and Political Praxis, American Political Science Association*, 6 PERSPECTIVES ON POLITICS 347–48, 350 (June 2008), *available at* http://www.apsanet.org/imgtest/POPJune08CounterInsurgency2.pdf. The four contributors to this symposium were Stephen Biddle (347–50), Stathis N. Kalyvas (351–53), Wendy Brown (354–57), and Douglas A. Ollivant (357–60).

79. *Id.* at 348. See also the excellent contribution of Stathis N. Kalyvas, who argues that by adopting the people's war model, the authors of the manual assume that the population interacts with either the government or the insurgents. *Id.* at 352. This leads them (the authors) to conclude, incorrectly, that if the insurgents are removed from the equation the people will move closer to the government.

80. *Id.* at 347–48 & 350.

81. US Army Field Manual 3-24, *supra* note 51, at 1-9 & 7-6. These brief references to Afghanistan do not describe the elements that make the Afghan conflict unique.

82. US Ambassador William B. Wood, Remarks at Media Roundtable, Kabul, Afghanistan (Dec. 30, 2008), http://kabul.usembassy.gov/amb_speech_3012.html.

83. Based on conversations with Bernard Fall and material in his writings. *See* BERNARD B. FALL, STREET WITHOUT JOY: INDOCHINA AT WAR, 1946–54 (1961); BERNARD B. FALL, VIET-NAM WITNESS 1953–1966, at 9 (1966) (which alludes to these issues). *See also* Dorothy Fall, *Preface to* BERNARD B. FALL, LAST REFLECTIONS ON A WAR 9–10 (1967) (his widow's remarkable writing).

84. Astri Suhrke, *Reconstruction as Modernisation: The 'Post-Conflict' Project in Afghanistan*, 28 THIRD WORLD QUARTERLY 1301 (2007), *available at* http://www.cmi.no/publications/file/?2742=reconstruction-as-modernisation.

85. Information from three UNHCR sources: UN REFUGEE AGENCY, STATISTICAL YEARBOOK 2006: TRENDS IN DISPLACEMENT, PROTECTION AND SOLUTIONS 36 (2007); UN REFUGEE AGENCY, 2007 GLOBAL TRENDS: REFUGEES, ASYLUM-SEEKERS, RETURNEES, INTERNALLY DISPLACED AND STATELESS PERSONS 8–9 (2008); and the UNHCR Statistical Online Population Database, http://www.unhcr.org/statistics/45c063a82.html. On November 3, 2008 UNHCR announced that so far in 2008 more than 276,000 refugees had returned to Afghanistan under its voluntary repatriation program. Press Conference, Ewen MacLeod, Acting UNHCR Representative in Afghanistan (Nov. 3, 2008), http://www.unama-afg.org/news/_pc/_english/2008/08nov03.html.

86. Adam B. Ellick, *Afghan Refugees Return Home, but Find Only a Life of Desperation*, NEW YORK TIMES, Dec. 2, 2008, at A17. Figure for IDPs from AFGHANISTAN INDEPENDENT HUMAN RIGHTS COMMISSION, ECONOMIC AND SOCIAL RIGHTS REPORT IN AFGHANISTAN – III 49 (2008), *available at* http://www.aihrc.org.af/2008_Dec/Ecn_soc/Eng_Eco_Soc_rep.pdf. *See also* Internal Displacement Monitoring Centre, http://www.internal-displacement.org (last visited Jan. 2009).

87. *See, e.g.*, Peter Beaumont, *Afghanistan: Fear, disillusion and despair: notes from a divided land as peace slips away*, OBSERVER (London), June 8, 2008, at 34–35.

88. The Secretary-General, *Report of the Secretary-General on the Situation in Afghanistan and Its Implications for International Peace and Security*, ¶ 2, U.N. Doc. A/63/372, S/2008/617 (Sept. 23, 2008).

89. *Id.*, ¶¶ 16, 18.

90. Ann Scott Tyson, *Commander in Afghanistan Wants More Troops*, WASHINGTON POST, Oct. 2, 2008, at A19. McKiernan described Afghanistan as "a far more complex environment than I ever found in Iraq."

91. *See, e.g.*, New NIE – Afghanistan in "Downward Spiral" (Oct. 9, 2008), http://www nsnetwork .org/node/1017 (reporting on the draft National Intelligence Estimate on Afghanistan).

92. Figures for casualties of coalition forces in Afghanistan from http://icasualties.org/oef/ (last visited Jan. 11, 2009).

93. Rory Stewart, *How to Save Afghanistan*, TIME, July 17, 2008, at 30.

94. For evidence that Taliban fighters in Afghanistan have learned from the mistakes of the period of Taliban rule up to 2001, see Ghaith Abdul-Ahad, *When I Started I Had Six Fighters. Now I Have 500*, GUARDIAN (London), Dec. 15, 2008, at 1, 4–5 (reporting from a Taliban-held area).

95. Robert Birsel, Pakistan Parliament Seen United against Militancy, Oct. 23, 2008, http://lite.alertnet.org/thenews/newsdesk/ISL355611.htm (Reuters report from Islamabad).

96. Thomas H. Johnson & M. Chris Mason, *All Counterinsurgency Is Local*, ATLANTIC, Oct. 2008, at 16–17, *available at* http://www.theatlantic.com/doc/200810/afghan.

97. John A. Nagl & Nathaniel C. Fick, *Counterinsurgency Field Manual: Afghanistan Edition*, FOREIGN POLICY, Jan.–Feb. 2009, at 42, *available at* http://www.foreignpolicy.com/story/cms .php?story_id=4587&page=3.

II

Terrorism and Afghanistan

Yoram Dinstein*

I. Terrorism as an Armed Attack

A. The "War on Terrorism"

The expression "war on terrorism" is merely a figure of speech or a metaphor: it is not different in principle from the parallel phrases "war on drugs" and "war on poverty." The reason is that the expression "war" is not used in either context as a legal term of art. This is easily grasped by anyone who knows international law. But the trouble with a catchy phrase is that it is apt to catch its users in a net: in time, they (especially if they are laypersons and not international legal experts) tend to believe that the figure of speech which they have coined actually reflects reality.

Metaphors aside, there are two types of war pursuant to international law: inter-State (international armed conflicts) and intra-State ("civil wars" or non-international armed conflicts). In an international armed conflict, two or more belligerent States are locked in combat with each other. Large numbers of States are currently engaged in the global "war on terrorism." Yet, the strife qualifies as war in the international legal sense only when hostilities are raging against an enemy State that has joined hands with the terrorists. As we shall see, this is true only in the case of Afghanistan.[1]

---

* Professor Emeritus, Tel Aviv University, Israel.

A "civil war" is an armed conflict between the central government of a State and a group (or groups) of domestic insurgents, or (absent a central government) between various factions vying for power in the State. Whether an internal disturbance crosses the threshold of a non-international armed conflict is a matter of gravity of scale and intensity. The United States, which has gone through the throes of a genuine "civil war" in its history, should know one when it sees it. In any event, the notion that the cross-border, worldwide "war on terrorism" is a non-international armed conflict—a notion that seems to have met with favor in the US Supreme Court, in the *Hamdan* case of 2006[2]—is manifestly incongruous.

B. Internal Terrorism

In any analysis of the struggle against terrorism, the point of departure must be a bifurcation between terrorism that is purely internal in character and that which is launched from a foreign country and perhaps warrants action in or against that foreign country. It is often forgotten that, until September 11, 2001, some of the most nefarious acts of terrorism were actually local in character. The mega-bombing in Oklahoma City as well as the lethal activities of terrorists in Europe (such as Irish Republican Army terrorists in the United Kingdom, Basque terrorists in Spain, the "Red Brigades" in Italy and the Baader-Meinhof gang in Germany) and in Asia (e.g., the Tamil "Tigers" in Sri Lanka, Moslem separatists in the Philippines and sarin gas–wielding terrorists in the Tokyo subway) were all products of domestic terrorism. Even when the atrocity of 9/11 occurred, it is symptomatic that for a while nobody knew for sure whether it was an external or an internal attack. Thus, when the NATO Council on September 12 decided for the first time ever to invoke Article 5 of the 1949 North Atlantic Treaty—whereby an armed attack against one or more of the allies in Europe or North America "shall be considered an attack against them all"[3]—this was qualified by a caveat that it be determined that the attack was directed from abroad against the United States.[4] Such a factual determination was made only subsequently, on the basis of additional information gathered.[5]

The answer to internal terrorism lies in law enforcement. In other words, domestic law enforcement agencies are expected to cope with the crime by searching for the terrorists (if they are not killed or captured in the act and are in hiding), arresting them, collating the necessary evidence, issuing an indictment, holding a trial (based, of course, on due process of law), securing a conviction, seeking a punishment that fits the crime and ensuring that the court's sentence is in fact carried out (so that a convicted terrorist is not pardoned or otherwise released from jail before the prescribed time). The law enforcement agencies—the police (in all its incarnations, embracing an agency like the FBI in the United States) and the judiciary—may act on the national (or federal) or local (including state, city or rural) level.

Even when terrorism is a matter of domestic law enforcement there may be a dire need of foreign cooperation. This may be the case either because some material witness or evidence is located abroad, or—if a terrorist manages to flee to a foreign country—because extradition (based on a treaty in force) or some other (less formal) means of rendition is required in order to bring the fugitive to justice. Success in the extradition of a terrorist may be contingent on the requested country not considering his/her act as "political" in character. Stripping terrorism of a political mantle is the thrust of the 1977 European Convention on the Suppression of Terrorism[6] and the bilateral 1985 US-UK Supplementary Extradition Treaty,[7] which has blazed the trail for a whole series of similar bilateral treaties concluded by the United States in later years.

International cooperation is also required in a concerted effort to stop or at least impede the financing of terrorism. This is the subject of the 1999 International Convention for the Suppression of the Financing of Terrorism.[8] More significantly, it is also the fulcrum of Security Council Resolution 1373 (2001),[9] an unprecedented landmark decision, whereby all UN member States (whether or not parties to the Convention) are obligated to suppress the financing of terrorism,[10] under the supervision of a special body (the Counter-Terrorism Committee) that monitors implementation.

C. Armed Attacks by Non-State Actors

The crux of the issue is whether an act of terrorism, launched from abroad by non-State actors, can be subsumed under the heading of an armed attack in the sense of Article 51 of the Charter of the United Nations (namely, as a trigger to the target State's exercising counterforce in self-defense). When a terrorist act originates outside the borders of the target State, a foreign State must somehow be implicated. The reason is that it is indispensable for the terrorists to have a base of operations as a springboard for their attack. Needless to say, such a base is not likely to be situated on the high seas, in outer space or in an unclaimed and uninhabited part of Antarctica.

Article 51 of the Charter opens with the following words: "Nothing in the present Charter shall impair the inherent right of individual or collective self-defence if an armed attack occurs against a Member of the United Nations." As can be seen, Article 51 talks about an armed attack occurring against a State (a member of the United Nations), but it does not say that the attack must be launched by another State. This is particularly notable given the comparable phraseology of Article 2(4) of the Charter, which mandates that all members (*i.e.*, States) shall refrain from the use of force in international relations.[11] It follows that, under Article 51, an armed attack need not be launched *by* a foreign State; it can also be launched by non-State actors *from* a foreign State. I have always (even prior to 9/11) pursued this line of thought,[12] but many other commentators were not convinced in the past.[13] These scholarly disagreements should now be regarded as moot, inasmuch as—since 9/11—the general practice of States has become crystal clear.

The international response to 9/11 was unequivocal. Preeminently, both in Resolution 1368 (2001)[14]—adopted a day after 9/11—and in the aforementioned Resolution 1373 (2001),[15] the Security Council recognized and reaffirmed in this context "the inherent right of individual or collective self-defence in accordance with the Charter." The NATO stand has already been referenced.[16] It may be added that in the September 2001 meeting of the Ministers of Foreign Affairs, acting as an Organ of Consultation, in application of the 1947 Inter-American Treaty of Reciprocal Assistance, it was resolved that "these terrorist attacks against the United States of America are attacks against all American States."[17] This must be understood in light of Article 3 of the Rio Treaty, which refers specifically to an armed attack and to the right of self-defense pursuant to Article 51.[18]

It is true that, in the 2004 advisory opinion on *Legal Consequences of the Construction of a Wall in the Occupied Palestinian Territory*, the International Court of Justice (ICJ) enunciated: "Article 51 of the Charter thus recognizes the existence of an inherent right of self-defence in the case of armed attack by one State against another State."[19] However, as correctly observed by Judge Higgins in her separate opinion: "There is, with respect, nothing in the text of Article 51 that *thus* stipulates that self-defence is available only when an armed attack is made by a State."[20] Similar criticism was expressed in the separate opinion of Judge Kooijmans[21] and in the declaration of Judge Buergenthal.[22] Indeed, the court itself noted without demur Security Council Resolutions 1368 and 1373, drawing a distinction between the situation contemplated by these texts (cross-border terrorism) and occupied territories.[23]

II. Action against Terrorists within a Foreign Territory

When terrorists perpetrate an armed attack against one State from within the territory of another State, there are three alternative scenarios of counteraction by the target State.

A. Action by Consent of the Foreign State

The first possibility is that the foreign State completely dissociates itself from the terrorists, who operate within its territory against its will. However, lacking the military wherewithal to eliminate the terrorist bases by itself, the local State invites the target State to send in its forces to accomplish (or assist in accomplishing) that mission. In such circumstances, the armed forces of the target State will deploy and operate against the terrorists on foreign soil with the consent of the government in charge. There is no doubt about the legality of such action, as long as the target State's expeditionary force carries out its mandate within the terms of the consent as granted. Article 20 of the 2001 Draft Articles on Responsibility of States for Internationally Wrongful Acts, as formulated by the International Law Commission (ILC), sets forth clearly: "Valid consent by a State to the commission of a given act by another State precludes the wrongfulness of that act in relation to the former State to the extent that the act remains within the limits of that consent."[24]

B. Action against the Foreign State

The second scenario is the antithesis of the first. The terrorists may act with the full approval and even instigation of the foreign State itself, which uses them as an irregular or paramilitary extension of its armed forces. In that case, the armed attack is deemed to have been launched by the foreign State itself. In the *Nicaragua* case of 1986, the ICJ pronounced that "it may be considered to be agreed that an armed attack must be understood as including not merely action by regular armed forces across an international border," but also the dispatch of armed bands or "irregulars" into the territory of another State.[25] "The sending by or on behalf of a State of armed bands, groups, irregulars or mercenaries, which carry out acts of armed force against another State" is specifically branded as an act of aggression in Article 3(g) of the General Assembly's consensus Definition of Aggression adopted in 1974.[26] In the *Nicaragua* judgment, the ICJ took paragraph (g) of Article 3 "to reflect customary international law."[27] In the post-*Nicaragua* period, the ICJ has come back to rely on Article 3(g) in its opinion in the 2005 Congo/Uganda *Armed Activities* case.[28] Interestingly, thus far, Article 3(g) is the only clause of the Definition of Aggression expressly held by the ICJ to be declaratory of customary international law.

The linkage between terrorists and a foreign State may be entangled and not easy to unravel. The cardinal question is whether the terrorists act as the de facto organs of that State. In the *Nicaragua* judgment, it was categorically proclaimed that, when the "degree of dependence on the one side and control on the other" warrant it, the hostile acts of paramilitaries can be classified as acts of organs of the foreign State.[29] Yet, the ICJ held that it is not enough to have merely "general control" by the foreign State. What has to be proved is "effective control"—in the sense of close operational control—over the activities of the terrorists.[30]

The ICJ's insistence on "effective control" by the foreign State over the local paramilitaries can hardly be gainsaid. However, the proposition that "general control" does not amount to "effective control"—and that a close operational control is always required—is not universally accepted. Indeed, in 1999, the Appeals Chamber of the International Criminal Tribunal for the former Yugoslavia (ICTY), in the *Tadic* case, sharply assailed the *Nicaragua* prerequisite of close operational control—as an absolute condition of "effective control"—maintaining that this is inconsonant with both logic and law.[31] The ICTY Appeals Chamber pronounced that "overall control" would suffice and there is no need for close operational control in every case.[32] The doctrine of overall control has been consistently upheld in successive ICTY judgments (both at the trial and the appeal levels) following the *Tadic* case.[33]

Article 8 of the ILC 2001 Draft Articles on Responsibility of States reads: "The conduct of a person or group of persons shall be considered an act of a State under international law if the person or group of persons is in fact acting on the instructions of, or under the direction or control of, that State in carrying out the conduct."[34] From the commentary one can draw the conclusion that the ILC endorsed the *Nicaragua* test of "effective control," although it conceded that the degree of control may "vary according to the factual circumstances of each case."[35]

The ICJ returned to the topic in the *Genocide* case of 2007, where the previous (*Nicaragua*) position was upheld and the *Tadic* criticism rejected.[36] Nevertheless, the ICJ set forth that the "overall control" test of the ICTY may be "applicable and suitable" when "employed to determine whether or not an armed conflict is international" (which was the issue in Tadic), but it cannot be presented "as equally applicable under the law of State responsibility for the purpose of determining . . . when a State is responsible for acts committed by paramilitary units, armed forces which are not among its official organs."[37] The ICJ added that

> the degree and nature of a State's involvement in an armed conflict on another State's territory which is required for the conflict to be characterized as international, can very well, and without logical inconsistency, differ from the degree and nature of involvement required to give rise to that State's responsibility for a specific act committed in the course of the conflict.[38]

It is doubtful whether the last word has been said on this theme.

C. "Extra-Territorial Law Enforcement"

There is a third scenario, intermediate between the two situations discussed so far. While the foreign State is not backing the terrorists (who cannot be regarded as its de facto organs, under either the *Nicaragua* test or even the *Tadic* test), it withholds consent from the target State to the dispatch of troops with a view to the eradication of the terrorists. The question is whether the target State is at an impasse—unable to act against the terrorists (absent consent) and having no ground to act against the foreign State (absent complicity with the terrorists)—or there is some other avenue open for action in conformity with international law.

As a rule, under international law, as per the 1949 ICJ judgment in the *Corfu Channel* case, every State is under an obligation "not to allow knowingly its territory to be used for acts contrary to the rights of other States."[39] Accordingly, a State must not allow knowingly its territory to be used for terrorist attacks against another State. The premise, of course, is that the local State is capable of rooting out the terrorists who are targeting another State. If the local State is incapable of doing that (for military or other reasons), the target State—invoking the right of self-defense—is entitled to respond to the terrorist armed attack. In other words, the target State is allowed to respond to the armed attack mounted from within the territory of the local State by doing what the local State should have done in the first place but failed to do. The emphasis is on the fact that, in these circumstances, the target State can employ force against the terrorists (in self-defense) within the territory of the local State, even without the consent of the government in charge. I call this exceptional state of affairs "extra-territorial law enforcement,"[40] but the nomenclature is not of major import: it is the normative substance that counts. The *fons et origo* of the norm in question is a famous dictum formulated by US Secretary of State Daniel Webster in resolving the *Caroline* incident of 1837.[41]

A paradigmatic illustration of the application in practice of "extra-territorial law enforcement" is the recent expedition of Turkish troops into northern Iraq, with a view to the elimination of Kurdish terrorists operating from that area against Turkey. Nobody is suggesting that the Iraqi government in Baghdad—or even the authority in control of the Kurdish enclave of northern Iraq—is in complicity with the terrorists, who belong to a renegade group. Nevertheless, since the terrorists are using Iraqi territory as their base of anti-Turkish operations, and the rather fragile government of Iraq is incapable of coming to grips with the problem at this time, Turkey has the right to do what the Iraqi government should have done but failed to do. There is no armed conflict between Turkey and Iraq. What we do have is "extra-territorial law enforcement" by Turkey in Iraq.

I am glad to note that in the ICJ 2005 decision in the *Armed Activities on the Territory of the Congo* case (Congo/Uganda), although the majority judgment glossed over the issue, two judges in their separate opinions—Judge Kooijmans and Judge Simma—cited my position on the subject.[42] In doing so, Judge Kooijmans said: "It would be unreasonable to deny the attacked State the right to self-defence merely because there is no attacker State, and the Charter does not so require."[43] And Judge Simma concurred.[44]

As for the majority position, all that I can say is that—in the past quarter of a century—the ICJ addressed the issue of self-defense four times, starting with the 1986 *Nicaragua* case[45] and going through the *Oil Platforms* case of 2003,[46] the *Wall* advisory opinion of 2004[47] and the 2005 *Armed Activities* case.[48] Self-defense was also mentioned on a fifth occasion (the *Nuclear Weapons* advisory opinion of 1996[49]). Is it merely a coincidence of bad luck that in all these separate proceedings the ICJ made serious blunders in the interpretation of the law of self-defense? In the *Nicaragua* judgment there were a number of flagrant flaws, e.g., as regards the distinction between more and less grave forms of use of force, the differentiation between an armed attack and mere frontier incidents, the non-mention of immediacy as a condition of self-defense, the denial of the right of a third State to act in collective self-defense on the basis of its own assessment of the situation and the ramifications of failure to report to the Security Council.[50] In the *Oil Platforms* case, apart from repeating uncritically earlier rulings, the court added some dubious new dicta about the need for an armed attack to be aimed specifically at a target State (as if indiscriminate but deliberate mine-laying in international shipping lanes is not enough).[51] In the *Wall* advisory opinion, we have the untenable brief statement on the need for an armed attack to be mounted by one State against another State.[52] In the *Armed Activities* case, the court ignored the issue of "extra-territorial law enforcement."[53] And in the *Nuclear Weapons* advisory opinion, the mention of self-defense comes in the most awkward fashion, in a notorious *dispositif* in which the court wrongly meshed the *jus in bello* with the *jus ad bellum*.[54]

The paradox is that, in 1986, scholars who critiqued the *Nicaragua* judgment (like me) thought that the ICJ plummeted to a nadir. But the *Nicaragua* judgment at least gave commentators an opportunity to chew on some juicy morsels of prime beef. A quarter of a century later, with decisions that are much more lean—to the point of being cryptic and even mystifying—we tend to think of the *Nicaragua* judgment, in retrospect, as the acme of the ICJ contribution on the subject.

III. The War in Afghanistan

A. Armed Attack and Self-Defense

Initially, Taliban-led Afghanistan was not directly involved in the armed attack unleashed by al Qaeda against the United States on 9/11. The Taliban regime in Kabul became tainted due to its subsequent behavior. In its judgment of 1980 in the *Tehran* case, the ICJ held that if the authorities of one State are required under international law to take appropriate acts in order to protect the interests of another State, and—while they have the means at their disposal to do so—completely fail to comply with their obligations, the inactive State bears international responsibility toward the other State.[55] By offering a haven to al Qaeda, in disregard of its obligations under international law—and disdaining binding Security Council resolutions adopted even before 9/11[56]—the Taliban regime assumed responsibility for the armed attack against the United States and opened the way to the exercise of forcible US response in self-defense.

Once the Taliban's brazen refusal to take the required steps against al Qaeda following 9/11 became evident, the United States issued an ultimatum, imperatively demanding that the al Qaeda bases be closed down and that its leaders be handed over.[57] When the Taliban ignored the ultimatum, the United States (with several allies) went to war on October 7, 2001. At that juncture, the Taliban regime—despite its failure to gain wide recognition—constituted the de facto government of Afghanistan because it was in actual control of more than 90 percent of the country.[58] A non-international armed conflict had independently flared up in Afghanistan long beforehand. This conflict was waged between the Taliban regime, on the one hand, and the Northern Alliance, on the other. Once the inter-State war (the United States and its allies versus Taliban-led Afghanistan and its al Qaeda ally) broke out, it was prosecuted simultaneously with the intra-State war (the Taliban versus the Northern Alliance) that went on until the fall of Kabul. The two wars (inter-State and intra-State), although connected, must be analyzed separately.

B. International and Non-International Armed Conflicts

Contrary to conventional opinion, I believe that the inter-State war in Afghanistan that started on October 7, 2001 continues unabated to this very day, despite the transformation in the status of the Taliban (who no longer form the de facto government of Afghanistan). When American and allied troops are fighting the Taliban (and their al Qaeda ally) on Afghan or adjacent (Pakistani) soil, this is a direct sequel to the hostilities that led to the ouster of the Taliban from the seat of power in Kabul. Both segments (past and present) of the hostilities are consecutive scenes in the same drama unfolding in Afghanistan. The inter-State war will not be over until it is over. And it will only be over once the Taliban are crushed.

We still have in Afghanistan—side by side with the inter-State war (the United States et al. versus the Taliban)—an intra-State war (the Taliban versus the Karzai government in Kabul). Except that, in terms of the intra-State war, the shoe is now on the other foot: the Karzai government is installed as the *de jure* government of Afghanistan, whereas the Taliban—originally the central government (if only de facto)—are the insurgents. For the credentials of the Karzai government, it is advisable to go back to Security Council Resolution 1386, adopted on December 20,

2001, which—acting under Chapter VII (i.e., in a binding manner)—(i) endorsed the Bonn Agreement, concluded earlier that month between various Afghan political factions, and (ii) gave its approval to the deployment of the International Security Assistance Force (ISAF) in consultation with the Afghan Interim Authority established by the Bonn Agreement.[59]

As long as the international armed conflict goes on in Afghanistan, the *jus in bello* in all its manifestations is applicable to the hostilities there. The singular feature of the inter-State war in Afghanistan is that it is conducted on Afghan soil with the consent of the Karzai government. This means that, at any point in time, the Karzai government (or, in the future, a successor Afghan government) may withdraw that consent and pull the rug out from under the feet of the United States and ISAF. The latter are fully conscious of the need to avert such an unwelcome development. If the United States (as heard at the conference) is applying in the field unusual constraints relating to collateral damage—compared to the general strictures imposed by the *jus in bello*—this is not an indication that the *jus in bello* is undergoing a metamorphosis. It simply shows that the United States is responsive to the concerns of the Afghan government, in whose territory the combat takes place. The government of Afghanistan is fully entitled to insist on the fighting against the Taliban (and al Qaeda) being conducted with minimal civilian casualties from among its citizenry.

Due to the special circumstances of the hostilities in Afghanistan—primarily, the intimate relationship characterizing the alliance between the Taliban and al Qaeda—US and allied combat operations against both (as long as they are conducted in and around Afghanistan, including in particular the lawless tribal lands of Pakistan), are clearly fused in a single inter-State armed conflict.

The differences from the vantage point of the *jus in bello* between the parallel international and non-international armed conflicts in progress in Afghanistan should not be exaggerated. Despite the profound disparity between the two types of armed conflicts from the angle of the *jus ad bellum*, there is a growing tendency to apply much of the *jus in bello* to both categories equally.[60] Apart from issues of semantics (exemplified by inappropriate usage of terms such as "belligerent parties" or even "combatants"), there are only three components of the *jus in bello* in international armed conflicts that—intrinsically—defy application in non-international armed conflicts. These are the entitlement to the status of prisoners of war, the law of neutrality and belligerent occupation.

Even in the last three respects, there may be some analogies or similarities. The rule of non-intervention on behalf of the insurgents by foreign States takes the place of the norms of neutrality. Detention of captured personnel in accordance with minimal requirements of human rights comes in lieu of the treatment of prisoners of war. But there is no avoiding the fact that—in the absence of recognition of belligerency—captured insurgents can be indicted and convicted for treason. In countries maintaining capital punishment, upon conviction defendants may be sentenced to death. In other jurisdictions, they may languish in jail for life.

Recognition of belligerency, issued by the central government in the face of large-scale rebellion (as happened in the American Civil War), denotes that a non-international armed conflict will be governed by exactly the same rules that are applicable in international armed conflicts.[61] It is occasionally alleged that recognition of belligerency has fallen into disuse and that, even if it were to occur, only "common Article 3 and not the [Geneva] Conventions as a whole will apply to the conflict."[62] However, Common Article 3 applies anyhow to any "armed conflict not of an international character occurring in the territory of one of the High Contracting Parties,"[63] and this is not contingent on any recognition of belligerency. Should such recognition be granted, it would undoubtedly signal that the conflict has to be treated as if it were an international armed conflict and that all the norms of the *jus in bello* (including those relating to the status of prisoners of war, neutrality and belligerent occupation) will become applicable.

The dilemma of recognition of belligerency is for the present Afghan government to wrestle with and resolve as it deems fit. This does not affect the United States, since—in any event, as stated[64]—its armed conflict with the Taliban (as well as their al Qaeda ally) has been and remains international in nature. When Taliban personnel are captured by American troops, they have to be treated in accordance with the *jus in bello*. These captives cannot be considered guilty of treason against the United States (although the Afghan perspective may be different). In principle, they would have been entitled to prisoner of war status. However, they may be denied that privilege due to the fact that they are unlawful combatants. I addressed in some detail the meaning and consequences of unlawful combatancy at the 2002 Newport conference on terrorism (shortly after the outbreak of the Afghan War),[65] and I do not wish to repeat here what I said there. I also do not wish to pursue the domestic-constitutional issue of the rights of unlawful combatants to *habeas corpus* within the American judicial system. I merely want to emphasize that Taliban internees held on Afghan soil in a US detention center (e.g., in Bagram) can be kept there only as long as the Afghan government allows the United States to maintain such facilities within Afghan territory.

C. Action against Terrorists outside Afghanistan

Action taken by the United States and numerous other countries against al Qaeda and diverse groups of terrorists in far-flung parts of the globe, beyond the borders of Afghanistan and its environs, do not constitute an integral part of the inter-State war raging in Afghanistan.

Al Qaeda has been active in many parts of the world, ranging from Mesopotamia to Somalia, from Hamburg to Madrid. In each instance, a discrete dissection of the legal situation is required. However, there is one common denominator, namely, the absence of any built-in nexus between the measures taken for the suppression of the local version of terrorism and the inter-State war in Afghanistan. In Iraq there is another war which, hopefully, is drawing to a close. In other places, the measures taken against the terrorists must be seen in the context of law enforcement,[66] leavened with sporadic injections of judicial and extrajudicial assistance and cooperation by foreign States.

IV. A New Paradigm?

I cannot resist adding a few words in response to a plea heard at the conference to come up with a new paradigm regarding the law of armed conflict. This is by no means the first occasion on which I have heard such an exhortation, and I am no longer surprised when it comes up. While all international wars are alike, no two wars are truly similar to each other. After every major war, it is perhaps natural that the international law of armed conflict is weighed and found wanting given the novel challenges specific to that war. When the challenges accumulate, it is frequently suggested that a new paradigm is required. After World War I, the international community was reeling from the carnage of trench warfare and the widespread use of gas warfare. After World War II, humankind was shocked by the horrors of the extermination camps and compelled to take into account the impact of atomic weapons. In both world wars it was contended that they were a category unto their own, since they constituted "Total Wars." Then came the Vietnam War, which was supposedly unique for it consisted of guerrilla warfare. Kosovo was singular, because it was exclusively an air campaign. And so it goes: each war leaves its special footprints in the sand of time.

As a matter of fact—and of law—I do not see any pressing need for a new paradigm. Of course, there are always new technologies, new weapons and new methods of warfare. What these novelties convey is that the law of warfare lags behind the actualities of the battleground. Yet, this is not an exclusive hallmark of the *jus in bello*. To a greater or lesser degree, all law lags behind reality. Lawyers always have to trail events, trying to close gaps that have opened up between real life and the law.

There is a great deal of reluctance on the part of most States today to close any such gap—when it becomes readily apparent—by means of a formal treaty, if only because most treaty making today in the field of the *jus in bello* is controversial. However, recent restatements[67] show that informal texts (if properly structured and formulated) may prove almost as effective as formal treaties.

In any event, the very difficulty of adopting new treaties only reinvigorates the argument against the practicability of setting up a new paradigm. With an old paradigm—even if it is far from perfect—at least we know where we stand. The need to have a *quid pro quo* of rights and obligations has been accentuated at this conference, and indisputably this is the rub. The advantage of the present law of both international and non-international armed conflicts is that, by and large, we stand on *terra firma*: we know who is bound or entitled to do what. Admittedly, the nuclei of legal clarity are surrounded by patinas of ambiguity and controversy. But this is the inevitable state of all legal norms. The trouble with an innovative legal paradigm is that it unbalances the existing paradigms. It is prone to plunge the entire legal system into a chaotic transition period in which legal certainty is eroded. Where the *jus in bello* is concerned, what is liable to happen is that the notorious "fog of war" will become the "fog of the law of war."

Notes

1. *See infra* p. 51.
2. Hamdan v. Rumsfeld, 126 S. Ct. 2749, 2796 (2006), *reprinted in* 45 INTERNATIONAL LEGAL MATERIALS 1130, 1153–54 (2006) (opinion of Stevens, J.).
3. North Atlantic Treaty, Apr. 4, 1949, 63 Stat. 2241, 34 U.N.T.S. 243.
4. Press Release, North Atlantic Treaty Organization (NATO), Statement by the North Atlantic Council (Sept. 12, 2001), *reprinted in* 40 INTERNATIONAL LEGAL MATERIALS 1267 (2001).
5. *See* Jack M. Beard, *America's New War on Terror: The Case for Self-Defense under International Law*, 25 HARVARD JOURNAL OF LAW AND PUBLIC POLICY 559, 568 (2001–2002).
6. European Convention on the Suppression of Terrorism, Jan. 27, 1977, 1137 U.N.T.S. 93.
7. Supplementary Extradition Treaty, June 25, 1985, US-UK, *reprinted in* S. EXEC. REP. No. 17, 99th Cong., 2d Sess. 15 (1986).
8. International Convention for the Suppression of the Financing of Terrorism, 1999, 39 INTERNATIONAL LEGAL MATERIALS 270 (2000).
9. S.C. Res. 1373, U.N. Doc. S/RES/1373 (Sept. 28, 2001).
10. Eric Rosand, *Security Council Resolution 1373, the Counter-Terrorism Committee, and the Fight against Terrorism*, 97 AMERICAN JOURNAL OF INTERNATIONAL LAW 333, 334 (2003).
11. *Id.* at 332.
12. *See* YORAM DINSTEIN, WAR, AGGRESSION AND SELF-DEFENCE 213–15 (3d ed. 2001).
13. *See, e.g.*, Oscar Schachter, *The Lawful Use of Force by a State against Terrorists in Another Country*, 19 ISRAEL YEARBOOK ON HUMAN RIGHTS 209, 216 (1989).
14. S.C. Res. 1368, U.N. Doc. S/RES/1368 (Sept. 12, 2001).
15. S.C. Res. 1373, *supra* note 9.
16. *See supra* p. 44.
17. Organization of American States (OAS), Resolution: Terrorist Threat to the Americas (Sept. 21, 2001), *reprinted in* 40 INTERNATIONAL LEGAL MATERIALS 1273 (2001).

18. Inter-American Treaty of Reciprocal Assistance, Sept. 2, 1947, 62 Stat. 1681, 121 U.N.T.S. 77, 95.

19. Legal Consequences of the Construction of a Wall in the Occupied Palestinian Territory, Advisory Opinion, 2004 I.C.J. 136 (July 9), 43 INTERNATIONAL LEGAL MATERIALS 1009, 1050 (2004).

20. *Id.* at 1063.

21. *Id.* at 1072.

22. *Id.* at 1079.

23. *Id.* at 1050.

24. Draft Articles on Responsibility of States for Internationally Wrongful Acts, Report of the International Law Commission on the Work of its Fifty-third Session, U.N. GAOR, 56th Sess., Supp. No. 10, at 48, U.N. Doc. A/56/10 (2001), *available at* http://untreaty.un.org/ilc/texts/instruments/english/draft%20articles/9_6_2001.pdf [hereinafter Report of the International Law Commission].

25. Military and Paramilitary Activities (Nicar. v. U.S.), 1986 I.C.J. 14, 103 (June 27) [hereinafter Nicaragua].

26. G.A. Res. 3314 (XXIX), U.N. Doc. A/9631 (Dec. 14, 1974).

27. Nicaragua, *supra* note 25, at 103.

28. Armed Activities on the Territory of the Congo (Dem. Rep. Congo v. Uganda), 2005 I.C.J. 19 (Dec. 19), 45 INTERNATIONAL LEGAL MATERIALS 271, 306 (2006) [hereinafter Armed Activities].

29. Nicaragua, *supra* note 25, at 62.

30. *Id.* at 64–65.

31. Prosecutor v. Tadic, Case No. IT-94-1, Judgment (July 15, 1999), *reprinted in* 38 INTERNATIONAL LEGAL MATERIALS 1518, 1540–45 (1999).

32. *Id.* at 1545.

33. For details, see EVE LA HAYE, WAR CRIMES IN INTERNAL ARMED CONFLICTS 19 (2008).

34. Report of the International Law Commission, *supra* note 24, at 45.

35. *Id.* at 106–08.

36. Application of the Convention on the Prevention and Punishment of the Crime of Genocide (Bosn. & Herz. v. Serb. & Mont.) (Feb. 27, 2007), 46 INTERNATIONAL LEGAL MATERIALS 185, 287–88 (2007).

37. *Id.* at 288.

38. *Id.*

39. Corfu Channel (U.K. v. Alb.), 1949 I.C.J. 4, 22 (Apr. 9).

40. *See* YORAM DINSTEIN, WAR, AGGRESSION AND SELF-DEFENCE 244–51 (4th ed. 2005).

41. Letter from Mr. Webster to Mr. Fox (Apr. 24, 1841), 29 BRITISH AND FOREIGN STATE PAPERS 1129, 1138 (1840–41).

42. Armed Activities, *supra* note 28, at 358, 370, 377.

43. *Id.* at 358.

44. *Id.* at 370.

45. Military and Paramilitary Activities, *supra* note 25.

46. Oil Platforms (Iran v. U.S.), 2003 I.C.J. 161 (Nov. 6).

47. *Wall* case, *supra* note 19.

48. *Supra* note 28.

49. Legality of the Threat or Use of Nuclear Weapons, Advisory Opinion, 1996 I.C.J. 226 (July 8).

50. *See* DINSTEIN, *supra* note 40, at 193–95, 208–09, 216–18, 268–70.

51. *See id.* at 209.
52. *See supra* p. 46.
53. *See supra* pp. 49–50.
54. *See* DINSTEIN, *supra* note 40, at 161–62.
55. United States Diplomatic and Consular Staff in Tehran (U.S. v. Iran), 1980 I.C.J. 3, 32–34, 44 (May 24).
56. *See especially* S.C. Res. 1267, U.N. Doc. S/RES/1267 (Oct. 15, 1999).
57. President George W. Bush, Address to a Joint Session of Congress and the American People (Sept. 20, 2001), *available at* http://news.findlaw.com/hdocs/docs/gwbush/bushspeech20010920.html.
58. *See* Christopher Greenwood, *International Law and the 'War against Terrorism,'* 78 INTERNATIONAL AFFAIRS 301, 312–13 (2002).
59. S.C. Res. 1386, U.N. Doc. S/RES/1386 (Dec. 20, 2001).
60. *See San Remo Manual on the Law of Non-International Armed Conflict* (Michael Schmitt, Charles Garraway & Yoram Dinstein eds.), 36 ISRAEL YEARBOOK ON HUMAN RIGHTS 333 (2006).
61. See LA HAYE, *supra* note 33, at 14.
62. LINDSAY MOIR, THE LAW OF INTERNAL ARMED CONFLICT 41–42 (2002).
63. Convention for the Amelioration of the Condition of Wounded and Sick in Armed Forces in the Field, Aug. 12, 1949, 6 U.S.T. 3114, 75 U.N.T.S. 31 [Geneva Convention I]; Convention for the Amelioration of the Condition of Wounded, Sick and Shipwrecked Members of Armed Forces at Sea, Aug. 12, 1949, 6 U.S.T. 3217, 75 U.N.T.S. 85 [Geneva Convention II]; Convention Relative to the Treatment of Prisoners of War, Aug. 12, 1949, 6 U.S.T. 3316, 75 U.N.T.S. 135 [Geneva Convention III]; and Convention Relative to the Protection of Civilian Persons in Time of War, Aug. 12, 1949, 6 U.S.T. 3516, 75 U.N.T.S. 287 [Geneva Convention IV]; all *reprinted in* DOCUMENTS ON THE LAWS OF WAR (Adam Roberts & Richard Guelff eds., 3d ed. 2000) at 197, 198; 222, 223; 244, 245; and 301, 302; respectively.
64. *See supra* p. 51.
65. Yoram Dinstein, *Unlawful Combatancy, in* INTERNATIONAL LAW AND THE WAR ON TERROR 151 (Fred Borch & Paul Wilson eds., 2003) (Vol. 79, US Naval War College International Law Studies).
66. *See supra* pp. 44–45.
67. The archetypical model is the *San Remo Manual on International Law Applicable to Armed Conflicts at Sea* (L. Doswald-Beck ed., 1995), *reprinted in* DOCUMENTS ON THE LAWS OF WAR, *supra* note 63, at 573.

III

International Legal Dynamics and the Design of Feasible Missions: The Case of Afghanistan

W. Michael Reisman*

I

Military missions must be accomplished within a political and legal environment. One often indistinct and elusive but nonetheless important dimension of that environment is comprised of the expectations held by politically relevant actors (some of whom may be far from the actual arena of operation) as to what constitutes or will constitute, in the circumstances, lawful action. Expectations which approve or disapprove a projected mission can be significant factors in determining the quantum of resources required for mission accomplishment or, indeed, in determining whether there will be a successful outcome. In some cases, these considerations may require adjustments in the mission's design or even its abandonment.

It is a truism that it is wise to consult your lawyers *before* you act, for they are expert in identifying authoritative expectations. In international law, such consultations do not always help, because expectations with respect to the lawfulness of current or projected actions in the contemporary international political system are not necessarily congruent with the stuff with which lawyers ordinarily work, the formal

* Myres S. McDougal Professor of International Law, Yale Law School.

texts of international law. For one thing, the jurymen of international law, the cast of politically relevant actors, have expanded from a small group of nation-State elites who produce those texts.[1] It now includes a wide range of non-governmental actors, whose activities and influence are amplified by easy mobility and a global network of communications. For another, the texts of international law which are produced by nation-State elites vary in their effectiveness and the extent to which they reflect or shape expectations; some of the texts, for all their legalistic language, are only aspirational, while others are "law-in-the-books" rather than "law-in-action." Still other texts are part of the "myth system" of international law rather than its "operational code."[2]

So although formal international legal texts can always be "crunched" in various logical exercises to reach desired "legal" conclusions, those conclusions may prove to be quite different from the expectations of lawfulness held by the actors whose expectations of lawfulness are actually relevant for a particular mission. Thus, the international legal specialist who plays a role in the design of a military mission and who appreciates the relevance of the legal variable as a factor in the mission faces two daunting professional challenges: first, in identifying who are the politically relevant actors in a specific context, and, second, in articulating and analyzing their operative expectations of lawfulness. The key values held by important actors in the institutions of, and outside of, contemporary international law can be critical factors in the cost or feasibility of a particular military mission. In designing or appraising missions against Al Qaeda, the collective views of the UN Security Council, other governments and non-State entities form parts of the legal environment. Al Qaeda's agents and franchisees often operate across political boundaries and may be independent of or have only shadowy relations with governments or components within them, instead deriving their support from non-governmental entities.

I believe that Afghanistan, the central focus of this workshop, provides an instructive example of my thesis. Because my purpose is to illustrate the relations between mission design and international legal and institutional environments, a cursory review of the modern history of Afghanistan is necessary.

II

Afghanistan is divided along geographic and ethnic lines which do not configure its political borders. Neither its demographic divisions nor its topography dispose it to effective and centralized control or internal stability. Still Afghanistan enjoyed an extended period of stability in the reign of Zahir Shah, from 1933 to 1973. That tranquility ended when Zahir Shah was overthrown by his brother-in-law, who terminated the monarchy and established a republic with, *mirabile dictu*, himself as its President. Five years later, he, in turn, was overthrown by the People's Democratic Party (PDPA). Nur Mohammed Taraki became President, the republic was rechristened the Democratic Republic of Afghanistan, and closer relations with the Soviet Union were forged. The Soviet Army intervened in Afghanistan in 1979 and installed Babrak Karmal in place of Taraki. In terms of internal order, it was more on the order of a personnel change than a regime change, as the political vocabulary and secular governmental program of Karmal's predecessor continued.

President Carter had begun to fund and train Mujahidin through Pakistan's secret service, the ISI (Inter-Services Intelligence agency), to fight the Soviet-backed government.[3] The policy was continued under President Reagan. The Mujahidin were a largely religiously-inspired resistance. That said and without minimizing the mobilizing potential of Jihadist Islam, any attempt to depict or comprehend the war or Afghan politics, in general, in exclusively ideological, nationalistic or religious terms without accounting for ethnicity, language, region, the pursuit of wealth or simple bare-knuckle power politics would oversimplify a dauntingly complex political system.

The Soviet occupation and the Afghan resistance cost the lives of over one million and perhaps as many as two million Afghans; five million Afghans fled the country.[4] When the Soviet Union withdrew from Afghanistan in 1989, the subtraction of the Soviet military from the Afghan equation did not produce the immediate collapse of the Najibullah government. The civil war continued. The factor that ultimately brought Dr. Najibullah down appears to have been the Soviet decision in 1992 to terminate the sale of petroleum to the Afghan government.

Even after the collapse of the Najibullah government, the civil war ground on, with great loss of life; by then, much of the fighting was being carried on between various Mujahidin factions, who broke along language, ethnic and regional lines. Beginning in 1994, however, the Taliban, a fundamentalist Sunni and Pashtun force based in the south, emerged as a more unified element. The Taliban seized Kandahar and then Kabul in 1996 and by 2000 had captured 95 percent of the country.[5] The erstwhile Democratic Republic of Afghanistan morphed into the Islamic Emirate of Afghanistan.

Only Pakistan, Saudi Arabia and the United Arab Emirates recognized and maintained diplomatic relations with the Taliban as the legitimate government. Nor did the Taliban fare better at the United Nations, where the General Assembly's Credentials Committee refused to seat the Taliban government, despite its effective control of the country. Instead, the Committee accredited the representatives of the ousted government of President Rabbani, the leader of a Mujahidin faction, who was not renowned for his commitment to secular values or to democracy.

There is no indication that withholding certification at the United Nations had any effect on the Taliban's control of the country. Indeed, it was only in its 2001 report *after* "Operation Enduring Freedom"[6] that the Credentials Committee took note of the agreement on provisional arrangements in Afghanistan which the Security Council had endorsed in Resolution 1383 (2001).[7] Thereupon, the Karzai government assumed the Afghan seat in the Assembly. Notwithstanding the potential fallacy of *post hoc ergo propter hoc*, it seems safe to say that the General Assembly's Credentials Committee was endorsing the regime change of Operation Enduring Freedom.

Osama bin Laden's organization, Al Qaeda, had been born and nurtured on the borders of Afghanistan during the war against the Soviet Union's occupation, but Al Qaeda is not a political movement indigenous to Afghanistan. It was formed as part of a pan-Islamic military effort to force the Soviet Union from Afghanistan. After the victory in 1989, Al Qaeda expanded its goals and relocated to Sudan. When Al Qaeda was subsequently expelled from Sudan as a result of US pressure, Osama bin Laden returned to and began to operate from Afghanistan. He established training and operational bases and his operatives conducted significant actions, *inter alia*, against US installations and forces. Those latter actions appear to have been the principal reason why the Security Council began taking a renewed interest in Afghanistan. Let me turn to them briefly.

In the late 1990s, though the General Assembly had refused to seat the Taliban government, Secretary-General Kofi Annan appointed a special representative who was charged with negotiating a political settlement. Meanwhile, the Security Council sought to influence events in the Afghan civil war through various resolutions which reflected different concerns. Security Council Resolution 1214 of December 8, 1998, for example, condemned many of the human rights violations of the Taliban but the Council registered, in particular, that it was "*deeply disturbed* by the continuing use of Afghan territory, especially areas controlled by the Taliban, for the sheltering and training of terrorists and the planning of terrorist acts."[8] In paragraph 13, the Council demanded "that the Taliban stop providing sanctuary and training for international terrorists and their organizations and that all Afghan factions cooperate with efforts to bring indicted terrorists to justice."[9]

A year later, the Council's focus on Al Qaeda became sharper. It

> *deplor*[*ed*] the fact that the Taliban continues to provide safe haven to Usama bin Laden and to allow him and others associated with him to operate a network of terrorist training camps from Taliban-controlled territory and to use Afghanistan as a base from which to sponsor international terrorist operations.[10]

In 2000, the Council reiterated this language and continued by "*strongly condemning* the continuing use of [Afghan territory, especially areas controlled by the Taliban], for the sheltering and training of terrorists and planning of terrorist acts . . . ."[11] The Council determined that the failure of the Taliban to respond to the demands of paragraph 13 of Resolution 1214 and of paragraph 2 of Resolution 1267 of the preceding years now "constitute[d] a threat to international peace and security."[12] Acting explicitly under Chapter VII, the Council essentially reiterated the demands which had been made in previous resolutions but also demanded that Osama bin Laden be surrendered either to the United States or to a country that would turn him over to the United States. The Council also imposed an array of economic sanctions in Resolution 1267, denying air access and freezing funds. A year later, in Resolution 1333 (2000), the Council reiterated its demands. At the end of July 2001, the Council ordered the Secretary-General to establish a monitoring mechanism for the implementation of all of the previous resolutions.[13]

Together, these were the measures which the Security Council members were able to agree to take during that period. None prescribed by its sequence of resolutions appears to have had any effect on the Taliban's control and administration of Afghanistan or Al Qaeda's freedom of operation within or beyond its borders. Quite the contrary: only forty-three days after the last Council resolution, on September 11, 2001, Al Qaeda mounted its infamous attacks on civilian and military targets in the United States.

The reaction of the Security Council on September 12, in Resolution 1368, is interesting and worth quoting in full, for its content tells much about the decision dynamics of the Council, its capacity to respond effectively to such crises and, as a result, its potential to facilitate—and restrain—such military actions as the United States concluded were necessary for its defense. Resolution 1368 provides, in its entirety:

> *The Security Council,*
>
> *Reaffirming* the principles and purposes of the Charter of the United Nations,
>
> *Determined* to combat by all means threats to international peace and security caused by terrorist acts,
>
> *Recognizing* the inherent right of individual or collective self-defence in accordance with the Charter,
>
> 1. *Unequivocally condemns* in the strongest terms the horrifying terrorist attacks which took place on 11 September 2001 in New York, Washington, D.C. and

Pennsylvania and *regards* such acts, like any act of international terrorism, as a threat to international peace and security;

2. *Expresses* its deepest sympathy and condolences to the victims and their families and to the people and Government of the United States of America;

3. *Calls* on all States to work together urgently to bring to justice the perpetrators, organizers and sponsors of these terrorist attacks and *stresses* that those responsible for aiding, supporting or harbouring the perpetrators, organizers and sponsors of these acts will be held accountable;

4. *Calls also* on the international community to redouble their efforts to prevent and suppress terrorist acts including by increased cooperation and full implementation of the relevant international anti-terrorist conventions and Security Council resolutions, in particular resolution 1269 (1999) of 19 October 1999;

5. *Expresses* its readiness to take all necessary steps to respond to the terrorist attacks of 11 September 2001, and to combat all forms of terrorism, in accordance with its responsibilities under the Charter of the United Nations;

6. *Decides* to remain seized of the matter.[14]

You will note that the "combat by all means" statement in the second considerandum and the "all necessary steps" in operative paragraph 5 refer to the Security Council and not to any single State; the single State (obviously the United States) is confined, in the third considerandum, to self-defense. But by characterizing, in the second considerandum, terrorist acts as "threats to the peace" rather than "breaches of the peace" or "acts of aggression," the Resolution kept them from falling under Article 51's right of self-defense.[15] As for the operative paragraphs of the Resolution, the third calls for judicial action, while the fourth refers back to the various economic and other means adopted in the previous resolutions. But their lack of success was painfully manifest in the ruins still smoking thirty blocks south of Turtle Bay.

On September 28, 2001, the Council revisited the problem in a somewhat calmer environment. Resolution 1373 (2001), again explicitly invoking Chapter VII, reiterated the pre-9/11 judicial and economic strategies but added that "all States shall . . . [t]ake the necessary steps to prevent the commission of terrorist acts, including by provision of early warning to other States by exchange of information."[16] By November 14, 2001, Resolution 1378 could refer, if vaguely, to the Council's support for "international efforts to root out terrorism,"[17] but it immediately made clear, as it had earlier, that this was to be done "in keeping with the Charter of the United Nations."[18] Those words are code for the Charter's prohibition on the unilateral use of force in any circumstance other than exigent self-defense. But in this Resolution, the Council inserted, in its fourth considerandum, an explicit condemnation of

> the Taliban for allowing Afghanistan to be used as a base for the export of terrorism by the Al-Qaida network and other terrorist groups and for providing safe haven to Usama Bin Laden, Al-Qaida and others associated with them, and in this context [the Council] *support[s] the efforts of the Afghan people to replace the Taliban regime.*[19]

This was the first mention of an internationally approved regime change in Afghanistan. But it would be more than overstatement to call this an *a priori* authorization or an authentic UN initiative. By the time the Resolution was agreed, US Special Forces were operating in northern Afghanistan, actively assisting the Northern Alliance, and they would shortly be in Kabul, where a new government would be installed. As for the Taliban, they would withdraw from the capital and the other cities. They were no longer the de facto government of Afghanistan but were far from defeated as a military force. So the Council was, in effect, only confirming and acceding to (or participating in the fruits of) a *fait accompli* which had been accomplished without prior Council authorization.

In Bonn, Germany, a conference, which brought together non-Taliban Afghans as well as warlords who had formerly been associated with the Taliban, was convened, essentially by the United States. On December 5, 2001, the conference concluded the Bonn Agreement, which put in place provisional arrangements for a new government.[20] A day later, on December 6, the Security Council, in Resolution 1383, endorsed the Bonn Agreement, called on all Afghan groups to support the new government and declared itself willing to support it.[21] On December 20, the Council, again, accommodated to rather than shaped events. In Resolution 1386, in effect, it acceded to the Bonn Agreement's request that the Council authorize an International Security Assistance Force, or ISAF; took note of the United Kingdom's willingness to organize and lead ISAF; and authorized ISAF to perform its mission in Afghanistan for 6 months.[22] It has been renewed semiannually.

III

The purpose of this rapid diachronic review of the actions of the Security Council from the late 1990s to the end of 2001 is not to belittle the contribution of the Security Council or of the United Nations to the US response to the attacks by Al Qaeda. Quite the contrary! I believe that the United Nations is an important institution for its member States and, when correctly and sensibly used, can be a critical instrument of policy for the United States.[23] But the United Nations is not a supple, multipurpose instrument that can be readily applied to all situations. The principles which the organization and its members value most—in particular national sovereignty, non-intervention and territorial inviolability—and the idiosyncratic structure of the Security Council limit the organization's effectiveness in managing and resolving conflicts with aggressive global Salafism. Or, to formulate it in more positive terms, the way a military mission is designed may influence whether the Security Council or, more generally, the United Nations will facilitate or constrain it; it may also determine the degree of that facilitation or obstruction.

Prior to 2001, the efforts of national actors who were threatened or were victims of Al Qaeda to work through the United Nations were of little effect. The problem was not that the Council's operational arsenal of diplomatic, economic and ideological instruments—which, after 1999, were even taken under its plenary Chapter VII powers—are inherently ineffective. In some cases, that arsenal has proved effective, either as a primary or adjunct instrument for securing desired political changes. The anti-Taliban sanctions *might* have worked over a very long period of time, especially if some of the governments contiguous to Afghanistan had fully complied with and implemented them.

The difficulty lies in that time factor. In the twenty-first century, governments, which anticipate the types of military attacks which actors such as Al Qaeda mount, cannot always afford the luxury of waiting for a very long period of time for Security Council measures to "bite." The most noxious of Salafist threats can operate on a much more accelerated timetable and with a greater potential for destructive impacts.

This is, of course, what happened in the case of the Taliban and Al Qaeda. While the Council fine-tuned and patiently waited for its sanctions program to work, the Taliban government, amply supplied with illicit drug money and benefitting from either indifferent or actively sympathetic elements in some contiguous States, reinforced its control over Afghanistan; as for Al Qaeda, comfortably cocooned in the Taliban system, it pursued its various programs, culminating in its operations on September 11.

The United Nations is neither world politics nor even its major arena; it is a part of it, a composite actor within it. Assessing the effectiveness of the UN role in this phase of the Afghan war requires us to look at the broader arena of world politics. There, what appears to have happened is that after September 11, the United States and those States cooperating with it, perforce, took their own initiatives. As for the other less supportive but indispensable members of the Security Council, they accommodated themselves to what appeared to be a *fait accompli*, trading a measure of Council authorization, by retrospective stamp of approval, in return for the validation of the Council's own relevance and a nominal share of supervision. In the coin of international political exchange, that validation was worth something.

But the Security Council does not control the market on international authority. It may not always deny lawfulness to an action by withholding its seal of approval; conversely, its seal of approval does not always assure that the actions in question will be viewed as lawful by other politically relevant actors in the international system. This is especially the case when the action involves invading and displacing an existing government—hence the tepid Security Council efforts prior to 9/11 and the limited authorizations (usually coming after the fact) thereafter.

IV

One of the lessons for the future here appears to be that where urgent action against entities like Al Qaeda and its affiliates is required, the responses which may, at the most, be expected from the Security Council—the sorts of measures ordered by the Council in the period before September 11, 2001—will not be sufficient in real time; in these circumstances, unilateral and, by its nature, anticipatory military action may be the only meaningful option. A confirmation of the international lawfulness of such unilateral action by the Security Council and the more diffuse international processes of decision should be sought. But it is not likely that such action, even when plausibly construed as a form of self-defense, will be authorized in advance by the Security Council or confirmed or celebrated after the fact. It appears clear, however, that the more ambitious, extensive and anti-governmental the unilateral action undertaken, the less likely will be Security Council or more general international support.

For the reasons set out in Part I, one of the considerations in the design of a unilateral action which a State feels it must take in either reactive or anticipatory self-defense[24] should be to increase its international legal acceptability and to decrease perceptions of the violation of international law. I would suggest that this be done even if addressing these considerations means ultimately that a less efficacious military action will be mounted. Missions which are designed so that they can be accomplished rather quickly, if unlikely to win formal and informal international approval, are more likely to provoke less, and less intense, international disapproval. By contrast, longer-term missions and, as I will explain in a moment, occupations will require international authorization and even if it does not erode, it may not be an assurance of success.

Thus, consideration of the legal perspective I sketched a moment ago leads to a general recommendation: where possible, narrow the focus of the mission to the neutralization or degrading of the specific terrorist threat and not to a regime change of the government which has served as the cocoon of the terrorist group.

V

Unquestionably, transforming a regime which is providing refuge and a launching pad for a terrorist group into a regime "enduring freedom" is a more comprehensive solution than simply degrading the capacities of the terrorist group itself. But aside from the formidable operational difficulties in effecting a regime change, which I have considered elsewhere,[25] planners cannot ignore the intense international political and legal resistance which a military mission of this sort will provoke.

A military action against a specific noxious target within a State is a finite and temporally limited military rather than an extended counterinsurgency action; with all the controversy it may excite (and I will consider it in a moment), it will still be less internationally controversial than an action to change the entire regime within the State.[26] If the jurisprudence of the International Court is taken as a reliable indicator of what formal international law currently considers lawful self-defense, the law of self-defense appears to be limited to response to and neutralization of an *immediate* threat,[27] and even within those narrow parameters, international appraisals of lawfulness may vary.

Contrast, first, the international legal reactions to the Clinton administration's periodic aerial actions against Iraqi air defenses with the objective confined to "degrading" them; and, second, the international legal reaction to the US invasion of Iraq in order to change the regime. Or, to take a rather wild hypothetical scenario, imagine the contrasting reactions to (I) unilateral ISAF or Afghan military action against Al Qaeda or Taliban bases in the frontier areas of Pakistan and (ii) unilateral ISAF military action to change the Pakistani government because elements high in the government or in ISI were believed to be supporting the Taliban or Al Qaeda.

Afghanistan, I concede, presented a difficult case for military planners. In 2001, Al Qaeda was effectively integrated in the Ministry of Defense of the Taliban government. But I am not sure that even this overlap required conflating the Taliban and Al Qaeda or that it precluded the United States from characterizing the adversary as Al Qaeda, reserving for the Taliban government the status of an obstacle to reaching the actual enemy, rather than an indistinguishable part of the enemy. Once Al Qaeda and the Taliban were conflated, however, and Afghan regime change became an ineluctable part of the mission, it was no longer possible to concentrate efforts on Al Qaeda; significant resources had to be diverted from the neutralization of Al Qaeda to creating and shoring up another Afghan government and then protecting it from the Taliban. In that difficult process, military planners had to accommodate the full range of civil, political and human rights standards of contemporary international law, which are demanded with ever greater intensity through myriad governmental and non-governmental channels. Regime change is perforce a comprehensive program and brings into the decision process a wide range of non-governmental organizations, insisting on objectives which, however worthy, detract from the prosecution of a more-focused military action; the more-focused military action would bring in far fewer and more-focused demands.

VI

A brief digression: Perhaps a more realistic understanding of how daunting a mission regime change is, especially in Afghanistan, might have led to a more focused military objective. A contemporary essay on Afghanistan appearing in the most popular online encyclopedia states:

> Once in power, the [People's Democratic Party of Afghanistan] moved to permit freedom of religion and carried out an ambitious land reform, waiving farmers' debts countrywide. They also made a number of statements on women's rights and introduced women to political life. A prominent example was Anahita Ratebzad . . . who wrote the famous *New Kabul Times* editorial which declared: "Privileges which women, by right, must have are equal education, job security, health services, and free time to rear a healthy generation for building the future of the country . . . educating and enlightening women is now the subject of close government attention."[28]

Incidentally, the online essay is not referring to the contemporary government of President Hamid Karzai but rather to the regime of Taraki, Amin, and Najibullah of the PDPA, the government which was then supported by the Soviet Union.

The essay from which I was reading a moment ago continues:

> The majority of people in the cities including Kabul either welcomed or were ambivalent to these policies. However, the secular nature of the government made it unpopular with religiously conservative Afghans in the villages and the countryside, who favoured traditionalist "Islamic" restrictions on women's rights and in daily life.[29]

Does it sound familiar?

Ronald Neumann, formerly the US ambassador in Kabul, reported that a recent poll taken in Afghanistan indicated that 55 percent of the respondents wanted the United States to remain.[30] That figure would be decisive in a normal civil situation where votes decide. But in a belligerent situation, it is raw power that decides. And if I may hazard an opinion, I would suggest that the balance of power in Afghanistan tilts in favor of the conservatizing and not the secularizing elements. Moreover, the relevant elite of the critical contiguous State most disposed to invest resources in trying to influence developments in Afghanistan also appears to tilt toward the conservatizing elements.

The would-be regime changer should bear in mind that, once such a mission is embarked upon, if military efforts prove indeterminative at acceptable cost levels, political solutions will have to be sought. In Afghanistan, a political solution would have to involve the Taliban. At a minimum, it would have to include some role in power for the Taliban in return for their commitment neither to host nor to support Al Qaeda. This would enable the United States to concentrate its resources on Al Qaeda. That could have been the principal objective of the mission from the outset.

I have taxed you with this little excursus from the subject of international law and expectations of international lawfulness to emphasize that outside powers, if they are willing to invest very great resources, could be influential factors in the Afghan political and military drama. But even then, the outside efforts could well prove indecisive, for Afghanistan is locked in its own historical process.

VII

I have recommended, from the standpoint of international law, the virtues of a "less-is-more" approach to the design of missions when international expectations of lawfulness appear unlikely to support a broader mission. But, in contexts like Afghanistan, is "less" really likely to be more acceptable to the institutions and jurymen of international law? In the context of Afghanistan and its unique geographical factors, can unilateral actions directed against entities like Al Qaeda, nesting in another State, ever be lawful? And how can one prospectively assess what expectations of lawfulness for such an action are likely to be?

I do not intend to crunch the familiar texts on the use of force but rather to focus on operative expectations of lawfulness. I quote from an online report of the Associated Press (AP) on June 15, 2008.

> Afghan President Hamid Karzai threatened Sunday to send Afghan troops across the border to fight militants in Pakistan, a forceful warning to insurgents and the Pakistani

> government that his country is fed up with cross-border attacks. Karzai said that in recent fighting in Helmand province, where hundreds of US marines have been battling insurgents for the last two months, most of the fighters came from Pakistan.[31]

Of interest to us is that President Karzai indicated that he believes that what he is threatening is a form of lawful self-defense. He stated that "Afghanistan has the right to self-defense, and because militants cross over from Pakistan 'to come and kill Afghan and kill coalition troops, it exactly gives us the right to do the same.'"[32] Karzai even threatened targeted assassinations in Pakistan of Baitullah Mehsud, the Taliban leader in Pakistan, and Mullah Omar, the leader of the Taliban in Afghanistan and de facto head of State from 1996 to 2001.

Pakistan's reaction to Karzai's statement (and, of course, it is not the first time he has made it) was interesting. Yousuf Raza Gilani, the Pakistani Prime Minister, insisted, according to the Associated Press, on Pakistani sovereignty over its territory but said that "the Afghan-Pakistan border is too long to prevent people from crossing, 'even if Pakistan puts its entire army along the border.'"[33] In the meanwhile, he said that Pakistan "is seeking peace deals with militants in its borders, including with Mehsud."[34] This particular Pakistani initiative has concerned the United States, the AP continues, "[b]ut Pakistan insists it's not negotiating with 'terrorists,' but rather with militants willing to lay down their arms."[35] Baitullah Mehsud seems to see it differently. He, the AP adds, "has said he would continue to send fighters to battle US forces in Afghanistan even as he seeks peace with Pakistan."[36]

And, one might add, he is not puffing. The Associated Press reports that "U.S. and NATO commanders say that following the peace agreements [between the Taliban and Pakistan] this spring, attacks have risen in the eastern area of Afghanistan along the border."[37]

NATO's ISAF declined to comment on Karzai's statement but unnamed US officials were willing to weigh in, on condition of anonymity. I quote their statement:

> U.S. officials have increased their warnings in recent weeks that the Afghan conflict will drag on for years unless militant safe havens in Pakistan are taken out. Military officials say counterinsurgency campaigns are extremely difficult to win when militants have safe areas where they can train, recruit and stockpile supplies.[38]

No one who has studied counterinsurgency will contest that. The Malayan Emergency, which is the poster child of successful counterinsurgencies—and which, incidentally, required three hundred thousand British and other troops and twelve years—was conducted in a peninsula whose surrounding waters could be controlled by the British; there was no contiguous friendly or passive State to provide safe redoubts like those available to the Taliban and Al Qaeda in the border areas of Pakistan. Moreover, the insurgents were racially distinct from the majority population. And the British public supported the mission.

In August 2007, Senator Barack Obama said, in a speech delivered in Washington: "If we have actionable intelligence about high-value terrorist targets and President Musharraf won't act, we will."[39] The claim of a right of "hot pursuit," even in maritime confrontations, is controversial. In the *I'm Alone* arbitration,[40] the right of pursuit was treaty-based and, hence, applied only to US and UK flag vessels. Moreover, it applied only to pursuit within one hour's sailing time of territorial waters. So the tribunal's holding, which is not distinguished by its coherence, relates to treaty interpretation rather than a pronouncement of customary international law.

Even more controversial is the claim of a right of hot pursuit across terrestrial borders. In terms of theory, the UN Charter obviates terrestrial hot pursuit, for the only unilateral action available to a State is self-defense against an armed attack; once the adversary has fled the attacked State's territory, the right of self-defense would exhaust itself. In theory, further prosecuting action that had commenced as legitimate self-defense might itself degenerate into an armed attack.

International politics and the use of the military instrument as part of it have proved to be more complicated than the simple theory of the Charter. Instances of hot pursuit of an adversary which has entered your territory as well as anticipatory interdiction of an enemy force sheltering in the contiguous territory of another State have been occurring. While the State whose territory has been invaded has almost always (there are some exceptions) issued a protest, it is harder to conclude that the international legal system, as a whole, has unequivocally condemned each of these pursuits or generally condemned all such actions in all circumstances. To take examples only from this *annus mirabilis*, consider (I) the Turkish pursuit of the Kurdistan Workers' Party in northern Iraq, (ii) the Colombian pursuit of the Revolutionary Armed Forces of Colombia in northern Ecuador and (iii) President Karzai's threat to send Afghan troops into Pakistan in pursuit of Taliban there. What was the operative judgment as to international lawfulness in these cases? What sanction was applied, if transgression there was?

Consider the paradigmatic problem of which the war in Afghanistan is a prime example: irregular non-State forces shelter in an uncontrolled area of State A from which they regularly conduct lethal raids into State B and then withdraw to the safety of State A. According to the International Court, the actions of the irregular forces are not deemed to fulfill the "armed attack" requirement of Article 51 of the Charter. Consequently, even if the Court were to expand its conception of the scope of self-defense so that it was available against non-State entities, State B may not respond with military force. State B is confined to bringing the matter to the Security Council. Assume that State B does bring the matter to the Security Council for ten consecutive attacks and, in each instance, the Security Council issues a resolution, condemning the attacks and ordering State A to act to prevent them. The attacks continue.

At a certain point, State B *will* enter the areas of State A where the irregulars shelter and seek to kill or capture them. Will the international community, through its various decision processes, condemn and effectively sanction the action?

The international legal system can speak with great subtlety and nuance. In *Corfu Channel*,[41] the International Court of Justice condemned the United Kingdom for having entered Albanian waters without the Albanian government's consent. It held that this condemnation was itself sufficient sanction and allowed the evidence which had been improperly seized to be admitted. My estimation of the situation with respect to cross-border pursuit is that there will always be a formal condemnation because of national pride and concern for the erosion of the principle of territorial integrity but there will only be meaningful and sanction-related condemnations by the international decision processes in those cases in which the cross-border action is deemed to have been unnecessary, disproportionate or in violation of the differentiation principle.

It is, of course, by the application of these criteria that the law of war has traditionally assessed the lawfulness of actions in new situations. Whether the UN Security Council or the International Criminal Court will look at it that way remains to be seen. But even a condemnation of an internationally unauthorized military action in another State which does not affect that State's territory or political independence will be less severe than a condemnation for a temporally extended and vigorously resisted regime change.

Notes

1. W. Michael Reisman, *The Democratization of Contemporary International Law-Making Processes and the Differentiation of Their Application*, *in* DEVELOPMENTS OF INTERNATIONAL LAW IN TREATY MAKING 15 R. Wolfrum & V. Röben eds., 2005), *reprinted in* 2 TRANSNATIONAL DISPUTE MANAGEMENT 3 (2005).

2. *See* W. Michael Reisman, *On the Causes of Uncertainty and Volatility in International Law*, *in* THE SHIFTING ALLOCATION OF AUTHORITY IN INTERNATIONAL LAW: CONSIDERING SOVEREIGNTY, SUPREMACY AND SUBSIDIARITY: ESSAYS IN HONOUR OF PROFESSOR RUTH LAPIDOTH 33 (Tomer Broude & Yuval Shany eds., 2008).

3. *See* JOHN K. COOLEY, UNHOLY WARS: AFGHANISTAN, AMERICA, AND INTERNATIONAL TERRORISM (2000).

4. *Refugees from Afghanistan: The world's largest single refugee group*, AMNESTY INTERNATIONAL, http://www.amnesty.org/en/library/asset/ASA11/016/1999/en/dom-ASA110161999en.html.

5. Afghanistan—Taliban Era, http://www.globalsecurity.org/military/world/afghanistan/taliban.htm (last visited Oct. 15, 2008).

6. Operation Enduring Freedom is the title given to the joint US-Afghan counterterrorism operations in Afghanistan from October 7, 2001 until October 6, 2005. *See* BENJAMIN S. LAMBETH, AIR POWER AGAINST TERROR: AMERICA'S CONDUCT OF OPERATION ENDURING FREEDOM (2005).

7. S.C. Res. 1383, considerandum 5, U.N. Doc. S/RES/1383 (Dec. 6, 2001).

8. S.C. Res. 1214, considerandum 13, U.N. Doc. S/RES/1214 (Dec. 8, 1998).

9. *Id.*, para. 13.

10. S.C. Res. 1267, considerandum 6, U.N. Doc. S/RES/1267 (Oct. 15, 1999).

11. S.C. Res. 1333, consideranda 10 and 7, U.N. Doc. S/RES/1333 (Dec. 19, 2000).

12. *Id.*, considerandum 14.

13. S.C. Res. 1363, para. 4, U.N. Doc. S/RES/1363 (July 30, 2001).

14. S.C. Res. 1368, U.N. Doc. S/RES/1368 (Sept. 12, 2001).

15. U.N. Charter art. 51.

16. S.C. Res. 1373, para. 2, U.N. Doc. S/RES/1373 (Sept. 28, 2001).

17. S.C. Res. 1378, para. 1, U.N. Doc. S/RES/1378 (Nov. 14, 2001).

18. *Id.*, considerandum 2.

19. *Id.*, considerandum 4 (emphasis added).

20. Agreement on Provisional Arrangements in Afghanistan Pending the Re-establishment of Permanent Government Institutions, Dec. 5, 2001, *available at* http://www.un.org/News/dh/latest/afghan/afghan-agree.htm.

21. S.C. Res. 1383, *supra* note 7, paras. 1–3.

22. S.C. Res. 1386, considerandum 8 & para. 1, U.N. Doc. S/RES/1386 (Dec. 20, 2001).

23. *See* W. Michael Reisman, *The United States and International Institutions*, 41 SURVIVAL 62 (1999).

24. *See* W. Michael Reisman & Andrea Armstrong, *The Past and Future of the Claim of Pre-emptive Self-Defense*, 100 AMERICAN JOURNAL OF INTERNATIONAL LAW 525 (2006).

25. W. Michael Reisman, *Why Regime Change Is (Almost Always) a Bad Idea*, 98 AMERICAN JOURNAL OF INTERNATIONAL LAW 516 (2004), *also available at* 2004 PROCEEDINGS OF THE AMERICAN SOCIETY OF INTERNATIONAL LAW 290.

26. It may even be viewed as lawful, as I will explain below.

27. *See, e.g.*, Military and Paramilitary Activities (Nicar. v. U.S.), 1986 I.C.J. 14 (June 27).

28. Wikipedia, Afghanistan, http://en.wikipedia.org/wiki/Afghanistan (last visited Aug. 30, 2008).

29. *Id.*

30. ABC News/BBC World Service Poll, Afghanistan: Where Things Stand, Dec. 7, 2006, *available at* http://abcnews.go.com/images/politics/afghanistan_poll_061205.pdf.

31. Carlotta Gall, *Karzai Threatens to Send Soldiers to Pakistan*, NEW YORK TIMES, June 16, 2008, at A6.

32. *Id.*

33. *Afghan President: I'll Send Troops to Pakistan*, THE ASSOCIATED PRESS, June 15, 2008, *available at* http://www.foxnews.com/story/0,2933,367184,00.html.

34. *Id.*

35. *Id.*

36. *Id.*
37. *Id.*
38. *Id.*
39. Statement of Barack Obama, *available at* http://factcheck.barackobama.com/factcheck/2008/06/19/bin_laden_death_penalty.php.
40. I'm Alone Arbitration (U.S. v. U.K.), 3 R. Int'l Arb. Awards 1609 (1935).
41. Corfu Channel (U.K. v. Alb.), 1949 I.C.J. 17 (Sept. 30, 1947).

PART II

THE LEGAL BASIS FOR MILITARY OPERATIONS

IV

Afghanistan: Hard Choices and the Future of International Law

John F. Murphy*

As I began my work on this article, the news out of, and the commentary about, Afghanistan was grim. For example, a United Nations human rights team has reportedly found "convincing evidence" that ninety civilians, including sixty children, were killed in airstrikes on a village in western Afghanistan.[1] According to a *Time* magazine article:

> There has been a dramatic series of recent attacks by the Taliban: a mass assault on jail freed hundreds of prisoners, and a suicide bombing outside the Indian Embassy on July 7 killed 40 and injured over 100. Many of these assaults are planned and supported from safe havens across the border in the tribal areas of Pakistan. Western casualties are climbing; the last two months exceeded the monthly death toll in Iraq. On July 13, nine U.S. soldiers were killed when Taliban fighters swarmed over their base in the eastern province of Kunar—the worst attack in three years.[2]

In response to the Taliban attacks from the tribal areas of Pakistan, President George W. Bush has reportedly authorized attacks by US special operations forces against the Taliban in Pakistan.[3] This in turn has precipitated a strong protest from the newly elected Pakistani government of Asif Ali Zardari, including a promise by Pakistan's top army officer to defend the country's sovereignty "at all costs."[4]

---

* Professor of Law, Villanova University School of Law.

There are also recent claims that Afghanistan has become a "narco-State."[5] According to these claims, Hamid Karzai, the President of Afghanistan, and the Afghan government are deeply involved in

> protecting the opium trade—by shielding it from American-designed policies. While it is true that Karzai's Taliban enemies finance themselves from the drug trade, so do many of his supporters. At the same time, some of our NATO allies have resisted the anti-opium offensive, as has our own Defense Department, which tends to see counternarcotics as other people's business to be settled once the war-fighting is over. The trouble is that the fighting is unlikely to end as long as the Taliban can finance themselves through drugs—and as long as the Kabul government is dependent on opium to sustain its own hold on power.[6]

Even if one would not go so far as to agree with a recent statement by a European diplomat with substantial experience in Afghanistan that Afghanistan is "in its worst shape since 2001,"[7] it seems clear that the United States and its allies are currently facing serious challenges in Afghanistan. It is also clear that many of the challenges raised by developments in Afghanistan constitute major challenges to international law and international institutions. The thesis of this article is that these challenges will require the United States and other members of the world community to make hard choices that will significantly affect the future of international law.

I will begin with a discussion of the backdrop to the current crisis in Afghanistan, starting with the events that led to the invasion by US and allied forces in 2001. In this section, as well as in subsequent sections of this article, the focus is primarily, but by no means exclusively, on issues of the *jus ad bellum*, the law of resort to the use of armed force; the *jus in bello*, the law regulating the way the armed force is employed, i.e., the law of armed conflict; and international human rights. I will also explore some issues of governance, the roles of the United Nations and NATO, problems created by the use of the tribal areas in Pakistan by the Taliban and al Qaeda as a safe haven, and the impact on Afghanistan of the current unstable political situation in Pakistan.

The Backdrop

It may come as a surprise to some in light of the highly negative images of Afghanistan created by the reign of the Taliban that Afghanistan enjoyed substantial periods of stability and enlightened governance.[8] The period of stability began after King Amanullah Khan (1919–29) launched attacks on British forces in Afghanistan shortly after taking power and won complete independence from Britain, a reality established by the Treaty of Rawalpindi on August 8, 1919. Reportedly, Khan was considered a secular modernizer presiding over a government in which all ethnic minorities participated. He was succeeded by King Mohammad Nadir Shah (1929–33), and then by King Mohammad Zahir Shah. "Zahir Shah's reign (1933–73) is remembered fondly by many older Afghans for promulgating a constitution in 1964 that established a national legislature and promoting freedoms for women, including freeing them from covering their face and hair."[9] He made, however, what was possibly a fatal mistake when he entered into a significant political and purchase relationship with the Soviet Union.

In the 1970s, Afghanistan slid into instability when the diametrically opposed Communist Party and Islamic movements grew in strength. As he was receiving medical treatment in Italy, Zahir Shah was overthrown by his cousin, Mohammad Daoud, a military leader who established a dictatorship with strong State involvement in the economy. The Communist Party overthrew Daoud in 1978, led by Nur Mohammad Taraki, who was displaced a year later by Hafizullah Amin, leader of a rival faction. They tried to impose radical socialist change, in part by redistributing land and bringing more women into government, sparking rebellion by Islamic parties opposed to such moves. On December 27, 1979, the Soviet Union sent troops into Afghanistan to prevent a seizure of power by the Islamic militias, known as the *mujahedin* (Islamic fighters). During their invasion, the Soviets replaced Hafizullah Amin with an ally, Babrak Karmal.

The Soviet occupation forces failed in their attempts to pacify the country. A major reason for this failure was that the *mujahedin* benefitted from US weapons and assistance, provided by the US Central Intelligence Agency (CIA) in cooperation with Pakistan's Inter-Services Intelligence directorate (ISI). Especially useful in combat were portable shoulder-fired anti-aircraft systems called "Stingers," which proved highly effective against Soviet aircraft. Also useful to the *mujahedin* was a large network of natural and man-made tunnels and caves throughout Afghanistan, in which they hid and stored weaponry.

As the Soviet losses mounted, Soviet domestic opinion turned against the war. In 1986, after Mikhail Gorbachev came into power, the Soviets replaced Karmal with the director of Afghan intelligence, Najibullah Ahmedzai (known by his first name). On April 14, 1988, Gorbachev agreed to a UN-brokered accord (the Geneva Accords) requiring the Soviet Union to withdraw. The withdrawal was completed by February 15, 1989, leaving in place the weak Najibullah government. On September 13, 1991, the Russian and US governments agreed to a cutoff of military aid to the Afghan combatants. With Soviet backing withdrawn, Najibullah's position became untenable. His government fell, and the *mujahedin* regime came into power on April 18, 1992.

There were major differences among the *mujahedin* factions, however, and civil war ensued (1992–96). Four years of civil war led to increased support for the Taliban as a movement that could deliver Afghanistan from the factional infighting. The Taliban took control of Kabul on September 27, 1996.[10]

It didn't take long for the Taliban regime to lose international and domestic support as it imposed strict adherence to Islamic customs in areas it controlled and employed harsh punishments, including summary executions. The Taliban authorized its "Ministry for the Promotion of Virtue and the Suppression of Vice" to use physical punishments to enforce strict Islamic practices, including bans on television, Western music and dancing. It prohibited women from attending school or working outside the home except in health care, and it publicly executed some women for adultery. In March 2001, the Taliban committed the act that gained the most international condemnation: it blew up two large statues carved into hills above Bamiyan city that were widely recognized as works of art, as representations of idolatry.

The Taliban's hosting of al Qaeda's leaders increasingly concerned the Clinton administration. In April 1998, then–US Ambassador to the United Nations Bill Richardson visited Afghanistan and asked the Taliban to hand over bin Laden, but the Taliban refused to do so. After the August 7, 1998 al Qaeda bombings of US embassies in Kenya and Tanzania, the Clinton administration increased the pressure on the Taliban, imposing US sanctions and gaining adoption of UN sanctions as well. On August 20, 1998, the United States fired cruise missiles at alleged al Qaeda training camps in eastern Afghanistan but failed to hit bin Laden. According to reports, Clinton administration officials said "they did not try to oust the Taliban from power with US military force because domestic US support for those steps was then lacking and the Taliban's opponents were too weak and did not necessarily hold US values."[11]

For its part, the George W. Bush administration initially largely continued the Clinton administration's policy toward Afghanistan—applying economic and political pressure while retaining dialogue with the Taliban, and refraining from providing military assistance to the Northern Alliance, the primary opponents of the Taliban. Its major deviation from the Clinton administration's policy was to intensify talks with Pakistan in an effort to end its support of the Taliban.

Although it was fighting with some Iranian, Russian and Indian financial and military support, the Northern Alliance continued to lose ground to the Taliban after it lost Kabul in 1996. By the time of the September 11 attacks, the Taliban controlled at least 75 percent of the country. The Alliance suffered a major setback on September 9, 2001, two days before the September 11 attacks, when Ahmad Shah

Masud, the leader of the Northern Alliance and a highly respected military strategist, was assassinated by alleged al Qaeda suicide bombers posing as journalists.

The September 11 Attacks and Operation Enduring Freedom

After the September 11, 2001 attacks, the policy of the Bush administration toward Afghanistan changed dramatically: it decided to overthrow the Taliban by military force when it refused to surrender bin Laden to the United States. Prior to the United States taking military action against Afghanistan, the UN Security Council adopted two resolutions: Resolution 1368[12] and Resolution 1373.[13] In the preamble of Resolution 1368 the Security Council recognizes "the inherent right of individual or collective self-defense in accordance with the Charter" and in its first operative paragraph its determination that such acts (i.e., the terrorist attacks of September 11) are "a threat to international peace and security." In its fifth operative paragraph the Council "*expresses* its readiness to take all necessary steps to respond to the terrorist attacks of 11 September 2001 . . . ." Declaring the September 11 attacks as a threat to international peace and security brings them within the scope of Chapter VII of the UN Charter and acts as a possible predicate to a UN enforcement action. Expressing its willingness to "take all necessary steps to respond" to the terrorist attacks implies that the Council might in the future, if necessary, establish a peace enforcement force or authorize the use of force by member States.[14] Recognizing that the inherent right of individual or collective self-defense applies to the September 11 attacks appears at first blush to be mere surplusage, but has significance for two reasons. First, under Article 51 of the UN Charter, the right to individual or collective self-defense is only an interim right—"until the Security Council has taken measures necessary to maintain international peace and security." The express recognition of the right in this instance arguably implies that the Council has no intention to intervene in such a way as to suspend the right[15] and would, of course, face a certain veto by the United States should it attempt to do so. Second, there are those who argue that the right of individual or collective self-defense applies only to an "armed attack" by a State and not to armed attacks by non-State actors. To the contrary it has been argued that in Resolution 1368 the Security Council has implicitly recognized that the right of individual or collective self-defense applies equally to attacks by non-State actors and attacks by States.[16]

In the preamble of Resolution 1373, the Security Council reaffirms Resolution 1368 and "its unequivocal condemnation" of the 9/11 terrorist attacks, its determination that the attacks constituted a threat to international peace and security, the inherent right of individual and collective self-defense, and "the need to combat by all means, in accordance with the Charter of the United Nations, threats to international peace and security caused by terrorist acts." In the rest of this landmark Resolution, however, the Council shifted its focus away from the 9/11 attacks and Afghanistan to actions that States must take to "prevent and suppress the financing of terrorist acts," a subject outside the scope of this article.

Major combat in Afghanistan began on October 7, 2001. The campaign was given the name "Operation Enduring Freedom."[17] Even before President Bush's September 20, 2001 address to a joint session of Congress, in which he issued an ultimatum to the Taliban that it deliver to US authorities all the leaders of al Qaeda "who hide in your land" or "share in their fate,"[18] the United States had entered into extensive diplomatic negotiations with its allies, seeking their understanding of, and ideally cooperation for, a military response. A key breakthrough was with then-president General Pervez Musharraf of Pakistan. Although Pakistan's intelligence services had supported the Taliban in its rise to power and Islamic groups in Pakistan objected to cooperation with the United States, Musharraf promptly condemned the attacks and the Taliban for harboring bin Laden, and agreed to allow the United States and its allies to use Pakistani airspace and eventually airbases. The former Soviet republics of Uzbekistan, Kyrgyzstan, and Tajikistan, which faced internal threats from al Qaeda–linked Islamist movements, agreed to permit US forces to operate from bases in their territory in exchange for increased US aid and closer political and security ties. Although several European States offered to provide military support, the United States decided to rely primarily on its own forces and those of the Northern Alliance, with limited military assistance from British, Canadian and Australian troops.

Combat operations in Afghanistan initially consisted primarily of US airstrikes on Taliban and al Qaeda forces, aided by joint efforts between small numbers (approximately one thousand) of US special operations forces and the Northern Alliance and Pashtun anti-Taliban forces. At the height of the fighting in October through December 2001, some US ground units (about thirteen hundred Marines) moved into Afghanistan to pressure the Taliban around Kandahar, but there were few pitched battles between US and Taliban forces. Most of the ground combat was between the Taliban and its Afghan opponents.[19]

A key turning point in the conflict came when Taliban forces lost Mazar-e-Sharif on November 9, 2001. The Taliban regime unraveled rapidly thereafter. Northern Alliance forces entered Kabul, the capital of Afghanistan, on November 12, 2001, to "general jubilation."[20] The Taliban subsequently lost the south and east to pro-US Pashtun leaders, such as Hamid Karzai, the current president of Afghanistan. The end of the Taliban regime is generally dated as December 9, when the Taliban surrendered Kandahar, leaving it under tribal law administered by Pashtun leaders.[21]

Some of the remaining Taliban and al Qaeda troops retreated to tunnel complexes built to house *mujahedin* fighting the Soviets, such as at Tora Bora, near the Pakistani border. On December 16, supported by US precision bombing, local forces the Americans dubbed the "Eastern Alliance" captured Tora Bora. There was no follow-up, however, by the Eastern Alliance and insufficient US ground forces, to prevent hundreds of al Qaeda members, possibly including bin Laden, from escaping into the relatively lawless tribal regions of Pakistan. A later attack on an al Qaeda cave complex in February and March 2002 was more successful. This time, over one thousand US infantrymen led the assault, called Operation Anaconda, against regrouping al Qaeda in the Shah-i-kot valley, and succeeded in preventing most of the al Qaeda fighters from escaping.

Thereafter, remnants of al Qaeda mostly scattered to tribal areas of Pakistan and Afghanistan. Cooperative combat operations between the US and allied forces and some local warlords continued, but these were small in comparison with the scale of Operation Anaconda or the campaign at Tora Bora. On May 1, 2003, then–Secretary of Defense Rumsfeld announced an end to "major combat operations."[22]

Before turning to the post-conflict efforts toward stabilization and reconstruction, let us consider a few *jus ad bellum* and *jus in bello* issues that arose prior to or during the major combat operations in Afghanistan. We have already briefly considered the claim that the United States and its allies violated the *jus ad bellum* because Article 51 of the UN Charter does not permit the use of armed force in self-defense against an armed attack by non-State actors.[23] Yoram Dinstein has noted that, "[i]n the past, many commentators admittedly argued that the expression 'armed attack' in Article 51 does not apply to every armed attack, 'regardless of the source,' but only to an armed attack by another State."[24] Dinstein goes on to state, however, that given the response of the international community to 9/11, "all lingering doubts on this issue have been dispelled." The responses of the international community to the 9/11 events cited by Dinstein include Security Council Resolutions 1368 and 1373; the invocation of Article 5 of the NATO Treaty, which provides that an armed attack against one or more of the Allies in Europe or North America "shall be considered an attack against them all," by the Atlantic Council;[25] and a resolution by the Ministers of Foreign Affairs, acting as an Organ of Consultation, in application of the 1947 Inter-American Treaty of Reciprocal Assistance, stating that "these terrorist attacks against the United States of America are attacks against all American States."[26]

Assuming that the shocking nature of the attacks of 9/11, and the international community's response to them, dispels any doubts that they constituted an armed attack within the scope of Article 51, it does not necessarily follow that any use of armed force by terrorists constitutes such an "armed attack." This remains a debatable issue, and we shall return to it later in this article when we consider the legality of the US use of armed force against the Taliban and al Qaeda in Pakistan.[27]

The increased use of high-technology warfare in Afghanistan, especially the use of so-called "smart bombs," guided by Global Positioning System satellites, resulted in relatively low civilian casualties. Nonetheless, there were some mistakes made,[28] and the US military was criticized for some operations that resulted in civilian casualties.[29] As noted at the beginning of this article, the issue of allegedly excessive civilian casualties has become especially acute recently, and we will return to it later.

Another self-defense issue arising out of Operation Enduring Freedom is whether the right of self-defense encompasses "regime change" or the removal of the government in power, in this case the Taliban. In the case of the Persian Gulf conflict of 1991 against Iraq, there was no "march to Bagdad" to remove the Saddam Hussein regime. Rather, President George H.W. Bush made the political decision to stop the attack in Iraq well short of an invasion of Bagdad. It is debatable whether Security Council Resolution 678, which authorized member States to use armed force against Iraq if it failed to comply fully with its resolutions on or before January 15, 1991, could have been interpreted to allow the removal of the Saddam Hussein regime.[30]

With respect to Operation Enduring Freedom, some have questioned whether self-defense under Article 51 of the UN Charter permitted the removal of the Taliban from power.[31] Arguably, while it was permissible for Enduring Freedom to eliminate the military capacity of the Taliban and al Qaeda, in order to prevent a future attack by them, "[e]liminating the whole government structure created by the Taliban, as a war aim, was beyond necessary self-defense" and therefore a disproportionate use of force.[32]

Interestingly, US Secretary of State Colin Powell reportedly indicated that the United States would not seek to eliminate the Taliban entirely[33] and that Northern Alliance forces had promised US officials they would not enter Kabul.[34] Under these circumstances, the United States "may not be responsible for a disproportionate use of force."[35]

From this account, however, it appears that, although the United States may not have intended to eliminate the Taliban entirely, because it hoped to attract moderate Taliban to the US side, it did intend to replace the radical Taliban leaders and to ensure that the new government of Afghanistan would not follow the policies of these Taliban leaders. It is questionable, at best, whether this goal would be incompatible with the right of self-defense.

Post-War Stabilization and Reconstruction

Despite George W. Bush's sharp criticism of "nation building" during his 2000 election campaign, it was immediately apparent to the Bush administration that nation building was urgently required in Afghanistan. Moreover, despite the distrust of the United Nations by many in the administration, President Bush called on the United Nations to help rebuild a post-war Afghanistan. During the 1990s, after playing a major role in ending the Soviet occupation, the United Nations employed a succession of mediators in an effort to achieve a government selected by a traditional assembly, or *loya jirga*.[36] These efforts were unsuccessful, however, because UN-mediated cease-fires between warring factions always broke down. Non-UN initiatives also made little progress, particularly the "Six Plus Two" multilateral contact group, which began meeting in 1997.[37]

Although he had resigned in frustration in 1999, immediately after the September 11, 2001 attacks, former UN mediator Lakhdar Brahimi was brought back. On November 14, 2001, the Security Council adopted Resolution 1378,[38] which called for a "central" role for the United Nations in establishing a transitional administration and invited member States to send peacekeeping forces to promote stability and the delivery of aid. After the fall of Kabul in November 2001, the United Nations invited major Afghan factions, most prominently the Northern Alliance and that of the former king—but not the Taliban—to a conference in Bonn, Germany.[39]

On December 5, 2001, the factions signed the Bonn Agreement.[40] It was endorsed by the Security Council on December 6, 2001.[41] Ironically, the Agreement was reportedly forged with substantial Iranian diplomatic help because of Iran's support for the Northern Alliance. According to Katzman, the Agreement, among other things:

- formed the interim administration headed by Hamid Karzai.
- authorized an international peacekeeping force to maintain security in Kabul and directed Northern Alliance forces to withdraw from the capital. (Security Council Resolution 1386 (December 20, 2001) provided formal Security Council authorization for the international peacekeeping force.)
- referred to the need to cooperate with the international community on counter-narcotics, crime and terrorism.
- applied the Afghan Constitution of 1964 until a permanent constitution could be drafted.[42]

Inside the United Nations, there was strong sentiment in favor of democratic reforms. During the 1990s, successive UN resolutions on Afghanistan called for "broad-based, representative government with a commitment to human rights and, increasingly, women's rights."[43] This sentiment, which was strongly supported by the US government, is reflected in the Bonn Agreement. Yet the international commitment to democratization was potentially a liability, as well. As noted by one commentator:

> The post-Taliban democratization process was from the outset more heavily internationalized than other reforms in Afghan history except under the communists. Reforms during the monarchy in the 1920s were certainly influenced by foreign ideas, but apart from a small number of foreign advisors they were very much an Afghan operation. The same applied to Zahir Shah's democratic reforms in 1964. This time, by contrast, the UN launched a visibly internationalized democratization process. Foreign experts virtually flooded into the country to help implement the transition schedule of the Bonn Agreement. The visibility of the foreign hand in the reforms was exemplified during the 2005 elections, when the UN had 40 million ballot papers printed in Europe and Australia and flown into Afghanistan. The foreign role was accentuated by the widespread presence of international consultants in the new administration as a whole. While many experts were Afghans returning from exile, often temporarily, they worked for international salaries. This hardened the distinction between "the locals" (on local salary) and "the internationalists" (on international salaries).[44]

This anti-foreigner sentiment continued and intensified to the point Afghans soon referred to foreign non-governmental organizations (NGOs) as "cows that drink their own milk."[45] Perhaps the most important policy impact of foreign involvement in Afghanistan was "the extreme dependence of the emerging Afghan state on international assistance."[46] The size of the US economic and military contribution in particular gave it paramount influence. By 2004, US aid accounted for over half of all recorded donor assistance to the government budget. As a result of its large financial contribution and extensive presence in Afghanistan, the United States "effectively underwrote the very survival of the government, as President Hamid Karzai publicly admitted, and wielded an implicit veto over all issues it considered important."[47]

President Karzai exercised decisive influence over the process of promulgating a new constitution. In accordance with established tradition, a small committee of experts prepared a first draft, which was reviewed by a larger commission. The final step would be the calling of a *loya jirga* to deliberate and approve a text. During the early drafting process, a critical issue emerged as to the form the government should take: a purely presidential system or a mixed structure with a prime minister. The debate divided along ethnic lines. The non-Pushtun minorities, including the Tajik, Uzbek, Hazara, Turkmen and Qizilbash, strongly favored the traditional position of a prime minister as a way to counter the influence of a Pashtun president. They, therefore, wanted a power-sharing mechanism and favored a mixed system with a president and a prime minister, the latter preferably to be elected by the parliament. The Pashtuns argued, however, that Afghanistan needed a strong executive in order to overcome the catastrophic divisions of the past and to provide a unifying leadership for the future. Hence, in their view, a purely presidential system was best. After a period of time, the drafting process was removed from the commission and "proceeded in a 'secretive and unaccountable manner' in the office of Karzai."[48] When the document was made public a couple of months later, in November 2003, the position of prime minister had been eliminated; instead, two vice presidents selected by the president had been added.[49] Karzai's success in overcoming a "varied and collectively powerful opposition during the constitutional process derived primarily from his relationship with the United States," but "the parliamentary issue left a deep scar among the minorities."[50]

Speaking of parliament, a controversial issue arose regarding the election system to be employed to select members of the parliament for Afghanistan. Although political parties were allowed—about sixty were registered with the Ministry of Justice—the government chose a system that prevented political parties from formally fielding candidates. The election system chosen is called the single non-transferable vote (SNTV). In the 2005 elections its use meant that voters could choose among individual candidates in multi-member constituencies, but there were no party lists and no party identification of candidates on the ballot. With no formal party affiliations allowed, there was no proportional representation according to party strength. As one commentator noted:

> As an institution of political democracy, the SNTV was deeply flawed. Without electoral recognition of political parties, the parliament was likely to be fragmented and weak, with little capacity to aggregate local interests, address national-level issues, provide clear lines of accountability to the voters and thus, in the end, check the power of the executive branch. . . . The limitations of a non-party election system were common knowledge. Most of the diplomatic community in Afghanistan, the UN mission in Kabul (UNAMA), and virtually all resident international experts and civil society groups warned against adopting the SNTV. . . . Yet Karzai resisted, and after a year-long debate pushed the SNTV through a final Cabinet decision in February 2005.[51]

The public argument made in favor of the SNTV by Karzai was that Afghanistan had historically had many bad experiences with political parties. The Communist Party had left a legacy of extreme violence, as had the civil war among the political factions during the early 1990s. According to Karzai, an election system that strengthened the role of political parties would likely institutionalize ethnic divisions and work against national reconciliation and unity. Therefore, it was preferable to have an election system where voters would vote for individuals rather than parties. Karzai's ability to have the SNTV adopted was reportedly dependent upon strong US support, including a brusque intervention by American Ambassador Zalmay Khalilzad at a meeting with UN officials and diplomats in Kabul, who declared that "he had just spoken to President Bush, who said 'SNTV is the choice. SNTV is going to happen.'"[52] Arguably, "[t]he institutional arrangement suited Washington's primary policy objective in Afghanistan, which was not to promote political democracy but to eliminate terrorists and Al Qaida."[53]

In any event, the process resulted in the election of a substantial number of alleged war criminals and drug traffickers in the parliament, which undermined the legitimacy of the democratic system. Moreover, as previously noted, the national budget was heavily dependent upon foreign funding. In 2005, around 90 percent of the total budget was based on foreign receipts. "Only the operating budget, which represented about one-fourth of the total, was managed by the government. The rest was the development, or 'external' budget, which the donors controlled more directly. As a result, the power of the parliament was extremely limited with regard to both taxation and spending."[54]

Not surprisingly, relations between Karzai and parliament have often been contentious. Nonetheless, they are both trying to improve and expand governance throughout the country. In testimony before the Senate Armed Services Committee on February 28, 2008, Director of National Intelligence Mike McConnell stated that the Karzai government controls only 30 percent of the country, while the Taliban controls 10 percent, and tribes and local groups control the remainder.[55] US and NATO officials in Kabul, however, told CBS in March 2008 that they disagreed with this assessment because it is too pessimistic.[56] There is a debate in Afghanistan over whether the focus should continue to be on strengthening the central government—the approach favored by the Karzai government and the United States and most of its partners—or to promote local solutions to security and governance problems, an approach some international partners, such as Great Britain, would like to explore.

Despite its relatively weak position, parliament has asserted itself on several occasions. For example, it exercised its prerogatives in the process of confirming a postelection cabinet and in forcing Karzai to remove several prominent conservatives from the Supreme Court and replacing them with jurists more experienced in modern jurisprudence.[57] In mid-2007, parliament promulgated a law granting amnesty to commanders who fought in the various Afghan wars since the Soviet invasion in an effort to improve the chances for greater stability as Afghanistan attempts to rebuild itself as a modern nation. In the course of debate on the legislation, the law was rewritten to give victims the right to bring accusations of past abuses forward. Its status, however, is unclear because, although Karzai did not veto the legislation, neither did he sign it.

In spite of the tensions between them, the executive and the parliament have cooperated with respect to less contentious issues, such as the adoption of a labor law, a mines law, a law on economic cooperatives and a convention on tobacco control. The legislature also confirmed Karzai nominees for a new Minister of Refugee Affairs, the head of the Central Bank and the final justice to complete the composition of the Supreme Court.[58]

The United Nations has been extensively involved in the post-war stabilization and reconstruction effort in Afghanistan. Some of the debate over the predominant role of the United States and its partners was reflected in a proposal to create a new position of "super envoy" that would represent the United Nations, the European Union and NATO in Afghanistan. The proposal would subsume the role of the head of the UN Assistance Mission in Afghanistan (UNAMA). In January 2008, with US support, UN Secretary-General Ban Ki-moon tentatively appointed British diplomat Paddy Ashdown to this "super envoy" position, but Karzai rejected the appointment, reportedly over concerns about the scope of the authority of Mr. Ashdown, especially whether it might dilute the US role in Afghanistan. There has also been speculation that Karzai wished to show his independence from the international community. Ashdown withdrew his name on January 28, 2008.[59]

On March 20, 2008, the Security Council adopted Resolution 1608,[60] which extended UNAMA's mandate for another year and expanded its authority to include some of the "super envoy" concept. UNAMA coordinates the joint Afghan–international community coordination body called the Joint Coordination and Monitoring Board, and Resolution 1806 directs UNAMA to coordinate the work of international donors and strengthen cooperation between the international peacekeeping force (ISAF, International Security Assistance Force; see below) and the Afghan government. The head of UNAMA, as of March 2008, is Norwegian diplomat Kai Eide. In April 2008, in Washington, D.C., Eide stated that additional capacity building resources are needed and that some efforts by international donors are redundant or tied to purchases by Western countries.[61]

There is little doubt that inadequate resources, both for security and reconstruction purposes, have been and remain a primary problem in Afghanistan. The problem, moreover, is lack of both financial resources and human capital in a country that is one of the poorest on earth, with a literacy rate estimated at only 30 percent. The recent deterioration in the security situation is especially disquieting.

Post-War Security Operations and Force Capacity Building

As noted previously, after the negotiation of the Bonn Agreement, the UN Security Council adopted Resolution 1386 on December 20, 2001, which established ISAF to aid the Afghan Interim Authority in maintaining peace and security in Kabul and its surrounding areas, "so that the Afghan Interim Authority as well as the personnel of the United Nations can operate in a secure environment."[62] To this end, the Resolution authorized ISAF to take "all necessary measures" to fulfill the peacekeeping mission.[63] Everyone recognized that "all necessary measures" might include the use of force. The Resolution also called upon member States "to contribute personnel, equipment and other resources to the [ISAF],"[64] and "calls on Member States participating in the [ISAF] to provide assistance to help the Afghan Interim Authority in the establishment and training of new Afghan security and armed forces."[65]

It is important to note that Resolution 1386 envisaged that ISAF would be a peacekeeping force in the classic sense. Although ISAF was authorized to take "necessary measures" to fulfill its mandate, which implied that force might have to be used, the initial limitation of its operations to Kabul and its surrounding areas indicated that the use of force contemplated would be in the nature of actions in self-defense, a use of force characteristic of *peacekeeping* operations. There is no language in the Resolution that implies the use of force to *enforce* peace. Rather, peace enforcement responsibility lay with separate US forces who sought to track down Taliban and al Qaeda remnants, which were largely located in the southern and eastern portions of the country near the border with Pakistan.

The composition of ISAF originally consisted of approximately forty-six hundred troops from 122 different States.[66] The leadership of ISAF initially rotated among the Western nations, but NATO took over leadership of ISAF in August 2003. This was NATO's first and so far only mission outside the Euro-Atlantic area in its history. At the time ISAF's primary goals were "to assist in maintaining security, develop Afghan national security structures, assist the nation's reconstruction, and aid the training of Afghan security forces."[67]

Although Resolution 1386 initially limited ISAF to Kabul, its area of responsibility had been expanded to include about 50 percent of the country before August 2006, when it further extended its role to take over the lead military role from US troops in southern Afghanistan. In other words, ISAF had evolved from a peacekeeping force to one clearly involved in enforcing the peace against rejuvenated Taliban and al Qaeda forces. As one European official in NATO reportedly stated, "When NATO agreed to expand its control to southern Afghanistan in 2006, no one really anticipated the difficulty in the fighting. Maybe we were in denial, but this has been a culture shock for a lot of us."[68]

For their part, US officials have been frustrated by what they perceive as a failure on the part of some NATO members to bear their fair share of the fighting. For example, the United States has been asking its NATO allies to provide more troops to stabilize the military situation in Afghanistan but has discovered that "some allies appear more eager to reduce their forces than to add to them."[69] US Secretary of Defense Robert Gates has credited the Netherlands, Britain, Australia and Canada with "doing their part in Afghanistan," but indicated that other NATO members have contributed far less.[70] For its part, Canada threatened to withdraw from the southern province of Kandahar early next year (2009) unless other NATO countries agreed to send one thousand additional combat troops there, a threat that was met when France agreed to contribute the extra troops.[71] Tensions within the alliance have also risen because of the unwillingness of some members, including Germany, Italy and Spain, to send troops to the south of Afghanistan, where the bulk of the fighting is taking place.[72]

Secretary Gates has recently emphasized "the direct threat posed to European security by extremists in and around Afghanistan" in a speech reflecting growing American concerns that weak public support risked undermining NATO's mission in the country.[73] As evidence of increased danger to Europe from terrorist attacks, Gates cited, among other things, the arrest of fourteen extremists in Barcelona, suspected of planning attacks against public transport systems in Spain, Portugal, France, Germany and Britain. On the reluctance of European States to commit more troops to Afghanistan, or to allow those already there to move to the south and other areas where the fighting was most intense, Gates warned against the alliance becoming a two-tiered coalition, of those willing to fight and those who were not. He reportedly added that "[s]uch a development, with all its implications for collective security, would effectively destroy the alliance."[74]

The same European official who reported that NATO members suffered "culture shock" when they realized how difficult fighting in southern Afghanistan would be, reportedly recognized the continuing frustration of American officials when he said, "American officials were frustrated when the alliance had 35,000 troops in Afghanistan but only 8,000 troops in the volatile south, and they are still unsatisfied with NATO's 52,000 troops in Afghanistan and 22,000 in the south."[75]

Both Barack Obama and John McCain, the contenders in the 2008 presidential elections, supported a troop "surge" in Afghanistan. Senator McCain proposed moving troops from Iraq to Afghanistan, conditional on continued progress in Iraq. Senator Obama's proposal is much more radical; he argues that we should have sent the 2007 surge to Afghanistan, not Iraq, that Afghanistan is the "central front" and that we must rebuild Afghanistan "from the bottom up along the lines of the Marshall Plan."[76] Secretary of Defense Gates has also supported the idea of a surge in Afghanistan. He has endorsed a $20 billion plan to increase substantially the size of Afghanistan's army, as well as the role and numbers of Western troops there to aid it.

Serious questions have been raised, however, about the validity of this thesis. For example, although denying sanctuary for terrorists—in Afghanistan and elsewhere—has been put forth as a rationale for increased troop strength, it has been argued that "[a]ccomplishing it . . . requires neither the conquest of large swathes of Afghan territory nor a troop surge there—nor even maintaining the number of troops NATO has in Afghanistan today. Counterterrorism is not about occupation. It centers on combining intelligence with specialized military capabilities."[77] Even if one maintains that counterterrorism in Afghanistan requires more troops than suggested by the above argument, the question remains, how many? Dan McNeill, the American general who was NATO's top commander in Afghanistan until he left in June 2008, reportedly said that "according to current American counterinsurgency doctrine, a successful occupation of Afghanistan, which is larger, more complex, more populous and very much less governable than Iraq, would require 400,000 troops."[78]

Strictly speaking, NATO is not an occupying force in Afghanistan because ISAF was established by Security Council resolution and President Karzai has given his permission for its presence. As noted previously, however, the large number of foreigners in Afghanistan has raised objections from the Afghans, who have a longstanding distrust of foreigners. Tensions have been greatly exacerbated by civilian casualties caused by NATO bombing. Karzai has demanded an end to civilian casualties. A surge of foreign troops along the lines suggested could greatly intensify these objections and likely provoke a serious backlash.

One possible answer to this objection might be to concentrate greater attention and resources on training an Afghan army and police. This has proven to be a difficult goal to achieve. American commanders remain frustrated by NATO's failure to deploy the promised number of Operational Mentor and Liaison Teams (OMLTs) ("Omelets" in NATO-speak). These are twelve- to nineteen-person training teams that serve as a vital link between forward-deployed Afghan army and police units and ISAF support such as airpower, medical evacuations and resupply. This is a dangerous mission, as was demonstrated in June 2008, when eighteen police trainers from the Security Transition Command were killed in action. It was the worst month of the conflict for that command.[79]

As a consequence, some NATO States, in particular Germany, now refuse to allow their OMLTs to accompany Afghan units into combat in the southern and eastern parts of the country. Others have failed to field the training teams at all, apparently because of the financial cost. The result is a shortage of twenty mentoring teams and twenty-three thousand trainers.[80] General John Craddock, NATO's supreme allied commander in Afghanistan, has expressed his frustration at this situation in vivid terms:

> I've talked at every meeting of the North Atlantic Council [NATO's governing body], and at every foreign ministers council. At one [meeting] I brought a big cup and labeled it "Contributions," and I reminded all the defense chiefs that their respective heads of state agreed to meet this requirement, so where is your bid? And I didn't get anything! So yeah, I'm frustrated.[81]

Building a quality police force in Afghanistan has so far proven to be a mission impossible because of pervasive corruption. The current seventy-nine thousand members of Afghanistan's national police force are "better known as shakedown artists than law enforcers."[82] Major General Robert Cone, who is in charge of the mission to train the Afghan army and national police, points out: "The problem is endemic corruption in a country that had virtually no economy for 30 years other than narco-trafficking, so the way cops made money was to stop vehicles at checkpoints and demand money."[83] Many of Afghanistan's governors are former warlords who put their cronies on the police rolls. As a result, they also are lukewarm to police reforms. According to Cone, "[i]f you gave them truth serum and asked if they wanted a good, non-corrupt police force, probably only 30 percent or so would say yes. For years, corrupt police is how they've made money."[84]

Military action against the Taliban and al Qaeda has not been going well the last two years. The toll among foreign troops in Afghanistan has reached a new high, with more than 230 deaths so far in 2008 among more than twenty NATO nations contributing troops. American commanders have said that the level of violence is up 30 percent in the past year. In July 2008, for the first time, American military casualties in Afghanistan exceeded those in Iraq.[85] A major reason for the increase of casualties in Afghanistan has been the ability of the Taliban and al Qaeda to cross the border between Pakistan and Afghanistan, launch an attack in Afghanistan and return to their safe haven in the tribal areas of Pakistan. After months of US criticism, behind the scenes and in public, against Pakistan for not doing enough to prevent such attacks, the United States launched drone strikes against targets in Pakistan and a raid by special operations forces in Pakistan's tribal areas. Pakistan reacted forcefully to these attacks and the risk grew of an armed confrontation between Pakistani and US forces. But as the Taliban went deeper into Pakistan proper and carried out major terrorist attacks like the Marriot Hotel bombing in

Islamabad on September 20, 2008, Pakistan reacted and escalated its attacks on Taliban strongholds like Swat, a settled area of the North-West Frontier Province that was once a middle class resort.[86] Fighting has been fierce, and success of the Pakistani effort is by no means assured.

For his part, President Karzai has repeatedly sought the intervention of the Saudi royal family to bring the Taliban to peace negotiations, but without success. Karzai has reportedly imposed conditions on bringing the Taliban into the government. These include a renunciation of violence, acceptance of Afghanistan's democratic constitution and a repudiation of al Qaeda—all terms the Taliban leadership has rejected.[87]

As noted earlier, there are recent claims that Afghanistan has become a "narco-State" and that Hamid Karzai and his government are deeply involved in protecting the opium trade and using proceeds from it to maintain themselves in power.[88] At this writing, there are further reports that President Karzai's brother, Ahmed Wali Karzai, is heavily involved in the heroin trade in Afghanistan and that President Karzai's government is protecting him. American officials in Kabul reportedly "fear that perceptions that the Afghan president might be protecting his brother are damaging his credibility and undermining efforts by the United States to buttress his government, which has been under siege from rivals and a Taliban insurgency fueled by drug money."[89]

I will now turn to a consideration of the international law issues raised by the current situations in Afghanistan and Pakistan, the hard choices faced by decision makers attempting to resolve these issues, and possible impacts on the future of international law of these choices.

Afghanistan, Pakistan, Hard Choices and the Future of International Law

A major problem that decision makers face in dealing with the currently unsatisfactory situations in Afghanistan and Pakistan is that both nations are sovereign States with governments selected in free elections. Although the United States and other foreign governments involved in Afghanistan can urge that President Karzai stop protecting drug lords and narco-farmers, they cannot order him to do so. Much less can they decide to remove him and his government from power. To be sure, they could, as suggested by Thomas Schweich, a former senior US Department of State counter-narcotics official, "inform President Karzai that he must stop protecting drug lords or he will lose US support."[90] The wisdom of this recommendation, however, is highly questionable. It would seem to call for a "nuclear option" in a situation not calling for it. As one commentator has noted:

> Neither [presidential] candidate has mentioned heroin use as a pressing domestic issue, and there is even less reason it should be a major international one. In any case, our demand for heroin is not the fault of the Afghan peasants who would take the financial hit for our interdiction efforts. Liberal democracies cannot win counterinsurgencies against the wills of local populations, and denying a livelihood to the poor farmers of southern and eastern Afghanistan is no way to persuade Afghans to our side.[91]

Tensions between the Karzai government and the US government over civilian casualties allegedly caused by airstrikes raise somewhat similar problems. Although the law of armed conflict clearly prohibits an intentional direct attack against the civilian population as such, and indeed categorizes it as a war crime,[92] "there can be no assurance that attacks against combatants and other military objectives will not result in civilian casualties in or near such military objectives."[93] In the latter case, the civilian casualties are known as "collateral damage" and do not give rise to accountability of the attacker. Nonetheless, as the head of the sovereign government of Afghanistan, President Karzai can order the complete cessation of airstrikes (he has done so on occasion), and, as a matter of international law, the United States and its allies are bound to comply—even though such airstrikes are a crucially important factor in the battle against the Taliban, and the Taliban regularly intermingles among the civilian population in order to use them as human shields (itself a violation of the law of armed conflict) and then uses civilian casualties as part of its war propaganda effort.[94] In short, the Taliban has been successfully engaging in so-called "lawfare," using false accusations of violations of the *jus in bello* in order to win public opinion to its side.

In a recent interview, Admiral Michael Mullen, Chairman of the US Joint Chiefs of Staff and the nation's highest-ranking military officer, has identified the problem of how to deal with attacks by the Taliban and al Qaeda across the border between Pakistan and Afghanistan, and their use of the tribal areas of Pakistan as a safe haven, as the gravest he faces.[95] Although he suggests that more military forces are needed, he states, "It's not just about [sending] additional combat forces to Afghanistan." Rather, he notes, "Afghanistan has a weak government and economy, a huge opium trade, and an inadequate army. If those problems aren't addressed, more troops won't help."

There is a serious question, however, whether these problems are surmountable. As raised starkly by one commentator:

> But what are the real prospects for turning fractious, impoverished Afghanistan into an orderly and prosperous nation and a potential ally of the United States? What true American interests are being insufficiently advanced or defended in its remote deserts

> and mountains? And even if these interests are really so broad, are they deliverable at an acceptable price? The answers to these questions put the wisdom of an Afghan surge into great question. . . . The invasion of Afghanistan was a great tactical success and the correct strategic move. Yet since then it seems as if the United States has been trying to turn the conflict into the Vietnam War of the early 21st century. Escalating in Afghanistan to "must-win" status means, according to General McNeil's estimate, deploying three times as many troops as were sent to Iraq at the height of the surge. If Americans really believe—as Senator Obama in particular argues—that Afghanistan is the right war and a place appropriate for Iraq-style nation-building, then they must understand both the cost involved and the remote likelihood of success.[96]

At this writing, Britain has reportedly backed a statement by a senior military commander that the war against the Taliban cannot be won.[97] According to the report, "the UK's ministry of defense 'did not have a problem' with warning the UK public not to expect a 'decisive military victory' and to prepare instead for a possible deal with the Taliban."[98] For its part, however, the United States is skeptical about any idea of negotiating with the Taliban. When asked about the British commander's statement, a White House spokesman reportedly said: "We plan on winning in Afghanistan. It's going to be tough and going to take some time, but we will eventually succeed."[99]

Even if there should be an eventual agreement that success in Afghanistan does not require a complete military victory, US Joint Chiefs Chairman Michael Mullen is surely right in suggesting that the problem along the Afghan-Pakistani border is the one to be most concerned about for the near future and will be "front and center on the agenda of the next president."[100] As noted earlier, US and coalition forces have been frustrated by Pakistan's failure to prevent Taliban and al Qaeda forces from crossing the border to launch attacks in Afghanistan and have recently attacked targets in the tribal areas of Pakistan either by drones or by special operations forces. Pakistan has protested vociferously and threatened military action against coalition forces. Most recently, however, Pakistan has reacted to Taliban and al Qaeda attacks in Pakistan by intensifying military action against them in Pakistan.[101]

A major issue arising out of this situation is whether US and coalition forces violated international law restraints on the use of force by launching their attacks in Pakistani territory. The answer to this question has to be a resounding "maybe." As noted previously, with respect to the 9/11 attacks and the issue of whether Article 51 of the UN Charter applies to armed attacks by non-State actors, Yoram Dinstein has concluded that "all lingering doubts on this issue have been dispelled as a result of the response of the international community to the shocking events" of September 11.[102] It is unclear, however, whether this conclusion would apply to cross-border attacks by "terrorists"—or less pejoratively, "irregular forces" of a non-State character—that do not have the extraordinary features of the 9/11 attacks and the global response to them. Dinstein himself notes that there is considerable scholarly comment in support of the proposition that there is no right of self-defense under Article 51 against an armed attack by a non-State actor. This proposition is also supported by the controversial statement in the 2004 International Court of Justice's Advisory Opinion on *Legal Consequences of the Construction of a Wall in the Occupied Palestinian Territory.*[103] There the court summarily dismissed Israel's claim that it was acting in self-defense against attacks by terrorist groups. In its view, Israel could not be acting in self-defense because Israel had not claimed that the terrorist attacks at issue were imputable to a foreign State and because those attacks were not transnational in nature, having occurred wholly within territory occupied by Israel. The opinion has been heavily criticized,[104] however, and the court arguably backed off its view in its 2005 case concerning *Armed Activities on the Territory of the Congo*, where the court stated that, given the circumstances of the case, there was "no need to respond to the contentions of the Parties as to whether and under what conditions contemporary international law provides for a right of self-defense against large scale attacks by irregular forces."[105]

Assuming *arguendo* that there is a right of self-defense against armed attacks by non-State actors, there is still the requirement that the use of force in self-defense be necessary for the object of defense and proportional to the injury threatened.[106] Although the drone attacks and special operations forces attack drew strong protests from the Pakistani government, they were arguably necessary in light of Pakistan's failure to prevent cross-border attacks and proportional to the injury they threatened. As noted by Admiral Mullen, there is no plan to invade Pakistan,[107] and there is evidence of a favorable shift in the Pakistani military's outlook after horrendous terrorist attacks on targets in its own country. He is also encouraged that a tribal leader in Bajaur, a Taliban and al Qaeda stronghold along the border, has mobilized several anti-Taliban fighters. At the same time he recognizes that the Pakistani military does not yet have the skills or the equipment it needs. If these can be provided, there is hope that no further cross-border attacks by US and coalition forces will be necessary.

Even a cursory review of the foregoing discussion leads to the unhappy conclusion that efforts toward "nation building" in Afghanistan are going very badly, and hard choices will have to be made that will have a major impact on the future of international law and international institutions. The first choice will have to be whether having a "surge" in Afghanistan of approximately ten thousand troops is a good idea and will contribute to winning the war against the Taliban and al Qaeda. Since both candidates in the US presidential election favor a surge, it is highly probable that such a surge will take place. As noted, however, the British government believes the war is unwinnable in the sense of a decisive military victory and favors instead President Karzai's efforts to broker a peace settlement with the Taliban—efforts apparently opposed by the US government. Some critics have gone much further and proposed a major drawdown of Western troops to a maximum of perhaps twenty thousand. In their view, this number would be sufficient, if coupled with an intelligence operation sufficient to collect the intelligence needed to allow special operations forces to eliminate terrorist threats as they appear.[108]

It will also be necessary to decide whether, in light of considerable evidence of pervasive corruption in the Karzai government, and considering the cost in lives and treasure already expended, the efforts toward nation building should be continued. On the topic of nation building in Afghanistan, James Kitfield of the *National Journal* had the following to say:

> The overwhelming theme of the Afghan nation-building at this time is a lack of coordination and coherence. Everyone seems to be doing their own thing based on different and occasionally conflicting or at least clashing agendas. The critical issue of who should be dealing directly with Taliban leaders in proposing reconciliation, and what they can offer them to jump to the government's side, is a case in point. The US pushed hard for the naming of a very high profile rep in Paddy Ashdown, precisely to instill more coherence in the effort. President Karzai apparently viewed that as a reproach and Ashdown as a potential competitor for influence, so he nixed the idea of a high profile UN "czar." The hopes for Ashdown's successor are more modest, but everyone seems to think someone is still needed who can be a one-stop contact for civil, international aid operations. The US military commanders in Afghanistan, and their NATO counterparts, are very anxious that someone fill such a role so that they can get the critical sequencing right in their "clear, hold, build" operations.[109]

Hard choices will also have to be made as to what to do about the drug lords and narcotics traffickers who are supporting the Taliban and al Qaeda insurgency. General David D. McKiernan, the top American commander in Afghanistan, has announced that ISAF forces will step up attacks on these drug lords and narcotics traffickers in situations where they are linked to the movement of weapons, improvised explosives or foreign fighters into Afghanistan.[110] American and NATO officials have vigorously rejected the suggestions of some NGOs that international security forces take an active role in eradicating the poppy crops, on the ground that such decisions should be left to the Afghan government, which would also have to develop alternate livelihoods for the farmers. But General McKiernan has proposed that perhaps this position should be reexamined because the fight in Afghanistan is now not only against the Taliban and al Qaeda, but also against "a very broad range of militant groups that are combined with the criminality, with the narco-trafficking system, with corruption, that form a threat and a challenge to that great country."[111] The major problem with increasing the mission of the military in this fashion is that there is substantial evidence that the Karzai government and its supporters are also receiving funds from the narco-traffickers.

With respect to the problem of cross-border attacks from Pakistan, the primary issue is whether the new Pakistani government will have the will and the ability to defeat the Taliban and al Qaeda forces in the tribal areas. General McKiernan has reported that he is "cautiously optimistic" that a continuing assault by Pakistani forces against militants in the tribal area of Bajaur could put a "dent in extremist operations in the border region." He also praised the appointment of the new head of Pakistan's top spy organization, saying Lieutenant General Ahmed Shuja Pasha was likely to reform the agency, which in the past had "institutional and historical ties to the Taliban and other militant networks."[112]

If, however, General McKiernan's cautious optimism turns out to be misplaced, and cross-border attacks by Taliban, al Qaeda and other militants become a major problem, then the choice facing US and coalition forces will be especially hard. As General John Craddock has acknowledged, insurgencies that enjoy uncontested sanctuary have rarely, if ever, been defeated.[113]

Similarly, General McKiernan, in addressing the question whether it is possible to have a positive outcome to the Afghanistan campaign without resolving the problem of insurgent sanctuaries in Pakistan, has answered that "while I won't say it will be impossible, it will be very, very difficult."[114] At the same time, McKiernan has stated categorically that "[f]ailure is not an option in Afghanistan."[115] Hence, the likelihood of US and NATO attacks on targets in Pakistan resuming under these circumstances would be great. Moreover, although Robert Gates has defended earlier such attacks as justified under international law in order to protect US troops in Afghanistan, as we have seen earlier, this is a debatable proposition, and Gates has recognized that "Pakistan probably did not agree that international law permitted unilateral action."[116] Indeed, as we also saw earlier, Pakistan vehemently objected to the US drone and special operations attacks in the tribal areas.

One should devoutly hope that failure in Afghanistan is in fact not an option. Robert D. Kaplan has recently suggested that "[s]trategically, culturally, and historically speaking, Afghanistan and Pakistan are inseparable."[117] Also, in his view:

> [F]ailure in Afghanistan would do India no favors. In Afghanistan we are not simply trying to save a country, but to give a whole region a new kind of prosperity and stability, united rather than divided by energy needs, that would be implicitly

pro-American. . . . What the Pentagon calls the "long war" is the defining geopolitical issue of our time, and Afghanistan is at its heart. The fate of Eurasia hangs in the balance.

But how long is this "long war" likely to be? A crucial issue, in both Iraq and Afghanistan, is the time required for a well-run counterinsurgency strategy to work. Sarah Sewall, a former Pentagon official who wrote the introduction to the University of Chicago edition of the new *U.S. Army/Marine Corps Counterinsurgency Field Manual,*[118] for one, is skeptical that the US public will be willing to "supply greater concentrations of forces, accept higher casualties, fund serious nation-building and stay many long years to conduct counterinsurgency by the book."[119]

If Ms. Sewall's gloomy prognosis should prove correct with respect to Afghanistan, the adverse impact on international law and international institutions would be substantial. Failure in Afghanistan would be a catastrophic failure on the part not only of the United States but of the world community as a whole. It would mean that the Taliban, al Qaeda and other militant Islamic forces had managed to defeat US and other NATO forces in ISAF, as well as US forces engaged in anti-terrorism missions under Operation Enduring Freedom. This would call into serious question the future viability of NATO and of UN peacekeeping efforts. Failure in Afghanistan would also call into question the continued viability of nation-building efforts, by the United Nations and others, and arguably support those skeptical of such efforts, such as the Bush administration in its early days.

At this writing, there are reports that the Bush administration has initiated a major review of its Afghanistan policy and that a nearly completed National Intelligence Estimate, a formal report that reflects the consensus judgments of all American intelligence agencies, will set forth an extremely grim assessment of the current situation in Afghanistan, especially of the Afghan leadership and its foreign allies. This should come as no surprise to those familiar with the developments and issues discussed in this article. One must hope, however, that issuance of the report after the 2008 presidential election will stimulate a searching review of these developments and issues. Avoiding failure in Afghanistan will depend in substantial measure upon a successful resolution of the many issues arising out of the situation there.

Notes

1. Carlotta Gall, *U.S. Killed 90 in Afghan Village, Including 60 Children, U.N. Finds,* NEW YORK TIMES, Aug. 27, 2009, at A6, col. 1. *See also* Alison Smale, *Afghanistan Is in Its Worst Shape Since 2001, European Diplomat Says,* NEW YORK TIMES, Sept. 15, 2008, at A11, col. 2.

2. Rory Stewart, *How to Save Afghanistan*, TIME, July 17, 2008, *available at* http://www.time.com/time/printout/0,8816,1823753,00.html.

3. *See* Eric Schmitt & Mark Mazzetti, *Bush Said to Give Orders Allowing Raids in Pakistan*, NEW YORK TIMES, Sept. 11, 2008, at A1, col. 1.

4. *See* Jane Perlez, *Pakistan's Military Chief Criticizes U.S. Over a Raid*, NEW YORK TIMES, Sept. 11, 2008, at A8, col. 3.

5. *See* Thomas Schweich, *Is Afghanistan a Narco-State?*, NEW YORK TIMES MAGAZINE, July 27, 2008, *available at* http://www.nytimes.com/2008/07/27/magazine/27AFGHAN-t.html?scp=1&sq=is%20afghanistan%20a%20narco-state&st=cse.

6. *Id.* at 1.

7. *See* Smale, *supra* note 1.

8. Much of the information in this section is taken from Kenneth Katzman, *Afghanistan: Post-War Governance, Security, and U.S. Policy*, CRS REPORT FOR CONGRESS 1–7 (July 11, 2008), *available at* http://www.fas.org/sgp/crs/row/RL30588.pdf.

9. *Id.* at 1.

10. After his government fell, Najibullah declined to flee Afghanistan. Instead, he, his brother and aides remained at a UN facility in Kabul until the Taliban movement gained control in 1996 and entered the facility to seize and then hang them. *Id.* at 4.

11. *Id.* at 5.

12. S.C. Res. 1368, U.N. Doc. S/RES/1368 (Sept. 12, 2001).

13. S.C. Res. 1373, U.N. Doc. S/RES/1373 (Sept. 28, 2001).

14. Compare the language the Security Council used in Resolution 678, adopted on November 29, 1990, which authorized member States, unless Iraq complied with a series of prior Council resolutions by January 15, 1991, to use "all necessary means" to "uphold and implement" these resolutions and "to restore international peace and security in the area."

15. It is debatable, however, whether the Security Council has ever acted in such a way as to supersede the right to individual or collective self-defense. *See, e.g.,* Eugene V. Rostow, *Until What? Enforcement Action or Collective Self-defense?*, 85 AMERICAN JOURNAL OF INTERNATIONAL LAW 506 (1991), in which the author argues that the Persian Gulf War of 1990–91 was not a UN enforcement action but rather "a campaign of collective self-defense approved, encouraged, and blessed by the Security Council." To the contrary, *see* Thomas M. Franck & Faiza Patel, *UN Police Action in Lieu of War: The Old Order Changeth*, 85 AMERICAN JOURNAL OF INTERNATIONAL LAW 63 (1991).

16. For a forceful defense of the proposition that "all lingering doubts on this issue have been dispelled as a result of the response of the international community to the shocking events of 9 [*sic*] September 2001 (9/11)," *see* YORAM DINSTEIN, WAR, AGGRESSION, AND SELF-DEFENSE 206–8 (4th ed. 2005).

17. This discussion of the early combat operations in Afghanistan is based primarily on Katzman, *supra* note 8, at 7 and BARRY E. CARTER ET AL., INTERNATIONAL LAW 80–84 (5th ed. 2007).

18. *See* excerpts from the President's speech in CARTER ET AL., *supra* note 17, at 80–81.

19. According to reports, "some critics believe that U.S. dependence on local Afghan militia forces in the war strengthened the militias in the post-war period." Katzman, *supra* note 8, at 7.

20. *Id.*

21. *Id.*

22. *Id.*

23. *See* DINSTEIN, *supra* note 16, and associated text.

24. *Id.* at 206–7.

25. As a condition precedent to its invocation of Article 5, for the first time in history, the Atlantic Council met and agreed that there had to be evidence that the attack against the United

States was directed from abroad. Evidence to support this condition was presented to and deemed sufficient by the Council.

26. Dinstein notes further that "[t]his must be understood in light of Article 3 of the Rio Treaty, which refers specifically to an armed attack and to the right of self-defence pursuant to Article 51 . . . ." DINSTEIN, *supra* note 16, at 208.

27. Michael Byers, for example, has described the US "expansion" of the definition of self-defense to include a military response against States, such as Afghanistan, that willingly harbor terrorist groups that have attacked the United States as "dangerous" because it might be extended to situations where the provocation is far less grave than the September 11 attacks. *See* MICHAEL BYERS, WAR LAW: UNDERSTANDING INTERNATIONAL LAW AND ARMED CONFLICT 67 (2005).

28. *See, e.g.,* David Usborne, *UN Raps U.S. Military after Afghan Wedding Deaths Cover-up,* THE INDEPENDENT (London), July 30, 2002, at 9.

29. *See* CARTER ET AL., *supra* note 17, at 82.

30. For discussion of this debate, see John F. Murphy, *Force and Arms,* in 1 UNITED NATIONS LEGAL ORDER 247, 286–88 (Oscar Schachter & Christopher C. Joiner eds., 1995).

31. *See e.g.,* Mary Ellen O'Connell, *Lawful Self-Defense to Terrorism,* 61 UNIVERSITY OF PITTSBURGH LAW REVIEW 889, 902–4 (2002).

32. *Id.* at 904.

33. *See* Pamela Constable, *U.S. Hopes to Attract Moderates in Taliban; Powell sees them in 'New Afghanistan,'* WASHINGTON POST, Oct. 17, 2001, at A24, *cited in id.* at 904 n.97.

34. Katzman, *supra* note 8, at 7.

35. O'Connell, *supra* note 31, at 904.

36. *See* Katzman, *supra* note 8, at 7.

37. The "Six Plus Two" group consisted of the United States, Russia, and the six States bordering Afghanistan: Iran, China, Pakistan, Turkmenistan, Uzbekistan, and Tajikistan. Other failed efforts included a "Geneva group" (Italy, Germany, Iran and the United States) formed in 2000; an Organization of the Islamic Conference contact group; and Afghan exile efforts, including one by the Karzai clan (including Hamid Karzai) and one centered on Zahir Shah, the former king of Afghanistan. *See id.* at 7–8.

38. S.C. Res. 1378, U.N. Doc. S/RES/1378 (Nov. 14, 2001).

39. Katzman, *supra* note 8, at 8. In most instances where the United Nations has sought to broker a post-conflict peace process, it has relied on existing administrative and political institutions. This could not be the case in Afghanistan, where the Taliban had been removed from power and what little it had in the way of an administrative and political infrastructure destroyed. *See* Marina Ottaway & Bethany Lacina, *International Interventions and Imperialism: Lessons from the 1990s,* 23 SAIS REVIEW OF INTERNATIONAL AFFAIRS 71, 82 (Summer–Fall 2003).

40. The text of the Bonn Agreement is *available at* http://www.ag-afghanistan.de/files/petersburg.htm.

41. S.C. Res. 1385, U.N. Doc. S/RES/1385 (Dec. 6, 2001).

42. Katzman, *supra* note 8, at 8.

43. *Id.*

44. *See* Astri Suhrke, *Democratizing a Dependent State: The Case of Afghanistan,* DEMOCRATIZATION, June 1, 2008, *available at* http://pdfserve.informaworld.com/974713_731198615_793225710.pdf.

45. *Id.* at 634.

46. *Id.* at 635.

47. *Id*

48. *Id.* at 638.
49. *Id.*
50. *Id.* at 639.
51. *Id.* at 640.
52. *Id.* at 641.
53. *Id.*
54. *Id.* at 644.
55. Katzman, *supra* note 8, at 10.
56. *Id.*
57. *Id.*
58. *Id.* at 11.
59. *Id.*
60. S.C. Res. 1608, U.N. Doc. S/RES/1608 (Mar. 20, 2008).
61. Katzman, *supra* note 8, at 12.
62. S.C. Res. 1386, U.N. Doc. S/RES/1386 (Dec. 20, 2001), operative para. 1.
63. *Id.*, operative para. 3.
64. *Id.*, operative para. 2.
65. *Id.*, operative para. 10.
66. CARTER ET AL., *supra* note 17, at 86.
67. *Id.*
68. *See* James Kitfield, *Backsliding*, NATIONAL JOURNAL, Sept. 13, 2008, at 30, 36.
69. *See* Yochi J. Deazen, *Troop Needs Open NATO Rift,* WALL STREET JOURNAL, Feb. 8, 2008, at A8, col. 1.
70. *Id.*
71. *See* Fidelius Schmid, Jon Boone & Stephen Fidler, *Paris comes to Canada's aid with extra troops*, FINANCIAL TIMES, Feb. 8, 2008, at 2, col. 1.
72. *Id.*
73. *See* Stephen Fidler, *US flags up Afghanistan terror dangers for Europe*, FINANCIAL TIMES, Jan. 11, 2008, at 4, col. 7.
74. *Id.*
75. Kitfield, *supra* note 68, at 36.
76. *See* Bartle Breese Bull, *The Wrong Force for the 'Right War,'* NEW YORK TIMES, Aug. 14, 2008, at A23, col. 2.
77. *Id.*
78. *Id.*
79. *See* Kitfield, *supra* note 68, at 36.
80. *Id.*
81. *Id.*
82. *Id.* at 33.
83. *Id.* at 40.
84. *Id.*
85. *See* John F. Burns, *Karzai Sought Saudi Help With Taliban*, NEW YORK TIMES, Oct. 1, 2008, at A12, col. 1.
86. *See* Jane Perlez & Pir Ubair Shah, *Confronting Taliban, Pakistan Finds Itself at War*, NEW YORK TIMES, Oct. 3, 2008, at A1, col. 4.
87. Burns, *supra* note 85, at A12, col. 1.
88. *See* Schweich, *supra* note 5.

89. *See* James Risen, *Reports Link Karzai's Brother to Afghanistan Heroin Trade,* NEW YORK TIMES, Oct. 5, 2008, at 1.
90. *See* Schweich, *supra* note 5, at 9–10.
91. *See* Bull, *supra* note 76.
92. *See* Statute of the International Criminal Court art. 8(2)(b)(i)–(ii), July 17, 1998, 2187 U.N.T.S. 90. For discussion of the problem of "collateral damage," see YORAM DINSTEIN, THE CONDUCT OF HOSTILITIES UNDER THE LAW OF INTERNATIONAL ARMED CONFLICT 115–16 (2004).
93. DINSTEIN, *supra* note 92, at 115, *quoting* Waldemar A. Solf, *Article 51, in* MICHAEL BOTHE, KARL J. PARTSCH & WALDEMAR A. SOLF, NEW RULES FOR VICTIMS OF ARMED CONFLICTS: COMMENTARY ON THE TWO 1977 PROTOCOLS ADDITIONAL TO THE GENEVA CONVENTIONS OF 1949, at 296, 300 (1982).
94. *See* Charles J. Dunlap Jr., *Using bad PR is Taliban's defense against airpower,* ATLANTA JOURNAL-CONSTITUTION, Sept. 17, 2008, *available at* http://www.ajc.com/opinion/content/opinion.stories/2008/09/17dunlaped. In his op-ed piece General Dunlap quotes a conversation between Taliban commanders, intercepted by US intelligence officers, in which one of the commanders says, "Tanks and armor are not a big deal—the planes are the killers. I can handle everything but the jet fighters."
95. *See* Trudy Rubin, *Danger on Remote Pakistan Border,* PHILADELPHIA INQUIRER, Oct. 5, 2008, at C1, col. 1.
96. *See* Bull, *supra* note 76.
97. *See* Jimmy Burns & Daniel Dombey, *Britain risks US rift in war against Taliban,* FINANCIAL TIMES, Oct. 6, 2008, at 9, col. 1.
98. *Id.*
99. *Id.*
100. *See* Rubin, *supra* note 95, at C1, C6.
101. *See* Perlez & Shah, *supra* note 86, and accompanying text.
102. *See* DINSTEIN, *supra* note 16, and accompanying text.
103. Legal Consequences of the Construction of a Wall in the Occupied Palestinian Territory, Advisory Opinion, 2004 I.C.J. 136 (July 9).
104. For sharply contrasting views on the opinion, *compare* Sean D. Murphy, *Self-Defense and the Israeli Wall Advisory Opinion: An Ipse Dixit from the ICJ?,* 99 AMERICAN JOURNAL OF INTERNATIONAL LAW 62 (2005), *with* Iain Scobbie, *Words My Mother Never Taught Me—In Defense of the International Court,* 99 AMERICAN JOURNAL OF INTERNATIONAL LAW 76 (2005).
105. Armed Activities on the Territory of the Congo (Dem. Rep. Congo v. Uganda), 2005 I.C.J. 116, para. 147 (Dec. 19).
106. Legality of the Threat or Use of Nuclear Weapons, Advisory Opinion, 1996 I.C.J. 226, para. 141 (July 8).
107. *See* Rubin, *supra* note 95.
108. *See, e.g.,* Bull, *supra* note 76.
109. E-mail from James Kitfield to John F. Murphy (Sept. 30, 2008) (on file with author).
110. *See* Thom Shanker & Eric Schmitt, *NATO Aims At Afghans Whose Drugs Aid Militants,* NEW YORK TIMES, Oct. 2, 2008, at A8, col. 1.
111. *Id.*
112. *Id.*
113. Kitfield, *supra* note 68, at 37.
114. *Id.* at 38.
115. *Id.* at 35.

116. *See* Demetri Sevastopulo, *Gates defends operations inside Pakistan*, FINANCIAL TIMES, Sept. 24, 2008, at 8, col. 1.

117. *See* Robert D. Kaplan, *A Manhunt Or A Vital War?*, NEW YORK TIMES SUNDAY OPINION, Oct. 5, 2008, at 10, col. 2.

118. *See* Sarah Sewall, *Introduction to* THE U.S. ARMY/MARINE CORPS COUNTERINSURGENCY FIELD MANUAL xxi (Univ. of Chicago Press 2007).

119. *Id.* at xxxviii–xxxix.

V

The International Legality of US Military Cross-Border Operations from Afghanistan into Pakistan

Sean D. Murphy*

Introduction

An aspect of US military involvement in Afghanistan since 2001 has been the use of cross-border US operations from Afghanistan into Pakistan, undertaken for the purposes of striking at the camps, compounds, and convoys of Al Qaeda and Taliban elements based in Pakistan, and of defending against cross-border attacks and infiltration by those militants from Pakistan into Afghanistan. As a matter of scale, US cross-border operations are far less momentous than operations that seek to topple a *de jure* government (as occurred when the United States intervened in Iraq in 2003, ousting the government of Saddam Hussein) or a de facto government (as occurred when the United States intervened in Afghanistan in 2001, displacing the largely-unrecognized government of the Taliban). Nevertheless, these smaller-scale cross-border attacks on non-State actors, though they entail less intrusive and more temporary projections of force, implicate important issues of sovereignty, stability, and self-defense, and raise difficult questions about the role of law in regulating low-intensity conflict.

This article discusses the nature of these cross-border operations for the purpose of assessing their legality under the *jus ad bellum*, meaning their consistency

* Patricia Roberts Harris Research Professor of Law, George Washington University Law School.

with the norms embodied in Articles 2(4) and 51 of the UN Charter. Attention is devoted to unpacking the complicated and evolving circumstances on the ground, but the facts at issue in many instances are quite difficult to discern, and hence can support only tentative legal conclusions. While the focus here will principally be on US operations from Afghanistan into Pakistan from 2002 to the present, the analysis is relevant in other contexts as well, such as Turkey's cross-border operations in northern Iraq against the Kurdistan Workers' Party or Colombia's recent forays into Ecuador against the Revolutionary Armed Forces of Colombia.

Among other things, this article assumes that analyzing the legality of US cross-border operations into Pakistan under the *jus ad bellum* is important to the United States. US law and policy generally call for compliance with international law in the conduct of US military operations. Further, US ability to secure the cooperation of other States may turn on whether US operations are in compliance with international law. Support from US allies includes support from Pakistan itself, in that most cargo and much fuel supporting the approximately thirty thousand US forces that are based in landlocked Afghanistan transit through Pakistan.[1] Indeed, in September 2008, the Pakistani government threatened to close down US supply routes into Afghanistan in response to US cross-border operations, prompting the United States to rethink its strategy in this area.[2] Broader US objectives of maintaining a stable Pakistan—an objective arguably paramount for the United States in combating terrorism[3]—may turn in part on internal Pakistani perceptions concerning the legality of US conduct. Moreover, though adjudication of the legality of US cross-border operations before an inter-State tribunal, such as the International Court of Justice, may not be likely, it is not impossible, and adverse rulings may affect the ability of the United States to maintain both domestic and international support for its policies.[4] Finally, the State parties to the Rome Statute[5] establishing the International Criminal Court (ICC), at their review conference in 2010, may activate the ICC's jurisdiction over the crime of aggression, thereby potentially exposing US military personnel engaged in such cross-border operations to international criminal liability.[6] For all these reasons, there is value in assessing the legality of US cross-border operations against Pakistan under the *jus ad bellum.*

US Cross-Border Operations from Afghanistan to Pakistan

The Afghan-Pakistan Border in Law

The 2,250-kilometer-long border between Afghanistan and Pakistan was essentially established in 1893 by Sir Henry Mortimer Durand, a civil servant and diplomat of colonial British India. The purpose of the line (which became known as the

"Durand Line") was to delimit British colonial holdings in India from Afghanistan, since Pakistan did not yet exist as a nation-State. The standard account is that the Durand Line was negotiated with and accepted by the Amir of Afghanistan, Abdur Rahman Khan, and when Pakistan achieved national independence in 1947, Pakistan succeeded to that border.[7]

The border, however, is not without some controversy. Given that the border divides the ancestral home of the Pashtun people, the Pashtuns have objected that the border was imposed by a strong colonial power (Britain) upon a weak State (Afghanistan), which was in no real position to object. In the years after Pakistani independence, Afghanistan began to voice a view that the Durand Line lapsed with the end of the British colonial rule,[8] a position that essentially rejects the internationally accepted principle of *uti possedetis juris* (which maintains that States newly formed out of colonies should have the same borders that they had before their independence). The Afghan position is widely accepted within Afghanistan, but has gained no traction in the international community, and would likely not be accepted by any authoritative decisionmaker, such as the International Court of Justice. By contrast, Pakistan has maintained that the border is of longstanding legality, is fully demarcated and largely follows a series of topographic features that provides for a natural divide.[9]

In short, the border as a legal construct is well known and accepted within the international community. As such, arguments in favor of significant cross-border operations cannot credibly be justified on grounds of uncertainty as to the location of the border or genuinely disputed territory; other justifications are necessary.

The Afghan-Pakistan Border in Practice

While the location of the Afghan-Pakistani border is relatively well settled, the functioning of that border as an effective barrier between the two States is far less so. The movement of peoples across the border is generally unchecked, with sizable populations of both Pashtuns and Baluch on both sides of the border moving freely and engaged in extensive smuggling operations that predate 2001.[10] The graphic[11] depicts the border area. On the Pakistani side of the border, there are certain groups that are the object of US cross-border operations.

First, there are the remnants of Al Qaeda and other extremist Islamic "foreign fighters" who fled across the border from Afghanistan after the US-led intervention in the fall of 2001. US defense officials and independent analysts place the number of Al Qaeda fighters in Afghanistan at somewhere between 150 and 500 persons.[12] Osama Bin Laden is thought to be hiding among those fighters in the Waziristan region of Pakistan, which is part of the Federally Administered Tribal

RAND *MG595-4.2*

Areas (FATA) immediately adjacent to the border,[13] but his whereabouts are not confirmed.

Second, there are remnants of the Afghan Taliban regime (a predominately Pashtun movement) that also fled into Pakistan in late 2001, but have reorganized and experienced a resurgence in fomenting guerrilla resistance to the new Afghan government and its foreign supporters, including the United States.[14] At present, Afghan insurgent groups based along the Afghan-Pakistani demarcation straddle both sides of the border, engaging in classic guerrilla warfare by attacking targets in Afghanistan and then retreating to mountain strongholds on both sides of the border.[15]

Third, there is Pakistan's own Taliban movement (called Tehrik-e-Taliban Pakistan), led by Baitullah Mehsud, and consisting of a cluster of Pashtun tribes and clans united principally by a shared goal of resistance to the Pakistani and US governments. Tehrik-e-Taliban Pakistan has established strongholds in North and South Waziristan, and at present there are concerns about "Talibanization" of the entire western region of Pakistan. While Pakistan's Taliban is principally focused on activities within Pakistan, it is also promoting fighting across the border with US forces in Afghanistan.[16]

The relationship among Al Qaeda, other militant groups, the Afghan Taliban and the Taliban in Pakistan is not entirely transparent, but connections clearly do exist. Many of the "foreign fighters" in the region take their guidance from senior Al Qaeda leaders and serve as "trainers, shock troops, and surrogate leaders for Taliban units in the field."[17] In this way, Al Qaeda is supporting militants who cross the border into Afghanistan, as well as insurgent groups in Afghanistan, in their attacks on US and coalition forces, as well as the Afghan government. A recent RAND report states:

> Al Qaeda played a critical role in the [Afghan] insurgency as a force multiplier, assisting insurgent groups such as the Taliban at the tactical, operational, and strategic levels. Groups such as the Taliban used support and training from jihadists to construct increasingly sophisticated IEDs [improvised explosive devices], including IEDs with remote-control detonators. For example, there were a handful of al Qaeda–run training facilities and IED assembly facilities in such places as North and South Waziristan. . . . al Qaeda received operational and financial support from local clerics and Taliban commanders in Waziristan.[18]

A Taliban commander characterized the Taliban and Al Qaeda in Pakistan as having "close ties," while a US military intelligence official stated that "trying to separate Taliban and al Qaeda in Pakistan serves no purpose. It's like picking gray hairs out of your head."[19]

In recent testimony before the US Senate Armed Service Committee, the Vice Chairman of the Joint Chiefs of Staff, General James Cartwright, testified that Islamic militant fighters crossing the border from the FATA region of Pakistan into Afghanistan account for about 30–40 percent of the guerrilla attacks taking place in Afghanistan against the Afghan government or its allies.[20] Further, those cross-border attacks (many of which are suicide attacks) from Afghanistan have been on the rise, from twenty a month in March 2007 to fifty-three a month in April 2008, with many attacks targeting troops from countries considering whether to withdraw their forces from Afghanistan, such as Canada and the Netherlands.[21] According to the RAND study:

> Several factors can be attributed to the rise in suicide attacks. First, the Taliban successfully tapped into the expertise and training of the broader jihadist community, especially al Qaeda. Jihadists imparted knowledge on suicide tactics to Afghan groups through the Internet and in face-to-face visits. With al Qaeda's assistance, these militants helped supply a steady stream of suicide bombers. Second, al Qaeda and the Taliban concluded that suicide bombing was more effective than other tactics in killing Afghan and coalition forces.[22]

The government of Pakistan generally does not control the FATA region, which is divided into largely autonomous provinces loosely linked to Islamabad by means of a "political agent" (a vestige of British colonialism). Indeed, the legal relationship is so attenuated that the ability of the Pakistani government, under Pakistani law, to authorize US military actions in the FATA is not entirely clear. Consequently, prior to the attacks of September 11, 2001, the border areas were almost entirely in the hands of local tribal groups. After 9/11 and the US-led intervention in Afghanistan, the United States urged Pakistan's central government to exercise greater control over the border areas, which resulted in the Pakistani army reluctantly conducting some counterterrorism operations in the FATA against Taliban and Al Qaeda operatives. Those operations were not effective in eliminating militant groups and caused significant collateral civilian casualties that inflamed local animosity toward the Pakistani government and army.[23] Most military operations have been left to the eighty-thousand-person "Frontier Corps," a poorly trained and underfunded paramilitary force consisting of recruits from local Pashtun tribes serving under regular Pakistani army officers. While these units have sometimes engaged in assaults on Taliban and Al Qaeda elements in the border areas, there are credible reports (denied by the Pakistani government) that elements of the Frontier Corps are closely aligned with the Taliban.[24] In response to Pakistani government military operations, the militant groups in the FATA began conducting a series of suicide attacks against various targets in other parts of Pakistan to show their strength and weaken the Pakistani government, though such attacks may have undermined support for the militants within the Pakistani population.[25]

Islamabad's efforts to "govern" the FATA have always entailed deals being struck between the government, its regional authorities, or the Pakistani army and the FATA tribal officials. In the post-9/11 period, the Pakistani government continued to pursue such deal making, including agreements not just with tribal groups but with Tehrik-e-Taliban Pakistan itself, addressing issues such as control of the border areas, militant terrorist attacks within Pakistan and militant cross-border attacks into Afghanistan.[26] As such, the strategy of the central Pakistani government in handling the western border areas has oscillated between military action and negotiation.

The opaqueness of the relationship among the Pakistani Army, the Frontier Corps and the militants in the FATA somewhat clouds the legal analysis that follows, since the cross-border militant attacks on Afghanistan might or might not be viewed as attributable to the Pakistani government, either due to that government's outright collusion with the Taliban or its failure to take the steps necessary to stop cross-border attacks. On the one hand, in some instances US intelligence officials, as well as independent researchers, have concluded that the Pakistani government has provided direct support to militants for operations in Afghanistan, such as logistical support for a militant car bombing at the Indian Embassy in Kabul in July 2008, a charge denied by Pakistan.[27] In light of those conclusions, it is no surprise that the *Washington Post* reported Central Intelligence Agency and US military officials as saying that they "now withhold intelligence about the suspected whereabouts of al-Qaeda commanders [in Pakistan] out of fear that the Pakistanis might tip them off."[28]

On the other hand, the Pakistani government's general indifference to militant attacks across the border into Afghanistan probably lies less in tacit support for those operations than in a simple belief that pursuing large-scale military operations in the FATA that kill Pashtuns, trample prior agreements providing for the FATA autonomy and incur significant Pakistani army casualties would be extremely unpopular with the Pakistani population and ultimately ineffective in stopping cross-border attacks. Moreover, some Pakistani officials apparently wish to preserve the possibility of a "Taliban option," one that might prove useful for future relations in Afghanistan.[29] Whatever the reason, by mid-2008 the *New York Times* was reporting that "Pakistani officials are making it increasingly clear that they have no interest in stopping cross-border attacks by militants into Afghanistan, prompting a new level of frustration from Americans who see the infiltration as a crucial strategic priority in the war in Afghanistan."[30]

US Cross-Border Operations into Pakistan

US cross-border operations into Pakistan to date have taken three forms: missile strikes from Predator drones, defensive actions in immediate response to a cross-border raid from Pakistan and covert missions by special operations forces against militant targets located deeper in Pakistan. Each should be considered separately when analyzing their legality under the *jus ad bellum*.

First, the United States has engaged in attacks against what are believed to be Al Qaeda and Taliban targets (such as training camps, compounds or convoys) in Pakistan, using Hellfire missiles launched from unmanned Predator aircraft. At least some of those aircraft are reportedly kept at a secret base in Pakistan, not Afghanistan, such that these are not necessarily cross-border operations.[31] Further, the Pakistani government apparently has tacitly agreed that these strikes may be undertaken without specific consent to each operation, so long as they target "foreign fighters" and not Pakistani Taliban, though the existence of that tacit consent is disputed.[32] While the United States does not disclose its strikes, the Pakistani government asserted that three strikes occurred in 2007, while eleven were conducted from January to August of 2008,[33] with perhaps another dozen or more in September and October.[34] The strikes reportedly have had some success, killing several senior Al Qaeda leaders.[35] Yet they have also been blamed for the deaths of dozens of civilians in Pakistan, collateral casualties that have fueled resentment among Pakistanis toward the United States. If relations between the United States and Pakistan were to deteriorate, and Predator aircraft were no longer allowed to be launched from within Pakistan, then presumably such aircraft might be based in Afghanistan for the purpose of undertaking cross-border missions into Pakistan.

Second, while US military forces engaged in military operations in Afghanistan are generally prohibited from crossing or firing into Pakistan, their rules of engagement apparently allow them to do so as a matter of "hot pursuit" when engaging in self-defense.[36] Hence, when US forces come under attack from militants (either by artillery fire from Pakistan or by militant units who cross over the border from Pakistan), US forces have responded forcibly against the militants both in Afghanistan and through pursuit of the militants back into Pakistan. For example, in June 2008, US officials asserted that Taliban fighters from Pakistan crossed over the border into Afghanistan (Kunar Province) and attacked US-led forces with small-caliber weapons and rocket-propelled grenades. The US-led forces returned fire, drove the militants back across the border, and then pursued them with US Air Force fighter-bombers and a B-1 bomber, which dropped twelve gravity bombs on them. Though US forces apparently alerted Pakistani forces in advance about the intended airstrike, Pakistani Frontier Corps personnel were present at a border checkpoint. Eleven were killed by the bombs (as were several of the militants), resulting in a strong protest by the Pakistani government that the US operation was "a gross violation of the international border."[37]

The determination that an attack from Pakistan against US forces in Afghanistan has occurred or is occurring has proven somewhat elastic. Hence, in at least one instance, when US forces received information that militants were on the move in Pakistan and heading toward US forces in Afghanistan, US forces preemptively attacked the militants even before they crossed the border, including striking a compound one mile within Pakistan with missiles.[38]

Third, US cross-border operations now apparently include covert missions by a US joint special operations task force likely consisting of Navy SEALs and the Army's Delta Force[39]) in pursuit of targets in Pakistan's tribal areas—missions not undertaken in immediate response to a cross-border raid from Pakistan. Such missions reportedly were planned but not undertaken up until mid-2008, due to concerns about the likely success of such missions, the effect on relations with the government of Pakistan, and the risks attendant to special forces being killed or captured.[40] In July 2008, however, President Bush reportedly issued secret orders for such operations to occur even in the absence of express and prior Pakistani government approval. According to the *New York Times*, which broke the story:

> The new orders reflect concern about safe havens for al Qaeda and the Taliban inside Pakistan, as well as an American view that Pakistan lacks the will and ability to combat militants. They also illustrate lingering distrust of the Pakistani military and intelligence agencies and a belief that some American operations had been compromised once Pakistanis were advised of the details.[41]

On September 3, 2008, the first operation occurred, involving US Navy SEALs crossing the border on helicopters, supported by an AC-130 gunship, landing in Angor Adda (in the South Waziristan tribal agency), killing about two dozen suspected Al Qaeda fighters and then returning to Afghanistan by helicopter.[42] Pakistani authorities strongly objected to the operation and threatened, if such attacks continued, to cut off US supply lines through Pakistan to US forces in landlocked Afghanistan.[43]

Potential Legal Bases for US Cross-Border Operations

Article 2(4) of the UN Charter provides that "[a]ll Members shall refrain in their international relations from the threat or use of force against the territorial integrity or political independence of any state, or in any other manner inconsistent with the Purposes of the United Nations."[44] The three forms of cross-border (or, with respect to drone aircraft, *potentially* cross-border) operations noted in the prior section would likely be regarded as violations of Article 2(4) in the absence of some form of justification, for they entail military personnel or weapons entering Pakistani territory and inflicting considerable violence upon persons present in Pakistan and their property. There are, however, four potential bases for justifying these cross-border operations under international law: (A) consent by the Pakistani government, (B) authorization by the UN Security Council, (C) inherent self-defense against non-State actors operating from Pakistan or (D) inherent self-defense against Pakistan itself. Each justification is briefly discussed in turn.

US Cross-Border Action Taken with the Consent of Pakistan

To the extent that the government of Pakistan has consented to US cross-border military operations from Afghanistan into Pakistan, that consent obviates any question about the legality of those operations under international law. Standard rules on State responsibility accept that conduct does not violate an obligation to a State if that State has consented to the conduct,[45] and that view applies in the area of the *jus ad bellum* as well.[46] While the legal justification for US cross-border operations appears heavily reliant on Pakistani consent, the existence of such consent to the three forms of US cross-border operations discussed above is not at all clear or may not prove enduring.

Media reports, largely based on off-the-record comments by senior US and Pakistani officials, indicate that Pakistan's civilian and military leadership are not prepared publicly to support US cross-border operations into Pakistan.[47] Yet that lack of public consent does not mean that Pakistani consent does not exist. Surveying the background to US cross-border operations, the *Washington Post* has noted that although Pakistan "formally protests such actions as a violation of its sovereignty, the Pakistani government has generally looked the other way when the CIA conducted Predator missions or US troops respond to cross-border attacks by the Taliban."[48] There may be internal documents or communications from the Pakistani government that clarify such consent and, if so, the United States will be in a strong position to establish the legality of these operations in whatever venue is necessary, assuming such information can be made public. Certainly the Pakistani government's knowledge of Predator drones being based in Pakistan, and its knowledge that such aircraft are being used for missile strikes, presents a strong picture of tacit consent so long as such knowledge can be established. However, if the claim of the Pakistani government's consent is based solely on a belief that the Pakistani government is "looking the other way," then establishing consent may be difficult in the face of the various public protests about US cross-border actions that have been made by Pakistan.

With respect to the more recent special operations missions, the *New York Times* reported that a "senior American official said that the Pakistani government had privately assented to the general concept of limited ground assaults by Special Operations forces against significant militant targets, but that it did not approve each mission."[49] Yet the public stance of the Pakistani government is that such operations are not permitted.[50] In the wake of the September 3, 2008 cross-border operation by US Navy SEALs, and the adverse reaction of the Pakistani army and public opinion to such raids, the Chief of the Army Staff, General Ashfaq Parvez Kayani, asserted: "There is no question of any agreement or understanding with the coalition forces whereby they are allowed to conduct operations on our side of the border."[51]

Confusion about the existence of consent stems in part from the fractured nature of the Pakistani government.[52] The President of Pakistan, Asif Ali Zardari, is the official head of State, while Prime Minister Syed Yousaf Raza Gillani is the head of government. The President and his designees would normally be looked to for Pakistani consent to the use of force by another State in Pakistan. Under Pakistani law, the President appoints the Chief of the Army Staff, currently General Ashfaq Parvez Kayani, an individual who might be seen as deputized to provide consent on behalf of the President. Yet, at present, there is a considerable divide in views between President Zardari and the Army leadership, including over Pakistani consent to US cross-border operations.[53] The Army's disagreements with the civilian leadership are not simply bureaucratic maneuvers; on several occasions the Army has overthrown the President and Prime Minister, most recently in October 1999 when the Army deposed the elected Prime Minister, Nawaz Sharif, in a bloodless coup.[54] Moreover, as indicated above, with the "Talibanization" of the western region, Pakistani sovereign power in the FATA is almost *de minimis,* suggesting a nascent insurgency that already contests Islamabad's authority in the west and that may ultimately contest it nationwide. Depending on how Pakistani politics unfold, discerning consent solely from the President may or may not reflect the true source of sovereign power in Pakistan.

Even if sovereign consent may be discerned, there are disadvantages to the United States in basing the *jus ad bellum* legality of its operations solely on the consent of the Pakistani government. That consent, whether given explicitly or implicitly, may be withdrawn at any time, unless it is expressed as a legally binding commitment for a specified period of time. With the changes in leadership within Pakistan in recent years, consent from the government cannot be relied upon as steadfast. Moreover, consent may always be predicated on certain requirements, such as prior notification of a given action to the Pakistani government, which may be difficult for time-sensitive operations or where concerns exist about maintaining confidentiality. Since the host government's consent only establishes the legality of action taken within the scope of the consent, any US operations taken outside that scope will implicate Article 2(4). For example, if it is true that Predator drone strikes are only authorized for attacks against Al Qaeda or foreign fighters, then pursuit of such strikes against the Taliban could be regarded as a violation of the *jus ad bellum*.

Finally, while consent is a valid justification when it is received from a *de jure* government fully in control of its territory, it might become invalid if that government no longer controls or only partially controls its territory. Traditional *jus ad bellum* doctrine regards support for a government as permissible until such point as an internal insurgency has risen to the level of being a co-belligerent with the government, at which point arguably the government is no longer "in a position to invite assistance in the name of the state."[55] If the apparent "Talibanization" of the western provinces of Pakistan continues apace, and spreads throughout Pakistan, at some point the ability of the *de jure* government to consent to US cross-border operations under international law may be regarded in the international community as insufficient to support the legality of those operations.[56]

In short, consent of the Pakistani government is a strong legal justification for the use of US Predator aircraft in Pakistan, so long as Pakistan continues to allow them to be launched from a Pakistani base. US *cross-border* operations, however, can only rely upon this justification if authoritative decisionmakers in Pakistan have formally consented to the type of operation at issue, and so long as that consent remains intact. The facts publicly available suggest Pakistani tolerance of, but not necessarily formal consent to, US cross-border operations undertaken in immediate response to attacks by militants staged from Pakistan. Even for these operations, Pakistan appears to expect notification and avoidance of actions that could harm Pakistani forces or civilians. By contrast, Pakistan publicly appears to have rejected cross-border operations by US special forces undertaken deeper in Pakistani territory and not in response to an immediate raid from Pakistan. Overall, given the potential difficulty in proving the existence of Pakistani consent to US cross-border operations, and the possibility of such consent ending, other justifications for US cross-border operations should be considered as well.

US Cross-Border Action Authorized by the UN Security Council

Assuming that Pakistani government consent cannot be found in support of all or some of the US cross-border operations, an alternative basis for legality might be pursued in the form of Security Council authorization. When acting under UN

Charter Chapter VII, the Security Council is empowered to decide upon measures necessary for maintaining or restoring peace and security, including measures that are forcible in nature.[57] The Security Council has adopted several resolutions relating to Afghanistan in the aftermath of the attacks of 9/11, but none of those resolutions appear to authorize US cross-border operations into Pakistan.

Prior to the overthrow of the de facto Afghan government of the Taliban, the Security Council adopted two resolutions that affirmed, in the context of the 9/11 attacks, the inherent right of individual and collective self-defense and the need "to combat by all means" the "threats to international peace and security caused by terrorist acts."[58] These resolutions did not constitute a Chapter VII authorization from the Security Council to use force; rather, they were a confirmation of an inherent right of self-defense that preceded and was preserved through passage of the resolutions.[59] The next subsection considers whether US cross-border operations into Pakistan can be justified on the basis of individual or collective self-defense.

After the de facto Taliban government was overthrown in late 2001, the United Nations facilitated negotiations in Bonn, Germany to establish a framework and timeline for the establishment of new Afghan political institutions. Moreover, Annex 1 of the Bonn Agreement provided that "the participants request the assistance of the international community in helping the new Afghan authorities in the establishment and training of new Afghan security and armed forces," and requested "the early deployment to Afghanistan of a United Nations mandated force."[60] In Resolution 1386, the Security Council endorsed the Bonn Agreement and authorized the establishment of the International Security Assistance Force (ISAF) "to assist the Afghan Interim Authority in the maintenance of security in Kabul and its surrounding areas, so that the Afghan Interim Authority as well as the personnel of the United Nations can operate in a secure environment."[61] The resolution also called upon "Member States participating in the International Security Assistance Force to provide assistance to help the Afghan Interim Authority in the establishment and training of new Afghan security and armed forces."[62] Shortly thereafter, the interim Afghan government concluded a bilateral agreement with the ISAF concerning the size of the deployment and the tasks it would undertake.[63] In 2002, the Security Council adopted Resolution 1413, authorizing "Member States participating in the International Security Assistance Force to take all necessary measures to fulfill the mandate of the International Security Assistance Force."[64] Subsequent resolutions have extended ISAF's mandate temporally[65] and geographically, such as allowing ISAF

> to support the Afghan Transitional Authority and its successors in the maintenance of security in areas of Afghanistan outside of Kabul and its environs, so that the Afghan

> Authorities as well as the personnel of the United Nations and other international civilian personnel engaged, in particular, in reconstruction and humanitarian efforts, can operate in a secure environment, and to provide security assistance for the performance of other tasks in support of the Bonn Agreement.[66]

From these instruments, it is apparent that the ISAF is a multinational security force authorized by the UN Security Council under Chapter VII of the UN Charter. The ISAF is not a UN force in the sense of being funded by, and under the command-and-control of, the United Nations; rather, it is a coalition of self-funding States authorized by the Security Council to engage in specified tasks in Afghanistan. Though the Security Council theoretically could authorize the ISAF to engage in cross-border operations into Pakistan, no such authorization exists in any of the Security Council resolutions either expressly or by implication. Indeed, while the ISAF sees its mission as including efforts to defeat the threat of insurgency in Afghanistan, NATO's 2005 Operational Plan, as revised, provides that ISAF's mission is the stabilization of Afghanistan, not counterterrorism.[67]

US cross-border operations are not undertaken through the ISAF. Rather, such operations occur as a part of the multinational coalition of States present in Afghanistan for Operation Enduring Freedom (OEF). US forces in Afghanistan for OEF are deployed as Combined Joint Task Force–82 (CJTF-82), which is based at Bagram Air Base. That task force reports to the US-led Combined Forces Command–Afghanistan, which is based in Kabul. CJTF-82 operates and supervises a Combined Joint Special Operations Task Force–Afghanistan, which consists of special operations forces. Yet there is also reportedly an "Other Coalition Forces" unit of special operations forces, which does not report to CJTF-82. This latter, more secretive unit may be the one responsible for the covert US cross-border missions into Pakistan.

In any event, all of these US forces deployed for OEF are separate from the US forces deployed in support of the UN-mandated and NATO-led ISAF which, as discussed above, is focused on providing security in Kabul and its surrounding areas for the Afghan government, and assisting the government in the establishment and training of Afghan security and armed forces. The ISAF and OEF have completely separate mandates and missions, with the ISAF focusing on a stabilization and security mission, while OEF focuses on the counterterrorism mission. None of the Security Council resolutions discussed above relate to OEF and hence cannot serve as a basis for a Security Council mandate for the United States to engage in cross-border operations into Pakistan.

US Cross-Border Action Taken in Self-Defense against Non-State Actors

A third basis for finding US cross-border operations into Pakistan permissible under the *jus ad bellum* relies upon the United States' inherent right of self-defense or its right to engage in collective self-defense at the request of Afghanistan. Article 51 of the UN Charter indicates that the prohibition on the use of force embedded in Article 2(4) may be overcome when acting in self-defense, since "[n]othing in the present Charter shall impair the inherent right of individual or collective self-defence if an armed attack occurs against a Member of the United Nations, until the Security Council has taken the measures necessary to maintain international peace and security."[68]

In considering this basis, there are several key and perhaps troubling questions that arise: What was the preceding use of force against which the United States is defending? Does that preceding use of force rise to the level of an "armed attack" within the meaning of UN Charter Article 51? Can the United States invoke Article 51 when defending against the conduct of a non-State actor? Are the US cross-border actions necessary and proportionate defensive responses? Each question is discussed in turn.

What Was the Preceding Use of Force against Which the United States Is Defending?

There are two candidates for the preceding use of force to which the United States is responding in self-defense. First, the United States might be seen today as still defending against Al Qaeda's attacks of 9/11 (as well as perhaps other actions taken by Al Qaeda globally against the United States, such as the 1998 bombing of US embassies in Tanzania and Kenya and the 2000 attack on the *USS Cole* in Yemen). If the initial US invasion of Afghanistan was a permissible act of self-defense against the perpetrators of 9/11, one designed to diminish or destroy Al Qaeda's network, then cross-border operations today might be seen as part of a continuous process to accomplish that objective, albeit years later. There has been no temporal interruption in the deployment of US forces for this purpose, nor has there been a geographic interruption given that Al Qaeda elements fled toward and across the Pakistani border.

One complicating factor, however, arises from the use of cross-border operations to diminish or destroy the Taliban instead of Al Qaeda. Even at the time of 9/11, there were some doubts expressed about the right of the United States to defend against the 9/11 attacks by using force for the purpose of ousting and destroying the Taliban.[69] While selective attacks on the Taliban that were necessary to defend US forces hunting down Al Qaeda elements post-9/11 were squarely within the notion of self-defending against Al Qaeda's 9/11 attacks, operations directed solely against the Taliban were seen as more problematic, since the Taliban was not directly involved in the 9/11 attacks, in the sense of planning, funding, sending persons or otherwise sponsoring those attacks.

An alternative preceding act triggering a right of US self-defense is the more recent cross-border raids into Afghanistan by militants based in Pakistan (mostly Taliban, but with support from Al Qaeda and other foreign fighters) to strike at US or coalition forces, or the government of Afghanistan. This approach does not emphasize the attacks of 9/11 but, rather, the contemporary cross-border operations that are harming coalition and Afghan interests in Afghanistan. So long as Afghanistan has consented to the presence of US forces as a means of assisting Afghanistan in defending against such attacks, US actions fall within the scope of either individual or collective self-defense, though they should be notified to the UN Security Council in accordance with UN Charter Article 51. Afghan President Hamid Karzai himself has asserted Afghanistan's right to defend itself from such attacks by crossing the border into Pakistan and destroying "terrorist nests."[70] Here, though, the complicating factor is the converse of that noted above; to the extent that the Taliban is principally responsible for such cross-border operations, then it is its conduct that may be seen as triggering a right of self-defense and it is its conduct against which defensive measures may be taken. Only to the extent that Al Qaeda is engaged in the cross-border attacks into Afghanistan can US defensive responses against those attacks target Al Qaeda elements.

The upshot is that the preceding acts at issue may be a hybrid. US cross-border actions against Al Qaeda in the form of covert special forces missions (as well as Predator attacks when launched from Afghanistan) are probably best viewed as a continuing defensive response to the attacks of 9/11, whereas actions against Taliban and other militants infiltrating Afghanistan are best viewed as defensive responses against attacks occurring today on coalition forces in Afghanistan, as well as the Afghan government.

Do Those Preceding Uses of Force Rise to the Level of an "Armed Attack" within the Meaning of UN Charter Article 51?

Article 51, by its terms, preserves a pre-existing right of self defense "if an armed attack occurs." Scholars and States differ over whether such language necessarily requires that an "armed attack" occur before the resort to self-defense,[71] but governments typically argue that such an attack has occurred whenever they resort to self-defense.[72] As such, a key question is whether the preceding actions that justify US cross-border operations rise to the level of being an "armed attack" within the meaning of Article 51. In the case concerning *Military and Paramilitary Activities in and against Nicaragua (Nicaragua v. United States of America)*, the International Court of Justice provided some guidance on this point. On the one hand, a

State's deployment of regular armed forces across a border, or the sending by a State of "armed bands, groups, irregulars or mercenaries which carry out acts of armed force," can constitute an armed attack; on the other hand, a State's "assistance to rebels in the form of the provision of weapons or logistical or other support" does not constitute an armed attack.[73] Hence, there is a sliding scale by which one assesses the level of intrusiveness and gravity of the act at issue to determine whether it rises to a level of "armed attack" that triggers a right of self-defense under Article 51.

With respect to the preceding act of Al Qaeda's conduct on 9/11, there should be little doubt that such coercion constitutes an "armed attack," given the scale of destruction and loss of life that occurred, as well as the reactions of the United States and relevant international organizations, all of which characterized the conduct as attacks triggering a right of self-defense.[74]

With respect to the preceding act of Taliban cross-border operations into Afghanistan, the gravity of those actions to date are of a much different character, in terms of the loss of life and destruction. Nevertheless, as indicated previously, the attacks are occurring at a rate of from twenty a month in March 2007 to fifty-three a month in April 2008, causing considerable injury and deaths to Afghans and the coalition forces that are in Afghanistan with Afghan consent. While any given cross-border raid into Afghanistan by militants from Pakistan might be said to fall below the threshold of an armed attack, and instead constitute merely a "frontier incident,"[75] the cumulative effect of all these cross-border attacks by militants would likely be seen as constituting an "armed attack" within the meaning of Article 51.

Can the United States Invoke Article 51 When Defending against the Conduct of a Non-State Actor?

Article 2(4) prohibits uses of force by one State against another State. Article 51 is less clear in speaking solely to conduct between two States, since its language simply speaks of a UN member's inherent right of self-defense against an armed attack, without indicating whether it is a State that must be undertaking that attack. Even so, it might be argued that the Charter was designed solely to speak to rights and obligations as between States, and any act of self-defense must be in response to an armed attack committed by or attributable to another State.[76] In the *Military and Paramilitary Activities* case, the International Court of Justice regarded attribution of non-State actor conduct to a State as the critical factor when weighing the permissibility of defensive action against that State, but did not directly address the issue of defensive action against the non-State actor itself.[77] However, in the *Advisory Opinion on the Israeli Wall*, the Court—without much analysis—rejected Israel's claim that it was acting in self-defense against attacks by terrorist groups. The Court opined that Israel could not be acting in self-defense under Article 51 because (1) Israel had not claimed that the terrorist attacks at issue were imputable to a foreign State and (2) those attacks were not transnational in nature, having occurred wholly within territory occupied by Israel.[78]

If the advisory opinion is correctly interpreting the *jus ad bellum*, then it may not be possible to engage in Article 51 self-defense against a non-State actor; rather, self-defense is reserved for actions against another State, perhaps in situations where the acts of the non-State actor have been imputed to that other State. The Court's opinion, however, has been subjected to considerable criticism, much of which notes the fact that the global community (including the Security Council, NATO, and the Organization of American States (OAS)) appears to have regarded the attacks by Al Qaeda of 9/11 as justifying a response in self-defense.[79] Such criticisms may explain a possible retreat by the Court in its 2005 case concerning *Armed Activities on the Territory of the Congo*. In that case, rather than repeat its legal position from the advisory opinion, the Court stated that, given the *facts at issue in the case*, there was "no need to respond to the contentions of the Parties as to whether and under what conditions contemporary international law provides for a right of self-defense against large-scale attacks by irregular forces."[80] Both Judges Kooijmans and Simma stated in separate opinions that, if the Court still views Article 51 as restricted to self-defense only against an attack by another State, then the Court is out of step with both the Security Council and State practice.[81]

While this area of the law remains somewhat uncertain, the dominant trend in contemporary interstate relations seems to favor the view that States accept or at least tolerate acts of self-defense against a non-State actor. Turkey has engaged in various cross-border operations against the Kurdish separatist guerrilla organization known as the Kurdistan Workers' Party,[82] without being condemned by the Security Council, General Assembly, or International Court. In early 2008, Colombian military forces bombed and crossed into Ecuador to attack guerrillas of the Revolutionary Armed Forces of Columbia, which is regarded by Colombia as a terrorist and drug-trafficking organization. Again, none of the principal organs of the United Nations criticized the action; while the Organization of American States adopted a resolution declaring the Colombian raid to be a violation of Ecuador's sovereignty, the OAS stopped short of expressly condemning Colombia.[83] Israel in the summer of 2006 sent military forces into, and bombed portions of, southern Lebanon in an effort to strike at the Hezbollah movement, which has operated out of Lebanon to attack and kill Israeli nationals.[84] Similarly, in early 2008, Israel launched a major military ground operation, as well as airstrikes, against Hamas fighters in the Gaza Strip.[85] In neither instance did the principal UN organs declare the conduct unlawful self-defense. The United States undertook an airstrike inside Syria in October 2008 reportedly to stem the flow of foreign fighters and weapons from that country into Iraq.[86] As is the case for most customary law on the *jus ad bellum* norms, it is not possible to demonstrate through widespread and systematic State practice that the concept of self-defense embraces action against non-State actors, but the better view appears to be that it does.

Are the US Cross-Border Actions Necessary and Proportionate Defensive Responses? Although Article 51 of the UN Charter does not expressly require that self-defense be undertaken only as necessary and proportionate to the threat faced, those constraints present in customary international law on the use of force have been deemed applicable to the post-Charter *jus ad bellum*. As the International Court of Justice has stated:

> The submission of the exercise of the right of self-defence to the conditions of necessity and proportionality is a rule of customary international law. As the Court stated in the case concerning *Military and Paramilitary Activities in and against Nicaragua (Nicaragua v. United States of America)*: there is a "specific rule whereby self-defence would warrant only measures which are proportional to the armed attack and necessary to respond to it, a rule well established in customary international law" (*I.C.J. Reports 1986*, p. 94, para. 176). This dual condition applies equally to Article 51 of the Charter, whatever the means of force employed.[87]

In considering whether force is "necessary," the International Court of Justice and scholars typically first consider whether there are peaceful alternatives to self-defense, such as pursuing available diplomatic avenues.[88] This might entail determining whether the attacker has been asked to desist from further attacks and to make reparation for injuries it has caused. Assuming that no reasonable alternative means exist, the concept of "necessity" focuses on the nature of the target pursued by the defender; where the target is the source (or one of the sources) of the threat to the defender, it is considered necessary defense to attack that target. "Necessity" does not require a defender to limit itself to actions that merely repel an initial attack; a State may use force in self-defense to remove a continuing threat to future security,[89] such as pursuing action against Japan in the 1940s until its militarist regime had capitulated. An example of a lack of necessity may be seen in the International Court of Justice's *Oil Platforms* case, where the Court found that the United States did not complain to Iran about the military activities allegedly undertaken from the platforms, nor prove that the platforms were the source of the threat to the United States in the Gulf such that attacking them was necessary for eliminating that threat.[90]

"Proportionality" does not require that the force be a mirror image of the initial attack, or that the defensive actions be restricted to the particular geographic location in which the initial attack occurred. Rather than focus on the form, substance or strength of the initial attack, proportionality calls for assessing the result sought for eliminating that threat and the means being used to achieve that result.[91] As suggested by Professor Roberto Ago, a rapporteur for the International Law Commission on the rules of State responsibility and later judge on the International Court of Justice, "[I]n the case of action taken for the specific purpose of halting and repelling an armed attack, this does not mean that the action should be more or less commensurate with the attack. Its lawfulness cannot be measured except by its capacity for achieving the desired result."[92] Such reasoning is reflected in the national military manuals adopted by many States; for instance, the US *Commander's Handbook on the Law of Naval Operations* indicates that proportionality imposes a "requirement that the use of force be in all circumstances limited in intensity, duration, and scope to that which is reasonably required to counter the attack or threat of attack and to ensure the continued safety of U.S. forces."[93]

In the *Oil Platforms* case, the International Court signaled that, if it were proved that a shore-based missile had been launched by Iran against a US flag vessel, a proportionate defensive response could include destroying an Iranian oil platform elsewhere in the Gulf, so long as the platform was shown to be engaged in assisting attacks on US vessels in the Gulf. In other words, the Court found that a proportionate defensive response to a missile attack on a vessel was not limited to infliction of a missile attack in response, nor limited to the targeting of the facility from which the missile was launched. At the same time, the Court stated that, in a situation where the attack consists of the single mining of a ship (which was damaged but not sunk), a defensive response that destroys numerous vessels and aircraft of the attacker, as well as oil platforms, is disproportionate in scale to the threat.[94] While one might argue about the Court's treatment of the facts in that case, the thrust of the Court's *dicta* was to consider the nature of the threat being faced by the defender and whether the defensive conduct, by its nature and scale, was designed to eliminate that threat. Similarly, in *Armed Activities on the Territory of the Congo*, the Court indicated that the armed "taking of airports and towns many hundreds of kilometers from [the defending State's] border would not seem proportionate to the series of transborder attacks it claimed had given rise to the right of self-defence, nor to be necessary to that end."[95]

In considering the necessity and proportionality of US cross-border operations against Pakistan, it is important to focus on the two preceding threats that appear to have prompted those operations: the attacks of 9/11 and the more recent cross-border attacks from Pakistan into Afghanistan.

First, the Al Qaeda attacks of 9/11 serve as a preceding "armed attack" against the United States triggering a right of self-defense in the form of operations designed to remove the threat of Al Qaeda. Given that for years the United States had demanded that Al Qaeda desist from its activities and had sought extradition of Bin Laden and his lieutenants from Afghanistan, and given that the 9/11 attacks were attributable to planning, training and funding emanating from Afghanistan,[96] the defensive response taken against Al Qaeda personnel and camps *in Afghanistan* is properly regarded as both necessary and proportionate.[97]

Yet most international observers or courts would likely find that the same is not true with respect to the ability of the United States to pursue defensive actions against Al Qaeda across a national boundary into Pakistan or any other country. Here the use of force in self-defense in response to the attacks of 9/11 would likely be seen as both unnecessary and disproportionate, principally because Pakistan is a third country that in no sense harbored Al Qaeda elements at the time of 9/11. Such use of force is unnecessary given Pakistan's stated willingness to ally itself with the United States in its counterterrorism efforts to strike at Al Qaeda. The United States no doubt disagrees and distrusts aspects of Pakistani policy on how best to engage in counterterrorism; yet those disagreements alone do not provide the legal justification for the United States to engage in unilateral uses of force in Pakistan. While working in conjunction with the Pakistani government is no doubt a difficult diplomatic challenge, most observers would likely say that it is an available avenue that makes the unilateral resort to force unnecessary.[98]

For similar reasons, the unilateral use of force to strike at Al Qaeda in Pakistan in response to the 9/11 attacks would be found disproportionate, in that the spatial and temporal displacement of the threat of Al Qaeda to a different nation introduces important competing values, to wit the territorial integrity and political independence of a nation that did not knowingly support, sponsor or tolerate Al Qaeda in the years preceding 9/11. The violence that invariably accompanies unilateral uses of force, even those taken in self-defense, intrudes severely into the values of peace and stability to which Pakistan is entitled under the *jus ad bellum*, and does so without justification when the targeted State bears no responsibility for the initial armed attack against which defensive action is being deployed.[99] Certainly if Osama Bin Laden were to turn up in a nation such as Bulgaria or Tunisia, that circumstance would introduce multiple new variables for any proportionality analysis, such that the United States could not rely on the same analysis that justified intervening in Afghanistan in 2001. The same holds true for Pakistan, notwithstanding its existence as a neighbor to Afghanistan.

A final consideration is that, arguably, the threat to the United States from Al Qaeda itself has changed since 9/11; the Al Qaeda now in Pakistan is a considerably reduced and weakened entity, one forced to hide out in the hills, with difficulty in sustaining the same infrastructure it operated in Afghanistan. Some observers see Al Qaeda as having mutated into an almost headless hydra, such that the real threat of attacks to the United States now largely lies in numerous cells located worldwide.[100] If so, then the elements of Al Qaeda present in Afghanistan, including Osama Bin Laden, remain dangerous, but may not be seen as operationally threatening the United States in the same manner as they did in 2001. As such, the defensive action that may be taken against those elements, in order to be proportionate, could be viewed as of a lesser magnitude than what was regarded as permissible in the immediate aftermath of 9/11. Not all analysts, however, see the threat of Al Qaeda as having changed so significantly since 9/11. While there may be "a low-level probability that al Qaeda will be able to attack the United States in the next five years," Al Qaeda even based along the Afghan-Pakistani border is still able to train personnel for and direct attacks abroad, such as the July 2005 London bombings, the foiled August 2006 plot in the United Kingdom to blow up US airliners with liquid explosives and Al Qaeda attacks in Iraq.[101]

Could circumstances change in Pakistan that might generate a consensus favorable to the unilateral resort to armed force in Pakistan against Al Qaeda because the latter represents a broad threat to US national security? Certainly if the same circumstances arose as existed at the time of 9/11—with a radical Islamic government in Islamabad, one hostile to the United States and with close connections to Al Qaeda, resulting in a major Al Qaeda attack on the United States—then the unilateral use of force in self-defense against Al Qaeda in Pakistan would likely be seen as justified, just as it was in Afghanistan in 2001. A more difficult question might be whether such force would be justified in the period prior to Al Qaeda in Pakistan's attack on the United States, perhaps due to highly credible information concerning an imminent attack. At present, however, Pakistan simply is not like Afghanistan under the Taliban in 2001, and it is hoped that with proper support from the United States and other allies, and avoidance of tactics that fuel militancy, Pakistan will not descend to that level.

The second type of preceding armed attack are the cross-border raids by militants from Pakistan, principally Taliban but with support from Al Qaeda, against US and coalition forces and the Afghan government in Afghanistan. Here the *jus ad bellum* requirements of necessity and proportionality do not lend themselves to broad conclusions, but do provide guidance for analyzing confrontations as they arise along the border. For example, the necessity of US forces reacting to incursions by militants from Afghanistan will turn in part on whether the United States has pursued and continues to pursue all avenues possible to obtain Pakistani government support for preventing such incursions. Responses by US forces to militant incursions will be regarded as necessary if it is evident that Pakistani authorities are unwilling or unable to stem such incursions from their territory. Further, responses by US forces that react to an actual raid by militants into Afghanistan likely will be regarded as more necessary than those that act to interdict anticipated incursions, given that there is always uncertainty as to whether the anticipated event will actually occur. Responses by US forces that react to incursions by directly and immediately targeting those militants, using force of a comparable nature and scale, likely will be regarded as more proportionate than responses that target other militants in other places and times, using force of considerably greater magnitude, though even the latter can be proportionate if designed to remove the overall threat of cross-border incursions from Pakistan.

A perhaps harder question concerns the necessity and proportionality of striking at Al Qaeda officials, camps or convoys *as a response to Al Qaeda's support for militant cross-border raids into Afghanistan.* Such attacks are more removed temporally and spatially from the cross-border raids by militants. Yet if Al Qaeda is providing training and other support for such raids, and in some instances even commanding them, then most observers would likely regard it as proportionate to the threat posed to respond by attacking persons and entities behind-the-lines directly associated with the raids. The facts of Al Qaeda's association with these cross-border raids would have to be well understood and the acts of self-defense by the United States against Al Qaeda, in order to be proportionate, would need to be designed to prevent that association. As for whether such actions are necessary, they are not necessary in the sense of providing immediate defense to US forces in Afghanistan who are under attack, but they are necessary if it can be shown that, in the absence of such actions, the cross-border raids from Pakistan will continue.

The distinction drawn here may seem meaningless, if it allows the United States to strike at Al Qaeda not for purposes of responding to 9/11, but instead for purposes of responding to Al Qaeda's association with cross-border raids into Afghanistan. Yet the point is that while *jus ad bellum* requirements of proportionality and necessity do not preclude US cross-border operations in response to raids by militants from Pakistan, nor attacks on Al Qaeda elements in support of those raids, those requirements will likely be regarded as conditioning the manner in which the US operations may be conducted. Rather than testing the necessity and proportionality of US operations against the threat posed by Al Qaeda from its attacks of 9/11, they must be tested against the threat posed by Al Qaeda in its association with the cross-border raids, which, depending on the facts, can lead to considerable differences in the scope and intensity of US measures that may be undertaken.

US Cross-Border Action Taken in Self-Defense against Pakistan

At present, the United States has not regarded Pakistan itself as posing a threat to the security of the United States, but this may change in the future. As discussed above, while the Pakistani government's relationship with militant actors in the western part of Pakistan is obscure, it is reasonably clear that Pakistan's interests and objectives are not fully synchronized with those of the United States. Though Pakistani officials seem to have no particular sympathy for Al Qaeda, the same is not uniformly true with respect to Tehrik-e-Taliban Pakistan. Over time, Pakistan's tolerance if not support for Tehrik-e-Taliban Pakistan may lead to some level of indirect support for Al Qaeda, which would place Pakistan at considerable odds with US interests.

The *jus ad bellum* disfavors action taken in self-defense against a government that is simply associated with a malfeasant non-State actor. The lesson of the *Nicaragua* case is that when a State simply harbors or even funds a bad actor, and that bad actor engages in an act of extreme violence against another State, the first State is not viewed as itself having committed an armed attack against the attacked State. Rules of State responsibility on the attribution of conduct to a State would require the host State itself to order the bad actor to engage in the violent conduct, to empower the bad actor to act on the State's behalf, to endorse the violent conduct, or perhaps to fail to prevent the violent conduct knowing that it was about to happen and having the means to prevent it.[102] As such, imputing the armed attacks of Al Qaeda or of the Taliban as being armed attacks of Pakistan would be a significant leap, at least in the absence of far greater connections between the Pakistani government and those militants than is presently understood to exist.

Conclusion

To date, US cross-border operations from Afghanistan into Pakistan have taken three forms: the use of Predator drones to target Al Qaeda fighters (although such drones may be launched solely from within Pakistan); the "hot pursuit" of militants who engaged in raids from Pakistan against US and allied forces in Afghanistan, as well as the Afghan government; and the deployment of special operations forces into Pakistan as a means of striking at Al Qaeda.

These types of cross-border operations clearly implicate the *jus ad bellum*, in that they entail one State projecting highly coercive military force into another State. Arguably Pakistan has consented to at least some of these types of cross-border operations, but that consent is poorly documented, suffers from the conflicting and diffuse sources of authority within the Pakistani government, and ultimately may not endure given the vicissitudes of Pakistani domestic politics. As such, though consent is a powerful and useful basis for supporting the legality of US cross-border operations, other justifications should be considered as well.

Assuming Pakistani consent is lacking, other justifications for US cross-border operations must be considered. The UN Security Council has on several occasions addressed the legality of foreign forces in Afghanistan. Yet the Security Council's Chapter VII resolutions are best seen as either authorizing the presence of a multinational force designed to stabilize Afghanistan (without having as its mission counterterrorism operations, let alone operations outside Afghanistan), or simply recognizing the inherent right of self-defense of the United States and its allies. The inherent right of self-defense (individual and collective) does justify US cross-border operations that respond to raids by militants from Pakistan into Afghanistan, so long as the US operations remain necessary and proportionate to the threat of those raids, and so long as the Afghan government consents to the presence of US forces. Such self-defense would also support unilateral uses of US force against Al Qaeda in Pakistan, in the form of either covert operations by special forces units or the launching of Predators from Afghanistan to strike at targets in Pakistan, so long as it can be shown that those Al Qaeda targets are ones that are supporting the cross-border raids into Pakistan, and so long as Pakistan is unwilling or unable to prevent Al Qaeda's support for those raids.

A *broader* right of self-defense against Al Qaeda targets in Pakistan based on the attacks of 9/11, however, is far more problematic, since the requirements of necessity and proportionality likely preclude unilateral uses of force against a third State that was not implicated in those attacks. In general, the *jus ad bellum* recognizes important rights of a defending State to maintain its security against the violence of a non-State actor, but those values must coexist with the rights of other States to their own security, rights that are not lost simply because the remnants of a dangerous non-State actor turn up on their territory. While circumstances may change in the future that could justify unilateral uses of US force against Pakistan for the broader threat Al Qaeda poses to the United States, the *jus ad bellum* at present requires the United States, when pursuing that objective, to cooperate with the government of Pakistan in finding and neutralizing Al Qaeda, not launch unilateral attacks through covert missions and missile strikes by the United States without Pakistani consent.

Notes

1. *See* Congressional Research Service, *Pakistan-U.S. Relations* 24 (Aug. 25, 2008), *available at* http://www.fas.org/sgp/crs/row/RL33498.pdf [hereinafter "CRS Report"]; Ann Scott Tyson, *Gates Is Pessimistic on Pakistani Support*, WASHINGTON POST, Sept. 24, 2008, at A16 (reporting comments of Senators Carl Levin and John Warner).

2. *See* Sean D. Naylor, *Spec Ops Raids Into Pakistan Halted*, NAVY TIMES, Sept. 29, 2008.

3. *See* Polly Nayak, *The Impact of Pakistan's and Bangladesh's National Strategies on U.S. Interests*, *in* STRATEGIC ASIA 2008–09: CHALLENGES AND CHOICES 297, 318–20 (Ashley J. Tellis, Merch Kuo & Andrew Marble eds., 2008).

4. For instance, Pakistan might invoke against the United States the 1959 bilateral Treaty of Friendship and Commerce, U.S.-Pak., Nov. 12, 1959, 12 U.S.T. 110, which provides for International Court of Justice jurisdiction when disputes arise. Iran and Nicaragua have both invoked similar treaties against the United States in response to US military or paramilitary operations.

5. *See* Statute of the International Criminal Court, July 17, 1998, 2187 U.N.T.S. 90.

6. The exact mechanism for applying the crime of aggression in a given circumstance is not yet known, though ICC jurisdiction might be triggered based on decision making at the ICC itself (without affirmative action at the Security Council) in circumstances where the alleged aggression is undertaken from or against a party to the Rome Statute. At present, Afghanistan is a party to the Rome Statute, while the United States and Pakistan are not. *See* International Criminal Court, Assembly of States Parties, *available at* http://www.icc-cpi.int/asp/statesparties.html.

7. *See* PERCY SYKES, SIR MORTIMER DURAND 200–17 (1956); MARTIN EWANS, AFGHANISTAN: A NEW HISTORY 106–07 (2002).

8. *See* OWEN BENNETT JONES, PAKISTAN: EYE OF THE STORM 137 (2003) ("Ever since partition, Kabul has argued that the Durand Line was never meant to be an international boundary and has complained that it deprived Afghanistan of territory that had been historically under its control").

9. For a more detailed discussion of these points and the history of the border, see Barnett R. Rubin & Abubakar Siddique, *Resolving the Pakistan-Afghanistan Stalemate*, US Institute of Peace Spec. Rep. 176 (Oct. 2006), *available at* http://www.usip.org/pubs/specialreports/sr176.html.

10. *See* RIZWAN HUSSAIN, PAKISTAN AND THE EMERGENCE OF ISLAMIC MILITANCY IN AFGHANISTAN 55–92 (2005).

11. The graphic appears in Seth Jones, *Counterinsurgency in Afghanistan*, RAND Counterinsurgency Study Vol. 4, at 45 (June 9, 2008), *available at* http://www.rand.org/pubs/monographs/2008/RAND_MG595.pdf, and is reprinted with permission of RAND Corporation, Santa Monica, CA.

12. *See* Eric Schmitt & Mark Mazzetti, *Pakistan's Planned Accord With Militants Alarms U.S.*, NEW YORK TIMES, Apr. 30, 2008, at A10; *see also* CRS Report, *supra* note 1, at 20–21; Jones, *supra* note 11, at 43–44; National Intelligence Council, *National Intelligence Estimate: The Terrorist Threat to the US Homeland* 6 (July 2007), *available at* http://www.dni.gov/press_releases/20070717_release.pdf.

13. US cross-border operations at issue in this paper are focused on the FATA region, not the North West Frontier Province (NWFP) or Baluchistan. It should be noted, however, that Pakistani militants have also begun holding territory (and attacking Pakistani military and government targets) in certain areas of the NWFP.

14. *See* Jones, *supra* note 11, at 58–59 ("Afghan insurgents used Pakistan as a staging area for offensive operations. Taliban insurgents that operated in the southern Afghan provinces of Kandahar, Oruzgan, Helmand, and Zabol had significant support networks in such Pakistani provinces as Baluchistan and the Federally Administered Tribal Areas, including in Waziristan. . . . The Taliban conduct much of their financing and recruiting operations on the Pakistani side of the border").

15. *See id.* at 38, 50–51.

16. CRS Report, *supra* note 1, at 18–20 & 29. Some believe Baitullah Mehsud masterminded the assassination of former Pakistani Prime Minister Benazir Bhutto in December 2007. In early October 2008, unconfirmed reports began circulating of Mehsud's death from illness.

17. *See* Jones, *supra* note 11, at 46.

18. *Id.* at 62–63.

19. *Quoted in* Peter Bergen, Assessing the Fight Against Al Qaeda, Testimony before the House Permanent Select Committee on Intelligence, at 8 (Apr. 9, 2008), *available at* http://www.fas.org/irp/congress/2008_hr/040908bergen.pdf.

20. *See* Tyson, *supra* note 1, at A16 (reporting testimony of General Cartwright); *see also* Jones, *supra* note 11, at 64–65 ("The use of suicide attacks was encouraged by al Qaeda leaders in Pakistan . . . . Suicide bombers included Afghans, Pakistanis, and some foreigners. Most suicide bombers through 2007 came from Afghan refugee camps in Pakistan").

21. Jane Perlez, *Pakistan Defies U.S. On Halting Attacks*, NEW YORK TIMES, May 16, 2008, at A6 (referring to NATO and US sources); CRS Report, *supra* note 1, at 31.

22. *See* Jones, *supra* note 11, at 65; *see also* Bergen, *supra* note 19, at 7 ("The use of suicide attacks, improvised explosive devices and the beheadings of hostages—all techniques that al Qaeda perfected in Iraq—are methods that the Taliban has increasingly adopted in Afghanistan, making much of the south of the country a no-go area").

23. *See* HUSAIN HAQQANI, PAKISTAN: BETWEEN MOSQUE AND MILITARY 301–10 (2005); CRS Report, *supra* note 1, at 26–27; Jones, *supra* note 11, at 59–60.

24. *See* Jones, *supra* note 11, at 56 (finding that parts of the Pakistani government, especially members of the Inter-Services Intelligence Directorate and Frontier Corps, provide support to the Taliban in Pakistan); CRS Report, *supra* note 1, at 23; Ann Scott Tyson, *Border Complicates War in Afghanistan*, WASHINGTON POST, Apr. 4, 2008, at A1 (quoting a frontline US soldier as saying the "Frontier Corps might as well be Taliban . . . . They are active facilitators of infiltration").

25. *See* Jones, *supra* note 11, at 21.

26. *See* CRS Report, *supra* note 1, at 27–28; Jones, *supra* note 11, at 57–58; Schmitt & Mazzetti, *supra* note 12, at A10; *see also* Ismail Khan & Carlotta Gall, *Pakistan Lets Tribal Chiefs Keep Control Along Border*, NEW YORK TIMES, Sept. 6, 2006, at A8.

27. *See* Joby Warrick, *U.S. Officials: Pakistani Agents Helped Plan Kabul Bombing*, WASHINGTON POST, Aug. 1, 2008, at A1, *available at* http://www.washingtonpost.com/wp-dyn/content/article/2008/08/01/AR2008080100133.html; CRS Report, *supra* note 1, at 25; Jones, *supra* note 11, at 54–57.

28. *See* Craig Whitlock, *In Hunt for Bin Laden, a New Approach*, WASHINGTON POST, Sept. 10, 2008, at A1.

29. *See* Nayak, *supra* note 3, at 305–06.

30. Perlez, *supra* note 21.

31. In February 2009, US Senator Dianne Feinstein, chairwoman of the Senate Intelligence Committee, stated publicly that unmanned Predator aircraft engaging in attacks in Pakistan are flown from an air base in Pakistan, marking the first time a US official had publicly commented on where the Predator aircraft patrolling Pakistan take off and land. *See* Greg Miller, *Feinstein Comment on U.S. Drones Likely to Embarrass Pakistan*, LOS ANGELES TIMES, Feb. 13, 2009, at 1.

32. *See* CRS Report, *supra* note 1, at 36; Robin Wright & Joby Warrick, *U.S. Steps Up Unilateral Strikes in Pakistan*, WASHINGTON POST, Mar. 27, 2008, at A1.

33. *See* Whitlock, *supra* note 28.

34. *See Officials Report Airstrike*, WASHINGTON POST, Oct. 27, 2008, at A10.

35. *See* Saad Gul & Katherine M. Royal, *Burning the Barn to Roast the Pig? Proportionality Concerns in the War on Terror and the Damadola Incident,* 14 WILLAMETTE JOURNAL OF INTERNATIONAL LAW & DISPUTE RESOLUTION 49, 51 (2006).

36. *See, e.g.*, Reza Sayah, *Pakistan fury over U.S. 'hot pursuit' act*, CNN, June 11, 2008, http://www.cnn.com/2008/WORLD/asiapcf/06/11/pakistan.troops.killed/index.html.

37. *See* Carlotta Gall & Eric Schmitt, *Pakistan Angry as Strike by U.S. Kills 11 Soldiers*, NEW YORK TIMES, June 12, 2008, at A1; CRS Report, *supra* note 1, at 34–35. In at least one instance, Pakistani military forces may have fired warning shots to prevent US troops from crossing the border into Pakistan. *See* Candace Rondeaux, *Pakistan Allegedly Repulses U.S. Raid*, WASHINGTON POST, Sept. 16, 2008, at A12.

38. *See* Tyson, *supra* note 24.

39. *See* Naylor, *supra* note 2.

40. *See* Whitlock, *supra* note 28.

41. *See* Eric Schmitt & Mark Mazzetti, *Bush Said to Give Orders Allowing Raids in Pakistan*, NEW YORK TIMES, Sept. 11, 2008, at A1.

42. *Id.*; Whitlock, *supra* note 28, (reporting that "U.S. commandos crossed from Afghanistan into Pakistan in helicopters and killed about 20 people in a suspected Taliban compound in South Waziristan"). The rules of engagement for special operations forces operating in Afghanistan are classified.

43. *See* Naylor, *supra* note 2 (quoting an unnamed US government official that the raid was a "strategic miscalculation").

44. UN Charter art. 2(4).

45. *See, e.g.*, International Law Commission, *Articles on Responsibility of States for Internationally Wrongful Acts* art. 20, *in Report of the International Law Commission, Fifty-third Session*, U.N. Doc. A/56/10 (2001) ("Valid consent by a State to the commission of a given act by another State precludes the wrongfulness of that act in relation to the former State to the extent that the act remains within the limits of that consent").

46. *See, e.g.*, Oscar Schachter, *The Right of States to Use Armed Force*, 82 MICHIGAN LAW REVIEW 1620, 1644–45 (1984) (seeing no violation of UN Charter Article 2(4) "when a foreign force is invited by the government to help put down an attempted coup or assist in restoring law and order").

47. *See* Tyson, *supra* note 1, at A16 (reporting testimony of Secretary of Defense Gates).

48. *See* Whitlock, *supra* note 28; Eric Schmitt & David E. Sanger, *Pakistan Shift Could Curtail Drone Strikes*, NEW YORK TIMES, Feb. 22, 2008, at A1 (reporting that "American officials reached a quiet understanding with Pakistan's leader last month to intensify secret strikes against suspected terrorists by pilotless aircraft launched in Pakistan").

49. *See* Schmitt & Mazzetti, *supra* note 41.

50. *See* CRS Report, *supra* note 1, at 34 ("Permission for U.S.-led attacks on forces under the command of militant leaders . . . is not overtly forthcoming to date").

51. *See* Jane Perlez, *Pakistan's Military Chief Criticizes U.S. Over a Raid*, WASHINGTON POST, Sept. 10, 2008, at A8.

52. *See generally* STEPHEN PHILIP COHEN, THE IDEA OF PAKISTAN (2004).

53. *See, e.g.*, *id.* (recounting apparent disagreement between President Zardari and General Kayani over the permissibility of the September 3, 2008 cross-border special forces operation).

54. *See, e.g.*, JONES, *supra* note 8, at 34–35.

55. WOLFGANG FRIEDMANN, THE CHANGING STRUCTURE OF INTERNATIONAL LAW 266 (1964).

56. By way of example, some States expressed concern about Ethiopia's intervention in Somalia in 2006 for the purpose of suppressing the Union of Islamic Courts (UIC). While the intervention was conducted at the request of the Somali Transitional Government, which had been established with the backing of the United Nations, the African Union and the Arab League, the transitional government controlled only a small portion of southern Somalia at the time of the intervention, while the UIC controlled the Somali capital and much of the rest of the country. "In such a fragile situation and in a crisis mainly of an internal nature, military intervention by invitation may be very controversial indeed . . . ." Zeray W. Yihdego, *Ethiopia's Military Action Against the Union of Islamic Courts and Others in Somalia: Some Legal Implications*, 56 INTERNATIONAL & COMPARATIVE LAW QUARTERLY 666 (2008).

57. *See* UN Charter arts. 39 & 42.

58. S.C. Res. 1368, pmbl., U.N. Doc. S/RES/1368 (Sept. 12, 2001); S.C. Res. 1373, pmbl., U.N. Doc. S/RES/1373 (Sept. 28, 2001).

59. *See* MICHAEL J. MATHESON, COUNCIL UNBOUND: THE GROWTH OF UN DECISION MAKING ON CONFLICT AND POSTCONFLICT ISSUES AFTER THE COLD WAR 157 (2006).

60. Agreement on Provisional Arrangements in Afghanistan Pending the Re-establishment of Permanent Government Institutions, annex 1, Dec. 5, 2001, *printed in* Letter dated 5 December 2001 from the Secretary-General addressed to the President of the Security Council, U.N. Doc. S/2001/1154 (2001).

61. S.C. Res. 1386, ¶ 1, U.N. Doc. S/RES/1386 (Dec. 20, 2001).

62. *Id.* at ¶ 10. The Security Council also subsequently created a very modest UN Assistance Mission in Afghanistan of fewer than two thousand persons (mostly Afghan nationals) charged with assisting the Afghan government in rebuilding the country and strengthening the foundations of peace and constitutional democracy.

63. Military Technical Agreement, Afghan.-ISAF, Jan. 4, 2002, *available at* http://www.operations.mod.uk/isafmta.pdf. After NATO assumed control of the ISAF, a further bilateral agreement was concluded between NATO and the Afghan government on December 9, 2003.

64. S.C. Res. 1413, ¶ 2, U.N. Doc. S/RES/1413 (May 23, 2002).

65. *See* S.C. Res. 1833, U.N. Doc. S/RES/1833 (Sept. 22, 2008) (extending ISAF's mandate for a period of twelve months beginning October 13, 2008).

66. S.C. Res. 1510, ¶ 1, U.N. Doc. S/RES/1510 (Oct. 13, 2003).

67. *See* NATO Press Release, Revised Operational Plan for NATO's Expanded Mission in Afghanistan (updated July 4, 2007), *available at* http://www.nato.int/issues/afghanistan_stage3/index.html; *see also* MATHESON, *supra* note 59, at 116.

68. UN Charter art. 51.

69. *See, e.g.*, Jordan J. Paust, *Use of Armed Force against Terrorists in Afghanistan, Iraq, and Beyond*, 35 CORNELL INTERNATIONAL LAW JOURNAL 533, 540–43 (2002).

70. CRS Report, *supra* note 1, at 22.

71. *See, e.g.*, PREEMPTION: MILITARY ACTION AND MORAL JUSTIFICATION (Henry Shue & David Rodin eds., 2007); W. Michael Reisman & Andrea Armstrong, *The Past and Future of the Claim of Preemptive Self-Defense*, 100 AMERICAN JOURNAL OF INTERNATIONAL LAW 525, 525–26, 547–48 (2006) (finding that "the International Court of Justice and most international lawyers have steadfastly insisted on the strict application of the Charter regime" and that "[v]ery few of the more recent statements [of governments] seem to contemplate or claim a right to direct preemptive attacks against other states").

72. *See, e.g.*, CHRISTINE GRAY, INTERNATIONAL LAW AND THE USE OF FORCE 130 (2d ed. 2004).

73. Military and Paramilitary Activities (Nicar. v. U.S.), 1986 I.C.J. 14, 103–04 (June 27).

74. *See* Sean D. Murphy, *Terrorism and the Concept of "Armed Attack" in Article 51 of the U.N. Charter,* 43 HARVARD INTERNATIONAL LAW JOURNAL 41, 45–51 (2002).

75. Military and Paramilitary Activities, *supra* note 73, para. 195.

76. *See* Eric Myjer & Nigel White, *The Twin Towers Attack: An Unlimited Right to Self-Defence,* 7 JOURNAL OF CONFLICT & SECURITY LAW 1, 7 (2002) (arguing that "[t]he categorization of the terrorists attacks on New York and Washington as an 'armed attack' within the meaning of article 51 is problematic to say the least .... Self-defence, traditionally speaking, applies to an armed response to an attack by a state").

77. *Supra* note 73.

78. Legal Consequences of the Construction of a Wall in the Occupied Palestinian Territory, Advisory Opinion, 2004 I.C.J. 136, 194 (July 9).

79. *See, e.g.,* Sean D. Murphy, *Self-Defense and the Israeli Wall Advisory Opinion: An Ipse Dixit from the ICJ?,* 99 AMERICAN JOURNAL OF INTERNATIONAL LAW 62 (2005); *see also* YORAM DINSTEIN, WAR, AGGRESSION, AND SELF-DEFENCE 192 (3d ed. 2001) (stating that "for an armed attack to justify counter-measures of self-defense under Article 51, it need not be committed by another State"); Rein Müllerson, *Jus ad Bellum and International Terrorism, in* INTERNATIONAL LAW AND THE WAR ON TERROR 75, 107, 109 (Fred L. Borch & Paul S. Wilson eds., 2003) (Vol. 79, US Naval War College International Law Studies) (finding that "terrorism belongs to the domain of *jus ad bellum* as terrorist attacks may constitute a specific, non-traditional ... form of an armed attack that gives rise to the right of self-defense ..." and "the right to self-defense today includes measures undertaken against non-state entities").

80. Armed Activities on the Territory of the Congo (Dem. Rep. Congo v. Uganda), 2005 I.C.J. 168, 223 (Dec. 19).

81. *Id.,* Separate Opinion of Judge Kooijmans, para. 28; *id.,* Separate Opinion of Judge Simma, para. 11.

82. *See, e.g.,* Alissa J. Rubin & Sabrina Tavernise, *Turkish Planes Strike Iraqi Kurdistan,* NEW YORK TIMES, Feb. 5, 2008; Sabrina Tavernise & Richard A. Oppel Jr., *After 8 Days, Turkey Pulls Its Troops Out of Iraq,* NEW YORK TIMES, Mar. 1, 2008, at A8.

83. *See* Organization of American States, *Convocation of the Meeting of Consultation of Ministers of Foreign Affairs and Appointment of a Commission,* CP/Res. 930 (1632/08) (Mar. 5, 2008).

84. *See* Andreas Zimmerman, *The Second Lebanon War: Jus ad Bellum, Jus in Bello and the Issue of Proportionality,* 11 MAX PLANCK YEARBOOK OF UNITED NATIONS LAW 99 (2007); Human Rights Watch, *Civilians under Assault: Hezbollah's Rocket Attacks on Israel in the 2006 War* (Aug. 29, 2007), http://hrw.org/reports/2007/iopt0807/.

85. *See* Griff Witte, *60 Gazans Killed in Incursion By Israel,* WASHINGTON POST, Mar. 2, 2008, at A1.

86. *See* Ernesto Londono, *U.S. Airstrike Allegedly Kills 8 Inside Syria,* WASHINGTON POST, Oct. 27, 2008, at A9.

87. Legality of the Threat or Use of Nuclear Weapons, Advisory Opinion, 1996 I.C.J. 226, 245 (July 8).

88. *See, e.g.,* DINSTEIN, *supra* note 79, at 237.

89. *See* JUDITH GARDAM, NECESSITY, PROPORTIONALITY AND THE USE OF FORCE BY STATES 4–8 (2004).

90. *See* Oil Platforms (Iran v. U.S.), 2003 I.C.J. 161, 196–98 (Nov. 6).

91. *See* GARDAM, *supra* note 89, at 8–19; *see also* Enzo Cannizzaro, *The Role of Proportionality in the Law of International Countermeasures,* 12 EUROPEAN JOURNAL OF INTERNATIONAL LAW 889, 892 (2001) (finding that "even responses greatly exceeding the magnitude of the original

breach, and extrinsically unconnected therewith, could nevertheless be justified, if reasonably necessary to terminate it").

92. Roberto Ago, *Addendum to Eighth Report on State Responsibility*, U.N. Doc. A/CN.4/318 & Add. 104 (1979).

93. ANNOTATED SUPPLEMENT TO THE COMMANDER'S HANDBOOK ON THE LAW OF NAVAL OPERATIONS § 4.3.2 (A. Ralph Thomas & James C. Duncan eds., 1999) (Vol. 73, US Naval War College International Law Studies).

94. *Id.* at 198–99.

95. Armed Activities on the Territory of the Congo, *supra* note 80, para 147.

96. *See* Gilles Dorronsoro, *The Security Council and the Afghan Conflict*, *in* THE UNITED NATIONS SECURITY COUNCIL AND WAR: THE EVOLUTION OF THOUGHT AND PRACTICE SINCE 1945 (Vaughan Lowe, Adam Roberts, Jennifer Welsh & Dominik Zaum eds., 2008).

97. *See* Müllerson, *supra* note 79, at 109 (finding that when "terrorists operate from the territory of a state and that state is unable or unwilling to end the terrorist acts, military action by other states directed at the terrorists within the state where the terror operations are originating from can be justified as a state of necessity") & 113 (stating that "[o]nly the refusal of the Taliban regime to comply with US demands and their active defense of the Qaeda network led to the use of force in self-defense against both al Qaeda and the Taliban").

98. For policy recommendations on US support to Pakistan for counterinsurgency operations, see Bergen, *supra* note 19, at 22.

99. *See* GREGOR WETTBERG, THE INTERNATIONAL LEGALITY OF SELF-DEFENSE AGAINST NON-STATE ACTORS 221 (2007).

100. *See, e.g.*, Lieutenant General Michael D. Maples, US Army Director, Defense Intelligence Agency, *Current and Projected National Security Threats to the United States*, Statement for the Record before the Senate Armed Services Committee, at 8 (Feb. 27, 2007), *available at* http://armed-services.senate.gov/statemnt/2007/February/Maples%2002-27-07.pdf ("In 2006, al-Qaida remained a loose network, broadly defined by the strategic objective of re-establishing their version of an Islamic caliphate, and unified by a common ideology rooted in the violent rejection of Western influence, especially in traditionally Islamic countries").

101. *See, e.g.*, Bergen, *supra* note 19, at 4–6.

102. *See* International Law Commission, *supra* note 45; Müllerson, *supra* note 79, at 109 (indicating that "if the territorial state, which has itself been unable to prevent terrorists attacking other states or their nationals and interests, resists the victim-state (or its allies) in their efforts to eliminate the terrorists, it itself becomes an accomplice to the terrorist organization") & 113 (stating that "[o]nly the refusal of the Taliban regime to comply with US demands and their active defense of the al Qaeda network led to the use of force in self-defense against both al Qaeda and the Taliban").

VI

Legal Issues in Forming the Coalition

Alan Cole*

"'Tis our true policy to steer clear of permanent alliances, with any portion of the foreign world."

George Washington, on leaving office, 1796.

"Personally I feel happier now that we have no allies to be polite to and to pamper."

King George VI, on hearing Britain stood alone against Hitler, June 1940.

Unlike George Washington and George VI, those who contemplated military action in Afghanistan in 2001 were eager to be part of a broad, capable and committed coalition. As well as the obvious practical benefits in terms of additional military assets and the crucial staging and basing support, they wanted the Taliban and al Qaeda to know that the resolve to defeat them stretched across all continents and many governments. The attacks of September 11, 2001 were so extraordinary in both scale and ferocity that no nation was likely to hesitate in identifying a clear legal basis to come to the assistance of the United States.

In fact the earliest days of the coalition were characterized by general consensus among its members: consensus on the horror of the attacks of 9/11, consensus on the fact that they represented an armed attack for the purposes of Article 51,[1]

---

* Commander, Royal Navy. The views expressed in this article are those of the author and do not represent those of the Royal Navy, the United Kingdom Ministry of Defence or Her Majesty's Government.

consensus that for those in NATO the Article 5 right to act in defense of the United States was triggered[2] and consensus that there was sufficient nexus between al Qaeda and the Taliban for an invasion of Afghanistan to be a proper response. Indeed, it is difficult to find much divergence of approach at this point among those who came to the support of the United States. United Nations Security Council Resolution 1373[3] made it quite clear that the inherent right of individual and collective self-defense had been triggered.

The United Kingdom's position, set out in a letter to the United Nations Security Council on October 7, 2001,[4] seems to have reflected the view of most of those who took part in the early stages of the Afghan campaign. It identified that the attack triggered the United States' inherent right of self-defense and the right of allies to act in collective self-defense. That said, the United Kingdom government did not rely solely on the attacks of September 11, 2001 as a basis for acting in collective self-defense of the United States. It referred also to the need to avert attacks from the same source in the future, and the continuing threat posed by al Qaeda. There was also reference to the August 7, 1998 attacks on the US embassies in Tanzania and Kenya and the October 12, 2000 attack on the *USS Cole* at anchor in Aden, for all of which al Qaeda had claimed responsibility. The United Kingdom wanted to make it clear it was not retaliation it contemplated, but self-defense in response to a campaign of international terrorist violence.

The German government, who had until 1994 been constrained from deploying troops outside Germany and retained a reputation for being cautious in its interpretation of the international law right to act in self-defense, had no doubt of the lawfulness of US actions. On September 19, 2001, Chancellor Schröder stated that

> [t]he [North Atlantic] Council—like the Security Council—now also regards a terrorist attack as an attack on a Party to the Treaty. The attack on the United States thus constitutes an attack on all NATO partners. What rights do these decisions create for the United States? Based on the decision of the Security Council, the United States can take measures against the perpetrators, organizers, instigators and sponsors of the attacks. These measures are authorized by international law. And, under the terms of the resolution, which further develops international law, they can and may take equally resolute action against States which support and harbour the perpetrators.[5]

Similarly, there is no evidence that the connection between the perpetrators of the attacks and the government of Afghanistan troubled the coalition members for very long. Most, if not all, were satisfied that the Taliban were the de facto government of Afghanistan even if they were not recognized as the legitimate government by the United Nations. The generally held view was that the Taliban had failed over a period of two years to comply with Security Council resolutions[6] following the bombings of the embassies in Kenya and Tanzania and could be regarded both as inextricably linked with and sheltering al Qaeda. Certainly the Taliban did not seek assistance with removing al Qaeda from their territory, nor did they condemn it publicly. They were given a "last chance" by the United States to surrender Osama Bin Laden, which they refused.

Early coalition contributions to the invasion of Afghanistan also reflected the generally held view that this was an international armed conflict. The deployment of forces and the details of their rules of engagement (ROE) were based on the premise that this was a conflict between the "coalition of the willing" on the one hand and Taliban forces, al Qaeda and the Afghan army on the other. That left no doubt that the four 1949 Geneva Conventions[7] applied and, for those who were signatories, Additional Protocol I.[8]

Operation Enduring Freedom (OEF) began October 7, 2001, when President Bush made the following statement:

> On my orders, the United States military has begun strikes against Al Qaeda terrorist training camps and military installations of the Taliban regime in Afghanistan. These carefully targeted actions are designed to disrupt the use of Afghanistan as a terrorist base of operations, and to attack the military capability of the Taliban regime. We are joined in this operation by our staunch friend, Great Britain. Other close friends, including Canada, Australia, Germany and France, have pledged forces as the operation unfolds. More than 40 countries in the Middle East, Africa, Europe and across Asia have granted air transit or landing rights. Many more have shared intelligence. We are supported by the collective will of the world.[9]

President Bush's words set the scene for a coalition of broad international base and substantial military depth: the Afghan government had few friends in the international community. The coalition enjoyed rapid success and by November 2001 the Taliban had evacuated Kabul, melting back into the Pushtun populace in southern Afghanistan and the Pakistani tribal areas. With this short-term military objective complete, attention (particularly in Europe) turned to the form and purpose of an enduring presence in Afghanistan. It is at this point that the different understandings of the legal basis for presence, use of force, detention and other military activity begin to impact more noticeably on the conduct of operations.

Operation Enduring Freedom and International Security Assistance Force: Different Missions and Different Legal Frameworks

The United States continued to consider its activities in Afghanistan as one front in its Global War on Terror. Although it is not suggested that this term is to be taken literally as an indication that the law of armed conflict applied to all responses to terrorism, it was clear the United States saw the pursuit of al Qaeda, both within and outside Afghanistan, as primarily a military mission. As such, OEF was presented to other militaries as part of a regional international armed conflict. A number of the nations that had supported the invasion continued to provide forces to OEF, including the United Kingdom, Canada and Australia, albeit they may not have (and certainly the United Kingdom did not) endorsed the concept of a Global War on Terror. The OEF mission not only covered all parts of Afghanistan, but stretched across the entire region, although most coalition partners limited their military activity to the territory of Afghanistan. President Bush had set out the following aims of the mission on October 7, 2001, and they remained the basis of mission directives and rules of engagement:

> By destroying camps and disrupting communications, we will make it more difficult for the terror network to train new recruits and coordinate their evil plans. Initially, the terrorists may burrow deeper into caves and other entrenched hiding places. Our military action is also designed to clear the way for sustained, comprehensive and relentless operations to drive them out and bring them to justice.[10]

OEF activity included substantial air operations by forces based both in Afghanistan and elsewhere, along with operations on the ground. Certainly they extended across the whole of Afghanistan and were often similar in intensity to those that formed part of the invasion. The embryonic government in Kabul, which clearly supported efforts to eliminate remaining al Qaeda and Taliban forces, not least to secure its own position, was not in a position to supervise or approve the conduct of the military mission. It consented to OEF's continuation in principle, but had no veto or control of particular operations. The business of establishing a national democratic government for the first time in the nation's history did not allow for detailed involvement in OEF operational decisions. The extent to which it would have been consulted had it sought to be is not clear. The absence of direct involvement by the Afghan government in 2001–2 tends to support the premise that OEF remained the expression of an international armed conflict between the OEF forces and the remaining Taliban and al Qaeda forces, albeit the Taliban and al Qaeda were never capable of being high contracting parties for the purposes of the Geneva Conventions.[11]

In parallel and following the Bonn conference in December 2001, the International Security Assistance Force (ISAF) was established by Security Council Resolution 1386.[12] On December 20, 2001, a UK general, Lieutenant General John McColl, took command of forces from nineteen nations, including the United States, the

United Kingdom, Canada and Australia, that were contributing to OEF. For many nations, including the United Kingdom and Canada, this was the point at which they may have judged that the international armed conflict had come to an end. The Taliban government had been replaced by one drawn from the Northern Alliance, which had itself fought alongside the coalition and was very much NATO's preferred replacement. That government had sought the assistance of the United Nations in establishing security in its country and provided forces from the Afghan National Army to fight alongside ISAF and against the remaining Taliban/al Qaeda, who wished to see it fail.

The ISAF mission was much more narrowly drawn in both geographical and military terms. ISAF forces restricted their operations to Kabul and its environs:[13] they saw their role as the provision of support to the new government in Kabul in its continuing internal armed conflict with Taliban, al Qaeda and others who sought to overthrow it. The ISAF mission was generally based on self-defense activity (including the collective defense of Afghan government forces), with only exceptional recourse to the use of offensive force under the law of armed conflict: in part this reflected fear of "mission creep." The characterization of the conflict as "non-international" also seemed to find favor with the International Committee of the Red Cross (ICRC), which, in June 2002, used the same description.[14] Although positions on the legal basis for operations varied among ISAF contributing nations, most relied on a combination of the Security Council Resolution and the consent of the government of Afghanistan. In fact, many contributing nations were pleased to distance themselves from the US notion of the Global War on Terror, understanding it (rightly or wrongly) to be the concept of an international armed conflict against international terrorist organizations wherever they might be in the world. They judged counterterrorism to be a law enforcement issue and characterized those they engaged under the laws of armed conflict within the context of the non-international armed conflicts in Iraq and Afghanistan (and they had to be members of identified groups that were considered party to those conflicts) as insurgents.

In Afghanistan, the narrower mission of ISAF in supporting the fledgling government in Kabul, with its wide international support and Security Council resolution basis, was altogether more palatable for some of the European nations that had rarely engaged in expeditionary operations since 1945. It was also a crucial mission if that government was to survive. For some NATO nations, uncertainty remained as to whether the remaining operations in Afghanistan amounted to an armed conflict and, if so, whether it justified the scale of operations undertaken by OEF.

Beyond Security Council Resolution 1510: Caution and Caveat

In late 2003, Security Council Resolution 1510 vested command of ISAF in NATO and extended its remit beyond Kabul. "Stage 1 Expansion," as it became known, began in the north and followed a request from the Afghan Minister of Foreign Affairs for assistance with security in the wider country. Notwithstanding that NATO had celebrated its fiftieth birthday some years before, the coalition was now engaged in the most complex operations in its history. As it became clear there was still substantial fighting to be done if the conditions for political and physical reconstruction were to be created, member States found themselves having to determine how far they were prepared to commit their militaries in a nation well outside the North Atlantic area and on a type of operation that had not been contemplated in 1949. The result was the steady emergence of policy, legal and capability constraints that have characterized ISAF operations (although not always hindered them) to this day.

Targeting

One of the first areas in which differing national appetites became obvious was in the targeting process. Although nations were very clear as to their duty to come to the collective self-defense of coalition troops who found themselves in contact with the enemy, their positions regarding preplanned targeting under the law of armed conflict were less consistent. ISAF remained a wholly self-defense mission until 2005, but OEF operated a formal target clearance process, designed to ensure that where force was contemplated against the enemy ("target sets" to use the military jargon) it was going to be used in accordance with the principles set out in the law of armed conflict.

The first issue that arose was identifying the enemy. Soldiers who target a person who does not present an imminent threat to their lives[15] have to be satisfied that they are attempting to kill a person who falls within the definition of a combatant. In the context of a war between States, and in the early days of the Afghan campaign, this was a reasonably straightforward matter. The Taliban, al Qaeda and Afghan military were the combatants and tended to fight in conventional ways. But by 2003, it had become more complex. As well as the fighting elements of al Qaeda and the Taliban, there were other tribal groups that wished to see the government in Kabul fail. There were also groups that were apathetic toward the government but opposed to the presence of foreign troops. Finally there were others who appeared to enjoy the support of neighboring States or who had traveled to Afghanistan to fight. Different nations took different views of whom they were engaged with in an armed conflict, so coalition targeting arrangements had to ensure that the nation that owned the assets likely to be allocated to the particular target was satisfied that the individuals they were likely to kill were within its own national understanding of who was a combatant. It is fair to say that the United States took a wider view of whom might legitimately be targeted than some of its European allies. The US approach reflected the widespread political and public support at home, while the European position reflected their more cautious national positions.

The application of Additional Protocol I to the conflict (and particularly its continued application once the conflict arguably ceased to be an international armed conflict in June 2002) is an issue that has exercised academic minds but had little impact on the conduct of operations. Those States that are signatories to Protocol I applied it throughout their targeting operations (because it applied as a strict matter of law or because it is their policy to apply it) and those who are not applied their own understandings on the customary international law framework relating to the use of force in offensive operations. The application of a uniform targeting practice throughout the period from invasion to the current day is for two reasons. First, as a matter of national policy, many nations will say that the principles set out for use in an international armed conflict, be they in Additional Protocol I or a body of similar customary international law, ought to be applied in any offensive operations. It is difficult to make an argument that those who find themselves at risk of collateral damage, for example, in a non-international armed conflict are entitled to less consideration that those in the vicinity of an international armed conflict. The second reason is a purely practical one. Targeting processes have to be carefully constructed to meet international law requirements and to allow lawful targets to be engaged as quickly and effectively as possible. Once a process has been put in place, it has to be rehearsed and personnel trained in their roles. To import a separate set of standards for a commander to apply (albeit advised by a military lawyer) is simply to overcomplicate the process. The better approach is to settle on the highest standards that can be said to be applicable (those for an international armed conflict) and use them for all kinetic targeting operations. Quite apart from the practical benefits of the latter approach, it made determination of the point at which the conflict changed from international to non-international irrelevant to the tactical commander.

Furthermore, the application of the principle of proportionality varied among States. NATO developed its own position on what was an acceptable level of collateral damage for the air campaign in Afghanistan but some nations took a more restrictive view than NATO. Not only did that mean that assets of those nations would not conduct the mission, but officers of those nations embedded in the targeting process might be barred from contributing to its success. Although NATO is a legal entity for contractual and other purposes and was created by treaty, it cannot set out a single position on public international law matters which are reserved solely for States. NATO is not, nor can it be, a signatory to the Geneva Conventions, the Ottawa Treaty or other law of armed conflict treaties, but its member nations have individual treaty obligations which are reflected in the organization's planning and procedures.

The position was further complicated by the multinational staffs at ISAF headquarters (HQ) and regional HQs. Although brigade-level formations tended to be wholly or largely from a single nation, thereby making it obvious which national provisions would apply, HQ staffs were invariably mixed. At ISAF HQ, with officers of more than ten nations regularly involved in an operation, determining whose caveats applied was not straightforward. In fact, for the military lawyer, issues of State responsibility for the actions of others are some of the most complex that they encounter in coalition operations. The long-standing principle that a soldier will not assist a colleague from another nation to carry out an action he knows he is forbidden from doing himself is now reflected at the State level in the International Law Commission's Draft Articles on Responsibility of States for Internationally Wrongful Acts, notably at Articles 16 and 17.[16] But even the publication of these Articles, which are not binding, did little to settle an approach to the issue. Officers of some States when asked to authorize a mission which their national policy or legal positions prevented their authorizing would take the view that they were required to prevent the mission from taking place, because in the view of their governments it was unlawful. Officers of other States, faced with the same issue, would choose to step aside and hand their roles to officers whose nations allowed them to assist. Although this approach reduced the number of operations that were thwarted, it required the reorganization of command structures depending on the nature of the mission and the nationality of the post holder. The operational lawyer and targeteer needed to understand not only which nations were barred from assisting, but also whether their officers would thwart the mission or merely abstain.

A related issue is the commander's responsibility for the manner in which those who are of another nationality, but under his command, carry out their mission. Putting aside the issue of command responsibility for war crimes, which has been well addressed elsewhere, there remains the issue of the extent to which a commander is obliged to scrutinize the means by which troops under his command conduct their mission to ensure they comply with his own national legal position. A useful illustration is the use of anti-personnel mines (APM) in respect to which many nations are signatories to the Ottawa Convention,[17] although the use of this example should not be seen as an indication that any nation employed APM in Afghanistan. Is a commander whose nation has ratified the Ottawa Convention (noting particularly the requirement "[n]ever under any circumstances . . . [t]o assist, encourage or induce, in any way, anyone to engage in any activity prohibited to a State Party under this Convention")[18] obliged to ensure that those under his command do not employ them even if their own nations have not ratified the Convention?

A parallel example from the maritime environment is the exercise of the right of visit. Some nations take the view that the right to visit in the absence of one of the legal bases set out in Article 110 of the 1982 Convention on the Law of the Sea[19] requires the specific permission of the flag State in each instance. Others consider that consent to board can be given by the ship's master. If a naval commander from a nation that requires specific flag State permission wants to have a vessel boarded but is unable to obtain the consent of the flag State, he could direct a vessel of a nation that permits boardings on the basis of a master's consent to conduct the boarding on that basis. Alternatively, on what might be called the restrictive view, he might seek assurances from all vessels under his command that they will adopt the flag State consent approach for the duration of the time they are under his command. Each nation will reconcile these matters in a different way, but one approach that was seen in the ISAF structure was for the commander simply to ensure that any mission or direction he gives is capable of being carried out within his own nation's legal commitments and interpretations. Hence, an order by a commander from an Ottawa Convention signatory nation to troops from a non-signatory nation to lay APM would not pass the test, while an order to a ship to conduct enforcement and search operations in a particular sea area might do so: it does not presuppose an activity which the commander is not allowed to carry out himself.

Detention

The second area in which significant divergence in approach became evident was in respect to detention. Prior to June 2002 (the period in which all coalition nations agreed that the conflict was international in nature), those who were detained might have expected their custody to be governed by the 1949 Geneva Conventions. Combatants other than members of the armed forces of Afghanistan may have been entitled to prisoner of war status under Geneva Convention III, and the expectation was that this issue would be resolved by way of Article 5 tribunals. The ICRC persists to this day in the view that the Taliban were not de facto prisoners of war but ought to have had their status properly determined. Those who were determined not to have been entitled to prisoner of war status ought to have been prosecuted. In practice, significant numbers of those captured on the battlefield by US forces were adjudged to be unlawful combatants and held at US facilities in Afghanistan or elsewhere.

From June 2002, although the United States continued with the use of the "unlawful combatant" categorization, the other coalition members moved swiftly to a model which they considered better fit the recategorization of the conflict as a non-international armed conflict. Many ISAF nations were extremely uneasy about becoming involved in any kind of detention operation, and to this day will not arrest or detain Afghan nationals. Others accepted that the campaign would require some detention element if it was to succeed and settled on short-term detention on behalf of the Afghan government as the preferred concept. In practice, this involved detention for short periods (days rather than weeks) to facilitate transfer to the Afghan National Police or other law enforcement agency. The legal basis for detention was, like the basis for presence itself, considered to be the relevant Security Council resolutions and the consent of the government of Afghanistan. Although there has never been an explicit authority to detain in the resolutions, the term "all necessary means," notably in Resolution 1510[20] and subsequent resolutions, was considered to give the requisite authority for detention for the purposes of self-defense and mission accomplishment. The Afghan government supported ISAF detention operations, both in political and practical terms, by cooperating with arresting units and providing Afghan National Police to ISAF missions that included a detention element. Despite these two firm legal bases for detention, many ISAF nations were reluctant to take part in detention operations.

In terms of the legal framework that was judged to govern the detention arrangements, Common Article 3 of the 1949 Geneva Conventions, certain aspects of customary international law and applicable human rights law were most often cited. For most European nations that meant giving consideration to the application of the European Convention on Human Rights,[21] a regional human rights treaty widely ratified by European States.

The extent of application of the European Convention on Human Rights to deployed operations was (and remains) not entirely clear, but what was clear from the start was that some nations considered that it had a bearing on detention operations. So far as can be determined, no signatory State took the view that human rights law was suspended during an armed conflict. They took the position that human rights law, while only capable of binding the State (it does not for example bind al Qaeda), certainly continues to apply to some extent during armed conflict, a position subsequently approved by the International Court of Justice.[22] In fact, the Convention concerns appear to have been a factor in dissuading some States from taking any part in ISAF detention operations. The better view,[23] it is submitted, is that the "all necessary means" provision in the Afghan resolutions[24] gives an implied authority to conduct detention operations for the purposes of accomplishing the mission. That implied authority does not set aside obligations under applicable human rights law but it does give a basis for detention that is not defeated by human rights treaties. What the Afghan resolutions certainly did not give was a power of internment such as those in respect to Iraq had given.[25]

In any event, if detention remains for as short a period as necessary in order to effect a transfer to the Afghan authorities, those nations who take part in ISAF detentions may hope that by limiting their operations in such a way they are mitigating the risk of challenge under human rights law.

Conclusion

Given the extraordinary speed with which an ad hoc coalition was formed to invade Afghanistan in October 2001 and the wide range of nations that contributed to the mission, conflicts in legal positions appear to have been few. Perhaps it is to be expected that an attack such as that on September 11, 2001 will cause governments to set aside concerns about the strict interpretation of the UN or NATO Charters. Certainly the militaries of coalition nations, which concern themselves chiefly with *in bello* rather than *ad bellum* issues, were left in no doubt that they were taking part in an international armed conflict against Afghanistan. Once it became clear that ISAF, on the one hand, and OEF, on the other, had different visions for the nature of operations subsequent to the installation of the Northern Alliance in June 2002 as the governing body of Afghanistan, international law positions on a number of issues began to diverge. There were concerns then, and there remain concerns now, that operating two separate missions at two different tempos in the same country in an attempt to suppress the same enemy is a recipe for a conflict of laws, but the nations that contribute to both missions have generally learned to reconcile the legal differences to ensure they do not prejudice success.

Notes

1. Both S.C. Res. 1368, U.N. Doc. S/RES/1368 (Sept. 12, 2001) and S.C. Res. 1373, U.N. Doc. S/RES/1373 (Sept. 28, 2001) expressly authorized the right of self-defense at a time when it seemed certain that the attacks were not the direct actions of a State.

2. The North Atlantic Council issued a press statement on September 12, 2001 stating that the attack met the requirements of Article 5 of the Washington Treaty and would be considered an attack on all signatories.

3. S.C. Res. 1373, *supra* note 1, "*Reaffirming* the inherent right of individual or collective self-defence as recognized by the Charter of the United Nations as reiterated in resolution 1368 (2001)."

4. Letter dated October 7, 2001 from the Chargé d'affaires a.i. of the Permanent Mission of the United Kingdom of Great Britain and Northern Ireland to the United Nations addressed to the President of the Security Council, U.N. Doc. S/2001/947 (2001).

5. Deutscher Bundestag, Plenarprotokoll (Stenographischer Bericht) (BT-Pl.Pr. 14/187), Sept. 19, 2001, at 18302.

6. *See* S.C. Res. 1267, U.N. Doc. S/RES/1267 (Oct. 15, 1999), S.C. Res 1333, U.N. Doc. S/RES/1333 (Dec. 19, 2000) and S.C. Res. 1390, U.N. Doc. S/RES/1390 (Jan. 28, 2002), in which the Security Council obliged all member States to freeze the assets; prevent the entry into or the transit through their territories; and prevent the direct or indirect supply, sale and transfer of arms and military equipment with regard to individuals and entities belonging or related to the Taliban, Osama Bin Laden and the al Qaeda network.

7. Convention for the Amelioration of the Condition of the Wounded and Sick in Armed Forces in the Field, Aug. 12, 1949, 75 U.N.T.S. 31 [Geneva Convention I]; Convention for the Amelioration of the Condition of the Wounded, Sick and Shipwrecked Members of Armed Forces at Sea, Aug. 12, 1949, 75 U.N.T.S. 85 [Geneva Convention II]; Convention Relative to the Treatment of Prisoners of War, Aug. 12, 1949, 75 U.N.T.S. 135 [Geneva Convention III]; and Convention Relative to the Protection of Civilian Persons in Time of War, Aug. 12, 1949, 75 U.N.T.S. 287 [Geneva Convention IV]; all *reprinted in* DOCUMENTS ON THE LAWS OF WAR (Adam Roberts & Richard Guelff eds., 3d ed. 2000) at 197, 222, 244 and 301, respectively.

8. Protocol Additional to the Geneva Conventions of 12 August 1949, and Relating to the Protection of Victims of International Armed Conflicts, June 8, 1977, 1125 U.N.T.S. 3, *reprinted in* DOCUMENTS ON THE LAWS OF WAR, *supra* note 7, at 422.

9. President George W. Bush, Address to the Nation (Oct. 7, 2001), *available at* http://www.whitehouse.gov/news/releases/2001/10/20011007-8.html.

10. *Id.*

11. *See* Geneva Convention I, *supra* note 7, art. 2.

12. S.C. Res. 1386, U.N. Doc. S/RES/1386 (Dec. 20, 2001).

13. As they were required to do by S.C. Res. 1386, *id.*

14. International humanitarian law and terrorism: questions and answers, http://www.icrc.org/web/eng/siteeng0.nsf/html/5ynlev (last visited Jan. 15, 2009).

15. The lawfulness of the use of self-defense is a matter for domestic law but this expression broadly reflects the position in most NATO nations.

16. Draft Articles on the Responsibility of States for Internationally Wrongful Acts, Report of the International Law Commission on the Work of its Fifty-third Session, U.N. GAOR, 56th Sess., Supp. No. 10, U.N. Doc. A/56/10 (2001), *available at* http://untreaty.un.org/ilc/texts/instruments/english/draft%20articles/9_6_2001.pdf.

17. Convention on the Prohibition of the Use, Stockpiling, Production and Transfer of Anti-Personnel Mines and on Their Destruction, Sept. 18, 1997, *reprinted in* DOCUMENTS ON THE LAWS OF WAR, *supra* note 7, at 648.

18. *Id.*, art.1.1.c.

19. United Nations Convention on the Law of the Sea, Dec. 10, 1982, 1833 U.N.T.S. 3.

20. S.C. Res. 1510, S/RES/1510 (Oct. 13, 2003).

21. Convention for the Protection of Human Rights and Fundamental Freedoms, Apr. 11, 1950, 213 U.N.T.S. 221, *available at* http://www.pfc.org.uk/node/328.

22. Armed Activities on the Territory of the Congo (Dem. Rep. Congo v. Uganda), 2005 I.C.J. 116 (Dec. 19).

23. And the one adopted by the European Court of Human Rights in Behrami v. France; and Saramati v. France, Germany and Norway, Apps. Nos. 71412/01 and 78166/01, 45 Eur. Ct. H.R. 41 (2007), *available at* http://www.echr.coe.int./echr/en/hudoc.

24. Including S.C. Res. 1386, *supra* note 12; S.C. Res. 1390, *supra* note 6; S.C. Res. 1419, U.N. Doc. S/RES/1419 (June 26, 2002); S.C. Res. 1510, *supra* note 20; and those that extended ISAF to the present day.

25. *See* S.C. Res. 1546, U.N. Doc. S/RES/1546 (June 8, 2004) and annexed letters.

PART III

THE CONDUCT OF HOSTILITIES

VII

Afghanistan and the Nature of Conflict

Charles Garraway*

Introduction

The story is told of a traveler in the west of Ireland. Thoroughly lost, he stopped beside a field and asked the farmhand working there how to get to Limerick. The answer was somewhat disconcerting: "Well, if I was you, sir, I wouldn't start from here!" There have been times over the last seven years when that phrase has come to mind. Decisions have been made and consequences have followed—none more so perhaps than in the relationship between the "war on terror" and the law of armed conflict/laws of war. Much of this uncertainty arose out of the initial conflict in Afghanistan in 2001. While it may not be possible to change the start point, it may help to look back and try to ascertain why we are where we are. Perhaps then, we will be in a better position to plan that route to Limerick.

The End of the Beginning

Our story has to start somewhere and where better than in the White House and with a presidential decision. On February 7, 2002, President Bush issued his memorandum on the subject of humane treatment of al Qaeda and Taliban detainees.[1] In paragraph 1, he stated:

---

* Visiting Professor, King's College London; Associate Fellow, Chatham House; and Visiting Fellow, Human Rights Centre, University of Essex.

Our recent extensive discussions regarding the status of al Qaeda and Taliban detainees confirm that the application of Geneva Convention Relative to the Treatment of Prisoners of War of August 12, 1949, (Geneva) to the conflict with al Qaeda and the Taliban involves complex legal questions. By its terms, Geneva applies to conflicts involving "High Contracting Parties," which can only be states. Moreover, it assumes the existence of "regular" armed forces fighting on behalf of states. However, the war against terrorism ushers in a new paradigm, one in which groups with broad, international reach commit horrific acts against innocent civilians, sometimes with the direct support of states. Our nation recognizes that this new paradigm – ushered in not by us, but by terrorists – requires new thinking in the law of war, but thinking that should nevertheless be consistent with the principles of Geneva.

Although this memorandum was not released to the public until some time later, its effect upon the debates on both the classification of conflicts and the application of the laws of war has been immense. No study of Afghanistan, or of any other conflict since 2002 in which the United States has been involved, can take place without considering the effect of this memorandum. Indeed so pivotal has it become to many of the arguments that now rage over the US position on law of war issues that it should be read in full:

SUBJECT: Humane Treatment of Taliban and al Qaeda Detainees

1. Our recent extensive discussions regarding the status of al Qaeda and Taliban detainees confirm that the application of Geneva Convention Relative to the Treatment of Prisoners of War of August 12, 1949, (Geneva) to the conflict with al Qaeda and the Taliban involves complex legal questions. By its terms, Geneva applies to conflicts involving "High Contracting Parties," which can only be states. Moreover, it assumes the existence of "regular" armed forces fighting on behalf of states. However, the war against terrorism ushers in a new paradigm, one in which groups with broad, international reach commit horrific acts against innocent civilians, sometimes with the direct support of states. Our nation recognizes that this new paradigm – ushered in not by us, but by terrorists – requires new thinking in the law of war, but thinking that should nevertheless be consistent with the principles of Geneva.

2. Pursuant to my authority as commander in chief and chief executive of the United States, and relying on the opinion of the Department of Justice dated January 22, 2002, and on the legal opinion rendered by the attorney general in his letter of February 1, 2002, I hereby determine as follows:

a. I accept the legal conclusion of the Department of Justice and determine that none of the provisions of Geneva apply to our conflict with al Qaeda in Afghanistan or elsewhere throughout the world because, among other reasons, al Qaeda is not a High Contracting Party to Geneva.

b. I accept the legal conclusion of the attorney general and the Department of Justice that I have the authority under the Constitution to suspend Geneva as between the United States and Afghanistan, but I decline to exercise that authority at this time. Accordingly, I determine that the provisions of Geneva will apply to our present conflict with the Taliban. I reserve the right to exercise the authority in this or future conflicts.

c. I also accept the legal conclusion of the Department of Justice and determine that common Article 3 of Geneva does not apply to either al Qaeda or Taliban detainees, because, among other reasons, the relevant conflicts are international in scope and common Article 3 applies only to "armed conflict not of an international character."

d. Based on the facts supplied by the Department of Defense and the recommendation of the Department of Justice, I determine that the Taliban detainees are unlawful combatants and, therefore, do not qualify as prisoners of war under Article 4 of Geneva. I note that, because Geneva does not apply to our conflict with al Qaeda, al Qaeda detainees also do not qualify as prisoners of war.

3. Of course, our values as a Nation, values that we share with many nations in the world, call for us to treat detainees humanely, including those who are not legally entitled to such treatment. Our Nation has been and will continue to be a strong supporter of Geneva and its principles. As a matter of policy, the United States Armed Forces shall continue to treat detainees humanely and, to the extent appropriate and consistent with military necessity, in a manner consistent with the principles of Geneva.

4. The United States will hold states, organizations, and individuals who gain control of United States personnel responsible for treating such personnel humanely and consistent with applicable law.

5. I hereby reaffirm the order previously issued by the Secretary of Defense to the United States Armed Forces requiring that the detainees be treated humanely and, to the extent appropriate and consistent with military necessity, in a manner consistent with the principles of Geneva.

6. I hereby direct the Secretary of State to communicate my determinations in an appropriate manner to our allies, and other countries and international organizations cooperating in the war against terrorism of global reach.

/s/ George W. Bush[2]

Learned treatises have been written on almost every part of this memorandum, in particular on the issue of the application of what the President refers to as "Geneva" law. However, for the purposes of this article, it is necessary to go back beyond the application of the law to the facts. It is the issue of classification of the conflict itself that raises challenges to the existing legal framework. Was the situation in Afghanistan, and also in the wider context of worldwide terrorism emanating in part at least from that country, a "new paradigm," removing it from the framework of law that had been painstakingly constructed over the previous 150 years? Or was it a mutation of an existing structure and well capable of accommodation within the current framework?

In order to attempt to answer these questions, it is necessary to examine the current framework and also to examine the legal debate that raged within the Bush administration. This memorandum was not the product of a "Eureka moment" in the Oval Office but the result of a need for a decision by the President following conflicting legal advice from within the administration itself. As with the memorandum itself, much of the debate revolves around classified material, in terms both of evidence and of the written advice itself. There have been leaks and much of the advice given, in particular by the Department of Justice, is now in the public domain. Greenberg and Dratel have sought to bring these together in their compilation *The Torture Papers: The Road to Abu Ghraib.*[3] At a later date, some of the State Department advice also came into the public domain. However, it is clear that the full picture remains locked in the corridors of power and it is unlikely that it will emerge for some time to come. In the meantime, scholars and others must make do with what we have.

The History

The factual history is comparatively straightforward. On September 11, 2001, terrorists hijacked four airliners in US airspace and used them as missiles to attack targets in New York (the World Trade Center) and Washington (the Pentagon). One airliner was brought down short of its target when passengers fought to regain control of the aircraft. Within days, it was apparent that these attacks were instigated by al Qaeda, operating primarily out of Afghanistan. Afghanistan at the time was a lawless State. Its location had made it a battleground for the power struggles between the British Empire and Russia in the nineteenth century. Although never fully colonized, it had not regained full independence until after the First World War, in 1919, but even then its history was not a happy one. Since 1973, there had been a series of bloody coups, culminating in a Soviet invasion after Mohammed Daoud was murdered in 1978. The Soviet forces were themselves forced to withdraw in 1989 and in 1996 the Taliban movement claimed control of the country and imposed a rigid Shari'a regime. Despite having territorial control of most of the country, the Taliban regime was not recognized by the vast majority of the nations of the world and the "officially recognized" government was the Northern Alliance, which remained in control of a small enclave in the north of the country. The Taliban had provided support, refuge and facilities for the al Qaeda network, whose leader, Osama Bin Laden, a Saudi national, had been driven out of previous sanctuaries, including Sudan.

On October 7, 2001, following advice on his authority under the US Constitution to conduct military operations "against terrorists and nations supporting them"[4] President Bush, in conjunction with other allies, launched military attacks against both al Qaeda and Taliban targets in Afghanistan. In the letter sent by the Representative of the United States of America, John Negroponte, to the President of the Security Council, the United States invoked "its inherent right of individual and collective self-defense following armed attacks that were carried out against the United States on September 11, 2001."[5] After describing the background to the 9/11 attacks, the letter went on to say:

> The attacks on September 11, 2001, and the ongoing threat to the United States and its nationals posed by the Al-Qaeda organization have been made possible by the decision of the Taliban regime to allow parts of Afghanistan that it controls to be used by this organization as a base of operation. Despite every effort by the United States and the international community, the Taliban regime has refused to change its policy. From the territory of Afghanistan, the Al-Qaeda organization continues to train and support agents of terror who attack innocent people throughout the world and target United States nationals and interests in the United States and abroad.[6]

While this made clear the connection drawn by the administration between al Qaeda and the Taliban, the letter also contained a slightly more ominous phrase: "We may find that our self-defense requires further actions with respect to other organizations and other States."[7]

The "war on terror" had begun.

The Laws of War

The history of the laws of war had developed in treaty terms since the middle part of the nineteenth century. The laws had developed amid the Westphalian structure, where States were the principal subject of international law. International law governed relations between States and did not generally concern itself with activities within States, which were reserved to the jurisdiction of the States themselves.

War was an activity conducted between States and, as a result, the laws of war only applied to such wars.

That does not mean that there was nothing that happened that today would be classified as "terrorism." However, much of this was inevitably internal and thus considered beyond the boundaries of international law. Occasionally such matters spread across borders and indeed one of the best-known principles in international law, that of self-defense in the *ius ad bellum*, the *Caroline* case, arose out of cross-border raids by irregulars. This led to the famous exchange of correspondence between Lord Ashburton, representing the United Kingdom, and the Secretary of War for the United States, Daniel Webster.[8] It is perhaps interesting that one of the lesser-known parts of that particular incident was the fate of one Alexander McLeod, who was arrested and detained by the US authorities for his alleged participation in the destruction of the *Caroline*. He was tried, and acquitted, in New York and indeed it was his detention that led to the exchange of diplomatic correspondence.

As a matter of practice, terrorism had normally been considered a matter of law enforcement—at times extraterritorial. It was dealt with by domestic law rather than international law and certainly not by the laws of war.

In 1949, the text of the four Geneva Conventions of that year[9] extended the laws of war beyond the traditional inter-State conflict. Conflicts were divided into two types. The first were described in Common Article 2 as follows:

> In addition to the provisions which shall be implemented in peacetime, the present Convention shall apply to all cases of declared war or of any other armed conflict which may arise between two or more of the High Contracting Parties, even if the state of war is not recognized by one of them.
>
> The Convention shall also apply to all cases of partial or total occupation of the territory of a High Contracting Party, even if the said occupation meets with no armed resistance.
>
> Although one of the Powers in conflict may not be a party to the present Convention, the Powers who are parties thereto shall remain bound by it in their mutual relations. They shall furthermore be bound by the Convention in relation to the said Power, if the latter accepts and applies the provisions thereof.[10]

This requires an "armed conflict" between "two or more High Contracting Parties." As only States can be High Contracting Parties, this means inter-State conflicts. However, Article 3 Common to the four Conventions covered new ground:

In the case of armed conflict not of an international character occurring in the territory of one of the High Contracting Parties, each Party to the conflict shall be bound to apply, as a minimum, the following provisions:

(1) Persons taking no active part in the hostilities, including members of armed forces who have laid down their arms and those placed "hors de combat" by sickness, wounds, detention, or any other cause, shall in all circumstances be treated humanely, without any adverse distinction founded on race, colour, religion or faith, sex, birth or wealth, or any other similar criteria.

To this end, the following acts are and shall remain prohibited at any time and in any place whatsoever with respect to the above-mentioned persons:

(a) violence to life and person, in particular murder of all kinds, mutilation, cruel treatment and torture;

(b) taking of hostages;

(c) outrages upon personal dignity, in particular humiliating and degrading treatment;

(d) the passing of sentences and the carrying out of executions without previous judgment pronounced by a regularly constituted court, affording all the judicial guarantees which are recognized as indispensable by civilized peoples.

(2) The wounded and sick shall be collected and cared for.

An impartial humanitarian body, such as the International Committee of the Red Cross, may offer its services to the Parties to the conflict.

The Parties to the conflict should further endeavour to bring into force, by means of special agreements, all or part of the other provisions of the present Convention.

The application of the preceding provisions shall not affect the legal status of the Parties to the conflict.[11]

The key elements governing the application of this particular "mini-convention" are as follows: (1) "an armed conflict," (2) "not of an international character" and (3) "occurring in the territory of one of the High Contracting Parties." Clearly this excluded any armed conflict that fell within the confines of Common Article 2, a conflict between two or more High Contracting Parties. However, the term "armed conflict" remained undefined and it was unclear as to the status of a conflict primarily "occurring in the territory of one of the High Contracting Parties" when it crossed over international borders. It should be noted that the original intention of the International Committee of the Red Cross (ICRC) was that the whole of the Conventions should apply to non-international armed conflicts. Common Article 3 therefore was an irreducible minimum so far as it was concerned. Attempts were indeed made to define what was meant by "armed conflict" but these were abandoned and it was the view of the ICRC that this "wise" decision meant that the term should be interpreted "as widely as possible."[12] This meant avoiding the application of any threshold test.

Similarly, although the geographic restriction was designed to catch civil wars, there does not appear to have been any intention to exclude conflicts with cross-border elements. Few conflicts are contained entirely within the boundaries of one territory and it has generally been considered sufficient if the conflict is centered within the territory of a High Contracting Party, even if it does have certain cross-border features. Many rebel groups operate from "safe havens" on the other side of international borders. Those who argued consistently that Northern Ireland amounted to a Common Article 3 conflict during the "Troubles" of the late twentieth century would hardly have been amused to be told that the fact that elements of the Irish Republican Army operated from across the border in the Irish Republic excluded the application of Common Article 3.

However, regardless of these arguments, what was clear was the division of conflict into two separate categories. This division was confirmed by the adoption of the two Additional Protocols to the 1949 Geneva Conventions in 1977. The first applied primarily to international armed conflicts as defined by Common Article 2[13] and the second to non-international armed conflicts.[14] However, Additional Protocol II adopted a much more restricted field of application and also introduced a threshold—a negative definition of what does not amount to an armed conflict. Article 1 reads:

> 1. This Protocol, which develops and supplements Article 3 common to the Geneva Conventions of 12 August 1949 without modifying its existing conditions of application, shall apply to all armed conflicts which are not covered by Article 1 of the Protocol Additional to the Geneva Conventions of 12 August 1949, and relating to the Protection of Victims of International Armed Conflicts (Protocol I) and which take place in the territory of a High Contracting Party between its armed forces and dissident armed forces or other organized armed groups which, under responsible command, exercise such control over a part of its territory as to enable them to carry out sustained and concerted military operations and to implement this Protocol.

2. This Protocol shall not apply to situations of internal disturbances and tensions, such as riots, isolated and sporadic acts of violence and other acts of a similar nature, as not being armed conflicts.

The higher threshold rules out a number of low-intensity conflicts where territory is not held by the dissident armed forces and, equally importantly, where the conflict is between dissident armed groups themselves without any involvement of the national forces, if they exist. Thus "failed State" conflicts where the battles are between rival warlords would normally be excluded from the application of Additional Protocol II. However, that does not mean that Common Article 3 does not apply.

For our purposes, it is the lower threshold that is important. "[S]ituations of internal disturbances and tensions, such as riots, isolated and sporadic acts of violence and other acts of a similar nature" are excluded "as not being armed conflicts." Terrorism was generally deemed to fit within this exclusion. This is illustrated by the statement made by the United Kingdom on ratification of Additional Protocol I in 1998. It read: "It is the understanding of the United Kingdom that the term 'armed conflict' of itself and in its context denotes a situation of a kind which is not constituted by the commission of ordinary crimes *including acts of terrorism whether concerted or in isolation*"[15] (emphasis added). This statement came from a nation that had been plagued by cross-border terrorism for a generation.

Back to the Future

The events of 9/11 undoubtedly caused a rift within the Bush administration. The language was all of "war" but what was not clear was whether this was seen as political rhetoric or legal analysis. The sheer scale of the atrocity undoubtedly contributed to this, but war against whom? The term "war on terrorism" cannot be taken as a legal description. "Terrorism" is a tactic and one cannot wage war against a tactic in any meaningful legal sense. The planning obviously focused on Afghanistan, where Osama Bin Laden was based, and the United States, with support from many parts of the world, prepared for war in Afghanistan.

It seems that, at this point, there was growing confusion between US constitutional law and international law. This may be because of the trend for both to be taught together in universities in the United States. On September 25, 2001, John Yoo wrote the memorandum opinion to Timothy Flanagan, Deputy Counsel to the President, already mentioned.[16] In that memorandum, which runs to some twenty pages, there is only one reference in the main text to international law.[17]

That reference is in relation to declarations of war. It states: "Instead of serving as an authorization to begin hostilities, a declaration of war was only necessary to 'perfect' a conflict under international law."

Apart from that isolated instance, the whole of the remainder of the memorandum deals with the position under US constitutional law. There is, however, one sentence which possibly sums up the change of opinion in the United States and also shows that such a change predates the presidency of George W. Bush. This sentence refers to the address to the nation delivered by President Clinton on August 20, 1998 in relation to the strike which he had ordered that day on Afghanistan and Sudan following the bombing of the US embassies in Kenya and Tanzania. The sentence reads: "Furthermore, in explaining why military action was necessary, the President noted that 'law enforcement and diplomatic tools' to combat terrorism had proved insufficient, and that 'when our very national security is challenged . . . we must take extraordinary steps to protect the safety of our citizens.'"[18] Thus, it appears that, as early as 1998 under President Clinton, the United States was beginning to move away from treating terrorism as solely a matter of law enforcement. The "war on terror" had not arrived but the initial skirmishes were under way.

Hostilities

The legal debate took a backseat during the conduct of hostilities. While there was some discussion over the *ius ad bellum* issues, the campaign was conducted in accordance with the principles of the law of armed conflict. Regardless of whether there was one conflict or two, the Department of Defense directive provides that the armed forces should "comply with the law of war during all armed conflicts, however such conflicts are characterized, and with the principles and spirit of the law of war during all other operations."[19]

However, the issue became live again when prisoners began to be captured. Were they prisoners of war under the Third Geneva Convention or were they not? Was there any distinction to be made between al Qaeda and the Taliban? If so, what was it and what were the legal grounds for making any distinction?

The Debate Continues

As has been mentioned earlier, not all the relevant documentation is in the public domain and therefore the discussion must inevitably be tentative. However, a number of documents have either been released or leaked and these in themselves make very interesting reading and go some way to explaining the decision made by President Bush on February 7, 2002.

On January 9, John Yoo circulated a draft memorandum prepared by him and Special Counsel Robert Delahunty addressed to the General Counsel of the Department of Defense, William J. Haynes.[20] This memorandum, significantly, was based on the War Crimes Act, a domestic statute.[21] It sought to argue two main propositions: (1) "[N]either the Geneva Conventions nor the [War Crimes Act] regulate the detention of al Qaeda prisoners captured during the Afghanistan conflict" and (2) the Geneva Conventions did not apply to "captured members of the Taliban militia."[22] The simple argument was that neither al Qaeda nor Taliban fighters were entitled to prisoner of war status. Put in those terms, the statement, while controversial, would have fitted within the traditional law of war concept. However, it was not so much the propositions themselves but the arguments put forward to support them that were to cause controversy.

First, starting from the War Crimes Act, Yoo and Delahunty began to examine the nature of conflict. They drew the usual distinction between Common Articles 2 and 3 to the Geneva Conventions but sought to narrow the application of Common Article 3, stating it "should not be read to include all forms of non-international armed conflict."[23] Their argument was that, "in enacting the [War Crimes Act], Congress did not understand the scope of Common Article 3 to extend beyond civil wars to all other types of internal armed conflict."[24] In their view Common Article 3 only applied to "large-scale conflicts between a State and an insurgent group,"[25] a similar threshold to that later incorporated into Additional Protocol II.[26]

Second, they argued that "Al Qaeda's status as a non-State actor renders it ineligible to claim the protections of the treaties specified by the [War Crimes Act]."[27] The argumentation is confused as it is not made explicit whether the reason for this conclusion is the nature of al Qaeda or the nature of the conflict itself. There are elements of both arguments and certainly when discussing Common Articles 2 and 3, the memorandum states, "Our conflict with al Qaeda does not fit into either category."[28]

Yoo and Delahunty then move to the "Taliban militia." They argue that, as a matter of constitutional law, "the Executive has the plenary authority to determine that Afghanistan ceased at relevant times to be an operating State and therefore that members of the Taliban militia were and are not protected by the Geneva Conventions."[29] There follows detailed argument as to why Afghanistan was a "failed State" and a conclusion that "Afghanistan under the Taliban militia was in a condition of 'statelessness,' and therefore was not a High Contracting Party to the Geneva Conventions for at least that period of time."[30]

A secondary argument was that, even if the Geneva Conventions did apply to Afghanistan, the members of the Taliban militia themselves did not fall within the category of prisoner of war, outlined in Article 4 of the Third Geneva Convention.[31]

They argued that the Taliban "cannot even be considered 'a government or authority'" for the purposes of Article 4A(3), which covers "[m]embers of regular armed forces who profess allegiance to a government or an authority not recognized by the Detaining Power." It was accepted that the United States had never recognized the Taliban regime as the government of Afghanistan.[32]

The memorandum continued with a review of previous US campaigns, arguing that wherever the Geneva Conventions had been applied—Korea, Vietnam, Panama, Somalia, Haiti and Bosnia—a distinction needed to be drawn between their application as a matter of law and their application as a matter of policy.[33] It goes on to discuss whether, even if the Geneva Conventions were *prima facie* applicable, the President had the power to suspend their application either in whole or in part in relation to Afghanistan. They concluded that as a matter of constitutional law "the President may regard a treaty as suspended for several reasons."[34] They then justified such a course essentially on the basis that "Afghanistan under the Taliban could be held to have violated basic humanitarian duties under the Geneva Conventions and other norms of international law."[35] They agreed that there was no precedent for such a suspension by the United States but pointed out that after both the Korean War and the Persian Gulf War, the United States had deviated from the strict terms of the Convention by allowing voluntary repatriation of prisoners of war rather than the mandatory repatriation required by the letter of the law in Article 118 of the Third Geneva Convention.[36]

The position under international law was also considered but with a telling introduction:

> We emphasize that the resolution of that question [whether the Geneva Conventions were applicable], however, *has no bearing* on domestic constitutional issues, or on the application of the [War Crimes Act]. Rather, these issues are worth consideration as a means of justifying the actions of the United States in the world of international politics.[37]

Their conclusion was that "it appears to be permissible, as a matter of both treaty law and of customary international law, to suspend performance of Geneva Convention obligations on a temporary basis."[38] The reference to customary international law was necessary as the United States is not party to the Vienna Convention on the Law of Treaties[39] though, somewhat reluctantly, the memorandum accepted that "some lower courts have said that the Convention embodies the customary international law of treaties, and the State Department has at various times taken the same view."[40]

The memorandum concludes with a general examination of customary international law. It comes to the firm conclusion that it does not amount to federal law, citing Chief Justice Marshall, who described customary international law as "a guide which the sovereign follows or abandons at his will. The rule, like other precepts of morality, of humanity, and even of wisdom, is addressed to the judgment of the sovereign; and although it cannot be disregarded by him without obloquy, yet it may be disregarded."[41] However, somewhat unusually, the authors went on to hold that "the President can properly find the unprecedented conflict between the United States and transnational terrorist organizations a 'war' for the purposes of the customary or common laws of war."[42] The purpose of this, however, was to subject al Qaeda and the Taliban to those laws rather than US forces to them. This is one of the few examples of the wider conflict against "transnational terrorist organizations" being mentioned.

The final paragraph sums up the whole memorandum. It states:

> [W]e conclude that neither the federal War Crimes Act nor the Geneva Conventions would apply to the detention conditions in Guantanamo Bay, Cuba, or to trial by military commission of al Qaeda or Taliban prisoners. We also conclude that customary international law has no legal binding effect on either the President or the military because it is not federal law, as recognized by the Constitution. Nonetheless, we also believe that the President as Commander-in-Chief, has the constitutional authority to impose the customary laws of war on both the al Qaeda and Taliban groups and the U.S. Armed Forces.[43]

It should be noted again that the main subject of this memorandum is detention conditions and the role of the military commissions. As such, the nature of the conflict or conflicts in themselves is a secondary consideration other than as it impacts on the main issue. There is thus no argument specifically on the issue of whether the conflict within Afghanistan itself was a single conflict governed by the laws relating to international armed conflict or whether it was bifurcated into a war against al Qaeda and a war against the Taliban. Indeed, the main purpose of the memorandum seems to be to argue that the laws relating to armed conflict did not apply at all!

The State Department Response

The draft memorandum had been copied to, *inter alia*, the State Department and brought a swift response from William H. Taft IV, the Legal Adviser. In a covering note to his memorandum in response to the Yoo/Delahunty draft, he said that he found "the most important factual assumptions on which your draft is based and its legal analysis are seriously flawed."[44] Again, the main purpose of the response was to examine the issues relating to detention rather than the nature of the conflict. The comments were grouped into four sections. The first dealt with the continuing applicability of treaty relations and made the point that "the ability, inability or even unwillingness of a State to perform international treaty obligations is a question entirely separate from the question of its status. Afghanistan has continued to be a State and a party to the Geneva Conventions during the relevant period."[45] There followed detailed legal and factual argument including a specific reference to United Nations practice:

> The UN Security Council [UNSC] has also indicated that the Taliban and other parties to the Afghan conflict were bound to comply with the Geneva Conventions. In UNSC Resolution 1193(1998), the Security Council reaffirmed that: All parties to the conflict [in Afghanistan] are bound to comply with their obligations under international humanitarian law and in particular the Geneva Conventions of 12 August 1949 . . . .

UNSC Resolution 1214, also concerning the conflict in Afghanistan, uses essentially the same language in a preambular clause. The parties referred to in these instances are the Taliban and those forces fighting against the Taliban. These Resolutions, in which the United States joined the consensus, describe "obligations" to adhere to the Geneva Conventions. The Security Council could not have issued a resolution containing such a clause if it had not been convinced that there was a proper legal basis to apply international law obligations to the parties to the conflict within Afghanistan. Evidently, the Council—and the United States—did not believe that Afghanistan was a "failed State" where the Geneva Conventions had become inapplicable.

The second section addresses application of the Geneva Conventions and states: "This section concludes that the [Third Geneva Convention] applies because the situation as between the United States and the Taliban is one of an armed conflict arising between two or more High Contracting Parties under Article 2."[46] It should be noted that this refers solely to "the situation as between the United States and the Taliban."

The section makes clear that, in the view of the State Department, Common Article 2 to the Geneva Conventions applied and that Afghanistan "remained a High Contracting Party by virtue of accepted principles of international law."[47] In its opinion, "the United States' refusal to recognize the Taliban as the government was not a conclusion that the Taliban was not in effective control of the great part of Afghanistan territory."[48] The State Department also resisted the Justice Department argument that the Taliban and al Qaeda were indistinguishable.

The memorandum then examined whether, on the basis that the Geneva Conventions applied, the Taliban still qualified under Article 4A of the Third Geneva Convention as prisoners of war. The conclusion was reached that, *prima facie*, they qualified as "regular armed forces" under Article 4A(3) but that in cases of doubt, the appropriate course would be to hold tribunals under Article 5 of the Third Geneva Convention.[49] In this section, there is a very interesting footnote, which reads:

> For instance, one reason among many that the Al Qaeda forces may not be entitled to POW status is that their operations are *designed* to violate the laws of war – most particularly, to target and attack civilian populations as such, civilians and civilian property. It is this kind of systematic violation which excludes organized forces from Article 4(A)(3).[50]

This does not rule out judging al Qaeda by the standards of the Geneva Conventions but in order to do so, they would have to be applicable.

The section concludes by taking issue with some of the conclusions drawn in the Justice Department memorandum on US practice in previous military campaigns before taking further issue with the Justice Department position on the possibility of suspending obligations under the Geneva Conventions. As the State Department pointed out, the United States had not sought to invoke any breach at the time as grounds for suspension and it was somewhat late now.

The final section examined the position under customary international law and pointed out one basic tenet:

> Were the President, as contemplated by the Draft Opinion, to act lawfully under federal law in a manner that would be inconsistent with the obligations of the United States under customary international law, that action would, notwithstanding its lawfulness under U.S. domestic law, constitute a breach of an international legal obligation of the United States.[51]

The memorandum pointed out how often the United States invokes customary law in its relations with other States, outlining, somewhat mischievously, that "the United States relies upon customary international law to provide the President and his family with immunity from prosecution and legal process when he travels abroad, by virtue of the doctrine of head of State immunity, which is entirely a matter of customary international law."[52]

The memorandum concludes with an annex on possible consequences if the Bush administration were to decide against the application of the Geneva

Conventions, both in domestic and international fora. It is a clear warning that any such action would not be without consequences.

As will be seen, the Taft memorandum bases itself on refuting the specific legal arguments put forward by the Justice Department. It does not deal with the classification of the conflict except when it is directly relevant to the subject matter. There is nothing in the memorandum that indicates that the author takes the view that there is a bifurcated conflict in Afghanistan rather than a single conflict that covers all the various participants. Such indications as there are tend toward the "single conflict" point of view though it may be that the author never considered that particular point as an issue.

The Justice Riposte

There followed a strong response from John Yoo and Robert Delahunty in which they effectively maintained their previous position.[53] Interestingly, they commented, "Although we have similar bottom lines, we differ in reasoning on the way there."[54] Indeed the argument was not so much on the practical effect of any decision on whether or not al Qaeda or the Taliban should be granted prisoner of war status, but more on the legal reasoning that led to any such decision. The discussion on the conflict itself was limited though they did refer to "the unprecedented nature of our war with al Qaeda and the Taliban,"[55] the singular being important here. The result was a new version of the Yoo/Delahunty memorandum, issued on January 22, 2002.[56]

However, there had been a development in that, on January 18, the President, acting as Commander in Chief, had directed that al Qaeda and Taliban individuals under the control of the Department of Defense were not entitled to prisoner of war status. This was communicated by a memorandum to the Chairman of the Joint Chiefs of Staff from the Secretary of Defense.[57]

Although the Yoo/Delahunty memorandum had been restructured, there was little change to the main arguments. There was reference to "a conflict with al Qaeda," stating that it "is not properly included in non-international forms of armed conflict"[58] and later that it "does not fall within Article 2" of the Geneva Conventions.[59] "It is not an international war between nation-States because al Qaeda is not a State. Nor is this conflict a civil war under Article 3 because it *is* a conflict of 'an international character.'"[60] This last quote is in a section dealing with the application of the War Crimes Act and associated treaties to al Qaeda.

When the memorandum turns to discussing the application of the Geneva Conventions to the Taliban militia, it refers to "the present conflict with respect to the Taliban militia."[61] Later on, in discussing the possible suspension of the Geneva

Conventions, the authors talk of the suspension of the Conventions "as applied to the Taliban militia in the current war in Afghanistan."[62] Later still, when discussing the possible status of Taliban prisoners under Article 4 of the Third Geneva Convention, there is reference to the need, if the Geneva Conventions are to apply, for "the Afghanistan conflict" to be qualified as an international armed conflict.[63] This is followed up with a telling sentence: "At this point in time, we cannot predict what consequences this acceptance of jurisdiction would have for future stages in the war on terrorism."[64]

An overall study of the memorandum leaves the reader with a sense that, as a result of the confused debate on the application of the law, the issue of whether Afghanistan was one conflict or two was not really considered. At some stages, there is indeed reference to "a conflict with al Qaeda" but in others there seems to be an indication that the conflict in Afghanistan was homogeneous though the application of the law might differ in respect to al Qaeda and Taliban detainees. Part of this confusion seems to arise from the uncertainty as to whether al Qaeda was a party to the conflict (which seems to be the view taken) or whether it was merely a participant in a conflict. The issue of how many conflicts were coexisting was not directly addressed.

The Final Arguments

The Justice Department riposte led to a strong response from the State Department. On January 23, William Taft wrote to Judge Gonzales, Counsel to the President, attaching a further memorandum which he had sent that day to John Yoo.[65] This in fact referred to a second draft of the original Yoo/Delahunty memorandum though it actually followed the dispatch of the final version. In it, Taft made his position clear. He stated:

> As you know from our previous comments, our view is that, as a matter of international law, the Third Geneva Convention applies to the armed conflict in Afghanistan because it "arises between" two High Contracting Parties to the Convention under common Article 2. The legal status of both al Qaeda and Taliban detainees must therefore be assessed under the Third Convention.[66]

This is as close as it is possible to get to a clear statement that Afghanistan was a single conflict and could not be bifurcated between al Qaeda and the Taliban. He then went on to deal with the application of that Convention, confirming that al Qaeda members were not entitled to prisoner of war status, though invoking Common Article 3 as providing "minimal standards applicable in any armed conflict."[67]

On January 25, 2002, Judge Gonzales prepared a draft memorandum for the President entitled "Decision Re Application of the Geneva Convention on Prisoners of War to the Conflict with Al Qaeda and the Taliban."[68] The title itself is interesting as, though the memorandum allies itself almost entirely with the positions being taken by the Justice Department—and indeed affirms that its interpretation on legal issues of this sort is "definitive"—the heading refers to "the [c]onflict with Al Qaeda and the Taliban." This use of the singular seems to confirm that the issue of bifurcation simply was not considered.

The draft memorandum brought a swift response from the Secretary of State, Colin Powell, who himself wrote to Judge Gonzales.[69] In this he said:

> I hope that the final memorandum will make clear that the President's choice is between
>
> Option 1: Determine that the Geneva Convention on the treatment of Prisoners of War (GPW) does not apply to *the conflict* on "failed State" or some other grounds. Announce this position publicly. Treat all detainees consistent with the principles of the GPW;
>
> and
>
> Option 2: Determine that the Geneva Convention does apply to *the conflict in Afghanistan*, but that members of al Qaeda as a group and the Taliban individually or as a group are not entitled to Prisoner of War status under the Convention. Announce this position publicly. Treat all detainees consistent with the principles of the GPW.[70]

There followed three pages of argument, as well as a page of comment on the Gonzales draft memorandum, but it seems clear that, in the view of the Secretary of State, there was only one conflict and the debate was only as to how al Qaeda and the Taliban should be treated within whatever legal regime was deemed to apply to that conflict. If the Secretary of State had considered that there was an issue as to whether the "conflict in Afghanistan" was one or bifurcated, it might be reasonable to expect that there would be some argument on the point in his letter. There is none.

The intervention of the Secretary of State brought a riposte from the Attorney General, John Ashcroft, on February 1, 2002.[71] In his letter to the President, he argues strongly for Option 1, stating that "this will provide the United States with the highest level of legal certainty available under American law."[72] At no point does he take issue with the statement by the Secretary of State that the conflict is singular. The purpose of his letter is made clear when he states:

> [A] Presidential determination against treaty applicability would provide the highest assurance that no court would subsequently entertain charges that American military officers, intelligence officials, or law enforcement officials violated Geneva Convention rules relating to field conduct, detention conduct or interrogation of detainees. The War Crimes Act of 1996 makes violation of parts of the Geneva Convention a crime in the United States.[73]

William Taft, in a memorandum dated February 2, 2002,[74] made one last despairing effort to repair what he apparently saw as an obvious departure by the United States from its traditional stance on the laws of war. He began by saying: "The paper should make clear that the issue for decision by the President is whether the Geneva Conventions apply to the conflict in Afghanistan in which U.S. armed forces are engaged."[75] After arguing forcefully for the application of the Conventions, he continued tellingly: "It is not inconsistent with the DOJ [Department of Justice] opinion that the Conventions generally do not apply to our world-wide effort to combat terrorism and to bring al Qaeda members to justice."[76] He concluded by saying:

> The structure of the paper suggesting a distinction between our conflict with al Qaeda and our conflict with the Taliban does not conform to the structure of the Conventions. The Conventions call for a decision whether they apply to the conflict in Afghanistan. If they do, their provisions are applicable to all persons involved in that conflict – al Qaeda, Taliban, Northern Alliance, U.S. troops, civilians, etc. If the Conventions do not apply to the conflict, no one involved in it will enjoy the benefit of their protections as a matter of law.[77]

This is the first occasion that any argument is given on this specific issue. Attached to that memorandum are some notes entitled "Status of Legal Discussions."[78] The notes clearly state that:

> • DOJ lawyers have concluded as matter of law that our conflict with al Qaeda, regardless of where it is carried out, is not covered by GPW. Lawyers from DOD, WHC and OVP support that legal conclusion.
>
> > • DOJ, DOD, WHC, and OVP lawyers believe that this conclusion is desirable from a domestic law standpoint because it provides the best possible insulation from any misapplication of the War Crimes Act to the conflict with al Qaeda, whether in Afghanistan or elsewhere.
> >
> > • DOJ, DOD, WHC, and OVP lawyers further believe that this conclusion is appropriate for policy reasons because it emphasizes that the worldwide conflict with al Qaeda is a new sort of conflict, one not covered by GPW or some other traditional rules of warfare.

- DOS lawyers believe that GPW applies to our treatment of al Qaeda members captured in Afghanistan on the theory that GPW applies to the conflict in Afghanistan, not to particular individuals or groups.

  - DOS lawyers believe this conclusion is desirable from a domestic and international law standpoint because it provides the best legal basis for our intended treatment of the detainees and strengthens the Geneva Convention protections of our forces in Afghanistan and other conflicts.

  - DOS lawyers further believe this conclusion is appropriate for policy reasons because it emphasizes that even in a new sort of conflict the United States bases its conduct on its international treaty obligations and the rule of law, not just its policy preferences.

At last, the issue was out in the open after being the "elephant in the room" for so long. Five days later, President Bush issued his memorandum[79] and the die was cast.

Conclusion

Why was the matter not dealt with in detail in any of the earlier documentation? Surely, if the State Department had realized that it was a live issue, it would have featured in the earlier correspondence. For example, the Secretary of State's memorandum[80] seems to have taken for granted that the conflict in Afghanistan was one entity and so, intriguingly, does the memorandum for the President, written by Judge Gonzales on January 25.[81] However, it was clearly an issue—indeed perhaps the key issue—by the time that William Taft wrote on February 2.[82]

Was this a sudden realization by the State Department or did the issue crystallize in those few days at the end of January 2002? In any event, it would seem that one of the most fundamental rulings that President Bush made was the least subject to legal discussion. A further irony is that it might not have been necessary. Had the President followed the advice of the State Department in respect to Afghanistan, the creation of the detention facility at Guantanamo Bay would still have happened. Members of al Qaeda would still have been denied prisoner of war status and it is likely that the vast majority of Taliban detainees would have been in the same position. The argument would have been on a different issue—whether there is a gap between the Third and Fourth Geneva Conventions where "unprivileged belligerents" are concerned. That is a case where the United States would have been on far stronger legal ground. Would it have had an effect on the worldwide effort to combat terrorism or would it have actually helped the United States in enabling it to lead the effort from the moral high ground? Unfortunately, we will never know.

Now we struggle to deal with the issues caused by that fateful decision both in relation to Afghanistan and elsewhere in the world. We are still struggling to get to Limerick but we have no choice but to start from here.

Notes

1. Memorandum from George Bush to Vice President et al., Humane Treatment of al Qaeda and Taliban Detainees (Feb. 7, 2002), *reprinted in* THE TORTURE PAPERS: THE ROAD TO ABU GHRAIB 134 (Karen J. Greenberg & Joshua Dratel eds., 2005).

2. *Id.* at 134–35.

3. *Supra* note 1.

4. Memorandum Opinion from John Yoo to Timothy Flanagan, Deputy Counsel to the President, The President's Constitutional Authority to Conduct Military Operations against Terrorists and Nations Supporting Them (Sept. 25, 2001), *reprinted in* TORTURE PAPERS, *supra* note 1, at 3.

5. Letter from John Negroponte, Representative of the United States of America to the United Nations, to the President of the Security Council (Oct. 7, 2001), *available at* http://avalon.law.yale.edu/sept11/un_006.asp.

6. *Id.*

7. *Id.*

8. The relevant correspondence is available at Yale Law School Avalon Project, Webster-Ashburton Treaty – The Caroline Case, http://www.yale.edu/lawweb/avalon/diplomacy/britain/br-1842d.htm.

9. Convention for the Amelioration of the Condition of the Wounded and Sick in Armed Forces in the Field, Aug. 12, 1949, 6 U.S.T. 3114, 75 U.N.T.S. 31 [Geneva Convention I]; Convention for the Amelioration of the Condition of the Wounded, Sick and Shipwrecked Members of Armed Forces at Sea, Aug. 12, 1949, 6 U.S.T. 3217, 75 U.N.T.S. 85 [Geneva Convention II]; Convention Relative to the Treatment of Prisoners of War, Aug. 12, 1949, 6 U.S.T. 3316, 75 U.N.T.S. 135 [Geneva Convention III]; and Convention Relative to the Protection of Civilian Persons in Time of War, Aug. 12, 1949, 6 U.S.T. 3516, 75 U.N.T.S. 287 [Geneva Convention IV]; all *reprinted in* DOCUMENTS ON THE LAWS OF WAR (Adam Roberts & Richard Guelff eds., 3d ed. 2000) at 197, 222, 244 and 301, respectively.

10. Geneva Conventions I–IV, *supra* note 9, at 198, 222, 244 and 301, respectively.

11. Geneva Conventions I–IV, *supra* note 9, at 198, 223, 245 and 302, respectively.

12. 1 COMMENTARY ON THE GENEVA CONVENTIONS OF 12 AUGUST 1949, at 50 (Jean S. Pictet ed., 1952).

13. Protocol Additional to the Geneva Conventions of 12 August 1949, and Relating to the Protection of Victims of International Armed Conflicts art. 1(3), June 8, 1977, 1125 U.N.T.S. 3, *reprinted in* DOCUMENTS ON THE LAWS OF WAR, *supra* note 9, at 422.

14. Protocol Additional to the Geneva Conventions of 12 August 1949, and Relating to the Protection of Victims of Non-International Armed Conflicts art. 1, June 8, 1977, 1125 U.N.T.S. 609, *reprinted in* DOCUMENTS ON THE LAWS OF WAR, *supra* note 9, at 483.

15. Letter from Christopher Hulse, Her Majesty's Ambassador to Switzerland, to the President of the Swiss Confederation statement (d) (Jan. 28, 1998), *reprinted in* DOCUMENTS ON THE LAWS OF WAR, *supra* note 9, at 510.

16. *Supra* note 4.

17. *Id.* at 7.

18. *Id.* at 18.

19. Deputy Secretary of Defense, Department of Defense Directive 5100.7, DoD Law of War Program para. 5.3.1 (Dec. 9, 1998), *available at* http://biotech.law.lsu.edu/blaw/dodd/corres/html2/d510077x.htm.

20. Memorandum from John C. Yoo & Robert Delahunty to William J. Haynes II, General Counsel, Department of Defense, Re. Application of Treaties and Laws to al Qaeda and Taliban Detainees (Jan. 9, 2002), *reprinted in* TORTURE PAPERS, *supra* note 1, at 38 [hereinafter Yoo/Delahunty Memorandum].

21. 18 US Code sec. 2441 (Supp. III 1997).

22. Yoo/Delahunty Memorandum, *supra* note 20, at 39.

23. *Id.* at 47.

24. *Id.*

25. *Id.* at 44.

26. *Supra* note 14, and following text.

27. Yoo/Delahunty Memorandum, *supra* note 20, at 48.

28. *Id.* at 49.

29. *Id.* at 51.

30. *Id.* at 55.

31. Geneva Convention III, *supra* note 9, art. 4.

32. Yoo/Delahunty Memorandum, *supra* note 20, at 61.

33. *Id.* at 62–64.

34. *Id.* at 65.

35. *Id.*

36. Geneva Convention III, *supra* note 9, art. 118.

37. Yoo/Delahunty Memorandum, *supra* note 20, at 67.

38. *Id.* at 69.

39. Vienna Convention on the Law of Treaties, May 23, 1969, 1155 U.N.T.S. 331, *reprinted in* BASIC DOCUMENTS IN INTERNATIONAL LAW 270 (Ian Brownlie ed., 5th ed. 2002).

40. Yoo/Delahunty Memorandum, *supra* note 20, at 68.

41. *Id.* at 73, *citing* Brown v. United States, 12 U.S. (8 Cranch) 110, 128 (1814).

42. *Id.* at 77.

43. *Id.* at 79.

44. Memorandum from William H. Taft IV, Legal Adviser, Department of State, to John C. Yoo, Deputy Assistant Attorney General, Office of the Legal Counsel, United States Department of Justice, Your Draft Memorandum of January 9, at 1 (Jan. 11, 2002), *available at* http://hei.unige.ch/%7Eclapham/hrdoc/docs/TaftMemo.pdf [hereinafter Taft Memorandum].

45. *Id.*, attachment at 4.

46. *Id.* at 11.

47. *Id.* at 13.

48. *Id.* at 19.

49. Geneva Convention III, *supra* note 9, art. 5.

50. Taft Memorandum, *supra* note 44, attachment n.35, at 21.

51. *Id.* at 31.

52. *Id.* at 33.

53. Letter from John Yoo, Deputy Assistant Attorney General, Office of Legal Counsel & Robert J. Delahunty, Special Counsel, Office of Legal Counsel, to William H. Taft IV, Legal Adviser, US Department of State (Jan. 14, 2002), available at http://www.cartoonbank.com/newyorker/slideshows/02yootaft.pdf.

54. *Id.* at 1.
55. *Id.* at 4.
56. Memorandum from John Yoo & Robert Delahunty to Alberto R. Gonzales, Counsel to the President & William J. Haynes II, General Counsel of the Department of Defense, Re. Application of Treaties and Laws to al Qaeda and Taliban Detainees (Jan. 22, 2002), *reprinted in* TORTURE PAPERS, *supra* note 1, at 81 [hereinafter Yoo/Delahunty Memorandum of January 22, 2002].
57. Memorandum from the Secretary of Defense to Chairman of the Joint Chiefs of Staff, Status of Taliban and Al Qaeda (Jan. 19, 2002), *reprinted in* TORTURE PAPERS, *supra* note 1, at 80.
58. Yoo/Delahunty Memorandum of January 22, 2002, *supra* note 56.
59. *Id.* at 90.
60. *Id.*
61. *Id.* at 91.
62. *Id.* at 104.
63. *Id.* at 111.
64. *Id.*
65. Note from William H. Taft IV, Legal Adviser, Department of State, to Judge Gonzales covering Memorandum from William H. Taft IV, Legal Adviser, Department of State, to John C. Yoo, Deputy Assistant Attorney General, Office of the Legal Counsel, United States Department of Justice, Your Draft Memorandum of January 18 (Jan. 23, 2002), *available at* http://www.pegc.us/archive/State_Department/taft_yoo_20020123.pdf.
66. *Id.* at 1.
67. *Id.* at 2.
68. Memorandum from Alberto R. Gonzales to the President, Decision Re Application of the Geneva Convention on Prisoners of War to the Conflict with Al Qaeda and the Taliban (Jan. 25, 2002), *available at* http://www.humanrightsfirst.org/us_law/etn/gonzales/memos_dir/memo_20020125_Gonz_Bush.pdf.
69. Memorandum from Colin L. Powell to Counsel to the President & Assistant to the President for National Security Affairs, Draft Decision Memorandum for the President on the Applicability of the Geneva Convention to the Conflict in Afghanistan (Jan. 26, 2002), *reprinted in* TORTURE PAPERS, *supra* note 1, at 122.
70. *Id.* (emphasis added).
71. Letter from John Ashcroft to the President (Feb. 1, 2002), *reprinted in* TORTURE PAPERS, *supra* note 1, at 126.
72. *Id.* at 127.
73. *Id.* at 126.
74. Memorandum from William H. Taft IV, Legal Adviser, Department of State, to Counsel to the President, Comments on Your Paper on the Geneva Conventions (Feb. 2, 2002), *reprinted in* TORTURE PAPERS, *supra* note 1, at 129.
75. *Id.*
76. *Id.*
77. *Id.*
78. Status of Legal Discussions re Application of Geneva Convention to Taliban and al Qaeda, *in* TORTURE PAPERS, *supra* note 1, at 130. The notes reference discussions among lawyers from the DOJ (Department of Justice), DOD (Department of Defense), WHC (the White House Counsel's office) and OVP (Office of the Vice President).
79. *Supra* note 1.
80. *Supra* note 69.

81. *Supra* note 68.
82. *Supra* note 74.

VIII

Making the Case for Conflict Bifurcation in Afghanistan: Transnational Armed Conflict, al Qaida and the Limits of the Associated Militia Concept

Geoffrey S. Corn*

In response to a Committee for Human Rights inquiry related to the targeted killing of an alleged al Qaida operative in Yemen, the United States asserted:

> The Government of the United States respectfully submits that inquiries related to allegations stemming from any military operations conducted during the course of an armed conflict with Al Qaida do not fall within the mandate of the Special Rapporteur.
>
> . . .
>
> Al Qaida and related terrorist networks are at war with the United States . . . .
>
> Despite coalition success in Afghanistan and around the world, the war is far from over. The Al Qaida network today is a multinational enterprise with operations in more than 60 countries.[1]

---

* Associate Professor of Law, South Texas College of Law.

This assertion of the existence of an armed conflict between al Qaida and the United States was both clear and emphatic, specifically rejecting the proposition that the killing was governed by human rights norms. It also represents what many believe is a radical theory of law: that an armed conflict can exist between a State and a transnational non-State entity.[2]

In no location has this latter proposition been more contested than in Afghanistan. Although al Qaida may very well operate in over sixty countries around the world, the reality is that almost all the US military effort directed against that enemy has occurred in Afghanistan, where much of that effort has been intertwined with the effort to defeat the Taliban armed forces. Because of the contiguous nature of these operations, most scholars and law of armed conflict (LOAC) experts have asserted from the outset of Operation Enduring Freedom that operations directed against al Qaida in Afghanistan are subsumed within the broader armed conflict in Afghanistan. Accordingly, they reject categorically the suggestion that there was, or is, in Afghanistan a distinct armed conflict between the United States and al Qaida.[3] Instead, operations directed against al Qaida were initially just a component of the broader international armed conflict between the US-led coalition and the Taliban regime, and thereafter of the non-international armed conflict between the Kharzai government and its coalition backers and the remnants of the Taliban.

But if the premise asserted in the US response excerpted above is valid—that an armed conflict does exist between the United States and al Qaida—the question of the nature of that conflict in Afghanistan is arguably more complex. By staking out a new category of armed conflict, what I have labeled in previous articles as transnational armed conflict, the United States created the potential to treat the contiguous conflicts in Afghanistan as distinct.

Such a theory of conflict bifurcation has potentially profound consequences. If there was and is only one armed conflict in Afghanistan, then rights and obligations related to al Qaida operatives must be analyzed under the regulatory regime related to that broader conflict. This would impact a wide array of legal issues, ranging from status of detainees, transferability and command responsibility to jurisdiction related to criminal sanction for violation of the LOAC. If, in contrast, the conflict between the United States and al Qaida occurring in Afghanistan is treated as distinct from the conflicts related to the Taliban, a far more uncertain legal framework would dictate a distinct package of rights and obligations vis-à-vis al Qaida. This framework would be, at best, composed of general LOAC principles, perhaps supplemented by policy extension of conventional LOAC provisions.[4]

This article will analyze the two primary impediments to recognizing such a bifurcated conflict theory. The first of these is related to recognition in the context of an international armed conflict—that in such a context al Qaida is properly and exclusively treated as a militia or volunteer group associated with the Taliban armed forces. The second is related to recognition in the context of a non-international armed conflict—that unless al Qaida is an element of the insurgent forces fighting against the Kharzai government, operations conducted against al Qaida cannot be characterized as armed conflict but must instead be characterized as extraterritorial law enforcement.

A theory of bifurcated armed conflict is concededly unconventional. Even if such a theory is viable in the abstract, it is particularly problematic in relation to the conflict in Afghanistan. This is because of the unavoidable reality that unlike the type of "one off" operations exemplified by the Predator strike that generated the Department of State assertion above, operations in Afghanistan directed against al Qaida are geographically and often operationally contiguous with those directed against the Taliban. Further complicating the theory is that operations conducted *by* al Qaida were, and are often are, intertwined with those conducted by the Taliban. However, these complicating realities only highlight the ultimate question: does all this mean that the legal character of the armed conflicts themselves *must* be contiguous? It is precisely because the United States has asserted the existence of a distinct armed conflict with al Qaida that this question must be critically considered.

Transnational Armed Conflict: Has Reality Outpaced Legality?

Defining the nature of the armed conflict against al Qaida—if there can be such an armed conflict—is obviously critical to this analysis. As I have asserted in previous articles,[5] the traditionally understood law-triggering paradigm that evolved from the development of Common Articles 2 and 3 of the Geneva Conventions proved insufficient to respond to the need for battlefield regulation of counterterror combat operations.[6] These operations, particularly those conducted in response to the attacks of September 11, 2001 reflect the reality that the basic regulatory framework of the law of armed conflict must be triggered by *any* armed conflict. Because this is the critical predicate for the application of a bifurcated conflict theory to Afghanistan, this section (reproduced with light edits from my prior article, "Hamdan, Lebanon, and the Regulation of Armed Conflict: The Need to Recognize a Hybrid Category of Armed Conflict"[7]) will explain the underlying rationale for a transnational, or *any*, armed conflict theory.

The "either/or" law-triggering paradigm of Common Articles 2 and 3[8] proved generally sufficient to address the types of armed conflicts occurring up until 9/11. However, this fact no longer justifies the conclusion that no other triggering standard should be recognized. Instead, as the events since 9/11 have illustrated so convincingly, such recognition is essential in order to keep pace with the evolving nature of armed conflicts themselves. The prospect of an unregulated battlefield is simply unacceptable in the international community, a fact demonstrated by the response to the conflict in Lebanon.[9] The ultimate question, therefore, is whether it is best to continue to try and fit the proverbial square "armed conflict" peg into the round "Common Article 3" hole, or whether the time has come to acknowledge that the essential trigger for application of basic LOAC principles is just armed conflict, irrespective of the enemy or the location.

The stress on the existing paradigm of law of war application reflected in the diverging conclusions of both the DC Circuit and the Supreme Court in the *Hamdan* case is in no way fatal to the ability of the law to adapt to the necessities of the changing nature of warfare. All law is adaptive, but this is particularly true with regard to the LOAC, a conclusion illustrated by the fact that this law has endured for centuries. This area of international legal regulation has been historically resilient precisely because the law has always responded to the changes in the nature of warfare. Perhaps more importantly, these responses have been implemented in a manner considered credible by States and the armed forces called upon to execute military conflicts.

It is essential that the applicability of the principles of the laws of war—principles that operate to limit the brutality of war and mitigate the suffering of victims of war—not be restricted by an overly technical legal triggering paradigm. Accordingly, the ongoing evolution in the nature of warfare requires acknowledgment that *any* armed conflict triggers the foundational principles of the laws of war. If this outcome is achieved by characterizing such military operations as "Common Article 3" conflicts that trigger the humane treatment obligation *plus* additional customary LOAC principles, the regulatory purpose of the law can be achieved. However, because Common Article 3 conflicts have become generally synonymous with *internal* conflicts, it is more pragmatic to expressly endorse a hybrid category of armed conflict: *transnational* armed conflict.[10]

The recognition of this "hybrid" category would not render Common Articles 2 or 3 irrelevant. Instead, these articles would continue to serve as triggers for application of the treaty provisions to which they relate. But this new category would be responsive to the rapidly changing nature of warfare, a change that creates an increased likelihood that States will resort to the use of combat power to respond to threats posed by non-State armed entities operating outside their territory. Such armed conflicts justify a more precise interpretation of the de facto conditions that trigger the foundational principles of the laws of war, supporting the conclusion that any de facto armed conflict serves as such a trigger. Common Articles 2 and 3 would then serve to trigger layers of more defined regulation in some ways redundant to, and in other ways augmenting, these principles. This "layered" methodology will ensure no conflict falls outside the scope of essential baseline regulation, while preserving the technical triggers for more detailed regulation required by application of specific treaty provisions.

This bifurcated methodology of distinguishing between treaty provisions per se and the principles providing the foundation for these treaty provisions was an essential aspect of the first major international war crimes trial since the advent of Common Articles 2 and 3. In the seminal decision defining the jurisdiction of the first international war crimes tribunal since World War II, *Prosecutor v. Tadic*,[11] the International Criminal Tribunal for the former Yugoslavia (ICTY), an ad hoc war crimes court created by the United Nations Security Council to prosecute alleged war criminals from the conflict that followed the breakup of the former Yugoslavia, relied on a similar methodology. The Tribunal was able to sustain many war crimes allegations only by extending to the realm of non-international armed conflict fundamental principles of the laws of war derived from treaty articles applicable only to international armed conflicts.[12] According to this seminal decision, the requirements for application of individual criminal responsibility under Article 3 of its Statute (vesting the Tribunal with competence to adjudicate violations of the laws or customs of war) were that "(i) the violation must constitute an infringement of a rule of international humanitarian law" and "(ii) the rule must be customary in nature *or, if it belongs to treaty law*, the required conditions must be met . . . ."[13] Accordingly, the Tribunal relied on this methodology to fill a regulatory gap essential to establish individual criminal responsibility in relation to the armed conflict, the exact same logic that supports a further reliance on this methodology to regulate transnational armed conflicts.

The pragmatic logic of adopting an *ipso facto* application of these fundamental principles to *any* armed conflict suggested in the *Tadic* ruling has also been at the core of US military policy for decades. It also provided the *ratio decidendi* for the *Hamdan* majority holding that the principle of humane treatment applied to the armed conflict between the United States and al Qaida. The *Hamdan* majority endorsed a modified version of the Common Article 2/3 "either/or" paradigm. The scope of international armed conflict defined by Common Article 2 was left intact. However, instead of endorsing the intra-State qualifier to the alternate "type" of armed conflict, the Court concluded that the term "non-international" as used in Common Article 3 operates in juxtaposition to international armed conflicts, and therefore covers *all* armed conflicts falling outside the scope of Common Article 2. Accordingly, the Court determined that a non-international armed conflict includes the traditional category of internal armed conflicts, *but also* extraterritorial armed conflicts between a State and non-State forces. As Justice Stevens noted:

> The Court of Appeals thought, and the Government asserts, that common article 3 does not apply to Hamdan because the conflict with al Qaeda, being "'international in scope,'" does not qualify as a "'conflict not of an international character.'" That reasoning is erroneous. The term "conflict not of an international character" is used here in contradistinction to a conflict between nations. So much is demonstrated by the "fundamental logic [of] the Convention's provisions on its application." Common article 2 provides that "the present Convention shall apply to all cases of declared war or of any other armed conflict which may arise between two or more of the High Contracting Parties." High Contracting Parties (signatories) also must abide by all terms of the Conventions vis-à-vis one another even if one party to the conflict is a nonsignatory "Power," and must so abide vis-à-vis the nonsignatory if "the latter accepts and applies" those terms. Common article 3, by contrast, affords some minimal protection, falling short of full protection under the Conventions, to individuals associated with neither a signatory nor even a nonsignatory "Power" who are involved in a conflict "in the territory of" a signatory. The latter kind of conflict is distinguishable from the conflict described in common article 2 chiefly because it does not involve a clash between nations (whether signatories or not). *In context, then, the phrase "not of an international character" bears its literal meaning.*[14]

This interpretation of the scope of Common Article 3 was the essential predicate to the Court's holding that the procedures established by the President for the military commission violated the laws of war. It is also thoroughly consistent with the view that all situations of armed conflict require regulation, the view that has motivated US military policy for decades.

Recognition that combat is an endeavor that must trigger an effective regulatory framework is derived from a long-standing history of self-imposed regulatory codes adopted by professional armed forces. As is suggested by A.P.V. Rogers in his book *Law on the Battlefield*,[15] prior to the development of the legal "triggering mechanisms" controlling application of this regulatory framework, armed forces did not appear to consider "conflict typing" as an essential predicate for operating within the limits of such a framework. While it is true that throughout most of history this framework took the form of self-imposed limits on warrior conduct,[16] these limits provided the seeds for what are today regarded as the foundational principles of the laws of war.[17] Thus, the pragmatic military logic reflected in both the *Hamdan* decision and the Department of Defense law of war policy is deeply rooted in the history of warfare.

This history undoubtedly includes examples of combat operations conducted by the regular armed forces of States against non-State armed groups prior to the development of Common Article 3. These operations ranged from colonial expeditions to what would today be characterized as "coalition" operations, such as the multinational response to the Boxers in China. In his book *Savage Wars of Peace*,[18] Max Boot provides several examples of such combat operations conducted by the armed forces of the United States prior to the Second World War, ranging from the conflict against the Barbary Pirates to the punitive expedition against Pancho Villa. Armed forces executing such operations must have invoked what today would be characterized as the principle of military necessity, asserting the authority to take all measures not forbidden by international law necessary to achieve the prompt submission of their opponents. However, these forces must have also respected what would today be regarded as the principle of humanity, as understood in historical context.[19] While the nature of the constraint on the conduct of these operations may have been understood more in terms of "chivalry" and less in terms of law,[20] the basic premise that runs through this history to the contemporary battlefield is that combat operations trigger a framework of regulation necessary for disciplined operations. Today, this framework is best understood not in terms of a chivalric code, but in terms of compliance with the principles of necessity, humanity, distinction and the prohibition against inflicting unnecessary suffering.[21]

It is, of course, improper to assert that the pre-1949 history of military operations supports a conclusion that armed forces regarded such operations as triggering legal obligations. On the contrary, the international legal character of the laws of war in relation to contemporary warfare was based primarily on treaties that applied to conflicts between States. This point is emphasized by Professor Green in his book *The Contemporary Law of Armed Conflict:*

> Historically, international law was concerned only with the relations between states. As a result, the international law of armed conflict developed in relation to inter-state conflicts was not in any way concerned with conflicts occurring within the territory of any state or with a conflict between an imperial power and a colonial territory.[22]

However, this history does suggest that the seeds that grew into the foundational principles of the contemporary laws of war extended to the realm of internal armed conflict by the *Tadic* ruling and applied to all US military operations by way of policy were derived from these internal military codes. Indeed, the fact that the contemporary laws of war find their origins in the practices of armed forces is also highlighted by Professor Green: "the law of armed conflict is still governed by those principles of international customary law which have developed virtually since feudal times . . . ."[23] It therefore seems significant that armed forces did not historically qualify application of these internal codes of conflict regulation on the character of the armed conflict. Nor can it be legitimately asserted that armed forces bound by such internal codes were employed exclusively in the realm of State-versus-State conflict. While this may have been the most common type of their combat operations, the history of the nineteenth and twentieth centuries also include military engagements falling outside this category.[24]

Nonetheless, the historical context of the range of combat operations engaged in by regular armed forces during this critical period of legal development is significant when assessing appropriate scope of application of the contemporary principles of the laws of war. This history supports the inference that regular armed forces historically viewed combat operations—or armed conflict—as an *ipso facto* trigger for principles that regulated combatant conduct on the battlefield. This history is also instructive in exposing the fact that this "basic framework" concept was severely strained during the years between the First and Second World Wars. This strain was exacerbated by the fact that the scope of the emerging treaty-based regulatory regime was strictly limited to "war," which was understood in the classic terms of a contention between States.[25]

In this regard, it also seems relevant that even Common Article 2 was a response to a perceived failure of the traditional expectation that armed forces would apply a regulatory framework derived from either the laws and customs of war or internal disciplinary codes when engaged in "war" between States.[26] The rejection of "war" as a trigger for application of the laws of war during inter-State conflicts in favor of the "armed conflict" trigger was an attempt to prevent what one might understand as "bad faith avoidance" of compliance with the customary standards related to the *jus in bello*.[27] The qualifier of "international" was, as indicated in the International Committee of the Red Cross (ICRC) *Commentary*, an effort to emphasize that specific provisions of the Geneva Conventions were triggered by armed conflicts conducted under State authority.[28] However, as that same *Commentary* indicates, it is the "armed conflict" aspect of military operations that distinguish such activities—and the law that regulates them—from the wide range of government activities not involving the application of combat power by armed forces. It is therefore thoroughly consistent with the purpose and history of the Geneva Conventions to place principal emphasis on the existence of armed conflict when assessing the appropriate trigger for the foundational principles reflected in those and other law of war treaties.

This general concept—that the need to provide effective regulation of de facto armed conflicts warrants resort to foundational principles reflected in treaties that are technically inapplicable to a given conflict—was also endorsed by the International Criminal Tribunal for the former Yugoslavia. In *Prosecutor v. Tadic*,[29] the Tribunal held that "an armed conflict exists whenever there is a resort to armed force between States or protracted armed violence between governmental authorities and organized armed groups or between such groups within a State."[30] Of course, because the question before this Tribunal dealt with application of the laws of war to international and/or internal armed conflict, or a combination thereof, the significance of this language is primarily related to these traditional categories of armed conflict.[31] What was far more significant about this decision was the recognition that non-international armed conflicts trigger a regime of regulation more comprehensive than only humane treatment. In ruling on the obligations applicable to participants in such non-international armed conflicts that provide a basis for individual criminal responsibility, the Tribunal looked beyond the humane treatment mandate of Common Article 3. In addition to this obligation, the Tribunal concluded that many of the fundamental rules related to the methods and means of warfare applicable in international armed conflicts had evolved to apply as a matter of customary international law to non-international armed conflicts.[32] While the Tribunal noted that this evolution did not result in a "mechanical transfer" of rules from one category of armed conflict to the other, this ruling clearly encompassed what are characterized by many sources as the foundational principles of the law of war.[33] According to the ruling, these principles

> cover such areas as protection of civilians from hostilities, in particular from indiscriminate attacks, protection of civilian objects, in particular cultural property, protection of all those who do not (or no longer) take active part in hostilities, as well as prohibition of means of warfare proscribed in international armed conflicts and ban of certain methods of conducting hostilities.[34]

The wisdom of the *Tadic* judgment recognizing the necessity of extending principles originally associated with international armed conflicts into the realm of non-international armed conflict logically extends to both internal and transnational armed conflicts. Indeed, there seemed to be virtually no hesitation among legal scholars and diplomatic officials for demanding application of these principles to the recent conflict in Lebanon.[35] Obviously, the alternate was unthinkable—that intense combat operations could fall beyond the scope of any legal regulation. Nor would application of the *Hamdan* ruling satisfy the perceived necessity to regulate such a conflict, as that ruling in no way addressed application of principles regulating the methods and means of warfare. Instead, the reaction to the conflict indicated an emerging international expectation that participants in such conflicts—and especially State forces—would be legally bound to comply with a range of law of war principles intended to mitigate the suffering inflicted by combat operations. This evolution is achieving the imperative proposed below by Professor Roberts:

> [I]n anti-terrorist military operations, certain phases and situations may well be different from what was envisaged in the main treaties on the laws of war. They may differ from the provisions for both international and non-international armed conflict. Recognising that there are difficulties in applying international rules in the special circumstances of anti-terrorist war, the attempt can and should nevertheless be made to apply the law to the maximum extent possible.[36]

In short, the logic animating the Department of Defense law of war *policy*, first extended to the realm of internal armed conflicts by the *Tadic* Tribunal, had been further extended to the realm of transnational armed conflicts. This evolution essentially treats the foundational principles of the law of armed conflict as a layer of regulation upon which more comprehensive treaty regimes are built. In so doing, it addresses the pragmatic necessity of regulation of de facto armed conflicts, while preserving the continuing significance of the Common Article 2 applicability criteria.

The Contiguous Conflict Dilemma: Does Any Association Create a Unified Armed Conflict?

Acknowledging that certain military operations conducted by the United States against al Qaida trigger basic LOAC principles does not in and of itself mandate a bifurcated conflict approach to Afghanistan. Instead, the viability of a distinct conflict theory vis-à-vis al Qaida mandates analysis of whether the facts related to operations in Afghanistan render such operations under this category or under the broader category of the armed conflict against the Taliban. This analysis must then turn on the relationship between al Qaida in Afghanistan and the Taliban.

The LOAC, specifically Article 4A(2) of the Third Geneva Convention Relative to the Treatment of Prisoners of War (GPW), specifically addresses the status of militia or volunteer corps personnel associated with a State party to an international armed conflict. That article provides that so long as certain conditions are satisfied, such personnel are to be treated as prisoners of war upon capture, suggesting that their status is no different from that of members of the armed forces. This in turn suggests that such militia and volunteer corps personnel are essentially connected to the international armed conflict triggering application of the convention and Article 4.

This provision provides the strongest basis to assert a unified armed conflict theory for Afghanistan. Indeed, this is the conventional approach to addressing the conflict classification issue related to al Qaida. The logic of this unified conflict theory is quite simple: Article 4 provides a basis to treat militia or volunteer corps personnel as prisoners of war; this suggests that such personnel are connected to the international armed conflict triggering Article 4; accordingly, their treatment pursuant to Article 4 indicates that their operations must be within the context of the broader international armed conflict.

While this logic is certainly appealing, it has unquestionably been undermined by the emergence of a transnational armed conflict theory. Prior to this development in the law, the presumption that armed groups operating in association with a State party to a conflict were part of that international armed conflict was conclusive, because no alternate theory of armed conflict could apply to such groups. However, if it is conceptually possible that such groups can be involved in a distinct armed conflict with the State party opposing the forces with which they are associated, this presumption can no longer be considered conclusive, but is instead better understood as rebuttable.

It therefore seems more appropriate to treat al Qaida personnel operating in Afghanistan in association with the Taliban as presumptively part of the international armed conflict between the United States and Afghanistan. Pursuant to this presumption, the status and treatment of captured al Qaida personnel would be pursuant to Article 4A(2) of the GPW: if they met the express qualification requirements of that article they were prisoners of war; if they did not they were civilians who had taken part in hostilities (with all the targeting and liability consequences that flow from such participation). Was there, however, a legitimate basis to treat this presumption as rebutted? Answering this question requires consideration of the underlying purpose and meaning of the "associated militia" provision of the GPW.

Article 4A(2) of the GPW was developed for a very clear purpose: to ensure that individuals fighting on behalf of a party to an international armed conflict who met certain qualification conditions could claim the protections of prisoner of war status. The ICRC *Commentary* to this provision indicates that the primary source of disagreement among delegates to the drafting conference was the treatment of partisan and resistance groups in occupied territories. However, one aspect of the development of this provision seems clear: there is no disagreement that any organized group claiming the benefit of Article 4 must be fighting *on behalf* of a State party. According to the *Commentary*

> [i]t is essential that there should be a *de facto* relationship between the resistance organization and the party to international law which is in a state of war, but the existence of this relationship is sufficient. It may find expression merely by tacit

> agreement, if the operations are such as to indicate clearly for which side the resistance organization is fighting.[37]

Thus, while such a relationship need not take the form of a formal agreement or declaration, it is clear that the militia must be operating on behalf of the State. As the *Commentary* notes, organized militia groups that are *not* fighting on behalf of a party to the conflict do not benefit from Article 4, but instead "the provisions of Article 3 relating to non-international conflicts are applicable, since such militias and volunteer corps are not entitled to style themselves a 'Party to the conflict.'"[38] This comment seems to explicitly recognize that geographically contiguous armed conflicts are indeed subject to legal bifurcation.

The emphasis of connection to a State party is also manifest in the provision of Article 4 granting prisoner of war status to members of armed forces fighting on behalf of a belligerent State authority not recognized by an opponent State. Treatment of such individuals apparently did not generate disagreement among the delegates to the drafting sessions, precisely because it was clear the belligerent conduct of such forces was conducted on behalf of a de facto State authority:

> At the Conference of Government Experts, delegations immediately approved the International Committee's proposal for a special clause to cover "members of armed forces claiming to be under an authority not recognized by the enemy." It was feared, however, that the proposal might be open to abusive interpretation, and the Conference therefore decided to add that such forces must, in order to benefit by the Convention, be fighting "in conjunction" with a State recognized as a belligerent State by the enemy.[39]

This express "in conjunction" language was removed in subsequent drafts, but only because it was clear that the situation that motivated the provision—the treatment of forces fighting on behalf of the Free French authority during World War II—made it clear that the provision would only be applicable when the "in conjunction" component was satisfied. Accordingly, the significance of fighting on behalf of a "State" remained the *sine qua non* for such application.

Few experts would likely dispute the conclusion that fighting on behalf of a State party is a condition precedent to application of Article 4 of the GPW. However, what exactly does this mean? Unfortunately, the ICRC *Commentary* provides virtually no guidance, a likely result of the fact that the primary concern for the drafters at the time Article 4 was revised was not this condition, but the four "combatant qualification" conditions required by Article 4A(2). However, the lack of discussion on this condition does not justify the conclusion that it has no substantive meaning.

What does seem clear from the spirit and purpose of Article 4 is that the association of an organized militia group to a State party must be more than merely incidental. Simple geographic continuity of operations does not in itself seem to rise above the concept of incidental association, a fact implicitly acknowledged by the *Commentary* when it indicates that some militia groups might fall under the non-international armed conflict legal regime. However, does a shared operational objective suffice to move beyond incidental association to the type of association required to trigger Article 4? In the opinion of this author, the answer is no.

The "on behalf" of language used by the ICRC *Commentary* to explain the meaning of article 4A(2) suggests more than a shared operational objective; it suggests that the militia or volunteer group be seeking to achieve that objective for the primary purpose of contributing to the State's strategic objective. Thus, for a militia group to be operating "on behalf" of a State party, its operations must be "nested" within the strategic and operational objectives of the State and its regular armed forces. If the militia group is operating for the purpose of achieving its own independent strategic objectives, the mere fact that some of these objectives might be shared by the State party, or that the operational implementation of these distinct objectives leads the militia group to collaborate with the State party in tactical execution, does not warrant the conclusion that it is operating on behalf of the State.

There is a legitimate argument that it was this latter type of linkage that defined the Taliban–al Qaida association in Afghanistan when the United States initiated operations against both these entities. There is no indication that al Qaida was subordinate to the Taliban in either a *de jure* or de facto sense. On the contrary, all indicators suggest that al Qaida had established what could be characterized as a parasitic relationship with the Taliban—using the territory and resources offered by the Taliban to further its own independent strategic goals. In many ways, this reflects a perverse inversion of the type of association envisioned by the drafters of the GPW. Instead of al Qaida militia operating under the command and control of the Taliban, Taliban forces were ostensibly subordinated to al Qaida command and control to serve al Qaida interests.[40]

It also seems clear that the events that caused the United States to target al Qaida with combat power—the terror attacks of September 11—were not conducted "on behalf" of Afghanistan. While it is undisputed that al Qaida had exploited the safe haven provided to it by the Taliban, this was at the time merely the latest base of operations al Qaida had exploited.[41] There is no evidence to indicate that al Qaida launched the terror attacks of September 11 at the direction of the Taliban or to further some Taliban strategic objective. On the contrary, the independent nature of these attacks resulted in the destruction of the Taliban regime.

All of this supports the conclusion that the association between al Qaida and the State of Afghanistan was insufficient to support the presumption of Article 4 applicability discussed above. If al Qaida initiated an armed attack on the United States as a distinct strategic objective, the mere fact that the military response to that attack led the United States to engage in armed conflict with the State that provided safe haven to al Qaida does not necessarily justify the legal windfall of lodging the conflict with al Qaida within the realm of the international armed conflict against Afghanistan.

The alternate conclusion is, of course, not without merit. It is certainly plausible that at least within the confines of Afghanistan, the conflict between the United States and al Qaida should be treated as derivative of the broader conflict between the United States and Afghanistan. But proponents of this theory should be required to muster more than mere geographic continuity, or even shared tactical objectives. The linkage between these two entities must reflect that al Qaida operated in a derivative capacity to the Taliban armed forces, for only such evidence can confirm the presumption that al Qaida was in fact operating "on behalf of" a party to the conflict.

If al Qaida was not sufficiently connected to the Taliban in Afghanistan to qualify as operating on behalf of a party to the conflict, then what was the nature of military operations conducted by the United States against al Qaida forces in Afghanistan? As I have argued elsewhere and outlined above, the de facto conflict nature of such operations indicates that they should be considered to qualify as an armed conflict triggering the basic regulatory framework of LOAC principles. Others, however, argue that unless military operations against al Qaida fall within the broader context of an armed conflict with Afghanistan, such operations are nothing more than extraterritorial law enforcement. It is to the fallacy of this proposition that this article will now turn.

The Fallacy of Extraterritorial Law Enforcement as a Legal Model for Transnational Counterterrorism Military Operations

One of the most difficult issues related to military operations directed against transnational terrorist operatives (what I will refer to throughout this section as counterterror military operations) has been determining the appropriate legal framework applicable to such operations. Since the United States characterized its response to the terror attacks of September 11, 2001 as an "armed conflict," the well accepted standards for determining when the law of armed conflict is triggered have been thrown into disarray. In the years following that tragic attack, a variety of legal theories have been offered to identify the appropriate locus of such operations within the international legal regulatory continuum. These have ranged from the US position that such operations are armed conflicts triggering LOAC-derived authorities (although what type of armed conflict remains allusive), to the ICRC assertion that such operations are merely derivative of international armed conflicts triggered whenever a State conducts military operations in the territory of another State, to the assertion of human rights organizations that these operations fall under the human rights regulatory framework because armed conflict between States and transnational non-State entities is a legal impossibility.

The skeptical reaction to the US assertion of a LOAC-based legal framework is unsurprising considering the breadth of that assertion typified by the hyperbolic characterization of a "Global War on Terror." But just as the nature of the military component of the international struggle against highly organized terrorist groups is much more refined than the broad concept of a "global war," so must be the analysis of which legal framework operates to regulate such military operations. Suggesting that the struggle against terrorism justifies invoking the "authorities of war" for every aspect of counterterrorism operations—from detaining a terrorist "foot soldier" on what is in all respects a conventional battlefield to capturing a terrorist operative with law enforcement assets in the midst of a peaceful domestic environ—is unjustifiably overbroad. But it is also unjustifiably under-inclusive to demand that military operations launched for the purpose of employing combat power against terrorist targets cannot be conducted pursuant to the LOAC legal framework because those operations fail to satisfy a law-triggering paradigm that evolved with an almost exclusive focus on inter-State or intra-State armed conflicts.

The stakes related to determining the applicable legal regime to regulate counter-terror military operations are enormous. Not only do they have profound impact on the rights and liberties of individuals captured and detained in the course of such operations, but whether operations are conducted under the LOAC legal framework or under the alternate human rights framework fundamentally impacts the authority of State forces to employ combat power. Nor will pigeonholing every operation under the inter-State conflict framework always produce a logical result. While offering the benefit of application of the LOAC, such an approach—for example, treating the 2006 conflict between Israel and Hezbollah as a subset of an armed conflict between Israel and Lebanon—results in what many consider to be an unjustified benefit for non-State forces, namely the opportunity to qualify for the privilege of combatant immunity.

But determining the *nature* of an armed conflict is secondary to determining the very existence of armed conflict. It is this issue—i.e., whether an armed conflict can even exist outside the inter-State/intra-State paradigm—that generates the most fundamental debate related to the military component of the fight against international terror groups. For the United States, the answer is an unequivocal "yes." However, this in no way indicates a consensus on this issue; far from it. Instead, many experts in international law have insisted that such operations are not armed conflicts, but instead "extraterritorial law enforcement" operations.

This alternate legal framework was recently emphasized by Professor Yoram Dinstein, certainly one of the international community's most respected *jus belli* scholars. During the conference which inspired this article, Professor Dinstein articulated what he asserted was the clear and simple legal framework for the conduct of transnational counterterror military operations. According to Dinstein, such operations qualify as armed conflict under only two circumstances: first, when the operations are essentially derivative to an armed conflict with the State sponsor of the terrorist organization; second, when the actions of the terrorist organization can be attributed to a sponsoring State as the result of terrorist authority over organs of the State. All other uses of force against such a threat must, according to Dinstein, be regarded as what he labels extraterritorial law enforcement. Accordingly, he categorically rejected the proposition that such operations could amount to armed conflict.

I will attempt the unenviable task of challenging the clarity and simplicity of Professor Dinstein's extraterritorial law enforcement theory. I will do so because I believe his conception of the legal characterization of counterterror military operations employing combat power is fundamentally inconsistent with the underlying nature of such operations. A far more important motive, however, is my conviction that under appropriate circumstances treating such operations as events that trigger LOAC obligations is much more consistent with the logic, history and spirit of that law than attempting to characterize them as law enforcement missions.

Context for this argument is critical. I do not suggest that there cannot be certain uses of the armed forces that do appropriately fall under a law enforcement legal paradigm. Instead, the nature of military operations I will focus on involve the application of combat power by the armed forces against a designated target or group. For point of reference and clarity, the focus of this article are those military operations conducted by the armed forces against non-State actors operating outside the State's territory pursuant to what are essentially status-based rules of engagement. If, as suggested above, operations conducted by the United States against al Qaida personnel in the context of Operation Enduring Freedom in Afghanistan can legitimately be segregated from the broader armed conflict against the Taliban, they would fall into this category. Other examples include the 2007 US AC 130 strike against an alleged al Qaida base camp in Somalia and the Israeli campaign against Hezbollah in southern Lebanon during the 1990s and again in 2006.

Determining the nature of such military operations is central to the ongoing struggle against transnational terrorism. Past and future military operations conducted to destroy, disable or disrupt the capabilities of such organizations have and will remain operationally and legally complex. More significantly, they will continue to strain the accepted construct for determining LOAC applicability. The depth of entrenchment of this construct no doubt explains Professor Dinstein's hostility to the suggestion that such operations could, under certain circumstances, qualify as armed conflicts for purposes of triggering LOAC obligations. However, any assessment of the controlling legal framework for these military operations must contemplate not only the "accepted" scope of the current law-triggering paradigm, but also the underlying purpose that motivated that paradigm. Perhaps of equal importance is the necessity to consider the second- and third-order consequences of characterizing these operations as law enforcement.

This section will therefore focus on the following factors that I believe are essential to any analysis of the legal framework for military operations conducted against transnational terrorist operatives. These include the underlying nature and purpose of the existing law-triggering paradigm; the relationship between the basic nature of employment of combat power and the legal regime that should regulate that employment; how the nature of the authority invoked reveals a fundamental distinction between the authority derived from the law of armed conflict framework and that derived from the law enforcement framework; the importance of maintaining a bright-line distinction between the *jus ad bellum* and the *jus in bello*; and the comparative feasibility of applying each framework to such operations. I believe these factors indicate that, contrary to Professor Dinstein's assertion, relying on the LOAC framework to regulate these operations is not only more logical but more feasible than relying on a law enforcement legal framework.

The Nature and Purpose of the Traditional LOAC-Triggering Paradigm

All LOAC scholars and practitioners are versed in what I have previously characterized as the "either/or" law-triggering paradigm created by Common Articles 2 and 3 of the four Geneva Conventions and the interpretation of these articles that evolved since 1949. This paradigm may have proved generally sufficient to address the types of armed conflicts occurring up until 9/11. However, this fact no longer justifies the conclusion that no other triggering standard should be recognized. Instead, as the events since 9/11 have illustrated so convincingly, such recognition is essential in order to keep pace with the evolving nature of armed conflicts themselves. The prospect of an unregulated battlefield is simply unacceptable in the international community, a fact demonstrated by the response to the conflict in

Lebanon.[42] The ultimate question, therefore, is whether it is best to continue to try and fit the proverbial square "armed conflict" peg into the round "Common Article 3" hole, or whether the time has come to endorse a new category of armed conflict. It is the limited impact of Common Article 3 itself that compels the conclusion that recognizing a new law-triggering category is essential.

Both the military components of the US fight against al Qaida and the recent conflict between Israel and Hezbollah have strained this traditionally understood LOAC-triggering paradigm.[43] While this strain has produced international and national uncertainty as to the law that applies to such operations,[44] it has also provided what may actually come to be appreciated as a beneficial reassessment of the trigger for application of fundamental LOAC principles. As a result, the time is ripe to consider whether the pragmatic logic that has animated military policy on this subject for decades should not be regarded as something more, to wit a reflection of a general principle of law requiring that all military operations involving the employment of combat power fall under the regulatory framework of the LOAC.

Before the United States Supreme Court issued its highly publicized ruling in the case of *Hamdan v. Rumsfeld*,[45] the Court of Appeals for the District of Columbia ruled on Hamdan's challenge. In the judgment of *Hamdan v. Rumsfeld*,[46] Judge Williams articulated the logic motivating this reassessment in his concurring opinion. In that opinion, he responded to the majority conclusion that Common Article 3 did not apply to armed conflict with al Qaida because the President has determined that this conflict is one of international scope:

> Non-state actors cannot sign an international treaty. Nor is such an actor even a "Power" that would be eligible under Article 2 (¶ 3) to secure protection by complying with the Convention's requirements. Common Article 3 fills the gap, providing some minimal protection for such non-eligibles in an "armed conflict not of an international character occurring in the territory of one of the High Contracting Parties." The gap being filled is the non-eligible party's failure to be a nation. Thus the words "not of an international character" are sensibly understood to refer to a conflict between a signatory nation and a non-state actor. The most obvious form of such a conflict is a civil war. But given the Convention's structure, the logical reading of "international character" is one that matches the basic derivation of the word "international," i.e., *between nations*. Thus, I think the context compels the view that a conflict between a signatory and a non-state actor is a conflict "not of an international character." In such a conflict, the signatory is bound to Common Article 3's modest requirements of "humane" treatment and "the judicial guarantees which are recognized as indispensable by civilized peoples."[47]

Although the logic expressed by Judge Williams seems pragmatically compelling, his interpretation did not sway his peers. This reflected the influence of

Common Articles 2 and 3—and the legal paradigm they spawned—on conflict regulation analysis. But, as Judge Williams recognized, it is fundamentally inconsistent with the logic of the LOAC to disconnect the applicability of regulation from the necessity for regulation. Judge Williams looked beyond the traditional interpretation of Common Articles 2 and 3 because he recognized that what was needed was a pragmatic reconciliation of these two considerations. Ironically, it is the long-standing policy of the US military that validates this interpretation of the LOAC. That policy, as will be explained below, long ago rejected a formalistic interpretation of applicability of LOAC principles to military operations in favor of a pragmatic application based on the necessity of providing US forces with a consistent regulatory framework.

Recognizing the Regulatory Gap: How Military Policies Reflect the Necessity of a "Principled" Approach to Military Operations

The need to provide a LOAC-based regulatory framework for all combat operations, even those ostensibly falling outside the accepted law-triggering categories derived from Common Articles 2 and 3, is not something that critics of Israeli operations targeting Hezbollah have only recently suggested. For more than three decades prior to this conflict, the armed forces of the United States followed a clear and simple mandate codified in the Department of Defense Law of War Program:[48] comply with the principles of the law of war during all military operations. While this policy mandate has never explicitly articulated what precisely is meant by "principles,"[49] this term is generally understood to refer to the concepts that reflect the fundamental balance between the dictates of military necessity[50] and the obligation to mitigate the suffering associated with armed conflict, concepts that provide the foundation for the more detailed rules that have evolved to implement these principles. This foundational principle/specific rule relationship is explained by Professor Adam Roberts:

> Although some of the law is immensely detailed, its foundational principles are simple: the wounded and sick, POWs and civilians are to be protected; military targets must be attacked in such a manner as to keep civilian casualties and damage to a minimum; humanitarian and peacekeeping personnel must be respected; neutral or non-belligerent states have certain rights and duties; and the use of certain weapons (including chemical weapons) is prohibited, as also are other means and methods of warfare that cause unnecessary suffering.[51]

While the US Department of Defense has never explicitly defined the content of the term "principles," manuals for other armed forces do provide more clarity to the content of this term. For example, the recently revised United Kingdom Ministry of Defence Manual for the Law of Armed Conflict provides:

> Despite the codification of much customary law into treaty form during the last one hundred years, four fundamental principles still underlie the law of armed conflict. *These are military necessity, humanity, distinction, and proportionality.* The law of armed conflict is consistent with the economic and efficient use of force. It is intended to minimize the suffering caused by armed conflict rather than impede military efficiency.[52]

For US forces and their operations, the significance of the mandate to comply with these principles during all military operations is not diminished by the absence of a precise definition of this term. Instead, definition is left to operational legal advisors based on their training and experience. What is significant for purposes of this article is that the policy requires that US armed forces treat *any* military operation, and especially any operation involving the use of combat power (armed conflict), as the trigger for application of a LOAC-based regulatory framework.[53] This policy has provided the basis for following LOAC principles during every phase of the military component of what the Bush administration has characterized as the "Global War on Terror."[54]

The motive for this policy was twofold. First, it was intended to provide a common standard of training and operational compliance during the range of military operations.[55] Second, it responded to the reality that such operations are often initiated prior to a clear government determination of the legal applicability of the laws of war.[56] Ultimately, the armed forces value this policy because they intuitively understand that a framework for the execution of combat operations is essential to the preservation of a disciplined force. This is a critically important purpose of legal regulation of the battlefield, a consideration often overlooked by contemporary commentators. Although no longer commonly cited as a critical purpose of the LOAC, prior generations clearly understood this purpose. This is clearly evident by the emphasis of this purpose in one of the most important precursors to the twentieth-century evolution of the conventional laws of war, the *Oxford Manual of the Laws of War on Land*:[57]

> By [codifying the rules of war derived from State practice], it believes it is rendering a service to military men themselves. . . . A positive set of rules, on the contrary, if they are judicious, serves the interests of belligerents and is far from hindering them, since by preventing the unchaining of passion and savage instincts—which battle always awakens, as much as it awakens courage and manly virtues,—it strengthens the discipline which is the strength of armies; it also ennobles their patriotic mission in the eyes of the soldiers by keeping them within the limits of respect due to the rights of humanity.[58]

The compelling logic reflected in this extract finds contemporary manifestation in the policy mandates imposed on US and other armed forces that extend application of these principles to all military operations. These mandates indicate that the application of combat power must always be subject to a basic regulatory framework. The gap in the accepted scope of legally required LOAC application, coupled with this logic, led other nations to follow the practice of imposing such regulation by policy.[59] Even the United Nations, habitually called upon to use military forces in situations of uncertain legal classification, implemented an analogous mandate for forces operating under its control.[60] However, no matter how logical such mandates may be in terms of military efficiency and humanitarian protections, their policy characters reveal a perceived gap between situations necessitating LOAC application and the technical legal triggers for such application. Furthermore, their policy characters indicate that these mandates are ultimately subject to modification.[61]

The historical underpinnings of the LOAC and the contemporary application of LOAC principles to a wide spectrum of military operations as a matter of national policy indicate that the dispositive factor in determining when this regulatory framework should apply is the fundamental nature of the military operation in question. When armed forces conduct operations employing combat power against a defined enemy with authority to engage and subdue the enemy based solely on that defined status, such operations should be regarded as armed conflicts. Because of this, the underlying logic that has driven the historical application of LOAC principles to regulate such operations provides compelling evidence in support of extending this framework to counterterror military operations that fall into this category, even when the enemy is a non-State entity with no plausible link of attribution to the State in which it operates. As will be discussed below, an analytical focus on the fundamental nature of the authority invoked by the State indicates that the alternate proposition—to characterize such operations as law enforcement—is unsupported by any analogous logic.

The Fundamental Distinction between the Law of Armed Conflict Legal Framework and the Extraterritorial Law Enforcement Legal Framework

The discussion above reveals why the regulatory framework applicable to military operations must respond to the de facto existence of armed conflict. However, it also reveals why the existing understanding of this law-triggering paradigm has operated as an impediment to such application in any armed conflict not falling neatly within the inter-State/intra-State conflict categories. As a result, military operations conducted by States against non-State operatives who operate transnationally fall into a category of regulatory uncertainty. In response to this uncertainty, scholars like Professor Dinstein argue that such operations are best understood as extraterritorial law enforcement activities, and not as armed conflicts. This view presumably indicates that it is a law enforcement legal framework, and not LOAC principles, that functions to regulate such operations.

This is a significant assertion, for it dictates a scope of authority that is arguably inconsistent with the fundamental nature and purpose of such military operations. It is undoubtedly true that the ultimate objective of disabling the operational capabilities of terrorist organizations is the common purpose of any counterterror State action. However, the means by which law enforcement activities achieve this objective differs fundamentally from the means by which military operations do so, most significantly with regard to the use of deadly force. Indeed, the most fundamental distinction between law enforcement and armed conflict is manifested in the scope of use of deadly force authority—a distinction between use of deadly force as a last resort and use of deadly force as a first resort. Law enforcement activities, governed by international human-rights standards, reserve the use of deadly force as a measure of last resort. In contrast, use of deadly force against a military objective is a legitimate measure of first resort during armed conflict.

This basic distinction between relative authorities reveals in the starkest manner the fundamental fallacy of characterizing military operations directed against transnational terrorists as law enforcement operations, not based on an analysis of the nature of authority associated with such operations, but merely on the basis of incompatibility with the inter-State/intra-State law-triggering paradigm. In most instances, the choice by the State to resort to military force against such a threat is driven by the assessed need to employ deadly force as a measure of first, and not last, resort. Consider the example of an airstrike conducted against a terrorist training facility operating with impunity in the territory of another State. It is inconceivable that the authority to employ deadly force relied on by the air assets executing the mission will be contingent on a provocation from the terrorist target. Nor is it conceivable that the air assets will be obliged to offer the potential targets the opportunity to submit to apprehension as a condition precedent to the employment of combat power. Instead, the authority to employ that power will almost certainly be based on an inherent invocation of the principle of military objective, allowing the use of deadly combat power based solely on the identification of the target as one falling into the category of a defined terrorist enemy.

Employment of combat power under this type of authority is not law enforcement. It is, quintessentially, a use of deadly force as a measure of first resort. The LOAC provides the only legal justification for such a use of force. Accordingly, based on the nature of the authority related to the military operation, armed conflict best characterizes the de facto nature of such activities, if for no other reason than the State's implicit invocation of the principle of military objective as a justification for the use of deadly force. Characterizing such operations as law enforcement creates an immediate incongruity that undermines the fundamental nature of that characterization: the suggestion that the use of deadly force is limited to a measure of last resort and that less destructive means must be attempted prior to such use.

No such incongruity would result from acknowledging that operations targeting terrorist operatives with combat power are armed conflicts. Instead, such acknowledgment achieves a critical effect: the authority implicitly invoked by the State is counterbalanced by the limiting humanitarian principles of this law. In short, if such operations are categorized as armed conflicts, the law essentially creates a "package deal" for participants. While the principle of military necessity/military objective may justify the employment of deadly force as a measure of first resort, other principles limiting the methods and means of warfare and establishing baseline standards of treatment for captured and detained personnel also become applicable. Unless combat operations conducted against terrorist operatives are understood to trigger this "package" of principles, States will continue to be free to adopt a selective invocation of the fundamental authority derived from the LOAC to take measures necessary to disable terrorist capabilities, while disavowing legally mandated obligations derived from the same source of law.[62]

The Bright-Line Distinction between the **Jus ad Bellum** *and the* **Jus in Bello**: *Remembering That Application of the LOAC Should Not Be Influenced by Use of Force Legality*

Another significant objection to treating military operations directed against transnational terrorists as triggering LOAC rights and obligations is that doing so will somehow legitimize such uses of force. This argument, however, ignores the historic bright-line distinction between the *jus ad bellum* and the *jus in bello*. This distinction has long stood for the proposition that the legality *of* war must not be permitted to influence the applicability of the rules for conduct *during* war. This distinction can genuinely be considered a foundational principle of the Geneva Conventions and the de facto law-triggering provisions incorporated therein.

The *ad bellum/in bello* distinction is intended to achieve a critical effect: to ensure that the legal regime protecting the *participants* in armed conflict is not diluted or denied based on the choices of those who *decide* on armed conflict. It is a reflection of the basic tenet of the Geneva Conventions—all individuals impacted by armed conflict, civilian and warrior alike, are in essence "victims of war," for they are not responsible for the decision to wage war. Accordingly, the legal regime that operates to limit the harmful effects of war on both warrior and civilian must be triggered by a pure de facto standard: the existence of armed conflict.

Of course, the primary concern at the time of the drafting of the Conventions was preventing States from using the illegality of war as a justification for denial of humanitarian protections. The issue related to the application of the LOAC to military operations between a State and non-State entity is quite the opposite. In this context, the concern is that acknowledging that such operations trigger the LOAC legal framework will bolster the legal justification for the use of force by the State. Nonetheless, the underlying purpose of the *ad bellum/in bello* distinction is equally applicable to this context and indicates that the legal framework that regulates the conduct of military operations should in no way influence the assessment of the legality of those operations.

As I have written extensively elsewhere, this de facto standard is a core concept of the existing law triggers of the Geneva Conventions. The focus of these triggers is on the question of actual hostilities that rise above the level of law enforcement activities. In such circumstances, the LOAC is the appropriate legal framework to achieve the humanitarian objective of limiting unnecessary suffering.

In the context of inter-State or intra-State hostilities, the line between a use of State power for law enforcement purposes and armed conflict has been relatively well defined. However, once States began to employ power outside their territories for the purpose of combating terrorism, this line became much blurrier. I (with my co-author Eric Jensen) have addressed the problem of defining the line between law enforcement and armed conflict in this extraterritorial context in a prior article, asserting that the nature of the use-of-force authority employed by armed forces is the most effective means of definition. It is not my purpose to expand upon that theory here. Instead, the basic concept reveals why the *ad bellum/in bello* distinction is equally relevant in such a context. We argue that when a State authorizes the use of combat power based on an inherent invocation of the principle of military objective (in the form of status-based rules of engagement) a situation of de facto armed conflict exists. Even assuming that the use of force authorized by the State is in violation of the *jus ad bellum*, this in no way alters the basic reality that the State has implicitly invoked the LOAC for purposes of executing the operation. As a result, there is no justification to deprive the participants in associated hostilities of the benefit of the fundamental principles of that law.

What seems more appropriate, and certainly more consistent with the *ad bellum/in bello* distinction that is an integral element in determining LOAC applicability, is to treat the ad bellum/in bello issues as truly independent legal questions. Concluding a State's use of military force to target a terrorist entity is in violation of the *jus ad bellum* but is nonetheless armed conflict triggering fundamental LOAC rights and obligations seems more satisfactory than asserting the *jus ad bellum* violation requires denying the participants in the hostilities the benefits of the legal framework best suited to regulate such activities.

Of course, characterizing such operations as law enforcement avoids this issue entirely. Or does it? It is unlikely that a State will not be held to account for armed interventions in the territory of other States simply because the State asserts it is exercising "extraterritorial law enforcement." And here lies the potential irony. In assessing the *jus ad bellum* legality of State action, it is almost certain that the *de facto* nature of that action will be the focus, and not the characterizations adopted by the State. As a result, use of combat power under the rubric of extraterritorial law enforcement creates a double failure: it will be insufficient to avoid condemnation for a *jus ad bellum* violation, while at the same time it will deprive the forces engaged in the operation of the clarity provided by the legal framework developed to regulate the essential nature of their activities: armed conflict.

The Law of Armed Conflict: A Defined and Intuitive Regulatory Framework

As suggested above, the regulatory framework applicable to the conduct of military operations against transnational terrorist threats should not influence the assessment of the legality of such operations. Accordingly, the primary analytical consideration for determining which legal framework is most appropriate for the regulation of such operations is how effectively it achieves the regulatory purpose. It is here that applying LOAC principles offers substantial benefit over applying a law enforcement framework. This conclusion is supported by two primary considerations. First, fundamental LOAC principles are well established and well understood by professional armed forces. Indeed, these principles are so pervasive they have formed the foundation for policy regulation of many military operations that are not technically subject to the law. Second, because of this pervasive application, armed forces are well versed in compliance with these principles and as a result conducting operations pursuant thereto is relatively intuitive.

This is not the case with the law enforcement framework. As a general proposition, armed forces are not trained to conduct law enforcement operations. Unlike their law enforcement counterparts, demanding a careful escalation of force to ensure that resort to deadly force is only a measure of last resort is the exception to the mindset normally demanded of military personnel. That mindset requires the ability to engage an enemy with deadly combat power on command. This often involves the application of overwhelming, and not graduated, combat power. Imposing a law enforcement framework on military personnel requires a radical modification to the combat mentality, with all the training, planning and execution challenges associated therewith.

Ironically, one of the common criticisms of the assertion that military operations against transnational terrorist groups trigger LOAC principles is the uncertainty associated with determining what rules would apply to such operations. As Professor Dinstein noted during one presentation, "Where do the rules come from? Do you just make them up in a library in Texas?" There is, however, no need to "make up" any rules. Instead, as my co-author and I have noted elsewhere, the fundamental LOAC principles—military necessity, military objective, proportionality and humanity—are well enough understood as to provide an effective starting point for the regulation of these military operations. Nor is extending these principles to transnational armed conflicts a radical suggestion, but instead a process analogous to that which has led to the development of the regulation of internal armed conflicts (another point of particular irony, considering that Professor Dinstein has been central to the proposed application of regulatory provisions developed in the context of inter-State conflict to the realm of internal conflict).

What seems particularly invalid about this criticism is that it seems even more legitimately leveled against the extraterritorial law enforcement theory. Unlike fundamental LOAC principles, there is no well established source of regulatory principles that apply to the use of military force for extraterritorial law enforcement principles. If such operations are considered law enforcement, where do the rules that govern those operations come from? While rules applicable to domestic law enforcement activities are certainly well developed, there is no basis to assert that they can simply be transplanted to apply to extraterritorial military operations. Use of law enforcement would presumably be governed by the sending State's domestic policing statutes, an odd choice of laws in an extraterritorial use of force. Accordingly, such a suggestion seems far more fabricated than applying LOAC principles to combat operations against terrorist operatives. In the latter situation, the armed forces would apply a body of rules that form the foundation of military training and operations and were developed to limit the harmful consequence of a State unleashing combat power. In the former, armed forces would be expected to comply with a regulatory framework that was never developed nor intended to apply to armed hostilities.

Policy Application of the Law of Armed Conflict: Its Value and Limitations

Perhaps the most compelling evidence in support of the validity of applying the LOAC framework to the type of military operations addressed in this article is that reliance on this framework as a "default" standard has been the long-standing solution to the legal uncertainties associated with contemporary military operations. For several decades, the armed forces of major military powers have imposed an obligation to comply with LOAC principles during all military operations, even when those principles were not applicable as a matter of law. This practice was ultimately emulated by the United Nations as a solution to the dilemma of establishing a uniform regulatory standard for all UN forces engaged in peacekeeping operations.

The logic behind this policy application of LOAC principles reinforces the argument that the LOAC is better suited to provide for the regulation of counterterror military operations than the law enforcement framework. Military leaders have long understood that setting a LOAC-based default standard of regulation enhances the probability of disciplined operations by facilitating uniform training and planning criteria. Perhaps more important, because the LOAC is the only source of international law that evolved for the specific purpose of regulating military operations, its extension to all military operations was understood as pragmatically and operationally logical. In short, these policies indicate that military operations are best regulated by the law developed for such a purpose, and not by some artificial application of a body of law developed for an entirely different purpose.

Indeed, the past effectiveness of this policy application of LOAC principles has led some to assert that there is no need to wade into the controversial waters of conflict characterization in relation to counterterror military operations, but that compliance with these policies provides an effective solution to the regulatory dilemma. But this argument is flawed for two reasons. First, it is in effect an acknowledgment that these operations require the regulatory framework provided by the LOAC, with an effort to avoid the difficult question of *why* this framework should be applied. However, if the assumption is valid—that the nature of the operations requires LOAC regulation—then that issue must be addressed head on; and the reason for this is revealed in the second flaw of this argument.

Until the US response to the terror attacks of September 11, the "policy is enough" argument held great merit. This was because issues related to the regulation of military operations and treatment of individuals captured and detained during those operations were left almost exclusively to military decisionmakers. However, it is widespread knowledge that this paradigm shifted dramatically after those attacks. No longer was the military free to "apply the principles of the law of war" with little or no interference from civilian policy- and decisionmakers. Instead, the intervention of these individuals exposed the limits of policy application of these principles.

In what are now regarded as notorious legal opinions, senior US government lawyers and the decisionmakers they advised adopted policies related to the treatment of captured and detained personnel that deviated from the "principles" of the LOAC. The justification for these decisions was clear: unlike law, policy is malleable. Accordingly, Department of Defense policy became ineffective once the leadership of the department or the nation chose to adopt inconsistent courses of action. This process exposed why simply asserting a policy-based application of LOAC principles to counterterror military operations is insufficient to address the regulatory issue. Participants in these endeavors—and the individuals they engage with combat power, subdue, capture and detain—require a legally defined and mandated regulatory framework. While the long-standing policies requiring compliance with LOAC principles certainly indicate that these principles are the most logical and appropriate source of regulation for these operations, policy is ultimately insufficient to provide this certainty. Only by acknowledging the legally mandated applicability of LOAC principles to such operations will this certainty be achieved.

Case-by-Case Application and the Rejection of the Zero-Sum Game

What I have attempted to do in this article is expose why it is invalid and disingenuous to characterize counterterror military operations employing combat power under a "deadly force as a first resort" authority as extraterritorial law enforcement. Instead, these operations should be treated as triggering the foundational principles of the LOAC. However, I am not suggesting a zero-sum game analysis—that all uses of the military in the struggle against transnational terrorism must be characterized as triggering LOAC principles; far from it. What I have proposed here and previously is that the essential nature of the use-of-force authority related to any use of military power must dictate whether that use falls into the category of armed conflict or instead remains under the assistance-to-law-enforcement category. This may often be a difficult line to decipher. But rejecting the applicability of LOAC principles to those operations that cross this line simply because to do so deviates from the entrenched law-triggering paradigm seems to defy the underlying logic of the conventions that paradigm evolved from: a truly de facto law-triggering standard that ensured the assertion of authority derived from the LOAC required compliance with limiting principles of the same body of law.

Acknowledging that under the appropriate circumstances armed forces are bound to comply with LOAC principles when conducting counterterror operations will not dilute the effectiveness of this law. It will instead ensure a balance of authority and obligation. Nor will it result in a parade of horribles because of the uncertainty as to what rules apply to such operations. Applying the fundamental principles of the LOAC to such operations is a feasible first step for such regulation, and one with which many armed forces are familiar pursuant to the policy application of these same principles that has been required for decades. Furthermore, any uncertainty as to the content of regulatory provisions derived from application of the LOAC is insignificant in comparison to the subjection of such operations to a law enforcement regulatory framework designed for a radically different purpose.

Nor do I believe that such acknowledgment will increase the uses of combat power by States. While characterizing counterterror operations under the LOAC framework will undoubtedly trigger more expansive authorities than law enforcement operations, requiring compliance with LOAC principles of constraint will limit the scope of that authority. Furthermore, there are other significant factors that will offset any tendency to treat such operations as armed conflict simply for the benefit of expanded authority. These include not only *jus in bello* considerations, which, when dealing with a terror target in anything other than a failed State are profound, but also domestic political considerations, international relations considerations and, perhaps most important, assessment of the most feasible means to achieve the neutralization objective. All that is suggested here is that when a State, after considering all these factors, chooses to unleash combat power to achieve the national objective, the benefit of the LOAC regulatory framework should not be denied simply because the enemy is a transnational organization without traditional military structure.

Conclusion

Conflict classification is the essential first step in determining the rights and obligations of parties involved in armed hostilities. For decades, this classification process has been premised on the assumption that international law recognizes only two types of armed conflict: inter-State and intra-State. This led to the evolution of an "either/or" law-triggering paradigm: either the conflict was between two States, satisfying the triggering criteria of Common Article 2, or the conflict was between a State and a non-State armed entity within the territory of the State, satisfying the triggering criteria of Common Article 3.

The increasing prevalence of extraterritorial military operations conducted by States against non-State armed organized groups has resulted in an assertion that such operations can qualify as armed conflicts. This theory of law applicability is exemplified by the US treatment of the struggle against al Qaida as an "armed conflict," a position clearly reflected in the Department of State enunciation excerpted at the beginning of this article. Although controversial, it seems undeniable that this theory of what can be functionally characterized as "transnational" armed conflict is gaining legal momentum.

The assumption that such a category of armed conflict can exist calls into question the related assumption that military operations conducted by the United States against al Qaida in Afghanistan could only be categorized as falling within the broader armed conflict against the Taliban. While such a unified armed conflict theory is certainly plausible, and concededly the presumptive position, it need not be the only position. Instead, a careful assessment of the relationship between al Qaida and the Taliban is necessary to determine whether such an outcome is justifiable. If, as is suggested in this article, the facts reveal that al Qaida did not operate truly "on behalf" of the Taliban, but instead had established more of a parasitic relationship to serve its own independent strategic objectives, then this presumption becomes invalid. Such invalidity suggests that the conflict between al Qaida and the United States in Afghanistan can and should be characterized as distinct from the conflict between the United States and the Taliban.

This conflict bifurcation leads to another inevitable question: are extraterritorial counterterror operations armed conflicts? Or are they simply exercises of extraterritorial law enforcement? Resolving this question and determining the most appropriate legal framework for the regulation of extraterritorial military operations directed against transnational terror operatives is no easy task, but it is essential because of the increasing prevalence of such operations. Since the United States began asserting it was engaged in an armed conflict with al Qaida, scholars, legal advisors, policymakers and courts have struggled with this question, producing a wide variety of outcomes. Two major theories have evolved in response to this question. The first, epitomized by the US position, is that these operations qualify as "armed conflicts" within the meaning of international law, triggering a heretofore undefined package of legal authorities and obligations. The second is that armed conflict can only occur within the inter-State or intra-State law-triggering paradigm established by Common Article 2 and Common Article 3, and that military operations can be considered "armed conflicts" only if they can be pigeonholed into one of these categories. In all other cases, including the use of combat power to target terrorist operatives in the territory of another State, the military operations must be characterized as extraterritorial law enforcement activities, presumably regulated by law enforcement authorities and human rights obligations.

This article has asserted that this latter approach—rejecting the possibility of an armed conflict between a State and a transnational non-State entity—produces an illogical outcome disconnected from the underlying purpose of the LOAC. By essentially pushing a square peg into a round hole, it unjustifiably denies the armed forces and the people they encounter on what is indisputably a "battlefield" the benefit of the regulatory framework developed specifically to limit the harmful consequences produced when States unleash their combat power. While the overly broad reach of LOAC authority resulting from the Bush administration's assertion of a "Global War on Terror" certainly justifies a cautious approach to the question of legal characterization, an under-inclusive backlash is equally invalid.

What is necessary is a careful assessment of the fundamental nature of military operations on a case-by-case basis. When those operations are conducted pursuant to a "use of deadly force as a first resort" authority—normally revealed in the form of status-based rules of engagement—it indicates an inherent invocation of the authority of the LOAC. Under such circumstances, armed forces must operate under the obligations established by the fundamental principles of the same body of law. These principles are generally well understood and have formed the foundation for operational regulation of a multitude of military operations conducted by many armed forces for decades. Whatever uncertainty that may be inherent in these principles is relatively insignificant compared to the far more uncertain regulatory content of an extraterritorial law enforcement legal framework. What is much more problematic, however, is that military operations conducted pursuant to status-based rules of engagement are fundamentally inconsistent with a law enforcement legal framework, for the use of deadly force as a measure of first resort is the quintessential nature—and in all likelihood purpose for—such operations. As such, it is the principles of the LOAC, and not those related to law enforcement activities, that are most logically, pragmatically and appropriately suited for such operations.

Notes

1. *See* The Report of the UN Special Rapporteur on Extrajudicial, Summary or Arbitrary Executions, U.N. Doc. E/CN.4/2004/7/Add.1 (Mar. 24, 2004).

2. See International Committee of the Red Cross, International humanitarian law and terrorism: questions and answers (May 5, 2004), available at http://www.icrc.org/Web/eng/siteeng0.nsf/html/5YNLEV#a3, asserting that unless associated with a "traditionally" defined armed conflict (such as Afghanistan), the "war on terrorism" is not an armed conflict:

> However, much of the ongoing violence taking place in other parts of the world that is usually described as "terrorist" is perpetrated by loosely organized groups (networks), or individuals that, at best, share a common ideology. On the basis of currently available factual evidence it is doubtful whether these groups and networks can be characterised as a "party" to a conflict within the meaning of IHL.

3. This rejection was evident from the reaction of many of the distinguished experts assembled for the conference that generated this article. Included among those who explicitly rejected such a contention were Professor Michael Schmitt, Professor Charles Garraway, Professor

Yoram Dinstein and Professor Marco Sassòli. Other participants, including many military practitioners, seemed to find the proposition more appealing.

4. *See* Geoffrey S. Corn & Eric T. Jensen, *Transnational Armed Conflict: A 'Principled' Approach to the Regulation of Counter-Terror Combat Operations* (forthcoming in ISRAEL LAW REVIEW), *available at* http://papers.ssrn.com/sol3/papers.cfm?abstract_id=1256380.

5. *See* Geoffrey Corn, *Hamdan, Lebanon, and the Regulation of Armed Conflict: The Need to Recognize a Hybrid Category of Armed Conflict*, 40 VANDERBILT JOURNAL OF TRANSNATIONAL LAW 295, 316, 341 (2007); *see also* Geoffrey Corn & Eric Jensen, *Untying the Gordian Knot: A Proposal for Determining Applicability of the Laws of War to the War on Terror* (forthcoming in TEMPLE LAW REVIEW), *available at* http://papers.ssrn.com/sol3/papers.cfm?abstract_id=1083849; Corn & Jensen, *Transnational Armed Conflict, supra* note 4.

6. *See* Corn, *Hamdan, Lebanon, and the Regulation of Armed Conflict, supra* note 5, at 316, 341.

7. *Id.*

8. Articles 2 and 3 are referred to as "common" because they are found identically in each of the four Geneva Conventions. *See* Convention for the Amelioration of the Condition of the Wounded and Sick in Armed Forces in the Field, Aug. 12, 1949, 6 U.S.T. 3114, 75 U.N.T.S. 31; Convention for the Amelioration of the Condition of Wounded, Sick and Shipwrecked Members of Armed Forces at Sea, Aug. 12, 1949, 6 U.S.T. 3217, 75 U.N.T.S. 85; Convention Relative to the Treatment of Prisoners of War, Aug. 12, 1949, 6 U.S.T. 3316, 75 U.N.T.S. 135; and Convention Relative to the Protection of Civilian Persons in Time of War, Aug. 12, 1949, 6 U.S.T. 3516, 75 U.N.T.S 287; all *reprinted in* DOCUMENTS ON THE LAWS OF WAR (Adam Roberts & Richard Guelff eds., 3d ed. 2000) at 197, 198; 222, 223; 244, 245; and 301, 302; respectively. Article 2 provides in pertinent part that "the present Convention shall apply to all cases of declared war or of any other armed conflict which may arise between two or more of the High Contracting Parties . . . ," i.e., international armed conflict. Article 3 applies to all cases "of armed conflict not of an international character occurring in the territory of one of the High Contracting Parties . . .," i.e., non-international armed conflict.

9. *See* Human Rights Watch, Lebanon/Israel: U.N. Rights Body Squanders Chance to Help Civilians (Aug. 11, 2006), http://hrw.org/english/docs/2006/08/11/lebano13969_txt.htm (statements by Louise Arbour) [hereinafter Lebanon/Israel]; *see also* Human Rights Watch, U.N.: Open Independent Inquiry into Civilian Deaths (Aug. 8, 2006), http://hrw.org/english/docs/2006/08/08/lebano13939.htm (statements by Kofi Annan) [hereinafter Open Independent Inquiry].

10. Recognition of this new classification of armed conflict might be viewed by some as subsuming the continuing role for the "internal" armed conflict classification. Such a conclusion is somewhat justified, because the principles triggered by transnational armed conflict would essentially be synonymous with those triggered by internal armed conflicts. However, pragmatic considerations warrant caution in this regard. The entire rationale for proposing a *transnational* designation is to respond to the policy reality that States will continue to seek to match a characterization with the geographic scope of conflicts in which they engage.

11. Prosecutor v. Tadic, Case No. IT-94-1-AR72, Appeal on Jurisdiction, para. 94 (Oct. 2, 1995), *reprinted in* 35 INTERNATIONAL LEGAL MATERIALS 32 (1996).

12. *See* Anthony Cullen, *Key Developments Affecting the Scope of Internal Armed Conflict in International Humanitarian Law*, 183 MILITARY LAW REVIEW 66 (2005) (providing an excellent analysis of the significance of the *Tadic* ruling).

13. Tadic, *supra* note 11, para. 94.

14. Hamdan v. Rumsfeld, 548 U.S. 557 (2006) (citations omitted) (emphasis added).

15. *See* A.P.V. ROGERS, LAW ON THE BATTLEFIELD (1st ed. 1996).

16. *See generally* Leslie Green, *What Is—Why Is There—the Law of War, in* THE LAW OF ARMED CONFLICT: INTO THE NEXT MILLENNIUM 141 (Michael N. Schmitt & Leslie C. Green eds., 1998) (Vol. 71, US Naval War College International Law Studies).

17. *Id.*

18. *See generally* MAX BOOT, SAVAGE WARS OF PEACE: SMALL WARS AND THE RISE OF AMERICAN POWER (2003).

19. *See* LESLIE C. GREEN, THE CONTEMPORARY LAW OF ARMED CONFLICT 54–55 (2d ed. 2000).

20. *Id.*

21. *See* ROGERS, *supra* note 15.

22. GREEN, *supra* note 19, at 54.

23. *Id.* at 52.

24. Without even considering the colonial conflicts of this period (see *id.* at 54–55), examples of such "non inter-State" military operations include several campaigns conducted by the armed forces of the United States, such as the operations during the Boxer Rebellion, Pershing's campaign against Pancho Villa, and numerous "stability" operations in Haiti, the Dominican Republic, the Philippine Islands and Nicaragua. *See generally* BOOT, *supra* note 18.

25. During this period, brutal internal conflicts in Spain, Paraguay, Russia and China challenged this customary expectation that professional armed forces engaged in armed conflict would conduct themselves in accordance with principles of disciplined warfare. The estimated number of people killed in civil wars during the inter-war years are 18,800,000, Russian Civil War (1918–21); 3,000,000, Chaco War (Paraguay and Bolivia) (1932–35); 2,500,000, Chinese Civil War (1945–49) and 365,000, Spanish Civil War (1936–39). Historical Atlas of the Twentieth Century, http://users.erols.com/mwhite28/20centry.htm#FAQ (last visited Sept. 5, 2006).

This created a perceived failure of international law to provide effective regulation for non-international armed conflicts, ultimately providing the motivation for the development of Common Article 3. It is, however, worth questioning whether Common Article 3 is properly understood as "necessary" to ensure compliance with such foundational principles during non-State conflicts. Within the context of the history of armed conflicts—a history that was characterized up until the inter-war years by relative obedience to internally imposed regulatory frameworks during all combat operations—Common Article 3 might instead be legitimately viewed as a fail-safe to provide the international community a basis to demand compliance with the most fundamental component of such a framework: respect for the humanity of persons placed *hors de combat* when armed forces refuse to comply with the customary standards of conduct related to any combat operation, including non-international conflicts.

26. According to the *International Committee of the Red Cross Commentary:*

> Since 1907 experience has shown that many armed conflicts, displaying all the characteristics of a war, may arise without being preceded by any of the formalities laid down in the Hague Convention. Furthermore, there have been many cases where Parties to a conflict have contested the legitimacy of the enemy Government and therefore refused to recognize the existence of a state of war. In the same way, the temporary disappearance of sovereign States as a result of annexation or capitulation has been put forward as a pretext for not observing one or other of the humanitarian Conventions. It was necessary to find a remedy to this state of affairs and the change which had taken place in the whole conception of such Conventions pointed the same

> way. The Geneva Conventions are coming to be regarded less and less as contracts concluded on a basis of reciprocity in the national interests of the parties, and more and more as a solemn affirmation of principles respected for their own sake, a series of unconditional engagements on the part of each of the Contracting Parties 'vis-à-vis' the others. A State does not proclaim the principle of the protection due to prisoners of war merely in the hope of improving the lot of a certain number of its own nationals. It does so out of respect for the human person.
>
> . . .
>
> By its general character, this paragraph deprives belligerents, in advance, of the pretexts they might in theory put forward for evading their obligations. There is no need for a formal declaration of war, or for the recognition of the existence of a state of war, as preliminaries to the application of the Convention. The occurrence of de facto hostilities is sufficient.
>
> It remains to ascertain what is meant by "armed conflict." The substitution of this much more general expression for the word "war" was deliberate. It is possible to argue almost endlessly about the legal definition of "war." A State which uses arms to commit a hostile act against another State can always maintain that it is not making war, but merely engaging in a police action, or acting in legitimate self-defence. The expression "armed conflict" makes such arguments less easy. Any difference arising between two States and leading to the intervention of members of the armed forces is an armed conflict within the meaning of Article 2, even if one of the Parties denies the existence of a State of war.

See COMMENTARY ON GENEVA CONVENTION III RELATIVE TO THE TREATMENT OF PRISONERS OF WAR 19–23 (Jean S. Pictet ed., 1960) (emphasis added) [hereinafter ICRC COMMENTARY].

27. *Id.*

28. *Id.* at 32.

29. Prosecutor v. Tadic, Case No. IT-94-1-AR72, Appeal on Jurisdiction, paras. 96–127 (Oct. 2, 1995), *reprinted in* 35 INTERNATIONAL LEGAL MATERIALS 32 (1996). It is interesting to note that the Tribunal cites US policy in support of this conclusion:

> The Standing Rules of Engagement issued by the US Joint Chiefs of Staff spell this out:
>
> U.S. forces will comply with the Laws of War during military operations involving armed conflict, no matter how the conflict may be characterized under international law, and will comply with its principles and spirit during all other operations.

Id.

30. *Id.*, para. 70.

31. Nonetheless, it is interesting to note that the qualifying language of "within a State" was not applied to "protracted armed violence between governmental authorities and organized armed groups." *Id.* This does lend some support for application of the principles of the law of war to armed conflicts involving protracted violence outside either of these traditional categories of conflict.

32. *See id.*, paras. 96–127.

33. *See id.*, para. 126.

34. *See id.*

35. *See* Gaby El Hakim & Joe Karam, *Beirut Bleeding: Law Under Attack in Lebanon,* http://jurist.law.pitt.edu/forumy/2006/07/beirut-bleeding-law-under-attack-in.php; *see also* Anthony

D'Amato, *War Crimes and the Middle East Conflict*, http://jurist.law.pitt.edu/forumy/2006/07/war-crimes-and-mideast-conflict.php; Nick Wadhams, *Annan: Israel Raid May Be Part of Pattern*, http://apnews.myway.com/article/20060808/D8JC0D5O2.html.

36. Adam Roberts, *Counter-terrorism, Armed Force and the Laws of War*, SURVIVAL, Spring 2002, at 7, *available at* http://www.ssrc.org/sept11/essays/roberts.htm.

37. *See* ICRC COMMENTARY, *supra* note 26, at 57.

38. *Id.*

39. *Id.* at 62.

40. Comments of W. Hays Parks at the Naval War College Workshop, The War in Afghanistan: A Legal Analysis (June 25–27, 2008).

41. *See* Al Qaida and Taliban, BOOKRAGS, http://www.bookrags.com/research/al-qaida-and-taliban-aaw-04/ (last visited Jan. 30, 2009).

42. *See* Lebanon/Israel, *supra* note 9; Open Independent Inquiry, *supra* note 9.

43. *See* Kenneth Watkin, *Controlling the Use of Force: A Role for Human Rights Norms in Contemporary Armed Conflict*, 98 AMERICAN JOURNAL OF INTERNATIONAL LAW 1 (2004) (discussing the complex challenge of conflict categorization related military operations conducted against highly organized non-State groups with transnational reach); *see also* Kirby Abott, *Terrorists: Combatants, Criminals, or . . . ?*, *in* CANADIAN COUNSEL ON INTERNATIONAL LAW, THE MEASURES OF INTERNATIONAL LAW: EFFECTIVENESS, FAIRNESS, AND VALIDITY 366 (2004); JENNIFER ELSEA, CONGRESSIONAL RESEARCH SERVICE, TERRORISM AND THE LAW OF WAR: TRYING TERRORISTS AS WAR CRIMINALS BEFORE MILITARY COMMISSIONS (2001), *available at* http://www.au.af.mil/au/awc/awcgate/crs/rl31191.pdf (analyzing whether the attacks of September 11, 2001 triggered the law of war).

44. This uncertainty is clearly reflected in the analysis prepared by the Office of Legal Counsel in response to the terrorist attacks of September 11, 2001. *Compare* Memorandum from John C. Yoo, Deputy Assistant General Counsel & Robert Delahunty, Special Counsel, Office of Legal Counsel, Department of Justice, to William J. Haynes II, General Counsel, Department of Defense, Re: Application of Treaties and Laws to al Qaeda and Taliban Detainees (Jan. 9, 2002), *reprinted in* THE TORTURE PAPERS: THE ROAD TO ABU GHRAIB 38 (Karen J. Greenberg & Joshua Dratel eds., 2005), *available at* http://www.gwu.edu/~nsarchiv/NSAEBB/NSAEBB127/02.01.09.pdf (concluding, *inter alia*, that Common Article 3 was inapplicable to the armed conflict with al Qaida because Common Article 3 applied exclusively to intra-State conflicts and conflict with al Qaida was "international" in scope), *with* Memorandum from William H. Taft IV, Legal Adviser, Department of State, to Counsel to the President, Comments on Your Paper on the Geneva Conventions (Feb. 2, 2002), *reprinted in* TORTURE PAPERS, *supra*, at 129, *available at* http://www.fas.org/sgp/othergov/taft.pdf (arguing that the Geneva Conventions should be interpreted to apply to the armed conflict with both the Taliban and al Qaida); *see also* Report of the Commission of Inquiry on Lebanon Pursuant to Human Rights Council Resolution S-2/1, U.N. Doc. A/HRC/3/2 (Nov. 23, 2006), *available at* http://www.ohchr.org/english/bodies/hrcouncil/docs/specialsession/A.-HRC.3.2.pdf ("[t]he hostilities that took place from 12 July to 14 August 2006 constitute an international armed conflict to which conventional and customary international humanitarian law and international human rights law are applicable").

45. 548 U.S. 557 (2006).

46. Hamdan v. Rumsfeld, 415 F.3d 33 (D.C. Cir. 2005).

47. *Id.* at 44 (Williams, Sr. Judge, concurring).

48. *See* Department of Defense, DoD Directive 5100.77, DoD Law of War Program (1998).

49. The purported justification for this omission is that each subordinate service is then able to define the content of this term for purposes of its forces. Leaving definition of these principles

to the individual services creates obvious concerns of inconsistent practice. This concern is unacceptable in the contemporary environment of joint operations. However, it is likely that a joint standard will be established by the Department of Defense in a Department of Defense Law of War Manual, which is currently under development.

50. *See* UK MINISTRY OF DEFENCE, THE MANUAL FOR THE LAW OF ARMED CONFLICT para. 2.2 (2004) [hereinafter UK MANUAL] ("Military necessity permits a state engaged in an armed conflict to use only that degree and kind of force, not otherwise prohibited by the law of armed conflict, that is required in order to achieve the legitimate purpose of the conflict, namely the complete or partial submission of the enemy at the earliest possible moment with the minimum expenditure of life and resources"); *see also* William Downey, *The Law of War and Military Necessity*, 47 AMERICAN JOURNAL OF INTERNATIONAL LAW 251 (1953).

51. International Middle East Media Center & Agencies, *United Nations Official: Israeli Bombardment of Lebanon Violates Humanitarian Law*, IMEMC NEWS, July 23, 2006, http://www.imemc.org/index.php?option =com_content&task=view&id=20260&Itemid=173.

52. *See* UK MANUAL, *supra* note 50, para. 2.1 (emphasis added). The manual also provides an extensive definition of these principles.

53. *See* Department of Defense, DoD Directive 2311.01E, DoD Law of War Program (2006) [hereinafter Directive 2311.01E]. The exact language is "It is DoD policy that: Members of the DoD Components comply with the law of war during all armed conflicts, however such conflicts are characterized, and in all other operations." *Id.*, para. 4.1; *see also* Timothy E. Bullman, *A Dangerous Guessing Game Disguised as an Enlightened Policy: Untied States Laws of War Obligations During Military Operations Other Than War*, 159 MILITARY LAW REVIEW 152 (1999) (analyzing the potential that the US law of war policy could be asserted as evidence of a customary norm of international law).

Other armed forces have implemented analogous policy statements. For example, the German policy to apply the principles of the law of war to any armed conflict, no matter how characterized, was cited by the ICTY in the *Tadic* jurisdictional appeal as evidence of a general principle of law extending application of the law of war principles derived from treaties governing international armed conflict to the realm of internal armed conflict. *See* Tadic, *supra* note 29, para. 118 *(citing* HUMANITARES VOLKERRECHT IN BEWAFFNETEN KONFLIKTEN—HANDBUCH 211, DSK AV207320065 (1992)[hereinafter German Military Manual of 1992]); *reprinted in* 35 INTERNATIONAL LEGAL MATERIALS 32 J(1996); *see also* Bullman, *A Dangerous Guessing Game, supra.*

This policy has recently been updated, and has been made even more emphatic by omitting the "principles" qualifier to require compliance with the law of war during all military operations. According to the most recent version: "It is DoD policy that: Members of the DoD Components comply with the law of war during all armed conflicts, however such conflicts are characterized, and in all other military operations." Directive 2311.01E, *supra*, para. 4.

54. This term will be used throughout this article as a convenient reference for the variety of military operations conducted by the United States subsequent to September 11, 2001. Use of this term is not intended as a reflection on this author's position on the legitimacy of characterizing these operations as a "war." While the author acknowledges the hyperbolic nature of this term, it is intended to refer to combat military operations against armed and organized opposition groups.

55. Interview with W. Hays Parks, a senior attorney for the Defense Department and recognized expert on the law of armed conflict. Parks is the chair of the Department of Defense Law of War Working Group, and one of the original proponents of the Law of War Program.

56. For example, the uncertainty related to the application of the laws of war to Operation Just Cause in Panama is reflected in the following excerpt from a Department of State submission related to judicial determination of General Noriega's status: "[T]he United States has made no formal decision with regard to whether or not General Noriega and former members of the PDF charged with pre-capture offenses are prisoners of war, but has stated that each will be provided all prisoner of war protections afforded by the law of war." *See* Gov't Resp. to Def. Post-Hearing Memo. of Law, Sept. 29, 1992, at 8, *cited in* United States v. Noriega, 808 F. Supp. 791 (S.D. Fla. 1992).

In Somalia, although US forces engaged in intense combat operations against non-State organized armed militia groups (see MARK BOWDEN, BLACK HAWK DOWN: A STORY OF MODERN WAR (1999), there was never a formal determination of the status of the conflict. *See* Memorandum from Lieutenant General Robert B. Johnston, Commander, Unified Task Force Somalia, to All Subordinate Unified Task Force Commanders, Subj: Detainee Policy (Feb. 9, 1993).

57. INSTITUTE OF INTERNATIONAL LAW, THE LAWS OF WAR ON LAND (1880), *available at* http://www.icrc.org/ihl.nsf/FULL/140?OpenDocument.

58. *Id.*, Preface.

59. *See* Prosecutor v. Tadic, Case No. IT-94-1-AR72, Appeal on Jurisdiction, para. 118 (Oct. 2, 1995), *reprinted in* 35 INTERNATIONAL LEGAL MATERIALS 32 (1996) (citing the German Military Manual of 1992, the relevant provision of which is translated as follows: "Members of the German army, like their Allies, shall comply with the rules of international humanitarian law in the conduct of military operations in all armed conflicts, whatever the nature of such conflicts." German Military Manual of 1992); *see also* UK Manual, *supra* note 50, para. 14.10 (which indicates that during what it defines as "Peace Support Operations"—military operations that do not legally trigger application of the law of armed conflict—"Nevertheless, such fighting does not take place in a legal vacuum. Quite apart from the fact that it is governed by national law and the relevant provisions of the rules of engagement, the principles and spirit of the law of armed conflict remain relevant").

60. In 1999, the Secretary-General of the United Nations issued a bulletin titled "Observance by United Nations forces of international humanitarian law." This bulletin mandated compliance with foundational principles of the law of war (international humanitarian law) during any operation that qualified as an "armed conflict." No characterization qualification was included, and the application paragraph demonstrates an extremely expansive interpretation of the concept of armed conflict to which such principles apply:

> **Section 1**
> **Field of application**
> 1.1 The fundamental principles and rules of international humanitarian law set out in the present bulletin are applicable to United Nations forces when in situations of armed conflict they are actively engaged therein as combatants, to the extent and for the duration of their engagement. They are accordingly applicable in enforcement actions, or in peacekeeping operations when the use of force is permitted in self-defence.

UN Secretary-General, Bulletin on the Observance by United Nations forces of international humanitarian law, U.N. Doc. ST/SGB/1999/13, *reprinted in* 38 INTERNATIONAL LEGAL MATERIALS 1656 (1999).

61. *See* Noriega, *supra* note 56 (indicating that a policy-based application of the laws of war is insufficient to protect the rights of General Noriega because it is subject to modification at any time at the will of the executive).

62. A brief comment here about what some scholars have characterized as "militarized" law enforcement. Pursuant to this theory, the overarching legal framework for extraterritorial counterterror operations is best defined as a one derived from law enforcement authorities; but under certain circumstances when the use of combat power to augment law enforcement capabilities is required, the presumptive law enforcement activity would be considered "militarized." This theory seems to be consistent with the thesis of this article, if it suggests that *when* law enforcement activities become "militarized," that ratcheting up of means brings into effect a different legal framework, namely LOAC principles. If, however, the suggestion is that when a State "militarizes" law enforcement activities, the armed forces engaged in operations are bound to comply with a law enforcement legal framework, then it seems that the effectiveness of the "militarization" of the activity would be disabled due to an incongruous operational authority equation.

One middle ground that might also be suggested by this concept is that armed forces would be regulated by LOAC principles during the operational phase of "militarized" law enforcement, but that individuals captured and detained, once removed from the area of immediate conflict, would be subject to a law enforcement legal regime. Such a hybrid approach seems responsive to the primary objection leveled against the US invocation of LOAC authorities vis-à-vis captured terrorists—namely their indefinite detention without trial on the basis of military necessity. It also seems to accommodate the needs of the armed forces engaged in such operations by providing them with the most logical legal framework during those operations. One other potentially significant benefit of such a hybrid approach is that it would eliminate any incentive for an unjustified invocation of LOAC authority as a subterfuge for avoiding normal legal process related to detention.

It does, however, seem difficult to dispute the logic of detaining an individual who has acted in what is for all intents and purposes a belligerent capacity against a State. The legitimacy of this "militarized" law enforcement theory rests on the assumption that existing domestic legal authority for the trial and incapacitation of such an individual will satisfy the necessity of preventing a return to belligerent activities. If this assumption is valid, then the hybrid approach holds great merit. If, however, the assumption is invalid, it seems inconsistent with a LOAC-based authority that led to the capture of such an individual to require release with full knowledge of a likely return to belligerent activities.

IX

Law of War Issues in Ground Hostilities in Afghanistan

Gary D. Solis*

Introduction

British soldiers first came to Afghanistan in 1839, hoping to extend the Empire and counter growing Russian influence there. That four-year conflict ended in the massacre of most of the retreating British force of 16,500, demonstrating that, while Afghanistan could be conquered, holding it was another thing. In 1878, again fearing Russian influence in the region, England once more invaded Afghanistan from its base in India. Britain's early victory and regime change nearly proved Pyrrhic. With their occupation unexpectedly costly in men and treasure, the English gained control of Afghan foreign policy, then withdrew most of their forces to India. In 1919, when remaining British units were attacked by Afghan forces, the British initiated a third foray into Afghanistan, this one more successful than the prior two adventures. Afghanistan nevertheless gained its independence in 1921.

Reminiscent of the British incursions into Afghanistan, from 1978 to 1992 the Soviet Union sponsored an armed conflict between the communist Afghan government and anti-communist Muslim guerrillas. For their trouble, the Russians learned the grim lesson of the Kipling poem, "Young British Soldier": "When you're wounded and left on Afghanistan's plains, And the women come out to cut up what remains, Jest roll to your rifle and blow out your brains, An' go to your Gawd like a soldier. . . ."

* Adjunct Professor of Law, Georgetown University Law Center.

Now, prepared to overcome history with modern weapons and new tactics, the United States is in the seventh year of its war in Afghanistan. Challenges abound. It is a nation of massive mountain ranges and remote valleys in the north and east, with desert-like conditions on the plains to the south and west. Road and rail systems remain minimal and many of those that do exist are in disrepair. About the size of Texas, Afghanistan has a population of around twenty-four million. Now it has a visiting military population embedded in the International Security Assistance Force (ISAF) numbering about 45,000 ground personnel, including 15,000 US troops, with another 19,000 US troops assigned to Joint Task Force 101, a part of Operation Enduring Freedom forces assigned to Afghanistan.[1]

This article offers a summary examination of some of the law of armed conflict (LOAC) issues encountered in US ground combat in Afghanistan. These issues were discussed during the June 2008 Naval War College workshop, "The War in Afghanistan," which was the genesis of this volume of the "Blue Book." Although it is a conflict whose ending remains to be written, much of its LOAC outlines are already discernable. Difficult issues involving conflict and individual status, questions about prisoner of war (POW) status, arguments regarding targeted killing and "direct participation," the questionable deportation of individuals from Afghanistan to Guantanamo Bay, and a disturbing number of war crime allegations all arose in workshop discussions of ground combat in Afghanistan. This summary account reflects a few of those issues as seen through the lens of one participant. Not all attendees will agree with all of these assessments, but they provide departure points for discussion at future workshops.

Armed Conflict Commences

The genesis of America's war in Afghanistan is well known. Long before the attacks of September 11, 2001, the United States was concerned with the direction taken by Afghanistan, as the Department of State's Coordinator for Counterterrorism said in a 1999 Senate hearing:

> Afghanistan has become a new safehaven for terrorist groups. In addition to bin Ladin and al-Qa'ida, the Taliban play host to members of the Egyptian Islamic Jihad, the Algerian Armed Islamic [G]roup, Kashmiri separatists, and a number of militant organizations from Central Asia, including terrorists from Uzbekistan and Tajikistan.[2]

After the 9-11 attacks, President George W. Bush demanded that Afghanistan close its terrorist camps and hand over al Qaeda leaders in hiding there.[3] As Professor Dinstein points out, an ultimatum from one government to another, setting a deadline and warning that war will immediately commence once the deadline lapses, will, at the designated time, indicate the initiation of armed conflict. Although there was no deadline in the Bush demand, it was clear that the Taliban were required to act immediately or armed conflict would be initiated by the United States.[4] Such was the case. "[US] military operations against Taliban and Al Qaeda targets in Afghanistan commenced on October 7th. . . . There ought to be no doubt that October 7th—and not September 11th—is the date of the beginning of the war between the United States and Afghanistan."[5] In support of the American initiation of armed conflict, the United Nations Security Council passed Resolution 1386, authorizing establishment of an International Security Assistance Force to maintain security in and around Kabul, after the fall of the Taliban. States participating in the ISAF were authorized "to take all necessary measures to fulfil its mandate."[6]

Shifting Conflict Status

From the outset, a unique aspect of the ground war in Afghanistan has been the heavy use of Special Forces:

> Army Special Forces (SF) was tested to a degree not seen since the Vietnam War. With little time to prepare for this mission, SF teams were to land by helicopter deep in hostile territory, contact members of the Northern Alliance, coordinate their activities in a series of offensives . . . and change the government of Afghanistan so that the country was no longer a safe haven for terrorists.[7]

Army SF units were the first US military personnel in Afghanistan for Operation Enduring Freedom, as the invasion was denominated. A first twelve-man SF team was inserted on October 19, 2001, joining with a Northern Alliance Uzbek commander, Abdul Rashid.[8] SF forces would carry the brunt of US fighting for the brief Common Article 2[9] period of the Afghan conflict. The Northern Alliance (the United Islamic Front for the Salvation of Afghanistan) had battled the Taliban government since the Alliance's formation in 1996, in a non-international armed conflict. Now, in the north of Afghanistan, SF/Northern Alliance operations took place near Mazar-e Sharif, Kondoz and Taloqan. In other areas the Northern Alliance continued its independent conflict with the Taliban central government.

Meanwhile, in the south of Afghanistan, on the night of October 19–20, an international armed conflict opened when US SF and Ranger forces made a nighttime parachute drop to initiate a raid on Kandahar, fighting Taliban units. Common Article 2 and Common Article 3[10] conflicts were being fought at the same time in a single country. "The fact that a belligerent State is beset by enemies from both inside and outside its territory does not mean that the international and internal armed conflicts necessarily merge."[11] A few weeks later, on November 13, with the capture of Kabul by Northern Alliance, US and British forces, the international armed conflict began to ebb, but significant LOAC issues were beginning to emerge.

Individual Status and Prisoner of War Issues

The US Army's official history of Operation Enduring Freedom notes, "At this point the wholesale surrender of the Taliban forces began to cause problems."[12] More than 3,500 Taliban fighters had surrendered around Kondoz. Several thousand more were captured by Northern Alliance forces near Mazar-e Sharif. Douglas Feith, then Under Secretary of Defense for Policy, writes, "The Pentagon's leadership appreciated the importance of honoring the Geneva Conventions, but issues arose time and again that required the very difficult balancing of weighty but competing interests: on interrogation methods . . . and on whether to prosecute individuals as criminals or simply continue to hold them as enemy combatants."[13] US efforts to "balance" the Geneva Conventions against interrogation methods and prosecution choices did not meet with notable success.

What was the status of Taliban captives taken in the brief Common Article 2 phase of the armed conflict? Did they qualify as POWs? Were they members of the armed forces of a party to the conflict? Additional Protocol I defines an armed force to include

> all organized armed forces, groups and units which are under a command responsible to that Party for the conduct of its subordinates, even if that Party is represented by a government or an authority not recognized by an adverse party. Such armed forces shall be subject to an internal disciplinary system which, *inter alia*, shall enforce compliance with the rules of international law applicable in armed conflict.[14]

Considering that definition, but for their compliance with international law, the Taliban appear to qualify as the armed forces of Afghanistan, entitled to POW status if captured in a Common Article 2 conflict.[15]

Or were Afghanistan's Taliban akin to a post–World War I *Freikorps* in defeated Germany? Consisting of private paramilitary groups, ultraconservative and highly nationalistic, more than sixty *Freikorps* proliferated throughout Germany in 1919, one of them becoming the National Socialist German Workers' Party—the Nazi Party. But in 1920 the Nazis were just another *Freikorps*, with an allegiance not to any German government but to their own *Freikorps*.[16] There is an argument that Afghanistan's armed forces ceased to exist after the fall of the communist Najibullah government in September 1996 and were supplanted by rival *Freikorps*-like "armies," the Taliban being one of the more powerful. The argument continues that there is no showing that the Taliban became the armed forces of Afghanistan, professing allegiance to the government of the State.[17] The *Commentary* on the Additional Protocols notes, "[C]ombatant status is given to regular forces only which profess allegiance to a government or authority . . . which claims to represent a State which is a Party to the conflict."[18] Accordingly, under this construct the Taliban were not "the armed forces of a Party to the conflict."[19] Rather, the argument goes, they were merely the armed group in control of Afghanistan and its government.

But the stronger case is that the Taliban were indeed the armed forces of Afghanistan. Starting in 1954, the International Law Commission (ILC) developed guidelines for State responsibility. Article 8 of the ILC's 2001 document, Responsibility of States for Internationally Wrongful Acts, reads: "The conduct of a person or group of persons shall be considered an act of a State under international law if the person or group of persons is in fact acting on the instructions of, or under the direction or control of, that State in carrying out the conduct."[20] That guidance, combined with the plain language of Additional Protocol I's Article 43.1, leads to the conclusion that the Taliban were the armed forces of Afghanistan.

Accepting, *arguendo*, that the Taliban were Afghanistan's armed forces during the period of the Common Article 2 conflict, did its captured fighters merit POW status as members of "the armed forces of a Party to the conflict"?[21] Applying the four conditions for lawful combatancy and POW status upon capture, the answer is reasonably clear: although they were the armed forces of Afghanistan, they did not wear uniforms or other distinctive fixed sign. Black turbans, common to many males in the region, do not suffice.

> Since the [four] conditions are cumulative, members of the Taliban forces failed to qualify as prisoners of war under the customary law of war criteria. These criteria admit no exception, not even in the unusual circumstances of . . . the Taliban regime. To say that '[t]he Taliban do not wear uniforms in the traditional western sense' is quite misleading, for the Taliban forces did not wear any uniform in any sense at all . . . .[22]

Throughout the Common Article 2 phase of the conflict they failed to distinguish themselves and were not entitled to POW status. Although there are reasoned views in disagreement,[23] the Taliban captured during the Common Article 2

US invasion were not merely soldiers out of uniform—or out of a Western conception of a uniform. They were not POWs.

What then was their status? Given the definition of civilians in Article 50 of Additional Protocol I, they were simply civilians and, being directly involved in an international armed conflict, they were unprivileged belligerents, i.e., civilians who took a direct part in hostilities, to be captured and tried under military or Afghan domestic law—not for being unlawful combatants, which is not a crime in and of itself, but for the unlawful acts that rendered them unlawful combatants.

One may question whether it would not have been wise to have a competent tribunal determine the status of those Taliban captured during the international phase of the conflict since their presumptive status upon capture was POW.[24] But such tribunals are called for only in cases of doubt regarding the captive's status. Was there doubt?[25] The US Congressional Research Service specifies several reasons for *not* granting POW status:

> The Administration has argued that granting [al Qaeda or Taliban] detainees POW status would interfere with efforts to interrogate them, which would in turn hamper its efforts to thwart further attacks. Denying POW status may allow the Army to retain more stringent security measures . . . . The Administration also argued that the detainees, if granted POW status, would have to be repatriated when hostilities in Afghanistan cease, freeing them to commit more terrorist acts.[26]

Initially the US position on the status of both the Taliban and al Qaeda was seemingly based on such faulty reasoning. Clearly al Qaeda, a violent, transnational, non-State terrorist group, is in violation of all law, including the LOAC.[27] Acts of terrorism like those commonly perpetrated by al Qaeda are prohibited by Geneva law, including the 1977 Protocols.[28] Initial individual status determinations were needlessly complicated by the inexplicable US view that the fight against the Taliban was an armed conflict, yet was neither a Common Article 2 nor Common Article 3 conflict.[29] Despite warnings from the US Secretary of State[30] and the Department of State's Legal Adviser,[31] the Bush administration held that neither the Taliban nor al Qaeda was protected by the Geneva Conventions,[32] including Common Article 3 protection.[33] The view that captured Taliban and al Qaeda fighters were outside the protections of Common Article 3[34] was rejected by the Supreme Court in its 2006 *Hamdan* decision,[35] and the administration subsequently softened its position. Lieutenant General Ricardo Sanchez, former US commander of ground combat troops in Iraq, wrote of the presidential memorandum denying the Taliban the protections of the Geneva Conventions:

> This presidential memorandum constituted a watershed event in U.S. military history. Essentially, it set aside all of the legal constraints, training guidelines, and rules for interrogation that formed the U.S. Army's foundation for the treatment of prisoners on the battlefield . . . . According to the President, it was now okay to go beyond those standards with regard to al-Qaeda terrorists. And that guidance set America on a path toward torture.[36]

If not covered by the Geneva Conventions, even Common Article 3, what, in the pre-*Hamdan* US view, was the status of captured Taliban and al Qaeda fighters, and what treatment were they to be accorded? The murky answer was provided by Secretary of Defense Donald Rumsfeld: "The Combatant Commanders shall, in detaining Al Qaeda and Taliban individuals under the control of the Department of Defense, treat them humanely and, to the extent appropriate and consistent with military necessity, in a manner consistent with the principles of the Geneva Conventions of 1949."[37] No individual status was specified. A former Assistant US Attorney General wrote, "This formulation sounded good. But it was very vague, it was not effectively operationalized into concrete standards of conduct, and it left all of the hard issues about 'humane' and 'appropriate' treatment to the discretion of unknown officials."[38] Nor was it consistent with the law of armed conflict.

Captured Taliban were dubbed "enemy combatants." That phrase first appeared in the US Supreme Court opinion in the World War II Nazi saboteur case, *Ex parte Quirin*. Chief Justice Stone wrote for the majority:

> [A spy or] an enemy combatant who without uniform comes secretly through the lines for the purpose of waging war by destruction of life or property, are familiar examples of belligerents who are generally deemed not to be entitled to the status of prisoners of war, but to be offenders against the law of war subject to trial and punishment by military tribunals.[39]

Sixty-five years later, critics of *Quirin* note of the Court's phrase, "enemy combatant," that "the term's meaning is blurred by its failure to appear in the positive case law existing at the time of the case as well as in the current treaty-based law of war."[40] Another critic dismissively asserts that "[t]he concept of the 'unlawful combatant' was invented to explain the legal fate of the eight German saboteurs tried in *Quirin*. . . . The concept . . . explained why the saboteurs were entitled neither to a jury trial under the Constitution nor to POW status under the Hague Convention."[41] Although *Quirin* continues to be cited when supportive of a writers' position, the opinion is muddled, and a poor example of LOAC insight that lacks legal clarity.

Canadian Brigadier General Kenneth Watkin writes, "[C]onfusion has also been created by the United States' use of an even more generic term: 'enemy combatants.'"[42] Colonel Charles Garraway agrees:

> The term "enemy combatant" . . . merely adds to the confusion. Traditionally, the term "enemy combatant" refers to legitimate combatants who are entitled to prisoner of war status. It is a new usage to describe those who are deemed to be unlawful belligerents as such. What term is left for those legitimate combatants belonging to enemy armed forces?[43]

Today, "enemy combatant," like the term "combatant" itself, has come to represent a status rather than an activity. A definition of "enemy combatant" binding US Armed Forces is found in a Department of Defense (DoD) directive: "Enemy combatant. In general, a person engaged in hostilities against the United States or its coalition partners during an armed conflict. The term 'enemy combatant' includes both 'lawful enemy combatants' and 'unlawful enemy combatants.'"[44] No mention is made of the treatment due a captured enemy combatant and the definition appears tailored for the "war on terrorism," rather than for general LOAC use. Its melding of lawful and unlawful combatants, long-established separate LOAC statuses, is also notable since, upon capture in a Common Article 2 conflict, the two are entitled to significantly differing protections. Whether this definition survives to become State practice, or the subject of treaties, remains to be seen.

A competing US directive, Joint Publication 3-63, adopts the just-mentioned DoD directive's definition but, significantly, omits its last sentence: "Enemy combatant. In general, a person engaged in hostilities against the United States or its coalition partners during an armed conflict."[45] Again, the Joint Publication's definition does not mention the captive's individual status (unless "enemy combatant" is considered a discrete status), or presumptive POW status or protected person status, one or the other of which must be applicable in a Common Article 2 conflict. In Afghanistan, the United States has been at pains to avoid referring to captured opposing fighters as POWs. The unsatisfactory term "enemy combatant" is instead used.

Taxonomic issues aside, Operation Enduring Freedom continued, its participants oblivious to status issues. On November 16, 2001, the battle of Tora Bora began. In support of Afghan warlord Hazrat Ali, dozens of US SF operators guided airstrikes on al Qaeda mountain strongholds. Although the constant strikes and pressure from ground forces reduced the enemy presence, fighting came to a halt in mid-December. Most of the enemy had either fought to the death or had found refuge across the Pakistan border.[46]

Also in November, at Tarin Kot, US aircraft guided by SF ground controllers decimated Taliban fighters, killing an estimated one thousand. On November 25, the first US conventional forces entered Afghanistan when five hundred Marines of the 15th Marine Expeditionary Unit (MEU) debarked from *USS Peleliu* and landed at Kandahar. They had moved by helicopter from their shipboard base four hundred miles inland to Kandahar, so distant an inland objective not being the usual Marine ship-to-shore movement. The 15th MEU departed a few weeks later, replaced by the 26th MEU,[47] who themselves departed within two months. On the ground, Afghanistan was still essentially an SF/Northern Alliance show.

Also, on November 25, 2001, during a riot at a prison located at Mazar-e Sharif, CIA Special Activities Division officer Johnny M. Spann was the first American killed by Taliban enemy action.[48]

Unmanned Aerial Vehicles and Targeted Killing

Operation Enduring Freedom is notable for the use of unmanned aerial vehicles (UAVs). Their role in ground combat has been significant because at least one UAV, the MQ-1 Predator, can carry and fire two laser-guided air-to-ground Hellfire missiles, changing the fundamental nature of ground combat when it is employed.

Predator UAVs first deployed to the Balkans in 1995. Since then, the Predator's offensive capabilities have increased. Today, it carries a daytime television nose camera, a forward-looking infrared camera for low-light and night operations, and a laser designator. Cruising at eighty-five miles per hour at 25,000 feet, a Predator can loiter for in excess of forty hours.[49] The first armed Predator mission in Afghanistan was flown on October 7, 2001.

Employing the Predator, the US admitted engaging in targeted killing for the first time.[50] On November 3, 2002, over the desert near Sana, Yemen, a CIA-controlled Predator tracked an SUV containing six men. One of the six, Qaed Salim Sinan al-Harethi, was believed to be a senior al Qaeda lieutenant who had played a major role in the 2000 bombing of the American destroyer *USS Cole*. He "was on a list of 'high-value' targets whose elimination, by capture or death, had been called for by President Bush."[51] The United States and Yemen had tracked al-Harethi's movements for months. Now, away from any inhabited area, the Predator fired a Hellfire missile at the vehicle. Its six occupants, including al-Harethi, were killed.[52] There is no consensus definition of "targeted killing" in the LOAC or in case law.[53] However, a reasonable definition is offered by International Committee of the Red Cross (ICRC) legal advisor Nils Melzer: "The use of lethal force attributable to a subject of international law with the intent, premeditation and deliberation to kill individually selected persons who are not in the physical custody of those targeting them."[54]

Additional Protocol I, Article 51.3, usually considered to be customary law, appears to prohibit targeted killing: "Civilians shall enjoy the protection afforded by this Section, unless and for such time as they take a direct part in hostilities." Those interested in international law or the LOAC know that for several years the phrase "unless and for such time as they take a direct part in hostilities" has been the subject of debate and the focus of meetings of international experts sponsored by the ICRC and the Asser Institute.[55] The plain meaning of the phrase indicates that terrorists and terrorist accomplices, such as weapon makers and communications experts, cannot lawfully be targeted unless, at the time of targeting, they are actually directly engaged in hostilities. Those who argue against such a constricting limitation urge that such terrorists should be lawful targets whenever and wherever their locations can be confirmed.

But events on the ground in Afghanistan and Iraq are making the debate moot. As Melzer notes:

> Today, targeted killing is in the process of escaping the shadowy realm of half-legality and non-accountability, and [is] gradually gaining legitimacy as a method of counter-terrorism and "surgical" warfare. Several Governments have expressly or implicitly acknowledged that they have resorted to targeted killings in their respective efforts to curb insurgent or terrorist activities.[56]

Those governments include the United States, Israel, Russia, Pakistan, the United Kingdom, Germany and Switzerland.

For better or worse, in the United States the 9-11 attacks caused shifts in public opinion, and often shifts in public policy, relating to terrorism and terrorists. For example, torture, previously rejected out of hand, shockingly became acceptable. A 2005 survey indicated that sixty-one percent of the American public would not rule out torture,[57] and President George W. Bush said in a nationally televised address that "the CIA used an alternative set of procedures"[58] when interrogating certain captured terrorist suspects.

Another post-9-11 change in policy and attitude related to targeted killing. Once anathema to America (in public at least),[59] after 9-11 targeted killing became tolerated,[60] then embraced. Under a series of classified presidential findings, President Bush reportedly broadened the number of named terrorists who may be killed if their capture is impractical.[61] In early 2006, it was reported that since 9-11 the US had successfully carried out at least nineteen targeted killings via Predator-fired

Hellfire missiles. In June 2006, the targeted killing of Abu Musab al-Zarqawi, leader of al Qaeda in Iraq, was celebrated as a US strategic and political victory.

In October 2001, a US Predator killed the military chief of al Qaeda in Afghanistan. In June 2004, a senior Taliban planner, Nek Mohammad, was killed by a UAV-launched missile. In May 2005, on the Afghanistan-Pakistan border, a CIA-controlled UAV killed Haitham al-Yemeni, a suspected senior figure in Afghan al Qaeda operations.[62] In August 2008, an Afghan warlord's camp in the mountains of Pakistan was destroyed and nine insurgents reportedly killed by four missiles.[63] The roster continues to lengthen. Though it occasionally admits to targeted killing, the US government remains reticent and evasive in acknowledging employment of the tactic, but its value to ground combat operations is apparent.[64]

Even considering their inevitable collateral damage, the effectiveness of UAVs mated with Hellfire missiles, combined with their relatively low cost and zero exposure of friendly personnel, assures their continued use. Although targeting errors, actual or contrived, are media staples,[65] the international trend toward their legitimization, whether or not seen to be in compliance with Article 51.3, is all but assured.

Meanwhile, in April 2002, coalition members met in Geneva and agreed on five "pillars" of change in Afghanistan. The United States assumed responsibility for building the Afghan army; Germany agreed to build the Afghan police; Italy took on the judicial system; the United Kingdom was to take the lead on curbing illegal drug use; and Japan accepted responsibility for disarmament, demilitarization and reintegration of the Afghan warlords and militias.[66] Six years on, one can only smile ruefully at such ambitious plans.

By late 2002 an Afghanistan conflict timeline was discernable. The US invasion was in October 2001. Coalition forces removed the Taliban from power in December.[67] According to the 2001 Afghan Bonn Agreement, Afghan sovereignty re-arose in December 2001 with the establishment of the Interim Authority.[68] Accepting those dates, the international armed conflict phase of the "war" lasted sixty-two days and the US occupation a mere fifteen days. In June 2002 the Afghans created a transitional government referred to as a *Loya Jirga*, or grand assembly.

In terms of ground combat, one observer noted that "[d]uty in Afghanistan isn't turning out to be the low-key operation many expected."[69] An infantry officer reported, "Afghanistan is home to some of the most extreme terrain and environmental conditions in the world. During our time there we operated in mostly mountainous terrain in excess of 8,000 feet [above] mean sea level, with temperatures ranging during the day from 80 to 100 degrees."[70]

Through 2003 Afghanistan's stresses on troop availability were reflected in tour lengths: Army tours of duty were from nine to twelve months; Marine Corps units rotated into and out of country every seven months; Air Force personnel rotated every three or four months. Five years later, manning levels and tour lengths continue to bedevil Pentagon planners.

Transfer of Protected Persons from Afghanistan to Guantanamo Bay

During the Newport workshop, several of us wondered why more has not been made of the movement of prisoners from Afghanistan and Iraq to Guantanamo Bay, Cuba. The history of deportations in armed conflicts is familiar. During World War I Germany deported thousands of French and Belgian citizens to Germany as forced laborers. The German action was called "an act of tyranny, contrary to all notions of humanity."[71] Georg Schwarzenberger wrote: "In World War II, Nazi Germany resorted to deportation as part of its policies of terrorisation and extermination and, even more so, for the purpose of implementing its slave-labour programme."[72] In response, the Charter of the International Military Tribunal at Nuremberg specified that the deportation of civilians from occupied territories—for any purpose—was a crime against humanity and a breach of the laws and customs of war.[73] In the post-war "Subsequent Proceedings," tried under authority of Control Council Law No. 10, unlawful deportation was among the charges in several of the twelve military tribunals. National tribunals prosecuted individuals for deportation as well.[74]

Article 49 of Geneva Convention IV addresses the removal of protected persons: "Individual . . . transfers, as well as deportation of protected persons from occupied territory to the territory of the Occupying Power or to that of any other country, occupied or not, are prohibited, regardless of their motive . . . ."[75]

The *Commentary* to Convention IV explains, "There is doubtless no need to give an account here of the painful recollections called forth by the 'deportations' of the Second World War. . . . The prohibition . . . is intended to forbid such hateful practices for all time. . . . The prohibition is absolute and allows of no exceptions . . . ."[76] How then to explain the history of forced movement of individuals from Afghanistan and Iraq to Guantanamo in the "war against terrorism"?

In non-international conflicts, Additional Protocol II mandates that "[c]ivilians shall not be compelled to leave their own territory for reasons connected with the conflict."[77] The Statute of the International Criminal Court[78] renders deportations in non-international conflicts a war crime as well, while the statutes of the International Criminal Tribunal for the former Yugoslavia (ICTY) and International Criminal Tribunal for Rwanda denominate deportations as crimes against humanity.[79]

The ICRC's study, *Customary International Humanitarian Law*, states, "Numerous military manuals specify the prohibition of unlawful deportation or transfer of civilians in occupied territory."[80] The study goes on to specify the legislation of thirty-nine States, several applicable in non-international conflicts, making deportation of civilians a domestic offense. The ICRC study finds State practice to establish the rule against deportation, in both international and non-international armed conflicts, as customary international law.[81] Finally, Geneva Convention IV mandates that "[p]rotected persons accused of offenses shall be detained in the occupied country, and if convicted they shall serve their sentences there."[82]

These prohibitory sources against deportation indicate the incontrovertible nature of the prohibition. Throughout the armed conflict in Afghanistan and the US occupation, Article 49 applied, prohibiting the deportation of protected persons from the occupied State to Guantanamo.

Who is a "protected person" whose deportation is prohibited? Geneva Convention IV, Article 4, tells us that, essentially, a protected person is someone in an international armed conflict, other than a POW, who is in the hands of the other side. There are limitations on the application of protected person status, of course—notably the "nationality requirement" and cobelligerents. The cobelligerent's requirement of diplomatic representation is significant,[83] because at the time of the armed conflict with the United States, the Taliban government did not have such relations with the United States. The nationality and cobelligerent limitations on protected person status did not apply to nationals of Afghanistan vis-à-vis the United States.

Can extraordinary measures, such as deportation, be taken in the case of unlawful combatants, as many Afghan insurgents were? The "unprivileged belligerent" has been characterized by the ICRC "as describing all persons taking a direct part in hostilities without being entitled to do so and who therefore cannot be classified as prisoners of war on falling into the power of the enemy."[84]

Dinstein argues that

> [a] person who engages in military raids by night, while purporting to be an innocent civilian by day, is neither a civilian nor a lawful combatant. He is an unlawful combatant. He is a combatant in the sense that he can be lawfully targeted by the enemy, but he cannot claim the privileges appertaining to lawful combatancy. Nor does he enjoy the benefits of civilian status . . . .[85]

Captured unlawful combatants are entitled to the basic humanitarian protections of Common Article 3 and of Article 75 of Additional Protocol I.[86] While being an unprivileged belligerent is not a war crime, the unlawful combatant forfeits the combatant's privilege and potential POW status, and may be charged for law of war violations that made him an unlawful combatant.

What is "deportation" in the LOAC? William Schabas states that

> [d]eportation . . . involves the movement of individuals, under duress, from where they reside to a place that is not of their choosing. Deportation would involve such transfer when an international border is crossed. It must be proven that the accused intentionally perpetrated an act or omission to effect such deportation . . . that was not motivated by the security of the population or imperative military reasons.[87]

ICTY jurisprudence defines deportation simply as forcible transfer beyond one's home State borders,[88] and finds it an inhumane act.[89]

In the pertinent timeframe, the seventy-seven-day-long US-Afghanistan conflict, whose deportation to Guantanamo Bay was prohibited? Answer: captured unlawful combatants who were nationals of a State other than Afghanistan *and*, because Afghanistan lacked normal diplomatic relations with the United States, Afghan nationals held by the United States in occupied Afghanistan who were allegedly unlawful combatants. Individuals in both categories were protected persons.

The only discovered US government document addressing deportations to Guantanamo is a March 2004 draft opinion written by the Justice Department's Office of Legal Counsel. The fourteen-page memorandum to Alberto Gonzales, then–Counsel to the President, is entitled "Permissibility of Relocating Certain 'Protected Persons' from Occupied Iraq."[90] Relying on a definition of deportation taken from Roman times, the draft memorandum argues that Geneva Convention IV does not prohibit the deportation of protected persons who are illegal aliens—presumably meaning foreign fighters—captured in Iraq. Creating the LOAC from whole cloth, the memorandum argues that protected persons, even if nationals of the State in which captured, may be deported as long as they have not been formally accused of wrongdoing, apparently an effort to circumvent the requirement of Article 76 of the Fourth Convention that protected persons accused of offenses be detained in the occupied State.

The draft memorandum's conclusion is that the United States may remove—deport—protected persons when the intent is not to accuse them of wrongdoing but only to interrogate them. From the memorandum: "[A]rticle 49(1)'s prohibition of forcible transfers and deportations *out of* occupied territory . . . should not be construed to extend to temporary transnational relocations of brief but not indefinite duration" (emphasis in original). This would allow authorities to simply designate a protected person as destined for interrogation and deport him without further accountability.

The draft memorandum was never finalized,[91] although its conclusions were confirmed by Mr. Gonzales when he was nominated to be Attorney General of the United States.[92] "A related issue that has inexplicably escaped broader attention is the fate of persons apprehended in the 'war on terrorism' who were or are being held at undisclosed locations."[93] The draft memorandum was the basis for the secret removal by the CIA of at least a dozen detainees from Iraq.[94]

How many Afghan and Iraqi prisoners held by the United States were deported to Guantanamo in contravention of Article 49? It is unlikely there will ever be a satisfactory answer.

Increased War Crimes Prosecutions—Perception or Fact?

Large-scale ground operations in Afghanistan, e.g., the US Army's Operations Anaconda (March 1–16, 2002), Valiant Strike (March 20–25, 2003) and Mountain Viper (September 4–5, 2003), do not usually give rise to charges of LOAC violations. Day-to-day operations in urban Afghan settings, however, have seen many such allegations. War crime charges are even more frequent in Iraq, where urban operations are more common.

Anytime a government puts high-power weapons in the hands of very young men and women, bad things will inevitably happen.[95] In fighting terrorists who ignore customary battlefield norms, incite retaliation and hide within the noncombatant population, the spur for opposing forces to commit offenses is only heightened. The "CNN factor" often ensures that offenses are broadcast worldwide in near-real time. The armed forces are in a difficult position: fail to formally investigate even flimsy allegations of wrongdoing and be pilloried for covering up war crimes, or prefer court-martial charges with slim evidence and be pilloried as overly aggressive martinets.

But one may ask, as some workshop attendees did around Naval War College luncheon tables, have LOAC violations actually increased in Afghanistan, or have their reporting and prosecution increased? Are US armed forces members less controlled today or has a heightened awareness of the law of armed conflict resulted in greater command awareness and increased prosecutions? Either way, anecdotal evidence suggests that there have been proportionally more courts-martial for LOAC-related offenses than in previous armed conflicts.

One cannot obtain accurate numbers of courts-martial for such violations. Each of the military Services annually reports total numbers of convictions (as opposed to charges) to the Court of Appeals for the Armed Forces, but the convictions are not broken down by offense. Even if they were, the murder of a POW, for example, would simply be reported as a murder, with no victim, no grave breach and no LOAC violation indicated. There is no requirement in federal law or military regulation to do otherwise.[96] Nor are media reports reliable indicators of indiscipline or criminality.

In December 2004 the Department of Defense reported that 130 US combatants had been punished or charged with prisoner abuse in Afghanistan, Iraq or Guantanamo.[97] Numbers in other reports for specific geographic areas vary.[98] In any event, there is no base point to which any number may be compared. Is 130 an unusually high number or normal or unusually low? Figures recorded in the current conflict cannot be compared to similar offenses in prior conflicts because, even if numbers had been kept—and they were not—every conflict is unique, with fundamentally different conflict characteristics that would make comparisons meaningless.

In both Afghanistan and Iraq there have clearly been a disturbingly high number of deaths of detainees at the hands of US warders. The *New York Times* reported: "At least 26 prisoners have died in American custody in Iraq and Afghanistan since 2002 in what Army and Navy investigators have concluded or suspect were acts of criminal homicide, according to military officials."[99] A few months later the *Los Angeles Times* reported that "[a]utopsy reports on 44 prisoners who died in US custody in Iraq and Afghanistan indicate that 21 were victims of homicide, including eight who appear to have been fatally abused by their captors."[100] And a few months after that the *Philadelphia Inquirer* reported: "Ninety-eight detainees in Iraq and Afghanistan have died in US custody since August 2002, and 34 of them were suspected or confirmed homicides, a human-rights group reported yesterday. Only 12 cases have resulted in punishment of any kind . . . ."[101] Which media figures, all said to be based on armed forces figures, can be relied upon—if any?

There are media reports of combatant misconduct occurring in Afghanistan, most involving detainee mistreatment[102] but not all. A closely watched case arose in March 2007 in Jalalabad, when it was reported that ten to nineteen Afghan noncombatants were killed (the actual number has never been settled) and thirty-three more wounded by uncontrolled US fire when a Marine Corps convoy was hit by a car bomb that slightly wounded one Marine. As the convoy sped from the scene it allegedly continued to fire on Afghan civilians over the course of a six-mile "escape." The area's Army commander immediately ordered the Marine unit out of the country, initiated an investigation, paid $2,000 in compensation for each reported death and apologized to the victims and their families on behalf of the United States. The Marine commander of the convoy unit was relieved by his Marine Corps seniors. At the same time the Commandant of the Marine Corps, General James Conway, publicly expressed his anger at the Army commander's expressions of regret and acceptance of responsibility, which General Conway considered premature. The involved Marines disputed the initial account, insisting they had only returned fire after the initial car bombing and subsequent lengthy escape.[103]

In May 2008, a court of inquiry cleared all Marines involved of criminal charges. In a fourteen-month arc the incident moved from newspaper front pages to back pages to silence, leaving hard feelings between the Marines and the Army, and Afghans distrustful and embittered against the United States. If not typical, it was a not uncommon progression, initially raising the specter of Haditha-like horrific unlawful conduct, fading to anticlimax and no charges.

There have indeed been numerous courts-martial involving war crime charges and there have been instances in which prosecution was found unwarranted. There have been convictions in which sentences were not commensurate with the offenses of which the accused was convicted.[104] All that can be said with assurance is that, after seven years in Afghanistan, there is no documented answer to the question of whether there are more LOAC violations than in prior conflicts; only arguments. Several attendees suggested the Department of Defense should require that all formal allegations of violent offenses involving indigenous individuals and armed service personnel, including prisoners of any description, whether or not resulting in trial, be periodically reported by the armed Service involved to a common DoD authority.

Meanwhile, in mid-2006 the US Marine Corps departed Afghanistan, leaving ground fighting to the Army and NATO combatants, and fledgling Afghan National Army troops. The Marine units would move on to Iraq. One observer noted: "The end of the Corps' Afghan deployments comes as the overall U.S. commitment to that country is on the decline. Military officials have said that American forces will be reduced from the roughly 23,000 troops there now to 16,000 by the end of the summer [of 2006]."[105] Planning was underway for the so-called "surge" in Iraq, which began in February 2007. Even at some tactical cost, US troop drawdowns in Afghanistan were required to meet the manpower needs of the coming "surge." By 2007, Afghanistan was being referred to as the "forgotten war."[106] But, once the surge was over, the Marines were back,[107] to the consternation of the Marine Corps' Commandant.[108] But, almost immediately, new plans were announced indicating they would yet again leave Afghanistan, this time within a year.[109] Such undulating personnel requirements, presenting planners with constantly moving targets, are one more price of fighting two wars at once.

Conclusion

After more than seven years of ground combat in Afghanistan, at the cost of more than nine hundred lives, well over five hundred of them American, and having spent in excess of $175 billion,[110] where are we?

We have succeeded in deposing the Taliban government and installing an elected parliament. We have disrupted al Qaeda in Afghanistan. There has been a major increase in availability of basic health care. A central banking system and a stable currency are in place. Yet, mid-2008 reports, not all of which are media-based, present a discouraging picture. Among media reports were these: "Security in the provinces ringing the capital, Kabul, has deteriorated rapidly in recent months. Today it is as bad as at any time since the beginning of the war . . . ."[111] "[T]he Taliban are demonstrating a resilience and a ferocity that are raising alarm here [in Kabul], in Washington and in other NATO capitals."[112] "Al Qaeda is more capable of attacking inside the United States than it was last year . . . ."[113] "There were ten times as many armed attacks on international troops and civilian contractors in 2007 as there were in 2004. Every other measure of violence, from roadside bombs to suicide bombers, is also up dramatically."[114] In April 2006, a National Intelligence Estimate reported that "the global jihadist movement . . . is spreading and adapting to counterterrorism efforts."[115] In 2007, the last year for which totals are available, enemy encounters, roadside bombs, suicide bombers and casualty figures all reached new highs. In 2008, the *Baltimore Sun* reported: "The chairman of the House Armed Services Committee, Democratic Rep. Ike Skelton of Missouri, has said the United States 'risks strategic failure' in Afghanistan."[116]

Poppy crop eradication, once a primary US mission in Afghanistan, has been abandoned. The media has reported that "[t]he Marines don't want to antagonize the local population by joining US-backed efforts to destroy the crop. 'We're not coming to eradicate poppy,' [a Marine major] says. 'We're coming to clear the Taliban.'"[117]

An open Pakistan border combines with Pakistani perfidy and Afghan exhaustion to undercut coalition efforts against a resurgent Taliban. The invasion of Iraq eclipsed Afghanistan as the battleground against terrorism, stripping it of military resources, American funding and public interest. So far, efforts to deny sanctuary to terrorists in Afghanistan have been unsuccessful. One reporter alleges: "In a vicious cycle, narcotics, corruption and the absence of law and order are rotting the heart of the government and rippling the economy. Despite massive Western investment, Afghanistan is close to being a failed state."[118]

An August 2008 editorial in the *New York Times* reflected the widespread concern regarding the progress of Operation Enduring Freedom:

> The news out of Afghanistan is truly alarming. . . . Taliban and foreign Qaeda fighters are consolidating control over an expanding swath of territory sprawling across both sides of the porous Afghanistan-Pakistan border. . . .Unless the United States, NATO and its central Asian allies move quickly, they could lose this war. . . . [s]even years have already been wasted. . . . Afghanistan's war is not a sideshow. It is the principal military confrontation between America and NATO and the forces responsible for 9/11 . . . .[119]

Seven years of ground combat in Afghanistan have not gained control of Afghanistan's borders, which is critical to ultimate success. The Afghan government has not yet established its authority or credibility. The Taliban are far from defeated.

The United States is not at the point of taking Kipling's advice to "Jest roll to your rifle and blow out your brains An' go to your Gawd like a soldier." But there is a large measure of ground combat yet to come in Afghanistan.

Notes

1. Gerry J. Gilmore, Pentagon Proposes Change to U.S. Command Structure in Afghanistan (Aug. 8, 2008), *available at* http://www.defenselink.mil/news/newsarticle.aspx?id=50748.

2. *Extremist Movements and Their Threat to the United States, Hearing Before the Subcomm. on Near East and South Asian Affairs of the S. Foreign Relations Comm.*, 106th Cong. 3 (1999) (statement of Amb. Michael A. Sheehan, Coordinator for Counterterrorism, US Dept. of State), *available at* http://www.state.gov/www/policy_remarks/1999/991102_sheehan_terrorism.html.

3. Address by President George W. Bush, *The War Against Terrorism*, *in* DIGEST OF UNITED STATES PRACTICE IN INTERNATIONAL LAW 856–58 (Sally Cummins & David Stewart eds., 2001).

4. YORAM DINSTEIN, WAR, AGGRESSION AND SELF-DEFENCE 31 (4th ed. 2005).

5. *Id.*

6. S.C. Res. 1386, ¶ 3, U.N. Doc. S/RES/1386 (Dec. 20, 2001).

7. Richard W. Stewart, The United States Army in Afghanistan, Operation Enduring Freedom, October 2001–March 2002, at 8 (2003), *available at* http://www.history.army.mil/brochures/Afghanistan/Operation%20Enduring%20Freedom.htm.

8. DOUGLAS J. FEITH, WAR AND DECISION 104 (2008). Feith notes that there may have been Central Intelligence Agency paramilitary personnel on the ground in Afghanistan before October 19.

9. Convention for the Amelioration of the Condition of the Wounded and Sick in Armed Forces in the Field art. 2, Aug. 12, 1949, 6 U.S.T. 3114, 75 U.N.T.S. 31 [hereinafter Geneva Convention I]; Convention for the Amelioration of the Condition of Wounded, Sick and Shipwrecked Members of Armed Forces at Sea art. 2, Aug. 12, 1949, 6 U.S.T. 3217, 75 U.N.T.S. 85 [hereinafter Geneva Convention II]; Convention Relative to the Treatment of Prisoners of War art. 2, Aug. 12, 1949, 6 U.S.T. 3316, 75 U.N.T.S. 135 [hereinafter Geneva Convention III]; and Convention Relative to the Protection of Civilian Persons in Time of War art. 2, Aug. 12, 1949, 6 U.S.T. 3516, 75 U.N.T.S. 287 [hereinafter Geneva Convention IV]: all *reprinted in* DOCUMENTS ON THE LAWS OF WAR (Adam Roberts & Richard Guelff eds., 3d ed. 2000) at 197, 222, 244 and 301, respectively. Article 2 provides in pertinent part that "the present Convention shall apply to all cases of declared war or of any other armed conflict which may arise between two or more of the High Contracting Parties," i.e., international armed conflict.

10. Geneva Conventions I, II, III and IV, *supra* note 9, art. 3. Article 3 applies to all cases "of armed conflict not of an international character occurring in the territory of one of the High Contacting Parties," i.e., non-international armed conflict.

11. YORAM DINSTEIN, THE CONDUCT OF HOSTILITIES UNDER THE LAW OF INTERNATIONAL ARMED CONFLICT 14 (2004).

12. Stewart, *supra* note 7, at 16.

13. FEITH, *supra* note 8, at 165.

14. Protocol Additional to the Geneva Conventions of 12 August 1949, and Relating to the Protection of Victims of International Armed Conflicts art. 43(1), June 8, 1977, 1125 U.N.T.S. 3, *reprinted in* DOCUMENTS ON THE LAWS OF WAR, *supra* note 9, at 422 [hereinafter Additional Protocol I]. *See also* Geneva Convention I, *supra* note 9, art. 13(1).

15. Marco Sassòli, *Query: Is There a Status of "Unlawful Combatant"?*, *in* ISSUES IN INTERNATIONAL LAW AND MILITARY OPERATIONS 57, 61 (Richard B. Jaques ed., 2006) (Vol. 80, US Naval War College International Law Studies).

16. WILLIAM L. SHIRER, THE RISE AND FALL OF THE THIRD REICH 33–34, 42–43 (1960).

17. Posting of John B. Bellinger, Unlawful Enemy Combatants (Jan. 15, 2007), to http://opiniojuris.org/author/john-bellinger/.

18. COMMENTARY ON THE ADDITIONAL PROTOCOLS OF 8 JUNE 1977 TO THE GENEVA CONVENTIONS OF 12 AUGUST 1949, at 508 (Yves Sandoz, Christophe Swinarski & Bruno Zimmermann eds., 1987).

19. Geneva Convention III, *supra* note 9, art. 4A(1).

20. Draft Articles on the Responsibility of States for Internationally Wrongful Acts, Report of the International Law Commission on the Work of its Fifty-third Session, U.N. GAOR, 56th Sess., Supp. No. 10, U.N. Doc. A/56/10 (2001), *available at* http://untreaty.un.org/ilc/texts/instruments/english/draft%20articles/9_6_2001.pdf. Article 10 continues, "[t]he conduct of an insurrectional movement which becomes the new Government of a State shall be considered an act of that State under international law." Article 11 adds, "[c]onduct which is not attributable to a State under the preceding articles shall nevertheless be considered an act of that State under international law if and to the extent that the State acknowledges and adopts the conduct in question as its own." These articles appear to fairly encompass the Taliban's relation to the State of Afghanistan.

21. Geneva Convention III, *supra* note 9, art. 4A(1).

22. DINSTEIN, *supra* note 11, at 48. Footnote omitted.

23. Marco Sassòli argues, "This allegation may astonish those who remember that during Operation Enduring Freedom, the United States stressed that it attacked Taliban command and control centers and did not complain that it was impossible to distinguish the Taliban from civilians." Sassòli, *supra* note 15, at 61; *see also* Jennifer Elsea, Congressional Research Service, *Treatment of "Battlefield Detainees" in the War on Terrorism* (Jan. 13, 2005), at 7; Robert K. Goldman & Brian D. Tittemore, *Unprivileged Combatants and the Hostilities in Afghanistan: Their Status and Rights Under International Humanitarian and Human Rights Law*, ASIL TASK FORCE PAPERS (American Society of International Law), Dec. 2002, at 23–31, *available at* http://www.pegc.us/archive/Journals/goldman.pdf; George H. Aldrich, *Editorial Comments, The Taliban, Al Qaeda, and the Determination of Illegal Combatants*, 96 AMERICAN JOURNAL OF INTERNATIONAL LAW 891, 894 (2002).

24. Geneva Convention III, *supra* note 9, art. 5; Additional Protocol I, *supra* note 14, art. 45.1. George Aldrich writes,

> Without a doubt, the most difficult element to defend of the decisions made . . . with respect to the prisoners taken in Afghanistan is the blanket nature of the decision to

> deny POW status to the Taliban prisoners. By one sweeping determination, the president ruled that not a single Taliban soldier, presumably not even the army commander, could qualify for POW status under the Geneva Convention.

Aldrich, *supra* note 23, at 897.

25. Geneva Convention III, *supra* note 9, art 5.

26. Elsea, *supra* note 23, at 7.

27. Aldrich, *supra* note 23, at 893 ("Its methods brand it as a criminal organization under national laws and as an international outlaw").

28. *See* Geneva Convention IV, *supra* note 9, art. 33; Additional Protocol I, *supra* note 14, art. 51.2; Protocol Additional to the Geneva Conventions of 12 August 1949, and Relating to the Protection of Victims of Non-International Armed Conflicts arts. 4(2)(d) & 13(2), June 8, 1977, 1125 U.N.T.S. 609, *reprinted in* DOCUMENTS ON THE LAWS OF WAR, *supra* note 9, at 483 [hereinafter Additional Protocol II].

29. *See* Memorandum from John C. Yoo & Robert Delahunty to William J. Haynes II, General Counsel, Department of Defense, Re: Application of Treaties and Laws to al Qaeda and Taliban Detainees (Jan. 9, 2002), *reprinted in* THE TORTURE PAPERS: THE ROAD TO ABU GHRAIB 38 (Karen J. Greenberg & Joshua Dratel eds., 2005) [hereinafter Yoo Memorandum] ("Common Article 2 . . . is limited only to cases of declared war or armed conflict 'between two or more of the High Contracting Parties.' Al Qaeda is not a High Contracting Party . . . Al Qaeda is not covered by common Article 3, because the current conflict is not covered by the Geneva Conventions. . . . Article 3 . . . shows that the Geneva Conventions were intended to cover either: a) traditional wars between Nation States . . . or non-international civil wars . . . . Our conflict with al Qaeda does not fit into either category"). The same conclusion applied to the Taliban ("Article 2 states that the Convention shall apply to all cases of declared war or other armed conflict between the High Contracting Parties. But there was no war or armed conflict between the United States and Afghanistan . . . if Afghanistan was stateless at that time. No[r], of course, is there a state of war or armed conflict between the United States and Afghanistan *now*"). And "[e]ven if Afghanistan under the Taliban were not deemed to have been a failed State, the President could still regard the Geneva Conventions as temporarily suspended during the current military action."

30. *See* Memorandum from Colin L. Powell to Counsel to the President & Assistant to the President for National Security Affairs, Draft Decision Memorandum for the President on the Applicability of the Geneva Convention to the Conflict in Afghanistan (Jan. 26, 2002), *reprinted in* TORTURE PAPERS, *supra* note 29, at 122.

31. Memorandum from William H. Taft IV, Legal Adviser, Department of State, to Counsel to the President, Comments on Your Paper on the Geneva Convention (Feb. 2, 2002), *reprinted in id.* at 129.

32. Yoo Memorandum, *supra* note 29 ("The weight of informed opinion strongly supports the conclusion that . . . Afghanistan was a 'failed State' whose territory had been largely overrun and held by violence by a militia or faction rather than by a government. Accordingly, Afghanistan was without the attributes of statehood necessary to continue as a party to the Geneva Conventions, and the Taliban militia[,] like al Qaeda, is therefore not entitled to the protections of the Geneva Convention").

33. Memorandum from Jay S. Bybee to Alberto R. Gonzales, Counsel to the President, & William J. Haynes II, General Counsel of the Department of Defense, Re: Application of Treaties and Laws to al Qaeda and Taliban Detainees (Jan. 22, 2002), *reprinted in* TORTURE PAPERS, *supra* note 29, at 81 ("Further, common Article 3 addresses only non-international conflicts that occur within the territory of a single state party, again, like a civil war. This provision would not reach

an armed conflict in which one of the parties operated from multiple bases in several different states").

34. Exec. Order No. 13,440, 72 Fed. Reg. 40,707 (July 24, 2007), *available at* http://www.fas.org/irp/offdocs/eo/eo-13440.htm ("On February 7, 2002, I determined for the United States that members of al Qaeda, the Taliban, and associated forces are unlawful enemy combatants who are not entitled to the protections that the Third Geneva Convention provides to prisoners of war. I hereby reaffirm that determination . . .").

35. Hamdan v. Rumsfeld, 548 U.S. 557, 629–31 (2006).

36. RICARDO SANCHEZ, WISER IN BATTLE 144 (2008).

37. Memorandum from the Secretary of Defense to the Chairman of the Joint Chiefs of Staff, Status of Taliban and Al Qaeda (Jan. 19, 2002), *reprinted in* TORTURE PAPERS, *supra* note 29, at 80.

38. JACK GOLDSMITH, THE TERROR PRESIDENCY 120 (2007).

39. Ex parte Quirin, 317 U.S. 1 (1942).

40. Mark D. Maxwell & Sean M. Watts, *'Unlawful Enemy Combatant': Status, Theory of Culpability, or Neither?*, 5 JOURNAL OF INTERNATIONAL CRIMINAL JUSTICE 19, 21 (2007).

41. Marco Sassòli, *The Status of Persons Held in Guantánamo under International Humanitarian Law,* 2 JOURNAL OF INTERNATIONAL CRIMINAL JUSTICE 96, 123 (2004).

42. Kenneth Watkin, *21st Century Conflict and International Humanitarian Law: Status Quo or Change?, in* INTERNATIONAL LAW AND ARMED CONFLICT: EXPLORING THE FAULTLINES 265, 286 (Michael N. Schmitt & Jelena Pejic eds., 2007).

43. Charles H. B. Garraway, *'Combatants' – Substance or Semantics?, in id.*, at 327.

44. US Department of Defense, Directive 2310.01E, The Department of Defense Detainee Program (Sept. 5, 2006), *available at* http://www.dtic.mil/whs/directives/corres/pdf/231001p.pdf.

45. Chairman of the Joint Chiefs of Staff, Joint Publication 3-63, Detainee Operations, at I-4 (2008).

46. Stewart, *supra* note 7, at 10–16.

47. Staff Report, *26th MEU Tapped for Enduring Freedom*, MARINE CORPS TIMES (Nov. 26, 2001), at 9; Gordon Lubold, *Marines Prepare to Leave Afghanistan*, MARINE CORPS TIMES (Jan. 7, 2002), at 10.

48. Afghanistan's first US military killed in action was Army Sgt. 1st Class Nathan R. Chapman, killed in a January 1, 2002 firefight in Paktia.

49. For Predator characteristics, see MQ-1 Predator Unmanned Aircraft System, http://www.af.mil/factsheets/factsheet.asp?fsID=122; Predator RQ-1 / MQ-1 / MQ-9 Reaper - Unmanned Aerial Vehicle (UAV), USA, http://www.airforce-technology.com/projects/predator (both last visited Feb. 24, 2009).

50. It may be argued that the Vietnam War's Phoenix Program, Operation El Dorado Canyon (the 1986 bombing of Libyan leader Muammar Qadhafi), or the attacks on Osama Bin Laden in 1998 (when he was linked to the bombing of US embassies in Dar es Salaam and Nairobi), constituted targeted killing. Those attacks may also be argued to be assassinations and attempted assassinations, mounted with political rather than tactical motives.

51. Seymour M. Hersh, *Manhunt*, NEW YORKER, Dec. 23, 2002, at 66.

52. *No holds barred,* ECONOMIST, Nov. 7, 2002, at 49.

53. There are other definitions in scholarly articles. One, for example, is "[p]remeditated killing of an individual by a government or its agents." William C. Banks & Peter Raven-Hansen, *Targeted Killing and Assassination: The U.S. Legal Framework,* 37 UNIVERSITY OF RICHMOND LAW REVIEW 667, 671 (2003). Another is "the intentional killing of a specific civilian who cannot

reasonably be apprehended, and who is taking a direct part in hostilities, the targeting done at the direction and authorization of the state in the context of an international or noninternational armed conflict." Gary D. Solis, *Targeted Killing and the Law of Armed Conflict*, NAVAL WAR COLLEGE REVIEW, Spring 2007, at 127, 127.

54. NILS MELZER, TARGETED KILLING IN INTERNATIONAL LAW 5 (2008).

55. *See, e.g.*, Second Expert Meeting: Direct Participation in Hostilities under International Humanitarian Law (Oct. 25–26, 2004), *available at* http://www.icrc.org/Web/eng/siteeng0.nsf/htmlall/participation-hostilities-ihl-311205/$File/Direct_participation_in_hostilities_2004_eng.pdf.

56. MELZER, *supra* note 54, at 9–10.

57. Will Lester, *Poll Finds Support for Use of Torture in War on Terror*, WASHINGTON TIMES, Dec. 7, 2005, at A1.

58. *See* Press Release, The White House, President Discusses Creation of Military Commissions to Try Suspected Terrorists (Sept. 6, 2006), *available at* http://georgewbush-whitehouse.archives.gov/news/releases/2006/09/20060906-3.html ("In some cases, we determine that individuals we have captured pose a significant threat, or may have intelligence that we and our allies need . . . and they withhold information that could save American lives. In these cases, it has been necessary to move these individuals to an environment where they can be held secretly, questioned by experts, and—when appropriate—prosecuted for terrorist acts").

59. *Self-licensed to kill*, ECONOMIST, Aug. 4, 2001, at 12 ("Israel justifies these extra-judicial killings as self-defense. . . . But the usual context of such a discussion would be that the two sides involved were at war . . . ."); Editorial, *Assassination Ill Befits Israel*, NEW YORK TIMES, Oct. 7, 1997, at A24 ("[T]rying to assassinate Palestinian leaders in revenge is not the answer").

60. In 1989, Abraham D. Sofaer, then US State Department Legal Adviser, equivocated:

> While the U.S. regards attacks on terrorists being protected in the sovereign territory of other States as potentially justifiable when undertaken in self-defense, a State's ability to establish the legality of such an action depends on its willingness openly to accept responsibility for the attack, to explain the basis for its action, and to demonstrate that reasonable efforts were made prior to the attack to convince the State whose territorial sovereignty was violated to prevent the offender's unlawful activities from occurring.

Abraham D. Sofaer, *Terrorism, the Law, and the National Defense,* 126 MILITARY LAW REVIEW 89, 121 (1989).

61. James Risen & David Johnston, *Bush Has Widened Authority of C.I.A. to Kill Terrorists,* NEW YORK TIMES, Dec. 15, 2002, at A1.

62. MELZER, *supra* note 54, at 41, 409.

63. Associated Press, *9 Suspected Insurgents Killed in Missile Strike, Pakistan Says*, NEW YORK TIMES, Aug. 14, 2008, at A7.

64. Josh Meyer, *CIA Expands Use of Drones in Terror War*, LOS ANGELES TIMES, Jan. 29, 2006, at A1 ("The Predator strikes have killed at least four senior al Qaeda leaders, but also many civilians, and it is not known how many times they missed their targets").

65. *See, e.g.*, Candace Rondeaux, *Civilian Airstrike Deaths Probed*, WASHINGTON POST, July 25, 2008, at A12 ("78 have died in three incidents this month alone, Afghan officials say"); Carlotta Gall, *British Criticize U.S. Air Attacks in Afghan Region,* NEW YORK TIMES, Aug. 9, 2007, at A1.

66. US GOVERNMENT ACCOUNTABILITY OFFICE, AFGHAN SECURITY: EFFORTS TO ESTABLISH ARMY AND POLICE HAVE MADE PROGRESS, BUT FUTURE PLANS NEED TO BE BETTER DEFINED 5 (2005), *available at* http://www.gao.gov/new.items/d05575.pdf.

67. US Department of State, *Timeline — Key Events in Afghanistan's Political and Economic Reconstruction*, Jan. 26, 2006, http://www.america.gov/st/pubs-english/2006/January/20060126120012dpnosmoht0.9750482.html.

68. Agreement on Provisional Arrangements in Afghanistan Pending the Re-establishment of Permanent Government Institutions, attached to Letter from the Secretary-General addressed to the President of the Security Council para. I.3, U.N. Doc. S/2001/1154 (Dec. 5, 2001), *available at* http://www.afghangovernment.com/AfghanAgreementBonn.htm ("Upon the official transfer of power, the Interim Authority shall be the repository of Afghan sovereignty. . . . As such, it shall, throughout the interim period, represent Afghanistan in its external relations and shall occupy the seat of Afghanistan at the United Nations . . . ").

69. Christian Lowe, *Leathernecks Aim to Take Back a Province*, MARINE CORPS TIMES, June 28, 2004, at 10.

70. Paul Merida, *Dismounted Infantry Operations*, MARINE CORPS GAZETTE, Nov. 2004, at 39.

71. James W. Garner, *Contributions, Requisitions, and Compulsory Service in Occupied Territory*, 11 AMERICAN JOURNAL OF INTERNATIONAL LAW 106 (1917).

72. II GEORG SCHWARZENBERGER, INTERNATIONAL LAW AS APPLIED BY INTERNATIONAL COURTS AND TRIBUNALS: THE LAW OF ARMED CONFLICT 230 (1968).

73. Charter of the International Military Tribunal arts. 6(b) & 6(c), Aug. 8, 1945, 59 Stat. 1544, 82 U.N.T.S. 280, *available at* http://avalon.law.yale.edu/imt/imtconst.asp.

74. *See, e.g.*, Trial of Robert Wagner, Gauleiter and Six Others (Perm. Milit. Trib. at Strasboug, 1946, and Ct. of Appeal, July 24, 1946), III LAW REPORTS OF TRIALS OF WAR CRIMINALS 23 (UN War Crimes Commission, 1948); Trial of Jean-Pierre Lex (Perm. Milit. Trib. at Nancy, May 13, 1946), VII LAW REPORTS OF TRIALS OF WAR CRIMINALS 23 (UN War Crimes Commission, 1948).

75. Article 147 of Geneva Convention IV makes the unlawful transfer of protected persons from an occupied area a grave breach, as does Additional Protocol I. Additional Protocol I, *supra* note 14, art. 85.4(a).

76. COMMENTARY IV GENEVA CONVENTION RELATIVE TO THE PROTECTION OF CIVILIAN PERSONS IN TIME OF WAR 278–79 (Jean S. Pictet ed., 1958).

77. Additional Protocol II, *supra* note 28, art. 17.2.

78. Statute of the International Criminal Court art. 8(2)(e), July 17, 1998, 2187 U.N.T.S. 90, *available at* http://www.un.org/law/icc/statute/romefra.htm.

79. Statute of the International Criminal Tribunal for the former Yugoslavia art. 5(d), S.C. Res. 827, U.N. Doc. S/RES/827 (May 23, 1993), *available at* http://www.icls.de/dokumente/icty_statut.pdf; Statute of the International Criminal Tribunal for Rwanda art. 3(d), S.C. Res. 955, U.N. Doc. S/RES/955 (Nov. 8, 1994), *available at* http://www.un.org/ictr/statute.html.

80. 1 CUSTOMARY INTERNATIONAL HUMANITARIAN LAW 458 (Rule 129) (Jean-Marie Henckaerts & Louise Doswald-Beck eds., 2005). The study notes that Israel argues that Article 49 of Geneva Convention IV was not meant to apply to the deportation of selected individuals for reasons of public order and security, and that Article 49 is not customary international law and contrary deportation orders under Israeli domestic law were lawful. *Id.*

81. *Id.* at 459 & 457.

82. Geneva Convention IV, *supra* note 9, art. 76.

83. Article 4 of Geneva Convention IV provides in pertinent part that "nationals of a co-belligerent State, shall not be regarded as protected persons while the State of which they are nationals has normal diplomatic representation in the State in whose hands they are."

84. Knut Dörmann, *The Legal Situation of "Unlawful/Unprivileged Combatants,"* 85 INTERNATIONAL REVIEW OF THE RED CROSS 45 (2003). In US domestic law, in the Military Commissions Act of 2006, an unlawful combatant is defined as a person who has engaged in, or purposefully and materially supported another in engaging in, hostilities against the United States and its allies, and who does not qualify as a lawful combatant, or an individual who has been deemed an unlawful enemy combatant by a Combatant Status Review Tribunal or any other competent tribunal. Military Commissions Act of 2006 § 948 a(1), Pub. L. No. 109-366, 120 Stat. 2600 (Oct. 17, 2006) (codified in 10 U.S.C. § 47(A)).

85. DINSTEIN, *supra* note 11, at 29.

86. Jelena Pejic, *'Unlawful/Enemy Combatants': Interpretations and Consequences*, *in* INTERNATIONAL LAW AND ARMED CONFLICT, *supra* note 42, at 340; Department of the Army, FM 27-10, The Law of Land Warfare para. 31 (1956); UK MINISTRY OF DEFENCE, THE MANUAL OF THE LAW OF ARMED CONFLICT para. 9.18.1 (2004); Prosecutor v. Delalic, Case No. IT-96-21-T, Judgment, para. 271 (Nov. 16, 1998).

87. WILLIAM A. SCHABAS, THE UN INTERNATIONAL CRIMINAL TRIBUNALS 252–53 (2006), *citing* Prosecutor v. Naletilic et al., Case No. IT-98-34-T, Judgment, paras. 519–21 (Mar. 31, 2003).

88. Prosecutor v. Kristic, Case No. IT-98-33-T, Trial Chamber Judgment, paras. 521, 531–32 (Aug. 2, 2001). *See also* Prosecutor v. Naletilic, *supra* note 87, para. 519, where "forcible transfer" is defined as "the movement of individuals under duress from where they reside to a place that is not of their choosing."

89. Prosecutor v. Stakic, Case No. IT-97-24-T, Judgment, para. 662 (July 31, 2003).

90. Draft Memorandum from Jack I. Goldsmith, Assistant Attorney General, to Alberto R. Gonzales, Counsel to the President, Re: Permissibility of Relocating Certain "Protected Persons" from Occupied Iraq (Mar. 19, 2004), *reprinted in* TORTURE PAPERS, *supra* note 29, at 367.

91. John R. Crook, *Contemporary Practice of the United States Relating to International Law, Reported Removal of Prisoners from Iraq*, 99 AMERICAN JOURNAL OF INTERNATIONAL LAW 253, 266 (2005).

92. John R. Crook, *Contemporary Practice of the United States Relating to International Law*, 99 AMERICAN JOURNAL OF INTERNATIONAL LAW 479, 484 (2005).

93. Jelena Pejic, *Terrorist Acts and Groups: A Role for International Law?*, 75 BRITISH YEARBOOK OF INTERNATIONAL LAW 71, 94 (2004).

94. Dana Priest, *Memo Lets CIA Take Detainees Out of Iraq*, WASHINGTON POST, Oct. 24, 2004, at A1. Six of the initial detainees were Algerians captured in Bosnia and were reportedly turned over to the CIA.

95. In South Vietnam, from January 1965 to March 1973, 201 soldiers and 77 Marines were convicted by courts-martial of serious offenses against Vietnamese noncombatants. Ninety-five soldiers and twenty-seven Marines were convicted of murder or manslaughter of Vietnamese noncombatants. GUENTER LEWY, AMERICA IN VIETNAM 324–25 (1978).

96. During the US-Vietnam conflict, the US Army in Vietnam, at the direction of then-Colonel George Prugh, the Military Assistance Command–Vietnam Staff Judge Advocate, recorded the numbers of LOAC offenses referred to courts-martial. When he was transferred from theater, the accounting coasted to a close. *See* GEORGE S. PRUGH, LAW AT WAR: VIETNAM 1964–1973 (1975).

97. *130 Yanks Abused Inmates – Pentagon*, DAILY NEWS (New York), Dec. 16, 2004, at 1.

98. Eric Schmitt, *Pentagon Officials Are Hurrying to Correct Conditions in Iraqi Prisons*, NEW YORK TIMES, Sept. 9, 2004, at A14, citing 111 cases in Iraq.

99. Douglas Jehl & Eric Schmitt, *U.S. Military Says 26 Inmate Deaths May Be Homicide*, NEW YORK TIMES, Mar. 16, 2005, at A1.

100. John Hendren, *Autopsies Support Abuse Allegations*, LOS ANGELES TIMES, Oct. 25, 2005, at A1.

101. Drew Brown, *Report: U.S. Detainees' Deaths Go Unaccounted*, PHILADELPHIA INQUIRER, Feb. 23, 2006, at A2.

102. Carlotta Gall, *U.N. Monitor of Afghan Rights Accuses U.S. on Detentions*, NEW YORK TIMES, Apr. 23, 2005, at A4; Tim Golden, *Army Faltered in Investigating Detainee Abuse*, NEW YORK TIMES, May 22, 2005, at A1; Tim Golden, *Case Dropped Against U.S. Officer in Beating Deaths of Afghan Inmates*, NEW YORK TIMES, Jan. 8, 2006, § 1, at 13; Tim Golden, *Years After 2 Afghans Died, Abuse Case Falters*, NEW YORK TIMES, Feb. 13, 2006, at A1; Paul von Zielbauer, *Green Berets Face Hearing on Killing of Suspect in Afghan Village*, NEW YORK TIMES, Sept. 18, 2007, at A11.

103. Griff Witte, *Marines Open Fire After Afghan Ambush*, WASHINGTON POST, Mar. 5, 2007, at A11; Ann Scott Tyson, *Marine Unit Is Told to Leave Afghanistan*, WASHINGTON POST, Mar. 24, 2007, at A12; David S. Cloud, *U.S. Military Opens Inquiry Into Whether Marines Killed 10 Afghans After Attack on Convoy*, NEW YORK TIMES, Mar. 24, 2007, at A6; Carlotta Gall, *Marines' Actions Called Excessive in Afghanistan*, NEW YORK TIMES, Apr. 15, 2007, at A1; Paul von Zielbauer, *Criminal Charges Are Expected Against Marines, Official Says*, NEW YORK TIMES, Apr. 27, 2007, at A14; David S. Cloud, *U.S. Pays and Apologizes to Kin of Afghans Killed by Marines*, NEW YORK TIMES, May 9, 2007, at A12; Josh White, *69 Afghans' Families Get a U.S. Apology*, WASHINGTON POST, May 9, 2007, at A12; Peter Spiegel, *Apology Wrong, General Says*, LOS ANGELES TIMES, May 18, 2007, at A7; Paul von Zielbauer, *Marines to Conduct Inquiry Into the Killings of Afghan Civilians in March*, NEW YORK TIMES, Oct. 12, 2007, at A10; Paul von Zielbauer, *Marine Inquiry Into Afghan Killings to Look at 2 Officers, Lawyer Says*, NEW YORK TIMES, Oct. 21, 2007, at A10; David Zucchino, *Marines Were Shot At, Army Expert Testifies*, LOS ANGELES TIMES, Jan. 26, 2008, at A14; Thom Shanker, *Marines Won't Charge 2 Officers Whose Men Killed Afghans After Car Bombing*, NEW YORK TIMES, May 24, 2008, at A5; Andrew Tilghman, *No Criminal Charges*, MARINE CORPS TIMES, June 2, 2008, at 10.

104. Gary Solis, *Military Justice?*, US NAVAL INSTITUTE PROCEEDINGS, Oct. 2006, at 24.

105. Christian Lowe, *A Mission Ends*, MARINE CORPS TIMES, May 29, 2006, at 14.

106. *See, e.g.*, Thomas Harding, *Despatch*, DAILY TELEGRAPH (London), June 2, 2007, at 21; Norma Greenaway, *U.S. public wakens to forgotten war; Almost no debate on merits of involvement in Afghanistan except to beat up on Bush*, GAZETTE (Montreal), Aug. 13, 2007, at A14; *In Europe, Gates to push for NATO help in Afghanistan*, CHRISTIAN SCIENCE MONITOR, Dec. 23, 2007, § USA, at 2.

107. Ann Scott Tyson, *U.S. to Bolster Forces in Afghanistan*, WASHINGTON POST, Jan. 10, 2008, at A4 ("The United States now provides about 26,000 of the roughly 54,000 foreign troops in Afghanistan and has the lead combat role in the eastern part of the country, while U.S. Special Operations forces operate in all regions. British, Canadian, Australian and Dutch forces play key combat roles in southern Afghanistan, where violence has surged in the past year . . . ").

108. Kimberly Johnson, *Conway: 2-Front war will overstretch Corps*, MARINE CORPS TIMES, Feb. 4, 2008, http://www.marinecorpstimes.com/news/2008/02/marine_conway_080202/. The Commandant of the Marine Corps is quoted by Johnson as saying: "We can't have one foot in Afghanistan and one foot in Iraq. I believe that would be—an analogy would be having one foot in the canoe and one foot on the bank. You can't be there long."

109. Reuters, NATO seeks to replace U.S. Marine Afghan mission, Reuters AlertNet, June 13, 2008, http://www.alertnet.org/thenews/newsdesk/L13172622.htm.

110. Amy Balasco, Congressional Research Service, *The Cost of Iraq, Afghanistan, and Other Global War on Terror Operations Since 9/11* (July 14, 2008), at summary page.

111. Carlotta Gall, *Scars of a Deadly Insurgency Line Afghanistan's Main Road*, NEW YORK TIMES, Aug. 14, 2008, at A1.

112. Carlotta Gall, *Ragtag Taliban Show Tenacity in Afghanistan*, NEW YORK TIMES, Aug. 4, 2008, at A1.

113. Mark Mazzetti, *U.S. Analyst Depicts Al Qaeda as Secure in Pakistan and More Potent Than in 2007*, NEW YORK TIMES, Aug. 13, 2008, at A7.

114. Bartle B. Bull, *The Wrong Force for the 'Right War,'* NEW YORK TIMES, Aug. 14, 2008, at A23.

115. Press Release, National Intelligence Counsel, Declassified Key Judgments of the National Intelligence Estimate, 'Trends in Global Terrorism: Implications for the United States' dated April 2006, http://www.dni.gov/press_releases/Declassified_NIE_Key_Judgments.pdf (last visited Feb. 26, 2009).

116. David Wood, *Short-Term Strategies Threaten Success*, BALTIMORE SUN, Apr. 1, 2008, at 1.

117. Jason Straziuso, *Narrow Mission for Marines in Lush Afghan Poppy Fields*, HOUSTON CHRONICLE, May 3, 2008, at A24; Paul Wiseman, *In Afghanistan, Marines Begin Assault on Taliban*, USA TODAY, Apr. 29, 2008, at 6.

118. Rory Stewart, *How to Save Afghanistan*, TIME, July 28, 2008, at 30, 32.

119. *Afghanistan on Fire*, NEW YORK TIMES, Aug. 21, 2008, at A22.

X

Combatants

W. Hays Parks*

Law school professors are known for devising complex, convoluted examination questions with factual situations at best remotely associated with reality. The following, for a fictitious law of war course final examination, might be viewed as representative:

> State A is a sovereign State with a functioning government enjoying diplomatic relations with other nations. It is a member of the United Nations in good standing and since 1956 a State party to the 1949 Geneva Conventions. It is not a State party to the 1977 Protocols I and II Additional to the 1949 Geneva Conventions.
>
> State B invades State A, displaces its government, and installs its own government. States C, D, E and others covertly provide funding and other support, including weapons, to indigenous resistance movements within State A, eventually forcing State B to withdraw. Subsequently, the puppet government installed by State B during its occupation is overthrown by a tribal faction (Faction 1) covertly funded and supported by States C and D. Other tribes (Faction 2), with limited support from outside sources, oppose rule by Faction 1. Neither replaces the previous government as the factions compete for control. The situation deteriorates into a civil war.

---

* Senior Associate Deputy General Counsel, International Affairs Division, Office of General Counsel, US Department of Defense. Statements contained herein are the personal views of the author and may not necessarily reflect official positions of the Department of Defense or any other agency of the United States government.

Factions 1 and 2 are loose amalgamations of occasional if disparate indigenous tribal alliances. Following long-standing custom within State A, tribal groups change sides, and back again, as battle momentum shifts. Faction 1 replaces personnel casualties and tribal defections primarily from a pool of volunteer and dragooned men of the same tribe in neighboring State C, divided by an official but artificial border created by an unsuccessful colonial power a century earlier that bisects historic, common tribal territory.

Given their heavy financial investment in support of Faction 1 and, in the case of State C, for geopolitical reasons, States C and D decide they will recognize Faction 1 as the government of State A when Faction 1 gains control of the entire country. Each prematurely recognizes Faction 1 when it captures Faction 2's major city. Faction 1's success is short-lived. It suffers a significant military defeat, and retreats from Faction 2's major city and the territory Faction 2 controls. Resistance to Faction 1 continues with varying levels of intensity throughout State A except in its territory of origin, the southern one-third of State A.

Neither State C nor D withdraws its premature recognition of Faction 1. State F joins States C and D in recognizing Faction 1 in order to continue bird-hunting privileges its wealthy leaders enjoy in State A.

Faction 1 aggressively but unsuccessfully solicits recognition as the government of State A from the United Nations, the European Union or any of the remaining 190 nations. It hosts a transnational terrorist group, which trains and organizes foreign nationals within State A before the group attacks two embassies of State E in other nations, killing 224 civilians and injuring more than 4,000. State E responds with limited military action against training camps of the transnational terrorist group and requests that Faction 1 deliver to it the leader of the terrorist group. Faction 1 offers to do so if State E will recognize it. State E will not, and Faction 1 does not. State D support of and relations with Faction 1 deteriorate because of Faction 1's hosting the leader of the transnational terrorist group, a former citizen of State D. Faction 1 rapidly becomes an international pariah. Faction 1's power within the territory it controls declines.

Subsequently the transnational terrorist group hosted by Faction 1 launches a major attack on the territory of State E, a member of the North Atlantic Treaty Organization (NATO). Almost three thousand people, primarily civilians, representing more than ninety nations are killed or missing and presumed dead. The United Nations Security Council and NATO support military action against Faction 1 and the transnational terrorist group. State E joins with military forces of State G and those of other governments to engage in military operations in State A against tribal forces aligned with Faction 1 and the transnational terrorist group. States C, D and F withdraw their recognitions of Faction 1.

Throughout the fighting, Faction 1 tribes continue to operate in indigenous attire under tribal command and control rather than as conventional, highly structured, uniformed military forces. Members of the transnational terrorist group dress in all black or indigenous attire. Some special operations forces (SOF) from States E, G and other nations allied with them working with Faction 2 forces dress in Faction 2 tribal attire to avoid being targeted as high-value targets by Faction 1 and its transnational terrorist partners.

Tribal forces aligned with Faction 1 abandon their informal alliance with it to join with Faction 2 and military forces of States E and G to defeat Faction 1. The leaders of Faction 1 and the transnational terrorist group flee into tribal territorial areas in State C.

A new leader is identified to head a national, democratically elected government in State A. His government gains recognition from the United Nations and national governments (including States B, C, D, E, F and G) as the government of State A.

In the process of the military operations against Faction 1 and its transnational terrorist partner by States E and G, members of Faction 1 and the terrorist group are captured.

What is the law of war status of the members of Faction 1 and transnational terrorist group forces captured during operations by States E and G? Had States E and G special operations forces wearing Faction 2 attire been captured by Faction 1 forces or its transnational terrorist partners, would they have been entitled to prisoner of war status?

Before the al-Qaeda attack on the United States on September 11, 2001, and the military response of the United States against the Taliban and al-Qaeda, the scenario would have qualified as humorously improbable enough to have been a law school examination question. But it was precisely the situation faced by US and coalition military forces as they entered Afghanistan to commence offensive military operations against the Taliban and al-Qaeda in October 2001.

A simple—or perhaps better said, simplistic—approach would be to review the four 1949 Geneva Conventions to determine their applicability to Taliban and al-Qaeda fighters or to the SOF of States E and G wearing indigenous attire of the faction with which they were aligned.[1] However, as the fictitious professor's examination question suggests, the situation is far from simple. More information is necessary from factual, cultural and historical standpoints prior to determining the legal statuses of the individuals in question.

In an essay published in 2003, this author concluded that the Taliban was not the government of Afghanistan at the time coalition operations began against it in late 2001.[2] Three highly respected colleagues argued that the Taliban was the de facto government of Afghanistan.[3] Subsequent scholarship by historians, regional experts, military officers who served in Afghanistan during the period in question, official military histories and others provide more information than did contemporary media reports, enabling a clearer picture from which to conduct a fresh analysis of Taliban status. Moreover, media accounts in large do not understand legal nuances, such as the distinction between physical presence of armed groups in an area, international law conditions for a group to be regarded as a government or law of war criteria for *occupation*. "Occupation" in media parlance is a general term significantly different from the latter.

Following is a summary of the situation that existed during the period in question; analysis of the Taliban's status as a government and the combatant status of Taliban and al-Qaeda fighters; brief consideration of the law of war issue of US and other nations' special operations forces' wear of indigenous attire as they fought the Taliban and al-Qaeda; and analysis of the Bush administration's legal rationale for denial of prisoner of war status to captured al-Qaeda and Taliban.

In considering the fact situation and legal determinations one may draw from it, two leading scholars have emphasized the importance of information beyond the face of applicable treaties. Writing in his classic 1911 *War Rights on Land*, James Moloney Spaight argued:

> War law has never been presented to officers in an attractive form, as it might have been (I submit with diffidence) if the writers had insisted on the historical, human, and practical side rather than on the legal and theoretical one. But the difficulty of the subject, and the necessity for a careful study of it have not been brought home to officers: they underestimate its importance and complexity.[4]

More than eight decades later, Spaight's view was shared by Sir Adam Roberts:

> The laws of war are strange not only in their subject matter, which to many people seems a contradiction in terms, but also in their methodology. There is little tradition of disciplined and reasoned assessment of how the laws of war have operated in practice. Lawyers, academics, and diplomats have often been better at interpreting the precise legal meaning of existing accords or at generalizing about the circumstances in which they can or cannot work. In short, the study of the law needs to be integrated with the study of history: if not, it is inadequate.[5]

While the present author agrees with Spaight and Sir Adam as to the necessity to know and understand relevant history in order to apply the law, in cases such as the conflict in Afghanistan knowledge of more than history is necessary. An appreciation of a nation's history, its culture, its geography and other local factors may be necessary. Interpreting and applying the law of war is not always a matter of mirror imaging or "one size fits all." These factors are relevant in interpreting nuances in law of war treaties in order to determine their application. Understanding Afghanistan's regional and national history, its geography, its culture, political structure and law of war history are important in determining whether captured Taliban were entitled to prisoner of war status. So, too, are the history of the law of war and the history of (and therefore the meaning and intent of) specific treaty provisions. There is no evidence any of these factors were considered by senior political leaders and legal advisers in providing advice to President George W. Bush with regard to prisoner of war entitlement for captured Taliban. Looking at the conflict in Afghanistan between the Taliban and the United States and its coalition partners as one might consider an armed conflict in (for example) Norway, Switzerland or Australia is akin to considering the most common way to core an apple while holding a baseball; each may have the same shape, but otherwise they are uniquely different. Political and military leaders and their legal advisers must be mindful of the risk of automatically assuming all opponents and all situations fit neatly within the same treaty template. In the opening stages of US operations in Afghanistan, ignorance and skepticism of the law of war by some within the Bush administration resulted in errors of law and judgment with respect to the legal basis for law of war protection for captured Taliban and al-Qaeda, and the legal rationale for denial of prisoner of war status to them.[6]

In this regard this author has heard it said, "As all 194 nations are State parties to the 1949 Geneva Conventions, they have universal applicability." This statement, while factually and legally accurate, fails to recognize that legal *applicability* differs from *application* in fact. The quoted statement tends to suggest a perfect mirror imaging in *application.* The title of the volume in which Sir Adam's comments are contained—*The Laws of War: Constraints on Warfare in the Western World*—acknowledges not only the predominately Western European origins of the law of war but the challenges that may be faced in its application outside nations of Western European tradition.[7]

It is in this context that the question of the statuses of combatants in the war fought by the United States and its allies against the Taliban and al-Qaeda in Afghanistan in late 2001 is examined. The specific time frame will be from the arrival of the first US military ground force elements in Afghanistan on October 20, 2001,[8] to the signing of a memorandum by President George W. Bush on February 7, 2002 which, *inter alia,* accepted the conclusion of the Department of Justice denying prisoner of war status to captured Taliban and al-Qaeda.[9]

Afghanistan

Afghanistan has been described as having "three constants: perpetual internal fighting between tribal ethnic groups, the dominance of Islam in society, and intervention by external actors using this discord to achieve influence in the country."[10] A nation divided by mountainous terrain, limited in modern transportation development and with few large cities contributes to emphasis on tribal loyalty, a highly decentralized form of government and strong resistance to central authority by its citizens.[11] Understanding its culture and local dynamics is critical to understanding Afghanistan; in contrast to Western European nations, controlling Afghanistan's capital city of Kabul does not necessarily equal control of the entire nation, for example.[12] Even within tribes, rivalries and blood feuds were and are a constant. Historian Louis Dupree observed, "No Pashtun [the ruling class in Afghanistan for more than two centuries[13]] likes to be ruled by another . . . particularly someone from another tribe, sub-tribe, or section."[14] As is the case in other tribal-centric nations, tribes in Afghanistan historically have been inclined to suspend tribal rivalries and blood feuds to resist foreign invasion, if only briefly enough to defeat them before returning to their internal competition.[15] Shultz and Dew offer a Somali proverb that could be said to apply equally well to Afghanistan tribal warrior ways:

> Me and my clan against the world;
> Me and my family against my clan;
> Me and my brother against my family;
> Me against my brother.[16]

In the same context, the same authors, while again referring to clan tradition in Somalia, quote I. M. Lewis's observation that applies equally well to Afghanistan's tribal traditions: "Although they esteem fighting so highly, the pastoralists have no standing military organization or system of regiments. Armies and raiding parties are *ad hoc* formations and while feuds often last for years, and sometimes generations, they are generally waged in guerrilla campaigns."[17]

Afghanistan's history has included invasion by foreign powers and competition for its control as a commercial route or "buffer zone" by foreign governments, most commonly known for the nineteenth-century competition between England and Russia first named "The Great Game" by Captain Arthur Conolly of the Bengal Cavalry, later popularized by Rudyard Kipling in his 1901 novel *Kim*.[18] In fighting one another or foreign invaders, alliances often were based on bargaining more than loyalties, and loyalties were fleeting. Tribal forces changed sides frequently as each saw the tide of battle shifting or if offered "a better deal" by the opposing force or a better chance for post-conflict success.[19]

Interim History: The British Colonial Period

British military history in Afghanistan is long in period of time, extensive, but for the most part beyond the scope of this author's topic.[20] However, it contains one point germane to understanding the situation on the ground in October 2001 and through the period in question.

The artificiality of Afghanistan's borders, particularly with respect to its eastern border with Pakistan, is the result of an arbitrary nineteenth-century colonial division of tribal territory for British security purposes. It is named for Sir Henry Mortimer Durand, who negotiated and drew a line dividing Wazari tribal territory to establish a border between Afghanistan and what today is Pakistan. In addition to the fact that a line drawn on a map seldom is easy to find with precision on the ground, particularly in terrain as rugged as that between Pakistan and Afghanistan, the "backdoor" it offered between the two nations played heavily in *mujahidin* support in fighting the Soviet occupation and Wazari support for the Taliban following the Soviet departure. Permanently resentful of the British-established border and accustomed to traveling unfettered by multiple footpaths between the two nations,[21] tribal traditions and support in armed conflict against opposing forces—whether indigenous or foreign—meant more to determining the way the Taliban manned, formed and commanded its forces than Western concepts of defined and marked borders, their sanctity, and military command and control. Tribal loyalty remained paramount.[22]

Afghanistan enjoyed relative stability and modernization during the reign of King Muhammed Zahir Shah (1933–1973). A "constitutional monarchy" was established on October 1, 1963.[23] On July 17, 1973, his cousin Daoud executed a bloodless coup during the king's absence from the country to abolish the monarchy and become Afghanistan's first president and head of the communist People's Democratic Party of Afghanistan (PDPA). Unable to achieve nationwide economic and agricultural reform,[24] he was murdered five years later by PDPA members. His assassination and other PDPA failures eventually led to the overt Soviet invasion on December 22, 1979.[25]

The Soviet occupation, Afghan resistance and US covert assistance to the latter against the former have been well told and became the subject of a popular movie.[26] Soviet forces faced a *mujahidin* resistance repeating the historic practice of indigenous foes joining forces to resist a foreign invader.[27] Unable to defeat the *mujahidin* resistance funded and supplied by China, Egypt, Iran, Pakistan and the

United States and strongly supported by the indigenous population, the Soviet 40th Army withdrew on February 15, 1989.[28]

US and other foreign support to the *mujahidin* led to a case of unintended consequences, as it left heavily-armed forces in Afghanistan, described by one author as "a network of jihadis without a jihad."[29] Refugee male children from the Soviet war in Afghanistan were placed in Saudi-funded *madrassas* in Pakistan teaching the conservative Wahhabi rejection of "all modern interpretations of Islam as well as the mystical Sufi form of Islam,"[30] in essence providing a "farm club" of holy warriors for the Taliban in its eventual effort to seize control of Afghanistan even before the Taliban existed in name. Foreign financing of the *mujahidin* resistance funneled through Pakistan's Inter-Services Intelligence Directorate (ISID) reversed religious toleration and other modern, liberal practices that existed in the 1970s, replacing them with narrow Islamic views.[31]

Soviet military withdrawal from Afghanistan left in place remnants of the weak Afghan (PDPA) Army and the PDPA puppet regime headed by President Mohammed Najibullah. While the PDPA demise was regarded as inevitable, it was delayed until 1992 as *mujahidin* allies against the Soviet occupation endeavored to agree to a power-sharing agreement, without success. Following Afghan custom, they resumed fighting one another.[32] Continued fighting led to a civil war between the various factions, collapse of the PDPA, and the replacement of the Najibullah government by one headed by President Burhanuddin Rabbani of the Islamic Council of Afghanistan. Tribal fighting continued and lawlessness increased, leading to Taliban emergence in 1994.[33] President Rabbani's departure in 1996 resulted in collapse of the remaining limited central government infrastructure, leaving Afghanistan in the position of a failed State, existing in name only.[34]

Taliban characteristics and origins arguably can be traced to the Wahhabi sect founded by Mohammed ibn Abd al-Wahhab in the eighteenth century,[35] but its contemporary formation originated in 1994 in Pashtun-dominated southern Afghanistan.[36] The Taliban sought to "work with the deep social grain of rural conservatism, not interfering with the power of tribal elders and landowners, as long as the people followed Taliban religious practices."[37] Its inability to gain international recognition, discussed *infra*, lay in part in the philosophy of its leader, Mullah Mohammed Omar, who departed from Afghanistan's traditional international role, expressing indifference with respect to international relations and foreign policy and their necessity for Afghanistan.[38] Equally important, Loyn observes,

> [a]t the core of the new antimatter soul being formed for Afghanistan was "anti-education", in which boys were taught not about culture or the natural world, and

> certainly not to think for themselves—the bedrock of education in the developed world—but to believe that this was all taken care of for them by Islam.
>
> The madrassas became factories turning out Taliban fighters, many of them war orphans who knew no other life. "Talib" simply means "student", although the word came to mean specifically "religious student", and the madrassa system provided a formidable old-boy network, giving a sinuous strength and flexibility to the Taliban army, *which otherwise lacked a formal command structure.*[39]

In the battles of the mid- to late 1990s, momentum ebbed to and fro and, in Afghan tradition, tribal warlords and individual tribes switched sides frequently. Personnel replacements for Taliban lost in battle or through defections to anti-Taliban forces were drawn from volunteers from tribal areas in Pakistan and non-Afghan volunteers.[40] Efforts in 1996 by the Pakistani interior minister to have the Taliban join in consolidated opposition to the Northern Alliance were rebuffed by Taliban leader Mullah Omar. As a result, when the Taliban eventually recaptured the Afghan capital of Kabul on September 26, 1996, "they had few friends, and never secured the international recognition they craved."[41]

Taliban recapture of Kabul did not bring formal recognition from its primary financial backers, Saudi Arabia and Pakistan. It did result in a new warlord alliance called the "Supreme Council for the Defence of the Motherland" to oppose the Taliban.[42] The following spring the Taliban began its advance north. Concentration of agriculture, industry, mineral and gas resources in northern Afghanistan made a Taliban offensive critical to its consolidation of power.[43] Political leaders in Pakistan and Saudi Arabia agreed they would extend formal recognition to the Taliban as the government of Afghanistan when and if it controlled the entire country, then advanced recognition following Taliban seizure of the Northern Alliance city of Mazar-i-Sharif on May 24, 1997, optimistically but incorrectly concluding control of the entire country would follow soon thereafter.

In a set of circumstances reflecting the Byzantine nature of the Pakistani government and despite the fact that ISID agency Chief of Staff Ahmed Badeeb acknowledged that the Taliban "had no clue how to run a country,"[44] at ISID urging the Pakistani foreign ministry announced Pakistan's recognition of the Taliban as the government of Afghanistan on May 25, 1997, a decision Pakistani Prime Minister Nawaz Sharif learned of from a television news announcement. His aide recalled Sharif was "furious," wondering out loud who had made a decision that was his to make.[45]

The ISID, heavily invested in the Taliban in part to provide a safe haven for Pakistan's insurgency operations in Kashmir,[46] pressed Saudi Arabia to join it in recognition of the Taliban. "Due to Pakistani [ISID] insistence and to the lack of any other options so as to fill the obvious vacuum" in Afghanistan, Saudi Arabia followed suit the next day.[47] The United Arab Emirates (UAE), whose leadership enjoyed special hunting privileges in Pakistan and Taliban-controlled western Afghanistan, recognized the Taliban two days later.[48]

These announcements were premature. Taliban seizure of Mazar-i-Sharif lasted only hours following Pakistan's recognition announcement,[49] and became a deathtrap for Taliban forces. Mazar-i-Sharif's Uzbek/Shia population, joining forces with the Northern Alliance, killed three hundred Taliban and captured another thousand. Taliban killed or captured included its top ten leaders in the assault on Mazar-i-Sharif.[50] Anti-Taliban forces increased in strength as warlords switched sides in an anti-Taliban offensive that killed, captured, or wounded another six thousand Taliban, including 250 Pakistani fighters killed and another 550 captured. The Taliban swiftly retreated toward Kabul, en route destroying crops and poisoning wells,[51] relinquishing any claim to control of northern Afghanistan. The civil war intensified as aid and support to anti-Taliban forces increased from Iran, Turkey, India, Russia, Uzbekistan, Kazakhstan, Kyrgyzstan and Tajikistan.[52]

Nonetheless, and bolstered by the premature recognition by Pakistan, Saudi Arabia and the UAE, the Taliban sought US recognition. The Clinton administration declined. Following a confrontation between pro- and anti-Taliban factions within the Afghanistan embassy in Washington in August 1997, the State Department ordered the embassy closed, informing its representatives that "[a]s far as the United States was concerned, Afghanistan's existence as a government in the international system had been suspended."[53] No other nation joined Pakistan, Saudi Arabia and the UAE in their recognition of the Taliban as the government of Afghanistan. Taliban efforts to gain UN recognition were equally unsuccessful,[54] in large measure due to its ignorance of "U.N. procedures and even the U.N. Charter" and its own counterproductive actions against UN agencies attempting to provide humanitarian aid in Afghanistan, such as the High Commissioner for Refugees and the World Food Program. An increase in funding by Pakistan and Saudi Arabia for the Taliban and drafts of young jihadists from tribal areas in Pakistan enabled the Taliban to reconstitute its forces and in 1998 commence another attack into northern Afghanistan, including a renewed effort to capture Mazar-i-Sharif. While militarily successful, international antipathy toward the Taliban increased owing to Taliban actions against UN officials and non-government organizations; massacres of Uzbek, Tajik and Hazaras civilians in Mazar-i-Sharif; murder of captured opposing-force fighters;[55] and the murder of eleven Iranian diplomats taken from the Iranian consulate in Mazar-i-Sharif.[56]

The Taliban had become an international pariah. Its status was exacerbated by the al-Qaeda attack on US embassies in Nairobi, Kenya and Dar es Salaam, Tanzania, on August 7, 1998, killing 213 civilians in the former and eleven in the latter, and wounding more than four thousand civilians in the two attacks.[57] The US response included a cruise-missile attack on the suspected al-Qaeda training camp at Zawhar Kili on August 20, 1998[58] and an end of any further argument of pragmatism toward the Taliban within the State Department.[59] International outrage increased with the Taliban's September 18, 1998 destruction of the two thousand-year-old Buddha statues in Bamiyan.[60] The murder of the Iranian diplomats led to Iran moving a military force of two hundred thousand to its border with Afghanistan; a meeting between Taliban leader Mullah Omar and UN envoy Lakhdar Brahimi in Kandahar on October 14, 1998; a strong UN Security Council resolution threatening and eventually imposing international sanctions against the Taliban;[61] and Saudi Arabia's withdrawal of its diplomatic representation in Kabul and its termination of official funding to the Taliban because of its protection of al-Qaeda leader Usama bin Laden.[62] Additional UN Security Council resolutions condemning the Taliban and imposing sanctions followed through 1999, 2000 and into 2001 prior to the September 11 al-Qaeda attack on the United States as the Security Council "remain[ed] seized" with the matter.[63] By 2000, Taliban support for Islamic fundamentalist groups from Central Asia, Iran, Kashmir, China and Pakistan had led to its further international isolation, increased support to anti-Taliban forces[64] and increasing signs of the Taliban's weakening grip on territory within Afghanistan.[65] Reports by the United Nations Secretary-General in April and July 2001 requested by the General Assembly and Security Council, respectively, are revealing in their conclusions as to the Taliban's failures to act in any way as a governing authority within Afghanistan.[66]

Throughout the period in which the UN Security Council and the Secretary-General weighed or took actions against the Taliban, at no time did either refer to or suggest recognition of the Taliban as the government of Afghanistan.[67]

The al-Qaeda attacks in the United States on September 11, 2001 brought a rapid military response by the United States, acting under the authority of UN Security Council Resolution 1368,[68] and concurrent political reactions by the three nations previously aligned with the Taliban. The United Arab Emirates withdrew its recognition of the Taliban on September 22; Saudi Arabia, three days later; and Pakistan on November 22.

As previously noted, US offensive ground force operations against the Taliban and al-Qaeda formally commenced on the evening of October 19–20, 2001, with insertion of two US Army Special Forces detachments.[69] In less than two months, Taliban and al-Qaeda resistance had collapsed. Usama bin Laden and his al-Qaeda fled into Pakistan.[70] Taliban leader Mullah Omar survived, and fighting would continue, but the Taliban as a viable entity had disintegrated.[71]

Was the Taliban Entitled Legally to Recognition as the Government of Afghanistan?

The actions of Pakistan, Saudi Arabia and the United Arab Emirates are illustrative of political recognition of a nation or a new government. But recognition by three nations out of the 185 members of the United Nations does not warrant the conclusion that the Taliban constituted the de facto much less the *de jure* government of Afghanistan for the following reasons:

- The Taliban was a faction in a civil war in a failed State, that is, a State in which no central authority existed capable of carrying out the duties and responsibilities of a national government to its citizens.
- As established in the preceding pages, the Taliban
  - Had no organized, uniformed military, no strategic military plans, and no formal command and control structure characteristic of a regular military;
  - Consisted of tribal forces with little to no formal military instruction;[72]
  - Was composed of individuals loosely organized along tribal lines who rotated between civilian (tribal or family) obligations and serving as fighters on a daily or seasonal basis; and
  - Lacked the capacity to fulfill traditional responsibilities of a government, such as providing essential services (security, welfare and representation) to the people of Afghanistan.
- The United Nations, the European Union and 181 of the 185 nations declined to recognize the Taliban as the government of Afghanistan.
- The Afghanistan seat in the United Nations remained reserved for the government of Burhanuddin Rabbani which for all intents and purposes ceased to exist in 1994.
- The civil war did not end with the Taliban as a clear victor occupying, much less controlling, Afghanistan. At the time of commencement of US and coalition operations on October 20, 2001, the civil war continued, and Taliban power had eroded significantly.
- As the 2001 Secretary-General's report observed, the Taliban was unable to consolidate its military successes outside the predominately Pashtun southern Afghanistan region from which it originated.

• The Taliban refused to acknowledge Afghanistan's pre-existing international obligations, such as those of being a member of the United Nations, or through its actions as a State party to the 1949 Geneva Conventions.[73]

International law requirements for existence as a State are historic:

> First, there must be a people. . . .
>
> Second, there must be a fixed territory which the inhabitants occupy. . . .
>
> Third, there must be an organized government exercising control over, and endeavoring to maintain justice within, the territory.
>
> Fourthly, there must be capacity to enter into relations with the outside world.
>
> Fifthly, the inhabitants of the territory must have attained a degree of civilization such as to enable them to observe with respect to the outside world those principles of law which are deemed to govern the members of the international society in their relations with each other.[74]

The State of Afghanistan previously joined and was accepted into the community of nations as a member of the United Nations. Its ratification of the 1949 Geneva Conventions in 1956 was accepted by Switzerland, the depositary. No State objected to its ratification of the 1949 Geneva Conventions. Hence it may be presumed that each State regarded Afghanistan as having met statehood criteria one and two. Were all other questions answered in the affirmative, a question would remain as to whether in its time as a failed State and with the ascendancy of the Taliban it continued to meet the third, fourth and fifth criteria. The third criterion does not say "exercise control over a substantial portion of" a nation's territory, or suggest a percentage of territorial control as threshold criteria, but the territory as a whole. As to "maintaining justice within the territory," Professors Goldman and Tittemore acknowledge "the Taliban exercised few, if any, of the traditional activities of government."[75] This cannot be dismissed entirely as a characteristic of Afghan culture; more likely it is affirmation of the fact that the resources for the Taliban to govern were unavailable because they had been diverted to fighting the continuing civil war. In turning inward under the leadership of Mullah Omar, the Taliban defaulted on the fourth. In the wholesale murder of foreign diplomats, representatives of non-governmental organizations, its civilians because of different religious beliefs, and captured fighters—violations of human rights law and the law of war—there is no evidence the Taliban met the fifth criterion essential to its qualification as the government of Afghanistan.[76]

Assuming for sake of argument the five criteria could be met for the failed State of Afghanistan to restore its place among its peers, there remains the question of whether the Taliban itself became the rightful government of Afghanistan at any time prior to its defeat and collapse in December 2001. Changes internal to a nation are regarded as matters of domestic concern.[77] That said,

> [i]nasmuch, however, as the government of a State is the instrument through which it has official contact with the outside world and undertakes to respond to official obligations, a change of government and the methods by which it is wrought are matters of concern to foreign countries. They are concerned primarily with a question of fact—whether the regime seeking recognition is in actual control of the reins of government. No difficulty presents itself when a change is wrought through normal processes and the result is accepted as a mere incident in the life or growth of the State concerned. The situation may be obscure, however, when a contest for governmental control is waged by force of arms or by other processes not contemplated by the local law; the completeness of the success of a contestant may be fairly open to doubt for a protracted period, and even after its adherents assume to exercise the functions of a government. In such case foreign States may, and oftentimes do, withhold recognition until they are themselves assured where the victory really lies. The sufficiency of such assurance depends obviously upon the circumstances of the particular case; and it may follow close upon the heels of a *coup d'état*. The matter is unrelated to the mode whereby the success of a régime is achieved, except in so far as recourse to a particular method may breed doubt as to the security or permanence of the control that has been won.[78]

The decision as to whether or not to recognize a State, or a new government in a State, resides in governments of other sovereign nations, and, within a government, with the executive branch of each.[79]

By analogy, the law of war provides a way in which to determine whether the Taliban had gained de facto or *de jure* status. State A invades State B. In doing so, its military forces physically seize a portion of State B's territory. Under the law of belligerent occupation State A becomes an occupying power only when the territory State A's forces physically occupy "is actually placed under the *authority* of the hostile army."[80] Further, the occupation "extends only to the territory where such authority has been established and can be exercised."[81] A claimant must be able to exercise effective control; that is, an occupying power must be in a position to enforce the authority he is asserting over the territory and meet the obligations of an occupying power, which includes governing and providing various services (such as security and welfare) to the civilian population necessary to meet its day-to-day requirements.[82] Assuming this analogy is reasonable, the history of the civil war between Taliban and anti-Taliban factions from 1994 to 2001 never resulted in a situation in which the Taliban was able to enforce the authority it may have asserted over the territory it physically occupied, much less all of Afghanistan. The Secretary-General's July 13, 2001 report that "[a]ll regions of the country, with the exception of the southern [Pashtun] region, now include active conflict zones"[83] confirms the conclusion that while the Taliban may have enjoyed a physical presence in a large portion of Afghanistan, it was unable to consolidate its military gains and exercise effective control over these areas, much less establish the infrastructure to govern them. These are critical legal distinctions that media reports failed to make.

The facts on the ground and international law do not support a conclusion that the Taliban was the de facto, much less *de jure*, government of Afghanistan at any time from its emergence in 1994 to October 20, 2001, when US and coalition military operations commenced against al-Qaeda and the Taliban.[84]

Combatant and Prisoner of War Status and the Taliban and Al-Qaeda

Accepting *arguendo* the US position that its intervention in Afghanistan was an international armed conflict, entitlement to the combatant's privilege and, therefore, prisoner of war status upon capture is determined by provisions contained in Article 4 of the Geneva Convention (III) Relative to the Treatment of Prisoners of War of August 12, 1949 (hereinafter GPW).[85] Relevant GPW provisions provide entitlement to humane treatment to captured individuals entitled to the *combatant's privilege.*

Combatants are members of the established armed forces of a government who have a legal right to engage in combat operations. Combatants enjoy "combatant immunity" under international law, protecting them from prosecution for death or injury to persons or damage or destruction of property resulting from combatant acts that otherwise comply with the law of war in an armed conflict.[86] A combatant

- Has the right to carry out lawful attacks on enemy military personnel and military objectives;
- Is at risk of attack by enemy military forces at any time, wherever located, regardless of the duties or activities in which he or she is engaged;
- Bears no criminal responsibility (a) for killing or injuring (i) enemy military personnel or (ii) civilians taking a direct part in hostilities, or (b) for causing damage or destruction to property incidental to lawful military operations,

provided his or her acts, including the means employed to commit those acts, have been in compliance with the law of war; and

- If captured:
    - Is entitled to prisoner of war status,
    - May be detained indefinitely until cessation of active hostilities,
    - Is entitled to humane treatment,
    - May be tried for violations of the law of war, and
    - May only be punished for violations of the law of war as a result of a fair and regular trial.

Limitations on entitlement to the combatant's privilege are historic and an essential component of the equally historic law of war principle of *discrimination*. Although the origins of the modern law of war can be traced to classical Greek and Roman times, the Middle Ages provided its greatest development prior to the mid-nineteenth century. Today's law of war began as an amalgamation of the *jus militaire*, recognized military practice contained in rules of chivalry, and canon law known as the just war tradition.[87] Both *jus militaire* and the just war tradition included a requirement for "public war," that is, war authorized by *right* (that is, competent) *authority*. In the *jus militaire*, "public war" was the "antithesis of perfidy and cowardly assassinations, actions repugnant to the conception of chivalry and the membership of the various knightly orders in which knights belonged."[88] Individuals engaging in unauthorized acts of war were acting outside "faith and the law of nations." They were regarded as "marauders and freebooters," treated as war criminals if captured, and usually summarily executed.[89]

Paralleling *right authority* was the principle of discrimination/noncombatant (civilian) immunity. In the conduct of military operations, commanders were obligated to exercise reasonable care to protect innocent civilians from the harmful effects of combat operations. It also obligated combatants to distinguish themselves from the civilian population, and obligated civilians not to engage in combatant acts.

Through the near century and a half of development of the modern law of war, governments have retained exclusive authority to wage war for practical, political and humanitarian reasons. First is the responsibility of a government to protect its citizens. Second, a desire for stability in international relations necessitates a prohibition of unilateral acts by a civilian or civilians that may lead to war between nations.[90] Third, the prohibition on civilians engaging in combatant acts serves to implement and enforce the law of war principle of *discrimination*.[91] The private citizen who engages in battle is not entitled to the combatant's privilege and forfeits his or her protection as a civilian from direct attack for such time as he or she takes a direct part in hostilities.[92] If captured, he or she is not entitled to prisoner of war status and may be prosecuted for his or her actions.

Codification of the modern law of war and these distinctions originated in the midst of the US Civil War (1861–65). Dr. Francis Lieber, a Columbia College law professor, offered to draft a document for the Union Army delineating in practical terms existing law of war rules. President Lincoln accepted Lieber's offer. Signed by President Lincoln on April 24, 1863, as US General Orders No. 100, Lieber's *Instructions for the Government of Armies of the United States in the Field* became the primary source for treaty law developed over the next century.

Of direct relevance to the present discussion is a less-known product requested of Professor Lieber. On August 6, 1862, Henry Wager Halleck, General-in-Chief of the Union armies, wrote to Lieber seeking his advice and assistance in addressing the issue of private citizens engaging in unauthorized acts of war and Union law of war obligations toward captured Confederate guerrillas. General Halleck viewed partisans and guerrillas as synonymous. Professor Lieber made a distinction between the two in his essay reply, "Guerrilla Parties Considered with Reference to the Laws and Usages of War." Lieber argued that partisans enjoy a formal association with a government and its military forces (and entitlement to prisoner of war status), while guerrillas were

> self-constituted sets of armed men, in times of war, who form no integrant part of the organized army, do not stand on the regular pay-roll of the army, or are not paid at all, take up arms and lay them down at intervals, and carry on petty war (guerrilla) chiefly by raids, extortion, destruction, and massacre, and who cannot encumber themselves with many prisoners, and will therefore generally give no quarter.[93]

While Lieber does not identify opposing forces that might have been illustrative of each category, the Virginia cavalry unit commanded by Confederate Colonel John S. Mosby[94] is regarded as meeting Lieber's category of *partisans,* and therefore lawful combatants, while William C. Quantrill's private group of raiders in Missouri[95] were *guerrillas* (as he used the term in his analysis), and, as such, not entitled to the combatant's privilege or prisoner of war status.[96]

Lieber maintained this distinction in General Orders No. 100. Article 57 states, "[s]o soon as a man is armed by a sovereign government and takes the soldier's oath of fidelity, he is a belligerent; his killing, wounding, or other warlike acts are not individual crimes or offenses . . .," while acknowledging in Article 59 that "[a] prisoner of war remains answerable for his crimes committed against the captor's army or people . . . ." Article 81 of General Orders No. 100 states:

> Partisans are soldiers armed and wearing the uniform of their army, but belonging to a corps which acts detached from the main body for the purpose of making inroads into the territory occupied by the enemy. If captured, they are entitled to all the privileges of the prisoner of war.

In contrast, Article 82 declares:

> Men, or squads of men, who commit hostilities, whether by fighting, or inroads for destruction or plunder, or by raids of any kind, without commission, without being part and portion of the organized hostile army, and without sharing continuously in the war, but who do so with intermitting returns to their homes and avocations, or with the occasional assumption of the semblance of peaceful pursuits, divesting themselves of the character or appearance of soldiers—such men, or squads of men, are not public enemies, and, therefore, if captured, are not entitled to the privileges of prisoners of war, but shall be treated summarily as highway robbers or pirates.

Franc-tireur actions in the Franco-Prussian War and the debate over military operations by Boer farmers dressed in civilian clothing in the Anglo-Boer War (1899–1902) brought the issue to international attention at the First International Peace Conference, held in The Hague in 1899.

Hague Convention II with Respect to the Laws and Customs of War on Land was among the treaties adopted by the 1899 Hague Peace Conference. Article 3 of its Annexed Regulations Respecting the Laws and Customs of War on Land states: "The armed forces of the belligerent parties may consist of combatants and non-combatants."[97] In case of capture by the enemy both have a right to be treated as prisoners of war.

Following Professor Lieber's lead, recognition as armed forces was provided not only to the regular forces of a belligerent but also to other forces in Article 1:

> The laws, rights, and duties of war apply not only to armies, but also to militia and volunteer corps fulfilling the following conditions:
>
> 1. To be commanded by a person responsible for his subordinates;
> 2. To have a fixed distinctive emblem recognizable at a distance;
> 3. To carry arms openly; and
> 4. To conduct their operations in accordance with the laws and customs of war.

> In countries where militia or volunteer corps constitute the army, or form a part of it, they are included under the denomination "army."

Entitlement to lawful combatant and prisoner of war status for organizations other than the regular forces of a nation was provisional. It was dependent upon these forces acting under government authority and complying strictly with the four conditions listed. Failure of compliance resulted in denial of the combatant's privilege. Individuals acting unilaterally outside an organization were not entitled to the combatant's privilege.

Development of railroads in the late nineteenth century facilitated rapid deployment of military forces, prompting fear by smaller nations such as Belgium and the Netherlands of threats posed by stronger powers such as France and Prussia. Article 2 of the Annex to the 1899 Hague II provided conditional combatant status to what is referred to as a *levée en masse*, as follows:

> The population of a territory which has not been occupied who, on the enemy's approach, spontaneously take up arms to resist the invading troops without having time to organize themselves in accordance with Article 1, shall be regarded as belligerent, if they respect the laws and customs of war.

The Martens Clause

The participating nations appreciated that Hague Convention II was a first effort at international codification of the law of war for ground forces. Of particular importance to the topic of this chapter is language contained in the main treaty:

> It has not . . . been possible to agree forthwith on provisions embracing all the circumstances which occur in practice. On the other hand, it could not be intended by the High Contracting Parties that the cases not provided for should, for want of a written provision, be left to the arbitrary judgment of the military commanders. Until a more complete code of the laws of war is issued, the High Contracting Parties think it right to declare that in cases not included in the Regulations adopted by them, populations and belligerents remain under the protection and empire of the principles of international law, as they result from the usages established between civilized nations, from the laws of humanity, and the requirements of public conscience.

This provision, referred to as the Martens Clause,[98] was the result of a debate over the status of private citizens who took up arms following enemy occupation. Delegations representing major European military powers argued that such individuals should be treated as unlawful combatants subject to summary execution if captured. Smaller European nations argued that they should be regarded as lawful combatants as each citizen has a duty to his nation to resist enemy presence. The argument essentially was one for *levée en masse "plus,"* a continuous resistance to enemy occupation. In the end, private citizens who took up arms in resistance to enemy occupation remained unprivileged combatants.[99] This prompted incorporation of the Martens Clause.[100]

These provisions were repeated verbatim or without substantive change in Hague Convention IV Respecting the Laws and Customs of War on Land adopted by the Second International Peace Conference in The Hague, on October 18, 1907.[101]

A humanitarian basis existed for the decision taken by delegations to the two Hague Peace Conferences. As one international lawyer commented:

> The separation of armies and peaceful inhabitants into two distinct classes is perhaps the greatest triumph of International Law. Its effect in mitigating the evils of war has been incalculable.... But if populations have a war right as against armies, armies have a strict right against them. They must not meddle with fighting. The citizen must be a citizen and not a soldier.[102]

The law of war principle of *discrimination* prohibits military forces from engaging in direct attack of innocent enemy civilians and the enemy civilian population in general. In addition to obligating military forces to distinguish themselves physically and in appearance from the civilian population, the principle of *discrimination* obligates civilians to refrain from engaging in combatant acts, as such actions may place the general civilian population at risk. That said, the Martens Clause acknowledged the existence of unspecified but minimum standards of protection and humane treatment for unprivileged combatants upon capture. The Bush administration's express rejection of Common Article 3 application in US operations in Afghanistan neglected to acknowledge that the United States, as a State party to the 1907 Hague Convention IV, was bound by the Martens Clause in the 1907 Hague Convention IV. The Bush administration's focus solely on the last four (of six) criteria in Article 4A, paragraph 2, GPW, discussed *infra,* also neglected the possible legal significance of the Martens Clause.

World War II

The 1939 invasion of major portions of Europe by Germany that began with the German invasion of Poland on September 2, 1939, and of Asia by Japan following its attack on Pearl Harbor on December 7, 1941, eventually brought organized resistance against Axis occupation on a scale previously unseen. The resistance movement within the Soviet Union was massive and well organized by the Soviet government.[103] The British Special Operations Executive (SOE) and US Office of Strategic Services (OSS) provided organization, training, equipment and other support to indigenous resistance movements in twenty nations under Axis control.[104] Resistance to enemy occupation argued for in 1899 by Belgium and other smaller nations, all victims of German or Japanese occupation in World War II, became reality. The World War II resistance experience prompted revisitation of the 1899 debate regarding law of war recognition of a *levée en masse "plus"* and a major change at the 1949 Geneva Diplomatic Conference in entitlement to combatant and prisoner of war status.

1949 Geneva Diplomatic Conference

The 1949 Geneva Diplomatic Conference met in 1949, completing (from drafts) and adopting four conventions:

- Geneva Convention (I) for the Amelioration of the Condition of the Wounded and Sick in Armed Forces in the Field of August 12, 1949;[105]
- Geneva Convention (II) for the Amelioration of the Condition of Wounded, Sick and Shipwrecked Members of Armed Forces at Sea;[106]
- Geneva Convention (III) Relative to the Treatment of Prisoners of War;[107] and
- Geneva Convention (IV) Relative to the Protection of Civilian Persons in Time of War.[108]

The Geneva Conventions are specific and exclusive in providing entitlement to protection. Thus the first convention provides protection for *military* wounded and sick and medical units, personnel, and transport, while the second convention protects *military* wounded, sick and shipwrecked and their associated facilities, units, and transport. Legal obligations with respect to protection of and care for civilian sick or wounded, civilian medical facilities, and civilian medical transport are not included.[109]

Similarly, Article 4 of the GPW is specific in identifying and limiting individuals entitled to prisoner of war status, while the civilians convention is equally specific in identifying the circumstances in which civilians in enemy hands are entitled to protection. The prisoner of war and civilians conventions did not provide all-encompassing, seamless entitlement to protection, but are quite specific in their respective applications to particular individuals.

With respect to private civilians engaged in combat actions, the prisoner of war convention is directly relevant to the topic at hand.

The criteria for prisoner of war entitlement were reconsidered in light of the World War II experience with State-sponsored organized resistance movements.

Paragraph 1 of Article 4A of the prisoner of war convention reconfirms entitlement to prisoner of war status for members of the regular armed forces and militias or volunteer corps of a government.[110] Paragraph 2 amended the criteria for combatant and prisoner of war status for groups not falling within paragraph 1:

> Members of other militias and members of other volunteer corps, *including those of organized resistance movements, belonging to a party to the conflict* and operating in or outside their own territory, even if this territory is occupied, provided that such militias or volunteer corps, including such organized resistance movements, fulfill the following conditions:
>
> (a) that of being commanded by a person responsible for his subordinates;
>
> (b) that of having a fixed distinctive sign recognizable at a distance;
>
> (c) that of carrying arms openly;
>
> (d) that of conducting their operations in accordance with the laws and customs of war.[111]

The International Committee of the Red Cross's (ICRC) Jean S. Pictet acknowledges that recognition of entitlement to combatant and prisoner of war status for State-sponsored resistance groups in enemy-occupied territory "was an important innovation which grew out of the . . . Second World War."[112] Fully cognizant of the World War II resistance experience, government delegations to the 1949 diplomatic conference declined to expand protection to all private armed groups. The historic criteria of *right authority* remained fundamental to entitlement to combatant and prisoner of war status.

A common mistake by lay persons, non–international law lawyers, some international law lawyers and, in the case at hand, by senior legal advisers and policymakers in the Bush administration is to recite the four criteria in (a) through (d) of Article 4A(2) as the criteria for any armed group to be eligible for combatant and prisoner of war status. This is a fundamental misunderstanding of the law of war and, in particular, of Article 4A(2), GPW, and the rationale and history behind it. Extension of combatant and prisoner of war status in Article 4A(2) is intentionally and expressly narrower. Combining Articles 2 and 4A(2), there are seven criteria, all of which must be met:

First, there must be an international armed conflict, that is, an armed conflict between two or more nations.[113]

Second, the individual who falls into enemy hands after engagement in combatant activities must be a member of an organized resistance movement, that is, he or she cannot be acting unilaterally or as a member of a *levée en masse* in which private citizens respond spontaneously.[114]

Third, the organized resistance movement to which the individual belongs must be operating under the authority and support of a government that is a party to the conflict, that is, it must have *right authority*. In World War II, this authority was manifested through training, logistical, communications and other support, provided by governments-in-exile with the assistance of the British SOE and American OSS, and military forces supporting them, such as with sealift and airlift for delivering supplies and agents,[115] as well as overtly through official pronouncements.[116]

The preceding criteria are prerequisites before the four remaining criteria in Article 4A(2) are applicable. The first two criteria in Article 4A(2) are a threshold that must be crossed before the last four can be considered.[117] If an armed group meets the threshold criteria, consideration must be given to whether or not the armed group meets each and every one of the remaining criteria listed in Article 4A(2).[118]

The 1949 change entitled members of an organized resistance movement operating under the authority of a government—but only organized armed groups operating under government authority—to prisoner of war status. The requirement for such movements to "conduct their operations in accordance with the laws and customs of war" confirmed the combatant's privilege and provided lawful combatant status.

The change in entitlement reflected the experience of World War II resistance movements while codifying the distinction between organized, State-sanctioned *partisans* and private *guerrillas* made by Francis Lieber during the American Civil War. Equally important, delegates to the 1949 Geneva Diplomatic Conference declined to provide lawful combatant or prisoner of war status to private citizens acting without government authority.

Geneva Convention (IV) Relative to the Protection of Civilian Persons in Time of War (GC) by its title and the language of Common Article 2 applies only in an international armed conflict between two or more nations. The GC filled a gap (that is, protection for civilians in enemy hands, including in enemy-occupied territory). Article 5, paragraph 3, provides limited protection to a civilian "suspected of or engaged in activities hostile to the State" in an international armed conflict as it is defined in Article 2. Private citizens who engage in combatant-like actions other than in occupied territory or enemy territory do not receive protection under the Geneva civilians convention. This excludes transnational terrorists from protection under that treaty.

Governments participating in the 1949 diplomatic conference did not intend that the four 1949 Geneva Conventions provide a seamless "safety net" of protection for all persons, in particular private individuals or organizations who conduct armed attacks without government authority. The negotiating record of the 1949 Geneva Conventions is clear that the conventions were not intended to and do not provide protection to unprivileged belligerents. In the course of the 1949 diplomatic conference, the delegate representing the ICRC stated that "although the two conventions might appear to cover all categories concerned, irregular belligerents were not actually protected."[119] Similarly, the representative of the United Kingdom stated "the whole conception of the . . . [Geneva civilians convention] was the protection of civilian victims of war, and not the protection of illegitimate bearers of arms."

In the development of the law of war from the mid-nineteenth century through the four 1949 Geneva Conventions, combatant status and prisoner of war protection was extended to members of a *levée en masse* (as noted, limited in scope and time) and to organized resistance movements operating in enemy-occupied territory under the authority of a government provided each met rigid conditions for distinguishing themselves from the civilian population and carrying out their operations in accordance with the law of war. In keeping with the centuries-old standards that originated in *jus militaire* and the just war tradition, governments steadfastly have refused to provide legitimacy to or legal recognition for private armed individuals or groups acting without government authority and responsibility. The historic condemnation of private armed groups remains through their exclusion from combatant or prisoner of war status for the overall protection of the civilian population. Governments over the centuries consistently have given greater priority to the protection of their civilian populations and individual civilians over entitlement to prisoner of war status for private armed groups, in part to dissuade private citizens from taking up arms and waging war without government authority and in respect for the law of war principle of *discrimination*.

With this history in mind, the status of members of the Taliban and al-Qaeda may be weighed.

Al-Qaeda

The history of Afghanistan and the fighting in the two decades prior to al-Qaeda's attack on the United States on September 11, 2001 focused on the Taliban. Al-Qaeda's history within Afghanistan and overall is loosely intertwined with the Taliban. Al-Qaeda was founded by Usama bin Laden, scion of a wealthy Saudi family, in protest against Saudi Arabia's consent to US bases in Saudi Arabia in the buildup to, and execution of, the 1991 coalition liberation of Kuwait from Iraq.[120]

Bin Laden, a veteran of the *mujahidin* battles of the 1980s against Soviet occupation of Afghanistan, arrived in Jalalabad, Afghanistan, on May 18, 1996, an area not under Taliban control and without invitation from the Taliban.[121] He had an agenda separate from, and broader than, the Taliban's battle within Afghanistan: a transnational jihad against the West and, in particular, the United States.

An extended discussion of Usama bin Laden and al-Qaeda's activities is unnecessary. Professors Goldman and Tittemore describe al-Qaeda as "a quintessential non-State actor," stating, "President [Bush] and Defense Secretary [Rumsfeld] are unquestionably correct in their depiction of al-Qaeda as an international terrorist organization."[122] Professor Toman agrees with Professors Goldman and Tittemore with respect to their first conclusion, declaring, "On the basis of this very short practical analysis, we can easily conclude, that al-Qaeda members cannot benefit—in any circumstances—from the status of prisoners of war." Nor does a law of war basis exist for al-Qaeda members to enjoy the combatant's privilege.[123]

The Taliban

Article 4 of the 1949 Geneva prisoner of war convention identifies persons entitled to prisoner of war status. Prisoner of war entitlement differs from combatant status, the latter being narrower in scope.[124]

The preceding pages establish that the Taliban was not the government of Afghanistan. That said, it is necessary to review the relevant provisions in Article 4 to determine whether captured Taliban are entitled to prisoner of war status.[125]

Article 4A(1)

Article 4A(1) provides prisoner of war status to "[m]embers of the armed forces of a Party to the conflict as well as members of militias or volunteer corps forming part of such armed forces."

In the 1949 Geneva Conventions, the term "Party to the conflict" means a "Contracting Party" or "High Contracting Party," in each case referring to a government that has ratified or acceded to the conventions. As noted in the ICRC *Commentary*,

> Each State contracts obligations *vis-à-vis* itself and at the same time *vis-à-vis* the others. The motive of the Convention is so essential for the maintenance of civilization that the need is felt for its assertion, as much out of respect for it on the part of the signatory State itself as in the expectation of such respect from all parties.[126]

As only governments may contract on behalf of a nation or, said differently, only governments may agree to become parties to the conventions, the term

"Party to a conflict" refers to an armed conflict between the military forces of two or more nations. An armed private group may choose to participate in an international armed conflict on one side or another, but its participation does not make it a "Party to the conflict" in the sense that phrase is used in the 1949 Geneva Conventions.[127]

In the same vein, the term "armed forces" refers to "all members of the regular armed forces of a nation,"[128] to include members of its reserve or militia forces. It is left up to each government to determine how its military is to be composed. In the United States, this includes the reserve component of each of its four military services and the National Guard when the latter have been activated by the President. The term "militia" in Article 4A(1) does not refer to private armed groups.

As the Taliban was not the government of Afghanistan in fact or in law, it was not a "Party to the conflict" as that term is used in the 1949 Geneva Conventions. Nor were the Taliban part of the military of Afghanistan, as it no longer existed. Neither a national government (other than perhaps in name only with respect to the Rabbani government) nor a national military force existed during the period in question.

Two issues arose in the debate over the Taliban and its status. As noted in the factual summary, the Taliban did not have the formal unit structure of a Western army. Similarly, some Taliban fighters ("non-Afghan Taliban") were from Pakistani tribes, while other fighters came from other nations. Were this a case in which the Taliban had been the government of Afghanistan and its military the regular military of Afghanistan, and therefore members of its forces falling under Article 4A(1), neither issue would have been a basis for denial of entitlement to prisoner of war status. Other than in the most general terms, such as command responsibility, the GPW does not specify force structure requirements. Further, the GPW is silent and State practice extensive with respect to the national origin of a member of the regular military forces. For example, US citizens joined British Commonwealth military forces and served in World Wars I[129] and II,[130] and the US military routinely enlists foreign nationals residing in the United States in its armed forces, often through the enticement of US citizenship following completion of a successful initial enlistment tour.[131] While Pakistan covertly supplied the Taliban with arms and ammunition and other support during the 1994–2001 Afghan civil war, and to a degree facilitated the movement of Pakistani tribesmen to join the Taliban, it was not an acknowledged party to the conflict in Afghanistan. As such, Pakistani and other non-Afghans who joined the Taliban were entitled to no greater status under the law of war than were Afghan members of the Taliban.

Article 4A(2)

As noted earlier, Article 4A(2), GPW, was an outgrowth of the World War II experience of organized resistance movements operating under the authority and with the support of the former governments of nations under Axis control.[132] It does not provide entitlement to prisoner of war status to all private armed groups, but only to those operating with government authority. In this respect it repeated the formula articulated by Dr. Francis Lieber in his 1863 "Guerrilla Parties Considered with Reference to the Laws and Usages of War,"[133] and proposed in the form of an extended *levée en masse* at the First Hague Peace Conference in 1899 by Belgium and other smaller military powers, without success.[134] The World War II government-sanctioned resistance movement experience prompted reconsideration of the issue and a guarded and highly conditioned broadening of entitlement to prisoner of war status only to organized armed groups acting under government authority.

Assuming *arguendo* that there was an international armed conflict upon commencement of US and coalition offensive ground operations against the Taliban and al-Qaeda on October 20, 2001, the Taliban did not meet the six criteria in Article 4A(2). Arguably it was an organized armed group, but loosely organized along tribal lines. Prior to commencement of US and coalition military operations, the Taliban had been financially and to some extent logistically supported by the Pakistan ISID and Saudi Arabia in the civil war in Afghanistan. Saudi Arabia had withdrawn its support and Pakistan withdrew support.[135] As noted, neither was a "Party to the conflict" in the Afghan civil war. The Taliban were not entitled to prisoner of war status under Article 4A(2), as it failed to meet all six criteria therein.

Article 4A(3)

Article 4A(3) entitles "[m]embers of regular armed forces who profess allegiance to a government or an authority not recognized by the Detaining Power" to prisoner of war status and entitlement.

This provision, new in the 1949 Convention, was based upon the experience of World War II, as members of the armed forces of nations conquered and occupied by Germany continued the fight under their respective governments-in-exile.[136] Jean S. Pictet, in the *Commentary* on the GPW he edited on behalf of the International Committee of the Red Cross, makes it clear that the point of reference for Article 4A(3) was the Free French: "This provision must be interpreted, in the first place, in the light of the actual case which motivated its drafting—that of the forces of General de Gaulle which were under the authority of the Free French National Liberation Committee."[137]

Pictet continues:

> The expression "members of the regular armed force" denotes armed forces which differ from those referred to in subparagraph (1) of this paragraph[[138]] in one respect only: the authority to which they profess allegiance is not recognized by the adversary as a Party to the conflict. These "regular armed forces" have all the material characteristics of armed forces in the sense of subparagraph (1): they wear uniform[s], they have an organized hierarchy and they know and respect the laws and customs of war. The delegates to the 1949 Diplomatic Conference were therefore fully justified in considering that there was no need to specify for such armed forces the requirements stated in subparagraphs (2) (a), (b), (c), and (d).[[139]]
>
> The distinguishing feature of such armed forces is simply the fact that in view of their adversary, they were not operating or are no longer operating under the direct authority of a Party to the conflict in accordance with Article 2 of the Convention.[[140]]
>
> One solution in order to bring these armed forces *legally* within the scope of the Convention was to associate them with a belligerent fighting against the Power concerned. During the Second World War the German authorities accepted this solution and stated they would consider the Free French Forces to be "fighting for England". The conference of Government Experts also supported this solution.[[141]]
>
> Another procedure which was proposed by the [ICRC] was that the forces should be recognized provided they were *constituted* in a regular manner "irrespective of the Government or authority under whose orders they might claim to be." In order to preclude any abusive interpretation which might have led to the formation of armed bands such as the "Great Companies" of baneful memory,[[142]] the drafters of the 1949 Convention specified that such armed forces must "profess allegiance to a Government or authority not recognized by the Detaining Power." It must be expressly stated that this Government or authority must, as a minimum requirement, be recognized by third States, but this condition is consistent with the spirit of the provision, which was founded on the specific case of the forces of General de Gaulle.
>
> It is also necessary that this authority, which was not recognized by the adversary, should either consider itself as representing one of the High Contracting Parties, or declare that it accepts the obligations stipulated in the Convention and wishes to apply them.[143]

The Taliban did not meet the criteria contained in Article 4A(3) inasmuch as it was never the *de jure* government of Afghanistan. Throughout the Taliban era and the period in question, the government of Afghanistan recognized by the United Nations, the United States and by all nations other than Pakistan, Saudi Arabia and the United Arab Emirates was that of Burhanuddin Rabbani.[144] His regime retained "title" to the Afghanistan seat in the United Nations throughout the ensuing events in Afghanistan set forth in this article. As previously noted, Saudi Arabia, the UAE and Pakistan withdrew their recognition of the Taliban as the United States and its coalition partners commenced military operations in Afghanistan.

A distinction exists between the "Free French" case as envisioned by Article 4A(3), GPW, and the situation in Afghanistan. For Article 4A(3) to have applied to captured Taliban, the Taliban at some point would have had to have been the *de jure* government of Afghanistan, a status it never achieved.

Article 4A(6)

Article 2 of the Annex to the 1907 Hague Convention IV entitled citizens "who, on the approach of the enemy, spontaneously take up arms to resist the invading troops without having had time to organize themselves" into regular armed forces to status as a *levée en masse* and to prisoner of war status if captured provided its members "carried their arms openly" and respected the law of war. Article 4A(6), GPW, reconfirmed the Hague provision, though Pictet acknowledges that a *levée en masse* "almost never occurred during the Second World War."[145] Entitlement to *levée en masse* exists only in territory not under enemy occupation. Pictet also notes that a *levée en masse* "can only be considered to exist during a very short period of time, that is, during the actual invasion period."[146] Thereafter, such individuals are entitled to prisoner of war status only if they meet the six criteria in Article 4A(2), GPW.[147]

The Taliban, however loosely structured, was an armed faction engaged in a civil war with other warlords or factions. Its resistance to the initial US/coalition assault would not have been a spontaneous, informal taking up of arms by individual private citizens of the sort contemplated by the language either of the 1907 Hague Convention or the 1949 GPW.

Special Operations Forces in Non-Standard Uniforms

Entry of US and allied SOF into Afghanistan in October 2001 brought to the fore the law of war issue of dress of some SOF in indigenous attire. It is a matter this author examined at length,[148] but which by necessity must be addressed briefly here. In addition to the legal issue as such, it exposes an inconsistency in the Bush administration's arguments for denial of prisoner of war status to captured Taliban.

US and allied SOF were members of the regular forces of their nations and, consistent with Article 4A(1), GPW, entitled to prisoner of war status if captured by military forces of an enemy nation. The entitlement to prisoner of war status of individuals who fall within Article 4A(1) is absolute; it is not conditional, as is the case with militia and organized resistance endeavoring to gain prisoner of war entitlement under Article 4A(2), GPW.[149]

As noted, governments involved in drafting the 1949 GPW were fully cognizant of the World War II resistance experience. It was the basis for broadening the protection contained in Article 1, Annex to the 1907 Hague Convention IV and Article 1, paragraph 1, Geneva Convention Relative to the Treatment of Prisoners of War of July 27, 1929,[150] to include members of State-sponsored organized resistance movements as individuals entitled to prisoner of war status provided they met the four criteria contained in each of those treaties and in Article 4A(2) of the 1949 GPW. Had governments in 1899, 1907, 1929 or 1949 regarded the wearing of a uniform a prerequisite for captured regular forces' entitlement to prisoner of war status, it would not have been difficult to have said so. They did not.[151] That said, a general assumption exists that members of a State's armed forces (as that term is used in the GPW), including SOF, will meet the four criteria contained in Article 4A(2) in their operations. In practical terms, this has been accomplished by regular forces, including SOF.[152]

A distinction exists, however, between the requirement in Article 4A(2)(b) to have a "fixed distinctive sign recognizable at a distance" and an assumption that regular forces, including SOF, must wear full uniforms in order to remain entitled to prisoner of war status. This distinction is not supported by treaty text or State practice, as this author has shown.[153]

Several problems arise with an assumption that uniforms are required for entitlement to prisoner of war status: (a) no such requirement exists in the 1899 Hague Convention II, 1907 Hague Convention IV, 1929 GPW, nor in the 1949 GPW; (b) the term "uniform" is not used in any of these treaties;[154] (c) "uniform" is undefined in the law of war;[155] and (d) requiring SOF to wear a complete uniform would impose upon them a higher standard than that imposed upon members of an organized resistance movement entitled to prisoner of war status under Article 4A(2), GPW.

The issue was clarified in the diplomatic history of the 1974–77 diplomatic conference that produced the 1977 Additional Protocol I and II. The criteria for combatant and prisoner of war status were relaxed in Articles 43(1) and 44(3), for non-State actors in conflicts of the type defined in Article 1(4). As neither the United States nor Afghanistan is a party to Additional Protocols I and II, these provisions are not directly germane to the issue at hand. However, Article 44(7) and its legislative history are. Article 44(7) states "[t]his Article is not intended to change the generally accepted practice of States with respect to the wearing of the uniform by combatants assigned to the regular, uniformed armed units of a Party to the conflict."

An authoritative commentary on this provision, prepared by individuals directly involved in its drafting and negotiation, explains the meaning of this provision:

> Within the Working Group the initial enthusiasm for a single standard applicable both to regular and independent armed forces was dampened when concern was expressed that the [new] rules . . . might encourage uniformed regular forces to dress in civilian clothing. . . . Accordingly, para. 7 was developed to [overcome this concern]. . . . The report of the Working Group, however, states that "regulars who are assigned to tasks where they must wear civilian clothes, as may be the case . . . with advisers assigned to certain resistance units, are not required to wear the uniform." The implication of para. 7, construed in the light of the Working Group report is that uniforms continue to be the principal means by which members of regular uniformed units distinguish themselves from the civilian population . . . but that members of regular armed forces assigned or attached to duty with the forces of resistance or liberation movements may conform to the manner in which such irregulars conform to the requirements of para. 3.[156]

The situation US and other coalition SOF faced upon entry into Afghanistan was not new. Special operations forces working with indigenous resistance forces frequently find themselves singled out as high-value targets by opposing forces.[157] With the precedent of the consequences of the 1993 Battle of Mogadishu, following which US forces were withdrawn from Somalia, and fearing a similar withdrawal in the event of US casualties, Northern Alliance warlords insisted on US and other SOF wearing indigenous attire in the opening phase of operations against al-Qaeda and the Taliban so they would blend in with the forces with whom they served.[158] Opposing sides generally had no difficulty identifying one another as fighters.[159]

The issue at hand with respect to al-Qaeda, the Taliban and coalition SOF in Northern Alliance dress was twofold: first, whether they met any of the criteria in Article 4, GPW, for entitlement to prisoner of war status, and second, if they were lawful combatants, whether they engaged in "treacherous killing," prohibited by Article 23(e), Annex to the 1907 Hague Convention IV,[160] and otherwise referred to as *perfidy*. In the case at hand the prohibition on *perfidy* is defined in part in Article 37, 1977 Additional Protocol I, as follows:

> 1. It is prohibited to kill, injure or capture an adversary by resort to perfidy. Acts inviting the confidence of an adversary to lead him to believe that he is entitled to, or is obliged to accord, protection under the rules of international law applicable in armed conflict, with intent to betray that confidence, shall constitute perfidy. The following acts are examples of perfidy:
>
> (c) the feigning of civilian or non-combatant status . . . .[161]

With the exception of acts by individual members of al-Qaeda or the Taliban, perfidy was not an issue in the course of the operations during the time frame in question. As noted, both sides readily identified opposing forces.

President Bush's Decision

On February 7, 2002, President George W. Bush signed a memorandum to the Vice President, Secretary of State, Secretary of Defense, Attorney General, Director of Central Intelligence, Chairman of the Joint Chiefs of Staff and others concerning humane treatment of al Qaeda and Taliban detainees.[162] The memorandum, by acknowledgment based upon a legal opinion rendered by the Attorney General, concluded:

1. None of the provisions of the 1949 Geneva Conventions apply to "our conflict with al Qaeda in Afghanistan or elsewhere throughout the world because, among other reasons, al Qaeda is not a High Contracting Party."

2. While the Attorney General advised the President that he has the constitutional authority to "suspend [*sic*] Geneva as between the United States and Afghanistan," President Bush declined to do so with respect to the conflict with the Taliban.

3. The conflict with al Qaeda and the Taliban was an international armed conflict in which Common Article 3 to the four 1949 Geneva Conventions (non-international armed conflicts) did not apply.

4. Taliban detainees are unlawful combatants. Neither Taliban nor al-Qaeda detainees are entitled to prisoner of war status.

5. Detainees will be treated "humanely and, to the extent appropriate and consistent with military necessity, in a manner consistent with the principles of Geneva."

The President's decision was preceded by considerable interagency debate, primarily between the Departments of Justice and State.[163] Professors Goldman, Tittemore and Toman provide analyses of the President's decision and details of the views taken within the executive branch to the extent they were available at the time each article was written.[164] The details of the debate are worthy of separate analysis beyond the scope of this article and, moreover, have been resolved more by decisions of the US Supreme Court since February 7, 2002, than by the President's

February 7 memorandum.[165] It is sufficient to note that the Department of Justice and the Attorney General aggressively sought suspension of the 1949 Geneva Conventions, while the Secretary of State argued for a decision consistent with long-standing US practice of providing humane treatment to individuals captured on the battlefield consistent with the GPW, even where an individual's precise status may not always be clear.[166]

In the debate between the Departments of Justice and State over the law of war status of captured Taliban, disagreements over facts played a large role. When Justice Department officials offered as one option the conclusion that Afghanistan was a failed State,[167] Secretary of State Colin L. Powell's response did not disagree, but contained an attachment with a diplomatically obscure and factually evasive rebuttal that "any determination that Afghanistan is a failed State would be contrary to the official US government position. The United States and the international community have consistently held Afghanistan to its treaty obligations and identified it as a party to the Geneva Conventions."[168] Similarly, White House Counsel Alberto R. Gonzales argued that "[t]he argument that the United States has never determined that GPW did not apply is incorrect. In at least one case (Panama in 1989) the United States determined that GPW did not apply even though it determined for policy reasons to adhere to the convention."[169] This assertion was incorrect as the US position during Operation Just Cause was that Article 3 Common to the 1949 Geneva Conventions applied at a minimum. Panamanian Defense Forces captured during Operation Just Cause were provided prisoner of war protections pending formal determination by individual Article 5, GPW, tribunals, if deemed necessary.[170]

A memorandum prepared by the late Edward R. Cummings, a senior and highly respected Department of State lawyer with extensive law of war experience, notes that his consultations determined that "[t]he lawyers involved [Departments of Justice, State, and Defense, White House Counsel, Office of the Vice President, and Legal Counsel to the Chairman, Joint Chiefs] all agree that al Qaeda or Taliban soldiers are presumptively not POWs [prisoners of war]."[171] However, it emphasized that Department of Defense, Joint Chiefs of Staff and Department of State

> lawyers believe that, in the unlikely event that "doubt should arise" as to whether a particular detainee does not qualify for POW status, we should be prepared to offer additional screening on a case-by-case basis, either *pursuant to* Article 5 of GPW (to the extent the convention applies) or *consistent with* Article 5 (to the extent it does not).[172]

The memorandum notes that lawyers at the Department of Justice, White House Counsel and Office of the Vice President did not agree.

The President's decision attempted to split the difference, but in a way that was less politically and legally defensible than had the law been strictly applied, as has been the long-standing practice of the United States in armed conflicts in which captured enemy personnel may not have met the criteria contained in Article 4, GPW, for entitlement to prisoner of war status.

Public statements offering a rationale for President Bush's decision contained a flawed law of war analysis. On February 7, 2002, the following White House announcement explained the legal basis for President Bush's decision:

> The President has determined that the Geneva Convention applies to the Taliban detainees, but not to the al Qaeda detainees.
>
> Al Qaeda is not a state party to the Geneva Convention; it is a foreign terrorist group. As such, its members are not entitled to POW status.
>
> Although we never recognized the Taliban as the legitimate Afghan government, Afghanistan is a party to the Convention, and the President has determined that the Taliban are covered by the Convention. Under the terms of the Geneva Convention, however, the Taliban detainees do not qualify as POWs.
>
> Therefore, neither the Taliban nor al Qaeda detainees are entitled to POW status.[173]

At a White House press briefing that same day, White House Press Secretary Ari Fleischer stated:

> [T]he national security team . . . has always said that these detainees should not be treated as prisoners of war, because they don't conform to the requirements of Article 4 of the Geneva Convention, which detailed what type of treatment would be given to people in accordance with POW standards. That's a very easily understood legal doctrine of Article 4. For example, the detainees in Guantanamo did not wear uniforms. They're not visibly identifiable. They don't belong to a military hierarchy. All of those are prerequisites under Article 4 of the Geneva Convention, which will be required in order to determine somebody is a POW.[174]

The following day Secretary of Defense Donald H. Rumsfeld repeated Fleischman's comment, stating the GPW "requires soldiers to wear uniforms that distinguish them from the civilian population."[175] Continuing, he stated, "The Taliban did not wear distinctive signs, insignias, symbols or uniforms. To the contrary, far from seeking to distinguish themselves from the civilian population of Afghanistan, they sought to blend in with civilian non-combatants, hiding in mosques and populated areas."[176]

The Fleischer and Rumsfeld statements contain two fundamental discrepancies. First, each fails to articulate the primary threshold for entitlement to prisoner of war status: al-Qaeda and the Taliban were private armed groups lacking any authorization or support from a State party to the armed conflict. Failing this, the four criteria cited by Fleischer and Rumsfeld are not relevant; they and the balance of the GPW do not apply to al-Qaeda, the Taliban or any other armed private group. As explained, the concept of *right authority* dates back more than eight centuries; it is expressly stated in Article 4A(2), GPW; yet it is missing from the Gonzales memorandum to President Bush, the Bush memorandum, and the Fleischer and Rumsfeld statements. The key element (*right authority*) was completely missed or ignored in the official decision-making process and explanations of the Bush administration.

Second, emphasis on captured al-Qaeda and Taliban not wearing a "uniform" not only was factually incorrect, but ignored the fact that US forces fought alongside anti-Taliban forces who also did not wear a "uniform" in the Western European tradition.[177] Moreover, the term "uniform" is not the prerequisite in Article 4A(2), GPW, which is "having a fixed distinctive sign recognizable at a distance." As previously noted, "uniform" is neither used nor defined in the relevant law of war treaties.[178] The distinctive apparel worn by Taliban and anti-Taliban forces and, in the case of the latter, by some US special operations forces working with them, met the "distinctive sign recognizable at a distance" test contained in Article 4A(2).[179]

Finally, in emphasizing the erroneous "uniform" test while ignoring the "organized resistance movement of a Party to the conflict" requirement, Fleischer and Rumsfeld not only ran afoul of the treaty provision but appeared to suggest that al-Qaeda and the Taliban represented the government of Afghanistan, contrary to the President's decision that "[b]y its terms, Geneva applies to conflicts involving 'High Contracting Parties,' which can only be states." This inconsistency was not missed by critics of the administration's approach to law of war application with respect to captured members of these two organizations.[180] Whether one agrees or disagrees with President Bush's decision, these statements were an incredible stumble given the degree to which this issue was discussed within the executive branch prior to the President's February 7 decision.

President Bush's principal conclusion that neither al-Qaeda nor the Taliban was entitled to combatant or prisoner of war status was legally correct, but its supporting statements were contradictory and factually and legally incorrect, as follows:

Bush administration rationale for denial of prisoner of war status to captured al-Qaeda and Taliban	Factual or legal discrepancy, or contradictory statements or actions by the Bush administration
"The President has determined that the [GPW] applies to the Taliban detainees, but not to the al-Qaida detainees."[181] "[T]he President has determined that the Taliban are covered by the [GPW] . . . . [H]owever, the Taliban detainees do not qualify as POWs."[182]	Legally incorrect and contradictory. As noted in subsequent statements and the six conditions contained in Article 4A(2), GPW, captured Taliban were not entitled to prisoner of war status. Therefore GPW did not apply to Taliban detainees. Inconsistent with the President's statement that "[b]y its terms, [GPW] applies to conflicts involving 'High Contracting Parties,' which can only be states." Inconsistent with statement 3 (below). US followed GPW as a matter of policy in past conflicts where status of captured individuals was undetermined. The Bush administration did not continue this practice, resisting application of Common Article 3 humane treatment provisions until mandated by US Supreme Court.[183]
"Al Qaeda is not a High Contracting Party."[184] "Al Qaeda is not a state party to the [GPW]; it is a foreign terrorist group. As such, its members are not entitled to POW status."[185]	Legally vague and inaccurate. It would have been more accurate to say "al-Qaeda is a private armed group that meets none of the GPW categories for POW status."
"Under the terms of the [GPW], neither the Taliban nor al-Qaida detainees are entitled to POW status."[186]	Inconsistent with first statement (above) that "GPW applies to Taliban detainees." GPW applies to captured individuals who meet one of the categories contained in Article 4. If captured personnel do not fall within one of those categories, GPW is legally inapplicable.
"We never recognized the Taliban as the legitimate Afghan government."[187] "The Taliban was not the government of Afghanistan."[188]	Contradictory statements. The first implies that the Taliban was the *de jure* government. The second contradicts the first. First statement is not supported factually.

Bush administration rationale for denial of prisoner of war status to captured al-Qaeda and Taliban	Factual or legal discrepancy, or contradictory statements or actions by the Bush administration
Captured al-Qaeda and Taliban "did not wear uniforms. They're not easily identifiable."[189] GPW "requires soldiers to wear uniforms that distinguish them from the civilian population. The Taliban did not wear distinctive signs, insignias, symbols, or uniforms."[190]	Assuming reference by each was to Article 4A(2), GPW, there is no requirement to wear uniform, but to wear "a fixed distinctive sign recognizable at a distance." "Distinctive sign" one of six requirements in Article 4A(2), GPW, all of which must be met. Factually incorrect: SOF reported both al-Qaeda and Taliban wore distinctive attire and by and large were easily identifiable when assembled as fighting units.[191] US/coalition SOF worked with and wore indigenous (Northern Alliance) attire that met the "distinctive sign" criteria. Hypocritical to emphasize "failure to wear uniform" as the basis for denial of POW status when coalition forces were similarly attired in non-standard (Northern Alliance) uniforms.
Al-Qaeda and Taliban "don't belong to a military hierarchy."[192]	Statement is factually incorrect, ambiguous, incomplete. Taliban had tribal hierarchy. GPW establishes no specific organizational criteria. Statement fails to emphasize that there are six criteria in Article 4A(2), GPW, each of which must be met for entitlement to POW status.
Taliban hid in mosques.[193]	Taking up position in a mosque is not a violation of the law of war. It may result in the mosque relinquishing its normal status as a civilian object and becoming a military objective,[194] but is not necessarily a law of war violation or a basis for denial of prisoner of war status.

Conclusions and Lessons to Be Learned

This author's remit was to examine the issue of al-Qaeda and the Taliban entitlement to combatant and prisoner of war status. As concluded herein, neither al-Qaeda nor the Taliban were entitled to lawful combatant or prisoner of war status.

The author believes the paper would be incomplete if it did not identify lessons to be learned from the actions taken by the Bush administration and others with respect to this process. Several conclusions or lessons may be drawn from the situation as it existed and the decision-making process related to the law of war status of al-Qaeda and Taliban captured in Afghanistan between the beginning of US/coalition offensive operations in October 2001 and President George W. Bush's decision memorandum of February 7, 2002:

- President George W. Bush was legally correct in concluding that neither al-Qaeda nor the Taliban met the prerequisites for prisoner of war status, but for the wrong reasons.
    - Both al-Qaeda and the Taliban were private armed groups. Neither operated as an agent of a government. As such, both groups lacked *right authority,* the centuries-old prerequisite for entitlement to lawful combatant and prisoner of war status that is continued in the 1949 Geneva Convention Relative to the Treatment of Prisoners of War. This point was completely overlooked or ignored in the Bush administration's rationale for denial of prisoner of war status to captured al-Qaeda and Taliban.
    - The Taliban was one faction in a civil war in a failed State. It had achieved neither status nor international recognition as the de facto or *de jure* government of Afghanistan. As was the case with captured al-Qaeda, Taliban fighters did not meet any of the categories within Article 4, GPW, for entitlement to prisoner of war status.
    - The Bush administration rationale for denial of prisoner of war status to captured Taliban was fundamentally flawed in its focus exclusively on the last four criteria of the six criteria contained in Article 4A(2), GPW, and inconsistent given US active support of and alliance with Northern Alliance forces that did not meet the same four criteria.
- Arguments by administration officials to "suspend" or minimize GPW application, and language used to accomplish this in the administration's rationalization for denial of prisoner of war status, ignored the historic leadership the United States has exercised in law of war application in general and in providing humane treatment for captured personnel, even those not entitled to prisoner of war status.
- The law of war is a highly esoteric subject. It requires careful research, reading and understanding of treaty texts, their diplomatic history and State practice, rather than cursory reading and selective use of treaty phrases in a manner inconsistent with their meaning. No competent lawyer would cite a case

without reading it in its entirety nor would he or she cite to a court a statutory provision without researching its law of war history. Making decisions related to law of war issues requires the same level of research, diligence and competence. This was not manifested in administration documents related to the determination of the status of al-Qaeda and the Taliban.

- The flawed arguments offered in support of the President's February 7, 2002 decision were politically based rather than based on the law. They ignored the fact that the 1949 Geneva Conventions were submitted to the Senate for its advice and consent to ratification by a Republican president who, as a military officer, led the Allied campaign to victory against Germany in World War II; that the 1949 Geneva Conventions have been applied in every armed conflict since their ratification without hesitation by successive administrations (four Republican and four Democrat), even where questions existed as to their formal application, because of US leadership in applying the law of war; and that these decisions did not hinder US military operations or place national security at risk.

- While his decision on the key point may have been correct, President Bush erred in accepting the advice of individuals who lacked military experience and in-depth knowledge of the law of war, but possessed skepticism, if not disdain, for the law of war, over that of individuals with military, combat and substantial law of war expertise and experience. This error affected the credibility of the decision and damaged the public diplomacy aspect of fighting the transnational terrorist threat posed by al-Qaeda and other terrorist groups associated with it.

- The executive branch possesses the subject-matter expertise capable of producing a legally accurate, credible and correct document to explain the rationale for denial of lawful combatant and prisoner of war status to private armed groups like al-Qaeda and the Taliban. The unnecessarily secretive decision-making process leading up to the President's February 7, 2002 memorandum failed to utilize the expertise available to it, to its detriment.

- The assertion of "universal applicability" of the 1949 Geneva Conventions (by virtue of their ratification or accession by all governments) is in sharp conflict with the significant failure of their application and implementation by the majority of State parties. The fundamental inconsistency of Afghanistan's tribal warfighting culture and history of abuse of innocent civilians and persons *hors de combat* with the law of war should have been apparent to and recognized by the International Committee of the Red Cross in eliciting Afghanistan's ratification of the 1949 Geneva Conventions, and by the government of Switzerland, as the depositary of the Geneva Conventions, in accepting Afghanistan's instrument of ratification or accession. Law of war treaty ratification should be a matter of quality of and capability for implementation, respect and adherence, rather than mere quantity of State parties. "Universal applicability" means nothing if there is not universal application.

- Afghanistan's cultural history does not relieve it of its treaty obligations. If the law of war is to have any relevance, State parties must be held accountable for their failures to take steps beyond merely being a name on the list to implement them.

- If the International Committee of the Red Cross is to maintain its claim as the "guardian of the Geneva Conventions," it must do more to gain "universal application" of law of war treaties to which each State is a party.

Notes

1. Afghanistan, the United States and every other nation involved is a party to the four 1949 Geneva Conventions. Neither the United States nor Afghanistan is a State party to the 1977 Protocols I and II Additional to the 1949 Geneva Conventions. Protocol Additional to the Geneva Conventions of 12 August 1949, and Relating to the Protection of Victims of International Armed Conflicts, June 8, 1977, 1125 U.N.T.S. 3 [hereinafter Additional Protocol I]; Protocol Additional to the Geneva Conventions of 12 August 1949, and Relating to the Protection of Victims of Non-International Armed Conflicts, June 8, 1977, 1125 U.N.T.S. 609 [hereinafter Additional Protocol II]; both *reprinted in* THE LAWS OF ARMED CONFLICTS (Dietrich Schindler & Jiri Toman eds., 4th rev. ed. 2004), at 785 and 791 respectively.

2. W. Hays Parks, *Special Forces' Wear of Non-Standard Uniforms*, 4 CHICAGO JOURNAL OF INTERNATIONAL LAW 493, 505–06 n.21 (2003), republished by the same title in abridged form in ISSUES IN INTERNATIONAL LAW AND MILITARY OPERATIONS 69, 74 (Richard B. Jaques ed., 2006) (Vol. 80, US Naval War College International Law Studies).

3. ROBERT K. GOLDMAN & BRIAN TITTEMORE, UNPRIVILEGED COMBATANTS AND THE HOSTILITIES IN AFGHANISTAN: THEIR STATUS AND RIGHTS UNDER INTERNATIONAL HUMANITARIAN AND HUMAN RIGHTS LAW 23 (2002), *available at* http://asil.org/taskforce/goldman.pdf; Jiri Toman, *The Status of Al Qaeda/Taliban Detainees under the Geneva Conventions*, 32 ISRAEL YEARBOOK ON HUMAN RIGHTS 271 (2003).

4. JAMES MOLONEY SPAIGHT, WAR RIGHTS ON LAND 17 (1911).

5. Adam Roberts, *Land Warfare: From Hague to Nuremberg*, *in* THE LAWS OF WAR: CONSTRAINTS ON WARFARE IN THE WESTERN WORLD 117 (Michael Howard, George J. Andreopoulos & Mark R. Shulman eds., 1994).

6. For an analysis of the basis for the Bush administration philosophy, see Stephanie Carvin, *Linking Purpose and Tactics: America and the Reconsideration of the Laws of War During the 1990s*, 9 INTERNATIONAL STUDIES PERSPECTIVES 128 (2008).

7. See, e.g., RICHARD H. SHULTZ JR. & ANDREA J. DEW, INSURGENTS, TERRORISTS, AND MILITIAS 5 (2006), where the authors correctly comment that "the Somali clan warriors that took on Task Force Ranger in 1993 either did not agree with or had never heard of strategist [Karl von] Clausewitz or international lawyer [Hugo] Grotius," referring to the Battle of Mogadishu on October 3–4, 1993, between the forces of local Somali warlord Mohammad Fawiz Aidid and US Army and Navy personnel. Accounts of the battle are KENT DELONG & STEVEN TUCKEY,

MOGADISHU! HEROISM AND TRAGEDY (1994) and MARK BOWDEN, BLACK HAWK DOWN (1999). *See also* SHULTZ & DEW, *supra*, at 47, 48–54, 86–87; MICHAEL SCHEUER, MARCHING TO HELL: AMERICA AND ISLAM AFTER IRAQ 108 (2008).

Sir Adam Roberts acknowledged this problem in his 2003 Naval War College International Law Studies analysis:

> In wars in Afghanistan over the centuries, conduct has differed markedly from that permitted by the written laws of war. These wars always had a civil war dimension, traditionally subject to fewer rules in the laws of war; and guerrilla warfare, already endemic in Afghanistan in the nineteenth century, notoriously blurs the traditional distinction between soldier and civilian that is at the heart of the laws of war. Some local customs, for example regarding the killing of prisoners and looting, are directly contrary to long-established principles of the law. Other customs are different from what is envisaged by the law, but are not necessarily a violation of it: for example, the practice of soldiers from the defeated side willingly joining their adversary rather than being taken prisoner. In some cases, conduct has been consistent with international norms: for example, the ICRC had access to some prisoners during the Soviet intervention. Overall, however, compliance with the laws of war has been limited.

Adam Roberts, *The Laws of War in the War on Terror, in* INTERNATIONAL LAW AND THE WAR ON TERROR 191 (Fred L. Borch & Paul S. Wilson eds., 2003) (Vol. 79, US Naval War College International Law Studies).

8. The first US military ground forces to arrive in Afghanistan following the September 11, 2001 al-Qaeda hijacking of four commercial airliners and their use in attacks on the twin towers of the World Trade Center, the Pentagon and an unconfirmed third target were US special operations forces (SOF) who engaged in ground reconnaissance missions preceding US and British air and cruise-missile attacks against Taliban communication and air-defense targets on October 7, 2001. STEPHEN BIDDLE, AFGHANISTAN AND THE FUTURE OF WARFARE: IMPLICATIONS FOR ARMY AND DEFENSE POLICY 8 (2002). Offensive ground operations began with arrival of US Army Special Forces Operational Detachments Alpha 555 and 595, 5th Special Forces Group, which were inserted on the night of October 19–20, 2001. CHARLES H. BRISCOE ET AL., WEAPON OF CHOICE: U.S. ARMY SPECIAL OPERATIONS FORCES IN AFGHANISTAN 96 (2003). Their entry was preceded by US and British air and cruise-missile attacks on Taliban positions on October 7, 2001. GARY BERNTSEN & RALPH PEZZULO, JAWBREAKER 77 (2005). During the period covered, US SOF were joined by SOF from Australia, Canada, Denmark, the Netherlands and the United Kingdom. The role of British SOF is described in DAMIEN LEWIS, BLOODY HEROES (2006).

9. Memorandum from George Bush to Vice President et al., Humane Treatment of Al Qaeda and Taliban Detainees (Feb. 7, 2002), *reprinted in* THE TORTURE PAPERS: THE ROAD TO ABU GHRAIB 134 (Karen J. Greenberg & Joshua Dratel eds., 2005), *available at* http://www.pegc.us/archive/White_House/bush_memo_20020207_ed.pdf [hereinafter Bush Memorandum].

10. BRISCOE ET AL., *supra* note 8, at 2.

11. *Id.* Professor Frank L. Holt observes:

> The long rhythms of Afghan history do show some periods of relative calm during which cities grew, trade routes pulsed, irrigated agriculture expanded, and the arts flourished, but between each renaissance we find an era of ruin brought on or exacerbated by the parochialism, tribalism, fierce independence, and mutual hostility. . . . These social conditions, not to mention physical challenges of a harsh terrain and environment, stretch back as far as our earliest written sources will carry us. In these

respects, the twenty-first century C.E. differs very little from the fifteenth or fifth C.E. or even the fourth B.C.E.

FRANK L. HOLT, INTO THE LAND OF BONES: ALEXANDER THE GREAT IN AFGHANISTAN 9–10 (2005). *See also* BYRON FARWELL, QUEEN VICTORIA'S LITTLE WARS 143 (1973); JOHN H. WALLER, BEYOND THE KHYBER PASS: THE ROAD TO BRITISH DISASTER IN THE FIRST AFGHAN WAR ix (1990); DAVID LOYN, BUTCHER & BOLT: TWO HUNDRED YEARS OF FOREIGN ENGAGEMENT IN AFGHANISTAN xxxvii, 12, 20, 46, 57, 238 (2008); AHMED RASHID, TALIBAN 9–10 (2001); STEVE COLL, GHOST WARS 110–11 (2004); DALTON FURY, KILL BIN LADEN 139 (2008). In explaining tribal allegiance and its sustainment in today's world, Shultz and Dew offer the following:

> [Sir Edward] Evans-Pritchard's segmentary-lineage theory was particularly applicable when the tribal setting was egalitarian. Such tribal groupings are decentralized and relatively small, numbering no more than several thousand. Building larger units was difficult because such tribes did not accept the authority of an outside chieftain. Leader status was gained through charisma, military prowess, negotiation skills, and moral status. Consequently, establishing larger tribal organizations in a segmentary-lineage system was likely only in the event of an external threat. Otherwise, larger political units existed, at best, as quasi-states. A ruling lineage can come to be recognized as providing leadership for a larger group consisting of other lineages—subtribes or clans. However, the establishment of such a centralized political relationship is complicated and delicate. Tribal organizations are based on kinship ties and patrilineal descent, making more centralized political organizations atypical.

SHULTZ & DEW, *supra* note 7, at 50, *citing* EDWARD EVANS-PRITCHARD, THE NUER, A DESCRIPTION OF THE MODES OF LIVELIHOOD AND POLITICAL INSTITUTIONS OF A NILOTIC PEOPLE (1940) and EDWARD EVANS-PRITCHARD, THE SANUSI OF CYRENAICA (1949). Continuing:

> Why, despite the crushing forces of modernity, do [traditional societies] continue to endure? The answer lies in what Ibn Khaldun, writing in the fourteenth century, said about *asabiyya*. The strength of that solidarity depends on the extent to which a tribe was segmentary, egalitarian, decentralized, and autonomous. Thus, the underlying foundation for those forces is the social principle of kinship, which is central to a tribal society's maintenance of its union. Tribes endure when the ties that bind them endure.

Id. at 51.

With respect to Afghanistan in particular, Shultz and Dew note that "[t]he Afghan tribes have tolerated state power for the advantages it provides over other tribal rivals. However, the state does not command the Afghan tribes and in the best of times has only limited authority over them." *Id.* at 157.

12. RASHID, *supra* note 11; SCHEUER, *supra* note 7, at 108; LOYN, *supra* note 11, at xxxiv, xxxvii, 12, 20. David Loyn offers an example of the philosophy of decentralized rule in relating that in 1838, following British support for Shah Shuja as king, "[n]one could give a response to Jabar Khan when he said, 'If Shah Shuja is really a king . . . leave him now with us Afghans, and let him rule if he can.'" Continuing, Loyn declares: "Afghans would make similar challenges in the wars that followed, up to and including the appointment of President [Hamid] Karzai by the U.S." *Id.* at 46.

13. See SHULTZ & DEW, *supra* note 7, at 150–54, for an excellent description of the tribal system within Afghanistan and the critical distinctions within and between tribes. *See also* FARWELL, *supra* note 11, at 147–48.

14. LOUIS DUPREE, AFGHANISTAN 316 (1973), as *cited in* BRISCOE ET AL., *supra* note 8, at 3.

15. As Loyn (*supra* note 11, at 147) notes:

> The ability of Muslims with different views of Jihad and various political ends to join against a common enemy would have profound importance when the frontier again became the front line, a crucible of violence, in the conflict that began in the late twentieth century. The frontier villages in Waziristan and Tirah that gave the best support to the Taliban and the foreign fighters in al-Qaeda were the same ones that had supported the mujahidin a decade before in the US-backed fight against the Soviet Union, and had been the quickest to rise against Britain in the nineteenth century—finding common cause against a common enemy—first Britain, later the USSR, then the US-led invasion.

Similarly, STEPHEN TANNER, AFGHANISTAN: A MILITARY HISTORY FROM ALEXANDER THE GREAT TO THE FALL OF THE TALIBAN 243 (2002), states: "The Soviet invasion achieved that rarity in Afghanistan history: a unifying sense of political purpose that cut across tribal, ethnic, geographic, and economic lines." On the concept in general, see SHULTZ & DEW, *supra* note 7, at 154; FARWELL, *supra* note 11, at 5, 47, 153–54. On Afghanistan and its history, see SHULTZ & DEW, *supra* note 7, at 151–54; WALLER, *supra* note 11, at x; LOYN, *supra* note 11, at 145–47; BRISCOE ET AL., *supra* note 8, at 11. *See also* Anon., *The Liberation of Mazar-e Sharif: 5th SF Group Conducts UW [Unconventional Warfare] in Afghanistan*, SPECIAL WARFARE, June 2002, at 34, which reports with respect to the US Special Forces experience:

> The situation on the ground presented challenges. . . . Although the major factions were united in their opposition to the Taliban, they had significant differences with each other, and they felt no allegiance to anything higher than their own party or ethnic group. At one time or another during the previous decade, the groups had taken up arms against one another or supported each other's rival factions. Although none of these events were uncommon in internal Afghan politics, they created a significant level of distrust between the factions . . . .

Id. at 39. The anonymous authors are members of 5th Special Forces Group.

16. SHULTZ & DEW, *supra* note 7, at 59.

17. *Id.* at 62, *quoting* IOAN M. LEWIS, A PASTORAL DEMOCRACY 27 (1999). Professor Toman recognizes this with respect to the Taliban, acknowledging, "Knowledgeable experts consider the Taliban's armed forces were not comparable to an organized army, since they had no strategic military plans, or decision-making power and they resorted to guerrilla tactics." Toman, *supra* note 3, at 284.

18. PETER HOPKIRK, THE GREAT GAME (1992); TANNER, *supra* note 15, at 129–54; WALLER, *supra* note 11, at x; FARWELL, *supra* note 11, at 153–54; LOYN, *supra* note 11, at 145–47; BRISCOE ET AL., *supra* note 8, at 34.

19. RASHID, *supra* note 11, at 9–10; LOYN, *supra* note 11, at xxxvii, 249; FURY, *supra* note 11, at 105–06, 124, 129, 139; Anon., *supra* note 15, at 38. An example is General Abdul Rashid Dostum, who

> rose to power after the Soviet invasion in 1979, forming a militia made up mainly of Uzbeks, who had grown to respect his leadership supporting union workers in the oil fields. He supported the communist-run government in Kabul until 1992, when he flip-flopped and joined his former opponent Ahmad Shah Massoud. Mr. Massoud, known as the "Panshjer Lion" and head of the Northern Alliance, convinced Gen. Dostum that the communists were losing ground and that he should fight for the winning side. . . . In 1994, Gen. Dostum again switched sides, joining Gulbuddin Hekmatyar, a mujahadeen accused of fighting his own people more than the Soviets and who is now wanted by the

> U.S. for supporting al Qaeda and the Taliban. . . . Gen. Dostum's decision to join Mr. Hekmatyar was a major factor in the collapse of a government led by Burhanuddin Rabbani and Mr. Massoud. Yet, less than two years later, Gen. Dostum switched again, realigning with Mr. Rabbani and Ismail Khan, the warlord from Herat, to fight the ascendant Taliban regime. However, Gen. Dostum was betrayed by one of his own commanders, who sided with the Taliban. The general fled to Turkey in fear for his life.
>
> Gen. Dostum returned in April 2001 at the urging of Mr. Massoud and reconstituted his militia to attack the Taliban in the north.

Sara A. Carter, *The Art of a Warlord: Flip-flopping General a Mixed Blessing to U.S. in Afghanistan*, WASHINGTON TIMES, Oct. 12, 2008, at 4–5. *See also* BRISCOE ET AL., *supra* note 8, at 2, 95; COLL, *supra* note 11, at 234, 236, 348.

20. Readers with greater curiosity or interest would benefit from SHULTZ & DEW, *supra* note 7, at 159–66; FARWELL, WALLER and LOYN, each *supra* note 11; HOPKIRK, *supra* note 18; and TANNER, *supra* note 15, at 129–54.

21. LOYN, *supra* note 11, at 23; SCHEUER, *supra* note 7, at 113; RASHID, *supra* note 11, at 54. These footpaths afforded al-Qaeda leader Usama bin Laden, his forces and Taliban the opportunity to enter Pakistan, evading capture in late 2001; FURY, *supra* note 11, at 277–78; TANNER, *supra* note 15, at 218–19.

22. *See* SHULTZ & DEW, *supra* note 7, at 166: "The British presence in Afghanistan had an important impact on the modern state of Afghanistan because the British left a legacy of political boundaries based on their strategic interests rather than on the historical location of tribal peoples." Similarly, RASHID, *supra* note 11, at 187, describes the Durand Line as "the disputed boundary line between the two countries [Pakistan and Afghanistan] created by the British and which no Afghan regime has recognized." Interpretations are being offered today by Afghan Pashtun nationalists that the Durand Line agreement is good for only one hundred years; LOYN, *supra* note 11, at 145–47, 167, 182.

23. BRISCOE ET AL., *supra* note 8, at 8–9.

24. Disregarding Afghan culture, the PDPA attempted to impose communist agricultural redistribution measures contrary to the long-standing clan and tribal system, providing another point for resistance to the regime; LOYN, *supra* note 11, at 184.

25. *Id.* at 188–93; SHULTZ & DEW, *supra* note 7, at 167–68.

26. GEORGE CRILE, CHARLIE WILSON'S WAR (2003), and the very entertaining 2008 movie of the same name. *See also* RUSSIAN GENERAL STAFF, THE SOVIET-AFGHAN WAR (Lester W. Grau & Michael A. Gress trans., 2002); COLL, *supra* note 11; SHULTZ & DEW, *supra* note 7, at 168–76; and LOYN, *supra* note 11, at 194–207.

27. SHULTZ & DEW, *supra* note 7, at 177–79, identify and describe in detail four major factions as the *mujahidin* who allied themselves to fight the Soviets: "(1) fundamentalist Sunni clerics, (2) moderate and radical Sunni Islamists affiliated with the Muslim Brothers, (3) Wahhabis, and (4) Shi'ia Islamists," *citing* OLIVIER ROY, AFGHANISTAN: FROM HOLY WAR TO CIVIL WAR 43–46 (1995). Nonetheless the war lasted almost a decade in part owing to factional differences within the *mujahidin*, illustrating again the primacy of tribal loyalties; LOYN, *supra* note 11, at 202. The term *mujahidin* has been traced to the holy man and "religious adventurer" Sayyid Ahmed Shah Brelwi, who returned from a pilgrimage to Mecca to preach war against infidels. Forming a sect called Mujahidin, he and his followers captured Peshawar in 1829. He was killed in 1831. The sect continued, but *mujahidin* eventually evolved into a term to describe indigenous fighters. FARWELL, *supra* note 11, at 150. In the war against Soviet occupation, the *mujahidin* were not limited to Afghan resistance but included volunteers from Chechnya and most Arab nations.

28. CRILE, *supra* note 26, at 504; SHULTZ & DEW, *supra* note 7, at 171, 176; and COLL, *supra* note 11, at 185. Shultz and Dew's observation that "[t]he Red Army's . . . conventional military doctrine and analysis was of no help in analyzing or fighting the asymmetrical guerrilla tactics of a traditional tribal culture" (*supra* note 7, at 149) applies equally well to the US Army in the Vietnam War and, more recently, in the first four years of Operation Iraqi Freedom as it failed to recognize it was faced with an insurgency, seeking to apply and unsuccessfully applying conventional war tactics against its "asymmetrical" threat, then waited until it had written and published new doctrine jointly with the Marine Corps before beginning to conduct counterinsurgency operations. For a critique of the Army in the Vietnam War and the Iraq conflict that began in 2003, see JOHN A. NAGL, COUNTERINSURGENCY LESSONS FROM MALAYA AND VIETNAM: LEARNING TO EAT SOUP WITH A SPOON (2002). The new doctrine is contained in Headquarters, Department of the Army & Headquarters, Marine Corps Combat Development Command, FM 3-24/MCWP 3-33.5, Counterinsurgency (2006). The same failure to properly assess the situation occurred with regard to the Bush administration's rationale for its determination as to the legal status of the Taliban, discussed *infra*.

29. LOYN, *supra* note 11, at 208.

30. RASHID, *supra* note 11, at 32–33; BRISCOE ET AL., *supra* note 8, at 19; LOYN, *supra* note 11, at 182, 238–39; SHULTZ & DEW, *supra* note 7, at 177–78; COLL, *supra* note 11, at 283–84.

31. LOYN, *supra* note 11, at 215.

32. RASHID, *supra* note 11, at 9–10; HUMAN RIGHTS WATCH, AFGHANISTAN: THE FORGOTTEN WAR, HUMAN RIGHTS ABUSES AND VIOLATIONS OF THE LAW OF WAR SINCE SOVIET WITHDRAWAL (1991). LOYN, *supra* note 11, at 114, observes:

> Of all of the foreign attempts to control Afghanistan in the two centuries after [British envoy Mounstuart] Elphinstone's first meeting in 1808, the Soviet invasion in 1979 was the one that came closest to success. And when the Soviet-backed government finally crumbled, the disunity of the forces that had ousted it flared into open civil war. Power had spun out of Kabul, and could not be drawn back. In Afghanistan imposing power from the center has always been temporary—like gathering together sand or water—since local loyalty outweighs any other.

See also SHULTZ & DEW, *supra* note 7, at 179–80; COLL, *supra* note 11, at 262–63.

33. LOYN, *supra* note 11, at 211–46, 253–54. In the 1994 battle for Kabul, Najibullah was forcibly taken by the Taliban from the United Nations compound in Kabul where he sought asylum in 1972. He and his brother were tortured and castrated before being hanged. BRISCOE ET AL., *supra* note 8, at 95; COLL, *supra* note 11, at 333; HOLT, *supra* note 11, at 44.

34. Rabbani remained the recognized ruler of Afghanistan, entitled to Afghanistan's seat in the United Nations during the Taliban period. He formally handed over power to an interim government headed by Hamid Karzai on December 22, 2001. *See* Burhanuddin Rabbani, GLOBALSECURITY.ORG, http://globalsecurity.org/military/world/afghanistan/rabbani.htm (last visited Feb. 27). RASHID, *supra* note 11, at 10, observes:

> Afghanistan was in a state of virtual disintegration just before the Taliban emerged at the end of 1994. The country was divided into warlord fiefdoms and all the warlords had fought, switched sides and fought again in a bewildering array of alliances, betrayals and bloodshed. The predominantly Tajik government of President Burhanuddin Rabbani controlled Kabul, its environs and the north-east of the country, while three provinces in the west centring on Herat were controlled by Ismael Khan. In the east on the Pakistan border three Pashtun provinces were under the independent control of a council or Shura (Council) of Mujaheddin commanders based in Jalalabad. A small region to the south and east of Kabul was controlled by Gulbuddin Hikmetyar.

In the north the Uzbek warlord General Rashid Dostum held sway over six provinces and in January 1994 he had abandoned his alliance with the Rabbani government and joined with Hikmetyar to attack Kabul. In central Afghanistan the Hazaras controlled the province of Bamiyan. Southern Afghanistan and Kandahar were divided up amongst dozens of petty ex-Mujaheddin warlords and bandits who plundered the population at will. With the tribal structure and the economy in tatters, no consensus on a Pashtun leadership and Pakistan's unwillingness to provide military aid to the Durranis as they did to Hikmetyar, the Pashtuns in the south were at war with each other.

35. RASHID, *supra* note 11, at 90–92. *See also* SHULTZ & DEW, *supra* note 7, at 180–81.

36. SHULTZ & DEW, *supra* note 7, at 86, 208, 235–36. Not all Taliban were Pashtun, nor were all Pashtun aligned with the Taliban. For example, Afghanistan's President, Hamid Karzai, is Pashtun. Dr. Stephen Biddle's excellent study of Operation Enduring Freedom identified three major components of enemy fighters facing the US-led coalition: (a) native Afghan Taliban, (b) predominantly foreign al-Qaeda and (c) non-al-Qaeda foreign allies of the Taliban. BIDDLE, *supra* note 8, at 13. For law of war purposes and as will be explained, only two categories existed: al-Qaeda and Taliban, and in cases where al-Qaeda served with or led Taliban elements, arguably only one.

37. SHULTZ & DEW, *supra* note 7, at 238.

38. *Id.* at 236.

39. LOYN, *supra* note 11, at 239 [emphasis provided]. In this regard, see the quotation from LEWIS, *supra* note 17.

40. RASHID, *supra* note 11, at 39, 53, 59. Dr. Biddle notes, "The Afghan Taliban were often poorly trained soldiers. Many had little or no formal military instruction, and Afghan ranks swelled and shrank with the seasons and the fortunes of war as troops went home to their villages or took up arms depending on the crop cycle and apparent military need." BIDDLE, *supra* note 8, at 15. *See also* Anon., *supra* note 15, at 36:

> Few of the factional commanders, at any level, possessed any experience in the conduct of large coordinated offensives. Most were extremely proficient at performing small-unit actions. But combining their forces (three separate and distinct major formations and numerous subordinate commands) into a coordinated offensive under one major formation was clearly uncharted territory and a distinct challenge.

On the Afghan practice of switching sides, the article continues:

> The Afghan tradition of surrender and transfer of loyalty is not unlike what the US experienced during the Civil War [1861–65], with prisoner exchanges, paroles and pardons. The Afghans, in keeping with their custom, expect soldiers who have surrendered to abide by the conditions of their surrender agreement and to behave honorably. But the vast numbers of Arabs, Pakistanis, Chechens, Uighers and other foreign nationals who were members of al-Qaeda ignored the Afghan custom. They used individual surrenders as a means of furthering their cause, often creating treacherous conditions.

Id. at 38.

41. SHULTZ & DEW, *supra* note 7, at 253.

42. RASHID, *supra* note 11, at 52–53.

43. *Id.* at 54.

44. COLL, *supra* note 11, at 349.

45. *Id.*

46. *Id.* at 475–76; LOYN, *supra* note 11, at 259–62; RASHID, *supra* note 11, at 26, 28–29, 39, 44–45, 52–53; SCHEUER, *supra* note 7, at 111, 113.

47. COLL, *supra* note 11, at 349.

48. *Id.* at 445–46 comments on the rationale for UAE recognition:

> One of the most passionate hunters was Sheikh Khalifa bin Zayed al-Nahayan, the billionaire crown prince of Abu Dhabi in the United Arab Emirates. . . . Scores of equally rich U.A.E. notables flew to Pakistan each season to hunt. So entrenched did the alliance with Pakistan around houbara hunts become that the Pakistani air force agreed secretly to lease one of its northern air bases to the [UAE] so that the sheikhs could more conveniently stage the aircraft and supplies required for their hunts. Pakistani personnel maintained the air base, but the U.A.E. paid for its upkeep. They flew in and out on C-130s and on smaller planes that could reach remote hunting grounds.
>
> Some of the best winter houbara grounds were in Afghanistan. Pakistani politicians had hosted Arab hunting trips there since the mid-1990s. They had introduced wealthy sheikhs to the leadership of the Taliban, creating connections for future finance of the Islamist militia. Bin Laden circulated in this Afghan hunting world after he arrived in the country in 1996. So the CIA report that he had joined a large, stationary camp in western Afghanistan that winter seemed consistent with previous reporting about bin Laden.

The UAE's Afghanistan western hunting camp played a key part in target selection for the August 20, 1998 US cruise-missile strike against al-Qaeda training camps in response to the al-Qaeda attacks on the US embassies in Nairobi and Dar es Salaam, discussed *infra.* Despite its relationship with the Taliban, the UAE royal family was cooperative with US planners in providing information to facilitate identification of the royal family western Afghan hunting camp, while disavowing its use by al-Qaeda leader Usama bin Laden. *Id.* at 448–49.

49. RASHID, *supra* note 11, at 251 n.4.

50. BRISCOE ET AL., *supra* note 8, at 21; LOYN, *supra* note 11, at 257–58.

51. BRISCOE ET AL., *supra* note 8, at 21.

52. *Id.*; RASHID, *supra* note 11, at 5, 44–45, 52–53, 58, 61–63, 72–73, 80, 188–89; COLL, *supra* note 11, at 349.

53. COLL, *supra* note 11, at 350–51; *see also* RASHID, *supra* note 11, at 64–66. The principal pro-Taliban proponent within the former Afghanistan embassy, Seraj Jamal, left Washington for New York to be the Taliban's unofficial (unrecognized) delegation at the United Nations; COLL, *supra*, at 351.

54. The government of President Burhanuddin Rabbani continued to hold Afghanistan's United Nations seat during the Taliban period.

55. BRISCOE ET AL., *supra* note 8, at 95.

56. RASHID, *supra* note 11, at 64–74; LOYN, *supra* note 11, at 253–54; BRISCOE ET AL., *supra* note 8, at 22; HUMAN RIGHTS WATCH, AFGHANISTAN: THE MASSACRE IN MAZAR-I-SHARIF (1998). Taliban actions prompted European Union suspension of all humanitarian aid to areas of Afghanistan controlled by the Taliban. RASHID, *supra*, at 72. The Human Rights Watch report contains a minor error in interchangeably referring to Taliban conduct in Mazar-i-Sharif as acts of "reprisal" or "revenge" for Taliban losses in its unsuccessful 1997 battle for Mazar-i-Sharif. The terms are not synonymous, with the former having a very specific meaning in the law of war. Although there may be questions as to whether the full range of protections against reprisal was applicable in Afghanistan's civil war, nonetheless the basic preconditions for executing reprisal did not exist. *See* FRITS KALSHOVEN, BELLIGERENT REPRISALS 339–44 (1971). The present author has identified the following criteria for a reprisal:

1. A reprisal is an act which would be unlawful if not committed for the purpose of a reprisal.

2. It must be done for the purpose of compelling the other belligerent to observe the law of war.

3. It must not be done before other means have been reasonably exhausted.

4. It may be executed only on the express order of higher authority.

5. It must be committed against persons or objects whose attack as a reprisal is not otherwise prohibited.

6. It must be proportional to the original wrong.

W. Hays Parks, *A Few Tools in the Prosecution of War Crimes*, 149 MILITARY LAW REVIEW 73, 84 (1995). *See also* UNITED KINGDOM MINISTRY OF DEFENCE, THE MANUAL OF THE LAW OF ARMED CONFLICT 65, ¶ 5.18 and 418–19, ¶¶ 16.16, 16.17 (2004) [hereinafter UK MANUAL]. As noted in this author's article, the term "reprisal" often is misused when other terms, such as "retaliation," "retorsion" or even "lawful attack of a military objective," might be more accurate. In the case of Taliban conduct in 1998 in Mazar-i-Sharif, the substantial delay between anti-Taliban forces in 1997's and Taliban actions does not suggest its actions were taken "for the purpose of compelling the other belligerent to observe the law of war," but were more in line with tribal acts of revenge in blood feuds. *See* SHULTZ & DEW, *supra* note 11, at 157. In this respect Taliban actions manifest the distinction between a "soldier" and a "warrior" made by Professor Hugh Turney-High in his classic PRIMITIVE WAR 149–52 (1949) in describing the revenge mode of a warrior, a trait discussed in the context of Somalia and Afghanistan in SHULTZ & DEW, *supra*, at 5–7, 57–100, 147–95.

57. RASHID, *supra* note 11, at 75; BERNTSEN & PEZZULO, *supra* note 8, at 1–27; COLL, *supra* note 11, at 403–05.

58. COLL, *supra* note 11, at 411.

59. LOYN, *supra* note 11, at 267. US State Department officials met with Taliban leader Mullah Omar, requesting that he turn over Usama bin Laden. A *quid pro quo* of US recognition of the Taliban in return for the Taliban to turn bin Laden over to it did not materialize; COLL, *supra* note 11, at 430; BRISCOE ET AL., *supra* note 8, at 24.

60. RASHID, *supra* note 11, at 76; COLL, *supra* note 11, at 548–49.

61. S.C. Res. 1214, U.N. Doc. S/RES/1214 (Dec. 8, 1998), discussed *infra*.

62. RASHID, *supra* note 11, at 77. UAE recognition had been token at best. As Rashid notes, following Saudi withdrawal from Afghanistan and its dealings with the Taliban, Pakistan remained the Taliban's sole financial provider. *Id.*

63. S.C. Res. 1333, U.N. Doc. S/RES/1333 (Dec. 19, 2000); S.C. Res. 1363, U.N. Doc. S/RES/1363 (July 30, 2001).

64. Rashid reports:

> Not surprisingly, Iran, Turkey, India, Russia and four of the five Central Asian Republics—Uzbekistan, Kazakhstan, Kyrgyzstan and Tajikistan—have backed the anti-Taliban Northern Alliance with arms and money to try and halt the Taliban's advance. In contrast Pakistan and Saudi Arabia have backed the Taliban. . . . The Taliban victories in northern Afghanistan in the summer of 1998 . . . set in motion an even fiercer regional conflict as Iran threatened to invade Afghanistan and accused Pakistan of supporting the Taliban. . . .

RASHID, *supra* note 11, at 5.

65. *Id.* at 80; COLL, *supra* note 11, at 513–15; Report of the Secretary-General on the humanitarian implications of the measures imposed by the Security Council resolutions 1267 (1999)

and 1333 (2000) on Afghanistan 2–8, U.N. Doc. S/2001/695 (July 13, 2001). See also The situation in Afghanistan and its implications for international peace and security: Report of the Secretary-General 4, 5–9, particularly ¶ 25, U.N. Doc. A/55/907–S/2001/384 (Apr. 19, 2001) (reporting on the Secretary-General's visit to South Asia), which refers to "fighting throughout Afghanistan," belying media assertions that the Taliban controlled as much as 80 percent of Afghanistan. So, too, does the Secretary-General's July 13, 2001 report, which states, "All regions of the country, with the exception of the southern [Pashtun] region, now include active conflict zones." *Supra*, ¶ 48.

66. U.N. Doc. A/55/907–S/2001/384, *supra* note 65; U.N. Doc. S/2001/695, *supra* note 65. Within Afghanistan, the Taliban did not enjoy popular support. BIDDLE, *supra* note 8, at 16. Continuing, Dr. Biddle notes that the Taliban was (a) poorly trained, (b) had poor morale and (c) had a cultural willingness to defect. *Id.* at 13.

67. See, e.g., S.C. Res. 1267, U.N. Doc. S/RES/1267 (Oct. 15, 1999), demanding that "the Taliban turn over Usama bin Laden without further delay to appropriate authorities in a country where he has been indicted," and further actions by UN members, which refer only to "the Taliban." See also S.C. Res. 1333, *supra* note 63, which refers to "areas of Afghanistan under the control of the Afghan faction known as Taliban, which also calls itself the Islamic Emirate of Afghanistan (hereinafter known as the Taliban)"; S.C. Res. 1363, *supra* note 63, refers to "States bordering the territory of Afghanistan under Taliban control." U.N. Doc. A/55/907–S/2001/384, *supra* note 65, reporting on the Secretary-General's visit to South Asia and his meeting with Taliban Foreign Minister Wakil Ahmad Mutawakkil, refers to the Taliban only and not as the Taliban "regime," much less as the government of Afghanistan.

68. S.C. Res. 1368, U.N. Doc. S/RES/1368 (Sept. 12, 2001).

69. Northern Alliance warlords Dostum and Atta Mohammed renewed offensive operations one day later; BIDDLE, *supra* note 8, at 8–10.

70. BRISCOE ET AL., *supra* note 8, at 188–89; FURY, *supra* note 11, at 275. Biddle states that "[o]n the night of December 6, Mullah Omar and the senior Taliban leadership fled the city [Kandahar] and went into hiding, ending Taliban rule in Afghanistan," then continues:

> Allied forces subsequently tracked a group of al Qaeda survivors thought to include Osama bin Laden to a series of redoubts in the White Mountains near Tora Bora. The redoubts were taken in a 16-day battle ending on December 17, but many al Qaeda defenders escaped death or capture and fled across the border into Pakistan.

BIDDLE, *supra* note 8, at 11.

71. BRISCOE ET AL., *supra* note 8, at 203–16; generally, SEAN NAYLOR, NOT A GOOD DAY TO DIE (2005) and PETE BLABER, THE MISSION, THE MEN, AND ME 262–95 (2008), describing Operation Anaconda, March 2–13, 2002. Taliban restoration and resurgence and the present situation in Afghanistan are beyond the scope of this article. As noted, this article considers the status of the Taliban from the time of commencement of US military operations on October 20, 2001, to February 7, 2002, when President George W. Bush issued his memorandum concerning the law of war status of captured al-Qaeda and Taliban. The issue of treatment of captured al-Qaeda and Taliban is the subject of separate articles in this volume by Stephane Ojeda, Matthew Waxman and Ryan Goodman.

72. Captured aircraft, tanks and anti-aircraft equipment had become inoperable due to the Taliban's inability to maintain them. In disbanding the PDPA army, the Taliban also disbanded the PDPA units responsible for their maintenance and operation. BLABER, *supra* note 71, at 161.

73. David Loyn offers this following anecdote related to the Taliban's Mullah Omar and his refusal to accept the basic obligations of UN membership:

> The UN made an effort to engage with the new administration, taking a copy of the UN Charter translated into Pashtu to Kandahar to show the Taliban what it meant to be a country. An envoy went through it page by page, sitting cross-legged on the ground, as he was asked what it meant when it talked of "human rights and fundamental freedoms for all, without distinction as to race, sex, language or religion." But Mullah Omar refused to meet the UN envoy then or at any other time.

LOYN, *supra* note 11, at 253.

74. *Id.* at 22–23; *see also* IAN BROWNLIE, PRINCIPLES OF PUBLIC INTERNATIONAL LAW 66–67 (1966).

75. GOLDMAN & TITTEMORE, *supra* note 3, at 24 n.84.

76. The Taliban was not alone in its failure to follow the law of war in Afghanistan's civil war, a point acknowledged by Colonel John Mulholland, 5th Special Forces Group commander, in advising his command that "[n]o one [the Afghan warlords] here is clean." BRISCOE ET AL., *supra* note 8, at 95. This demonstrates this author's earlier point of a distinction between legal *applicability* of law of war treaties and *application* in fact.

77. CHARLES CHENEY HYDE, I INTERNATIONAL LAW CHIEFLY AS INTERPRETED AND APPLIED BY THE UNITED STATES 158–59 (2d rev. ed. 1951).

78. *Id.* at 159–60.

79. *Id.* at 156–57.

80. Regulations Respecting the Laws and Customs of War on Land, Annex to Hague Convention No. IV Respecting the Laws and Customs of War on Land art. 43, Oct. 18, 1907, 36 Stat. 2227, *reprinted in* THE LAWS OF ARMED CONFLICTS, *supra* note 1, at 66 (emphasis provided) [hereinafter Hague IV Annex]. *See also* LASSA OPPENHEIM, II INTERNATIONAL LAW, DISPUTES, WAR AND NEUTRALITY 434–45, § 167 (Hersch Lauterpacht ed., 7th ed. 1952) [hereinafter LAUTERPACHT].

81. Hague IV Annex, *supra* note 80, art. 43.

82. SPAIGHT, *supra* note 4, at 327; UK MANUAL, *supra* note 56, at 275, ¶ 11.3, states:

> To determine whether a state of occupation exists, it is necessary to look at the area concerned and determine whether two conditions are satisfied: first, that the former government has been rendered incapable of publicly exercising its authority in that area; and, secondly, that the occupying power is in a position to substitute its own authority for that of the former government.

Applying by analogy this test to the Taliban, while the Taliban may have physically occupied substantial areas of Afghanistan, persistent resistance to the Taliban—as acknowledged in UN reports—precluded it from meeting the second part of the test. The first part occurred through the meltdown of the PDPA between 1992 and 1994. The second part never took place.

The challenge the Taliban faced has historical precedent. A Russian analysis of British failures in its Second Anglo-Afghan War concluded, "English commanders understood that they had not gained possession of all these strips of country over which the troops had passed, but only of the actual ground on which their forces were encamped." LOYN, *supra* note 11, at 114. This was the predicament the Taliban faced and suggests the media's failure to appreciate the distinction between physical presence and control sufficient to govern.

83. *Supra* note 65.

84. The present author may have contributed to Professor Toman's conclusion that the Taliban was the de facto government. As he notes in his article, *supra* note 3, in reply to an e-mail from Professor Toman, the present author stated, "An argument might be made that the Taliban was the *de facto* government of Afghanistan until early October 2001, as it occupied 80%

of Afghanistan." This informal response was based entirely on media reports, as the present author had not been involved in Operation Enduring Freedom issues or had access to official reports or analyses. The additional information obtained in research for and presented in this article presents a substantially different and more accurate picture.

Even were one to argue that at the time of Taliban recognition by Pakistan, Saudi Arabia and the UAE the Taliban was the de facto government, Professor Brownlie notes that "[i]t is sometimes said that *de jure* recognition is irrevocable while *de facto* recognition can be withdrawn." BROWNLIE, *supra* note 74, at 87.

85. Aug. 12, 1949, 6 U.S.T. 3316, T.I.A.S. 3364, 75 U.N.T.S. 135, *reprinted in* THE LAWS OF ARMED CONFLICTS, *supra* note 1, at 507 [hereinafter GPW Convention]. This section is derived from W. Hays Parks, *Jus in Bello in the Struggle against Terrorism*, *in* LEGAL ISSUES IN THE STRUGGLE AGAINST TERROR (John Norton Moore & Robert Turner eds., forthcoming).

86. *See* U.S. v. Lindh, 212 F. Supp. 2d 541, 552–58 (E.D. Va. 2002).

87. The just war tradition is an historic articulation of *when* (*jus ad bellum*) it is justifiable for a State to resort to arms, and *what* (*jus in bello*) use of force is legally permissible. *See* JAMES TURNER JOHNSON, JUST WAR AND THE RESTRAINT OF WAR (1981).

88. Gerald I.A.D. Draper, *The Status of Combatants and the Question of Guerrilla Warfare*, BRITISH YEAR BOOK OF INTERNATIONAL LAW 173, 176 (1971); Gerald I.A.D. Draper, *The Present Law of Combatancy*, *in* REFLECTIONS ON LAW AND ARMED CONFLICTS: THE SELECTED WORKS ON THE LAWS OF WAR BY THE LATE PROFESSOR COLONEL G.I.A.D. DRAPER, OBE 195 (Michael A. Meyer & Hilaire McCoubrey eds., 1998). *See also* MAURICE H. KEEN, THE LAWS OF WAR IN THE LATE MIDDLE AGES 13–15, 69 *et seq*. (1965).

89. KEEN, *supra* note 88, at 50.

90. The classic example is the assassination of Archduke Franz Ferdinand, heir to the Austrian throne, by the Slav Gavrilo Princip, in Sarajevo on June 28, 1914, generally regarded as the spark that ignited World War I. This principle is made clear in the US Constitution, which vests in the President of the United States the authority to act as commander in chief of US armed forces (Article II, § 2) and in the US Congress the authority to raise armies and navies and to declare war (Article I, § 8). 18 U.S.C. § 960 (2000) (Neutrality Act) makes it a criminal offense for a person within the United States to begin, set on foot, provide for or prepare "a means for or [furnish] the money for, or [take] part in, any military or naval expedition or enterprise to be carried on . . . against the territory or dominion of any foreign . . . state . . . with whom the United States is at peace . . . ." See, e.g., United States v. Stephen E. Black and Joe D. Hawkins, 685 F.2d 132 (5th Cir. 1982), a case in which US citizens were convicted of violation of the Neutrality Act. A narrative history of the case is STEWART BELL, BAYOU OF PIGS (2008).

91. HYDE, *supra* note 77, at 1692, 1797; LAUTERPACHT, *supra* note 80, at 203–05.

92. Additional Protocol I, *supra* note 1, art. 51(3); Additional Protocol II, *supra* note 1, art. 13(3).

93. Denial of quarter includes refusal to accept an offer to surrender and summary execution upon capture.

94. Mosby's unit operated under a commission issued by the Governor of Virginia. State commissions were a practice common for Union and Confederate forces. Receipt and retention of a governor's commission were dependent upon a unit carrying out its operations in uniform under a commander responsible for its actions, and compliance with the law of war. JEFFRY D. WERT, MOSBY'S RANGERS 62–63, 69–71, 76, 77–78, 124, 151, 157 (1990).

95. MICHAEL FELLMAN, INSIDE WAR: THE GUERRILLA CONFLICT IN MISSOURI DURING THE CIVIL WAR (1989), describes Quantrill's actions and *modus operandi*.

96. *See* RICHARD HARTIGAN, LIEBER'S CODE AND THE LAW OF WAR 2–16, 31–44, 56, 60 (1983). A traditional term is *unprivileged belligerent*, meaning a private individual not entitled to the combatant's privilege. Other commonly used terms are *unprivileged combatant* and *unlawful combatant*. The term adopted by the Bush administration—*enemy combatant*—was counter to its own arguments, as it incorrectly equated captured Taliban and al-Qaeda to lawful enemy combatants. The term "unlawful enemy combatant" is potentially misleading, as it suggests a member of regular military forces of a government may be denied prisoner of war status because he or she has acted in a manner inconsistent with the law of war or committed other criminal acts. In accordance with Article 85, GPW, a pre-capture offense does not provide a basis to deny prisoner of war status to an individual who meets any of the categories in Article 4. As was the case with many law of war decisions by Bush administration officials during the period in question, "enemy combatant" was selected more for political purposes than for legal accuracy.

97. As used in Article 3, "noncombatants" refers to military medical personnel and chaplains rather than civilians.

98. Named for its sponsor, Russian delegate Fyodor Fyodorovich Martens (1845–1909).

99. The debate was limited to a form of extended *levée en masse* following enemy occupation. A private citizen who took up arms against his or her own government or against another government with which his or her nation was at peace remained an unprivileged combatant.

100. FRITS KALSHOVEN, CONSTRAINTS ON THE WAGING OF WAR 14 (1987). Professor Kalshoven notes that "[t]his phrase, although formulated especially with a view to the thorny problem of armed resistance in occupied territory, has acquired a significance far exceeding that particular problem." Continuing, he says that "[i]t implies no more and no less than that, no matter what States may fail to agree upon, the conduct of war will always be governed by existing principles of international law."

101. THE LAWS OF ARMED CONFLICTS, *supra* note 1, at 70. Article 2 providing lawful combatant status to members of a *levée en masse* was amended to require that its members carry their arms openly in addition to respecting the laws and customs of war.

102. SPAIGHT, *supra* note 4, at 37.

103. *See* EARL F. ZIEMKE & MAGNA E. BAUER, MOSCOW TO STALINGRAD: DECISION IN THE EAST 199–219, 252–54, 330, 434–35 (rev. ed. 1985).

104. Representative histories are HENRI MICHEL, THE SHADOW WAR: EUROPEAN RESISTANCE, 1939–1945 (Richard Barry trans., 1972); MICHAEL R.D. FOOT, RESISTANCE: EUROPEAN RESISTANCE TO NAZISM, 1940–1945 (1977); JØRGEN HÆSTRUP, EUROPE ABLAZE (1978); DAVID STAFFORD, BRITAIN AND EUROPEAN RESISTANCE, 1940–1945 (1980); CHARLES CRUICKSHANK, S.O.E. IN THE FAR EAST (1983); WILLIAM MACKENZIE, THE SECRET HISTORY OF SOE: THE SPECIAL OPERATIONS EXECUTIVE, 1940–1945 (1948, 2000); FRANCIS B. MILLS, ROBERT MILLS & JOHN W. BRUNNER, OSS OPERATIONS IN CHINA (2002). The present author has identified organized resistance movements authorized by exiled governments and provided SOE and OSS assistance in Albania, Belgium, Burma, China, Czechoslovakia, Denmark, Finland, France, Greece, Indo-China, Italy, Malaya, Norway, Poland, Rumania, Serbia, Singapore, Sumatra, Thailand and Yugoslavia.

105. Aug. 12, 1949, 6 U.S.T. 3114, T.I.A.S. 3362, 75 U.N.T.S. 31, *reprinted in* THE LAWS OF ARMED CONFLICTS, *supra* note 1, at 459.

106. Aug. 12, 1949, 6 U.S.T. 3217, T.I.A.S. 3363, 75 U.N.T.S. 85, *reprinted in* THE LAWS OF ARMED CONFLICTS, *supra* note 1, at 485.

107. *Supra* note 85.

108. Aug. 12, 1949, 6 U.S.T. 3516, T.I.A.S. 3365, 75 U.N.T.S. 287, *reprinted in* THE LAWS OF ARMED CONFLICTS, *supra* note 1, at 575.

109. The absence of treaty protection for civilian medical facilities and transport and wounded, sick or shipwrecked civilians was corrected in the 1977 Additional Protocols I and II. *See, e.g.*, Additional Protocol I, *supra* note 1, arts. 8–31; MICHAEL BOTHE, KARL JOSEF PARTSCH & WALDEMAR A. SOLF, NEW RULES FOR VICTIMS OF ARMED CONFLICTS 89–167 (1982).

110. In the United States, this includes activated reserve and National Guard forces.

111. GPW Convention, *supra* note 85, art. 4A(2) (emphasis provided).

112. COMMENTARY III GENEVA CONVENTION RELATIVE TO THE TREATMENT OF PRISONERS OF WAR 50 (Jean S. Pictet ed., 1960) [hereinafter Pictet GPW].

113. Article 2 Common to the four 1949 Geneva Conventions states in part: "[T]he present Convention shall apply to all cases of declared war or any other armed conflict which may arise between two or more of the High Contracting Parties, even if the state of war is not recognized by one of them." "High Contracting Parties" means nations who are State parties to the Geneva Conventions. "High Contracting Parties" distinguished between nations who had ratified or acceded to the Geneva Conventions and those who were not yet party to and bound by the Geneva Conventions. As all 194 nations are now parties to the 1949 Geneva Conventions, they have universal applicability. As this author notes herein, *applicability* does not necessarily translate into *application* by State parties.

Article 2 Common to the four 1949 Geneva Conventions does not define *war*. It establishes the threshold for application of the four Conventions to, *inter alia*, "all cases of declared war or any other armed conflict which may arise between two or more of the High Contracting Parties, even if the state of war is not recognized by one of them." In contrast, the judgment in *United States v. Wilhelm von Leeb et al.* (The High Command Case, XI TWC 485 (1948)) defines *war* more broadly as "the exerting of violence by one state *or politically organized body* against another. In other words, it is the implementation of a political policy by means of violence." There are two points of significance to the current discussion. First, the authors of the 1949 Geneva Conventions, and particularly the prisoner of war convention, were very deliberate in declining to recognize combat operations by a government against a private, politically organized body such as the Taliban as an armed conflict in which the Geneva Conventions technically or formally applied. Second, ignorance of history by the Bush administration resulted in faulty analysis and justification for its actions with respect to captured Taliban and al-Qaeda.

114. Prisoner of war entitlement for actions as a *levée en masse* cease following enemy occupation. Article 4A(6), GPW, expressly states, "Inhabitants of a non-occupied territory, who on the approach of the enemy spontaneously take up arms to resist the invading forces, without having had time to form themselves into regular armed units, provided they carry their arms openly and respect the laws and customs of war." Thereafter members of a *levée en masse* cease to exist as such and must meet each of the six criteria in Article 4A(2), GPW, to receive entitlement to prisoner of war status.

115. Pictet GPW, *supra* note 112, at 57, states, "It is essential that there should be a *de facto* relationship between the resistance organization and the party [*sic*] to international law which is in a state of war, but the existence of this relationship is sufficient," commenting further that such a relationship "may be indicated by deliveries of equipment and supplies, as was frequently the case during the Second World War, between the Allies and the resistance networks in occupied territories." In addition to the general histories noted *supra* note 104, British and US sealift and airlift support to organized resistance movements in Axis-occupied nations is described in DAVID HOWARTH, THE SHETLAND BUS (1951); III THE ARMY AIR FORCES IN WORLD WAR II EUROPE: ARGUMENT TO V-E DAY, JANUARY 1944 TO MAY 1945, at 493–524 (Wesley Frank Craven & James Lea Cate eds., 1951); GIBB MCCALL, FLIGHT MOST SECRET: AIR MISSIONS FOR SOE AND

OSS (1981); BEN PARNELL, CARPETBAGGERS: AMERICA'S SECRET WAR IN EUROPE (1987); BROOKS RICHARDS, I SECRET FLOTILLAS: CLANDESTINE SEA OPERATIONS IN BRITTANY, 1940–1944 (2004); BROOKS RICHARDS, II SECRET FLOTILLAS: CLANDESTINE SEA OPERATIONS IN THE MEDITERRANEAN, NORTH AFRICA, AND THE ADRIATIC, 1940–1944 (2004).

116. Pictet GPW, *supra* note 112, at 57 n.2, offers the example of the July 15, 1944 declaration by US General Dwight D. Eisenhower, Supreme Headquarters, Allied Expeditionary Force (SHAEF) commander, recognizing the Free French Forces of the Interior and taking them under his command.

117. Toman, *supra* note 3, at 290–94; Draper, *The Status of Combatants and the Question of Guerrilla Warfare*, *supra* note 88, at 176.

118. The four criteria were relaxed in Articles 43(1) and 44(3) of 1977 Additional Protocol I, the latter requiring only that an individual entitled to combatant status under that treaty "carry his arms openly (a) during each military engagement, and (b) during such time as he is visible to the adversary while he is engaged in a military deployment preceding the launching of an attack in which he is to participate." This change is not relevant to the current discussion, as neither Afghanistan nor the United States is a party to Additional Protocol I.

119. 2A FINAL RECORD OF THE DIPLOMATIC CONFERENCE OF GENEVA OF 1949, at 433. Other delegations offered similar comments.

120. *See generally*, YOSSEF BODANSKY, BIN LADEN: THE MAN WHO DECLARED WAR ON AMERICA (2001); ROHAN GUNARATNA, INSIDE AL QAEDA (2002); BRISCOE ET AL., *supra* note 8, at 23; Toman, *supra* note 3, at 287–89. YAROSLAV TROFIMOV, THE SIEGE OF MECCA 7, 246–47 (2007), attributes Saudi Arabia's attack on Muslim extremists, led by Juhayman al Uteyhi, who seized the Grand Mosque in Mecca on September 20, 1979, as the point at which Usama bin Laden began to separate himself from the Saudi royal family.

121. LOYN, *supra* note 11, at 262–63.

122. GOLDMAN & TITTEMORE, *supra* note 3, at 29.

123. Toman, *supra* note 3, at 294. Professor Toman characterizes al-Qaeda through the following words of other experts:

> A question under the Hague Regulations and the Third [Geneva] Convention involves the status of an independent force, which has no factual link to a Party to an international armed conflict. In general, it may be said that such a force would probably be viewed as waging a private war. In any event, it would have no status better than that of insurgents in a non-international armed conflict, unless the movement they represent has such *de facto* objective characteristics of belligerency that the movement itself could be recognized as a Party to an international armed conflict.

Id. at 291–92, *quoting* BOTHE, PARTSCH & SOLF, *supra* note 109, at 235. Professor Toman's conclusion is that al-Qaeda does not meet the objective characteristics of belligerency. *Id.* at 294.

124. For example, civilians who accompany the armed forces are entitled to prisoner of war status under Article 4, paragraph 4, GPW, but do not enjoy the combatant's privilege.

125. In such an analysis, the first question should be whether there is an international armed conflict, as defined in Article 2 Common to the four 1949 Geneva Conventions ("all cases of declared war or of any other armed conflict which may arise between two or more of the High Contracting Parties, even if the state of war is not recognized by one of them"). Failing to meet the prerequisites in Common Article 2, there is no basis for considering provisions contained in Article 4, GPW.

126. Pictet GPW, *supra* note 112, at 18.

127. "Party to the conflict" was broadened to include a limited range of private armed groups in Articles 1(4) and 43(1) of the 1977 Additional Protocol I, *supra* note 1. As noted *supra* note 1,

as neither Afghanistan nor the United States is a party to Additional Protocol I, the change is not applicable. Had it been applicable, the Taliban would not have qualified as a party to the conflict as it met none of the criteria in Article 1(4). Since Additional Protocol I's entry into force on December 7, 1978, no private armed group has qualified as a "Party to the conflict."

128. HOWARD S. LEVIE, PRISONERS OF WAR IN INTERNATIONAL ARMED CONFLICT 36 (Vol. 59, US Naval War College International Law Studies, 1979).

129. See, e.g., HERBERT W. MCBRIDE, A RIFLEMAN WENT TO WAR (1935), detailing the account of a US citizen who joined and fought as a member of the 21st Battalion, Canadian Expeditionary Force, in World War I.

130. For example, on July 14, 1940, the *New York Herald Tribune* contained a British advertisement inviting individuals with aircraft experience to join the Royal Air Force (RAF); others already had joined and fought in the RAF in the Battle for France. Others quickly followed. RICHARD HOUGH & DENIS RICHARDS, THE BATTLE OF BRITAIN 187–88 (2008). In total, 547 men from thirteen nations, including seven US citizens, served as aircrew with the RAF during the 1940 Battle of Britain. *Id.* at 191. Similarly, Draper Kauffman attended the US Naval Academy but was screened out as the result of his pre-commissioning eye examination. Seven years later, as an ambulance driver in the American Volunteer Ambulance Corps of the French Army, he was captured by invading German forces. Eventually released, he was commissioned in the Royal Navy, where he served as a bomb disposal officer. That he was an American citizen serving first with French military and later with British naval forces would not have been a basis for German denial of prisoner of war status. (Returning to the United States on convalescent leave, he received a commission in the US Navy. He earned a Navy Cross as a result of his clearing Japanese bombs dropped during the December 7, 1941 attack on Pearl Harbor, then was assigned to establish training for and to form up naval combat demolition units, forerunner of the Navy's underwater demolition teams and today's SEALs.) *See* ELIZABETH KAUFFMAN BUSH, AMERICA'S FIRST FROGMAN: THE DRAPER KAUFFMAN STORY ix, x, 1–12, 19, 23–25, 32–43, 62–63, 78–82 (2004).

131. *See, e.g.*, Pauline Jelinek, *Pentagon Seeks Recruits on Visas*, WASHINGTON TIMES, Dec. 11, 2008, at B8.

132. Pictet GPW, *supra* note 112, at 53–58, contains an excellent summary of the negotiating history.

133. FELLMAN, *supra* note 95.

134. Parks, *supra* note 85.

135. BIDDLE, *supra* note 8, at 22, states that the ISID ceased its logistical support to the Taliban on October 12, 2001, while acknowledging that it may have continued after that date.

136. Its history is contained in INTERNATIONAL COMMITTEE OF THE RED CROSS, 1 REPORT OF THE INTERNATIONAL COMMITTEE OF THE RED CROSS ON ITS ACTIVITIES DURING THE SECOND WORLD WAR (September 1, 1939–June 30, 1947) (General Activities) 519–20, 532–33 (1948).

137. Pictet GPW, *supra* note 112, at 62. While ICRC focus was on the Free French, actual practice was far broader. *See, e.g.,* POLISH AIR FORCE ASSOCIATION, DESTINY CAN WAIT: THE POLISH AIR FORCE IN THE SECOND WORLD WAR (1949).

138. GPW Convention, *supra* note 85, art. 4A(1).

139. *Id.*, art. 4A(2).

140. *Id.*, art. 2.

141. *Citing* INTERNATIONAL COMMITTEE OF THE RED CROSS, REPORT ON THE WORK OF THE CONFERENCE OF GOVERNMENT EXPERTS 106–07 (1948).

142. A specific reference/mention of "[m]ercenaries who devastated France in the XIVth century, during the peaceful periods of the Hundred Years War." Pictet GPW, *supra* note 112, at 63 n.3.

143. *Id.* at 62–64.

144. *See supra* note 34 and accompanying text.

145. Pictet GPW, *supra* note 112, at 67.

146. *Id.* at 68.

147. Having resolved the issue that prompted the original Martens Clause in the 1907 Hague IV, the Martens Clause was relegated to the article common to the four 1949 Geneva Conventions dealing with denunciation of (withdrawal from) the Geneva Conventions by a State party. *See, e.g.*, GPW Convention, *supra* note 85, art. 42(4); Pictet GPW, *supra* note 112, at 648.

148. Parks, *supra* note 2.

149. Yoram Dinstein, *Unlawful Combatancy*, *in* INTERNATIONAL LAW AND THE WAR ON TERROR, *supra* note 7, at 159, discussed *infra*. However, under Article 85, GPW, they retain their entitlement to prisoner of war status.

150. Convention Relative to the Treatment of Prisoners of War, July 27, 1929, 47 Stat. 2021, 118 L.N.T.S. 343, *reprinted in* THE LAWS OF ARMED CONFLICTS, *supra* note 1, at 421. Article 1, paragraph 1 states: "The present Convention shall apply without prejudice . . . (1) To all persons referred to in Articles 1, 2 and 3 of the Regulations to the Hague Convention (IV) of 18 October 1907 . . . who are captured by the enemy."

151. A legal requirement that regular forces wear uniforms in order to enjoy entitlement to prisoner of war status would have exceeded the requirement in the 1899 and 1907 Hague treaties and Article 4A(2), GPW, which does not specify a "uniform" but merely "a fixed distinctive sign recognizable at a distance." As indicated in the previous discussion of Lieber's 1863 analysis and the argument put forward by Belgium and other nations in 1899, delegates were aware of the existence of irregular forces based upon the experience of the Franco-Prussian War and Anglo-Boer War. Expansion of special operations forces in World War II brought the issue to the fore.

152. Dinstein, *supra* note 149, at 164; Roberts, *supra* note 7, at 212.

Department of the Army, FM 27-10, The Law of Land Warfare para. 63 (1956) states: "Commando forces and airborne troops, although operating by highly trained methods of surprise and violent combat, are entitled, so long as they are members of the organized armed forces of the enemy and wear uniforms, to be treated as prisoners of war upon capture, even if they operate singly." That language is ambiguous in its failure to explain what constitutes a "uniform," and potentially more restrictive than the text contained in earlier editions of the US manual. For example, Chief of Staff, Department of War, Rules of Land Warfare, at 22, para. 33 (1914) states: "*The distinctive sign*. This requirement will be satisfied by the wearing of a uniform or even less than a complete uniform." This text was deleted, apparently for brevity, in the 1940 edition; the 1914 edition contained 221 pages, while the 1940 edition was reduced to 123. The necessity for paragraph 33 of the 1914 edition may have not been recognized in light of the US World War I experience in fighting uniformed enemy forces in conventional military operations on well-defined fronts; nor is it likely organized resistance movements were contemplated. The 1940 US manual contains an official publication date of October 1, 1940. The British SOE was established under highly classified circumstances on July 22, 1940; the US OSS did not follow until two years later, on July 21, 1942. Parks, ISSUES IN INTERNATIONAL LAW AND MILITARY OPERATIONS, *supra* note 2, at 84 and 85 n.69. As SOE historian M.R.D. Foot points out, "A dense veil of secrecy was indispensable to SOE, a body for mounting surprise attacks in unexpected places: no secrecy, no surprise. The fact that the body existed at all was for long a closely guarded secret." MICHAEL R.D. FOOT, SOE IN FRANCE 13 (2d rev. ed. 2004). That SOE and OSS operations and tactics, techniques and procedures were highly classified may have played a part in incorporation of the erroneous language contained in paragraph 63 of the 1956 edition of the manual. But its author(s) should have been cognizant of the change made in article 4A(2), GPW, and the rationale for it.

Due to its ambiguity and inconsistency with State practice, including US practice in World War II, the 1956 text is clarified in the forthcoming Department of Defense Law of War Manual.

153. Parks, ISSUES IN INTERNATIONAL LAW AND MILITARY OPERATIONS, *supra* note 2, annex at 92–99.

154. *See, e.g.*, ALLAN ROSAS, THE LEGAL STATUS OF PRISONERS OF WAR: A STUDY IN INTERNATIONAL HUMANITARIAN LAW APPLICABLE IN ARMED CONFLICTS 349 (1976) ("The concept of uniforms has never been explicitly defined in international law).

155. *Id.* at 78–81. As noted therein, the ICRC *Commentary* on the 1977 Additional Protocols I and II states:

> What constitutes a uniform, and how can emblems of nationality be distinguished from each other? The Conference in no way intended to define what constitutes a uniform. . . . "[A]ny customary uniform which clearly distinguished the member wearing it from a non-member should suffice." Thus a cap or an armlet etc. worn in a standard way is actually equivalent to a uniform.

COMMENTARY ON THE ADDITIONAL PROTOCOLS OF 8 JUNE 1977 TO THE GENEVA CONVENTIONS OF 12 AUGUST 1949, at 468 (Yves Sandoz, Christophe Swinarski & Bruno Zimmermann eds., 1987).

156. BOTHE, PARTSCH & SOLF, *supra* note 109, at 257.

157. See, e.g., JEREMY WILSON, LAWRENCE OF ARABIA 1043 (1990), relating the death of British Army captain William H.I. Shakespear, easily identified, targeted, and killed in 1915 by a sniper in the forces of pro-Turkish leader Ibn Rashid, as Shakespear insisted on wearing his British uniform rather than dressing in indigenous attire to appear like the forces to which he was assigned. This prompted British Army Captain T.E. Lawrence to don Arab clothing as he led the Arab revolt against Ottoman rule. *Id.* at 1043 n.4, and further discussion in Parks, ISSUES IN INTERNATIONAL LAW AND MILITARY OPERATIONS, *supra* note 2, at 100–01 n.5.

158. Parks, ISSUES IN INTERNATIONAL LAW AND MILITARY OPERATIONS, *supra* note 2, at 101 n.6; FURY, *supra* note 11, at 100, 167.

159. According to one SOF commander, Taliban wore black on black, with turbans; al Qaeda, all black, with hoods to mask their faces; Northern Alliance, a pakol (chitrali hat) and the Massoud scarf; US SOF, partial US uniform and Northern Alliance attire. FURY, *supra* note 11, at 119, 167; see also Parks, ISSUES IN INTERNATIONAL LAW AND MILITARY OPERATIONS, *supra* note 2, at 101; BLABER, *supra* note 71, at 243, 247 for the US SOF rationale, which did not involve perfidy. Anon., *supra* note 15, at 36, acknowledged, "[B]ecause the disparate forces lacked any semblance of a uniform, visual identification, *particularly at long distances*, was virtually impossible. The tasks of preventing fratricide and synchronizing multiple combat elements fell to the SF [Special Forces] detachments" (emphasis supplied). A distinction existed in Taliban operations when a single or a few Taliban would conceal himself/themselves within a crowd of innocent civilians in order to carry out an attack; such an act would be perfidy. US SOF wear of Northern Alliance attire, though much publicized, was limited as to time, unit, specific unit personnel, location of operations and mission. Parks, *supra*, at 84.

160. Hague IV Annex, *supra* note 80, art. 23 states, "In addition to the prohibitions provided by special Conventions, it is especially forbidden: . . . (b) To kill or wound treacherously individuals belonging to the hostile nation or army."

Afghanistan is not a State party to the 1907 Hague Convention (IV) nor its 1899 predecessor, Hague Convention II with Respect to the Laws and Customs of War on Land, which contained the same prohibition.

161. The official English text states "the feigning of civilian, non-combatant status." The official French text correctly states "feindre d'avoir le statut de civil *ou* de non-combatant," that is, "the feigning of civilian *or* non-combatant status," the two categories being distinctive. BOTHE, PARTSCH AND SOLF, *supra* note 109, at 206 n.21. As noted, neither the United States nor Afghanistan is a party to the 1977 Additional Protocol I. However, the definition of perfidy (using the French text) is consistent with State practice and has been applied by US military forces in conflicts since 1977.

As the present author has noted, the legal approach of the prerequisite of perfidy is not new; see Parks, ISSUES IN INTERNATIONAL LAW AND MILITARY OPERATIONS, *supra* note 2, at 82.

162. Bush Memorandum, *supra* note 9.

163. Key documents in the interagency debate are Memorandum from John C. Yoo & Robert Delahunty to William J. Haynes II, General Counsel, Department of Defense, Re: Application of Treaties and Laws to al Qaeda and Taliban Detainees (Jan. 9, 2002), *reprinted in* TORTURE PAPERS, *supra* note 9, at 38, *available at* http://www.slate.com/features/whatistorture/LegalMemos.html [hereinafter Yoo]; Memorandum from Alberto R. Gonzales to the President, Decision Re Application of the Geneva Convention on Prisoners of War to the Conflict with Al Qaeda and the Taliban (Jan. 25, 2002), *available at* http://www.slate.com/features/whatistorture/LegalMemos.html [hereinafter Gonzales]; Memorandum from Colin L. Powell to Counsel to the President & Assistant to the President for National Security Affairs, Draft Decision Memorandum for the President on the Applicability of the Geneva Convention to the Conflict in Afghanistan (Jan. 26, 2002), *reprinted in* TORTURE PAPERS, *supra*, at 122, *available at* http://www.slate.com/features/whatistorture/LegalMemos.html [hereinafter Powell]; Letter from John Ashcroft to the President (Feb. 1, 2002), *reprinted in id.* at 126, *available at* http://www.slate.com/features/whatistorture/LegalMemos.html [hereinafter Ashcroft]; Memorandum from William H. Taft IV, Legal Adviser, Department of State to Counsel to the President, Comments on Your Paper on the Geneva Conventions (Feb. 2, 2002), *reprinted in id.* at 129, *available at* http://www.slate.com/features/whatistorture/LegalMemos.html [hereinafter Taft].

164. GOLDMAN & TITTEMORE, *supra* note 3; Toman, *supra* note 3.

165. *See, e.g.*, Boumediene v. Bush, 128 S. Ct. 2229 (2008). The present author's assignment was to establish the status of those persons captured during the specified time frame. Their treatment and US Supreme Court cases dealing with their treatment are beyond the scope of this author's remit.

166. The US military provided prisoner of war protection (if not status per se) to individuals it captured on the battlefield in its operations in the Republic of Vietnam (1964–72), Grenada (1983), Panama (1989–90), Iraq (1990–91), Somalia (1992–94) and Haiti (commencing in 1994); personal knowledge of author, who was responsible for the legal aspects of this issue within the Office of the Judge Advocate General of the Army from 1979 to 2003.

167. Yoo, *supra* note 163, at 2; Ashcroft, *supra* note 163, at 1; Gonzales, *supra* note 163, at 1.

168. Powell, *supra* note 163, at "Comments on the Memorandum of January 25, 2002." The statement undoubtedly is factually correct, but does not respond to the conclusion reached by Yoo, Ashcroft and Gonzales. The United States may have opted not to comment with regard to the situation in Afghanistan (a) for fear of jeopardizing the fragile status of the government of Burhanuddin Rabbani and its entitlement to the Afghan seat in the United Nations coveted by the Taliban, (b) to avoid interference in the civil war and/or (c) to resist the conclusion that a "failed State" would be relieved of its treaty obligations.

169. Gonzales, *supra* note 163, at 3.

170. Powell, *supra* note 163, at "Comments on the Memorandum of January 25, 2002"; and personal knowledge of the present author, who was directly involved in issues related to prisoner of war treatment for captured members of the Panamanian Defense Forces; *see supra* note 166. Judge Gonzales' statement also errs in suggesting a separate policy decision was made for Operation Just Cause (Panama, 1989–90).

171. Taft, *supra* note 163, as attachment thereto.

172. *Id.*

173. Press Release, Office of the White House Press Secretary, Fact Sheet: Status of Detainees at Guantanamo (Feb. 7, 2002), *available at* http://geneva.usmission.gov/press2002/0802detainees.htm [hereinafter White House Fact Sheet].

174. Ari Fleischer, Press Briefing (Feb. 7, 2002), transcript available at http://www.presidency.ucsb.edu/ws/index.php?pid=61628.

175. Secretary of Defense Donald H. Rumsfeld and General Richard Myers, DoD News Briefing (Feb. 8, 2002), transcript available at http://www.defenselink.mil/transcripts/transcript.aspx?transcriptid=2624 [hereinafter Rumsfeld].

176. *Id.*

177. The rationale offered by Bush administration officials incorrectly listing a uniform requirement neglects a key historical point from the Ronald Reagan and George H.W. Bush administrations—which included key participants in developing the erroneous "uniform" rationale for denial of prisoner of war status to captured al-Qaeda and Taliban—i.e., that both administrations supported (with weapons and funding) the *mujahidin* resistance against the Soviet occupation. The *mujahidin* wore the same or similar attire as the Taliban and the Northern Alliance, and in many instances were the same persons who fought for the Taliban or the Northern Alliance. As the United States was not a party to the conflict against the Soviet occupation, and the Soviet Union had established a belligerent occupation, the *mujahidin* were not entitled to prisoner of war status under Article 4A(2) (organized resistance movement of a party to the conflict) or 4A(6) (*levée en masse*). If one follows the natural logic of the George W. Bush administration regarding the status of the Taliban, then arguably it is condemning the support of the previous administrations for the *mujahidin* or acting with hypocrisy.

178. Parks, ISSUES IN INTERNATIONAL LAW AND MILITARY OPERATIONS, *supra* note 2, at 516–19.

179. *Id.* at 496–98, 517, 522–23. US SOF who were involved in these operations and with whom the author has spoken have indicated there was no difficulty by either side in identifying opposing forces when operating as units.

180. *See, e.g.*, GOLDMAN & TITTEMORE, *supra* note 3, at 25–26, 28; and Toman, *supra* note 3, at 281.

181. White House Fact Sheet, *supra* note 173.

182. *Id.*

183. Boumediene v. Bush, 128 S. Ct. 2229 (2008).

184. Bush Memorandum, *supra* note 9.

185. Fleischer, *supra* note 174.

186. *Id.*

187. *Id.*

188. White House Fact Sheet, *supra* note 173.

189. Fleischer, *supra* note 174.

190. Rumsfeld, *supra* note 175.

191. *See, e.g.*, FURY, *supra* note 11, at 93.

192. Fleischer, *supra* note 174.

193. Rumsfeld, *supra* note 175.

194. Article 52(2) of Additional Protocol I defines *military objective* as "those objects which by their nature, location, purpose or use make an effective contribution to military action and whose total or partial destruction, capture or neutralization, in the circumstances ruling at the time, offers a definite military advantage." The same definition is contained in Article 2(6) of the Amended Mines Protocol (II), Convention on Certain Conventional Weapons (CCW) and Article 1(3) of CCW Protocol III (Incendiary Weapons). As the United States is a party to CCW Amended Mines Protocol, it accepts this definition. Protocol on Prohibitions or Restrictions on the Use of Mines, Booby-Traps and Other Devices, as amended May 3, 1996, 2048 U.N.T.S. 133; Protocol on Prohibitions or Restrictions on the Use of Incendiary Weapons, Oct. 10, 1980, 1342 U.N.T.S. 171; both *reprinted in* THE LAWS OF ARMED CONFLICTS, *supra* note 1, at 196 and 210, respectively.

XI

Targeting and International Humanitarian Law in Afghanistan

Michael N. Schmitt*

Experience has demonstrated, time and again, that the application of international humanitarian law (IHL) on the battlefield is an exercise of extreme intricacy. No aspect of this body of law has proven more difficult to apply than that governing targeting—the use of force against enemy forces, material and facilities. Combat operations in Afghanistan since October 7, 2001, the date on which the United States and its coalition partners launched Operation Enduring Freedom, have aptly illustrated the complexity of targeting in modern warfare.

This article examines targeting practices during the Operation Enduring Freedom campaign through 2008, with emphasis on US operations. Specifically, it explores the role law played in the calculations of those responsible for planning, approving and conducting "attacks," defined in IHL as "acts of violence against the enemy, whether in offence or defence."[1] As will become apparent, their decisions were determined less by law than by either the operational realities of the battlefield or, in a Clausewitzian sense, the policy dictates underpinning the conflict.

Reference is largely to the law applicable in international armed conflict, that is, the law governing hostilities between States.[2] Although debate continues over whether the terrorist attacks of September 11, 2001 launched a conflict of this

---

* Charles H. Stockton Professor of International Law, US Naval War College, Newport, Rhode Island.

character,[3] the October 7 coalition strikes against Taliban and terrorist forces based in Afghanistan unquestionably did so, one between Afghanistan and the States participating in the US-led coalition.[4] Arguably, the conflict became non-international in June 2002, when the *Loya Jirga* elected Hamid Karzai President of the Transitional Authority, an act which the United Nations recognized as establishing legitimate indigenous governance over a sovereign Afghanistan.[5] Today, the "war" in Afghanistan comprises a non-international armed conflict between the Afghan government (supported by foreign States) and various armed groups, most notably the remnants of the Taliban and Al Qaeda.[6]

Although the conflict has become non-international, it must be understood that the IHL norms governing attacks during international armed conflicts, on one hand, and non-international armed conflicts, on the other, have become nearly indistinguishable. In particular, the foundational IHL principle of distinction, which requires those involved in hostilities to "at all times distinguish between the civilian population and combatants and between civilian objects and military objectives," applies equally in all conflicts.[7] That being so, the humanitarian law governing international armed conflict always serves as an appropriate benchmark against which to measure targeting practices.

The Operational Environment

Afghanistan presented a multifarious environment in which to apply targeting law.[8] The country's physical and human terrains are of unparalleled complexity. At nearly 650,000 square kilometers, it is roughly the size of Texas. Much of the country is mountainous and few roads or other means of transportation exist. The 5,500-kilometer border is ill-defined and porous. These features often compelled US forces to employ airpower in lieu of ground operations. Habitation is widely scattered and predominantly rural, and combatants are seldom distinguishable from civilians by dress. The operational result was an unusually heavy reliance on intelligence, surveillance and reconnaissance (ISR) capabilities, rather than visual identification by an attacker. Complex ethnic and tribal relationships, characterized by shifting alliances, complicated matters. Indeed, Afghans typically have less sense of identity as such than as Tajiks, Pashtuns, Hazaras, Turkmens, Uzbeks or members of other similar groups. In many cases, these ethnic groups straddle borders with Afghanistan's neighbors—Pakistan, Turkmenistan, Uzbekistan, Tajikistan and China.

Perhaps most significantly, Afghanistan's recent history has been one of constant warfare, from the internal conflict and ensuing Soviet invasion of 1979, through the Soviet withdrawal a decade later, and into the war that led to the 1996

Taliban victory. Defeat of the Taliban by the US-led coalition in late 2001 ushered in the period of hostilities considered here. Many Afghans have known nothing but war, and many have found themselves on both sides of the battle lines at different times. A massive illegal narcotics infrastructure financially fuels these conflicts. Afghanistan is presently the world's largest producer of opium, with an output of eight thousand metric tons in 2008. Since unemployment runs at 40 percent, and in light of a per capita gross domestic product of a meager $800, both the drug trade and conflict offer attractive means of subsistence.[9]

As noted, terrain, distance and infrastructure led the coalition forces to rely heavily on air attacks. Political demands for a quick response to September 11, the practical difficulty of rapidly deploying ground forces and fear of repeating the disastrous Soviet experience further led to an emphasis on air operations.[10] During the initial phase of hostilities, friendly indigenous armed groups, supported by US and coalition special forces, shouldered responsibility for most ground operations. However, once the conflict morphed into a classic insurgency, ground operations assumed increasing importance. Nevertheless, air attack remains a dominant feature of the war in Afghanistan.

Targeting in a Counterinsurgency

Within months, the conflict in Afghanistan became an insurgency in which traditional methods of warfare no longer sufficed.[11] As US military doctrine recognizes, the application of force to defeat an insurgency must be but part of a broader strategy that incorporates paramilitary, political, economic, psychological and civic actions.

> The application of a purely military approach to irregular warfare [IW] has not proved successful in the past. IW is about winning a war of ideas and perception. Its battles are fought amongst the people and its outcomes are determined by the perceptions and support of the people. The campaign must change the perception and offer viable alternatives, rather than specifically kill an enemy or destroy his resources in isolation.[12]

This reality necessitates carefully measured use of force, lest the complementary components of the strategy suffer. The current US counterinsurgency (COIN) manual accordingly cautions,

> [a]ny use of force generates a series of reactions. . . . Counterinsurgents should calculate carefully the type and amount of force to be applied and who wields it for any operation. An operation that kills five insurgents is counterproductive if collateral damage leads to the recruitment of fifty more insurgents. . . . [Thus,] it is vital for

> commanders to adopt appropriate and measured levels of force and apply that force precisely so that it accomplishes the mission without causing unnecessary loss of life or suffering.[13]

Sensitivity to the reverberating consequences of an attack that causes civilian casualties lies at the heart of counterinsurgency strategy, for "using substantial force . . . increases the opportunity for insurgent propaganda to portray lethal military activities as brutal, [while] using force precisely and discriminately strengthens the rule of law that needs to be established."[14]

Ultimately, the key is legitimacy with the population, the support of which constitutes the ultimate objective of all counterinsurgencies. The term "legitimacy" unsurprisingly appears 131 times in the COIN manual. In 2008, it was elevated to a "principle of war" for US joint operations. Along with perseverance and restraint, similarly relevant in the context of targeting, legitimacy joined the nine traditional principles: objective, offensive, mass, economy of force, maneuver, unity of command, security, surprise and simplicity.[15]

The legitimacy imperative undergirds US targeting doctrine. As an example, the Air Force requires consideration of the following factors during the "target validation" phase of planning.[16]

> - Does the target meet [combined force air component commander] or higher commanders' objectives, guidance, and intent?
> - Is the target consistent with [law of armed conflict] and [rules of engagement]?
> - Is the desired effect on the target consistent with the end state?
> - Is the target politically or culturally "sensitive?"
>   - What will the effect of striking it be on public opinion (enemy, friendly, and neutral)?
> - What are the risks and likely consequences of collateral damage?
> - Is it feasible to attack this target? What is the risk?
> - Is it feasible to attack the target *at this time*?
> - What are the consequences of *not* attacking the target?
> - Will attacking the target negatively affect friendly operations due to current or planned friendly exploitation of the target?

Clearly, counterinsurgency targeting planners must be especially sensitive to issues beyond the immediate military utility of a strike and the legal norms governing it.

The collateral damage estimate methodology (CDEM) employed by US forces reflects this sensitivity.[17] "Collateral damage" refers to incidental injury to civilians and damage to civilian objects caused during an attack on a lawful target. CDEM sets forth "standardized procedures for determining potential collateral damage, options available to mitigate that damage, and approval authorities for strikes based on the anticipated collateral damage during the conduct of operations."[18] Although the precise parameters of CDEM are classified, in general terms the methodology involves using computer-assisted modeling, intelligence analysis, weaponeering and human vetting to assess likely collateral damage and determine the level at which a preplanned strike must be approved.[19] It further requires particular caution when attacking dual-use targets, when employing cluster munitions or when civilians are present within military objectives.

The Law of Targeting in Brief

The law of targeting is, from a theoretical and undeconstructed perspective, fairly straightforward.[20] Consistent with the principle of distinction, attacks may only be conducted against military objectives, including members of the armed forces and other organized armed groups participating in the conflict.[21] Objects which by "nature, location, purpose, or use make an effective contribution to military action and whose total or partial destruction, capture, or neutralization, in the circumstances ruling at the time, offers a definite military advantage" qualify as military objectives.[22] By the "use" criterion, civilian objects may become military objectives when the enemy employs them for military ends. Analogously, civilians may be targeted should they "directly participate in hostilities."[23] Attacks must not be indiscriminate; that is, they must be directed against a specific military objective and may not treat "as a single military objective a number of clearly separated and distinct military objectives located in a city, town, village or other area containing a similar concentration of civilians or civilian objects."[24]

When engaging a lawful target, the attacker may be barred from employing certain weapons. Such restrictions derive either from the customary law forbidding the employment of indiscriminate weapons[25] and those which cause unnecessary suffering or superfluous injury,[26] or from specific treaty restrictions, such as the Dublin Treaty on cluster munitions, for States party.[27]

Even assuming a lawful target and permitted weapon, an attacker must take "feasible precautions" to minimize collateral damage. Specifically, "the commander must decide, in light of all the facts known or reasonably available to him, including the need to conserve resources and complete the mission successfully, whether to adopt an alternative method of attack, if reasonably available, to reduce civilian casualties and damage."[28] Considerations include weapon and tactic options, as well as alternative targets that can be attacked to attain a "similar military advantage."

Finally, attacks that violate the principle of proportionality are unlawful. An attack will breach the standard if it is "expected to cause incidental loss of civilian life, injury to civilians, damage to civilian objects, or a combination thereof, which would be excessive in relation to the concrete and direct military advantage anticipated."[29] The rule of proportionality is often misconstrued as either prohibiting "extensive" collateral damage or as a test which balances collateral damage against military advantage. In fact, it bars attack only when no proportionality at all exists between the ends sought and the expected harm to civilians and civilian objects. Restated, the linchpin term "excessive" indicates unreasonable collateral damage in light of the reasonably anticipated military advantage expected to result from the attack.[30]

Law and Targeting in Afghanistan

That law limits targeting options is self-evident. However, the nature of a conflict equally affects application of the law, sometimes by necessitating policy and operational limitations that exceed those found in international humanitarian law. Nowhere has this dynamic been more apparent than during operations in Afghanistan.

The legitimacy imperative, so prominent in counterinsurgency doctrine, was the driving force behind targeting practices in the conflict. Early high-visibility mistakes drew international attention to the US operations. Of particular note were two mistaken strikes on an International Committee of the Red Cross (ICRC) warehouse in the first month of the conflict and an attack on a wedding party in November.[31] Resultantly, the incentive to avoid future mistakes and, indeed, even lawful collateral damage, grew quickly.

Intent on avoiding unintended harm to the civilian population, commanders imposed strict restrictions on the conduct of operations. For instance, the International Security Assistance Force Commander directed his forces to employ precision munitions whenever possible; humanitarian law imposes no such requirement. Additionally, he directed on-scene commanders to make every effort to ensure houses from which their troops received fire were free of innocent civilians before responding,[32] even though, as a matter of IHL, returning fire in such circumstances is governed by the rule of proportionality and the requirement to take feasible precautions in attack, not by the mere presence of civilians. Further, in 2007 the United States and NATO restricted the use of airstrikes during troops-in-contact (TIC) situations, often opting for withdrawal rather than engagement. US forces also increasingly employed small-diameter bombs (low-collateral-damage bombs). Again, IHL would not necessarily mandate such practices.

Despite such efforts, civilian casualties continued to occur. Human Rights Watch estimates that in 2007 over 1,600 civilians were killed in the conflict. Nine hundred fifty died as a result of Taliban and Al Qaeda actions, whereas 434 of the casualties were attributable to US and NATO actions (312 in airstrikes and 113 during ground action). Another fifty-seven died in crossfire between the warring parties and the circumstances surrounding the deaths of 192 were unclear.[33]

President Karzai, struggling with the public-opinion fallout of civilian casualties, repeatedly addressed the issue. Following a particularly tragic attack in 2007 that killed fifty-one civilians, he stated that while "the intention is very good in these operations to fight terrorism . . . five years on, it is very difficult for us to continue to accept civilian casualties."[34] Karzai continues to demand greater care in executing attacks endangering civilians.

A number of obstacles dramatically hindered attempts to avoid collateral damage. The enemy was scattered across the country and often operated in small groups. The non-linear nature of this battlespace meant that operations had to be conducted over vast areas in which the mere position of a group, vehicle or other mobile target seldom served as a reliable indicator of its enemy character. Moreover, because neither the Taliban nor Al Qaeda fielded a classic military force, with corresponding fixed military facilities, coalition forces quickly exhausted known targets, thereby necessitating a shift to fleeting targets, which were harder to identify because of time constraints. Most targeting consequently became "dynamic." In dynamic targeting, targets are passed to aircraft already airborne as hostile forces are identified, thereby limiting the opportunity for comprehensive target analysis, and requiring use of whatever weapons the aircraft happen to be armed with at the time.

The difficulty of identifying the enemy complicated matters. Enemy forces wore no uniforms or other distinctive clothing that allowed immediate visual identification. Merely being armed was an insufficient indicator, as Afghans in remote areas often carry weapons for protection, and because friendly indigenous armed groups were usually indistinguishable from the Taliban and Al Qaeda. General T. Michael Mosely, the combined force air component commander, highlighted the operational murkiness when he noted that "in any given space—ground space—out there, you had regular and unconventional forces, humanitarian assistance guys, maybe regular guys and not one of us in the command authority knew where all those guys were."[35]

Determined to avoid incidents which might delegitimize their operations, US and coalition forces imposed wide-ranging targeting restrictions through myriad mechanisms. These included coalition and national rules of engagement (ROE),[36] no-strike lists (for reasons such as IHL or host-nation sensitivities), restricted target lists (in which attack requires special preapproval, e.g., due to negative cultural implications), individual target folder[37] restrictions (such as a requirement to use a particular munition or strike a particular "desired point of impact"), Joint Air Operations Plans,[38] execute orders,[39] fragmentary orders,[40] fire support coordination measures[41] and soldier cards.[42] The net result was a dense and oft confusing normative environment, one in which IHL played a minor role relative to policy and operational considerations.[43]

Such restrictions deviated measurably from customary practices attendant to attacks on individuals. The traditional approach in conventional conflict is straightforward. Typically, enemy armed forces, including organized armed groups supporting the enemy, are "declared hostile," either at the outset of the conflict or, in the latter case, once their involvement in the conflict becomes evident. Declaring forces hostile operationalizes the principle of distinction, which permits attacks on combatants. It matters not whether the combatants are threatening the attacker, or even whether they represent a potential threat; status alone renders them a lawful target. For instance, an unarmed cook may be attacked on sight if he or she is a member of the armed forces.

By the principle of distinction, civilians may not be attacked unless, and for such time as, they directly participate in hostilities.[44] Accordingly, although they may not be declared hostile per se, rules of engagement and other targeting guidance allow them to be attacked while engaging in actions that constitute direct participation. Much controversy exists over the reach of the qualifying activities, as well as the meaning of the phrase "for such time." These issues will be dealt with later; the point here is that it is customary for targeting guidance to permit attacks on direct participants.

Beyond declaring forces hostile and incorporating direct participation into the ROE, the third typical form of engagement authority addresses violence with no nexus to the conflict—criminal acts. Soldiers faced with such criminality may employ force consistent with the law of self-defense (and defense of others). Specifically, they may use deadly force to protect themselves and others against an imminent threat of death or serious injury, when less extreme measures are unavailable.[45] Operationally, the US rules of engagement provide that US military personnel may use force in the face of a hostile act or a demonstration of hostile intent.[46] They may only do so when force is the sole viable option for addressing the situation (principle of necessity). No more force than that required to repel the attack, or prospective attack, is permitted.

This typical three-tiered paradigm was notably altered during operations in Afghanistan. Although targeting practices shifted somewhat over time to meet emerging battlefield realities, in broad terms they have been relatively constant. When the conflict began, the United States and its coalition partners declared no enemy forces hostile, to include the Taliban and Al Qaeda. Instead, the "enemy" had to represent a "likely and identifiable threat" (LIT) before being attacked. Those not meeting this standard could only be engaged if they had committed a hostile act or demonstrated hostile intent, the self-defense rule traditionally employed to respond to actions unconnected to the hostilities. During Operation Iraqi Freedom, by contrast, the Iraqi military was declared hostile from the outset of hostilities. Similarly, "designated terrorist groups" could generally be engaged in the same fashion.[47]

Afghanistan represented the first use of the LIT standard in an armed conflict. It was less permissive than the practice of declaring forces hostile because potential targets had to manifest some degree of threat. Paradoxically, the standard was more permissive than the designated-terrorist-group approach applicable in Iraq because it included no status criterion, i.e., circumstances alone justified engagement even in the absence of intelligence as to membership.

The adoption of this untested approach to engagement authority begs the question of why the standard declaration of forces hostile, combined with direct participation and self-defense ROE, was judged insufficient. Apparently, concern over the liberality of declaring forces hostile, combined with apprehension over the potential for friendly-fire incidents, underpinned the standard. According to one key participant in its development at US Central Command (CENTCOM), the military headquarters for Afghanistan and Iraq operations,

> I intentionally designed it to allow the guys in contact (Ground Forces) the ability to engage the "enemy," such as they were, without actually being shot at first, while at the same time limiting the ability of the guys flying at 21,000 feet and 210 knots to drop bombs everywhere they wanted (potentially on our allies). As you know, when we began operations targets (deliberate targets) were intentionally held at the highest levels and this was a way to provide some flexibility to the guy in the field. "Self Defense Plus" is how I describe it. In theory, this gave the Air Force the ability to strike as well (e.g. SAM batteries, anti-aircraft guns, etc). Based on the "OPLAN" I knew there would be people (ally and enemy alike) all over the country that looked exactly the same (white robes/turbans[,] on horses/pickup trucks, etc).

> Identification of the enemy was everything during this conflict. There wasn't even a FLOT [forward line of own troops]. Eventually, the best we could do was create small zones/boxes where we could say none of our people were located. You simply couldn't tell who the enemy was from the lawn darts [slang for an F-16] and this was a way of empowering the guys in contact to shoot or call air strikes based upon "Positive Identification" (the totality of the circumstances). And, even with these tight rules the conflict didn't go without incident.[48]

The less candid, but official, CENTCOM explanation focused on the conflict's unique nature. Central Command was intent on maintaining strict control over attacks because it well understood the downside of collateral damage during an insurgency. Recall also the difficulties of verifying targets, both because identification based solely on appearance was problematic and because it was often difficult to determine to which side the various armed groups owed their allegiance at any particular time. With its comprehensive access to ISR assets, and fuller grasp of operational and strategic considerations, CENTCOM believed that it was best situated to distinguish friendly from hostile targets.

Yet, the command realized that a conflict of this magnitude required more than self-defense rules. One scenario cited to justify the new standard involved US forces encountering sleeping Taliban soldiers; another posited aircraft spotting anti-aircraft systems along the route of attack. Self-defense rules alone would not permit attack in such situations, and it clearly would make no sense for soldiers in the field or airborne aircraft to have to "call home" for engagement authorization, merely because these lucrative targets were neither committing a hostile act nor demonstrating hostile intent. For CENTCOM, the answer lay in the LIT standard.[49]

The level of certainty required to determine that a target qualified as a likely and identifiable threat was also a novel feature, at least in ground operations. Likely and identifiable threat required more than merely "suspicious people in a questionable location."[50] Rather, the rules of engagement mandated positive identification (PID) of the target as a threat before attacking it. Previously, this standard had only been applied in the no-fly-zone-enforcement context of Operations Northern and Southern Watch.[51] Afghanistan represented its first use in ground operations, and it unsurprisingly caused confusion. The meaning of PID was eventually clarified in an unclassified format during Operation Iraqi Freedom on the Combined Forces Land Component ROE Card: "PID is a reasonable certainty that the proposed target is a legitimate military target."[52] Interestingly, PID had meant something much more in the no-fly-zone context—almost a no-mistakes standard.[53]

Accounts from soldiers and airmen, as well as judge advocates, indicate that LIT generated confusion, in great part because it was not a standard to which combat forces had trained. Numerous subordinate commands urged CENTCOM to issue guidance.[54] The new terminology also elevated form over substance, at least to an extent. For instance,

> [r]eservations of targeting authority to higher levels made it extremely important for team members calling for fires to use the right terms to avoid any delays. In addition to using terms like "positively identified" and "likely and identifiable threat" in the request, the team members needed to indicate the situation requiring the fires so that the approval was obtained at the most immediate level possible.[55]

One US officer cut to the chase: "When lawyers can easily argue about what [LIT] means or doesn't mean as far as engaging targets, we have failed[,] because the 21-year-old corporal doesn't have the luxury of such an academic exercise."[56]

Likely and identifiable threat represented a standard exceeding that required by the relevant norms of international humanitarian law. Most significantly, it rejected the universally accepted premise that combatants, whether members of the armed forces or of other organized armed groups, can be attacked on sight. Under IHL, their mere status as combatants rendered them targetable. By contrast, act (or imminent act) replaced status in the LIT standard.

LIT is a genre of the direct participation in hostilities—one without an express "for such time" component. This should be unsurprising, since the absence of classic conventional operations by the Taliban and Al Qaeda, combined with the difficulty of identifying fighters as members of a particular group, meant that application of the direct-participation notion, in some form, was destined to loom large.

As mentioned earlier, disagreement exists over the scope of direct participation. For instance, while all agree that conducting an attack and gathering tactical intelligence qualify, disagreement prevails as to whether directly financing insurgents does. An ICRC-sponsored multiyear project to clarify matters is nearing completion. Although the final interpretive guidance on direct participation has yet to be released, indications are that three cumulative criteria will emerge.[57]

The act in question must first adversely affect (or be likely to do so) enemy military operations or capacity, or harm civilians or civilian objects. Second, there must be a direct causal link between the act and the harm caused the enemy, or the harm must derive from a coordinated military operation of which the act is an integral part. This causality criterion excludes actions that may contribute in some way to the enemy's military efforts, but which do not directly enhance its combat actions. Finally, the act must be designed to negatively affect the enemy in support of its opponent. This belligerent nexus requirement would exclude mere criminality unconnected to the conflict. The LIT standard meets all three criteria: the threat is to

US forces, the anticipated actions amount to hostile activity and the forces acting are not mere criminals.

The absence of a "for such time" element in LIT raises several legal issues. Before discussing them, it is useful to recall that they are not raised as to any individuals who are members of an organized armed force, for, as noted, members of such groups may be attacked regardless of whether they are directly participating.[58] There is no temporal issue—as a matter of law—vis-à-vis them.

Those who are not members of an organized armed group, but meet the direct participation scope threshold, may only be attacked "for such time" as they directly participate in the hostilities. The notion of "for such time" is the source of much contention. The ICRC *Commentary* to the relevant provision of Additional Protocol I, Article 51.3, provides that direct participation includes "preparations for combat and return from combat," but that "[o]nce he ceases to participate, the civilian regains his right to the protection . . . ."[59] Individuals who have not set out to attack their enemy are immune from attack; those who manage to make it home following an operation regain civilian protection until they set out on another operation. Certain experts of the working group on direct participation embraced the strict approach set forth in this non-binding commentary.

Other experts point out that this narrow approach creates a "revolving door" through which the direct participant passes as he or she begins and completes each mission.[60] They propose an alternative which locks the door after exit: once an individual has opted into the hostilities, he or she remains targetable until unambiguously opting out. Opting out can occur either through extended non-participation demonstrating an intention to desist from further involvement, or an affirmative act of withdrawal. Although it may be difficult to determine whether a potential target has opted out, since the individual did not enjoy any privilege to engage in hostilities in the first place, it is reasonable that he or she bear the risk that the other side is unaware of withdrawal.

This is the better interpretation of direct participation. In international humanitarian law, gray areas must be interpreted in light of the law's underlying purposes—achieving balance between military necessity and humanitarian concerns.[61] A revolving door would throw off this balance. It would frustrate combatants charged with combating the direct participants, and combatants frustrated with legal norms constitute a risk to the civilian population. Additionally, the restrictive approach would paradoxically create a situation in which those entitled to use force—lawful combatants—would enjoy less protection than those not so entitled but nevertheless doing so; the former could be attacked at any time, whereas the latter could only be attacked while deploying to and from an operation and during the operation itself. From a military necessity perspective, enemy direct participants would unacceptably enjoy a temporal sanctuary.[62]

The LIT standard runs counter to the revolving-door interpretive approach. For instance, the approach begs the question of how one responds to the sleeping-fighters scenario posed by those responsible for LIT's adoption. By strict application of the revolving-door approach, the sleeping fighters could not be engaged. LIT imposes no such constraint. Albeit sleeping, the fighters are a likely and identifiable threat. There need be no debate as to whether their sleeping falls within the confines of deploying to or from an operation. By contrast, the alternative liberal interpretation of direct participation tracks LIT neatly. Both allow attack in this and similar situations in which the direct participant is taking a tactical pause. Indeed, these are precisely the sorts of scenarios posed by critics of the revolving-door approach to convincingly point out its impracticality.

As can be seen, LIT is roughly comparable to the liberal standard of direct participation.[63] Yet, beyond questions as to the scope of the standard lies the issue of certainty. With LIT, individuals must be positively identified as likely threats before being attacked. This requirement poses a number of practical and legal questions. Central among them is the requisite type and degree of certainty. What does "positive" mean in practice? How positive? Beyond a reasonable doubt? More likely than not? And does positive identification mean that the individual in question is likely to be a potential threat or, instead, likely to actually threaten?

Consider the requirement's application on the bewildering battlefield that is Afghanistan. What indicators should suffice in making a positive identification? Perhaps carrying weapons? Yet, many non-participants carried weapons in Afghanistan for self-protection. Perhaps the weapons (e.g., crew-served weapons) evidenced their status as a threat. However, recall that there were friendly indigenous forces armed with the same type of weapons, and that identity and allegiances were difficult to discern. And what type of intelligence should be required to determine that someone was a likely and identifiable threat? Many were available in Afghanistan, but which sufficed? Satellite imagery, unmanned aerial vehicle (UAV) imagery transmitted in real time, human eyes on target, cell phone intercepts, human intelligence? Finally, there is the critical matter of whether positive identification is contextual. That is, does the criterion represent a constant in low- and high-risk environments, or does high risk lower the threshold necessary for positive identification? In Afghanistan, both environments existed at various times and places.

Uncertainty is hardly a novel phenomenon on the battlefield. That being so, States have tended to mandate the only level of certainty that is practicable in the fog of war—would a reasonable warfighter in the same circumstances hesitate to act? The US position is representative. *The Commander's Handbook on the Law of*

Naval Operations provides that "[c]ombatants in the field must make an honest determination as to whether a particular person is or is not taking a direct part in hostilities based on the person's behavior, location, and attire, and other information available at the time."[64]

International humanitarian treaty law also addresses battlefield uncertainty. Article 50.1 of Additional Protocol I provides that "in case of doubt whether a person is a civilian, that person shall be considered to be civilian."[65] Obviously, the article does not rule out doubt altogether. This is clear from the ICRC *Commentary* on the provision, which notes, in an example particularly appropriate to Afghanistan, "if combatants do not clearly distinguish themselves from the civilian population . . ., this could result in a weakening of the immunity granted civilians and the civilian population."[66] Such weakening could occur only if engagement in the face of some doubt was contemplated by the commentary. The UK understanding accompanying its ratification of the Protocol similarly adopts a contextual reading. It states that "the rule . . . applies only in cases of substantial doubt still remaining after [the required assessment of the attack], and [it does not override] a commander's duty to protect the safety of troops under his command or to preserve his military situation, in conformity with the other provisions of the protocol."[67] The determinative term is "substantial." Finally, the ICRC's *Customary International Humanitarian Law* study reasonably finds that "it is fair to conclude that when there is a situation of doubt, a careful assessment has to be made under the conditions and restraints governing a particular situation as to whether there are sufficient indications to warrant attack. One cannot automatically attack anyone who might appear dubious."[68] Use of the phrase "sufficient indications" suggests that absolute certainty was not required.

It is unclear what LIT required beyond IHL's "reasonable warfighter in same or similar circumstances" threshold. Its positive-identification requirement, absent clear explication to the contrary, could be interpreted as suggesting that the established IHL frame of reference had been rejected in lieu of a more restrictive standard. But, if so, how? Complicating matters even further is the fact that the concept of positive identification had been adopted in other contexts. For instance, it was adopted for "kill or capture" operations to heighten the preconditions over those applying during a "capture or detain" operation.[69] So, does PID mean different things in different types of operations? Whatever it does mean, it is clear that PID was at least as restrictive as IHL—in all likelihood more so in application.

Another aspect of targeting in Afghanistan relevant to an IHL analysis was the requirement that attacks be cleared at specified levels of command. As noted by one director of combat operations in the Combined Air Operations Center during Operation Anaconda,

> [t]he ROE was not there to go out and do a conventional fight. Under the rules of engagement for Operation Enduring Freedom, pre-planned strikes, interdiction targets and time-sensitive targets all had to be approved by USCENTCOM; and for the most part, the USCENTCOM/J-2 and legal advisors . . . drove what we did and did not target.[70]

His comments exemplified the concerns senior leadership had about operations going awry, even in the remotest of areas.[71]

This raises the issue of approval level. The Anaconda requirements exceeded even those found in the CDEM approval process. Yet, IHL imposes no level of strike approval tied to likely levels of civilian harm. In great part, this is because law is contextual. The degree of lawful civilian harm is determined by reference to the military advantage accruing from the attack in question. "Those who plan or decide upon an attack" must also take feasible (practical in the circumstances) precautions in attack.[72] In other words, the law lies where it falls—on those planning, approving or executing attacks, whoever they might be. This tightening of the restrictions over and above what IHL required demonstrated the extent to which Afghanistan ROE and CDEM approval levels reflected an understanding that unintended civilian harm can have extra-normative consequences.

The two remaining IHL issues raised by targeting operations in Afghanistan are the principle of proportionality and requirement to take feasible precautions in attack. For a number of practical reasons, proportionality posed few concerns. From an operational perspective, the population was widely dispersed, engagements often occurred in remote areas and no major urban battles took place. Precision munitions were generally available when called for and intelligence, surveillance and reconnaissance assets, particularly unmanned aerial vehicles, could be used to assess and monitor target areas, often in real time.

Counterinsurgency doctrine and practices also minimized the play of the proportionality principle in the conflict. As noted, counterinsurgency doctrine puts a high premium on the avoidance of collateral damage; in Afghanistan, even attacks which were clearly proportionate were often avoided. However, counterinsurgency affects application of the principle in a less obvious fashion.

> In conventional operations, proportionality is usually calculated in simple utilitarian terms: civilian lives and property lost versus enemy destroyed and military advantage gained. But in COIN operations, advantage is best calculated not in terms of how many insurgents are killed or detained, but rather which enemies are killed or detained. If certain key insurgent leaders are essential to the insurgents' ability to conduct operations, then military leaders need to consider their relative importance when determining how best to pursue them. In COIN environments, the number of civilian lives lost and property destroyed needs to be measured against how much harm the

> targeted insurgent could do if allowed to escape. If the target in question is relatively inconsequential, then proportionality requires combatants to forego [*sic*] severe action, or seek noncombative means of engagement.[73]

This extract from the COIN manual is overstated. As a matter of law, the military importance of the individuals targeted is always relevant, whether in conventional or counterinsurgency operations. However, the fact that the goal of an insurgency is not attrition of enemy forces means that the military advantage of killing a simple fighter is likely not as high as during attrition warfare, in which victory is achieved through serial destruction of enemy forces.

Reduced to basics, in Afghanistan the operational concern was the mere fact of collateral damage, not whether that damage expected to be caused was excessive relative to military advantage. Rules of engagement so embraced this casualty aversion that the legal principle of proportionality never loomed large.

The case of human shields exemplifies the extent to which, in the context of proportionality, policy and operational considerations swallowed legal requirements. Human Rights Watch has documented the Taliban's widespread use of human shields,[74] acts which undeniably violated international humanitarian law.[75]

Many experts correctly argue that voluntary shields are direct participants in hostilities who, therefore, do not factor into proportionality calculations. As to involuntary shielding, the practice most prominent in Afghanistan, the weight of opinion holds that its victims remain civilians factored fully into any proportionality analysis.[76] This approach reflects Additional Protocol I, Article 51.8's caveat that "any violation of . . . [*inter alia*, the provision prohibiting the use of shields] shall not release the Parties to the conflict from their legal obligations with respect to the civilian population and civilians . . . ."[77]

There have been no serious allegations that US forces ever ignored the presence of human shields. On the contrary, CDEM specifically mandates consideration of the presence of human shields; such presence elevates the required approval level. Recall also that rules of engagement and other operational guidelines in Afghanistan often required US forces to withdraw if the enemy was collocated with civilians. Because US forces were already bound by policy and operational requirements exceeding those of IHL, the use of human shields neither complicated application of the existing legal norms nor created pressure for a relaxed interpretation thereof.

Counterinsurgency operations raise a final theoretical question as to proportionality: Does collateral damage directly influence the degree of military advantage accruing from an attack (as distinct from the determination of whether collateral damage is excessive relative to military advantage)? An analogous issue is force protection. During Operation Allied Force, NATO aircraft flew at altitudes outside the threat envelope of Federal Republic of Yugoslavia air defenses. Albeit counterfactual, allegations surfaced that this tactic heightened risk to the civilian population. The affair has generated a lively academic debate over whether survival of the aircrew and aircraft should be considered military advantage when making proportionality calculations.[78]

The case of Afghanistan presents the opposite case. If aircrew and aircraft survival enhance military advantage, does the counterproductive nature of collateral damage during a counterinsurgency detract from it? After all, avoidance of collateral damage constitutes an express objective in such conflicts.

Although it is not the place to resolve this complex issue, it is important to understand that, as a rule, military advantage is typically viewed as advantage benefiting friendly operations or hindering the enemy's.[79] The notion does not extend to winning hearts and minds, a point illustrated by agreement that destroying enemy civilian morale does not qualify as advantage vis-à-vis the definition of military objective.[80] Rather, military advantage is purely military in nature; there must be some direct contribution to military operations. Political, economic or social advantage does not suffice.

This being so, any assertion that collateral damage should diminish military advantage would have to be supported by a direct nexus to military factors. While true that collateral damage motivates civilian sympathy for the enemy, such general effects are too attenuated. As a general rule, then, collateral damage plays no part in proportionality calculations beyond being measured against the yardstick of excessiveness.

The final area of consideration is the requirement to take precautions in attack. Codified in Additional Protocol I, Article 57, it requires an attacker to minimize collateral damage by taking feasible steps to avoid and, in any event, minimize "incidental loss of civilian life, injury to civilians and damage to civilian objects." Precautions include both target verification and choosing among available targets, weapons and tactics so as to lessen the impact of an attack on the civilian population.

In modern conflicts, critics increasingly condemn targeting operations for failure to comply with the requirement. This phenomenon results, in part, from the fact that the globalized media and non-governmental organizations, employing modern communications technology, have a powerful ability to focus attention on civilian casualties and harm to civilian objects. Collateral damage is easily grasped when viewed in the media; understanding the complexity of mounting a modern attack is not. Thus, perceptions can become distorted.

Further, the availability of advanced intelligence, surveillance and reconnaissance assets, especially UAVs and precision weaponry, such as the small-diameter bomb,[81] has created the false impression that technology makes "zero collateral damage" attacks possible. The result is a recurring sense that failure to take precautions is the only possible explanation for civilian damage, injuries and deaths.[82]

Reports on US and coalition operations in Afghanistan exemplify this tendency. For instance, the Human Rights Watch report on the conflict, *Troops in Contact*, asserts that "[t]he cases described here raise concerns as to whether the attacking forces acted in accordance with their obligation under the laws of war to exercise 'constant care to spare the civilian population' and take 'all feasible precautions' to minimize loss of civilian life."[83]

Human Rights Watch displayed a sophisticated understanding of targeting procedures during the conflict. The organization found that "when aerial bombing is planned, mostly against suspected Taliban targets, US and NATO forces in Afghanistan have had a very good record of minimizing harm to civilians . . . ."[84] It explained,

> [p]lanned attacks allow the US and NATO to use civilian risk mitigation procedures, including formal risk estimates to model and minimize civilian casualties. This includes a "pattern of life analysis," which looks for civilians in the area for hours or days before an attack using "eyes on the target" ranging from ground observers to technical reconnaissance. According to NATO Judge Advocate General (JAG) staff, the US and NATO also require positive visual identification of the target during a planned strike, allowing the pilot to look for civilians and call off an attack based on those observations. Planned strikes also allow the US and NATO to develop a target over time, thereby using far more detailed intelligence to understand who is and is not in the target area.[85]

Most casualties were caused, by contrast, during non-preplanned strikes. These TIC situations occurred when US or coalition forces came upon the enemy unexpectedly. Although the rules of engagement provided that forces should withdraw when civilians were in the vicinity of an attack, doing so was not always possible. For instance, it might expose them to greater risks or the path of retreat may have been cut off by the enemy. The report also pointed to cases which "began as TICs but lasted for several hours or days, with airstrikes used to support small troop numbers on the ground resulting in civilian deaths."[86]

Human Rights Watch expressed numerous concerns about such engagements. With regard to TICs that developed into prolonged battles, the organization opined that the resulting civilian casualties "suggest[ed] that the US is not taking all feasible precautions during prolonged battles, including using adequate forces to minimize civilian harm, employing low–collateral damage bombs, and positively identifying the locations of combatants and civilians."[87] It also suggested that while preplanned attacks involved intricate procedures to determine the presence of civilians, during a TIC the "tactical collateral damage assessment performed by the Joint Terminal Attack Controller (JTAC), a service member qualified in directing airstrikes on the ground[,] is one of the only checks done, and, of necessity, such assessments often are made under the stress of hostile fire."[88]

While *Troops in Contact* is the best report produced by the organization on international humanitarian law in recent conflicts,[89] its analysis of the precautions in attack norms misses several key points. As it did in its report on Operation Iraqi Freedom, Human Rights Watch appears to have imposed a rebuttable presumption that collateral damage evidences a failure to take sufficient precautions in attack. This shifts the burden to the attacker, who by this approach must demonstrate that it complied with precautions norms. That this is so is illustrated by a flawed tendency to allege failure to take feasible precautions without identifying or developing those which were presumably available, but ignored.

"Feasible precautions" have been defined as "precautions which are practicable or practically possible taking into account all circumstances ruling at the time, including humanitarian and military considerations."[90] Consider the suggestions cited above. Albeit reasonable in the abstract, there is no support in the report for the proposition that they were feasible in the sense of being practical in the circumstances at hand. For instance, were additional troops on hand that could have been deployed to minimize civilian harm? Or were low-collateral-damage bombs readily available, either at bases from which aircraft launched or aboard the attacking aircraft (since many attacks were conducted by aircraft to which targets were passed while already airborne)? As to the fact that only JTACs generally had eyes on target, one must query what the alternative might have been. What seems to have been missed is that, as a matter of law, the feasible-precautions-in-attack requirements only apply when there are practical alternatives available to the attacker. The burden of demonstrating non-compliance lies with those asserting violation of the requirements, not the forces executing the attack.

In contrast to the LIT criterion for engagement, self-defense was much clearer, since it is a standard to which US and other forces train and with which they are, therefore, familiar. Self-defense presents no status issues because anyone against whom self-defense is necessary can be engaged. Further, it poses no direct-participation-in-hostilities concerns, because only those who are actually attacking, or about to attack, are liable to being engaged defensively. Accordingly, neither the scope nor the timing debates infecting direct-participation analysis, and, correspondingly, the LIT criterion, surface.

Be that as it may, even self-defense proved troublesome in Afghanistan. As is often the case with application of rules of engagement, mission accomplishment standards tended to slip into application of self-defense principles.[91] The condition precedent for acting in self-defense is either a hostile act or a demonstration of hostile intent.[92] For US forces, this standard is codified in the Standing Rules of Engagement. Both criteria reflect the self-defense concept of military necessity, by which force may only be used if lesser means of addressing the threat are likely not to suffice.

In preparing for combat in Afghanistan, "considerable time and effort was spent attempting to create training packages aimed at developing a specific level of identification before either returning fire or taking other actions in response to a hostile act or demonstration of hostile intent."[93] Identification has no place in self-defense situations, other than to locate the source of the hostile act or demonstration of hostile intent. It is instead an element of mission accomplishment rules of engagement, by which forces are authorized to attack combatants and direct participants only once they have been reliably identified as such.

It is well-accepted that intermingling mission accomplishment and self-defense notions in rules of engagement risks causing those who need to act in self-defense to hesitate, thereby endangering themselves and others in their units. Moreover, US training emphasizes that there is no need to seek higher approval in self-defense situations, for delay may impede the ability of troops to defend themselves. It is only in mission accomplishment rules of engagement that engagement approval levels appear. Conflating the two types of rules of engagement can confuse troops at the tactical level, causing them to act precipitously when they should be seeking higher approval in a mission accomplishment engagement.

A further self-defense complication derived from the fact that US and NATO forces operated in the same theater. Both used "hostile intent" as a criterion for employing airpower in defensive operations employing airpower.[94] However, NATO defined the term as "manifest and overwhelming" force, whereas the US standard was "the threat of imminent use of force."[95] In other words, the NATO standard placed greater emphasis on the necessity criterion of self-defense and was more restrictive temporally. Employing the same term differently created confusion regarding the availability of air support in TIC situations, especially when US and NATO forces were supporting each other. It also created an impression that the US forces were quick to pull the trigger. As one ambassador in the country told Human Rights Watch, "[s]ome Afghans think the US is worse than the Russians. The problem is in the TIC they call in air support in a hurry, and special forces go too far on the ground and call in airstrikes too often. There is a cultural problem with the US—they are cowboys."[96] Since counterinsurgencies seek support of the population, such perceptions, whether correct or not, prove costly.

Finally, the mere notion of a self-defense rule of engagement is misplaced in armed conflicts. This is so not only because combatants are always lawful targets, but also due to the fact that the concept of direct participation already permits engaging anyone who is attacking or about to attack. The debate over the scope of direct participation has no bearing in this regard; all sides agree that acts which constitute a hostile act or a demonstration of hostile intent in the self-defense sense qualify as acts of direct participation. The controversy over the "for such time" criterion is equally irrelevant, since the term undeniably includes the period when an attack is imminent or under way (the self-defense period).

Consequently, the only legally relevant circumstance for self-defense during an armed conflict is defense against those who do not meet the scope requirements of direct participation, specifically that requiring a belligerent nexus to the hostilities. Expanding self-defense beyond such situations by giving it a central role in engagement guidance was, therefore, unusual as an operational matter and unnecessary as a matter of law. Doing so represented yet another policy and operational decision ratcheting back what was allowed by international humanitarian law.

Concluding Thoughts

What is fascinating about the application of IHL in Afghanistan (and other recent conflicts) is that its foundational premise seems to have been turned on its head. International humanitarian law is designed for classic attrition warfare, where each side tries to so wear down the enemy forces that they can no longer continue fighting. The St. Petersburg Declaration principle that law fixes the "limits at which the necessities of war ought to yield to the requirements of humanity" comported neatly with warfare along such lines.[97] Both sides sought to avoid excessive restrictions on their military actions, but both also wanted to ensure the protection of their civilian populations. Military necessity and civilian harm were counterpoised in a zero-sum game.

However, this traditional balance began to be stressed by the emergence of coercive warfare, in which the objective is not to defeat the enemy, but rather to affect a decisionmaker's calculations. NATO's air campaign in 1999 (Operation Allied Force), during which the goal was to convince Slobodan Milosevic to stop slaughtering the Kosovar Albanians and return to the negotiating table, best illustrates coercive warfare in the contemporary context.[98] The dilemma was that some of those assets, the destruction of which would most effectively have such effects (such as property owned by the State's leader), qualified as protected civilian property under international humanitarian law. The ensuing calls for a relaxation of the *lex lata* should have come as no surprise.[99]

Counterinsurgency warfare, in that it seeks to win hearts and minds, constitutes "persuasive" warfare, that is, warfare designed to influence the population of the State in which an insurgency is under way, and, to a lesser extent, international public and governmental opinion. Since collateral damage hinders military operations by undercutting domestic and international support and by increasing insurgent strength, strict compliance with IHL norms actually complements military necessity. Accordingly, as in Afghanistan, counterinsurgent forces often adopt restrictions on their operations that far outstrip those found in the law. Humanitarians and counterinsurgency warfighters paradoxically find themselves in lockstep.

Their perspectives on the practices may, nevertheless, conflict. Although the restrictions originate as context-specific operational and policy choices, humanitarians tend to style them as normative. As a matter of law, the crux of the issue is whether such restrictions comprise State practice bearing on the emergence of customary international law norms.

The ICRC's *Customary International Humanitarian Law* study notes that "both physical and verbal acts of States constitute practice that contributes to the creation of customary international law. Physical acts include, for example, battlefield behavior. . . . Verbal acts include military manuals . . . instructions to armed and security forces, military communiqués during war . . . ."[100] But what must be emphasized is that State practice matures into customary law only when it evidences *opinio juris sive necessitatis*, a belief on the part of States engaging in said practice that it is legally obligatory.[101] Clearly, the extensive restrictions placed on US and coalition forces in Afghanistan did not result from legal concerns, but rather apprehension that even legal collateral damage would prove counterproductive in the specific context of Afghanistan. In other words, they did not rise to the level of State practice which would evidence the emergence of international humanitarian law norms more restrictive than those already extant.

Be that as it may, warfighters, commentators and judge advocates often conflate the distinction between humanitarian law and rules of engagement (and other engagement mandates). The latter include not only elements of law, but also operational and policy dictates. Because ROE are the actual norms applicable on a battlefield, many observers lose sight of the difference, thereby distorting assessments of State practice.[102] One can imagine that the CDEM process, for instance, might foster expectations that greater collateral damage requires a higher level of approval authority. Similarly, the LIT concept risks suggesting that there is no longer any military necessity in declaring combatants hostile, as permitted in IHL.

Ultimately, the conduct of hostilities in Afghanistan illustrated a shift from law toward legitimacy. As governments, non-governmental organizations, academics and others raise expectations, there is decreasing emphasis on strict legal analysis. In Afghanistan, for instance, authorization to conduct attacks which would otherwise comport with the proportionality principle was sometimes denied as risking "bad press" or negative communicative consequence. The requirement to take *feasible* precautions in attack seems to be slowly slipping toward a standard of *all possible* precautions.

Clearly, law is playing a lesser role in targeting than it has in past conflicts. This lesson has not been lost on enemy forces, who increasing employ lawfare—the use of law as a "weapon" employed to create the impression, correct or not, that an opponent acts lawlessly, thereby undercutting support for the war effort.[103] In the face of this strategy, there is even greater motivation for operating at levels of caution far exceeding the IHL's mandates. But doing so only exacerbates the blurring of legal, policy and operational practices.

Prosecuting a conflict to the limit of the law to prevent erosion of the military necessity aspect of international humanitarian law is self-evidently not the answer. At least in a counterinsurgency doing so would sacrifice victory on the altar of principle. Nevertheless, rules of engagement and other targeting restrictions should be crafted in a way that reflects the content, structure, function and accepted terminology of this body of law. Afghanistan should serve as a warning that understanding and communicating the difference between law, on the one hand, and operational and policy choices, on the other, remains imperative.

Notes

1. Protocol Additional to the Geneva Conventions of 12 August 1949, and Relating to the Protection of Victims of International Armed Conflicts art. 49.1, June 8, 1977, 1125 U.N.T.S. 3, *reprinted in* DOCUMENTS ON THE LAWS OF WAR 422 (Adam Roberts & Richard Guelff eds., 3d ed. 2000) [hereinafter AP I].

2. The accepted definition of international armed conflict is found in Common Article 2 of the four 1949 Geneva Conventions: "[A]ll cases of declared war or of any other armed conflict which may arise between two or more [States], even if the state of war is not recognized by one of them." Convention for the Amelioration of the Condition of the Wounded and Sick in Armed Forces in the Field art. 2, Aug. 12, 1949, 6 U.S.T. 3114, 75 U.N.T.S. 31 [hereinafter GC I]; Convention for the Amelioration of the Condition of Wounded, Sick and Shipwrecked Members of Armed Forces at Sea art. 2, Aug. 12, 1949, 6 U.S.T. 3217, 75 U.N.T.S. 85 [hereinafter GC II]; Convention Relative to the Treatment of Prisoners of War art. 2, Aug. 12, 1949, 6 U.S.T. 3316, 75 U.N.T.S. 135 [hereinafter GC III]; and Convention Relative to the Protection of Civilian Persons in Time of War art. 2, Aug. 12, 1949, 6 U.S.T. 3516, 75 U.N.T.S. 287 [hereinafter GC IV]: all *reprinted in id.* at 197, 222, 244 and 301, respectively.

3. *See, e.g.*, Derek Jinks, *The Applicability of the Geneva Conventions to the "Global War on Terrorism,"* 46 VIRGINIA JOURNAL OF INTERNATIONAL LAW 165, 177–90 (2005). In 2002, President George Bush concluded that the conflict with Al Qaeda was "international in scope." Memorandum from George W. Bush to the Vice President et al., Subject: Humane Treatment of Al Qaeda and Taliban Detainees para. 2(c) (Feb. 7, 2002), *reprinted in* THE TORTURE PAPERS: THE ROAD TO ABU GHRAIB 134 (Karen J. Greenberg & Joshua Dratel eds., 2005). Four years later, the Supreme Court disagreed, finding a conflict with transnational terrorists to be "not of an international character," as that term is employed in Common Article 3 to the 1949 Geneva Conventions. Hamdan v. Rumsfeld, 126 S.Ct. 2749, 2795–97 (2006). The International Committee of the Red Cross takes the position that transnational terrorism, absent a nexus to either an international or non-international armed conflict, fails to qualify as an armed conflict in the first place. *See* INTERNATIONAL COMMITTEE OF THE RED CROSS, INTERNATIONAL HUMANITARIAN LAW AND THE CHALLENGES OF CONTEMPORARY ARMED CONFLICTS 7–8, *available at* http://www.icrc.org/Web/eng/siteeng0.nsf/htmlall/ihl-30-international-conference-101207/$File/IHL-challenges-30th-International-Conference-ENG.pdf [hereinfter IHL and the Challenges of Contemporary Armed Conflicts].

4. Despite its illegitimacy, and non-recognition by most States, the Taliban constituted the de facto government of Afghanistan in that it controlled the greatest amount of territory and generally exercised the normal functions of governance. As noted by Yoram Dinstein, "[n]o formal recognition is required by a belligerent State as to the statehood of the opposing side. As long as the adversary satisfies objective criteria of statehood under international law, any armed conflict between two belligerent Parties would be characterized as inter-State." YORAM DINSTEIN, THE CONDUCT OF HOSTILITIES IN THE LAW OF INTERNATIONAL ARMED CONFLICT 16 (2004). Therefore, in humanitarian law terms, the conflict in Afghanistan between the Taliban forces (and organized armed groups supporting the Taliban) and the US-led coalition was an international armed conflict.

5. S.C. Res. 1419, U.N. Doc. S/RES/1419 (June 26, 2002). Additional Protocol II to the Geneva Conventions, which addresses non-international armed conflict, does not apply to the conflict because Afghanistan is not a party to the instrument; even if it was, the conflict would not meet the threshold criteria set forth in Article 1.1. Protocol Additional to the Geneva Conventions of 12 August 1949, and Relating to the Protection of Victims of Non-International Armed Conflicts art. 1.1, June 8, 1977, 1125 U.N.T.S. 609, *reprinted in* DOCUMENTS ON THE LAWS OF WAR, *supra* note 1, at 483. However, the conflict does meet the threshold criteria of Common Article 3, to which Afghanistan is a party, as an "armed conflict not of an international character," as well as those contained in customary international law. GC I, II, III, IV, *supra* note 2, art. 3; MICHAEL N. SCHMITT, CHARLES H.B. GARRAWAY & YORAM DINSTEIN, THE MANUAL ON THE LAW OF NON-INTERNATIONAL ARMED CONFLICT, Rule 1.1.1 and accompanying commentary (2006), *reprinted in* 36 ISRAEL YEARBOOK ON HUMAN RIGHTS (2006) (Special Supplement), *available at* http://www.michaelschmitt.org/images/Manual%5B1%5D.Final.Brill..pdf [hereinafter NIAC Manual].

6. This is the position taken by the International Committee of the Red Cross (ICRC). *See* IHL and the Challenges of Contemporary Armed Conflicts, *supra* note 3, at 8. However, some experts see a continuing international armed conflict, existing beside the non-international one, with Al Qaeda and related transnational terrorist groups.

7. AP I, *supra* note 1, art. 48. In the *Tadic* case, the International Criminal Tribunal for the former Yugoslavia Appeals Chamber held that the principle of distinction, which lies at the heart of the law of targeting, applies in non-international armed conflict. By the decision, customary rules had developed to govern "internal strife," covering

> such areas as protection of civilians from hostilities, in particular from indiscriminate attacks, protection of civilian objects, in particular cultural property, protection of all those who do not (or no longer) take active part in hostilities, as well as prohibition of means of warfare proscribed in international armed conflicts and ban of certain methods of conducting hostilities.

Prosecutor v. Tadic, Case No. IT-94-1, Decision on Defence Motion for Interlocutory Appeal on Jurisdiction para. 127 (Oct. 2, 1995). The Tribunal cited General Assembly Resolution 2444, which recognized the "necessity of applying basic humanitarian principles in *all* armed conflict." *Id.*, para. 110, *citing* G.A. Res. 2444 (XXIII), U.N. Doc. A/7218 (Dec. 19, 1968), Respect for Human Rights in Armed Conflicts, *reprinted in* THE LAWS OF ARMED CONFLICT 511 (Dietrich Schindler & Jiri Toman eds., 4th ed. 2004). The United States later recognized the Resolution as "declaratory of existing customary international law." Letter from J. Fred Buzhardt, General Counsel of the Department of Defense, to Senator Edward Kennedy (Sept. 22, 1972), *excerpted in* A. Rovine, *Contemporary Practice of the United States Relating to International Law*, 67 AMERICAN JOURNAL OF INTERNATIONAL LAW 118, 122 (1973). See also NIAC Manual, *supra* note 5, at 11; CUSTOMARY INTERNATIONAL HUMANITARIAN LAW 25–29 (Rule 7 and accompanying commentary) (Jean-Marie Henckaerts & Louise Doswald-Beck eds., 2005) [hereinafter CIHLS]; COMMENTARY ON THE ADDITIONAL PROTOCOLS OF 8 JUNE 1977 TO THE GENEVA CONVENTIONS OF 12 AUGUST 1949 para. 4761 (Yves Sandoz, Christophe Swinarski & Bruno Zimmermann eds., 1987) [hereinafter AP I Commentary].

8. The US Army has cited complexity as a major factor in future operations. In particular, it points to three especially relevant manifestations: complex physical terrain, complex human terrain and complex informational terrain.

> In the face of overwhelming U.S. combat power, future adversaries can be expected to conduct operations more frequently from the shelter of *complex physical terrain* (urban, jungle/forest, and mountain). Such terrain typically comprises a mosaic of open patches and highly restrictive terrain, with the potential to minimize exposure to superior firepower, inflict higher U.S. casualties, and prolong the conflict. Urban defenses, in particular, will tend to reduce U.S. advantages in overhead information collection, tactical mobility, and long-range precision fires, instead placing a premium on dismounted maneuver, direct fires, ground reconnaissance, HUMINT, and the troop strength needed to conduct them.
>
> An urban setting also invites adversaries to exploit public sensitivities to collateral damage and civilian casualties, and tends to magnify the perceived costs of protracted conflict. . . .
>
> *Complex human terrain* exists where numerous population groups coexist in the same physical space—often a city or an urbanized area. These might include ethno-linguistic groups, political factions, tribes or clans, religious sects, or ideological movements. Identification of combatants in complex human terrain is extraordinarily difficult; applying force in such an environment imposes a high risk of counterproductive or unintended consequences.
>
> Finally, *complex informational terrain* is the multiple sources or transmission paths for communications, data, or information—including news media. A force operating in complex informational terrain will not have the ability to control information flow.

U.S. Army Training and Doctrine Command, TRADOC Pam. 525-3-0, The Army in Joint Operations: The Army's Future Force Capstone Concept 2015–2024, at 44 (2005).

9. For a general description of Afghanistan, see Central Intelligence Agency, The World Factbook, Afghanistan (2008), https://www.cia.gov/library/publications/the-world-factbook/geos/af.html (last visited Mar. 11, 2009).

10. This approach reversed the standard tactic of ground forces driving the enemy into areas where it can be attacked by airpower. In Afghanistan, air attacks often did the opposite, with air forces driving the enemy into areas where it could be engaged by ground forces.

11. "An organized movement aimed at the overthrow of a constituted government through use of subversion and armed conflict." Chairman of the Joint Chiefs of Staff, Joint Publication 1-02, Dictionary of Military and Associated Terms (Apr. 12, 2001, as amended through Oct. 17, 2008), http://www.dtic.mil/doctrine/jel/doddict/ [hereinafter DoD Dictionary]. Security Council resolutions setting forth mandates on Afghanistan illustrate the counterinsurgency nature of operations. *See, e.g.*, S.C. Res. 1386, U.N. Doc. S/RES/1386 (Dec. 20, 2001); S.C. Res. 1413, U.N. Doc. S/RES/1413 (May 20, 2002); S.C. Res. 1444, U.N. Doc. S/RES/1444 (Nov. 20, 2002); S.C. Res. 1510, U.N. Doc. S/RES/1510 (Oct. 13, 2003); S.C. Res. 1563, U.N. Doc. S/RES/1563 (Sept. 17, 2004); S.C. Res. 1623, U.N. Doc. S/RES/1623 (Sept. 13, 2005); S.C. Res. 1659, U.N. Doc. S/RES/1659 (Feb. 15, 2006); S.C. Res. 1707, U.N. Doc. S/RES/1707 (Sept. 12, 2006); S.C. Res. 1746, U.N. Doc. S/RES/1746 (Mar. 23, 2007); S.C. Res. 1776, U.N. Doc. S/RES/1776 (Sept. 19, 2007); S.C. Res. 1817, U.N. Doc. S/RES/1817 (June 11, 2008); S.C. Res. 1833, U.N. Doc. S/RES/1833 (Sept. 22, 2008).

12. US Marine Corps & US Special Operations Command, Multi-Service Concept for Irregular Warfare Version 2.0, USMC Combat Development Command and US Special Operations Command Center for Knowledge and Futures, at 5–6 (2006), *available at* http://www.dtic.mil/cgi-bin/GetTRDoc?AD=ADA454228&Location=U2&doc=GetTRDoc.pdf.

13. Headquarters, Department of the Army & Headquarters, Marine Corps Combat Development Command, FM 3-24/MCWP 3-33.5, Counterinsurgency, at 1-141–1-142 (2006), *available at* http://www.usgcoin.org/library/doctrine/COIN-FM3-24.pdf [hereinafter COIN Manual]. The manual was drafted in part by General David Petraeus, who presently commands US Central Command (CENTCOM). The command exercises responsibility over the conflicts in both Iraq and Afghanistan.

14. *Id.* at 1-150.

15. Chairman of the Joint Chiefs of Staff, Joint Publication 3-0, Joint Operations, at II-1 (2006, incorporating change 1 (Feb. 13, 2008)), *available at* http://www.dtic.mil/doctrine/jel/new_pubs/jp3_0.pdf.

16. Headquarters, Air Force Doctrine Center, AFDD 2-1.9, Targeting, at 35 (2006), *available at* http://www.dtic.mil/doctrine/jel/service_pubs/afdd2_1_9.pdf [hereinafter AFDD 2-1.9]. The target validation phase ensures vetted targets

> achieve the effects and objectives outlined in a commander's guidance and are coordinated and deconflicted with agencies and activities that might present a conflict with the proposed action. It also determines whether a target remains a viable element of the target system. During the development effort, the targets may also require review and approval based on the sensitive target approval and review process, coordinated through the combatant commander to national authorities.

Id. at 34.

17. The CDEM methodology is set forth in Chairman of the Joint Chiefs of Staff, CJCSM 3160.01B, Joint Methodology for Estimating Collateral Damage and Casualties for Conventional Weapons: Precision, Unguided and Cluster (Aug. 31, 2007). The document is "For Official Use Only" and unavailable to the public. For open-source discussions of the topic, see Colin H. Kahn, Boots on the Ground or Bolts from the Blue? Risks to Civilians from U.S.

Counterinsurgency Operations in Iraq and Afghanistan 3–4 (unpublished memo prepared for the Cornell University "Human Rights at War" Workshop, Nov. 9–10, 2007); DWIGHT A. ROBLYER, BEYOND PRECISION: ISSUES OF MORALITY AND DECISION MAKING IN MINIMIZING COLLATERAL CASUALTIES, PAPER FOR THE PROGRAM IN ARMS CONTROL, DISARMAMENT, AND INTERNATIONAL SECURITY 18 (2003), *available at* http://acdis.illinois.edu/assets/docs/246/BeyondPrecisionIssuesofMoralityandDecisionMakinginMinimizingCollateralCasualties.pdf.

18. 1 Center for Law and Military Operations, Judge Advocate General's Legal Center and School, Lessons Learned from Afghanistan and Iraq, Major Combat Operations (11 September 2001–1 May 2003), at 84 (2004) [hereinafter 1 Lessons Learned].

19. The CENTCOM CDEM for both Operation Enduring Freedom and Operation Iraqi Freedom is illustrative. It sets forth a series of questions to be addressed during the CDEM process:

1. Can I positively identify the object or person I want to attack as a legitimate military target authorized for attack by the current rules of engagement?
2. Is there a protected facility (i.e. No Strike), civilian object or people, or significant environmental concern within the effects range of the weapon I would like to use to attack the target?
3. Can I avoid damage to that concern by attacking the target with a different weapon or with a different method of approach?
4. If not, how many people do I think will be injured/killed by my attack?
5. Do I need to call my higher commander for permission to attack this target?

Id. at 103, *citing* US Central Command, Collateral Damage Estimation Policy and Methodology para. 2 (2003).

20. However, the law of targeting contains many unresolved issues. On some of them, see Michael N. Schmitt, *Targeting*, *in* PERSPECTIVES ON THE ICRC STUDY ON CUSTOMARY INTERNATIONAL HUMANITARIAN LAW 131 (Susan Breau & Elizabeth Wilmshurst eds., 2007); Michael N. Schmitt, *Fault Lines in the Law of Attack*, *in* TESTING THE BOUNDARIES OF INTERNATIONAL HUMANITARIAN LAW 277 (Susan Breau & Agnieszka Jachec-Neale eds., 2006).

21. AP I, *supra* note 1, art. 51; CIHLS, *supra* note 7, ch. 1; US Navy, Marine Corps & Coast Guard, The Commander's Handbook on the Law of Naval Operations, NWP 1-14M/MCWP 5-12.1/COMDTPUB P5800.7A paras. 8.2.1, 8.2.2 (2007) [hereinafter NWP 1-14M]; UK MINISTRY OF DEFENCE, THE MANUAL OF THE LAW OF ARMED CONFLICT para. 5.32 (2004) [hereinafter British Manual]; NIAC Manual, *supra* note 5, Rules 2.1.1, 2.1.1.1 & 2.1.1.2.

22. AP I, *supra* note 1, art. 52.2. "Nature" denotes intrinsic military significance, thereby including objects like ammunition depots, tanks, combat aircraft, headquarters or military barracks. "Location" refers to areas that have "special importance to military operations." The classic example is a mountain pass that can be blocked to foil the enemy's advance. When reliable intelligence or other information indicates that the enemy intends to use an object militarily in the future, the object qualifies as a military objective through "purpose." Finally, "use" means that the enemy is presently utilizing an object militarily. AP I Commentary, *supra* note 7, paras. 2020–24. *See also* British Manual, *supra* note 21, para. 4.4.

23. AP I, *supra* note 1, art. 51.3: "Civilians shall enjoy the protection afforded by this Section, unless and for such time as they take a direct part in hostilities." *See also* CIHLS, *supra* note 7, at 19 (Rule 6); NWP 1-14M, *supra* note 21, para. 8.2.2; British Manual, *supra* note 21, para. 5.3.2.

24. AP I, *supra* note 1, arts. 51.4(a) & 51.5(a). *See also* CIHLS, *supra* note 7, at 37 (Rule 11), 40 (Rule 12), 43 (Rule 13); British Manual, *supra* note 21, para. 5.24.

25. CIHLS, *supra* note 7, at 244 (Rule 71). *See also* AP I, *supra* note 1, arts. 51.4(b) & (c); NWP 1-14M, *supra* note 21, para. 9.1.2; British Manual, *supra* note 21, para. 6.4.

26. CIHLS, *supra* note 7, at 237 (Rule 70). *See also* AP I, *supra* note 1, art. 35.2; NWP 1-14M, *supra* note 21, para. 9.1.1; British Manual, *supra* note 21, para. 6.2.

27. Convention on Cluster Munitions, May 30, 2008, *available at* http://www.icrc.org/ihl.nsf/FULL/620?OpenDocument.

28. NWP 1-14M, *supra* note 21, para. 8.3.1. The requirement is codified in AP I, *supra* note 1, art. 57. *See also* CIHLS, *supra* note 7, ch. 5; British Manual, *supra* note 21, para. 5.32.

29. AP I, *supra* note 1, arts. 51.5(b) & 57.2(b); CIHLS, *supra* note 7, ch. 4; NWP 1-14M, *supra* note 21, para. 8.3.1; British Manual, *supra* note 21, paras. 2.6–2.8.

30. The commentary to Article 51 suggests that damage which is "extensive" is not proportionate. AP I Commentary, *supra* note 7, para. 1980. See discussion in DINSTEIN, *supra* note 4, at 120–21.

31. For a discussion of the incidents, see Sean D. Murphy, *Contemporary Practice of the United States Relating to International Law*, 96 AMERICAN JOURNAL OF INTERNATIONAL LAW 237, 247 (2002).

32. HUMAN RIGHTS WATCH, TROOPS IN CONTACT 22 (2008) [hereinafter TROOPS IN CONTACT], *citing* e-mail communication from NATO Media Operations Center to Human Rights Watch (May 6, 2008).

33. *Id.* at 14.

34. Karzai Denounces Reported Civilian Deaths from U.S., NATO Raids, Online NewsHour (May 2, 2007), http://www.pbs.org/newshour/updates/asia/jan-june07/afghanistan_05-02.html.

35. Headquarters United States Air Force, Operation Anaconda: An Airpower Perspective 42–43 (2005), *available at* http://www.af.mil/shared/media/document/AFD-060726-037.pdf.

36. "Directives issued by competent military authority that delineate the circumstances and limitations under which United States forces will initiate and/or continue combat engagement with other forces encountered." DoD Dictionary, *supra* note 11.

37. "A folder, hardcopy or electronic, containing target intelligence and related materials prepared for planning and executing action against a specific target." *Id.*

38. "A plan for a connected series of joint air operations to achieve the joint force commander's objectives within a given time and joint operational area." *Id.*

39. "An order to initiate military operations as directed." *Id.*

40. "An abbreviated form of an operation order issued as needed after an operation order to change or modify that order or to execute a branch or sequel to that order." *Id.*

41. "A measure employed by land or amphibious commanders to facilitate the rapid engagement of targets and simultaneously provide safeguards for friendly forces." *Id.*

42. A card distributed to soldiers bearing simple rules regarding the use of force and other matters.

43. 1 Lessons Learned, *supra* note 18, at 86–88. *See generally* AFDD 2-1.9, *supra* note 16, at 94–95.

44. AP I, *supra* note 1, art. 51.3; CIHLS, *supra* note 7, at 19 (Rule 6); NWP 1-14M, *supra* note 21, para. 8.2.2; British Manual, *supra* note 21, para. 5.3.2. See also the reports of meetings of a group of international experts advising the ICRC on interpretive guidance regarding the notion of direct participation, available at http://www.cicr.org/Web/Eng/siteeng0.nsf/htmlall/participation-hostilities-ihl-311205. The guidance will be issued in 2009.

45. The United Nations Office of the High Commissioner for Human Rights issued what is effectively a model standard in 1990. The Basic Principles on the Use of Force and Firearms by Law Enforcement Officials provides that

> [l]aw enforcement officials shall not use firearms against persons except in self-defense or defense of others against the imminent threat of death or serious injury, to prevent

> the perpetration of a particularly serious crime involving grave threat to life, to arrest a person presenting such a danger and resisting their authority, or to prevent his or her escape, and only when less extreme means are insufficient to achieve these objectives. In any event, intentional lethal use of firearms may only be made when strictly unavoidable in order to protect life.

U.N. Doc. A/CONF.144/28/Rev.1, prov. 9 (1990), *available at* http://www.unhchr.ch/html/menu3/b/h_comp43.htm. On this and other use-of-force standards, see Michael N. Schmitt, *Targeted Killings in International Law: Law Enforcement, Self-Defense and Armed Conflict, in* INTERNATIONAL HUMANITARIAN LAW AND HUMAN RIGHTS LAW: TOWARDS A NEW MERGER IN INTERNATIONAL LAW 525 (Roberta Arnold & Noelle Quenivert eds., 2008).

46. Chairman of the Joint Chiefs of Staff, CJCSI 3121.01B, Standing Rules of Engagement for US Forces, encl. A, paras. 2a & 3a (2005). A hostile act is "an attack or other use of force against the United States, US forces or other designated persons or property." Hostile intent is "the threat of imminent use of force" against the same entities. *Id.*, paras. 3e & f.

47. Various interviews with US military personnel with Operation Iraqi Freedom experience (May–Aug. 2008).

48. E-mail to author (June 17, 2008) (on file with author).

49. 1 Lessons Learned, *supra* note 18, at 100–102 and accompanying footnotes.

50. 2 Center for Law and Military Operations, Judge Advocate General's Legal Center and School, Lessons Learned from Afghanistan and Iraq, Full Spectrum Operations (2 May 2003–30 June 2004), at 137 (2004) [hereinafter 2 Lessons Learned].

51. 1 Lessons Learned, *supra* note 18, at 96.

52. *Id.* This definition was the result of a series of meetings between operators and judge advocates at the CENTCOM level. The standard was applauded by some judge advocates, while criticized by others. *Id.* at 96 n.59.

53. Personal experience of author while Staff Judge Advocate, Operation Northern Watch, 1997.

54. A Marine after-action report expressed the frustration:

> Upon 26th [Marine expeditionary unit (special operations capable)]'s arrival in the 5th Fleet [area of responsibility], I immediately began requesting guidance and clarification on the intent and meaning of this new concept, "likely and identifiable threat." My concerns were primarily that "likely and identifiable threat" was introducing an unfamiliar concept to our Marines immediately before the commencement of combat operations. I had trained our Marines on the concepts of hostile act, hostile intent and declared hostile, as well as other U.S. Standing ROE concepts, and was certain as to their ability to implement them in any context; however, on its face, "likely and identifiable threat" appeared to beg further elaboration and clarification.
>
> . . . .
>
> [I]f judge advocates and commanders have relative difficulty in defining ROE terms, it goes without saying that the Marines charged with implementing the ROE will likely have similar difficulties.

1 Lessons Learned, *supra* note 18, at 100 n.77, *citing* Staff Judge Advocate, 26th Marine Expeditionary Unit (Special Operations Capable), After Action Report: Operation Enduring Freedom/Operation Swift Freedom (Mar. 22, 2002). Similar frustrations were expressed by others, including US Army judge advocates. *Id.*

55. *Id.* at 106 n.91, *citing* Memorandum, Dean L. Whitford, former Group Judge Advocate, 5th Special Forces Group (Airborne), Staff Judge Advocate, Joint Special Operations Task Force–

North (Task Force Dagger) (OEF), and Staff Judge Advocate, Combined Joint Special Operations Task Force–West and successor CJSOTF–Arabian Peninsula (OIF), for Major Daniel P. Saumur, Deputy Director, CLAMO, subject: Task Force Dagger OEF/OIF ROE AAR (June 14, 2004).

56. *Id.* at 100, *citing* Major Thomas A. Wagoner, Staff Judge Advocate, 15th Marine Expeditionary Unit (Special Operations Capable), After Action Report of the 15th MEU(SOC) West Pac 01 (2002).

57. This discussion is based on the experience of the author as a member of the group of experts participating in the ICRC effort to produce Interpretive Guidance on the Notion of Direct Participation. The ICRC Interpretive Guidance is expected to be released in March 2009.

58. Some controversy exists over whether the standard applies equally in non-international armed conflict. The author believes it should. Others would add a requirement that the individual be performing a "combat function."

59. AP I Commentary, *supra* note 7, para. 1944.

60. *See, e.g.*, Michael N. Schmitt, *Humanitarian Law and Direct Participation in Hostilities by Private Contractors or Civilian Employees*, 5 CHICAGO JOURNAL OF INTERNATIONAL LAW 511, 535–36 (2005). The Israeli Supreme Court addressed the issue in Public Committee Against Torture in Israel et al. v. Government of Israel et al., HCJ 769/02, Judgment, para. 30 (Dec. 13, 2006), *reprinted in* 46 INTERNATIONAL LEGAL MATERIALS (2007), *available at* http://elyon1.court.gov.il/files_eng/02/690/007/a34/02007690.a34.pdf. It rejected an argument that the "for such time" criterion was not customary law, but then proceeded to interpret it liberally.

61. The Vienna Convention provides that "[a] treaty shall be interpreted in good faith in accordance with the ordinary meaning to be given to the terms of the treaty in their context and in the light of its object and purpose." Vienna Convention on the Law of Treaties art. 31.1, *opened for signature* May 23, 1969, 1155 U.N.T.S. 331. On the balance between military necessity and humanitarian concerns, see note 97 *infra* and accompanying text.

62. For criticism, see Schmitt, *supra* note 60, at 535–36. Lest the impact of the differing interpretations of direct participation on assessments of the appropriateness of LIT cause excess concern, it is important to emphasize that under both approaches (and LIT) an individual seeking temporary sanctuary in an inhabited area during an operation still qualifies as an attackable direct participant if the mission in question is ongoing.

63. Any concern that it is overly liberal would have to be tempered by the fact that the decision not to declare forces hostile already meant that operations in Afghanistan commenced with a higher standard than that required in IHL.

64. NWP 1-14M, *supra* note 21, para. 8.2.2. Note that the United States does not see the same rule regarding objects as customary in nature, for it risks shifting the burden as to determining the precise use of an object to the attacker from the person controlling the object. *See* US DEPARTMENT OF DEFENSE, FINAL REPORT TO CONGRESS: CONDUCT OF THE PERSIAN GULF WAR 616 (1992).

65. AP I, *supra* note 1, art. 50.1.

66. AP I Commentary, *supra* note 7, para. 1921.

67. Statement made by the United Kingdom at time of ratification, *reprinted in* DOCUMENTS ON THE LAWS OF WAR, *supra* note 1, at 510–11.

68. CIHLS, *supra* note 7, at 24.

69. Author interview with judge advocate responsible for providing legal advice in such situations (May 2008).

70. Operation Anaconda, *supra* note 35, at 40.

71. Anaconda was the first operation to involve significant US conventional ground forces.

72. AP I, *supra* note 1, art. 57.

73. COIN Manual, *supra* note 13, para. 7-32.

74. TROOPS IN CONTACT, *supra* note 32, at 25–28.

75. AP I, *supra* note 1, art. 51.7; CIHLS, *supra* note 7, at 337 (Rule 97); NWP 1-14M, *supra* note 21, para. 8.3.2; British Manual, *supra* note 21, para. 15.14.2; NIAC Manual, *supra* note 5, para. 2.3.8.

76. But see DINSTEIN, *supra* note 4, at 131, arguing that "the test of excessive injury must be relaxed."

77. AP I, *supra* note 1, art. 51.8. On human shields, see generally Michael N. Schmitt, *Human Shields and International Humanitarian Law*, 38 ISRAEL YEARBOOK ON HUMAN RIGHTS 17 (2008).

78. But all sides of the debate agree it is a factor in determining whether precautions are feasible.

79. In terms of the quantum of advantage, the ICRC *Commentary* notes that "it is not legitimate to launch an attack which only offers potential or indeterminate advantages." AP I Commentary, *supra* note 7, para. 2024.

80. *See* DINSTEIN, *supra* note 4, at 85–86; Schmitt, *Fault Lines*, *supra* note 20, at 295.

81. The small-diameter bomb is a guided munition that relies on the Global Positioning System of satellites to provide navigation to target. Because it is accurate, it does not need the explosive force that would otherwise be required to ensure destruction of the target. Its small size (currently in the 250 lb. class) reduces the likelihood of collateral damage. Factsheet, GBU-39B Small Diameter Bomb, Air Force Link, http://www.af.mil/factsheets/factsheet.asp?id=4500 (last visited Mar. 11, 2009). An upgrade replaces the steel casing with a composite casing to reduce the fragmentation effects of the weapon. Small Diameter Bomb/Small Smart Bomb, GlobalSecurity.org, http://www.globalsecurity.org/military/systems/munitions/sdb.htm (last visited Mar. 11, 2009).

82. *See, e.g.*, HUMAN RIGHTS WATCH, OFF TARGET: THE CONDUCT OF THE WAR AND CIVILIAN CASUALTIES IN IRAQ 21–22, 40 (2003). For a discussion of the report's conclusion on precautions in attack, see Michael N. Schmitt, *The Conduct of Hostilities During Operation Iraqi Freedom*, 6 YEARBOOK OF INTERNATIONAL HUMANITARIAN LAW 90–92 (2003).

83. TROOPS IN CONTACT, *supra* note 32, at 4.

84. *Id.* at 29. Doctrine distinguishes among three types of targeting. Deliberate targeting is that which is preplanned (scheduled). Dynamic targeting occurs when a target was not anticipated or when, although anticipated, it was not identified in sufficient time to perform deliberate mission planning. Time-sensitive targeting occurs when there is a need for an immediate response because of a threat to friendly forces or in cases involving important lucrative fleeting targets. AJP-3.9, Allied Joint Doctrine for Targeting (2008).

85. TROOPS IN CONTACT, *supra* note 32, at 29.

86. *Id.* at 30.

87. *Id.*

88. *Id.* A life-pattern analysis looks at the pattern of civilian activity in the target area in an effort, for instance, to determine the times at which a strike will risk the least incidental injuries to civilians.

89. For a discussion of the organization's earlier report on Iraq, see Schmitt, *supra* note 82.

90. Protocol on Prohibitions or Restrictions on Use of Mines, Booby Traps and Other Devices art. 3(1), Oct. 10, 1980, as amended May 3, 1996, 2048 U.N.T.S. 133, *reprinted in* DOCUMENTS ON THE LAWS OF WAR, *supra* note 1, at 536.

91. Mission accomplishment rules of engagement are guidelines for performing an assigned mission, as distinct from those relating to defense of oneself and the force. For instance, mission

accomplishment rules of engagement would establish guidelines for the conduct of a preplanned attack.

92. See definitions at note 46 *supra*.

93. 2 Lessons Learned, *supra* note 50, at 131, *citing*, for Operation Enduring Freedom, CJCS Message (S) 212315Z NOV 01, para. 3.H, and, for Operation Iraqi Freedom, USCENTCOM Message (S/REL AUS/GBR/USA) 121917Z MAR 03, para. 3.J.

94. TROOPS IN CONTACT, *supra* note 32, at 31.

95. *Id.*

96. *Id.* at 32, *citing* Human Rights Watch interview with an ambassador (name withheld) in Kabul (July 22, 2007).

97. St. Petersburg Declaration Renouncing the Use, in Time of War, of Explosive Projectiles Under 400 Grammes Weight, Nov. 29, 1868, 138 Consol. T.S. 297, *reprinted in* DOCUMENTS ON THE LAWS OF WAR, *supra* note 1, at 54.

98. On coercive strategies, also labeled compellance strategies, see Michael N. Schmitt, *Targeting and Humanitarian Law: Current Issues*, 34 ISRAEL YEARBOOK ON HUMAN RIGHTS 59, 60–69 (2004).

99. *See, e.g.*, Charles J. Dunlap Jr., *The End of Innocence: Rethinking Noncombatancy in the Post-Kosovo Era*, STRATEGIC REVIEW, Summer 2000, at 14.

100. CIHLS, *supra* note 7, at xxxii. This approach has been criticized as overbroad by the United States. Letter from John B. Bellinger III, Legal Adviser, US Department of State, and William J. Haynes, General Counsel, US Department of Defense, to Dr. Jacob Kellenberger, President, International Committee of the Red Cross (Nov. 3, 2006), 46 INTERNATIONAL LEGAL MATERIALS 514 (2007).

101. Article 38 of the Statute of the International Court of Justice is universally accepted as a restatement of the sources of international law. Paragraph 1(b) includes "international custom, as evidence of a general practice accepted as law" in such sources. Statute of the International Court of Justice art. 38(1), June 26, 1945, 59 Stat. 1055, 33 U.N.T.S. 993. According to the International Court of Justice,

> [n]ot only must the acts concerned amount to a settled practice, but they must also be such, or be carried out in such a way, as to be evidence of a belief that this practice is rendered obligatory by the existence of a rule of law requiring it. The need for such a belief, i.e., the existence of a subjective element, is implicit in the very notion of the *opinio iuris sive necessitatis*. The States concerned must therefore feel that they are conforming to what amounts to a legal obligation.

North Sea Continental Shelf (F.R.G. v. Den.; F.R.G. v. Neth.), 1969 I.C.J. 3, 44 (Feb. 20). *See also* Continental Shelf (Libya v. Tunis.), 1985 I.C.J. 13, 36 (June 3). For an excellent summary of the nature and sources of customary international humanitarian law, see Jean-Marie Henckaerts, *Study on Customary International Humanitarian Law: A Contribution to the Understanding and Respect for the Rule of Law in Armed Conflict*, 87 INTERNATIONAL REVIEW OF THE RED CROSS 175 (2005). On customary international law generally, see Yoram Dinstein, *The Interplay between Customary International Law and Treaties*, 322 RECUEIL DES COURS 246 (2006).

102. On the law relevant to precision attacks, see Michael N. Schmitt, *Precision Attack and International Humanitarian Law*, 87 INTERNATIONAL REVIEW OF THE RED CROSS 445 (2005).

103. On lawfare, see Charles Dunlap Jr., *Law and Military Interventions: Preserving Military Values in 21st Century Conflicts* (Working Paper, Harvard Kennedy School, Carr Center for Human Rights Policy, 2001), *available at* http://www.hks.harvard.edu/cchrp/programareas/nshr_publications.php (follow "Working Papers Volume 1 Part 1" hyperlink). In Iraq, for instance, insurgents quickly learned that coalition forces employ counter-battery fire against mortar

attacks. They, thus, adopted a "shoot and scoot" tactic in which they fired from an area containing civilians (often with little likelihood of hitting coalition forces), hoping the coalition response would cause civilian deaths and injuries that would generate negative public and international reaction. Author interviews with senior US Marine Corps and Army officers (June 2008). Hezbollah employed the same tactics in Lebanon in 2006, firing Katyusha rockets from populated areas in the hope of baiting the Israelis into a response. *See* Israel Ministry of Foreign Affairs, Hizbullah's Exploitation of Lebanese Population Centers and Civilians: Photographic Evidence (2006), http://www mfa.gov.il/MFA/MFAArchive/2000_2009/2006/Operation+Change +of+Direction+Video+Clips.htm.

PART IV

DETENTION OPERATIONS

XII

The Law of Armed Conflict and Detention Operations in Afghanistan

Matthew C. Waxman*

In reflecting on the arc of US and coalition detention operations in Afghanistan, three key issues related to the law of armed conflict stand out: one substantive, one procedural and one policy. The substantive matter—what are the minimum baseline treatment standards required as a matter of international law?—has clarified significantly during the course of operations there, largely as a result of the US Supreme Court's holding in *Hamdan v. Rumsfeld*.[1] The procedural matter—what adjudicative processes does international law require for determining who may be detained?—eludes consensus and has become more controversial the longer the Afghan conflict has continued. And the policy matter—in waging counterinsurgency warfare, how do foreign military forces transition military detention operations to effective civilian institutions?—has emerged as a critical strategic priority for which the law of armed conflict provides little instructive guidance.

President Barack Obama's determination to close Guantanamo while expanding US military commitments in Afghanistan will draw new public attention to these questions. After briefly explaining the basis of US and coalition detention operations, this article addresses each of these issues in turn. Viewing them together,

---

* Associate Professor of Law, Columbia Law School; Adjunct Senior Fellow, Council on Foreign Relations; Member, Hoover Institution Task Force on National Security and Law.

it concludes with some general observations about the convergence of law and strategy.

US and Coalition Detention Operations in Operation Enduring Freedom

In late 2001, the United States launched operations in Afghanistan, and almost immediately began capturing and holding suspected enemy fighters. The US legal authority for detention operations in Afghanistan began from the propositions that

> [t]he United States and its coalition partners are engaged in a war against al-Qaida, the Taliban, and their affiliates and supporters. There is no question that under the law of armed conflict, the United States has the authority to detain persons who have engaged in unlawful belligerence until the cessation of hostilities. Like other wars, when they start we do not know when they will end. Still, we may detain combatants until the end of the war.[2]

Although many US allies participated in military operations, US forces took the lead in conducting detention operations in Afghanistan,[3] eventually consolidating theater detention operations at Bagram air force base facilities.

As explained by a commander of US detention forces in Operation Enduring Freedom (OEF), "[d]uring the execution of this campaign, the U.S. Armed Forces and allied forces have captured or procured the surrender of thousands of individuals believed to be members or supporters of either al Qaeda or the Taliban."[4] Detentions were intended to

> [prevent] them from returning to the battlefield and engaging in further armed attacks against innocent civilians and U.S. and coalition forces. Detention also serves as a deterrent against future attacks by denying the enemy the fighters needed to conduct war. Interrogations during detention enable the United States to gather important intelligence to prevent future attacks.[5]

Nearly eight years after the initial invasion, US detention operations go on, and the US military is modernizing its facilities in the expectation of their further continuation.[6]

In some respects US and coalition detention operations in Afghanistan are a valuable case study for examining contemporary application of the law of armed conflict. Aside from the thousands of individual detentions, the "data" include publicly released and declassified documents of internal US government legal and policy decision-making, as well as litigation that has pushed the US government to clarify its legal positions and has produced judicial interpretations of the law of armed conflict.

In other respects, however, it is difficult to examine the law of armed conflict in the Afghanistan setting because of some peculiar aspects of detention operations there. First, most US allies participating in coalition operations in Afghanistan have done so not as part of anti-Taliban and anti-al Qaida combat operations (Operation Enduring Freedom) but as part of the International Security Assistance Force (ISAF). The latter, which assists the Afghan government in maintaining security in certain parts of the country, is authorized by a series of Chapter VII UN Security Council resolutions that authorize participating contingents to "take all necessary measures to fulfil its mandate."[7] Participating military forces therefore derive authority to detain certain captured militants from this UN Security Council mandate independent of the law of armed conflict. Second, US allies participating in both OEF and ISAF have almost entirely "opted out" of detention operations. In 2005, NATO adopted guidelines, which the European partners follow, calling for transferring detainees to the Afghan government within ninety-six hours of capture.[8] As explained further below, this has meant that US detentions form the only significant body of State practice in Afghanistan to measure against or help interpret the law of armed conflict related to detention.

Detention Treatment Standards

In the early phases of military operations in Afghanistan, but especially after the Abu Ghraib crisis in Iraq, followed by exposure of detainee abuses in Afghanistan and Guantanamo, the most intense public controversy focused on the issue of treatment standards. Much of this debate centered on the appropriate classification of captured Taliban and al Qaida fighters, because most protagonists in this debate believed that the appropriate treatment baseline turned in part on captured individuals' legal statuses.[9]

Shortly before conventional combat operations began, US military commanders in charge of Afghanistan operations issued an order instructing that the Geneva Conventions were to be applied to all captured individuals. Belligerents would be screened according to standard doctrine to determine whether or not they were entitled to prisoner of war status.[10] This was consistent with existing military regulations and recent US military practice.

On February 7, 2002, however, the President determined that Taliban and al Qaida detainees were "unlawful combatants,"[11] and therefore protected by neither the custodial standards of the Third Geneva Convention applicable to prisoners of war nor Common Article 3 of the Geneva Conventions.[12] Prisoner of war protections did not cover al Qaida detainees because al Qaida was not a "High Contracting Party" to the Conventions, and they did not cover Taliban because those forces failed the tests of Article 4 of the Third Convention, which stipulates requirements for legitimate military forces.[13] Common Article 3 did not apply, by its own terms, because this was believed to be an international armed conflict, whereas Common Article 3 rules apply in conflicts "not of an international character."[14]

The President further directed in his February 2002 instructions, however, that "[a]s a matter of policy, the United States Armed Forces shall continue to treat detainees humanely and, to the extent appropriate and consistent with military necessity, in a manner consistent with the principles of Geneva."[15] While ostensibly protective, this directive also opened holes in the law of armed conflict's barriers. First, it applied by its terms only to armed forces, hinting that intelligence services might not be similarly constrained. Second, by emphasizing humane treatment as a matter of policy, it suggested that humane treatment was not required as a matter of law. And, third, it suggested that the Geneva Conventions' principles could validly be compromised in pursuit of security requirements.

Well known is the storm of criticism that erupted over the initial US government position that the Geneva Conventions—and, presumably, customary law of armed conflict—provided no legal guarantee of minimum treatment standards for enemy combatants captured in OEF. Many critics have attributed detainee abuses in Afghanistan to these foundational legal decisions. Critics of the US position consistently rejected the notion that unlawful combatants fall into a "legal gap" in protection. They asserted a range of alternatives, including that captured fighters (at least Taliban) were entitled to prisoner of war status; that all captured fighters are entitled at least to minimum protections of Common Article 3, Article 75 of the first Additional Protocol to the Geneva Conventions,[16] and the customary law of armed conflict; and/or that any detainees are protected by international human rights law, including prohibitions on "cruel, inhuman and degrading" treatment.[17]

In June 2006 the US Supreme Court resolved much of this debate, at least as a matter of international law incorporated into US law. It held in *Hamdan v. Rumsfeld*, a petition brought by a Yemeni detained during OEF and transferred to Guantanamo, that Common Article 3 affords minimal protections to individuals captured within the territory of a signatory but engaged in a conflict not between two nations. This would include not only civil wars (as Common Article 3 is more traditionally understood) but also conflicts with transnational actors like al Qaida.[18] Soon after, on July 7, 2006, the Deputy Secretary of Defense directed that "all DoD personnel adhere to [Common Article 3] standards" and that each department component "review all relevant directives, regulations, policies, practices, and procedures . . . to ensure that they comply with [them]."[19]

Hamdan's holding that Common Article 3's minimum treatment standards apply to enemy combatants captured in Afghanistan significantly narrowed the scope of controversy over international legal constraints on US detention operations. Common Article 3 demands that detainees "in all circumstances be treated humanely," and it prohibits, among other things, "cruel treatment and torture" as well as "outrages upon personal dignity, in particular, humiliating and degrading treatment."[20] Although vague, these provisions contain basic care and custody requirements that match closely the basic treatment standards of human rights law that some critics argued applied. While not matching the enhanced protections afforded prisoners of war, this holding nevertheless answered the criticism of those critics who argued that the Geneva Conventions contain no "gaps" in their coverage of individuals detained in armed conflict. Perhaps most important, this holding clarified that these minimum treatment standards apply as a matter of treaty law of armed conflict, not merely policy.

Detention Adjudicatory Process

The *Hamdan* holding helped clarify the minimal treatment standards applicable to OEF detention operations in Afghanistan, but the sparse terms of Common Article 3 do little to clarify the separate issue of what minimum procedural requirements govern decisions to detain or continue to detain individuals in Afghanistan.[21] Procedural mechanisms for reviewing detention decisions in Afghanistan have received remarkably little public scrutiny compared with those at Guantanamo, even though in many respects—at least as initially characterized by the US government—the detainees in both are similarly situated. Thus far the war in Afghanistan does more to highlight the difficult issue of procedural safeguards in the law of armed conflict than it does to answer it.

In the early phases of OEF operations in Afghanistan, much of the legal debate about procedural detention issues focused on Article 5 of the Third Geneva Convention, the Prisoner of War Convention. It provides that "[s]hould any doubt arise as to whether persons, having committed a belligerent act and having fallen into the hands of the enemy," qualify as prisoners of war, "such persons shall enjoy the protection of the present Convention until such time as their status has been determined by a competent tribunal."[22] Then, as now, however, little State practice or detailed authoritative commentary existed interpreting these terms. US military regulations previously called for a three-officer panel that would take testimony from reasonably available witnesses, including the detainee, and make judgments.[23] And US military forces were preparing to conduct such tribunals for individuals captured in Afghanistan until they were directed otherwise, eventually by the President's February 7, 2002 legal determinations which rendered any captured Taliban and al Qaida fighters "unlawful combatants" as a matter of law; hence there was not "any doubt" as to their status for Article 5 tribunals to adjudicate.[24]

Many critics contested this claim, arguing that Article 5 requires case-by-case determinations; that group designations of this sort are impermissible.[25] Others have argued that this provision means that when there is doubt whether a captured individual is even an enemy fighter or not, he is entitled to a hearing before a tribunal; therefore, the argument goes, suspected al Qaida and Taliban combatants in US custody should have been entitled upon capture to such review.[26] Article 5's language begins with the notion that a subject detainee has "committed a belligerent act," suggesting that the drafters intended to mandate minimum procedures for resolving factual doubt as to a subject's *type* of combatant or belligerent act, not the prior question whether he is or is not a combatant. But in practice any process to adjudicate an individual's type of combatancy, and hence the Geneva protections to which he is entitled, would likely uncover some cases of mistaken identity or otherwise erroneous detentions.[27]

Regardless of its precise meaning, it is quite clear that Article 5 was drafted with very different circumstances in mind from those of the Afghanistan conflict. In particular, it was intended for a conflict pitting professional armies and of limited duration.[28] A relatively simple front-end adjudicatory review was sufficient in such conflicts because sorting combatants from noncombatants (for detention purposes) was relatively easy and conflicts would likely end within a few months or years, whereupon any remaining captives would be released. Afghanistan, by contrast, involves a set of conflicts already lasting almost eight years and likely to continue many more, and an enemy force (especially al Qaida forces, but also residual Taliban) that routinely obscures its identity among civilian populations.[29]

In contexts such as this, the more important issue than appropriate front-end status screening is to what form of review (and perhaps adversarial process) are detainees entitled to contest the factual basis of their detention, given the relatively high probability and cost of errors. Three main positions have emerged, though there are many sub-positions within each.

The US government has generally taken the position that the law of armed conflict is the exclusive body of international law dictating procedural constraints on detention of captured fighters in Afghanistan. This position assumes the continued existence of armed conflict (in the US view, it remains an international armed conflict, though *Hamdan* at least adds new questions to this view), and that the law of armed conflict operates as *lex specialis,* displacing otherwise applicable legal norms.[30] Beyond consistently arguing against the reach of judicial habeas corpus protections to Afghanistan,[31] however, the US government has not articulated any clear procedural mandates imposed by the law of armed conflict for sorting out who is or is not a combatant. Instead it has sought to maintain flexibility, adopting procedural protections as a matter of policy.

Some human rights organizations have argued that, especially since the establishment of the new Afghan government following the 2002 *Loya Jirga*, international human rights law, not the law of armed conflict, governs procedural protections, along with Afghan domestic law.[32] This view generally assumes that the war in Afghanistan evolved at that time from an international armed conflict to an internal armed conflict and that the law of armed conflict provides no independent authorization for detention in the latter category. Holders of this view look to, among other sources, the International Covenant on Civil and Political Rights, which states:

> No one shall be deprived of his liberty except on such grounds and in accordance with such procedure as are established by law. . . . Anyone who is deprived of his liberty by arrest or detention shall be entitled to take proceedings before a court, in order that that court may decide without delay on the lawfulness of his detention and order his release if the detention is not lawful.[33]

Under the strictest form of this view, any long-term detention of suspected Taliban or al Qaida fighters in Afghanistan requires criminal trial with universally recognized due process safeguards—a standard that leaves US practice in Afghanistan falling far short.[34]

A third view holds that neither the law of armed conflict nor human rights treaty law provides sufficiently clear or comprehensive procedural safeguards to persons detained for security reasons. The International Committee of the Red Cross (ICRC) has developed a set of principles and safeguards that it argues should govern security detention in all circumstances, i.e., both in armed conflicts and outside of them. The guidelines are based on law of armed conflict and human rights treaty rules, as well as on non-binding standards and best practice, and are to be interpreted on a case-by-case basis. According to the ICRC guidelines, detainees are entitled—among other things—to challenge the lawfulness of their detention and to have an independent and impartial body decide on continued detention or release.[35] The ICRC considers that Afghanistan is a situation of non-international armed conflict: it would argue that detainees in US or other international-force hands should enjoy far more robust procedural rights than currently afforded and that detainees in Afghan custody should be granted judicial review.[36]

Experience in Afghanistan offers intuitive support for the third approach, but it does little to resolve the difficult issue of exactly which international human rights law provisions should apply. The fact that the nature of fighting there—

against an enemy that deliberately obscures its identity and moves in and out of local communities—creates a high likelihood of some erroneous, long-term detentions supports the call for thorough screening procedures.[37] But combat conditions, resource constraints and the weak state of Afghan justice would complicate efforts to establish formal judicial mechanisms by either coalition or the Afghan governments.[38]

Meanwhile, the US Supreme Court recently held in *Boumediene v. Bush* that enemy combatants at Guantanamo are entitled to constitutional habeas corpus rights.[39] The issue of *Boumediene*'s reach beyond Guantanamo, especially to Afghanistan, will be litigated for some time, and that case turned on interpretation and application of US domestic law. In any event, the Supreme Court did not clarify exactly what procedural structures and protections apply even in habeas cases for Guantanamo detainees, and the Court seemed to have Afghanistan in mind when it cautiously suggested that practical considerations and exigencies of foreign combat zones might limit the reach of constitutional habeas rights to enemy combatant detainees held outside Guantanamo.[40]

Legal requirements aside, US forces have gradually instituted more formalized procedural mechanisms for adjudicating detention decisions as time has gone on. The little detail on review processes in Afghanistan shared openly by the US government appears mostly in court filings in habeas corpus actions brought by Bagram detainees. These public documents explain that by 2006 all individuals brought to theater detention facilities for long-term confinement have their cases reviewed by a five-officer panel, sitting as an Enemy Combatant Review Board, usually within seventy-five days of capture and thereafter every six months. The review board may recommend by a majority vote to the commanding general or his designee whether the individual should continue to be detained.[41] Although the US government maintains that the Fourth Geneva Convention is inapplicable as a matter of law to Afghanistan detainees because that Convention applies to civilians, not combatants, the processes US forces eventually put in place roughly track the requirements of Article 78, which calls for, among other things, regular processes and periodic review (at least every six months) for security internees.[42]

So far, the Afghanistan case has produced little legal consensus on minimum procedural requirements in part because the spectrum of views spans differing judgments on such basic questions as what type of conflict exists (international versus internal), what body of law applies (law of armed conflict versus human rights law versus domestic Afghan law, or some combination) and what specific minimum requirements those bodies of law impose (mandatory provisions versus a sliding scale depending on practicability). Meanwhile, US forces have adopted increasingly robust processes for adjudicating cases, suggesting at least *some*—

though still far from complete—convergence between the aspirations of restrictive legal views and the pragmatic and ethical inclinations of those charged with waging the conflict.

Transitioning Detention Operations to Local Civilian Institutions

A final issue to consider is the transition from a military detention to a civilian justice system in Afghanistan. Unlike the substantive and procedural issues discussed above, this is not a law of armed conflict issue in a strict sense (except for Geneva Convention rules governing repatriation). But it is entwined with the other legal issues, and the strategic necessity of resolving it effectively may impact the future development of the law of armed conflict.

The law of armed conflict is generally designed to minimize unnecessary suffering in wartime and to facilitate a return to peace and public order. In the context of conventional warfare, the law of armed conflict's detention authorities and rules generally serve well these goals: until order is restored through victory or settlement of the conflict they allow—with sparse procedural requirements compared to peacetime justice systems—the incapacitation of captured individuals presumed (or assessed) likely to fight again if released and they protect those individuals from mistreatment. For the most part, the rules align with the law's policy objectives, including the strategic necessities of detention during combat.

US detention operations have taken place in Afghanistan amid a more complex strategic environment. Operations have evolved to include a major counterinsurgency component against Taliban and al Qaeda forces conducting guerrilla-style and terrorist operations aimed to undermine the new Afghan government. Of course, the role and rules of detention in counterinsurgency conflicts are not new problems or unique problems. One aspect that distinguishes the Afghanistan case, however, is the weakness or nascent condition of State institutions, including law and order systems, which needed to be almost completely reconstituted after coalition and Afghan forces overthrew the Taliban in 2001. Indeed, the collapse or weakness of governance in many parts of the country and the inability of the State to provide basic State services like policing and criminal justice create an environment hospitable to insurgent forces.[43] Moreover, the Afghan government lacks effective institutions of governance, including a police and justice sector capable of maintaining order. This is not just a counterinsurgency campaign to save a mature government; it is a counterinsurgency campaign while building a new government in a region long accustomed to internal strife and warlordism.

Amid this setting, a 2004 Pentagon inspection and assessment of US detention operations in Afghanistan concluded that "US detainee operations can only be normalized by the emergence of an Afghan justice and corrections system that can assume the responsibility for the long-term detention of low level enemy combatants currently held by the US."[44] The report continued:

> The value of continuing to keep low-level enemy combatants in custody is simply to keep individuals that represent a proven threat to coalition forces off the battlefield. This is a function that can and should be undertaken by the Afghan government. . . . Despite efforts to improve the process, the press of a growing detainee population without an Afghan solution or continued transfer to [Guantanamo] will continue to create the potential for bad choices to be made at several points in that process.[45]

In 2005 the governments of the United States and Afghanistan reached diplomatic agreements to "allow for the gradual transfer of Afghan detainees to the exclusive custody and control of the Afghan Government."[46] But this gradual transition has been slowed since then by the shakiness of Afghan security institutions and inability to install domestic legal authorities and processes capable of handling or prosecuting captured militants.[47]

These factors raise several policy questions onto which the law of armed conflict no longer maps so neatly: Does the long-term reliance on foreign military detention strengthen versus deplete or build versus undermine public confidence in domestic civilian justice institutions? As coalition forces turn over more and more security and governance functions to Afghan authorities, how should responsibility for detaining militants, including those already in custody, be transferred? Many features of this conflict are unique to Afghanistan, but these basic problems resemble those faced in Iraq and could likely recur in other areas where governance collapses, such as Somalia.

One lesson that the US military appears to have drawn in Afghanistan, as well as in Iraq, is the strategic imperative of high substantive and procedural standards of detainee treatment, especially when seeking to bolster rule-of-law institutions.[48] The new Army and Marine Corps *Counterinsurgency Field Manual* emphasizes this principle, not only for legal and ethical reasons, but also for military effectiveness.[49] After noting, for example, that the "nature of [counterinsurgency] operations sometimes makes it difficult to separate potential detainees from innocent bystanders, since insurgents lack distinctive uniforms and deliberately mingle with the local populace,"[50] the manual goes on to warn that "treating a civilian like an insurgent is a sure recipe for failure."[51] It continues:

> [Counterinsurgency] operations strive to restore order, the rule of law, and civil procedures to the authority of the [host nation] government. . . . Multinational and U.S. forces brought in to support this objective must remember that the populace will

> scrutinize their actions. People will watch to see if Soldiers and Marines stay consistent with this avowed purpose. Inconsistent actions furnish insurgents with valuable issues for manipulation and propaganda.[52]

Although the law of armed conflict has little to say directly on the issue of transferring detention responsibilities from military to civilian systems, the substantive and procedural legal issues described earlier affect this transition process insofar as adherence to their standards helps lay a foundation of support and legitimacy upon which local rule of law can be built.

Conclusion

The operational and strategic significance of detention standards imply several conclusions about the future development and refinement of the law of armed conflict, returning the discussion to the legal controversies discussed earlier. As to substantive treatment standards, the strategic rationale is likely to reinforce strongly the idea of universally applicable minimum requirements, despite initial efforts by the Bush administration to reserve greater flexibility. As to procedural requirements, in thinking about the future trajectory of the law of armed conflict (or the application of human rights law in armed conflict), the more that rule-of-law promotion features as a strategic objective, the more robust procedural protections for detainees will align with military necessity, rather than collide with it.

Notes

1. Hamdan v. Rumsfeld, 548 U.S. 557 (2006).
2. UN Committee against Torture, Consideration of Reports Submitted by States Parties under Article 19 of the Convention, Second Periodic Reports of States Parties Due in 1999, Addendum (United States of America) Annex 1, at 47, U.N. Doc. CAT/C/48/Add.3 (May 6, 2005), *available at* http://www.state.gov/g/drl/rls/45738.htm#part_one; *see also* Hamdi v. Rumsfeld, 542 U.S. 507, 518–21 (2004) (recognizing the executive branch's authority to detain enemy combatants—at least those captured in the course of operations in Afghanistan—pursuant to the congressional "Authorization for Use of Military Force" against those responsible for the September 11 attacks).
3. As well as transferring several hundred detainees from Afghanistan to Guantanamo, though I do not discuss those legal issues here.
4. Declaration of Colonel Rose M. Miller ¶ 8, Ruzatullah v. Rumsfeld, No. 06-CV-01707 (GK) (D.D.C. Nov. 20, 2006).
5. *Id.*
6. Eric Schmitt & Tim Golden, *U.S. Planning Big New Prison in Afghanistan*, NEW YORK TIMES, May 17, 2008, at A01.
7. *See* S.C. Res. 1707, ¶ 2, U.N. Doc. S/RES/1707 (Sept. 12, 2006); S.C. Res. 1386, ¶ 3, U.N. Doc. S/RES/1386 (Dec. 20, 2001).

8. *See* Ashley S. Deeks, *Starting from Here*, *in* INTERNATIONAL LAW AND MILITARY OPERATIONS (Michael D. Carsten ed., 2008) (Vol. 84, US Naval War College International Law Studies).

9. *See* Adam Roberts, *The Prisoner Question: If the U.S. Has Acted Lawfully, What's the Furor About?*, WASHINGTON POST, Feb. 3, 2002, at B1.

10. *See* JAMES R. SCHLESINGER ET AL., FINAL REPORT OF THE INDEPENDENT PANEL TO REVIEW DOD DETENTION OPERATIONS 80 (2004), *available at* http://news.findlaw.com/wp/docs/dod/abughraibrpt.pdf.

11. *See* Memorandum from George Bush to Vice President et al., Humane Treatment of Al Qaeda and Taliban Detainees (Feb. 7, 2002), *reprinted in* THE TORTURE PAPERS: THE ROAD TO ABU GHRAIB 134 (Karen J. Greenberg & Joshua Dratel eds., 2005), *available at* http://www.washingtonpost.com/wp-srv/nation/documents/020702bush.pdf [hereinafter President's Memo].

12. Article 3 is referred to as "Common" because it is found identically in each of the four Geneva Conventions. *See* Convention for the Amelioration of the Condition of the Wounded and Sick in Armed Forces in the Field art. 3, Aug. 12, 1949, 6 U.S.T. 3114, 75 U.N.T.S. 31; Convention for the Amelioration of the Condition of Wounded, Sick and Shipwrecked Members of Armed Forces at Sea art. 3, Aug. 12, 1949, 6 U.S.T. 3217, 75 U.N.T.S. 85; Convention Relative to the Treatment of Prisoners of War art. 3, Aug. 12, 1949, 6 U.S.T. 3316, 75 U.N.T.S. 135 [hereinafter Geneva III]; and Convention Relative to the Protection of Civilian Persons in Time of War art. 3, Aug. 12, 1949, 6 U.S.T. 3516, 75 U.N.T.S 287 [hereinafter Geneva IV]; all *reprinted in* DOCUMENTS ON THE LAWS OF WAR (Adam Roberts & Richard Guelff eds., 3d ed. 2000) at 197, 222, 244 and 301, respectively. Article 3 applies to all cases ". . . of armed conflict not of an international character occurring in the territory of one of the High Contacting Parties . . . ."

13. *See* President's Memo, *supra* note 11. For a contrary view, see Memorandum from William H. Taft IV, Legal Adviser, Department of State, to Counsel to the President, Comments on Your Paper on the Geneva Conventions (Feb. 2, 2002), *reprinted in* TORTURE PAPERS, *supra* note 11, at 129, *available at* http://www.nytimes.com/packages/html/politics/20040608_DOC.pdf.

14. *See* President's Memo, *supra* note 11.

15. *Id.*

16. Protocol Additional to the Geneva Conventions of 12 August 1949, and Relating to the Protection of Victims of International Armed Conflicts art. 4, June 8, 1977, 1125 U.N.T.S. 3, *reprinted in* DOCUMENTS ON THE LAWS OF WAR, *supra* note 12, at 422.

17. *See* John B. Bellinger, US State Department Legal Advisor, Oxford Leverhulme Programme Lecture on the Changing Character of War (Dec. 10, 2007).

18. Hamdan v. Rumsfeld, 548 U.S. 557, 629–31 (2006).

19. Memorandum from Gordon England, Deputy Secretary of Defense, to the Secretaries of the Military Departments et al., Application of Common Article 3 of the Geneva Conventions to the Treatment of Detainees in the Department of Defense (July 7, 2006), http://www.defenselink.mil/home/dodupdate/For-the-record/documents/20060711.html.

20. *Supra* note 12.

21. Some of the sparse State practice on this issue, for example, US practice during the Vietnam War and procedures employed by Canadian and British militaries, is described in Robert Chesney & Jack Goldsmith, *Terrorism and the Convergence of Criminal and Military Detention Models*, 60 STANFORD LAW REVIEW 1079, 1090–92 (2008).

22. Geneva III, *supra* note 12, art 5.

23. *See* Headquarters, Departments of the Army, the Navy, the Air Force and the Marine Corps, Army Regulation 190-8/OPNAVINST 3461.6/AFJI 31-304/MCO 3461.1, Enemy

Prisoners of War, Retained Personnel, Civilian Internees and Other Detainees § 1-6(a) (1997), *available at* http://www.au.af.mil/au/awc/awcgate/law/ar190-8.pdf.

24. *See* Katharine Q. Seelye, *Detainees Are Not P.O.W.'s, Cheney and Rumsfeld Declare*, NEW YORK TIMES, Jan. 28, 2002, at A6.

25. *See* Michael Ratner, Letter to the Editor, *When Are Captives Prisoners of War?*, NEW YORK TIMES, Jan. 16, 2002, at A18.

26. *See, e.g.*, W. Michael Reisman, *Rasul v. Bush: A Failure to Apply International Law*, 2 JOURNAL OF INTERNATIONAL CRIMINAL JUSTICE 973 (2004).

27. In the 1991 Persian Gulf War, the US military conducted about twelve hundred such hearings for captured Iraqi individuals thought to be pro-Saddam fighters, and found about nine hundred of them to be displaced civilians, who were promptly released. *See* Department of Defense, Conduct of the Persian Gulf War Final Report to Congress 578 (2002).

28. COMMENTARY ON GENEVA CONVENTION III RELATIVE TO THE TREATMENT OF PRISONERS OF WAR (Jean S. Pictet ed., 1960) [hereinafter ICRC COMMENTARY].

29. *See* Matthew C. Waxman, *Detention as Targeting: Standards of Certainty and Detention of Suspected Terrorists*, 108 COLUMBIA LAW REVIEW 1365 (2008).

30. *See* John B. Bellinger, US State Department Legal Advisor, Remarks to the Committee Against Torture (May 5, 2006), *available at* http://www.state.gov/g/drl/rls/68557.htm; Bellinger, *supra* note 17.

31. *See, e.g.*, Government's Motion to Dismiss, Al Maqaleh v. Gates, No. 06-CV-01669 (JDB) (D.D.C. March 5, 2007); Government's Response to Order to Show Cause and Motion to Dismiss for Lack of Jurisdiction, Ruzatullah v. Rumsfeld, No. 06-CV-01707 (GK) (D.D.C. Nov. 20, 2006).

32. *See* Human Rights First, *Arbitrary Justice: Trials of Bagram and Guantanamo Detainees in Afghanistan* (Apr. 2008), *available at* http://www.humanrightsfirst.info/pdf/USLS-080409-arbitrary-justice-report.pdf; Tim Golden & David Rohde, *Afghans Hold Secret Trials for Men That U.S. Detained*, NEW YORK TIMES, Apr. 10, 2008, at A6 (citing criticisms from human rights organizations).

33. International Covenant on Civil and Political Rights art. 9, Dec. 16, 1966, 999 U.N.T.S. 171.

34. *See, e.g.*, *US Detentions in Afghanistan: An* Aide-Mémoire *for Continued Action* (Amnesty International), June 7, 2005, *available at* http://www.amnesty.org/en/library/asset/AMR51/093/2005/en/dom-AMR510932005en.pdf ("When [the] armed conflict ended [in 2002], those who were captured by the USA during hostilities . . . were required to be released, unless charged with criminal offences. Civilians detained in that conflict . . . too were required, when that conflict ended, to be released, unless charged with recognized criminal offences.")

35. *See* ICRC, International Humanitarian Law and the Challenges of Contemporary Armed Conflicts, Official Working Document of the 30th International Conference of the Red Cross and Red Crescent, Geneva, Nov. 2007, annex 1; Jelena Pejic, *Procedural Principles and Safeguards for Internment/Administrative Detention in Armed Conflict and Other Situations of Violence*, 87 INTERNATIONAL REVIEW OF THE RED CROSS 375 (2005).

36. *See* ICRC, US Detention Related to the Events of 11 September 2001 and Its Aftermath – The Role of the ICRC, July 30, 2008, *available at* http://icrc.org/web/eng/siteeng0.nsf/htmlall/usa-detention-update-121205?opendocument.

37. *See* Waxman, *supra* note 29, at 1402–29.

38. How much these efforts would be complicated is the source of significant debate between the US government and human rights organizations.

39. 128 S. Ct. 2229 (2008).

40. *See id.* at 2259–62.

41. *See* Declaration of Colonel James W. Gray ¶¶ 11–13, Al Maqaleh v. Gates, No. 06-CV-01669 (JDB) (D.D.C. March 3, 2007) (discussing review process for detainees in Afghanistan); Declaration of Colonel Rose M. Miller ¶¶ 10–12, Ruzatullah v. Rumsfeld, No. 06-CV-01707 (GK) (D.D.C. Nov. 19, 2006) (discussing detention procedures and review process for enemy combatants detained in Afghanistan).

42. *See* Geneva IV, *supra* note 12, art. 78.

43. *See* Seth G. Jones, *The Rise of Afghanistan's Insurgency*, 32 INTERNATIONAL SECURITY 7 (2008).

44. Combined Forces Command–Afghanistan Area of Operations, Detainee Operations, Report of Inspection, June 26, 2004, at 20.

45. *Id.*

46. Press Release, US Embassy, Kabul, Afghanistan, Detainee Transfers to Afghanistan (Aug. 4, 2005), *available at* http://kabul.usembassy.gov/pr080405.html.

47. *See* Human Rights First, *supra* note 32; Schmitt & Golden, *supra* note 6.

48. *See* Carlotta Gall, *U.S.-Afghan Foray Reveals Friction on Antirebel Raids*, NEW YORK TIMES, July 3, 2006, at A9; Alissa Rubin, *U.S. Remakes Jails in Iraq, but Gains Are at Risk*, NEW YORK TIMES, June 2, 2008, at A1.

49. Headquarters, Department of the Army & Headquarters, Marine Corps Combat Development Command, FM 3-24/MCWP 3-33.5, Counterinsurgency ¶¶ 7-38, 7-40 (2006).

50. Id., ¶ 7-38.

51. Id., ¶ 7-40.

52. Id., ¶ 8-42.

XIII

US Detention of Taliban Fighters: Some Legal Considerations

Stephane Ojeda*

During the last seven years detention activities by US forces involved in the Afghanistan conflict[1] have raised numerous questions from the perspective of international law, in particular international humanitarian law (IHL);[2] this article addresses some of them. The focus will be on identifying the applicable law throughout the various stages of the hostilities (Part I) and issues related to the deprivation of liberty of Taliban fighters that entails its practical application (Part II).[3]

No issues pertaining to *ius ad bellum*, i.e., related to the lawfulness of the use of force, are discussed in this article. Given that there is often some confusion as to the relationship between the *ius ad bellum* and IHL (*ius in bello*), it must be stressed that IHL applies equally to all parties to an armed conflict, and that this is independent of whether the use of force has been lawful or not under the *ius ad bellum*.[4]

IHL only applies in situations of armed conflict. Treaty law has traditionally distinguished between international armed conflicts and non-international armed conflicts, the former being regulated in far more detail than the latter as can be seen in the core IHL treaties, the 1949 Geneva Conventions[5] and their two 1977 Additional Protocols.[6] The last years have, however, seen a growing tendency to regulate

* Legal Adviser to the Operations at the Legal Division of the International Committee of the Red Cross (ICRC) in Geneva. The article reflects the views of the author alone and not necessarily those of the ICRC.

international and non-international armed conflicts in the same way in treaty law, and customary international law has developed in a way as to largely apply the same rules in both types of conflicts.[7] However, there are still important differences between the two situations concerning the applicable law. To give two examples, the concept of combatant status, which entails, *inter alia*, the privilege of exclusion from criminal prosecution for lawful acts of war, and prisoner of war (POW) status only exist in international armed conflicts.

Following the terrorist acts of September 11, 2001 (9/11), President Bush declared that the United States was at "war against terrorism."[8] On October 7, the United States led a military campaign against the de facto government of Afghanistan—the Taliban—accused of harboring the al-Qaeda group, which was held responsible for 9/11. Since the commencement of this military campaign, the United States has detained thousands of people. Some suspected Taliban and al-Qaeda members, as well as other individuals suspected of supporting them or of being associated with them, were transferred beginning in January 2002 to the US internment facilities at Guantanamo Bay, Cuba. Between 2002 and 2005, the United States brought about eight hundred individuals to Guantanamo. For various reasons those transfers almost completely ceased by the end of 2004. Since that time, the great majority of persons captured have been held in Afghanistan, mainly in the Bagram Theatre Internment Facility;[9] the United States has brought only about twenty individuals to Guantanamo.[10]

At the time this is written, about 240 persons are held at Guantanamo Bay and about 600 at Bagram. The closure of Guantanamo is due to take place no later than January 22, 2010,[11] while the building of a new Bagram facility in Afghanistan with a greater detention capacity has been reported in the media.[12]

I. The Law Applicable to the Situation in Afghanistan

In order to determine the applicable law and standards governing any military activity, such as deprivation of liberty, a legal determination of the situation existing at the time the persons were captured is necessary. From October 7, 2001 to date, two phases in the Afghanistan situation can clearly be identified: a first phase in which the US-led coalition forces fought against the Afghan authorities and non-State armed groups, followed by a phase in which the US and other foreign forces assisted the Afghan authorities in fighting non-State armed groups.[13]

A. The Situation from October 7, 2001 to June 18, 2002

Even though only recognized by a few States[14] as the legitimate authorities of Afghanistan, the Taliban were controlling and ruling over about 95 percent of the

Afghan territory in October 2001. Afghanistan clearly had a functioning Taliban government and its armed wing was the country's regular armed forces. The airstrikes by the US-led coalition that started on October 7, 2001 thus clearly constituted an international armed conflict between the coalition States and Afghanistan.

An international armed conflict is generally defined as "any difference arising between two States and leading to intervention of members of the armed forces,"[15] or, as the International Criminal Tribunal for the former Yugoslavia has put it, as a situation where "there is a resort to armed force between States."[16]

The four Geneva Conventions of 1949 were thus applicable, but not Additional Protocol I (AP I) to which neither the United States nor Afghanistan was a State party. While the Geneva Conventions focus almost entirely on the protection of persons in the hands of the enemy, AP I contains detailed rules on the conduct of hostilities, including air-to-ground operations. Consequently, the airstrikes, which were the predominant feature at the beginning of the military operations, were essentially subject to the rules of customary international law. However, these rules of customary international law now correspond largely to those of AP I. These include the principle of distinction and the fundamental rules derived from it, such as

- the prohibition of direct attacks on civilians or civilian objects;
- the prohibition of indiscriminate attacks, including those that may be expected to cause excessive incidental civilian casualties or damages (principle of proportionality);
- the prohibition on attacking objects indispensable for the survival of the civilian population;
- the prohibition on attacking cultural property;
- the obligation to take precautions in attacks;
- the obligation to take precautions against attacks; and
- the prohibition on the use of human shields.[17]

In addition, the rules contained in the 1907 Hague Regulations,[18] which are considered as reflecting customary international law,[19] have also been of primary importance to the international armed conflict in Afghanistan.

B. The Situation from June 19, 2002 to Date

The fall of the Taliban did not necessarily mean the cessation of active armed hostilities. There are certainly still active armed hostilities in Afghanistan; however, the nature of the armed conflict has changed.

Following the convening of the *Loya Jirga* in Kabul in June 2002, an Afghan transitional government was established on June 19, 2002. It received unanimous recognition by the international community of States and could also claim broad-based recognition within Afghanistan through the *Loya Jirga* process. This new government of Afghanistan has been leading an armed struggle against an insurgency (i.e., the remnants of the Taliban and other non-State armed groups), which can be qualified as a non-international armed conflict. Indeed, the criteria usually used in IHL to define non-international armed conflicts seem to be met: the hostilities have reached a minimum level of intensity, and non-governmental groups involved in the conflict can be considered as "parties to the conflict" since they possess organized armed forces, operate under a certain command structure and have the capacity to sustain military operations.[20]

This non-international armed conflict is "internationalized" by the participation of foreign forces, including those of the United States, but because those foreign forces are assisting the Afghan government, it still cannot be characterized as an international armed conflict since it does not involve opposing States.

Recent developments in the conduct of the hostilities, in particular the US cross-border operations into Pakistan, might raise further questions about the legal qualification of the nature of the situation, i.e., is there an international armed conflict between the United States and Pakistan? According to the information available at the time of writing, it is the author's opinion that those operations represent a "spill-over" of the armed hostilities in the Afghan non-international armed conflict into Pakistan and do not represent a separate armed conflict.

Common Article 3 (CA3) of the four Geneva Conventions of 1949 and customary IHL rules are thus applicable to this situation,[21] but not Additional Protocol II (AP II) to which neither the United States nor Afghanistan are State parties.

II. Deprivation of Liberty of Taliban Fighters

The two phases in the Afghanistan conflict have direct consequences on the status given to the Taliban deprived of liberty and the legal standards governing their deprivation of liberty.

A. Taliban Captured before June 19, 2002

In an international armed conflict governed by the Geneva Conventions, such as the one in Afghanistan between October 2001 and June 2002, there are two main categories of persons deprived of liberty: either they are captured combatants entitled to POW status and protected by the Third Geneva Convention (GC III),[22] or they are civilians interned or detained and protected by the Fourth Geneva Convention (GC IV).[23]

Article 4, GC III identifies several groups of persons that, having fallen into the power of the enemy, are to be considered POWs. The first group of persons includes members of the armed forces of a party to the conflict. As stated earlier, given that the Taliban government was not recognized by a large part of the international community, including the United States, members of the Taliban regular armed forces fell into the category of persons described in Article 4(A)(3) of GC III, i.e., "members of regular armed forces who profess allegiance to a government or an authority not recognized by the Detaining Power." These "members of regular armed forces" differ from those referred to in Article 4(A)(1) ("members of the armed forces of a Party to the conflict") in one respect only: the authority to which they profess allegiance is not recognized by the adversary as a party to the conflict.

As pointed out in the International Committee of the Red Cross (ICRC) *Commentary*, the "regular armed forces"—be they of recognized or unrecognized governments—are assumed to have all the material characteristics and all the attributes of the armed forces falling within Article 4(A)(1), GC III: they wear uniforms, they have an organized hierarchy, and they know and respect the laws and customs of war.[24] Therefore, the delegates to the 1949 Diplomatic Conference thought that it was not necessary to expressly specify that such armed forces had to satisfy the requirements laid down in Article 4(A)(2)(a), (b), (c) and (d): that of being commanded by a person responsible for his subordinates, that of having a fixed distinctive sign recognizable at a distance, that of carrying arms openly and that of conducting operations in compliance with IHL.[25] It was presumed that States' regular armed forces complied with these requirements.[26]

While it recognized the application of GC III in the conduct of armed hostilities against the Taliban, the US administration reached the conclusion, as set forth in a 2002 White House memorandum, that the Taliban collectively were not entitled to POW status because they were not fulfilling the necessary criteria under Article 4 of GC III.[27] This collective denial of POW status for the adversary armed forces is highly problematic. The main reasons invoked were that the Taliban did not distinguish themselves from the general population and did not obey the laws and customs of war.[28]

It is highly unlikely that none of the Taliban fighters complied with these requirements. This is particularly evident with regard to the obligation to distinguish oneself during an attack. Indeed, it has been argued that the Taliban fighters were clearly distinguishable from the civilian population because they wore black turbans and had scarves indicating to which force they belonged.[29] Thus, the requirement to distinguish oneself could not be assessed in a generalized manner, but had to be decided for each captured person. According to Article 5, GC III,[30] a "competent tribunal" is to decide in each individual case whether a person was indeed distinguishing her/himself. An individualized factual assessment was also necessary for the other requirements. Given that there was debate about whether these conditions were fulfilled, there was reason for doubt and thus a competent tribunal—and not the executive authorities in Washington—should have made a finding on the facts and ruled on whether the person in question was or was not a POW. This competent tribunal could have been either civilian or military.[31] Until the tribunal has given its ruling, the person deprived of his or her liberty must be treated as a POW.

Because of the position enunciated in the 2002 White House memorandum competent tribunals were never established in Afghanistan. But in response to a US Supreme Court decision in June 2004, according to which US courts have jurisdiction to hear legal challenges on behalf of persons detained at Guantanamo,[32] the US Department of Defense (DoD) established administrative hearings, called Combatant Status Review Tribunals (CSRTs).[33] The purpose of the CSRTs is to review whether each person meets the criteria to be designated as an enemy combatant and to allow those persons to contest such designation.[34] US authorities have stated that CSRT procedures provide a process similar to that of a competent tribunal under Article 5, GC III.[35] In this regard, it must be argued that the CSRT and Article 5 hearings serve different purposes and operate under different circumstances. Article 5 hearings are meant to take place on or near the zone of combat, immediately after capture, thereby maximizing availability of witnesses and evidence. They are designed to swiftly determine a detainee's legal status, i.e., if he or she is entitled to POW status. In contrast, CSRTs started to operate in July 2004, two and a half years after the arrival of the first detainees at Guantanamo from Afghanistan and thousands of miles from the combat zone. Moreover, CSRTs may only confirm the enemy combatant designation or conclude it was an error; they do not have the authority or the option of declaring a detainee a lawful combatant, i.e., a POW.

What would be the main consequences if a Taliban fighter had received POW status after an Article 5 hearing? In those circumstances, he could lawfully be deprived of liberty until the end of active hostilities of the international armed conflict.[36] He could not be prosecuted for his mere participation in hostilities, unless he had committed a war crime. If prosecuted for war crimes, the concerned POW should be sentenced by the same courts and according to the same procedures as in the case of members of the armed forces of the detaining power, i.e., by "court martial" if prosecuted by the United States.[37]

An Article 5 tribunal could also have decided that an individual was not entitled to POW status. In that scenario, the concerned Taliban fighter would then be protected by GC IV as a detainee or internee[38] (if he fulfilled the criteria of nationality found in Article 4, GC IV).[39] A person protected by GC IV may be detained until the end of active hostilities unless released earlier because this person is deemed to no longer pose a security threat. He may be deprived of certain rights and privileges while in detention (but must be humanely treated), and may be prosecuted for the mere fact of having taken up arms under the domestic law of the United States.

For the individuals who did not fulfill the criteria of GC III or GC IV to benefit from their respective protections, they would still benefit from the rules of existing customary IHL as reflected in CA3[40] and Article 75, AP I,[41] which lay down fundamental guarantees. Thus, there is no category of persons affected by or involved in international armed conflict that fall outside the scope of IHL protection.

B. Taliban Captured before June 19, 2002 and Still Held by the United States

Taliban captured during the period of the international armed conflict in Afghanistan and still in the power of the United States are not held in Afghanistan but in Guantanamo. With the end of the international armed conflict, GC III and IV no longer provide a valid legal basis for continuing to hold, without charge, persons captured before June 19, 2002. Because armed hostilities are ongoing in Afghanistan, it would not be realistic to require that every person held by the United States in Guantanamo who is not facing a criminal proceeding be released; such a person might still constitute a security threat to the United States in the context of the ongoing non-international armed conflict in Afghanistan. The United States could, therefore, continue to hold these persons for the same reason(s) that it currently interns persons in connection with the non-international armed conflict in Afghanistan (see Part C below). As GC III and IV no longer provide a legal basis for continuing to hold them, these persons should be placed within another legal framework to regulate their internment, including, in particular, a regular, independent and impartial review of the reasons for their continued deprivation of liberty.[42] In its June 2008 decision concerning those held at Guantanamo, the US Supreme Court granted internees access to US civilian courts.[43] This access would allow the concerned individuals to benefit from judicial supervision of the lawfulness of their continued deprivation of liberty. Such judicial supervision seems to be the most adequate means of ensuring a genuine independent and impartial review process.

Those who are suspected of having committed war crimes or other criminal offenses can and should be prosecuted. Some have argued that the US federal criminal justice system has proven itself highly adequate and adaptable to the challenges of prosecuting complex terrorism cases, while the possible use of "new" military commissions on US soil has been reported in the media.[44] But whatever system is eventually used, those prosecuted must be afforded essential judicial guarantees such as the presumption of innocence, the right to be tried by an impartial and independent tribunal, the right to effective legal counsel and the exclusion of any evidence obtained as a result of torture or other cruel, inhumane or degrading treatment.

An appropriate approach would be to consider that these persons are now protected by CA3, customary rules applicable to non-international armed conflict and relevant rules of human rights law since their deprivation of liberty is no longer linked to the former international armed conflict but rather to the current non-international one. From an analytical perspective, these persons would be viewed as though they had been released at the end of the international armed conflict and simultaneously re-arrested at the beginning of the non-international conflict, with the legitimacy and conditions of their continued detention reevaluated in accordance with this approach.

C. Taliban Captured after June 19, 2002 and Still Held by the United States

Combatant status, which entails the right to participate directly in hostilities, and POW status do not exist in non-international armed conflict, such as the one that began on June 19, 2002 and is ongoing. Therefore, upon capture the Taliban do not, as a matter of law, enjoy POW status and may be prosecuted by US authorities under domestic law for any acts of violence committed during the conflict, including, of course, war crimes. In terms of IHL, their rights and treatment during detention are governed by CA3 and customary rules applicable to non-international armed conflicts.

Following the June 2006 *Hamdan* decision,[45] the DoD issued a memorandum requiring all DoD personnel to adhere to the standards of CA3 with regard to the treatment of detainees and that all relevant directives, regulations, policies, practices and procedures be reviewed "no later than three weeks from the date of this memorandum" in order to comply with the CA3 standards.[46] In January 2009 the Secretary of Defense was tasked with undertaking a review of the conditions of confinement of those held at Guantanamo to ensure they meet humane standards, notably those required by CA3.[47]

The vast majority of the Taliban captured after June 2002 are held in Afghanistan, but almost none of them have been charged with any crime. Therefore, they must be considered as internees. As for those interned in Guantanamo (see Part II B above), a wide range of procedural principles and safeguards should be implemented by the US detaining authorities, including a regular independent and impartial review of the reasons for their continued deprivation of liberty.

One particular issue that needs to be tackled and clarified by US authorities is the legal basis for their internment activities at Bagram for individuals detained by US forces operating as part of Operation Enduring Freedom. Indeed, there is no UN Security Council resolution (unlike in Iraq until December 31, 2008), no agreement with the Afghan authorities and no US domestic legislation or executive order governing this type of deprivation of liberty.[48]

While internment is clearly a measure that can be taken in a non-international armed conflict, as evidenced by the language of AP II, which mentions internment in Articles 5 and 6,[49] CA3 contains no provisions regulating internment apart from the requirement of humane treatment. Therefore, reliance on international human rights law as a complementary source of law in situations of non-international armed conflict is necessary. Moreover, even though not applicable per se, the principles and rules of GC IV might serve as guidance.[50]

It can be argued that the basis for the detention/internment activities of US forces assigned to the International Security Assistance Force (ISAF) can be found in UN Security Council Resolution 1386 of December 20, 2001 and subsequent resolutions. Those resolutions authorize the ISAF to assist Afghan authorities in the maintenance of security and ISAF-participating States to take "all necessary measures to fulfil its mandate."[51] The wording "necessary measures" could be interpreted as encompassing deprivation of liberty activities. However, this wording remains vague and definitely needs more details regarding the grounds and process governing the use of internment as a form of deprivation of liberty.

Conclusions

In the aftermath of 9/11, the armed conflict in Afghanistan has raised many questions concerning the application of IHL, in particular with regard to deprivation of liberty. Nothing in existing IHL prevents US authorities from capturing, detaining or interning persons in the fight against terrorism, or from prosecuting persons suspected of having committed criminal offenses when appropriate. Thus, it is the author's opinion that, if properly implemented, the existing conventional and customary rules of IHL adequately address most, if not all, of these questions. Seven years after the beginning of the conflict, and on the verge of the closure of Guantanamo, it is time to think on how better compliance can be achieved. The January 2009 White House executive order establishing a special task force to identify "lawful options for the disposition of individuals captured or apprehended in connection with armed conflicts and counterterrorism operations"[52] seems to be a significant step in the right direction.

Notes

1. US forces have been deployed in Afghanistan under the banner of Operation Enduring Freedom since 2001 and under the NATO-led International Security Assistance Force operation since 2002.

2. The term "IHL" is used as synonymous with the "law of armed conflict" and the "laws and customs of war."

3. It is not the aim of the author to identify and attribute specific violations that may have been committed by the parties to the conflict.

4. *See* Yoram Dinstein, *Jus in Bello Issues Arising in the Hostilities in Iraq in 2003*, 33 ISRAEL YEARBOOK ON HUMAN RIGHTS 2 (2003).

5. Convention for the Amelioration of the Condition of the Wounded and Sick in Armed Forces in the Field, Aug. 12, 1949, 6 U.S.T. 3114, 75 U.N.T.S. 31; Convention for the Amelioration of the Condition of Wounded, Sick and Shipwrecked Members of Armed Forces at Sea, Aug. 12, 1949, 6 U.S.T. 3217, 75 U.N.T.S. 85; Convention Relative to the Treatment of Prisoners of War, Aug. 12, 1949, 6 U.S.T. 3316, 75 U.N.T.S. 135 [hereinafter GC III]; Convention Relative to the Protection of Civilian Persons in Time of War, Aug. 12, 1949, 6 U.S.T. 3516, 75 U.N.T.S. 287; all *reprinted in* DOCUMENTS ON THE LAWS OF WAR (Adam Roberts & Richard Guelff eds., 3d ed. 2000) at 197, 222, 244 and 301, respectively.

6. Protocol Additional to the Geneva Conventions of 12 August 1949, and Relating to the Protection of Victims of International Armed Conflicts, June 8, 1977, 1125 U.N.T.S. 3 [hereinafter AP I]; Protocol Additional to the Geneva Conventions of 12 August 1949, and Relating to the Protection of Victims of Non-International Armed Conflicts, June 8, 1977, 1125 U.N.T.S. 609 [hereinafter AP II]; both *reprinted in* DOCUMENTS ON THE LAWS OF WAR, *supra* note 5, at 422 and 483, respectively.

7. *See* Jean-Marie Henckaerts, *Binding Armed Groups Through Humanitarian Treaty Law and Customary Law, in* RELEVANCE OF INTERNATIONAL HUMANITARIAN LAW TO NON-STATE ACTORS 132 (Marc Vuijlsteke, Christine Reh & Christopher Reynolds eds., 2003), *available at* http://www.coleurop.be/content/publications/pdf/Collegium27.pdf; Jean-Marie Henckaerts, *The Conduct of Hostilities: Target Selection, Proportionality, and Precautionary Measures under International Humanitarian Law, in* PROTECTING CIVILIANS IN 21ST CENTURY WARFARE: TARGET SELECTION, PROPORTIONALITY AND PRECAUTIONARY MEASURES IN LAW AND PRACTICE 11–12 (Mireille Hector & Martine Jellema eds., 2006).

8. *See* President George W. Bush, Address to the Nation (Sept. 11, 2001), *available at* http://www.nationalcenter.org/BushGW91101Address.html.

9. Bagram is a place of detention located on the US military base in the ancient city of Bagram, north of Kabul. The US base was originally built and used by the Soviet Union during its war in Afghanistan in 1979–89. The detention center was set up at the end of 2001 and was used by the US military as a temporary screening facility until the end of 2004. Detainees were either released, or sent to US places of detention at Kandahar, Afghanistan or at Guantanamo Bay, Cuba.

10. For a list of US detainee transfers to and from Guantanamo, see http://www.globalsecurity.org/military/facility/guantanamo-bay_detainees.htm (last visited Feb. 24, 2009).

11. *See* Exec. Order No. 13492, § 3, 74 Fed. Reg. 4897 (Jan. 27, 2009) (Review and Disposition of Individuals Detained at the Guantanamo Bay Naval Base and Closure of Detention Facilities) [hereinafter White House Executive Order].

12. *See* Eric Schmitt, *Two Prisons, Similar Issues for President*, NEW YORK TIMES, Jan. 27, 2009, at A1.

13. While not of direct interest for this article, at the time of the launching of the coalition military campaign, years of armed hostilities in Afghanistan between the Northern Alliance armed group and the Taliban constituted a non-international armed conflict, thus were subject to the rules of IHL.

14. Pakistan, Saudi Arabia and the United Arab Emirates.

15. COMMENTARY IV RELATIVE TO THE PROTECTION OF CIVILIAN PERSONS IN TIME OF WAR 20 (Jean S. Pictet ed., 1958).

16. Prosecutor v. Tadic, Case No. IT-94-1-A, Decision on Defence Motion for Interlocutory Appeal on Jurisdiction, ¶ 70 (Oct. 2, 1995). This definition has been adopted by other international bodies since then.

17. *See* AP I, *supra* note 6, arts. 48, 51, 53, 54, 57 & 58.

18. Regulations Respecting the Laws and Customs of War on Land, annex to Hague Convention No. IV Respecting the Laws and Customs of War on Land, Oct. 18, 1907, 36 Stat. 2227, *reprinted in* DOCUMENTS ON THE LAWS OF WAR, *supra* note 5, at 69.

19. Legal Consequences of the Construction of a Wall in the Occupied Palestinian Territory, Advisory Opinion, 2004 I.C.J. 136, ¶ 89 (July 9); 1 Trial of the Major War Criminals Before the International Military Tribunal at Nuremberg, 14 November 1945–1 October 1946, at 253–54 (1947).

20. *See* ICRC Opinion Paper, How is the term "armed conflict" defined in International Humanitarian Law (Mar. 2008), http://www.icrc.org/web/eng/siteeng0.nsf/htmlall/armed-conflict-article-170308/$file/Opinion-paper-armed-conflict.pdf

21. For more information on customary law and for a complete description of the rules of IHL applicable in non-international armed conflict as a matter of customary law, see the ICRC study on customary international humanitarian law. JEAN-MARIE HENCKAERTS & LOUISE DOSWALD-BECK, CUSTOMARY INTERNATIONAL HUMANITARIAN LAW (2005) (2 volumes: Volume I, Rules; Volume II, Practice (2 Parts)).

22. There are some exceptions such as Article 46 of AP I, which is of customary nature. It provides that combatants who engage in espionage do not have the right to POW status.

23. There are some categories of persons who are not combatants but who are granted POW status (e.g., war correspondents as provided in Article 4, GC III).

24. COMMENTARY III RELATIVE TO THE TREATMENT OF PRISONERS OF WAR 63 (Jean S. Pictet ed., 1958) [hereinafter ICRC COMMENTARY III].

25. *Id.* at 59–61.

26. Whether these criteria must also be met by a State's regular armed forces has generated some controversy in literature with arguments based on textual logic, i.e., the conditions are only mentioned in Article 4(A)(2) and not in Article 4(A)(1) and (3) of GC III. *See, e.g.*, George H. Aldrich, *The Taliban, Al Qaeda, and the Determination of Illegal Combatants*, 96 AMERICAN JOURNAL OF INTERNATIONAL LAW 895 (2002); Yoram Dinstein, *Unlawful Combatancy*, 32 ISRAEL YEARBOOK ON HUMAN RIGHTS 255 (2002).

27. *See* Memorandum from George Bush to Vice President et al., Humane Treatment of Al Qaeda and Taliban Detainees (Feb. 7, 2002), *reprinted in* THE TORTURE PAPERS: THE ROAD TO ABU GHRAIB 134 (Karen J. Greenberg & Joshua Dratel eds., 2005); Press Release, Office of the Press Secretary, White House Fact Sheet: Status of Detainees at Guantanamo (Feb. 7, 2002), *available at* http://www.aiipowmia.com/wh/wh06_07feb02.html.

28. *See, e.g.*, Posting of John B. Bellinger, Unlawful Enemy Combatants (paras. 6 & 7 of Jan. 17, 2007 posting), to http://opiniojuris.org/author/john-bellinger/.

29. *See* Rüdiger Wolfrum & Christiane E. Philipp, *The Status of the Taliban: Their Obligations and Rights under International Law*, 6 MAX PLANCK YEARBOOK OF UNITED NATIONS LAW 559 (2002).

30. Article 5(2) of GC III states that

> [s]hould any doubt arise as to whether persons having committed a belligerent act and having fallen into the hands of the enemy belong to any of the categories enumerated in Article 4, such persons shall enjoy the protection of the present Convention until such time as their status has been determined by a competent tribunal.

31. ICRC COMMENTARY III, *supra* note 24, at 77.

32. Rasul v. Bush, 542 U.S. 466 (2004).

33. *See* Memorandum from the Deputy Secretary of Defense to the Secretary of the Navy, Order Establishing Combatant Status Review Tribunal (July 7, 2004), *available at* http://www.defenselink.mil/news/Jul2004/d20040707review.pdf.

34. *See* Memorandum from the Secretary of the Navy to Distribution, Implementation of Combatant Status Review Procedures for Enemy Combatants at Guantanamo Bay Naval Base, Cuba (July 9, 2004), *available at* http://www.dod.mil/news/Jul2004/d20040730comb.pdf.

35. *See, e.g.*, Brief for the Respondents at 50, Boumediene v. Bush, No. 06-1195 (U.S. Oct. 9, 2007).

36. *See* GC III, *supra* note 5, art. 118.

37. *See id.*, art. 102.

38. Internment is defined as the deprivation of liberty of a person that has been initiated/ordered by the executive branch, not the judiciary, without criminal charges being brought against the internee.

39. For more details, see Knut Dörmann, *The Legal Situation of "Unlawful/Unprivileged Combatants,"* 85 INTERNATIONAL REVIEW OF THE RED CROSS 45 (2003).

40. The International Court of Justice recognized the customary nature of CA3 not only in non-international armed conflict but also in the event of international armed conflict. Military and Paramilitary Activities (Nicar. v. U.S.), 1986 I.C.J. 14 (June 27).

41. *See* Christopher Greenwood, *International Law and the "War Against Terrorism,"* 78 INTERNATIONAL AFFAIRS 316 (2002).

42. For an elaboration on the procedural principles and safeguards governing internment, see INTERNATIONAL COMMITTEE OF THE RED CROSS, IHL AND THE CHALLENGES OF CONTEMPORARY ARMED CONFLICTS Annex 1 (2007), *available at* http://www.icrc.org/Web/eng/siteeng0.nsf/htmlall/ihl-30-international-conference-101207/$File/IHL-challenges-30th-International-Conference-ENG.pdf [hereinafter ICRC Report].

43. Boumediene v. Bush, 553 U.S. 7 (2008).

44. *See* Richard B. Zabel & James J. Benjamin, Jr., Human Rights First, In Pursuit of Justice: Prosecuting Terrorism Cases in Federal Court (2008), *available at* http://www.humanrightsfirst.info/pdf/080521-USLS-pursuit-justice.pdf. *See also* Peter Finn, *Obama Set to Revive Military Commissions, Changes Would Boost Detainee Rights*, WASHINGTON POST, May 9, 2009.

45. Hamdan v. Rumsfeld, 548 U.S. 557 (2006).

46. Memorandum from the Deputy Secretary of Defense to the Secretaries of the Military Departments et al., Application of Common Article 3 of the Geneva Conventions to the Treatment of Detainees in the Department of Defense (July 7, 2006), *available at* http://www.fas.org/sgp/othergov/dod/geneva070606.pdf.

47. *See* White House Executive Order, supra note 11, § 6. See the outcome of this review in Review of Department Compliance with President's Executive Order on Detainee Conditions of Confinement (2009), *available at* http://www.defenselink.mil/pubs/pdfs/REVIEW_OF_DEPARTMENT_COMPLIANCE_WITH_PRESIDENTS_EXECUTIVE_ORDER_ON_DETAINEE_CONDITIONS_OF_CONFINEMENTa.pdf.

48. It is arguable whether the Authorization for the Use of Military Force (Pub. L. No. 107-40, (codified at 50 U.S.C. § 1514), which authorizes the President to use "all necessary and appropriate force" against "nations, organizations, or persons" associated with 9/11, provides an adequate basis for US detention abroad. In this regard, see Hamdi v. Rumsfeld, 542 U.S. 507 (2004). See also the Respondents' Memorandum Regarding the Government's Detention Authority Relative to Detainees Held at Guantanamo Bay, in Re: Guantanamo Bay Detainee Litigation, filed by the US Department of Justice on March 13, 2009. At the time this is written, it is unclear whether the US administration would rely on the Authorization for the Use of Military Force authority with regard to detention in Afghanistan.

49. AP II, *supra* note 6, art. 5(1) ("the following provisions shall be respected as a minimum with regards to persons deprived of their liberty for reasons related to the armed conflict, whether they are interned or detained"); *id.*, art. 6(5) ("At the end of hostilities, the authorities in power shall endeavour to grant the broadest possible amnesty to persons who have participated in the armed conflict, or those deprived of liberty for reasons related to the armed conflict, whether they are interned or detained").

50. For more details, see ICRC Report, *supra* note 42.

51. S.C. Res. 1386, ¶ 3, U.N. Doc. S/RES/1386 (Dec. 20, 2001).

52. Exec. Order No. 13493, § 1, 74 Fed. Reg. 4901 (Jan. 27, 2009) (Review of Detention Policy Options).

XIV

Rationales for Detention: Security Threats and Intelligence Value

Ryan Goodman*

In the armed conflict with Al Qaeda inside and outside Afghanistan,[1] the US government has had to grapple with difficult legal issues concerning who can be detained. In this brief essay, I discuss whether US practices have been consistent with the law of armed conflict (LOAC). Three specific issues are considered. The first is a threshold question: Does LOAC regulate who can be detained in a non-international armed conflict? After concluding that it does, I address two questions that implicate the substantive criteria for detention. First, is it lawful to detain civilians who have not directly participated in hostilities? Second, is it lawful to detain individuals for a long or indefinite period for the purpose of gathering intelligence? Since September 11, the US government has adjusted its detention practices to overcome various legal defects. These three issues remain among the fundamental challenges to the detention regime.

It is not obvious that LOAC regulates the substantive grounds for detention in non-international armed conflict. Neither Common Article 3 nor Additional Protocol II explicitly addresses the subject. They contain no language expressly prohibiting arbitrary detention or unlawful confinement. Similarly, the Rome Statute for the International Criminal Court includes "unlawful confinement" in a list of

* Rita E. Hauser Professor of Human Rights and Humanitarian Law, Harvard Law School.

war crimes in international armed conflict.[2] Unlawful confinement, however, is conspicuously absent from the Statute's list of war crimes in non-international armed conflict. Additionally, a 2004 expert meeting—which included Louise Doswald-Beck, Knut Dörmann, Robert Goldman, Walter Kälin, Judge Theodore Meron, Sir Nigel Rodley and Jelena Pejić—concludes that LOAC does not contain rules precluding unlawful confinement in non-international armed conflicts:

> *Non-International Armed Conflicts*
> The experts noted that there are no provisions requiring certain reasons for detention, nor any procedures to prevent unnecessary detention. It was further observed that there are no specific supervisory mechanisms other than the minimal requirement that the ICRC [International Committee of the Red Cross] be allowed to offer its services. It was stated, therefore, that only national law is relevant, as well as international human rights law.[3]

Some legal advisers at the International Committee of the Red Cross (ICRC) have helped support this view. A presentation at the 2004 meeting by Dörmann, Deputy Head of the Legal Division of the ICRC, states: "International humanitarian law applicable to non-international armed conflicts contains no provisions requiring certain grounds for detention/internment nor are there any procedures defined to check the need for such detention."[4] An important article in the *International Review of the Red Cross* by Jelena Pejić, Legal Adviser in the ICRC Legal Division, is more equivocal. She states:

> In non-international armed conflicts there is even less clarity as to how administrative detention is to be organized. Article 3 common to the Geneva Conventions, which is applicable as a minimum standard to all non-international armed conflicts, contains no provisions regulating internment, i.e. administrative detention for security reasons, apart from the requirement of humane treatment.[5]

Pejić does not elaborate whether or to what extent the requirement of humane treatment might directly regulate the use of security rationales or other grounds for confinement.

Many of these experts find some solace in the notion that gaps in LOAC are intolerable (else a legal black hole) and that those gaps would be filled by international human rights law. The 2004 expert meeting, in which Pejić, Dörmann and others participated, concludes:

> The experts stated that as IHL does not provide procedural guarantees to persons detained during non-international armed conflict, human rights standards must always apply . . . . The general view was that instead of trying to amend humanitarian

> law to remedy its failings, the standards applicable to non-international armed conflict should be those of human rights law and subject to human rights remedies.[6]

International human rights law, however, is not accorded the same legal (or symbolic) weight in US law and practice as the Geneva Conventions or customary international humanitarian law. Hence, the exclusion of LOAC from this domain would leave a substantial void in the definition and regulation of impermissible behavior.

According to the weight of legal authority, however, no such gap exists. Unlawful confinement is prohibited by Common Article 3 (e.g., as a form of inhumane treatment) and by customary international humanitarian law. Under the framework set forth in Common Article 3, the power to detain is subject to a number of substantive constraints. First, individuals cannot be detained on discriminatory grounds such as "race, color, religion or faith, sex, birth or wealth, or any other similar criteria."[7] Second, parties to a conflict are prohibited from taking hostages. According to the ICRC *Commentary*, that prohibition is based on a fundamental principle of justice:

> The taking of hostages, like reprisals, to which it is often the prelude, is contrary to the modern idea of justice in that it is based on the principle of collective responsibility for crime. Both strike at persons who are innocent of the crime which it is intended to prevent or punish.[8]

In other words, if a person does not bear individual responsibility for a security threat to the State, he should not be deprived of his liberty, even if confining him could prevent the threat from materializing. Third, Common Article 3 prohibits the passing of a sentence without affording fundamental judicial guarantees, and that provision implicitly restricts the use of administrative detention for punitive purposes.

More generally, unlawful confinement is prohibited by a broad-based obligation under Common Article 3: *hors de combat* "shall in all circumstances be treated humanely."[9] Indeed, the recent 2005 ICRC study on customary international humanitarian law states that, as a matter of treaty law, "arbitrary deprivation of liberty is not compatible" with humane treatment under Common Article 3.[10] Joanna Dingwall argues persuasively that Common Article 3 prohibits unlawful confinement as a form of "cruel treatment."[11] And, the overriding obligation of humane treatment is even more clearly and directly connected to the sources that Dingwall invokes.[12] As an analytic matter, these interpretations of humane treatment are not precluded by the existence of text explicitly prohibiting unlawful confinement in international conflicts, but the absence of text referring to unlawful confinement in Common Article 3. Rape is not explicitly prohibited by Common Article 3 either; yet it is well understood that rape is covered by the article.[13] The protections codified in Common Article 3 are simply written in broader terms.

International authorities also suggest that unlawful confinement is prohibited in non-international armed conflict as a matter of customary international law. In considering the practices of armed opposition groups in Colombia's civil war, the Inter-American Commission on Human Rights stated: "International humanitarian law also prohibits the detention or internment of civilians except where necessary for imperative reasons of security."[14] Liesbeth Zegveld also reports that the UN Commission on Human Rights drew from international humanitarian law applicable to international armed conflicts in demanding armed opposition groups refrain from arbitrary detention in Afghanistan (1993) and in the Sudan (1995).[15] In addition, Article 3 of the Turku Declaration of Minimum Humanitarian Standards proscribes the disappearance of individuals, "including their abduction or unacknowledged detention."[16] And Article 11 of the Turku Declaration includes an implicit restriction on substantive grounds for detention: "If it is considered necessary for imperative reasons of security to subject any person to assigned residence, internment or administrative detention, such decisions shall be subject to a regular procedure prescribed by law . . . ."[17]

Once the question whether LOAC prohibits arbitrary detention is resolved in the affirmative, a second-order question is whether LOAC permits the administrative detention of civilians, including civilians who do not directly participate in hostilities.[18] That question has arisen in recent litigation, and federal judges have been divided on the issue.[19] The Fourth Geneva Convention rules on internment are the most directly relevant in this regard.[20] And, in accordance with Articles 5, 27, 41–43 and 78 of the Civilians Convention, States are permitted to detain not only civilians who directly participate in hostilities (e.g., unlawful combatants) but also civilians whose *indirect* participation in hostilities poses a security threat. At first blush, US practices in the conflict with Al Qaeda do not necessitate making such distinctions. The US government has formally claimed the authority, in legislation[21] and in executive action,[22] to detain only "unlawful *combatants.*" However, the government's peculiar definition of "combatants" and its actual detention decisions betray a contrary policy of detaining civilians who have, at most, indirectly participated in hostilities.[23]

Although LOAC does not forbid the detention of this broader class of civilians, domestic law might. For example, an important constitutional distinction may exist with respect to classes of individuals who can be subject to military jurisdiction. The constitutional line may be drawn between "combatants" (including direct participants in hostilities) and civilians, and LOAC should help define the boundaries of those groups for constitutional purposes. Indeed, if the government wishes to detain individuals in the latter group, it may be required to adopt laws explicitly subjecting "civilians" to detention. The basis for that clear statement rule would derive from domestic law, however, and not LOAC itself.

A remaining question is whether the United States can detain individuals, on a long-term or indefinite basis, for the purpose of gathering intelligence. Before analyzing that question of law, first consider the record of US detention practices following September 11. The government has used intelligence value as a ground for initial internment decisions, as well as for denying release. Former Deputy Assistant Secretary of Defense for Detainee Affairs Professor Matthew Waxman recently wrote: "Intelligence gathering through questioning of those in custody constitutes another important reason for detention in warfare, and especially in fighting terrorist networks."[24] With respect to the global sphere of operations, the 2006 *Counterinsurgency Field Manual* states that information gathering provides a reason for detaining two classes of individuals: (1) "persons who have engaged in, or assisted those who engage in, terrorist or insurgent activities" and (2) "persons who have incidentally obtained knowledge regarding insurgent and terrorist activity, but who are not guilty of associating with such groups."[25] Notably, information gathering appears to be an independent basis for detaining the first category of individuals even if they no longer pose a security threat.[26] However, for the second category, the *Counterinsurgency* manual states: "Since persons in the second category have not engaged in criminal or insurgent activities, they must be released, even if they refuse to provide information."[27] It stands to reason that individuals in the first category could be denied release if they refuse to provide information. As another component of global operations, President George Bush announced that under the CIA's secret detention program "[m]any are released after questioning, or turned over to local authorities—if we determine that they do not pose a continuing threat and no longer have significant intelligence value."[28]

With respect to detention in Guantanamo specifically, in determining whether a detainee should be transferred to the base, US military screening teams and the combatant commander must consider "the possible intelligence that may be gained from the detainee."[29] And administrative review boards (ARB) may consider whether a detainee "is of continuing intelligence value" in deciding whether to recommend release.[30] That standard appears to regularize practices that predated the ARB process.[31] Although stated in a summary fashion, a joint report by UN human rights officials concerning Guantanamo concludes "that the objective of the ongoing detention is not primarily to prevent combatants from taking up arms against the United States again, but to obtain information and gather intelligence on the Al-Qaeda network."[32]

Within the United States, the cases of individuals such as José Padilla and Ali Saleh Kahlah al-Marri suggest that intelligence value may constitute a dominant rationale for detention. In Padilla's case, the Solicitor General argued before the Supreme Court that "[t]he detention of enemy combatants serves two vital purposes directly connected to prosecuting the war. First, detention prevents captured combatants from rejoining the enemy and continuing the fight. Second, detention enables the military to gather critical intelligence from captured combatants concerning the capabilities and intentions of the enemy."[33] For the latter proposition, the Solicitor General cited and included, as an appendix to his brief, a declaration by Vice Admiral Lowell Jacoby, Director of the Defense Intelligence Agency.[34] The Jacoby Declaration focuses on the need to obtain information from the detainee as the basis for military confinement outside of the criminal justice system.[35] In al-Marri's case, federal judges expressed concern over the apparent interrogation–based reasons for transferring the petitioner from criminal jurisdiction to military administrative detention:

> [N]ot only has the Government offered no other explanation [than interrogation purposes] for abandoning al-Marri's prosecution, it has even propounded an affidavit in support of al-Marri's continued military detention, stating that he "possesses information of high intelligence value." *See* Rapp. Declaration. Moreover, former Attorney General John Ashcroft has explained that the Government decided to declare al-Marri an enemy combatant only after he became a "hard case" by "reject[ing] numerous offers to improve his lot by . . . providing information." John Ashcroft, Never Again: Securing America and Restoring Justice 168-69 (2006).[36]

Professor Marty Lederman, a leading expert on US detention policy since September 11, summarizes his view of the overall scheme: "Unlike in past conflicts, when the purpose of detention was incapacitation of actual combatants so that they could not fight against us, the dominant purpose of this detention regime is intelligence-gathering."[37]

It is important to recognize that intelligence value has also constituted an independent basis for administrative detention in Iraq.[38] Consider Lieutenant Andru Wall's account of detainee operations:

> Officially, individuals could be detained for their intelligence value for no more than 72 hours; however, anecdotal evidence suggested that longer intelligence detentions were common. The argument in favor of intelligence detentions was that, for example, if an individual knew who was responsible for carrying out attacks on Coalition Forces . . . then withholding [this information] constituted an imperative threat to the security of Coalition Forces . . . . The argument against such detentions was that the individual himself did not pose an imperative security threat . . . .[39]

Other reports also find that intelligence value constituted a—formal and informal—ground for detention in Iraq.[40]

Three arguments might be raised to support the legality of US practice. First, the Geneva Conventions contain no express prohibition on the use of detention for intelligence-gathering purposes. Second, detention is permitted if obtaining the relevant information serves an imperative security interest. Third, if a State has the authority to detain an individual until the cessation of hostilities, the State has the prerogative to release her earlier if she provides valuable intelligence information.

At the outset in addressing these arguments we should note that an express provision of the Geneva Conventions may not be necessary if the regime implicitly contemplates that the only basis for detention is to prevent individuals returning to the fight. A customary norm may also suffice if treaties do not. And, even if LOAC permits interrogation incidental to detention, it does not necessarily permit detention for the purpose of interrogation. Nor does it permit coercive interrogation. Let's turn to an elaboration of some of these points and other points as well.

First, all three arguments are contradicted by legal authorities that have addressed the subject with respect to the general LOAC regime. The ICRC publicly criticized the use of Guantanamo for interrogation purposes.[41] The joint report of UN officials declared: "The indefinite detention of prisoners of war and civilian internees for purposes of continued interrogation is inconsistent with the provisions of the Geneva Conventions."[42] And a plurality of the US Supreme Court stated in dicta: "Certainly, we agree that indefinite detention for the purpose of interrogation is not authorized."[43] Some commentators have suggested that the plurality's statement is conclusory and without citation to legal authority. However, in earlier passages, the opinion references authorities suggesting that detention is permitted exclusively to prevent individuals returning to the battlefield.[44] US policy, accordingly, contradicts the collective judgment of the US Supreme Court (in a plurality opinion), the ICRC and UN human rights officials.

Second, other provisions of the Geneva Conventions indirectly support the conclusion that indefinite or long-term detention is permitted only to prevent individuals returning to the battlefield. In general, detaining powers argue against early release of prisoners of war on the ground that the individuals might return to the fight. However, some detainees are too sick or wounded to return to the battlefield.[45] A valuable question for our purposes is whether the detaining power could nevertheless hold the individual to gather intelligence. The Prisoner of War (POW) Convention is clear; it places a categorical obligation to repatriate such individuals to their home countries.[46] There is no exception for detaining or precluding release of individuals on any other grounds such as intelligence value.

Third, the most relevant rules may not be found directly in provisions regulating detention. The most relevant source may be found in rules governing interrogation. And those interrogation rules preclude the initial decision to detain an individual, as well as the purported prerogative to order release of a detainee who provides information. More specifically, the use of intelligence value violates Article 17 of the POW Convention and Article 31 of the Civilians Convention. Both articles strictly prohibit physical and moral coercion to obtain information from detainees.[47] Accordingly, individuals who are interrogated should not receive better treatment (release from detention) or worse treatment (continued confinement) on the basis of whether they provide or withhold information. In short, the relevant LOAC rules are found more directly in provisions regulating methods of interrogations, rather than provisions regulating grounds for detention. Notably, the former constitutes an independent basis for the application of LOAC in non-international armed conflicts. That is, even if LOAC does not regulate unlawful confinement in non-international armed conflict, it undoubtedly regulates coercive interrogations.

Fourth, an individual's possession of information does not constitute a valid security rationale for internment under the Civilians Convention. According to the ICRC *Commentary*, States have significant discretion to define activities that threaten their security.[48] The *Commentary*, however, also suggests that the individuals must themselves directly pose the threat. The paradigmatic examples provided by the *Commentary* include "[s]ubversive activity carried on inside the territory of a Party to the conflict or actions which are of direct assistance to an enemy Power."[49] More specific examples include "members of organizations whose object is to cause disturbances, or ... [individuals who] may seriously prejudice its security by other means, such as sabotage or espionage."[50] Moreover, as described above, various authorities, including the ICRC, UN human rights officials and the Supreme Court, have repudiated intelligence-based grounds for detention. Those rejections were absolute and were issued in the context of security-based reasons for gathering intelligence.

Finally, the implications of allowing intelligence value as an independent ground for long-term or indefinite detention are intolerable. Doing so might permit the confinement of individuals, such as the children or other family members of combatants, who have no engagement in hostilities but have personal knowledge about the combatants. It might also permit the confinement of innocent detainees who do not have information themselves but are held as bargaining chips to coerce other individuals to provide information. And, a further implication is suggested by the declaration of Admiral Jacoby. He contends that "the intelligence cycle is continuous. This dynamic is especially important in the War on Terrorism.

There is a constant need to ask detainees new lines of questions as additional detainees are taken into custody and new information is obtained from them and from other intelligence-gathering methods."[51] That justification essentially provides for continuing to hold individuals even if they have exhausted their current intelligence value. In sum, it is not too much of a stretch to suggest that "detaining individuals on the basis of what they were believed to know could be a slippery slope leading to mass, unwarranted detentions."[52]

Since September 11, the United States has adjusted its detention practices in response to powerful objections. Some of the remaining objections are valid and others not. As a threshold matter, an important point is that the laws of war prohibit unlawful confinement in non-international armed conflict. The Obama administration provides a new opportunity to reassess detention policy through that legal framework.

Notes

1. I work with the assumption that since September 11, 2001, the United States has been engaged in an armed conflict with Al Qaeda—a proposition that all three branches of the US government now accept. *See, e.g.*, Hamdan v. Rumsfeld, 548 U.S. 557, 630–31 (2006); Memorandum from Gordon England, Deputy Secretary of Defense, to the Secretaries of the Military Departments et al., Application of Common Article 3 of the Geneva Conventions to the Treatment of Detainees in the Department of Defense (July 7, 2006), http://www.defenselink.mil/home/dodupdate/For-the-record/documents/20060711.html; Military Commissions Act of 2006 § 948a(1), Pub. L. No. 109-366, 120 Stat. 2600 (Oct. 17, 2006) (codified in 10 USC 47(A)). *See also* Derek Jinks, *September 11 and the Laws of War*, 28 YALE JOURNAL OF INTERNATIONAL LAW 1 (2003).

2. Statute of the International Criminal Court art. 8, July 17, 1998, 2187 U.N.T.S. 90.

3. EXPERT MEETING ON THE SUPERVISION OF THE LAWFULNESS OF DETENTION DURING ARMED CONFLICT 17 (The Graduate Institute of International Studies, 2004), *available at* http://www.ruig-gian.org/ressources/communication_colloque_rapport04.pdf [hereinafter 2004 Expert Meeting].

4. *Id.* at 15.

5. Jelena Pejić, *Procedural Principles and Safeguards for Internment/Administrative Detention in Armed Conflict and Other Situations of Violence*, 858 INTERNATIONAL REVIEW OF THE RED CROSS 375 (2005).

6. 2004 Expert Meeting, *supra* note 3, at 41.

7. Convention Relative to the Protection of Civilian Persons in Time of War art. 3(1), Aug. 12, 1949, 6 U.S.T. 3516, 75 U.N.T.S. 287, *reprinted in* DOCUMENTS ON THE LAWS OF WAR 301 (Adam Roberts & Richard Guelff eds., 3d ed. 2000) [hereinafter Civilians Convention].

8. COMMENTARY: IV GENEVA CONVENTION RELATIVE TO THE TREATMENT OF CIVILIANS IN TIME OF WAR 39 (Jean S. Pictet ed., 1958) [hereinafter ICRC COMMENTARY IV].

9. Civilians Convention, *supra* note 7, art. 3(1).

10. I CUSTOMARY INTERNATIONAL HUMANITARIAN LAW 344 (Jean-Marie Henckaerts & Louise Doswald-Beck eds., 2005); cf. James G. Stewart, *Rethinking Guantánamo: Unlawful*

Confinement as Applied in International Criminal Law, 4 JOURNAL OF INTERNATIONAL CRIMINAL JUSTICE 12 (2006); ICRC, *US Detention Related to the Events of 11 September 2001 and Its Aftermath—The Role of the ICRC*, July 30, 2008, http://www.icrc.org/web/eng/siteeng0.nsf/htmlall/usa-detention-update-121205?opendocument [hereinafter Role of the ICRC].

11. Joanna Dingwall, *Unlawful Confinement as a War Crime: The Jurisprudence of the Yugoslav Tribunal and the Common Core of International Humanitarian Law Applicable to Contemporary Armed Conflicts*, 9 JOURNAL OF CONFLICT AND SECURITY LAW 133 (2004).

12. *Id.* For an argument that Article 5 of the Civilians Convention provides evidence that "humane treatment" includes a prohibition on unlawful confinement, see DEREK JINKS, THE RULES OF WAR: THE GENEVA CONVENTIONS IN THE AGE OF TERROR (forthcoming 2009).

13. Dingwall, *supra* note 11, at 159.

14. Inter-American Commission on Human Rights, Third Special Report on the Human Rights Situation in Colombia, OEA/Ser.L/V/II.102, Doc. 9, rev. 1 (1999), ¶ 122; *id.*, ¶ ¶ 128–29 ("The Commission notes that the vast majority of these detentions relating to the election boycott constituted breaches of international humanitarian law. The armed dissident groups repeatedly captured and held civilians, although they did not pose any direct threat to the military operations of the guerrillas . . . . Armed dissident groups are also responsible for arbitrary deprivations of liberty carried out against civilians, outside of the context of the elections.").

15. *See* LIESBETH ZEGVELD, THE ACCOUNTABILITY OF ARMED OPPOSITION GROUPS IN INTERNATIONAL LAW 65–66 (2002); *see also* I CUSTOMARY INTERNATIONAL HUMANITARIAN LAW, *supra* note 10, at 348–49.

16. Turku Declaration, art. 3, U.N. Doc. E/CN.4/Sub.2/1991/55 (1990).

17. *Id.*, art. 11.

18. *See* Ryan Goodman, *The Detention of Civilians in Armed Conflict*, 103 AMERICAN JOURNAL OF INTERNATIONAL LAW 48 (2009).

19. *See, e.g.*, al-Marri v. Pucciarelli, 534 F.3d 213 (4th Cir. 2008) (en banc), *cert. granted*, 77 U.S.L.W. 3148 (U.S. Dec. 5, 2008) (No. 08-368).

20. One reason to examine the rules that apply in international conflict is due to their use as an analogy. It is commonplace for commentators to draw implicitly and explicitly on the Third and Fourth Conventions in discussing the conflict with Al Qaeda (e.g., with respect to detaining fighters and holding them until the cessation of hostilities). We must, therefore, understand the referent—the rules governing international conflict—simply to assess those types of claims. A stronger reason is that the Fourth Geneva Convention, indeed, generally constitutes the most closely analogous rules concerning detention of civilians. It thus provides the best approximation of LOAC rules when interpretive gaps arise.

More fundamentally, LOAC in international armed conflict is directly relevant because it establishes an outer boundary of permissive action. If States have authority to engage in particular actions in an international armed conflict, they a fortiori possess the authority to engage in those actions in non-international conflict. That proposition results from the general relationship between State sovereignty and international law. And LOAC is no exception. The scope of LOAC is uniformly less restrictive in internal armed conflicts (where State sovereignty is stronger) than in international armed conflicts (where State sovereignty is weaker). Hence, if LOAC permits States to detain civilians in international armed conflicts, LOAC surely permits States to take those actions in non-international conflicts.

21. Military Commissions Act of 2006 § 948 a(1), Pub. L. No. 109-366, 120 Stat. 2600 (Oct. 17, 2006) (codified in 10 USC 47(A)).

22. Memorandum from Deputy Secretary of Defense Paul Wolfowitz to the Secretary of the Navy, Order Establishing Combatant Status Review Tribunals 1 (July 7, 2004), *available at* http://www.defenselink.mil/news/Jul2004/d20040707review.pdf.

23. Department of Defense, Fact Sheet: Guantanamo Detainees 2 (Feb. 13, 2004) (including among "representative examples" of detained combatants individuals "involved in terrorist financing," "with links to a financier of the September 11th plots," and "who served as an al Qaida translator and managed operating funds"), *available at* http://www.defenselink.mil/news/Apr2004/d20040406gua.pdf; *see also* News Release, Office of the Assistant Secretary of Defense (Public Affairs), Guantanamo Provides Valuable Information (June 12, 2005), *available at* www.defenselink.mil/releases/release.aspx?releaseid=8583 ("Guantanamo houses enemy combatants ranging from terrorist trainers and recruiters to bomb makers, would-be suicide bombers and terrorist financiers"). Also consider the principal charges against individuals held at Guantanamo and later designated for prosecution before military commissions. According to the initial charge sheets, one detainee allegedly served as an "accountant and treasurer" and "provided logistical support such as food, shelter and clothing;" he also "assisted in loading and transporting" weapons and ammunition. Charge Sheet at 3–4, United States v. al Qosi (US Military Commission), *available at* http://www.defenselink.mil/news/Feb2008/d20080208qosi.pdf (last visited Feb. 10, 2009). A second detainee "created several instructional and motivational recruiting video tapes." Charge Sheet at 3, United States v. al Bahlul (US Military Commission), *available at* http://www.defenselink.mil/news/Jun2004/d20040629ABCO.pdf (last visited Feb. 10, 2009). These allegations alone clearly would not support a finding of "direct participation" under LOAC. Instead, these facts fall squarely within expressly identified examples of indirect participation or nonparticipation. *See* MICHAEL BOTHE ET AL., NEW RULES FOR VICTIMS OF ARMED CONFLICTS 672 (1982) (noting that "transporting supplies, serving as messengers or disseminating propaganda" does not constitute direct participation). *See also* Ryan Goodman & Derek Jinks, *International Law, U.S. War Powers, and the Global War on Terror*, 118 HARVARD LAW REVIEW 2653 (2005).

24. Matthew C. Waxman, *Detention as Targeting: Standards of Certainty and Detention of Suspected Terrorists*, 108 COLUMBIA LAW REVIEW 1365, 1375 (2008).

25. Headquarters, Department of the Army & Headquarters, Marine Corps Combat Development Command, FM 3-24/MCWP 3-33.5, Counterinsurgency ¶ 7-40 (2006).

26. *See also* Department of Defense, Fact Sheet: Guantanamo Detainees, *supra* note 23, at 6 ("The commander of US Southern Command, or his designee, then makes a recommendation in each individual case . . . . Continued detention of enemy combatants is appropriate not only when a detainee is identified as posing a significant threat if released, but also when . . . there is a substantial law enforcement or intelligence interest").

27. Counterinsurgency, *supra* note 25.

28. President George W. Bush, Remarks on the War on Terror, 42 WEEKLY COMPILATION OF PRESIDENTIAL DOCUMENTS 1569 (Sept. 6, 2006); *see also id.* at 1573 ("[O]nce we've determined that the terrorists held by the CIA have little or no additional intelligence value, many of them have been returned to their home countries for prosecution or detention by their governments").

29. Deputy Secretary of Defense Paul Wolfowitz, OSD Order 06942-04, Administrative Review Procedures for Enemy Combatants in the Control of the Dep't of Def. at Guantánamo Bay, Cuba (May 11, 2004), at 1-2, *available at* http://www.defenselink.mil/news/May2004/d20040518gtmoreview.pdf.

30. Administrative Review Board Process § 3(f)(1)(c) (attached to Memorandum from Gordon England, Deputy Secretary of Defense, to the Secretary of State et al., Implementation of

Administrative Review Procedures for Enemy Combatants Detained at US Naval Base Guantanamo Bay, Cuba (Sept. 14, 2004), *available at* http://www.defenselink.mil/news/Sep2004/d20040914adminreview.pdf).

31. General Tommy Franks, Press Conference in Tampa, Florida (Jan. 18, 2002), http://www.globalsecurity.org/military/library/news/2002/01/mil-020118-dod01.htm ("When we have them in Guantanamo Bay, that sort of interrogation will continue, and then determinations will be made as to whether these—a given detainee may be retained for intelligence value or may be handed over for prosecution within legal channels."); Neil A. Lewis, *Red Cross Criticizes Indefinite Detention in Guantanamo Bay*, NEW YORK TIMES, Oct. 10, 2003, at A1 ("General [Geoffrey] Miller[, Commander of Joint Task Force Guantanamo Bay,] said the inmates had been kept in custody because they had valuable information to impart.").

32. U.N. Economic and Social Counsel, Commission on Human Rights, Situation of Detainees at Guantanamo Bay, Report of the Chairperson-Rapporteur of the Working Group on Arbitrary Detention; the Special Rapporteur on the independence of judges and lawyers; the Special Rapporteur on torture and other cruel, inhuman or degrading treatment or punishment; the Special Rapporteur on freedom of religion or belief; and the Special Rapporteur on the right of everyone to the enjoyment of the highest attainable standard of physical and mental health, ¶ 23, U.N. Doc. E/CN.4/2006/120 (Feb. 2006), *available at* http://daccessdds.un.org/doc/UNDOC/GEN/G06/112/76/PDF/G0611276.pdf?OpenElement [hereinafter Joint Report on Situation of Detainees at Guantanamo Bay].

33. Brief for the Petitioner at 28–29, Rumsfeld v. Padilla, 542 U.S. 426 (2004) (No. 03-1027).

34. Declaration of Vice Admiral Lowell E. Jacoby, *id.*, *available at* http://www.pegc.us/archive/Padilla_vs_Rumsfeld/Jacoby_declaration_20030109.pdf.

35. For further analysis on this point, see Marty Lederman, *The Rosetta Stone of the Detention/Interrogation Scandal*, http://balkin.blogspot.com/2007/08/rosetta-stone-of-detentioninterrogation.html (Aug. 14, 2007, 11:32 EDT).

36. al-Marri v. Pucciarelli, 534 F.3d 213, 237 n.19 (2008) (Motz, J., concurring in part and dissenting in part).

37. Lederman, *supra* note 35.

38. On the theory that the US conflict with Al Qaeda extends into Iraq, US detention practices in that area are relevant to our discussion.

39. *See* Andru E. Wall, *Civilian Detentions in Iraq*, *in* INTERNATIONAL LAW AND ARMED CONFLICT: EXPLORING THE FAULTLINES: ESSAYS IN HONOUR OF YORAM DINSTEIN 413, 431 (Michael N. Schmitt & Jelena Pejic eds., 2007).

40. *See, e.g.*, JAMES R. SCHLESINGER ET AL., FINAL REPORT OF THE INDEPENDENT PANEL TO REVIEW DETENTION OPERATIONS 60 (2004), *available at* http://news.findlaw.com/wp/docs/dod/abughraibrpt.pdf ("The security detainees were either held for their intelligence value or presented a continuing threat to Coalition Forces."); *id.* at 61 ("Interviews indicated area commanders were reluctant to concur with release decisions out of concern that potential combatants would be reintroduced into the areas of operation or that the detainees had continuing intelligence value.").

41. Lewis, *supra* note 31 (Christophe Girod, senior Red Cross official in Washington, "said that it was intolerable that the [Guantanamo] complex was used as 'an investigation center, not a detention center.'").

42. Joint Report on Situation of Detainees at Guantanamo Bay, *supra* note 32, ¶ 23; cf. Role of the ICRC, *supra* note 10 ("Persons detained in relation to an armed conflict may be detained for either imperative reasons of security or on suspicion of having committed a crime.").

43. Hamdi v. Rumsfeld, 542 U.S. 507, 521 (2004).

44. *Id.* at 518.

45. COMMENTARY: III GENEVA CONVENTION RELATIVE TO THE TREATMENT OF PRISONERS OF WAR 515 (Jean S. Pictet ed., 1960) (explaining in similar terms the categorical obligation to repatriate).

46. Convention Relative to the Treatment of Prisoners of War art. 110, Aug. 12, 1949, 6 U.S.T. 3316, 75 U.N.T.S. 135, *reprinted in* DOCUMENTS ON THE LAWS OF WAR, *supra* note 7, at 244.

47. *Id.*, art. 17(3) ("No physical or mental torture, nor any other form of coercion, may be inflicted on prisoners of war to secure from them information of any kind whatever. Prisoners of war who refuse to answer may not be threatened, insulted, or exposed to unpleasant or disadvantageous treatment of any kind."); Civilians Convention, *supra* note 7, art. 31 ("No physical or moral coercion shall be exercised against protected persons, in particular to obtain information from them or from third parties.").

48. ICRC COMMENTARY IV, *supra* note 8, at 257.

49. *Id.* There is a possible exception with respect to information, but of a wholly different character. An individual may possess information which makes her a danger to the detaining power (e.g., knowledge of vulnerabilities in the detaining power's defense system). A plausible reading of *Commentary IV* would permit the employment of administrative detention—if it is absolutely necessary—to prevent her directly assisting the enemy with that type of knowledge. *See id.* at 258 ("To justify recourse to such measures the State must have good reason to think that the person concerned, by his activities, knowledge or qualifications, represents a real threat to its present or future security.").

50. *Id.* at 258. *See also* Prosecutor v. Delalić et al., ICTY Trial Chamber, Case No. IT-96-21, Judgment, ¶ 568 (Nov. 16, 1998), upheld by Prosecutor v. Delalić et al., ICTY Appeals Chamber, Case No. IT-96-21-A, Judgment (Feb. 20, 2001); Prosecutor v. Kordić and Čerkez, Case No. IT-95-14/2-T, Judgment, ¶ 280 (Feb. 26, 2001), upheld by Prosecutor v. Kordić and Čerkez, ICTY Appeals Chamber, Case No. IT-95-14/2-A, Judgment, ¶¶ 72–73, 620 (Dec. 17, 2004).

51. Declaration of Vice Admiral Jacoby, *supra* note 34, at 5.

52. Wall, *supra* note 39, at 431.

PART V

STABILITY OPERATIONS

XV

Jus ad Pacem in Bello? Afghanistan, Stability Operations and the International Laws Relating to Armed Conflict

David Turns*

Introduction

One of the more notorious quotations widely attributed to George W. Bush, when he was campaigning for the presidency of the United States in 2000, was something to the effect that "[w]e don't do nation-building." As with many attributed quotations, the actual remark he made was less curt and slightly more nuanced. What actually happened was that in the course of a presidential debate with his opponent, Vice President Al Gore, Bush was asked if he would have supported US military involvement in the ill-fated expanded United Nations Operation in Somalia (UNOSOM II) in 1993–94[1] had he been president at the time. This is what he actually said in reply:

> [Somalia] [s]tarted off as a humanitarian mission and it changed into a nation-building mission, and that's where the mission went wrong. The mission was changed. And as a result, our nation paid a price. And so I don't think our troops ought to be used for what's called nation-building. I think our troops ought to be used to fight and

* Senior Lecturer in International Laws of Armed Conflict, Defence Academy of the United Kingdom (Cranfield University). All opinions stated herein are personal to the author and are in no way to be taken as necessarily representing the official views of the government, Ministry of Defence or Armed Forces of the United Kingdom. Responsibility for any errors is mine alone.

win war. I think our troops ought to be used to help overthrow the dictator when it's in our best interests. But in this case [i.e., Somalia] it was a nation-building exercise, and same with Haiti.[2] I wouldn't have supported either.[3]

This antipathy notwithstanding, and despite former President Bush's best efforts amid the rhetoric of the "Global War on Terror," the realities of the transnational military operational environment in the first decade of the twenty-first century have produced an exponential growth in the importance of what are now generally termed stability (or stabilization) operations, to such an extent that even US military doctrine now acknowledges such operations as "a core U.S. military mission . . . [to] be given priority comparable to combat operations."[4] The Ministry of Defence in the United Kingdom, whose long experience with so-called "small wars" in the postcolonial context during the withdrawal from Empire (approximately during the period 1945–65, including conflicts in Palestine, Malaya, Cyprus, Kenya and Aden) has led some foreign observers to suggest a particular mastery of nation-building and counterinsurgency campaigns,[5] has only recently—in January 2009—circulated a working draft of what will eventually become the first promulgation of a British doctrine on such operations.[6]

The current campaign in Afghanistan has been described as "a test case for international development assistance and bi- and multilateral cooperation"[7] even in the midst of sustained combat operations in substantial parts of the country, whereby "the main problems . . . are restoring security and establishing a functioning state."[8] Stability operations seem to have become the catchphrase for a new generation of military actions: indeed, they have come to be viewed as an essential stage in the type of conflicts most prevalent today, namely, asymmetric conflicts between State and non-State actors. In order to win the war it has become essential, in places like Iraq and Afghanistan, to win the peace, and that is done by stabilizing the situation in theater after the initial opposition has been defeated or at least contained.[9] The moment of hubris, when President Bush landed on the aircraft carrier *USS Abraham Lincoln* on May 1, 2003 and declared that major combat operations in Iraq had ended, did not in fact herald the conclusion of hostilities in Iraq: the coalition merely swapped one enemy (the State armed forces of the defeated Saddam Hussein regime) for another (various assorted non-State militias representing different sectors of Iraqi society, along with groups affiliated with Al Qaeda). In Afghanistan, by way of contrast, the main enemy has stayed the same—i.e., the Taliban—but its status changed from being the de facto government in control of up to 90 percent of Afghan territory in September 2001, to that of an insurgency dispersed in (mainly) the southern provinces of Kandahar and Helmand. Although intensive military operations against the Taliban continue, international coalition forces in Afghanistan, acting in concert with the Afghan government of President Hamid Karzai, are attempting at the same time to continue apace with the reconstruction and development of the country: in a word, nation-building.[10]

Military operations in circumstances such as those prevailing in Afghanistan are situated at the intersections of two major fault lines in public international law: namely, they are at the junction of the *jus ad bellum* and the *jus in bello*, and simultaneously (within the *jus in bello*) at the junction of international and non-international armed conflicts. This article will, first, define stability operations in doctrinal terms and situate them within an international legal context. The significance of their legitimacy under the *jus ad bellum* will be briefly considered and related to the context of Afghanistan before their classification in terms of the international law of armed conflict (LOAC) will be analyzed. The application of the *jus in bello* to such operations will then be discussed, with reference to some specific operational problems such as the status and treatment of insurgents captured by coalition forces in Afghanistan, and the targeting of such insurgents. Finally, some tentative conclusions will be suggested as to the international law applicable to stability operations.

From Peacekeeping to Stability Operations

The phrase "stability operations" may represent, to some extent, new terminology; but it does emphatically not refer to a new phenomenon in the continuum of military operations. The military doctrinal term previously applied in the United States and United Kingdom was "military operations other than war" (MOOTW), a term that somehow always seemed to carry a faint hint of derision but nevertheless was undeniably useful as a catch-all phrase: in effect, it covered practically the entire spectrum of military operations, excluding only all-out "war."[11] From the mid-1950s until the early 1990s the principal manifestation of MOOTW was in "classic" peacekeeping operations undertaken pursuant to UN mandates.

Starting in 1992 with the situation in Somalia, the United Nations began to use two new terms—"peace enforcement" and "peace building"—which were distinguished from traditional peacekeeping. While *peacekeeping* involved the interposition of a military force with host State consent in order to supervise ceasefire or peace agreements already in place, typically with very restrictive rules of engagement that extended no further than authorizing the use of force in self-defense, *peace enforcement* came to be used to refer to what might be described as a "beefed-up peacekeeping operation," namely one in which the situation remained unstable enough to allow for an expansion of the permitted use of force in order to maintain the peace. This would generally occur in situations where the parties to the conflict might have reached a ceasefire or interim peace accord, but its observance was too fragile for the interpositional force to preserve a passive role. Peace enforcement, in other words, was proactive and essentially involved the international force taking sides in the enforcement of obligations already entered into by the belligerents.[12] *Peace building*, on the other hand, encompassed a much wider range of activities designed to prevent the resumption or proliferation of a particular conflict, from disarmament and demobilization of the warring parties to election monitoring, from the strengthening of State institutions to the promotion of human rights and from the repatriation of refugees to the provision of humanitarian aid.[13] UN-mandated missions throughout the 1990s in Somalia, Haiti, Bosnia and Herzegovina, and Kosovo all had various combinations of the above list of activities taking place simultaneously. Their salient feature for the purposes of this discussion was that they all took place in conditions of continuing armed conflict or, at the very least, serious civil unrest.

Strangely, however, although the range of activities being assigned to these missions grew and although there was often manifestly no peace to keep, few outside the United Nations adopted the new terminologies outlined above: within the US government, for example, Congress continued to use the generic term "peacekeeping" to refer to all such operations, while the executive branch adopted the similarly generic "peace operations." In both cases, the inclusion of the word "peace" was manifestly misplaced since it created the misleading impression that such operations involved comparatively little risk for the military personnel assigned to them, whereas in fact they often saw soldiers in what amounted to full-scale warfighting operations. This, coupled with the stigma of failure that came in many circles to be attached to "peace operations" in 1990s, contributed—at least on a psychological level—to the shift in language away from peace and toward stability. Peace became the endgame, the ultimate objective to be achieved; hence, *jus ad pacem*. But the realities on the ground in places like Iraq and Afghanistan, with all their complexities and ambiguities, forced a general recognition that in order to have peace, it is necessary to have stability.

The US Department of Defense currently characterizes stability operations as "[m]ilitary and civilian activities conducted across the spectrum from peace to conflict to establish or maintain order in States and regions."[14] The US doctrinal definition of stability operations ("missions, tasks and activities [that] seek to maintain or reestablish a safe and secure environment and provide essential government services, emergency infrastructure reconstruction, or humanitarian relief"[15]) is situated within the following contemporary context:

> The character of this conflict [i.e., the post-2001 security environment] is unlike any other in recent American history, where military forces operating among the people of

> [the] world will decide the major battles and engagements. The greatest threats to our national security will not come from emerging ambitious states but from nations unable or unwilling to meet the basic needs and aspirations of their people. Here, the margin of victory will be measured in far different terms from the wars of our past. However, time may be the ultimate arbiter of success: time to bring safety and security to an embattled populace; time to provide for the essential, immediate humanitarian needs of the people; time to restore basic public order and a semblance of normalcy to life; and time to rebuild the institutions of government and market economy that provide the foundations for enduring peace and stability. This is the essence of stability operations.[16]

It is very telling—and very relevant for the assumption of this author, that the conduct of stability operations must be subject to the international law of armed conflict—that this description of the context for stability operations explicitly places them within a continuum of military operations, that is to say, in a spectrum of activity that in itself is closer to war than to peace.

In the United Kingdom, despite the lack at present of a formally promulgated doctrine on stability operations, military thinking is very much on the same lines as that of our US counterparts. Stability operations are understood to be those that impose security and control in a defined area while restoring and developing infrastructure and services, in collaboration with appropriate civilian agencies. They may involve kinetic or non-kinetic applications of force and may occur before, during or after major combat operations; or indeed, they may in themselves be the primary objective of a campaign. Their desired endgame, ultimately, is always to secure a transition of power and control to the civilian authorities of the host State. Recently the Chief of the UK General Staff characterized stability operations as involving "several different lines of operation—ensuring security, rebuilding essential services, promoting good governance and facilitating economic regeneration."[17] Discussing future trends for the British armed forces, he said:

> Instead of adapting each time we deploy, it is clear from recent experiences that we should be structured and trained to conduct an Intervention and Stabilisation operation almost as the default setting, with the right forces and the correctly qualified personnel with the right training to deliver the right effect from the outset.
>
> And this will require both kinetic and non-kinetic means—there will always be a need for soldiers who are trained to fight a hostile and implacable enemy, but there will also be a need for soldiers who are trained to deliver essential services until the situation is safe enough for civil agencies to engage; so there will be a need for soldiers trained to deliver humanitarian assistance, to assist with the delivery of local governance[,] and for soldiers who are experts in the local politics and culture of the area, and who can therefore initiate the early stages of reconciliation and peace-building.[18]

Perhaps the most significant aspect of General Dannatt's remarks is his suggestion that stability operations be regarded "almost as the default setting" for future British military capabilities. This reflects the British view that "major combat operations"—full-scale inter-State armed conflicts which have as their objective the total defeat of a governmental enemy, leading to its removal from power—are very much the exception in the contemporary paradigm of "fourth-generation warfare." In both the Afghanistan (2001) and Iraq (2003) campaigns, operations directed against the State (the Taliban in the former case, Saddam's armed forces in the latter) were over remarkably quickly; yet counterinsurgency fighting continues to this day, alongside attempts to transform the institutions and infrastructure of these failing States into stable, functioning authorities that are able to maintain law and order. Whether or not one accepts *in abstracto* the Bush administration's characterization of the contemporary security environment for America and her allies as a "long war,"[19] ongoing stability operations in Afghanistan and Iraq have aspects that definitely amount in effect to "war," even while the stated objective is peace.

Stability operations are nowhere mentioned in international law; neither the *jus ad bellum* nor the *jus in bello* explicitly recognizes the concept. Nevertheless, in light of the foregoing, it must be stated categorically that a key feature of contemporary stability operations is international legitimacy (as will be seen in the next section with specific reference to Afghanistan). While legitimacy is not the same thing as legality, the prevalent view in both the United States and the United Kingdom is that the main framework for international legitimacy *is* international legality: stability operations must take place on the basis of sound authority in international law, and must be conducted (in their specifically military aspects) in accordance with the international law of armed conflict.

Stability Operations and the Legality of the Use of Force

Two salient features of contemporary stability operations are that they tend to be (1) multilateral, i.e., conducted by coalitions, whether ad hoc or (preferably) within the framework of an established military alliance, like the North Atlantic Treaty Organization (NATO); and (2) legitimate, i.e., constituting a lawful use of force under either the UN Charter or customary international law—normally the former, since no stability operations as presently understood have taken place on such a controversial legal basis as the doctrine of humanitarian intervention, for instance. Current operations in Afghanistan will hereinafter be taken as the case study for discussion of stability operations and international law.

Although US and coalition forces first commenced military action against the Taliban militia and Al Qaeda elements in Afghanistan in Operation Enduring

Freedom (OEF) on October 7, 2001 pursuant to the right of individual and collective self-defense as recognized in Article 51 of the UN Charter (for which no Security Council mandate is legally required), and OEF continues to this day primarily in southern and eastern Afghanistan, internationally-mandated forces were first deployed to the country only in December 2001, after the Taliban had been ejected from its seats of power. The last main Taliban urban stronghold, Kandahar, was captured by coalition forces on December 7, two days after the signing of the Bonn Agreement, in which delegations of various Afghan political factions committed themselves to cooperation in the establishment of an Interim Authority that would rebuild the Afghan State after decades of conflict.[20] The Bonn Agreement specifically requested the Security Council

> to consider authorizing the early deployment to Afghanistan of a United Nations mandated force. This force will assist in the maintenance of security for Kabul and its surrounding areas. Such a force could, as appropriate, be progressively expanded to other urban centres and other areas. . . . It would also be desirable if such a force were to assist in the rehabilitation of Afghanistan's infrastructure.[21]

On December 19 two letters arrived at UN headquarters: one from the Afghan Minister for Foreign Affairs and the other from his British counterpart. The former stated somewhat opaquely that the envisaged international security force "could be deployed under Chapter VI or VII of the Charter."[22] The latter expressed the UK's willingness to serve as the initial lead nation for the proposed deployment, known as the International Security Assistance Force (ISAF), with the core missions of (1) assisting the establishment of the Interim Administration of Afghanistan in liaison with the UN Secretary-General's Special Representative in Kabul; (2) providing advice and support to the Afghan administration and the United Nations in Kabul on security issues; and (3) preparing for the establishment and training of new Afghan national armed and security forces, key infrastructure development "and possible future expanded security assistance in other parts of Afghanistan."[23] The British letter did not refer to specific chapters or articles of the UN Charter as the legal basis for the proposed deployment, but stated that it would be "based on the willingness expressed [on the part of the Afghan administration] to receive such a force and an authorizing Security Council resolution."[24] The letter also emphasized that the proposed international force "will have a particular mission authorized by a Security Council resolution that is distinct from Operation Enduring Freedom."[25] One day later, the Security Council, acting under Chapter VII of the Charter, passed the resolution referred to in the British letter and authorized the establishment, for an initial six months, of ISAF.[26] Apart from assisting in the maintenance of security in Kabul and surrounding areas,[27] the only other task expressly mandated to ISAF at this stage was "to provide assistance to help the Afghan Interim Authority in the establishment and training of new Afghan security and armed forces."[28] As far as the use of force by the mission was concerned, the Resolution authorized ISAF troop-contributing nations (TCNs) to take "all necessary measures to fulfil its mandate."[29]

At this stage, therefore, ISAF was clearly an ad hoc "coalition of the willing" formed by mandate of the Security Council under Chapter VII of the Charter, with the use of force authorized in terms whose broad ambit recalls Article 42 of the Charter ("such action . . . as may be necessary"). The emphasis by the British—and other TCNs—on Afghan consent to the operation, however, would seem to militate against ISAF being an Article 42 enforcement action, since such actions are mandatory in nature and do not require host State consent. It would plainly be absurd to classify the ISAF mission as classic peacekeeping, because of the extent of actual fighting that was taking place in Afghanistan at the time of the force's initial deployment and that continues to this day. Perhaps better—albeit still imperfect—analogies might be the UN's enforcement actions in respect to Korea (1950), the Congo (1960) and Haiti (2004). The first case, that of Korea, was in fact the first instance in which the phrase "coalition of the willing" came to be used in the context of UN enforcement actions. Following the invasion of the Republic of Korea (ROK) by the forces of the Democratic People's Republic and the ROK's appeal to the UN for help, Resolution 83 of the Security Council recommended "that the Members of the United Nations furnish such assistance to the Republic of Korea as may be necessary to repel the [North Korean] armed attack and to restore international peace and security in the area."[30] The result was three years of intensive hostilities, but the UN-ROK forces were not organized into a UN mission as such, nor was their contribution mandatory: it should be remembered that Resolution 83 merely *recommended* that UN member States provide military assistance to the ROK. Moreover, there was no civilian component and the operation was a classic warfighting campaign, with none of the reconstruction and development activities associated with stability operations.

In the second case the United Nations, having received a request for military assistance from the Prime Minister of the newly-independent Congo in the face of Belgian military intervention and the attempted secession of the province of Katanga, authorized the Secretary-General "to take the necessary steps . . . to provide the Government with such military assistance as may be necessary until . . . the [Congolese] national security forces may be able, in the opinion of the [Congolese] Government, to meet fully their tasks."[31] A subsequent resolution on the same matter urged "that the United Nations take immediately all appropriate measures to prevent the occurrence of civil war in the Congo, including arrangements for cease-fires, the halting of all military operations, the prevention of clashes, and the use of force, if necessary, in the last resort."[32] Although the resulting force, the *Organisation des Nations Unies au Congo*, was officially a peacekeeping mission, it did become involved in actively suppressing the Katangese secessionists, thereby taking sides in a way that peacekeeping missions do not normally do. A remarkably complex operation for the time, with large civilian and technical components alongside military troops, it eventually came to number some twenty thousand officers and men.

The third case is perhaps the closest analogy to the deployment of ISAF: the Security Council created the *Mission des Nations Unies pour la stabilisation en Haïti* (MINUSTAH) in 2004,[33] a decade after authorizing a multinational force to intervene and effect "regime change." MINUSTAH is Brazilian-led and comprises some nine thousand personnel, with both military and civilian components; its wide-ranging tasks include ensuring a secure and stable environment (including reforming the Haitian National Police and protecting civilians from imminent threat of physical violence), supporting the constitutional and political process (including the administration of elections and the extension of State authority and good governance at all levels throughout Haiti), the promotion and protection of human rights[34] and the facilitation of humanitarian assistance.[35] Within that framework, in 2004–05 MINUSTAH personnel executed large-scale military raids, using lethal force, on the slum of Cité Soleil in the capital city of Port-au-Prince (an anarchic area in which armed gangs roam the streets shooting, looting, raping and kidnapping), with subsequent allegations of excessive collateral damage;[36] MINUSTAH soldiers have been killed, also.

In Afghanistan, strategic command, control and coordination of ISAF was assumed unilaterally by NATO on August 11, 2003,[37] and it remains a NATO operation to the present time—still separate from the American-led OEF, which has a far smaller number of TCNs and is not being executed within the framework of an international organization. The Afghan government immediately approved of NATO's assumption of the ISAF mandate and, indeed, addressed a formal request to the Security Council to expand the mandate so as to permit deployments of ISAF outside the Kabul area;[38] thus host State consent has continued to be a crucial element of the legal basis for stability operations in Afghanistan. This was then acknowledged and formalized by the Security Council in Resolution 1510, which authorized the expansion of ISAF's mandate and the continued use of all necessary measures to fulfill that mandate.[39] The ISAF mandate is renewable at yearly intervals, the latest Security Council authorization at the time of writing dating from September 22, 2008.[40] Current troop levels are approximately 55,100, supplied by a total of forty-one States under NATO leadership.[41] Particularly prominent among ISAF's activities for some years have been the Provincial Reconstruction Teams (PRTs), which operate at a local level to rebuild infrastructure.[42] With the increasing emphasis on the need to transfer more and more capability and power in the field of security to the Afghan National Army (ANA), a major aspect of ISAF's operations now is the Operational Mentor and Liaison Teams, which are deployed to ANA partner-units across the country, with the objective of training and mentoring the ANA in its capability for independent operational deployments, coordinating ISAF-ANA liaison and ensuring the provision of enabling support to ANA units.[43]

The basis of ISAF's stability operations in international law appears uncertain to the extent that such operations are nowhere mentioned in the UN Charter, nor do they exist as a clear concept recognized by customary international law. Rather, they are a military doctrinal construct that reflects the realities of the types of operations being carried out in environments like that of Afghanistan, where conflicts are ongoing but international efforts are being made to shore up the legitimate government and increase its capabilities. ISAF is characterized by NATO as deriving from a peace-enforcement mandate under Chapter VII of the Charter, despite the fact that it is a "coalition of the willing" rather than a UN force.[44] In that sense, it is quite different from the operations mandated in Congo and Haiti discussed earlier. Comparisons with the UN-ROK forces fighting in Korea, the original "coalition of the willing," would be more helpful were it not for the fact that the latter had no element of stabilization, but were simply charged with fighting a full-scale war against external aggression by other States: the intra-State, asymmetric and counterinsurgency aspects so prominent in Afghanistan were entirely absent in Korea. Official British pronouncements on the legal authority for ISAF are sparse, but emphasize the combination of an invitation from the democratically elected government of Afghanistan and the mandate provided by the UN Security Council in Resolution 1510.[45]

We may surmise from the above that stability operations are an emerging concept in the international law governing the use of force and are thus effectively *sui generis*: they have not been previously recognized in customary law and have no explicit basis in the UN Charter or other treaties—except for ad hoc specific cases like (in relation to Afghanistan) the Bonn Agreement. However, appreciation of their legitimacy, through a combination of post-conflict morality and executive legal authority, is regarded as essential by States that participate in such operations.[46] They in fact represent a peculiar combination of what might be termed "invited intervention" and "authorized intervention"—*invited* by the host State and *authorized* by an international organization. Therefore, we may suggest that the *jus ad bellum* legal basis of stability operations will differ from case to case, but will normally have in common the following features: (1) an invitation by the internationally legitimate government of the host State; (2) a mandate (even if postdating the actual start of the operation) from an international organization, ideally the United Nations; and (3) a multilateral coalition, either within the framework of an existing military alliance such as NATO, or on an ad hoc basis.

Whether stability operations could eventually take place absent one or more of the above features must be a matter of some legal uncertainty. In Operation Palliser in May 2000, the United Kingdom unilaterally planned and executed a limited military intervention in Sierra Leone, initially for the purpose of evacuating British, Commonwealth and European Union citizens at risk from the escalating threat to the capital, Freetown, from the advancing insurgent forces of the Revolutionary United Front (RUF). The noncombatant evacuation operation having been successfully accomplished, the British government then expanded the operation—again, unilaterally—and the troops retained control of the international airport, enabled the safe delivery of UN humanitarian aid into Sierra Leone, and provided security and stability in Freetown by patrolling the capital.[47] Operation Palliser was terminated on June 15, 2000, although the United Kingdom continued extensive involvement in ongoing multinational UN efforts to bring peace and security to Sierra Leone.

The government of Sierra Leone did not comment publicly on the British action; neither did the subsequent debates in the British House of Commons[48] and the House of Lords,[49] nor in the UN Security Council,[50] make any overt reference to the *legality* of the British intervention. Aside from the United Kingdom, eight States expressed approval of the British action in the Security Council,[51] as did Secretary-General Kofi Annan, although he made an oblique reference to the "limited mandate" of the British troops.[52] Following its last meeting to discuss the escalating crisis in Sierra Leone prior to the British deployment, the Security Council had issued a presidential statement in which it "call[ed] upon all States in a position to do so to assist" the UN forces already present in Sierra Leone, which might arguably have been a code that could reasonably have been interpreted as permitting State intervention without the need for any further authority from the UN,[53] although neither the Secretary-General nor any of the States in the Council expressed any views to that effect. None of the Council members that failed explicitly to endorse the British intervention actually commented on it at all publicly, so their real views on the matter must remain a subject of debate; but they clearly acquiesced in it. It should be noted that Operation Palliser was not a stability operation *ab initio*, although it did acquire characteristics thereof in the course of its execution. It was not requested by the host State, nor did it have a mandate from the

United Nations, although it was made in support of the UN peacekeeping mission already present in Sierra Leone (many of whose personnel were at the time being held hostage by the RUF). The element of morality—or perceived legitimacy—was undoubtedly present, and the operation was lawful on the basis that it was a limited humanitarian intervention for the protection of UK nationals and others for whom the United Kingdom had consular responsibilities; but its legality *qua* stability operation cannot be conclusively affirmed.

Stability Operations and the International Law of Armed Conflict

Just as stability operations are not mentioned in the international law governing the use of force, so, as a military doctrinal concept rather than a legal construct as such, they are equally absent from the international LOAC. To the extent that stability operations do not involve any actual armed hostilities, in their peaceful and civilian aspects, they evidently are not governed by the LOAC at all. The LOAC applies only in armed conflicts, which are generically defined in customary international law as existing

> whenever there is a resort to armed force between States or protracted armed violence between governmental authorities and organized armed groups or between such groups within a State. International humanitarian law applies from the initiation of such armed conflicts and extends beyond the cessation of hostilities until a general conclusion of peace is reached; or, in the case of internal conflicts, a peaceful settlement is achieved. Until that moment, international humanitarian law continues to apply in the whole territory of the warring States or, in the case of internal conflicts, the whole territory under the control of a party [to the conflict], whether or not actual combat takes place there.[54]

It would seem very clear, from the above descriptors, that an armed conflict continues to take place in certain parts of Afghanistan (primarily the south and east of the country) between the ANA and ISAF on the one hand, and insurgents (mostly Taliban) on the other. The law which governs the behavior of ISAF troops in other parts of the country, which have seen relatively sustained peace for some time now, will be considered further below. But to the extent that an armed conflict is taking place in certain parts of Afghanistan, it is governed by the LOAC and it is necessary to consider what type of conflict that might constitute, as the applicable rules differ to some extent between international and non-international armed conflicts.

International armed conflicts are defined in Common Article 2 of the 1949 Geneva Conventions as

> all cases of declared war or of any other armed conflict which may arise between two or more of the High Contracting Parties, even if the state of war is not recognized by one of them . . . [and] all cases of partial or total occupation of the territory of a High Contracting Party, even if the said occupation meets with no armed resistance.

There is patently no armed conflict between two or more States in Afghanistan, since ISAF forces are present in the territory at the invitation of the State itself and are assisting the State against the insurgents. Nor could it conceivably be said that there is a "partial or total occupation of the territory" by ISAF, since that would require that the territory be under the effective control of the occupier, either following the complete defeat of the lawful sovereign (*debellatio*) or because the invading force has temporarily asserted its authority over the territory (belligerent occupation). In Afghanistan, ISAF has not occupied the territory belligerently vis-à-vis the current Afghan government, with which it is allied; and in those areas where it operates, it does so emphatically in support of the Afghan government and not on its own account.

Protocol I Additional to the Geneva Conventions in 1977 extended the scope of application in respect to international armed conflicts to "armed conflicts in which peoples are fighting against colonial domination and alien occupation and against racist regimes in the exercise of their right to self-determination."[55] Article 96(3) then provides for an "authority representing a people engaged against a high contracting party in an armed conflict of the type referred to in [Article 1(4)]" to make a unilateral declaration undertaking to apply the Geneva Conventions and Additional Protocol I. The Taliban has not sought to take advantage of these provisions, and even if it did, the argument could be defeated easily enough on the basis that the rights and obligations of the 1949 Conventions and the 1977 Additional Protocol only take effect following a unilateral declaration under Article 96(3) on a basis of reciprocity, i.e., the high contracting party in question must also have assumed the same rights and obligations under the same instruments. In the case of Afghanistan, the State is not a party to Additional Protocol I, and it is hard to see how these provisions could be binding upon ISAF States, even to the extent that (like the United Kingdom) they are parties to the Protocol.

If a conflict is not international in nature, then it must—if only by default—be non-international in nature. Non-international armed conflicts are defined in Common Article 3 of the Geneva Conventions as "armed conflict[s] not of an international character occurring in the territory of one of the High Contracting Parties," which is essentially a negative definition. The notoriously high threshold of application for 1977 Additional Protocol II further requires that the conflict be

> in the territory of a High Contracting Party between its armed forces and dissident armed forces or other organized armed groups which, under responsible command, exercise such control over a part of its territory as to enable them to carry out sustained and concerted military operations and to implement this Protocol.[56]

Quite apart from the fact that Afghanistan is not a high contracting party to Additional Protocol II, it is doubtful, in any case, whether the conditions for the applicability of the Protocol would be met by the present stability operations in Afghanistan. Article 1(1) refers only to the armed forces of the high contracting party *on its own territory*, which would not cover ISAF; and while the Taliban undoubtedly does have control of some territory and carries out "sustained and concerted military operations," it is most unlikely that it could be considered to be "under responsible command" and it has given no sign of willingness to implement the Protocol.

The default position under the treaties that constitute the bulk of the LOAC—particularly the Geneva Conventions and their Additional Protocols—would therefore seem to be that stability operations in Afghanistan that involve "resort to armed force . . . or protracted armed violence" in terms of the *Tadic* formulation[57] are neither an international nor a non-international armed conflict, properly speaking. Instead, they amount to "armed conflict not of an international character" in terms of Common Article 3.[58] The trouble with that approach, logical though it may be on the text of the treaties, is that Common Article 3, being the "minimum yardstick" for humanitarian protection in all armed conflicts, as recognized by the International Court of Justice in the *Nicaragua* case,[59] is notoriously vague, imprecise and of the utmost generality. It is for this reason that the recent approach of the Supreme Court of Israel, to the effect that Israeli military operations against Palestinian militants are subject to the law of international armed conflicts,[60] is in the opinion of the present author much to be preferred.

The main basis for this finding, that the military capabilities of Palestinian militant organizations are such as to equate their threat with that which might emanate from a State's armed forces, is at least as true in respect to the Taliban as it is in respect to Hamas. The Israeli court also concluded that the conflict between Israel and the Palestinians should be treated as international in nature for the purposes of the LOAC on the basis of the transnational nature of the military operations in question: they were crossing the internationally recognized frontiers of the State of Israel and were related to the context of Israel's belligerent occupation of the Palestinian territories since 1967.[61] Although, as noted above, the aspect of belligerent occupation is not relevant in the case of ISAF and Afghanistan, the fact of deployment of NATO troops across international frontiers in the territory of another

State could, by analogy, arguably be sufficient to bring ISAF stability operations within the dictum of the Israeli court.

In light of the above theoretical observations, what practical conclusions may be drawn as to the LOAC rules or principles to be applied by ISAF during combat operations in Afghanistan? In respect to the conduct of hostilities by ISAF troops, the force commander has recently directed that "[a]ll responses [to clear and identified danger] must be proportionate and the utmost of care [*sic*] should be taken to minimize any damage."[62] No doubt sensitive to recurrent Afghan complaints of excessive collateral damage caused by airstrikes, he added:

> We are engaged in a counterinsurgency in an extremely demanding environment. We are fighting an enemy that often cannot be identified before he has struck and then once he has, he hides among the civilian population. The battle is often waged among civilians and their property. We must clearly apply and demonstrate proportionality, requisite restraint, and the utmost discrimination in our application of firepower. No one seeks or intends to constrain the inherent right of self defense of every member of the ISAF force. However, Commanders must focus upon the principles which attach to every use of force—be that self defense or offensive fires. Good tactical judgment, necessity, and proportionality are to drive every action and engagement; minimizing civilian casualties is of paramount importance.[63]

If there are difficulties in applying specific treaty instruments of the LOAC to multinational coalition operations, the directive just cited, in its emphasis on the fundamental principles of necessity, proportionality and discrimination, suggests that at a minimum the customary rules of the LOAC derived from those principles are applicable.[64]

In respect to the protection of victims and treatment of persons *hors de combat*, it may be suggested in line with the above reasoning that Common Article 3 of the Geneva Conventions applies as the "minimum yardstick" of humanitarian treatment:

> Persons taking no active part in the hostilities, including members of armed forces who have laid down their arms and those placed *hors de combat* by sickness, wounds, detention, or any other cause, shall in all circumstances be treated humanely, without any adverse distinction founded on race, colour, religion or faith, sex, birth or wealth, or any other similar criteria.

Although there have been reports recently of some unhappiness expressed by British service personnel at the fact that wounded Taliban fighters are being treated in the same operating theaters and in the same field hospital wards as wounded British soldiers,[65] it should be noted that this is no less than what is required by Common

Article 3 and Articles 12–15 of Geneva Convention I.[66] As regards civilians, Article 4 of Geneva Convention IV provides that "[p]ersons protected by the Convention are those who, at a given moment and in any manner whatsoever, find themselves, in case of a conflict or occupation, in the hands of a Party to the conflict or Occupying Power of which they are not nationals." Since the stipulation in Article 4 is disjunctive ("conflict *or* occupation"), it would seem clear that Afghan civilians detained by ISAF troops could be covered by its provisions. In respect to captured Taliban fighters, the simplest expedient under the scheme established in Geneva Convention III would be either to classify them as prisoners of war (POWs) under Article 4(A)(2) (which is most unlikely because of their probable failure to satisfy the conditions stated therein), or to treat them as if they were POWs pending adjudication of their status under the LOAC by a competent tribunal under Article 5.[67]

The above discussion has centered on the type of armed conflict, if any, that subsists during the present stability operations in Afghanistan, and the rules and principles of the law of armed conflict to be applied to the conduct of ISAF thereunder. But it is entirely possible that in any given place and at any given time in Afghanistan, the situation may be stable and secure, and ISAF troops may accordingly not be involved in any armed conflict at all for the purposes of application of the LOAC. Although detailed analysis of the law applicable to ISAF in such situations is essentially beyond the scope of this piece, recent case law from the United Kingdom, arising from obligations under the European Convention on Human Rights (ECHR) as incorporated into UK domestic law by the Human Rights Act 1998 (HRA), requires that the likely position should be at least briefly noted. The full implications of the House of Lords decision in *R (on the application of Al-Skeini) v. Secretary of State for Defence*,[68] already commented upon by the present author in a previous edition of this series,[69] remain a matter of some uncertainty. For all that, it seems fairly clear that British troops deployed outside the United Kingdom on combat operations may be subject, in certain circumstances, to the provisions of the ECHR and the HRA. However, none of the cases decided so far in the British courts concerning the application of human rights law arise from the specific situation of Afghanistan and, indeed, all are materially distinguishable from the Afghan situation in one way or another. The *Al-Skeini* case, for example, arose in the context of British operations in Iraq at a time when that country was generally recognized to be in a state of belligerent occupation; as already indicated above, belligerent occupation is not relevant to Afghanistan at all. In the *Behrami* and *Saramati* cases, the European Court of Human Rights found certain actions (and, therefore, potential violations of the ECHR) by the multinational force in Kosovo since 1999 to be directly imputable to the United Nations itself, rather than to the individual TCNs. But that was in the context of an operation over which the

Security Council retained ultimate authority and control, with very specific allocation of tasks (i.e., de-mining) in the relevant Security Council resolution and in a territory that had neither sovereignty nor effective government of its own at the material time.[70] In Afghanistan, by contrast, the relevant resolutions do not allocate detailed specific tasks, authority and control rests with NATO and the North Atlantic Council, and Afghanistan remains a sovereign State with a legitimate government. Finally, two recent English cases[71] concerning liability for human rights violations in circumstances where British troops had actual custody of civilian detainees in Iraq again largely turn on detailed obligations under relevant Security Council resolutions (which are not applicable in the case of Afghanistan), their interaction with broader obligations under customary international law and the effect of Article 103 of the UN Charter.[72]

The *Al-Skeini* case is currently on appeal to the European Court of Human Rights so its final legal effect is likely to remain of uncertain scope and ambit for some time yet. At present, therefore, the most that can be asserted on the basis of current case law is that British forces on stability operations will be required to apply the ECHR and HRA if they are in belligerent occupation of territory and to persons under their effective control for the purposes of jurisdiction under the human rights instruments (which, as the House of Lords decided in *Al-Skeini*, is a higher standard than effective control under the LOAC and will essentially require British troops to have actual custody of civilian detainees). For reasons explained below, these conditions do not obtain in current stability operations in Afghanistan and are most unlikely ever to do so.

Conclusion: The United Kingdom and Stability Operations

Every State will take a different view on the determination of the existence of a state of armed conflict and the nature thereof. Generally the approach of the United Kingdom is to be as vague as possible concerning the legal classification of military operations in which British forces are engaged and to concentrate instead on the legal basis for such operations. Thus, statements from the British Ministry of Defence on the deployment and use of British troops in Afghanistan do not refer to their participation in an armed conflict in that country, merely to the fact that they are present as part of ISAF under the aegis of NATO, with a brief to aid reconstruction and with the approval of the UN Security Council.[73] The general position in the United Kingdom is that the determination of a state of armed conflict is a policy decision to be made by the government and one that "depends upon the status of the parties to the conflict, and the nature of the hostilities."[74] Thus, each individual situation needs to be examined separately on the basis of its own facts—the actors and the nature of the hostilities—to determine if it amounts to an armed conflict or not. This decision may also be made by the judiciary in the course of legal proceedings, if relevant.[75]

As far as the British position on the nature of an armed conflict is concerned, again as a matter of both law and doctrine, any such determination must be done on a case-by-case basis, depending on the facts in each given situation.[76] The legal basis of the decision for UK authorities will be the international law definitions of international and non-international armed conflicts referred to above, in conjunction with the facts on the ground. If British forces are in action against the government or other official forces of any other State, the situation will be classified as one of international armed conflict—a decision made all the easier by the fact that virtually every State in the world is now a high contracting party to the Geneva Conventions. In any other situation in which British troops are deployed, the situation will be regarded as one of de facto non-international armed conflict. Thus, from the official point of view of the United Kingdom, the ongoing hostilities in Afghanistan and Iraq are in effect treated as internal conflicts in which UK forces are participating on the side of the governments of those States. The conflict in Afghanistan after the removal of the Taliban from de facto power in December 2001 is not considered to be a conflict between the British and Afghan States; it is between Afghan insurgents and the Afghan State, and the latter (with the sanction of the UN Security Council) invited British troops, along with those of other NATO States, to assist it in combating the insurgency, maintaining or restoring law and order, and assisting with reconstruction and development.

Although this position might seem counterintuitive—how can forces of one State be engaged in hostilities in another State, against foreign nationals, yet the conflict not be regarded as an international one?—it is in fact not devoid of sense from a strictly legal perspective. If the British and Afghan States are not at war with each other, but there is a conflict going on in Afghanistan, it cannot be international according to the definitions in the Geneva Conventions or Additional Protocol I; therefore, by default, it must be "not international." Whether it is then governed by Common Article 3 or by Additional Protocol II will depend, as far as British authorities are concerned, on whether the non-State party to the conflict is fighting under responsible command, has control of territory and is able to implement Additional Protocol II.[77] Again, this will be a policy decision made by the government.[78]

As for the specific rules of law applicable to British forces in Afghanistan, if those forces are engaged in actual armed hostilities, particular rules of the LOAC will apply as above. In respect to targeting operations, the United Kingdom as a matter of policy applies the rules concerning target selection and precautions in attack that are contained in Additional Protocol I to *all* military operations, irrespective of the classification of the armed conflict in question.[79] In respect to detainees, given the UN mandate and the general context of stability operations in Afghanistan, British policy is to surrender all detainees to the Afghan authorities as quickly as possible after processing.[80] This latter policy may in due course be exposed to legal challenge, on the basis of concerns that the detainees' human rights may be violated in Afghan custody and in light of the UK's obligation of *non-refoulement* under the ECHR, as discussed particularly in the very recent decision in *Al-Saadoon and Mufdhi*.[81]

Finally, is should be borne in mind that under the military law of the United Kingdom,[82] British troops remain subject to the ordinary criminal law of the land wherever in the world they may be deployed and irrespective of whether or not they are deployed in a situation of armed conflict. Throughout the so-called "Troubles" in Northern Ireland (1969–2007), the use of force by British troops providing support to the civil authority was regulated by the ordinary criminal law, resulting in periodic trials of individual British soldiers (who had been accused of using excessive force) on charges of murder or manslaughter. The same principles apply when the deployment is to a territory outside the United Kingdom. In *Bici v. Ministry of Defence*,[83] it was accepted in principle that aspects of civil law—notably the torts of negligence and trespass to the person—could also be applicable in situations where British troops deployed on certain types of operation abroad could be shown to have a duty of care toward any persons killed or wounded as a result of their actions. It was emphasized that this will not be the case in full combat operations,[84] but it may very well turn out to be relevant to stability operations.

Notes

1. UNOSOM II was created by the UN Security Council with a remarkably broad mandate that encompassed humanitarian relief operations in Somalia, disarming the various militias, restoring law and order, and assisting in the establishment of a representative government and in the restoration of infrastructure. S.C. Res. 814, U.N. Doc. S/RES/814 (Mar. 26, 1993). The mission was violently opposed by the Somali militias from the outset and US troops were withdrawn from the operation after American public opinion turned decisively against their continued involvement as a result of the deaths of eighteen US soldiers and the wounding of another eighty-three in the so-called First Battle of Mogadishu in October 1993.

2. Following a military coup displacing a democratically elected civilian government and ensuing political repression which resulted in an exodus of Haitian refugees across the Caribbean Sea toward the United States, the Security Council authorized the establishment of a US-led Multinational Interim Force "to use all necessary means to facilitate the departure from Haiti of the military leadership, . . . the prompt return of the legitimately elected President and the restoration of the legitimate authorities of the Government of Haiti, and to establish and maintain a secure and stable environment." S.C. Res. 940, U.N. Doc. S/RES/940 (July 31, 1994).

3. Commission on Presidential Debates, The Second Gore-Bush Presidential Debate (Oct. 11, 2000), *available at* http://www.debates.org/pages/trans2000b.html.

4. US Department of Defense, Directive 3000.05, Military Support for Stability, Security, Transition, and Reconstruction (SSTR) Operations para. 4.1 (Nov. 28, 2005), *available at* http://www.dtic.mil/whs/directives/corres/pdf/300005p.pdf [hereinafter DoD Directive 3000.05]. *See also* Bob Hubner, *Developing Joint Stability Operations Doctrine*, A COMMON PERSPECTIVE (Oct. 2004), at 9.

5. *E.g.*, Robert M. Cassidy, *The British Army and Counterinsurgency: The Salience of Military Culture*, MILITARY REVIEW (May–June 2005), at 53, 59.

6. United Kingdom Ministry of Defence, Joint Doctrine Publication 3-40, Security and Stabilisation: The Military Contribution (as of January 2009 available only on a restricted basis for consultation and discussion purposes, not yet adopted as an official document and with no official standing).

7. Resolution on Stabilisation of Afghanistan: Challenges for the EU and the International Community para. 2, EUROPEAN PARLIAMENT, Doc. P6_TA(2008)0337 (July 8, 2008).

8. *Id.*, para. 19.

9. *See* Peter W. Chiarelli & Patrick R. Michaelis, *Winning the Peace: The Requirement for Full-Spectrum Operations*, MILITARY REVIEW (July–August 2005), at 4.

10. US Defense Secretary Donald Rumsfeld declared an end to "major combat" in Afghanistan on May 1, 2003. Kenneth Katzman, Congressional Research Service, *Afghanistan: Post-War Governance, Security, and U.S. Policy*, No. RL30588 (Nov. 26, 2008), at 7, *available at* http://assets.opencrs.com/rpts/RL30588_20081126.pdf. On the actual combat situation in Afghanistan, see *id.* at 22–25.

11. The term "war" has, of course, been largely replaced in international legal discourse since 1945 with the term "armed conflict." This terminological shift was connected initially with the development of the UN Charter and its move to outlaw any use of force that did not constitute either an act of self-defense or an enforcement action under Chapter VII of the Charter. With the changing nature of warfare in the international relations context, it also came increasingly to reflect the reality that most conflicts were no longer being fought between States; and even when they were, the States concerned were no longer willing formally to declare war on each other, but preferred to maintain a *status mixtus* of neither war nor peace. In the *jus in bello*, the term "armed conflict" was also explicitly enshrined in the language of the 1949 Geneva Conventions and, subsequently, their Additional Protocols. (Although, as discussed later in this article, the 1949 instruments did retain the concept of "declared war" as part of their scope of application. *See, e.g.*, Convention for the Amelioration of the Condition of the Wounded and Sick in Armed Forces in the Field art. 2, Aug. 12, 1949, 6 U.S.T. 3114, 75 U.N.T.S. 31, *reprinted in* DOCUMENTS ON THE LAWS OF WAR 197, 198 (Adam Roberts & Richard Guelff eds., 3d ed. 2000)). For elaboration and discussion of these trends, see Georg Schwarzenberger, *Jus Pacis ac Belli? Prolegomena to a Sociology of International Law*, 37 AMERICAN JOURNAL OF INTERNATIONAL LAW 460, 465–74 (1943); Robert W. Tucker, *The Interpretation of War Under Present International Law*, 4 INTERNATIONAL LAW QUARTERLY 11 (1951); Philip C. Jessup, *Should international law recognize an intermediate status between peace and war?*, 48 AMERICAN JOURNAL OF INTERNATIONAL LAW 98 (1954); Christopher Greenwood, *Scope of Application of Humanitarian Law*, *in* THE HANDBOOK OF HUMANITARIAN LAW IN ARMED CONFLICTS 39, 39–45 (Dieter Fleck ed., 1995); LESLIE C. GREEN, THE CONTEMPORARY LAW OF ARMED CONFLICT 70–75 (2000).

12. *See* Nina M. Serafino, Congressional Research Service, *Peacekeeping and Related Stability Operations: Issues of U.S. Military Involvement*, No. RL33557 (Jan. 24, 2007), at 6, *available at* http://assets.opencrs.com/rpts/RL33557_20070124.pdf.

13. *Id.*

14. DoD Directive 3000.05, *supra* note 4, para. 3.1.

15. Chairman of the Joint Chiefs of Staff, Joint Publication 3-0, Doctrine for Joint Operations, at V-1 (Sept. 2006, with change 1, Feb. 13, 2008), *available at* http://www.dtic.mil/doctrine/jel/new_pubs/jp3_0.pdf.

16. Headquarters, Department of the Army, FM 3-07, Stability Operations (2008), *available at* http://downloads.army.mil/docs/fm_3-07.pdf.

17. General Sir Richard Dannatt, Chief of the General Staff, Address to the Institute for Public Policy Research, London (Jan. 19, 2009), *available at* http://www.mod.uk/DefenceInternet/AboutDefence/People/Speeches/ChiefStaff/20090119AddressToTheInstituteForPublicPolicyResearchLondon htm.

18. *Id.*

19. *See* US Department of Defense, Quadrennial Defense Review Report v, 9–18 (2006).

20. Agreement on Provisional Arrangements in Afghanistan Pending the Re-establishment of Permanent Government Institutions, attached to Letter from the Secretary-General addressed to the President of the Security Council, U.N. Doc. S/2001/1154 (Dec. 5, 2001).

21. *Id.*, Annex I, paras. 3–4.

22. Letter dated 19 December 2001 from the Permanent Representative of Afghanistan to the United Nations addressed to the President of the Security Council, U.N. Doc. S/2001/1223 (Dec. 19, 2001), Annex.

23. Letter from the Permanent Representative of the United Kingdom of Great Britain and Northern Ireland to the United Nations addressed to the President of the Security Council, U.N. Doc. S/2001/1217 (Dec. 19, 2001), Annex.

24. *Id.*

25. *Id.*

26. S.C. Res. 1386, operative para. 1, U.N. Doc. S/RES/1386 (Dec. 20, 2001).

27. *Id.*

28. *Id.*, operative para. 10.

29. *Id.*, operative para. 3.

30. S.C. Res. 83, U.N. Doc. S/RES/83 (June 27, 1950).

31. S.C. Res. 143, operative para. 2, U.N. Doc. S/RES/143 (July 17, 1960).

32. S.C. Res. 161, operative para. 1, U.N. Doc. S/RES/161 (Feb. 21, 1961); this was supplemented by S.C. Res. 169, operative para. 4, U.N. Doc. S/RES/169 (Nov. 24, 1961).

33. *See* S.C. Res. 1542, U.N. Doc. S/RES/1542 (Apr. 30, 2004).

34. *Id.*, operative para. 7 (I–III).

35. *Id.*, operative para. 9.

36. *See* BBC News, *UN peacekeepers storm Haiti slum* (Dec. 15, 2004), http://news.bbc.co.uk/1/hi/world/americas/4096841.stm; United Nations Stabilization Mission in Haiti, Statement Relating to the Operation Conducted on 06 July 2005 at Cité Soleil, *available at* http://www.un.org/Depts/dpko/missions/minustah/pb060705e.pdf (last visited Feb. 19, 2009); Andrew Buncombe, *UN admits civilians may have died in Haiti peacekeeping raid*, THE INDEPENDENT (London), Jan. 10, 2006, at 25, *available at* http://www.independent.co.uk/news/world/americas/un-admits-civilians-may-have-died-in-haiti-peacekeeping-raid-522317.html.

37. Letter from the Secretary-General of the North Atlantic Treaty Organization addressed to the Secretary-General, Annex I, U.N. Doc. S/2003/970 (Oct. 2, 2003).

38. Letter from the Minister for Foreign Affairs of Afghanistan addressed to the Secretary-General, attached to U.N. Doc. S/2003/986 (Oct. 10, 2003).

39. S.C. Res. 1510, U.N. Doc. S/RES/1510 (Oct. 13, 2003).

40. S.C. Res. 1833, U.N. Doc. S/RES/1833 (Sept. 22, 2008).

41. NATO Topics, NATO's Role in Afghanistan, http://www.nato.int/issues/afghanistan/index.html (last visited Feb. 19, 2009).

42. According to the British Foreign & Commonwealth Office, PRTs

> embody a joint military and civilian approach to stabilising Afghanistan. . . . They bring together civilian and police experts, under the security umbrella provided by the military, to help extend the authority of the Afghan central government and help to facilitate development and reconstruction. PRTs also aim to support the reform of the Afghan security sector . . . .

FCO, Provincial Reconstruction Teams, http://www.fco gov.uk/en/fco-in-action/uk-in-afghanistan/security/prt/ (last visited Feb. 19, 2009).

43. *See* Press and Media Service, NATO HQ Brussels, Fact Sheet, Operational Mentor and Liaison Team (OMLT) Programme – October 2008, *available at* http://www.nato.int/isaf/topics/factsheets/omlt-factsheet.pdf (last visited Feb. 19, 2009).

44. NATO, ISAF Mandate, *available at* http://www.nato.int/isaf/topics/mandate/index.html (last visited Feb. 19, 2009).

45. *See* UK Ministry of Defence, Defence Factsheet, Operations in Afghanistan: Background Briefing 2, *available at* http://www.mod.uk/DefenceInternet/FactSheets/OperationsFactsheets/OperationsInAfghanistanBackgroundBriefing2.htm (last visited Feb. 19, 2009).

46. *See* Jared Tracy, *Ethical Challenges in Stability Operations*, MILITARY REVIEW (Jan.–Feb. 2009), at 86. Tracy's article asserts, correctly, that Just War doctrine is of no use to consideration of the *jus ad bellum* of stability operations, because it only covers the rationale for going to war in the first place, while "there is nothing in *jus in bello* that compels the victorious nation to provide security, rebuild infrastructure, improve public services, and see to the establishment of a democratic form of government." *Id.* at 86. In consequence, Tracy posits that morality, rather than law, must be the basis of ethical understandings about what the military should or should not do in post-conflict operations. While I agree with Tracy that morality plays a part in contemporary military thinking, especially in situations as complex as that of Afghanistan, I consider that a strictly *legal* basis for stability operations does (and, indeed, must) exist.

47. *See* Kwaku Nuamah & I. William Zartman, *Intervention in Sierra Leone*, *in* MILITARY INTERVENTION: CASES IN CONTEXT FOR THE TWENTY-FIRST CENTURY 133, 145–49 (William J. Lahneman ed., 2004); Eric G. Berman & Melissa T. Labonte, *Sierra Leone*, *in* TWENTY-FIRST-CENTURY PEACE OPERATIONS 141, 181–82 (William J. Durch ed., 2006).

48. *See* Hansard (HC Debs) vol. 349, cols. 518–29 (May 8, 2000).

49. *See* Hansard (HL Debs) vol. 612, cols. 1233–40 (May 8, 2000).

50. *See* U.N. Doc. S/PV.4139 (May 11, 2000).

51. *Id.* at 8 (Canada), 9 (Malaysia), 11 (United States), 14 (Namibia), 15 (Argentina), 18 (Ukraine & France) and 22 (Portugal). Portugal did not have a seat on the Council at the time and attended as the representative of the European Union.

52. *Id.* at 3.

53. Statement by the President of the Security Council, U.N. Doc. S/PRST/2000/14 (May 4, 2000).

54. Prosecutor v. Tadic, Case No. IT-94-1-1, Decision on Defence Motion for Interlocutory Appeal on Jurisdiction, para. 70 (Oct. 2, 1995).

55. Protocol Additional to the Geneva Conventions of 12 August 1949, and Relating to the Protection of Victims of International Armed Conflicts art. 1(4), June 8, 1977, 1125 U.N.T.S. 3, *reprinted in* DOCUMENTS ON THE LAWS OF WAR, *supra* note 11, at 422, 423.

56. Protocol Additional to the Geneva Conventions of 12 August 1949, and Relating to the Protection of Victims of Non-International Armed Conflicts art. 1(1), June 8, 1977, 1125

U.N.T.S. 609, *reprinted in* DOCUMENTS ON THE LAWS OF WAR, *supra* note 11, at 483, 484 [hereinafter Additional Protocol II].

57. *Supra* note 54.

58. This is the default position supported by a plurality of the US Supreme Court, in relation to the treatment of detainees captured in the "Global War on Terror" (including in the Afghan theater of operations). Hamdan v. Rumsfeld, 548 U.S. 557 (2006).

59. Military and Paramilitary Activities (Nicar. v. U.S.), 1986 I.C.J. 14, para. 218 (June 27). In *Tadic*, the International Criminal Tribunal for the former Yugoslavia also held that "the character of the conflict is irrelevant" in terms of the application of Common Article 3. Tadic, *supra* note 54, para. 102.

60. Public Committee Against Torture in Israel et al. v. Government of Israel et al., HCJ 769/02, Judgment, para. 21 (Dec. 13, 2006), *available at* http://elyon1.court.gov.il/files_eng/02/690/007/a34/02007690.a34.pdf.

61. *Id.*, para. 18.

62. Headquarters, International Security Assistance Force, Tactical Directive para. 4(a) (Dec. 30, 2008), *available at* http://www.nato.int/isaf/docu/official_texts/Tactical%20Directive_090114.pdf.

63. *Id.*, para. 5.

64. *See* JEAN-MARIE HENCKAERTS & LOUISE DOSWALD-BECK, CUSTOMARY INTERNATIONAL HUMANITARIAN LAW (2005) (2 volumes: Volume I, Rules; Volume II, Practice (2 Parts)). Part I of the Rules ("The Principle of Distinction") contains many asserted customary rules of the LOAC that would be relevant to the conduct of hostilities by ISAF. These relate to the distinction between civilians and civilian objects on the one hand, and combatants and military objectives on the other (Rules 1–10); indiscriminate attacks (Rules 11–13); proportionality (Rule 14); precautions in attack (Rules 15–21); and precautions against the effects of attacks (Rules 22–24). *Id.* at 3–76.

65. *See* Jo Adetunji, *MoD defends hospital treatment for Taliban*, THE GUARDIAN (London), Jan. 23, 2009, at 2, *available at* http://www.guardian.co.uk/uk/2009/jan/23/military-afghanistan.

66. At the time of writing, a Canadian officer is to face a court-martial on a charge of illegally shooting a wounded and disarmed Taliban fighter in Afghanistan. Sean Chase, *Canadian soldier granted bail*, THE INTELLIGENCER, http://www.intelligencer.ca/ArticleDisplay.aspx?e=1377810&auth=SEAN%20CHASE,%20SUN%20MEDIA (last visited Feb. 19, 2009).

67. Although see further *infra*, text to note 80, concerning British practice in regard to persons detained by British forces in Afghanistan. The treatment of captured persons in Afghanistan has been the source of much controversy among the ISAF TCNs. *See, e.g.*, Vincent Morelli, Congressional Research Service, *NATO in Afghanistan: A Test for the Transatlantic Alliance*, No. RL33627 (Oct. 23, 2008), at 16–17, *available at* http://assets.opencrs.com/rpts/RL33627_20081023.pdf. This dissension has, moreover, been present from the outset of OEF, also in regard to the classification of such prisoners upon capture. *See* Robert Cryer, *The Fine Art of Friendship:* Jus in Bello *in Afghanistan*, 7 JOURNAL OF CONFLICT & SECURITY LAW 37, 68–82 (2002).

68. [2008] 1 APPEAL CASES 153.

69. *See* David Turns, *The Treatment of Detainees and the "Global War on Terror": Selected Legal Issues, in* INTERNATIONAL LAW AND MILITARY OPERATIONS 199 (Michael D. Carsten ed., 2008) (Vol. 84, US Naval War College International Law Studies).

70. Behrami v. France and Saramati v. France, Germany and Norway, 45 E.Ct. H.R. 41 (2007).

71. R (on the application of Al-Jedda) v. Secretary of State for Defence [2008] 1 APPEAL CASES 332; R (on the application of Al-Saadoon and Mufdhi) v. Secretary of State for Defence [2008] ENGLAND & WALES HIGH COURT 3098.

72. Whereby obligations arising under the Charter, such as those consequent upon mandatory Chapter VII resolutions of the Security Council, override inconsistent obligations arising from other international agreements.

73. *E.g.*, Adam Ingram, Minister of State, UK Military Operations in Afghanistan, Remarks to the All-Party Parliamentary Army Group (Oct. 24, 2006), *available at* http://www.mod.uk/DefenceInternet/AboutDefence/People/Speeches/MinAF/UkMilitaryOperationsInAfghanistan.htm; Defence Factsheet, *supra* note 45.

74. UK Ministry of Defence, Joint Doctrine Publication 1-10, Joint Doctrine Publication – Prisoners of War, Internees and Detainees para. 403 (2006) [hereinafter JDP 1-10].

75. In an extradition case in recent years, for example, an English judge was faced with a Russian government claim that the situation in Chechnya in 1995–96 "amounted to a riot and rebellion, 'banditry' and terrorism." It was held, however, that "the events in Chechnya . . . amounted in law to an internal armed conflict." In support of that determination, the judge listed the following factors: "the scale of the fighting—the intense carpet bombing of Grozny with in excess of 100,000 casualties, the recognition of the conflict in terms of a cease fire and a peace treaty." Government of the Russian Federation v. Akhmed Zakaev (Bow Street Magistrates' Court, Nov. 13, 2003, at 2) (unreported; copy on file with the author). The factors listed do not apply to Afghanistan, except in respect to the scale and intensity of the fighting.

76. *See* UK MINISTRY OF DEFENCE, THE MANUAL OF THE LAW OF ARMED CONFLICT paras. 3.1–3.13 (2004) [hereinafter UK MANUAL].

77. As required by Article 1(1) of Additional Protocol II, *supra* note 56.

78. JDP 1-10, *supra* note 74, paras. 403–04.

79. The United Kingdom is bound by treaty obligation to apply the Additional Protocol I rules on targeting in all international armed conflicts to which it is a party. These rules "should [also] be treated as applicable" in non-international armed conflicts. UK MANUAL, *supra* note 76, para. 15.9.1.

80. UK Ministry of Defence, Joint Doctrine Publication 1-10.3, Joint Doctrine Publication – Detainees, paras. 116–17 (2006).

81. *Supra* note 71, paras. 44–53 and 204.

82. Specifically, the Army Act 1955, the Royal Air Force Act 1955 and the Naval Discipline Act 1957 (which will in the course of 2009 be progressively repealed and replaced with the new tri-service Armed Forces Act 2006).

83. [2004] ENGLAND & WALES HIGH COURT 786. The court found the Ministry of Defence to have civil liability in tort for the accidental killing and wounding of four Kosovar Albanians by British soldiers on peacekeeping duties near a demonstration in Priština.

84. *Id.*, paras. 84–105, citing in particular the Australian case of *Shaw Savill and Albion Company Ltd v. The Commonwealth* (1940) 66 C.L.R. 344 (concerning the liability of the State in tort for a collision on the high seas between an Australian warship and an Australian civilian vessel, caused by the navigational negligence of the warship's officers). Furthermore, the House of Lords decision in *Al-Skeini*, *supra* note 68, which confirmed that the ECHR and HRA were applicable to the case of the detainee Baha Mousa, who died in British military custody, was made on such narrow grounds as at least implicitly to exclude any possibility of similar liability in combat situations, where the troops could not be said to have effective control of the territory in question.

XVI

Stability Operations: A Guiding Framework for "Small Wars" and Other Conflicts of the Twenty-First Century?

Kenneth Watkin*

[I]f international law is, in some ways, at the vanishing point of law, the law of war is, perhaps even more conspicuously, at the vanishing point of international law.[1]

Introduction

The ongoing armed conflict in Afghanistan provides a stark example of the challenging and complex operating environment in which the international community is seeking to establish and maintain the rule of law. Professor Hersch Lauterpacht's entreaty in the aftermath of World War II for lawyers to address the myriad of law of war issues not covered by the Geneva Conventions with a feeling of humility is no less applicable today regarding attempts to regulate contemporary conflict.[2] Twenty-first-century conflict rarely meets the traditional legal criteria of an international armed conflict. Instead, operational lawyers have to apply a normative framework primarily designed to regulate State-on-State conflict to increasingly complex security situations involving warfare both within States and across international borders. Such operations range from relatively benign

* Brigadier General, Canadian Forces. The opinions expressed in this article are solely those of the author and do not necessarily reflect the views of the government of Canada.

humanitarian relief operations to significant combat operations, such as those in Afghanistan involving the multinational forces assisting the Afghan government.

Lawyers should not feel isolated in this endeavor, as the challenge of categorizing conflict and operating in complex security situations is not a uniquely legal one. Military commanders are also seeking to have doctrine adapted, and where necessary developed, to address such conflicts. The doctrinal goal of attempting to categorize operations that do not fit within the classic notions of offensive or defensive operations between State armed forces has led to the development of the concept of "stability operations." This article explores the relationship between the law of armed conflict and what is largely a US-led initiative to place a myriad of military missions, often occurring at the lower end of the conflict spectrum, under one overarching doctrinal umbrella.[3] The analysis includes an outline of the limits of the contemporary normative legal framework in governing operations designed to bring stability to failed or failing States.

Stability operations will be assessed in four parts, commencing with an outline of the definition, scope and purpose of those operations. A key question is the degree to which such operations are actually new or whether the concept is in reality a catch-all term for a variety of missions that have always challenged both doctrine writers and lawyers alike. Secondly, the law governing operations at the lower end of the conflict spectrum will be explored. Emphasis will be placed on looking at whether international law has adapted to account for such conflict, or if it has, like military doctrine, focused on State-on-State conflict. Thirdly, the applicability of the term "stability operations" in a coalition environment will be explored. Given the prevalence of such operations, the adoption, or lack thereof, of this doctrinal approach by potential allies provides an important indicator of the maturity and potential viability of the concept.

Finally, potential limitations on this forward-thinking American doctrinal approach to addressing the contemporary "war amongst the people"[4] will be considered. While there is a possibility for failure, the significant potential this new categorization of conflict presents in seeking to articulate a realistic regime in which to conduct operations in the existing complex security environment will be explored.

Stability Operations

The Doctrine

The analysis will now turn to outlining the stability operations doctrine, exploring its scope and relationship with doctrine governing combat operations, and situating stability operations in a historical context regarding previous efforts to categorize such conflict. "Stability operations" is a relatively recent doctrine developed by the prolific US military doctrine production process. In its simplest form, such operations are defined as "[m]ilitary and civilian activities conducted across the spectrum from peace to conflict to establish or maintain order in States and regions."[5] This definition, found in Department of Defense (DoD) Directive 3000.05, elevates such operations to "a core U.S. military mission that the Department of Defense shall be prepared to conduct and support. They shall be given priority comparable to combat operations and be explicitly addressed and integrated across all DoD activities . . . ."[6] The goal of these operations is ambitious:

> The immediate goal often is to provide the local populace with security, restore essential services, and meet humanitarian needs. The long term goal is to help develop indigenous capacity for securing essential services, a viable market economy, rule of law, democratic institutions, and a robust civil society.[7]

Among the activities envisaged are rebuilding indigenous security forces, correctional facilities and judicial systems necessary to secure and stabilize the environment; reviving or building the private sector; and developing representative governmental institutions.[8] The partners for US military forces include "U.S. Departments and Agencies, foreign governments and security forces, global and regional international organizations . . . U.S. and foreign nongovernmental organizations . . . and private sector individuals and for-profit companies . . . ."[9] While the directive clearly anticipates that many stability operations are best performed by indigenous, foreign or US civilian professionals it clearly, and perhaps for many military planners ominously, states: "[n]onetheless, U.S. military forces shall be prepared to perform all tasks necessary to establish or maintain order when civilians cannot do so."[10]

The fulfillment of the "stability operations" mission presents a significant challenge. Indeed some might think it at best aspirational if it were not for the fact such operations comprise the types of missions presently being conducted, not just by the US military, but also by the wider international community. This is evident not only in Iraq, which is often cited as the most glaring example of what can go wrong when mission planning has not fully contemplated or provided for the maintenance of order and the re-establishment of governance institutions when traditional fighting has concluded, but also in Afghanistan. In Afghanistan, NATO, the United Nations, international organizations and nongovernmental organizations are all faced with the tremendous security, governance and organizational challenges of trying to rebuild or, perhaps more accurately, build a State. Both the Afghanistan and Iraq missions provide clear examples of the activities stability operations can encompass, as well as the policy and legal challenges they pose. Given the post-2001 emergence of the doctrine they appear to have been primary catalysts for its development.

However, there is a significant danger in looking at stability operations through the narrow lens of Iraq or Afghanistan. The activities captured under the stability operations doctrine are much broader than those two major conflicts. This idea is reflected in the foreword to the 2008 US Army Field Manual on "Stability Operations," where Lieutenant General William Caldwell notes, "America's future abroad is unlikely to resemble Afghanistan or Iraq."[11] It is the very breadth of the stability operations doctrine that highlights not only the complex nature of the existing security challenge, but also the deficiencies in the underlying legal framework within which contemporary security operations take place.

The "Catch-All" of Conflict

The complexity of stability operations results from a number of factors, including the wide scope of activities that fall within its definition. To fully understand that scope it is necessary to look at recent US Army doctrine. That doctrine has undergone a significant revision with the 2008 Army manual replacing an earlier version produced just in 2003.[12] The speed with which this doctrine has undergone that revision appears to reflect not only the dynamic environment within which such operations are conducted, but also the impact of "lessons learned" information being incorporated into military doctrine.

While not as specific as its predecessor in terms of identifying types of operations, the new doctrine indicates that stability operations occur across a spectrum of conflict from peace to general war and can include

> a wide range of stability tasks performed under the umbrella of various operational environments—
>
> • To support a partner nation during peacetime military engagement.
>
> • After a natural or man-made disaster as part of a humanitarian-based limited intervention.
>
> • During peace operations to enforce international peace agreements.
>
> • To support a legitimate host-nation government during irregular warfare.
>
> • During major combat operations to establish conditions that facilitate post-conflict activities.

- In a post-conflict environment following the general cessation of organized hostilities.[13]

Consistent with the 2003 version, the doctrine found in the 2008 manual envisages stability operations to be carried out during humanitarian disaster relief, peacetime support to other nations, peacekeeping and peace enforcement, counterinsurgency (COIN) operations and post-conflict occupation. Given the general wording provided in the new doctrine there is no reason to believe it would not also include operations identified in the earlier manual, such as support to counterdrug operations, combating terrorism and noncombatant evacuation operations.[14]

Significantly, in respect to terrorism, the 2008 doctrine notes that the greatest threat to American national security "comes not in the form of terrorism or ambitious powers, but from fragile states."[15] While terrorism remains a threat which must be addressed in the context of such operations, avoiding the impression of engagement in a "Global War on Terror" will undoubtedly remove a potential irritant with many coalition partners. The reference to humanitarian operations also highlights the degree to which dealing with humanitarian disaster is increasingly being seen in the same light as insurgency and other challenges to governance by State authorities.[16] Both humanitarian and many other types of stability operations, which are located well down on the conflict spectrum, often involve military forces in issues related to governance, including law enforcement. What remains to be seen is the degree to which military forces can or must adapt their operations to participate in a law enforcement role.

Significantly, the stability operations doctrine takes a bold step in addressing the primary security challenge of the twenty-first century by elevating such operations in DoD Directive 3000.05 to an equal footing with combat operations. In many ways this doctrine is revolutionary, visionary and long overdue. The Army manual seeks to reinforce this doctrinal advance by indicating the full spectrum of operations includes "continuous, simultaneous combinations of offensive, defensive, and stability tasks."[17] That relationship is depicted as follows:[18]

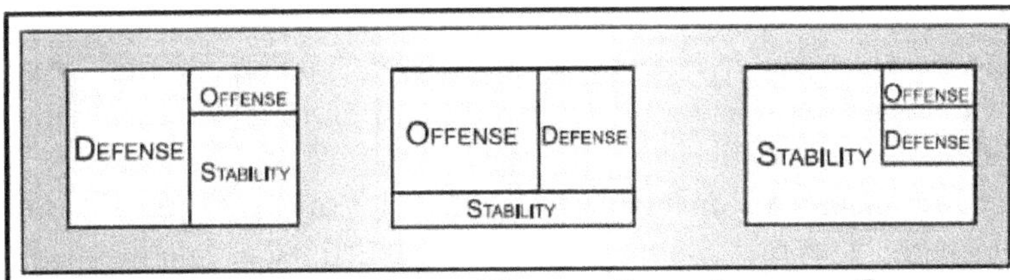

The Mission Determines the Relative Weight of Effort Among the Components

The question remains, however, whether the attempt to elevate stability operations to the level of combat operations will win out over the significant historical resistance to changing the focus on traditional "inter-State" armed conflict. To do so, such a change in status will have to address the significant effort that will be required in terms of training and education. The challenges that arise from focusing on armed conflict between States not only has plagued doctrine writers, but has also impacted on attempts to clearly outline the legal framework governing operations at the lower end of the conflict spectrum.

A Doctrinal Morass

The strength of military doctrine is that it provides an overall conceptual framework within which operations are conducted. One of the potential obstacles to gaining acceptance for the new doctrinal term "stability operations" is that it could appear to a cynical observer to simply be an attempt to provide a new name to an old problem. For well over a century efforts have been made to categorize small-scale and lower-intensity conflict. Such terms have included small wars,[19] imperial policing,[20] police action,[21] insurgency, low intensity conflict,[22] military operations other than war,[23] peacekeeping,[24] peace enforcement,[25] three block wars,[26] revolutionary war, irregular warfare, war amongst the people and, more recently, mosaic war.[27]

These categorizations can often be used to encompass one or more of the other doctrinal terms associated with conflict at the lower end of the conflict spectrum. For example, the 2007 US Army and Marine Corps counterinsurgency manual notes that "insurgency and COIN are two sides of a phenomenon that has been called revolutionary war or internal war."[28] Further, they are "included within a broad category of conflict known as irregular warfare."[29]

The development and use of the term "mosaic war" in the counterinsurgency manual[30] itself highlights the challenge of seeking just one term to categorize contemporary complex security operations. "Mosaic war" was introduced to highlight that contemporary COIN operations are more complicated than the 1990s concept of "three block war" on the basis that such warfare "is difficult for counter-insurgents to envision as a coherent whole."[31] The manual recognizes the term "stability operations" and identifies it as an essential component of COIN operations, along with offensive and defensive operations.[32] It is within this shifting doctrinal framework that stability operations will have to be interpreted.

The counterinsurgency manual also highlights a further complexity of contemporary conflict. In that manual "insurgency" is defined as "an organized, protracted politico-military struggle designed to weaken the control and legitimacy of an established government, *occupying power*, or other political authority while increasing insurgent control."[33] Counterinsurgency operations and as a result stability operations occur not only during internal armed conflicts, but also during periods of occupation.

Part of the challenge in applying the doctrinal term "stability operations" is that the underlying security situations which motivated its creation are not only not new, but have been and are the dominant form of warfare. As has been identified by Doctor Lawrence Yates for the Combat Studies Institute Press, "[i]f America's armed forces have fought fewer than a dozen major conventional wars in over two centuries, they have, during that same period, engaged in several hundred military undertakings that would today be characterized as stability operations."[34] It has been noted that in 2006 no State-sponsored opposing armies were engaged in armed conflict, while the number of civil wars increased.[35]

Although the potential for armed conflict between States continues, as was evidenced by the 2008 armed conflict between the armed forces of Russia and Georgia, there is increasing recognition within the US Department of Defense that "the main threat faced by the U.S. military overseas will be a complex hybrid of conventional and unconventional conflicts, waged by 'militias, insurgent groups, other non-State actors and Third World militaries.'"[36] It is within this complex security environment that the applicable law must be identified and applied in order to ensure that military operations, including stability operations, are conducted pursuant to the "rule of law."

The Law

Unfortunately, it appears that international law has been no more successful than military doctrine in definitively addressing the challenges associated with irregular warfare. Like military doctrine, the law of armed conflict has been more readily developed and applied to regulate conflict at the inter-State level. The lack of a comprehensive set of legal rules governing conflict outside the context of traditional inter-State warfare has been influenced by a number of interrelated factors: the post–World War II emphasis on prescribing the recourse to war between States, difficulty in categorizing conflict at the lower end of the conflict spectrum and a general reluctance to introduce international law of armed conflict rules to what are often viewed as internal security matters. This in turn results in considerable debate regarding what legal regime governs such conflict: the law of armed conflict or human rights law. The analysis will now turn to discussing this challenge.

Emphasis on Inter-State Conflict

While the immediate post–World War II period saw the almost concurrent development of the 1949 Geneva Conventions,[37] governing aspects of the conduct of warfare, particular legal emphasis was placed on stopping or limiting future inter-State wars. This was perhaps best evidenced by the increasing use of the terms *jus ad bellum* and *jus in bello*, which were designed to separate the legal analysis regarding conflict into two distinct analytical spheres.[38] The *jus ad bellum* branch focused on the replacement of the balance of power approach to inter-State relations with resurgence of the concept of *bellum justum*.[39] This is reflected in the UN Charter, which significantly prescribed the recourse to war.[40]

The extent to which war between States was to be limited is reflected in the fact that the very use of the term "war" has become problematic. While "war" continues as part of the everyday lexicon, including in the newly issued stability operations doctrine manual,[41] in a legal sense it has often been viewed since World War II as being "outlawed."[42] This sensitivity toward describing conflict as "war" is frequently reflected in legal articles where that term is often prefaced with the qualifier that it is being used in a de facto rather than a de jure sense.[43]

Even the new term "armed conflict," introduced in the 1949 Geneva Conventions to describe a broad range of conflicts between States,[44] came with limitations that reflected the inter-State bias of the drafters of those Conventions. The scope of "armed conflict" is effectively qualified in Common Article 3 of the Conventions with reference to "armed conflict not of an international character," mirroring the historic approach of distinguishing between public and private war. States were more willing to deal with international armed conflict than comprehensively identify rules to govern its non-international counterpart. In effect, there was significant armed conflict in terms of scope, frequency and levels of violence to which the rules governing conflict between States were not clearly stated to be applicable. This emphasis by the international community on inter-State conflict is understandable given the horrific human and material cost of the total wars of the twentieth century. However, the bias toward inter-State conflict has resulted in intra-State conflict not being provided as clear or rigorous a governing legal framework.

It is evident there has been an extreme reluctance on the part of States to codify the law governing armed conflict as it applies to warfare within a State. Certainly, the expansion of Additional Protocol I[45] to deal with "national liberation movements" and what otherwise would be an internal armed conflict has met with significant resistance. Efforts commenced by the International Committee of the Red Cross (ICRC) as early as 1912 to introduce law of armed conflict norms to internal conflict continued through the immediate post–World War II period to the present day with what realistically can only be described as having had limited success.

Common Article 3 of the Geneva Conventions, while representing a significant milestone in the twentieth-century efforts to codify the rules governing internal conflict, in reality represents the best that could be attained in a broader effort to have all of the Conventions apply to conflicts "not of an international character."[46] A quarter century later the success in negotiating Additional Protocol II[47] is tempered by both the lack of universal acceptance by States[48] and the relatively high threshold for its application that leaves significant internal conflict outside its scope.[49] Notwithstanding a trend in having law of armed conflict treaties address both international and non-international armed conflict[50] it undoubtedly was the long-standing reluctance by States to outline in codified form the rules to be applied to internal armed conflict which has resulted in efforts by the International Criminal Tribunal for the former Yugoslavia (ICTY)[51] and the ICRC to articulate what customary international law rules should apply to govern internal warfare.[52] These initial efforts are long overdue. However, there remains a lack of agreement regarding the scope and content of the customary law of armed conflict as it applies to non-international armed conflicts.

One example of the degree to which international law often focuses on inter-State conflict is reflected in *Legal Consequences of the Construction of a Wall in the Occupied Palestinian Territory*,[53] where the International Court of Justice ruled the invocation of Article 51 of the UN Charter required attacks that were imputable to a foreign State and a threat originating outside of occupied territory.[54] Even where there is a clash between State armed forces the *jus ad bellum* focus on limiting conflict has left considerable room for disagreement and, as a result, confusion as to when such clashes engage the law of armed conflict. This is evident in the assessment of the threshold of what constitutes an "armed attack."[55] The reference in *Military and Paramilitary Activities in and against Nicaragua*[56] to "frontier incidents" as a less grave use of force not constituting such an attack raises the question as to whether such incidents could constitute "armed conflict" where the law of armed conflict would apply.

The ICTY has stated armed conflict "exists whenever there is resort to armed force between States or protracted armed violence between governmental authorities and organized armed groups or between such groups within a State."[57] In that assessment, particular attention is paid to the intensity of the fighting and the organization of the armed groups.[58] However, the requirement for "protracted" armed violence between opposing armed forces still results in situations where armed forces may be engaged in fighting where it is not clear there is consensus that "armed conflict" exists such that the law of armed conflict would apply. If that is the case, it is not necessarily evident how the alternative legal framework of international human rights law is equipped to regulate such violence. The criteria established by the ICTY can be contrasted with that followed in *Abella v. Argentina*, where an isolated act of armed violence between State armed forces and a rebel armed group during a two-day period resulted in the application of the law of armed conflict.[59]

While the *Nicaragua* judgment has garnered considerable criticism, it highlights that in the context of the inter-State use of force and in respect to military action between State and non-State actors there is a wide range of activity that does not neatly fall within the parameters of traditional armed conflict. Such contemporary operations can include peacekeeping, noncombatant evacuations, hostage rescue, humanitarian intervention and attacks against terrorist groups. These types of operations fall within the scope of stability operations. Yet this is an area which has not garnered sufficient attention in terms of clearly identifying the law which applies to the conduct of those operations.

Identification of the applicable law can be further clouded by references to "policing" language when describing the types of operations. For example, referring to UN military operations as "police actions" or counterterrorist operations as "extra-territorial law enforcement"[60] does not mean such military activity is governed by a law enforcement legal framework. Those military operations would, to the extent they involve combat, be governed by the law of armed conflict regardless of whether such fighting is called a "war."[61]

Providing Clarity: Which Norms Apply?

The degree of uncertainty regarding what law applies to the wide range of international military operations falling within the scope of stability operations should raise significant concern. Whether perceived as a "gap" that must be filled, or simply a grey zone that must be clarified, the reality is that there is no clear international consensus as to what law applies to a wide range of international operations involving the use, or potential use, of armed force by State armed forces.

It is a problem often addressed by reference to the "spirit and principles" of the law of armed conflict[62] or to applying that law to all military operations as a matter of direction from national authorities.[63] While strong policy statements or national direction provides an important indication that the law of armed conflict should apply to operations outside the scope of traditional armed conflict, there is considerable room for confusion and debate, particularly in light of the continued application of human rights during armed conflict.[64]

The confusion results, in part, because of the complexity of such operations. Further, the requirement to interface with the civilian population during the conduct of many stability operations can significantly impact on the freedom to use force. For example, in terms of controlling the use of force the question will inevitably arise as to whether military forces are using force in a combat or law enforcement role. At some point the law of armed conflict as a *lex specialis* must be reconciled with the application of the norms associated with a human rights–based law enforcement framework. It is not completely clear how such reconciliation can occur if the law of armed conflict is only accepted as applying as a matter of policy or national direction.

The breadth of the potential tasks assigned to military forces under the stability operations doctrine also introduces other significant challenges. The rule of law tasks inherent in stability operations require an understanding of legal norms and standards well beyond a simple familiarity with the law of armed conflict. There has been significant debate regarding the impact of human rights norms during periods of occupation[65] and even a lack of consensus of what constitutes an occupation at law.[66] This can result in a potential broadening of situations in which the interface between occupation law and human rights may have to be considered.

To the extent the stability operations doctrine encompasses periods of occupation, that debate will continue to have relevance. However, the law of armed conflict and human rights interface might be seen to be less relevant to stability operations outside the context of occupation, although questions will continue to arise as to the impact of Common Article 3, Additional Protocol II or customary international law on human rights law during internal armed conflicts.[67] The ability to interpret and apply international human rights and host-nation laws will raise significant challenges for military commanders and their legal advisers, who likely will be more comfortable applying the law applicable to armed conflict.

Is it War or Policing?

A particular challenge for military forces is that stability operations are usually conducted among the people.[68] This interface often places those forces in the difficult situation of policing the local population in addition to fighting organized armed groups. This occurs regardless of whether those forces are operating under the legal framework of occupation during an international armed conflict or in respect to a multinational coalition effort engaged in combating the counterinsurgency in Afghanistan.

Perhaps the most graphic evidence of the unwillingness or inability of the international community to deal directly with this challenge is that neither the responsibility for, nor the conduct of, a policing function is directly addressed in the black-letter law governing occupation.[69] Perhaps the closest reference can be found in Article 43 of the 1907 Hague Regulations,[70] which provides that the occupying power "shall take all the measures in his power to restore, and ensure, as far as possible, public order and safety [civil life], while respecting, unless absolutely prevented, the laws in force in the country."[71]

The reality is that where a military force controls territory and comes in contact with the local population it may, particularly where the failing State is unable to do so, be required to perform a policing role. This occurs regardless of whether the force is operating on behalf of an occupying power, as part of a multinational coalition or at the invitation of a failing State. Reference to this policing task is found in FM 3-07 (2008), where it is noted that "[n]ormally the responsibility for establishing civil security tasks belongs to the military from the outset of operations through transition, when host-nation security and police forces assume this role."[72] This policing task can be problematic for two reasons. First, military forces may be neither trained nor equipped to perform a policing function. Secondly, performance of a policing function concurrently with ongoing operations against insurgent forces can create a complex and, at times, unclear interface between the law of armed conflict and the human rights–based norms governing policing.[73]

At this stage the international community is just coming to terms with how force should be regulated at the lower end of the conflict spectrum. One approach adopted by the Israeli High Court of Justice in the *Targeted Killing* decision[74] is a blended one based, in part, on Israeli "internal law" being applied in a law-of-armed-conflict targeting analysis which has a preference for "[a]rrest, investigation, and trial."[75] Here the domestic law requirements reflect the law enforcement norms of international human rights law in favoring capture over killing. An alternative approach is a "situation based" one which looks at the type of threat and then applies the appropriate legal regime to control the use of force by security forces. This means the law of armed conflict is applied to incidents of violence related to the armed conflict, while human rights–based law enforcement standards are applicable to policing scenarios.[76]

Whichever approach is applied, there are significant doctrine, training and operational deployment challenges for military forces. The question is not necessarily one of "targeting" or deciding when someone is taking a direct part in hostilities. For soldiers manning checkpoints or defending convoys against suicide bombers or improvised explosive devices their reaction will often be governed by self-defense rules. The inevitable restriction on the use of force in counterinsurgency operations points to an application of graduated minimum force not normally associated with armed conflict. The challenge of reacting to such threats is not helped by the present lack of clarity in the law, particularly in light of the decisions being asked of young coalition and International Security Assistance Force soldiers operating in complex security situations such as Afghanistan.

The United States and Coalition Partners: On the Leading Edge or Alone?

Having outlined a number of the doctrinal and legal challenges associated with the stability operations doctrine, there is also the question of how this US doctrine will resonate in a coalition environment. Given the likelihood that the United States will continue to conduct operations as the dominant member of international coalitions, it is evident that a common understanding among coalition partners of what stability operations are will be helpful in ensuring interoperability. Further, the military doctrine of the United States, as the major State on the international stage regarding military capability, is a significant factor in terms of developing customary international law.

In considering the approach of allied countries toward stability operations, it appears that the United States has a much more robust, well-developed and ambitious vision for such operations. For example, the Canadian Forces (CF) have no separate stability operations doctrine, although there is doctrine for CF operations generally, as well as peace support operations, humanitarian operations, disaster relief operations and noncombatant evacuation operations, that would fall under the US stability operations doctrine umbrella.[77]

As often occurs in situations where military forces are confronted with new operational challenges, Canadian doctrine appears to be driven by experiences gained at the tactical level in Afghanistan. The Canadian Army has developed two manuals that refer to stability operations.[78] The new doctrine focuses on counterinsurgency, with stability operations being addressed at the tactical level. Tactical activities comprise four parts: offensive, defensive, stability and enabling operations, thereby setting out "full-spectrum operations."[79] Stability operations are defined as "a tactical activity conducted by military and security forces, often in conjunction with other agencies to maintain, restore or establish a climate of order."[80] To the extent these manuals reflect the focus of Canadian Forces operations, it is clear this approach is not as comprehensive as that adopted by the United States.

At this stage NATO does not appear to have embraced stability operations as a separate strategic- or operational-level concept. It is perhaps telling that the 2006 *NATO Handbook* refers to the Afghanistan mission as an international peacekeeping effort.[81] One of the factors that may impact on a wider allied adoption of the term "stability operations" is found in the indication that part of the rationale for the US development of a separate stability operations doctrine may be the negative connotation attached to "peace operations." As is noted in a 2006 Congressional Research Service Issue Brief for Congress, "[p]eacekeeping has been the traditional generic term . . . . More recently, in an attempt to capture their ambiguity and complexity, and perhaps to avoid the stigma of failure attached to peacekeeping, they have become known as 'stabilization and reconstruction' operations, or more simply 'stability' operations."[82]

As a result, there may be a number of factors that may impact on the degree to which coalition partners embrace the US concept of stability operations. First, peacekeeping and other peace support operations do not necessarily have the same negative connotation outside the United States. Therefore, it may not necessarily be evident to other States why a new term is required. Second, the very "ambiguity and complexity" of such operations may cause other military forces to embrace more narrowly focused mission-specific doctrine. Third, other nations may neither be involved, nor plan to get involved, in as wide a variety of stability operations as the US doctrine appears to cover. Accordingly, potential coalition partners may continue to use separate doctrinal terms such as peace support operations or humanitarian operations. Finally, the traditional approach of State militaries in focusing on State-versus-State conflict may still be prevalent among the potential allies of the United States. This in turn may limit any acceptance that stability operations have an equal status with traditional combat operations. None of these factors will necessarily preclude the conduct of coalition operations within the wider stability operations doctrine. However, it may mean that the US military will have to be prepared to interface with coalition partners on a different level (e.g., tactical) and with terms that reflect only a partial acceptance by other States of subcomponents of the overarching stability operations doctrine.

The Future

The question remains as to whether this new doctrine is simply the latest attempt in a long history of short-lived efforts to definitively categorize unconventional conflict. While it is likely an answer to that question will only be provided with the passage of time, it is clear the US military has taken a significant step in creating the stability operations doctrine. It is an approach which seeks to break the historical reluctance to address warfare outside of State-versus-State conflict. Combined with other publications such as the counterinsurgency manual and the *Rule of Law Handbook: A Practitioner's Guide for Judge Advocates,*[83] there is evidence significant effort continues to be placed on developing doctrine and guidance that specifically addresses unique aspects of counterinsurgency operations, the dominant form of warfare in the twenty-first century.

Unfortunately, it does not appear the doctrine can point to a comprehensive, clearly articulated legal framework for such operations. Perhaps this is understandable given the inability of the international community to definitively come to grips with this challenge. This is graphically evidenced by the continued reliance on a "spirit and principles" or national-direction approach to applying the law of armed conflict to operations conducted at the lower end of the conflict spectrum. However, until clear direction on the legal framework can be provided, there is a danger such operations will be conducted at the "vanishing point" of the law of armed conflict. In this respect it could be the complexity and ambiguity inherent in the scope of stability operations doctrine that sows the seeds of its downfall.

Yet such an outcome can be avoided. The doctrine itself is visionary in that it shines a spotlight on the very type of operations that dominate the international scene today. Given the number, scope and complexity of such operations and the fact that international intervention, either under a UN mandate or otherwise, is a common occurrence, it may be time for a clear statement by States as to what law of armed conflict applies beyond general reference to Common Article 3 of the Geneva Conventions, Additional Protocol II (if it applies) or the suggested rules of the ICRC customary law study. It may very well be that the credibility of the doctrine of "stability operations," which is based upon establishing legitimacy and the rule of law, will itself be dependent on such a definitive articulation of customary norms.

As is noted in FM 3-07 (2008), intervening forces "carry with them an innate perception of legitimacy that is further strengthened by consistent performance conforming to the standards of national and international law."[84] However, unless this new doctrine is matched by an effort by individual States, and by the international community generally, to comprehensively outline the law of armed conflict that applies to conflict outside the context of inter-State warfare, and articulate how that law interfaces with the human rights norms, the ability of armed forces to conform with such legal standards may be at risk.

Notes

1. Hersch Lauterpacht, *The Problem of the Revision of the Law of War*, 29 BRITISH YEAR BOOK OF INTERNATIONAL LAW 360, 382 (1952).
2. *Id.* at 381–82.
3. Joint Doctrine Division, J-7, Joint Staff, Joint Publication 1-02, DOD Dictionary of Military and Associated Terms (as amended through 26 August 2008), *available at* http://www.dtic.mil/doctrine/jel/doddict/ (doctrine is defined as "[f]undamental principles by which the military forces or elements thereof guide their actions in support of national objectives. It is authoritative but requires judgment in application").
4. RUPERT SMITH, THE UTILITY OF FORCE: THE ART OF WAR IN THE MODERN WORLD 3–4 (2007).

5. Department of Defense, DoD Directive 3000.05, Military Support for Stability, Security, Transition, and Reconstruction (SSTR) Operations (2005), at 2, para. 3, *available at* http://www.dtic.mil/whs/directives/corres/pdf/300005p.pdf.

6. *Id.* at 2, para. 4.1.

7. *Id.* at 2, para. 4.2.

8. *Id.* at 2, paras. 4.3.1–4.3.3.

9. *Id.* at 3, para. 4.4.

10. *Id.* at 2, para. 4.3.

11. Headquarters, Department of the Army, FM 3-07, Stability Operations (2008), *available at* http://downloads.army.mil/docs/fm_3-07.pdf [hereinafter FM 3-07 (2008)].

12. Headquarters, Department of the Army, FM 3-07 (FM 100-20), Stability Operations and Support Operations (2003), *available at* http://cgsc.cdmhost.com/cgi-bin/showfile.exe?CISOROOT=/p4013coll6&CISOPTR=69&filename=70.pdf#search=%22Stability%20Operations%20and%20Support%20Operations%22 [hereinafter FM 3-07 (2003)].

13. FM 3-07 (2008), *supra* note 11, at 13, para. 1-11.

14. FM 3-07 (2003), *supra* note 12, at 1-4 (in that manual stability operations are defined also to include peace operations, foreign internal defense (e.g., counterinsurgency), security assistance, humanitarian and civic assistance, support to insurgencies and show of force).

15. *See* FM 3-07 (2008), *supra* note 11, Foreword.

16. *See* PHILIP BOBBITT, TERROR AND CONSENT: WARS FOR THE TWENTY-FIRST CENTURY 3 (2008) (In referring to the risks posed to civilians by nuclear or biological terrorism, it is noted that "these risks are in several important dimensions indistinguishable from those imposed by the terror that is the consequence of genocide and ethnic cleansing and also of metropolitan earthquakes, pandemics, tidal waves, and hurricanes").

17. FM 3-07 (2008), *supra* note 11, at 2-1, para. 2-1.

18. *Id.*

19. *See* C.E. CALDWELL, SMALL WARS: THEIR PRINCIPLES AND PRACTICE 21 (University of Nebraska Press, 3rd ed. 1996) (1906); *see also* US Marine Corps, Small Wars Manual: United States Marine Corps 1 (1940) and MAX BOOT, THE SAVAGE WARS OF PEACE: SMALL WARS AND THE RISE OF AMERICAN POWER xiv (2002).

20. *See* CHARLES W. GWYNN, IMPERIAL POLICING 3–4 (1934). (The author identifies three types of "police duties" performed by UK military forces: small wars, acting in aid of the civil power and "imperial policing." The latter type of operation occurs "when normal civil control does not exist, or has broken down to such an extent that the Army becomes the main agent for the maintenance of or for the restoration of order.").

21. *See* Josef Kunz, *The Chaotic Status of the Laws of War and the Urgent Necessity for Their Revision*, 45 AMERICAN JOURNAL OF INTERNATIONAL LAW 37, 54 n.41 (1951) (relying on a quote from P.C. JESSUP, A MODERN LAW OF NATIONS 188–89 (1948), where he also says, "It is a mistake to assume that the acceptance of the concept of an international police force . . . with its subsequent abolition of the concept of 'war' in a legal sense, eliminates the necessity for the legal regulation of the rights and duties of those who are active participants in the struggle").

22. *See* Headquarters Department of the Army and Air Force, FM 100-20/AFP 3-20, Military Operations in Low Intensity Conflict, at ch. 1 (1990) (superseded by FM 3-07 (2003), which in turn was replaced in 2008), *available at* http://www.globalsecurity.org/military/library/policy/army/fm/100-20/10020ch1.htm ("Low intensity conflict is a political-military confrontation between contending states or groups below conventional war and above the routine, peaceful competition among states. It frequently involves protracted struggles of competing principles and ideologies. Low intensity conflict ranges from subversion to the use of armed force. It is waged by

a combination of means, employing political, economic, informational, and military instruments. Low intensity conflicts are often localized, generally in the Third World, but contain regional and global security implications").

23. *See* FM 3-07 (2003), *supra* note 12, at 1-1 (where the relationship between stability operations and military operations other than war is noted as follows: "[t]he army conducts full spectrum operations to accomplish missions in both war and military operations other than war (MOOTW). Full spectrum operations include offensive, defensive, stability, and support operations . . . . Offensive and defensive operations normally dominate military operations in war, as well as some smaller scale contingencies. On the other hand, stability operations and support operations predominate in MOOTW that may include certain smaller scale contingencies and peacetime military engagements").

24. YORAM DINSTEIN, WAR, AGGRESSION AND SELF-DEFENCE 307–08 (4th ed. 2005).

25. *Id.* at 310–15 (for an explanation of non–Article 42 enforcement actions).

26. Charles C. Krulak, *The Strategic Corporal: Leadership in the Three Block War*, MARINES MAGAZINE, Jan. 1999, at 3, *available at* http://www.au.af.mil/au/awc/awcgate/usmc/strategic_corporal.htm ("Modern crisis responses are exceedingly complex endeavors. In Bosnia, Haiti and Somalia the unique challenges of military operations other than war (MOOTW) were combined with the disparate challenges of mid-intensity conflict. The Corps has described such conflicts as the three block war, contingencies in which Marines may be confronted with the entire spectrum of tactical challenges in the span of a few hours within the space of three adjacent city blocks").

27. *See* Headquarters, Department of the Army & Headquarters, Marine Corps Combat Development Command, FM 3-24/MCWP 3-33.5, Counterinsurgency (2006), at 1-8, para. 1-37, *available at* http://www.usgcoin.org/library/doctrine/COIN-FM3-24.pdf.

28. *Id.* at 1-1, para. 1-2.

29. *Id.*

30. *Id.* at 1-8, para. 1-37.

31. *Id.*

32. *Id.* at 2-5, para. 2-18 ("COIN draws heavily on a broad range of the joint force's capabilities and requires a different mix of offensive, defensive, and stability operations from that expected in major combat operations").

33. *Id.* at 1-1, para. 1-2 (emphasis added).

34. LAWRENCE A. YATES, THE US MILITARY'S EXPERIENCE IN STABILITY OPERATIONS, 1789–2005 (2006), *available at* http://www-cgsc.army.mil/carl/download/csipubs/yates.pdf.

35. *See* Daniel Smith, *World at War* (The Defense Monitor, Center for Defense Information, Washington, D.C.), Jan./Feb. 2007, http://www.cdi.org/PDFs/DM_JanFeb07.pdf.

36. Ann Scott Tyson, *Gates Criticizes Conventional Focus At Start of Iraq War*, WASHINGTON POST, Sept. 30, 2008, at A04.

37. Convention (I) for the Amelioration of the Condition of the Wounded and Sick in Armed Forces in the Field, Aug. 12, 1949, 6 U.S.T. 3114, 75 U.N.T.S. 31; Convention (II) for the Amelioration of the Condition of Wounded, Sick and Shipwrecked Members of Armed Forces at Sea, Aug. 12, 1949, 6 U.S.T. 3217, 75 U.N.T.S. 85; Convention (III) Relative to the Treatment of Prisoners of War, Aug. 12, 1949, 6 U.S.T. 3316, 75 U.N.T.S. 135; and Convention (IV) Relative to the Protection of Civilian Persons in Time of War, Aug. 12, 1949, 6 U.S.T. 3516, 75 U.N.T.S. 218 [hereinafter Fourth Geneva Convention]; all *reprinted in* DOCUMENTS ON THE LAWS OF WAR (Adam Roberts & Richard Guelff eds., 3d ed. 2000) at 197, 222, 244 and 301, respectively.

38. *See* Robert Kolb, *Origin of the Twin Terms Jus Ad Bellum/Jus in Bello*, INTERNATIONAL REVIEW OF THE RED CROSS 553, 560–62 (1997). (The terms *jus ad bellum* and *jus in bello* appear

to have first come into usage in the 1930s. Widespread use appears to have only started after World War II.).

39. IAN BROWNLIE, INTERNATIONAL LAW AND THE USE OF FORCE BY STATES 3 (1963) (in "which every sovereign entity may decide on the occasion for war").

40. CHRISTINE GRAY, INTERNATIONAL LAW AND THE USE OF FORCE 5 (2d ed. 2004).

41. *See* FM 3-07 (2008), *supra* note 11, at 1-1, para. 1-1. *See also* OXFORD ENGLISH DICTIONARY 950 (Catherine Soanes ed., 2002) ("war n. 1 a state of armed conflict between different nations, states, or armed groups. 2 a sustained contest between rivals or campaign against something undesirable: *a war on drugs. . . .*" (emphasis added)).

42. Quincy Wright, *The Outlawry of War and the Law of War*, 47 AMERICAN JOURNAL OF INTERNATIONAL LAW 365 (1953).

43. *See* Christopher Greenwood, *The Concept of War in Modern International Law*, 36 INTERNATIONAL AND COMPARATIVE LAW QUARTERLY 283, 283 (1987).

44. *See* COMMENTARY I GENEVA CONVENTION FOR THE AMELIORATION OF THE CONDITION OF THE WOUNDED AND SICK IN ARMED FORCES IN THE FIELD 32 (Jean S. Pictet ed., 1960) [hereinafter ICRC COMMENTARY]. A similar commentary was published for each of the four Geneva Conventions. Because Articles 2 and 3 are identical—or common—to each Convention, however, the commentary for these articles is also identical in each of the four commentaries. ("Any difference arising between two States and leading to the intervention of armed forces is an armed conflict within the meaning of Article 2, even if one of the Parties denies the existence of a state of war. It makes no difference how long the conflict lasts, or how much slaughter takes place.").

45. *See also* Protocol Additional (I) to the Geneva Conventions of 12 August 1949, and Relating to the Protection of Victims of International Armed Conflicts art. 3(b), June 8, 1977, 1125 U.N.T.S. 3, *reprinted in* DOCUMENTS ON THE LAWS OF WAR, *supra* note 37, at 422.

46. *See* ICRC COMMENTARY, *supra* note 44, at 38–48 (for an outline of the efforts to have the provisions of the Geneva Conventions apply to internal armed conflict). *See also* LINDSAY MOIR, THE LAW OF INTERNAL ARMED CONFLICT 23–29 (2002).

47. *See* Protocol Additional (II) to the Geneva Conventions of 12 August 1949, and Relating to the Protection of Victims of Non-International Armed Conflicts art. 1(2), June 8, 1977, 1125 U.N.T.S. 609, *reprinted in* DOCUMENTS ON THE LAWS OF WAR, *supra* note 37, at 483.

48. *See* International Humanitarian Law—Treaties & Documents, http://www.icrc.org/ihl.nsf/INTRO?OpenView (last visited Feb. 4, 2009) (where 164 countries are identified to be States party to Additional Protocol II).

49. *See* MOIR, *supra* note 46, at 101–03.

50. *See, e.g.*, the Chemical Weapons Convention; the Amended Protocol II to the Convention on Certain Conventional Weapons; the 1997 Convention on the Use, Stockpiling, Production and Transfer of Anti-Personnel Mines and on Their Destruction; the 1998 Rome Statute; and the 1999 Second Protocol to the 1954 Hague Convention for the Protection of Cultural Property.

51. *See* Prosecutor v. Tadic, Case No. IT-94-1-AR72, Appeal on Jurisdiction, para. 94 (Oct. 2, 1995), *reprinted in* 35 INTERNATIONAL LEGAL MATERIALS 32 (1996), *available at* http://www.un.org/icty/tadic/appeal/decision-e/51002.htm.

52. *See* JEAN-MARIE HENCKAERTS & LOUISE DOSWALD-BECK, CUSTOMARY INTERNATIONAL HUMANITARIAN LAW (2005) (2 volumes).

53. Legal Consequences of the Construction of a Wall in the Occupied Palestinian Territory, Advisory Opinion, 2004 I.C.J. 136 (July 9), *reprinted in* 43 INTERNATIONAL LEGAL MATERIALS

1009, 1050 (2004), *available at* http://www.icj-cij.org/docket/fil/131/1671.pdf [hereinafter Wall].

54. *Id.* (The court distinguished the terrorist threat by Palestinian groups as different than Al Qaeda attacks on the United States on the basis that Israel exercises "control" over the Occupied Territories.).

55. See GRAY, *supra* note 40, at 145–49 and DINSTEIN, *supra* note 24, at 195–96 for a discussion of the *Nicaragua* case and the issues raised by the concept of "frontier incidents."

56. Military and Paramilitary Activities (Nicar. v. U.S.), 1986 I.C.J. 14 (June 27).

57. *See* Tadic, *supra* note 51, para. 70.

58. *See* Prosecutor v. Boskoski, Case No. IT-04-82-T, Judgement, para. 176 (July 10, 2008), *available at* http://www.icty.org/x/cases/boskoski_tarculovski/tjug/en/080710.pdf.

59. Juan Carlos Abella v. Argentina, Case 11.137, Inter-Am. C.H.R., Report No. 55/97, OEA/ Ser.L./V./II.95, doc. 7 rev. 271 (1997), *reprinted in* 13 INTER-AMERICAN YEARBOOK ON HUMAN RIGHTS 602 (Inter-American Commission on Human Rights ed., 1999). This approach has been the subject of critical comment because it does not take into account the duration of the confrontation. *See* LIESBETH ZEGVELD, THE ACCOUNTABILITY OF ARMED OPPOSITION GROUPS IN INTERNATIONAL LAW 137–38 (2002).

60. DINSTEIN, *supra* note 24, at 247 (where the term "extra-territorial law enforcement" is used to describe a form of self-defense where recourse is made to cross-border counterforce against terrorists and armed bands).

61. *See* Kunz, *supra* note 21, at 54 n.41 ("It is a mistake to assume that the acceptance of the concept of an international police force . . . with its subsequent abolition of the concept of 'war' in a legal sense, eliminates the necessity for the legal regulation of the rights and duties of those who are active participants in the struggle").

62. *See* Office of the Judge Advocate General, Canadian Forces Doctrine Manual: The Law of Armed Conflict at the Operational and Tactical Level, B-GJ-005-104/FP-021 17-1, para. 1702 (2001), *available at* http://www.cfd-cdf.forces.gc.ca/sites/page-eng.asp?page=3481 (follow Law of Armed Conflict hyperlink) ("[t]oday a significant number of armed conflicts in which the CF may be involved are non-international in nature. As stated, the law applicable to such conflicts is limited. It is CF policy, however, that the CF will, as a minimum, apply the spirit and principles of the LOAC during all operations other than domestic operations") and the United Nations UN Secretary-General, Bulletin on the Observance by United Nations forces of international humanitarian law, U.N. Doc. ST/SGB/1999/13, *reprinted in* 38 INTERNATIONAL LEGAL MATERIALS 1656 (1999) (see section 1 where it is indicated the "fundamental principles and rules of international humanitarian law" are applicable in situations of armed conflict, which include "enforcement actions, or in peacekeeping operations when the use of force is permitted in self-defence"). For background to the introduction of the "spirit and principles" approach to applying humanitarian law during United Nations operations, see MOIR, *supra* note 46, at 76–77.

63. Department of Defense, Directive 2311.01E, DoD Law of War Program, para. 4.1 (2006) ("Members of the DoD Components comply with the law of war during all armed conflicts, however such conflicts are characterized, and in all other military operations").

64. Legality of the Threat or Use of Nuclear Weapons, Advisory Opinion, 1996 I.C.J. 226, para. 26 (July 8); and Wall, *supra* note 53, para. 106.

65. *See* Adam Roberts, *Prolonged Military Occupation: The Israeli-Occupied Territories Since 1967*, 84 AMERICAN JOURNAL OF INTERNATIONAL LAW 97–102 (1990).

66. *See* Adam Roberts, *What Is a Military Occupation?*, 55 BRITISH YEAR BOOK OF INTERNATIONAL LAW 249, 250 (1984) ("[o]ne might hazard as a fair rule of thumb that every time the

armed forces of a country are in control of foreign territory, and find themselves face to face with the inhabitants, some or all of the provisions of the law on occupations are applicable").

67. *See* MOIR, *supra* note 46, at 193–231 (for a discussion of the interface between law of armed conflict (Common Article 3 and Additional Protocol II) and human rights law).

68. *See* SMITH, *supra* note 4, at 3–4; and FM 3-07 (2008), *supra* note 11, at 1-2, para. 1-8 (for reference to war among the people).

69. The Fourth Geneva Convention does recognize the continuance in force of the laws of the occupied territory and the maintenance of the status of public officials or judges.

70. Convention No. IV Respecting the Laws and Customs of War on Land and its Annex: Regulations Concerning the Laws and Customs of War on Land, Oct. 18, 1907, 36 Stat. 2277, T.S. No. 539, *reprinted in* DOCUMENTS ON THE LAWS OF War, *supra* note 37, at 69.

71. Annex, *supra* note 70, art. 43. The reference here to "civil life" comes from the French version, which some have suggested was incorrectly phrased as "safety" in the first English translation. *See* EYAL BENVENISTI, THE INTERNATIONAL LAW OF OCCUPATION 7 n.1 (2004) (relying on E.H. Schwenk, *Legislative Power of the Military Occupant under Article 43, Hague Regulations*, 54 YALE LAW JOURNAL 393 (1945)).

72. *See* FM 3-07 (2008), *supra* note 11, at 2-10 to 2-11, para. 2-46.

73. *See* Kenneth Watkin, *Controlling the Use of Force: A Role for Human Rights Norms in Contemporary Armed Conflict*, 98 AMERICAN JOURNAL OF INTERNATIONAL LAW 1, 24–30 (2004).

74. *See* Public Committee Against Torture in Israel et al. v. Government of Israel et al., HCJ 769/02, Judgement (Dec. 13, 2006), *available at* http://elyon1.court.gov.il/files_eng/02/690/007/a34/02007690.a34.pdf.

75. *Id.*, para. 40.

76. Kenneth Watkin, *Maintaining Law and Order during Occupation: Breaking the Normative Chains*, 41 ISRAEL LAW REVIEW 175, 192–95 (2008).

77. *See* CF Doctrine Hierarchy, *available at* http://www.cfd-cdf.forces.gc.ca/websites/Resources/dgfda/Joint%20Doctrine%20Hierarchy/doctrineHierarchy.gif.

78. Land Operations, B-GL-300-001/FP-000 (Jan. 1, 2008) [hereinafter Land Operations Manual]; and Counter-Insurgency Operations, B-GL-323-004/FP-003 (Dec. 13, 2008).

79. Land Operations Manual, *supra* note 78, at 3-18 to 3-20.

80. *Id.* at 3-18.

81. PUBLIC DIPLOMACY DIVISION, NATO HANDBOOK 155 (2006).

82. Nina M. Serafino, Congressional Research Service, *Peacekeeping and Related Stability Operations: Issues of U.S. Military Involvement*, No. IB94040 (2006), *available at* http://www.fas.org/sgp/crs/natsec/IB94040.pdf.

83. Center for Law and Military Operations, The Judge Advocate General's Legal Center School & Joint Force Judge Advocate, United States Joint Forces Command, Rule of Law Handbook: Practitioner's Guide for Judge Advocates i–ii (July 2007) (see *id.* at ii where it is stressed the Handbook "is not intended to serve as US policy or military doctrine for rule of law operations. [Center for Law and Military Operations] has neither the resources, nor more importantly the mission, to propose or institute doctrine on a topic upon which no consensus has been achieved." However, it is also noted, *id.* at i, that military lawyers have been engaged in rule of law projects since the invasion of Afghanistan in 2001 and "have been on the cutting edge of the effort to bring stability and rule of law support to the embryonic and fragile democratic governments in both Afghanistan and Iraq. . . .").

84. FM 3-07 (2008), *supra* note 11, at 1-7, para. 1-32.

XVII

The International Legal Framework for Stability Operations: When May International Forces Attack or Detain Someone in Afghanistan?

Marco Sassòli*

I. Introduction

Whether we call the involvement of international forces in Afghanistan assistance to the Afghan government or a peace operation, a stability operation, part of the "war on terror," an armed conflict, a foreign occupation or a love affair, and whatever the legal basis of such involvement may be, two of the most important tactical and humanitarian issues confronting international forces are when they may attack or detain an "enemy." Concerning detention, the key issues are on what legal basis and according to what procedure the decision to arrest and detain may be taken. Two branches of international law govern attack and detention: international humanitarian law (IHL) (or the law of armed conflict) and international human rights law (IHRL). For both branches, first, a question of applicability arises: IHRL applies in every circumstance and to everyone, but are the armed forces of States bound by IHRL when acting outside their national territories? As for IHL, it certainly applies to armed forces acting extraterritorially, but

* Professor of International Law at the University of Geneva, Switzerland, and Associate Professor at the universities of Quebec in Montreal and of Laval, Canada. This article will also be published in volume 39 of the *Israel Yearbook on Human Rights* (forthcoming 2009).

it applies only to armed conflicts and its rules on the issues of attack and detention are probably different in international and non-international armed conflicts. Second, when applicable, for both IHL and IHRL the question arises as to when they allow (or rather, do not prohibit) international forces to deprive enemies of their life or their liberty. Third, if both branches apply and lead to differing results on the two issues, we must determine which of the two prevails.

In this article, I will try to discuss these three questions, putting the emphasis on the substance of the rules, as others in this volume have extensively discussed the classification of the conflict(s) in Afghanistan under IHL.

When I refer to the "enemies" who may or may not be attacked or detained under the rules to be discussed, I will call them "fighters." Who may be attacked or detained for what reasons is obviously one of the questions with which the legal framework must deal; even if the answer to that legal question were clear, one of the greatest practical difficulties would remain: to identify whether someone belongs to those categories. However, this article does not deal with thieves, with harmless civilians who may become incidental victims of attacks or are mistakenly targeted, or with civilians who oppose the government or the international presence without using force. These people are obviously covered by the rules to be explored, but they are not the hard cases and IHL and IHRL do not prescribe differing rules on them. The same is true for attacks directed against people who actually attack international forces while they are engaged in such attacks. The difficult cases, with regard to the legality of attacks and the legal basis for their detention, are persons whom international forces believe to be members of armed groups, such as Al Qaeda and the Taliban. I will explain why I consider that mere membership in such groups is not sufficient, but that the person must also have a fighting function to be a legitimate target of attack.[1]

II. Applicability of IHL to the Situation in Afghanistan

It is uncontroversial that in 2008 the level of violence and the degree of organization of the Taliban and, at least in Afghanistan, of Al Qaeda are sufficiently high to make IHL applicable, even if the higher requirements of intensity and organization of the parties of IHL of non-international armed conflicts are applied.[2] The United States agrees, indeed, that the conflict between the Taliban and the Afghan government is not of an international character and that this characterization is not altered by the fact that the latter is heavily supported (if not kept alive) by international forces. The only construction under which the entire conflict in Afghanistan could still (in 2008) be claimed to be of an international character would be to recall that the conflict was indeed international in 2001 because it was fought between the United States and the Taliban (who constituted the de facto government of Afghanistan) and to consider that this conflict continues until the defeat of the Taliban. Most, including the International Committee of the Red Cross (ICRC), consider that the international conflict turned into a conflict not of an international character in 2002 when the Karzai government was first appointed by the *Loya Jirga*[3] and then elected (since this new government of Afghanistan requested the foreign forces to support its continuing fight against the Taliban). Formally, however, one could consider that, until the Taliban are completely defeated, the conflict between the United States and the Taliban maintains its international character and the United States (or the UN Security Council) could not have altered this classification by establishing, recognizing or concluding agreements with a new local government in the territory it occupied following its invasion.[4] However, this is certainly not the thesis of the United States and it encounters different legal problems, *inter alia*, that it is difficult to consider free elections a change introduced by the occupying power, that the UN Security Council has given its blessing to the new arrangements and that UN Security Council resolutions prevail over any other international obligation under Article 103 of the UN Charter.

The United States argues, however, that beside the non-international armed conflict against the Taliban, a separate international armed conflict exists: the "war on terror" against Al Qaeda and its associates.

As far as treaty law is concerned, international armed conflicts are mainly governed by the Geneva Conventions and Additional Protocol I.[5] Neither the United States nor Afghanistan is a party to Protocol I, but they are bound by the many rules of the latter that correspond to customary international law. The Geneva Conventions apply to international armed conflicts. Common Article 2 to the Conventions states that they "shall apply to all cases of declared war or of any other armed conflict which may arise between two or more of the High Contracting Parties." Only States can be parties to the Conventions. Al Qaeda is not a State. Therefore, the Conventions do not apply to a conflict between the United States and its allies, on the one hand, and this non-State actor, on the other hand. As for customary international law, there is no indication confirming what seems to be the view of the US administration, i.e., that the concept of international armed conflict under customary international law is broader.[6] State practice and *opinio juris* do not apply the law of international armed conflict to conflicts between States and certain non-State actors. On the contrary, and in conformity with the tenets of the Westphalian system, States have always distinguished between conflicts against one another, to which the whole of IHL applied, and other armed conflicts, to which they were never prepared to apply those same rules, but only more limited humanitarian rules.

III. The Applicability of International Human Rights Law

1. Does International Human Rights Law Apply Extraterritorially?

International forces in Afghanistan do not act in their own territories. They are therefore bound by IHRL only if its obligations bind a State even when acting beyond that State's territory. Article 1 of both the American Convention on Human Rights and the European Convention on Human Rights (ECHR) clearly state that the State parties must secure the rights listed in those Conventions to everyone within their jurisdictions. Under the jurisprudence of the European Court of Human Rights (ECtHR) this includes an occupied territory.[7]

On the universal level, under the International Covenant on Civil and Political Rights (ICCPR) a party undertakes "to respect and to ensure to all individuals within its territory *and* subject to its jurisdiction the rights recognized . . ." (my emphasis). This wording and the negotiating history lean toward understanding territory and jurisdiction as cumulative conditions.[8] The United States and Israel therefore deny that the Covenant is applicable extraterritorially.[9] The International Court of Justice (ICJ),[10] the UN Human Rights Committee[11] and other States[12] are however of the opinion that the Covenant equally applies in an occupied territory.[13] From a teleological point of view it would indeed be astonishing that persons whose rights can neither be violated nor protected by the territorial State lose any protection of their fundamental rights against the State who can actually violate and protect their rights.

2. How Much Control Is Necessary to Be under the Jurisdiction of a Foreign State?

If IHRL applies extraterritorially, the next question that arises is when a person can be considered to be under the jurisdiction of a State. Analysis of this issue—the level of control a State must exercise in order to be bound by its international human rights obligations—has often been divided according to treaty. However, there has been a certain amount of convergence in the interpretation of jurisdiction in recent cases.[14] The Inter-American Court of Human Rights and the Inter-American Commission on Human Rights have tended to adopt broad views of what may give rise to a State having extraterritorial jurisdiction. The widely cited case of *Alejandre v. Cuba* illustrates that physical control over territory exercised through having "boots on the ground" is not necessary for jurisdiction to arise in the Inter-American system. In that case, the Commission held that the applicants came within Cuban jurisdiction when Cuba's airplanes fired on another airplane flying in international airspace.[15]

As for the European Court of Human Rights, from its strictest test articulated in *Bankovic*—that a State must exercise effective control over territory by being physically present on that territory in order to have jurisdiction[16]—the ECtHR has moved, over the past decade, to applying a standard that does not always require "boots on the ground." In *Issa*, the ECtHR looked for effective territorial control. It found, on the facts, that Turkish forces in northern Iraq did not exhibit that level of control and therefore, in its decision on the merits, held that in fact the Iraqi applicants' claim was inadmissible.[17] In a very recent case, however, the ECtHR has held that jurisdiction can flow from facts not unlike those in *Alejandre v. Cuba* (or indeed, in *Bankovic*). *Pad v. Turkey* involved a skirmish on the Turkish-Iranian border in which seven Iranians were killed by Turkish helicopter gunships. The Court held that

> it is not required to determine the exact location of the impugned events, given that the Government had already admitted that the fire discharged from the helicopters had caused the killing of the applicants' relatives. . . . Accordingly, the Court finds that the victims of the impugned events were within the jurisdiction of Turkey at the material time.[18]

This conclusion is clearly at variance with *Bankovic*, where, as one commentator put it, "the Court found that jurisdiction could not arise by the mere fact of dropping bombs on individuals."[19] It would be specious if, in the future, the Court were to distinguish *Pad* exclusively on the grounds that Turkey had not formally contested that it had jurisdiction over the applicants' relatives.

Conceivably, for all treaties, jurisdiction could arise through a State's extraterritorial exercise of control over persons. However, it seems likely that courts will at times also look for effective control over territory. The factors identified by the ECtHR in *Issa* as indicators of such control were (1) the number of soldiers on the ground, (2) the size of the area controlled, (3) the degree of control exercised (i.e., whether checkpoints, etc. were established) and (4) the duration of the exercise of control.[20] The first and third factors are valid indicators to measure something as nebulous as "control"; however, with all due respect to the Court, the second and fourth factors bring little to the analysis. All other things being equal, it is difficult to imagine why it would make a difference whether foreign forces controlled a vast area or only a village. The fourth factor, the duration of control, may be helpful for a Court reviewing actions long after the fact, but it fails to provide States and their forces or agents with a clear indication of when they begin to be responsible for respecting (and possibly even protecting) the human rights of the people in their care.

In my view, a solution could be found through a functional approach, distinguishing the degree of control necessary according to the right to be protected.[21] Such an approach would reconcile the object and purpose of human rights to protect everyone with the need not to bind States by guarantees they cannot deliver outside their territories and the protection of the sovereignty of the territorial State (which may be encroached upon by international forces protecting human rights against anyone other than themselves). For our two issues, this functional approach would mean that international forces have to respect the right to life of a person simply by omitting to attack that person as soon as those forces could affect that right by their attack, while they would have to respect the procedural guarantees inherent in the right to personal freedom only as long as they physically detain the person. The applicability of IHRL obviously does not yet determine whether its guarantees or those of IHL prevail in a given situation. All on the contrary, the *lex specialis* issue only arises if both branches apply to a certain situation.

3. What If Jurisdiction Is Shared by Different Coalition Partners and a Host Government?

If IHRL applies extraterritorially, even if we knew exactly what degree of control is necessary to put someone under the jurisdiction of a State, in the case of coalition operations such as those in Afghanistan additional questions arise. Can the degree of control necessary to exercise jurisdiction result from cumulative contributions by different States, including the host State? In such a case, does every contributing State have jurisdiction? These questions have been raised but not exhaustively examined before the ECtHR. In *Hussein v. Albania et al.*, the Court held that the applicant, Saddam Hussein, had failed to furnish sufficient proof that the respondent States had control over Iraq or over him at the time of his detention (or arrest) from which jurisdiction would flow.[22] The Court seemed to suggest that jurisdiction would not automatically exist for States participating in a "coalition with the US, when the impugned actions were carried out by the US, when security in the zone in which those actions took place was assigned to the US and when the overall command of the coalition was vested in the US."[23] Given the last-mentioned specificities, there is no *prima facie* reason to exclude that collective control could suffice to establish jurisdiction. A case that provides more guidance on this issue is *Hess v. United Kingdom*, which dealt with an application by Rudolph Hess' wife for his release from Spandau Prison. At the relevant time, the prison was under the control of the four Allied powers in Germany following the Second World War. The European Commission on Human Rights, in determining whether the prison came within the UK's jurisdiction, accepted *a priori* the premise that the ECHR could apply to the activities of British forces in Berlin. However, it took into account the fact that decision-making power regarding the prison was by unanimous agreement between all four Allied powers. As such, it held that:

> . . . the United Kingdom acts only as a partner in the joint responsibility which it shares with the three other Powers. The Commission is of the opinion that the joint authority cannot be divided into four separate jurisdictions and that therefore the United Kingdom's participation in the exercise of the joint authority and consequently in the administration and supervision of Spandau Prison is not a matter "within the jurisdiction" of the United Kingdom, within the meaning of Art. 1 of the Convention.[24]

This holding would seem to exclude the possibility of jurisdiction flowing from collective control during a multilateral operation. However, as one author has observed, the Commission was particularly troubled by the lack of executive decision-making power of the UK in regard to the prison.[25] Logically, if a State participating in a multilateral operation nevertheless retains executive decision-making power over its forces and personnel, there is no reason to deny jurisdiction.

Moreover, any agreement between States participating in a multilateral operation affecting that kind of decision-making power could run afoul of a State's obligations. In *Hess*, the Commission wrote:

> The conclusion by the respondent Government of an agreement concerning Spandau prison of the kind in question in this case *could raise an issue under the Convention* if it were entered into when the Convention was already in force for the respondent Government. The agreement concerning the prison, however, came into force in 1945.[26]

On the two issues dealt with in this article, I conclude as follows. No contributing State may make a deliberate causal contribution to a violation of the right to life of any person. However, a contributing State that is not an occupying power does not exercise the level of jurisdiction over a person that would oblige it to protect that person's right to life against other coalition partners or the host State.[27] Applying this reasoning to Afghanistan, the coalition and the Afghan authorities collectively exercise effective control, but, for the international coalition partners, this does not give rise to the positive obligations associated with the right to life (i.e., to protect it against third parties). The responsibility for ensuring the respect of that aspect of the right to life remains with the Afghan government, which, to give effect to it, may have a due diligence obligation regarding the conduct of coalition forces. As for detainees, even a State which is not an occupying power must offer any person it actually detains, independently of whether it also arrested that person or not,[28] the rights that detainee has during that phase of detention; however, such rights may also be respected by measures actually taken by another coalition partner or the host State.

In my view, the same analysis must be made when different coalition partners and a host State are bound by differing treaty obligations. Every State has to comply with its own obligations concerning its own contribution. In addition, a State actually detaining a person must protect the rights of that person even against States not bound to grant such rights.

4. Who Could Proceed to Admissible Derogations?

Under normal circumstances, a State's ability to derogate from its obligations under human rights treaties is limited to situations in which the security of the State itself is in jeopardy.[29] Can this requirement be met when a State's forces are involved in a multilateral operation abroad? Lord Bingham of Cornhill wrote in *Al-Jedda* that the power to derogate

> may only be exercised in time of war or other public emergency threatening the life of the nation seeking to derogate, and only then to the extent strictly required by the exigencies of the situation. . . . It is hard to think that these conditions could ever be met when a state had chosen to conduct an overseas peacekeeping operation, however dangerous the conditions, from which it could withdraw.[30]

Lord Bingham went on to add: "The Secretary of State does not contend that the UK could exercise its power to derogate in Iraq (although he does not accept that it could not)."[31]

In my view, one cannot simultaneously hold a State accountable because it has a certain level of control abroad and deny it the possibility to derogate because there is no emergency on that State's own territory. An emergency on the territory where the State has a certain limited control must be sufficient.

5. What Is the Impact of a UN Mandate?

Normally, the legality or illegality of an exercise of jurisdiction does not matter for the applicability of IHRL.[32] No one denies that human rights most typically apply to the most lawful exercise of jurisdiction: territorial jurisdiction. The ECtHR held that the responsibility of a State also arose "when as a consequence of military action—*whether lawful or unlawful*—it exercises effective control of an area outside its national territory."[33] Theoretically, UN Security Council resolutions could, under Article 103 of the UN Charter, prevail over IHRL obligations of States (however, the extent to which they may do so is controversial). In my view, any derogation from IHRL by the UN Security Council must, however, be explicit. In *Al-Jedda*, the UK House of Lords considered that UN Security Council Resolution 1546, authorizing "internment where . . . necessary for imperative reasons of security" qualified the UK's obligations under Article 5 of the ECHR.[34] In my view, the wording of this Resolution is not explicit enough to be considered a mandate to UN member States not to provide such internees with the procedural guarantees they are obliged to offer under IHRL. In any case, the UN Security Council resolutions concerning Afghanistan contain no language similar to that of Resolution 1546 which could be claimed to govern the admissible reasons of detention.

In my view, UN Security Council resolutions must be interpreted whenever possible in a manner compatible with the rest of international law. The mandate of the Security Council to maintain international peace and security includes the authorization of the use of force. How such force may be used is, however, governed by other branches of international law, including IHRL. No one would claim that a UN Security Council resolution urging States to prevent acts of terrorism implicitly authorizes torture or summary executions. Beyond that, it is often argued that even the Security Council must comply with *ius cogens*[35] and the human rights discussed here belong to *ius cogens.*

A distinct question relates to situations where foreign forces are participating in a peace operation in a way that their acts can be attributed only to the United Nations. A much-criticized recent judgment suggests that in such a case the sending State will not have jurisdiction for the purposes of its obligations under human rights treaties.[36] Indeed, this judgment runs counter to explicit statements by States and to practice.[37] In my view, here as elsewhere, everything depends on the facts. It may well be that a State contributes troops to a peace operation in such a way that it no longer has control over what those troops do and that the exclusive command and control is with the UN, with another international organization or with a third State. In fact, this is the situation the drafters envisaged in Articles 43–47 of the UN Charter, which have remained a dead letter. In reality, contributing States retain a very large degree of control over their forces. Everyone familiar with ISAF in Afghanistan knows of the national caveats discussed in other contributions to this volume. If UN Security Council resolutions and NATO rules allow a contributing State to opt out of a certain kind of operation, out of any given operation or out of certain methods to implement them, that State has enough control over the acts of its own troops to be responsible for their conformity with its human rights obligations. The case of joint control by a State and an international organization can be dealt with similarly to the case of joint control by several States.[38] However, a member State of an organization has a continuing responsibility to ensure that an organization, to which it delegates conduct that may have implications in terms of human rights, complies with the corresponding standards.[39]

IV. The Substantive Rules of International Humanitarian Law

1. On Attacks

a) The Traditional Answer of Humanitarian Law of International Armed Conflicts
In international armed conflicts, members of armed forces belonging to a party to the conflict are combatants. Combatants may be attacked at any time until they surrender or are otherwise *hors de combat*, and not only while actually threatening the enemy. Combatants are part of the military potential of the enemy and it is therefore always lawful to attack them for the purpose of weakening that potential. Beside combatants, civilians, too, may be attacked, but only for such time as they directly participate in hostilities.[40] The traditional understanding is that no rule restricts the use of force against combatants to only those circumstances when they cannot be captured. Within IHL, this view has been challenged based on the principle of military necessity as a restriction on all violence[41] and the prohibition of treacherous killings.[42] However, neither of these understandings has been translated into actual battlefield instructions, and even less into actual battlefield behavior.[43]

Even attacks directed at combatants are subject to the proportionality principle, but in IHL this principle protects only civilians incidentally affected[44] and does not require a proportionality evaluation between the harm inflicted on the combatant and the military advantage drawn from the attack. The same is true for precautionary measures in attack, which must only be taken for the benefit of the civilian population.

b) The Uncertain Answer of the Treaty Rules of IHL of Non-international Armed Conflicts
In contradistinction to international armed conflicts, it is not clear under the treaty law of non-international armed conflicts when an enemy fighter may be attacked. Indeed, neither Article 3 common to the Geneva Conventions nor Protocol II refers to "combatants" because States did not want to confer on anyone in non-international armed conflicts the right to participate in hostilities and the corresponding combatant immunity. Those provisions prohibit "violence to life and person, in particular murder," directed against "persons taking no active part in hostilities," including those who have ceased to take part in hostilities.[45] Specifically addressing the conduct of hostilities, Article 13 of Protocol II prohibits attacks against civilians "unless and for such time as they take a direct part in hostilities."[46]

One may deduce from these rules, and from the absence of any mention of "combatants," that everyone is a civilian in a non-international armed conflict and that no one may be attacked unless he or she directly participates in hostilities. However, first, it would be astonishing that Article 13 uses the term "civilian" instead of a broader term such as "person."[47] Second, if everyone is a civilian, the principle of distinction, which is a fundamental principle of IHL, becomes meaningless and impossible to apply.[48] Third, Common Article 3 confers its protection on "persons taking no active part in hostilities, including members of armed forces who have laid down their arms or are otherwise hors de combat." The latter part of the phrase suggests that for such members of armed forces[49] it is not sufficient to no longer take an active part in hostilities to be immune from attack. They must take additional steps and actively disengage. Fourth, on a more practical level, to prohibit government forces from attacking clearly identified fighters unless the latter engage government forces is militarily unrealistic as it would oblige them to act purely reactively while facilitating hit-and-run operations by the rebel group. These arguments may therefore lead to the conclusion of the ICRC *Commentary* to Protocol II that "[t]hose belonging to armed forces or armed groups may be attacked at any time."[50]

This conclusion that fighters may be attacked, as in international armed conflicts, at any time, until they disengage from the armed group, may be reconciled with the text of the treaty provisions in two ways. First, "direct participation in hostilities" can be understood to encompass the simple fact of remaining a member of the group[51] or of keeping a fighting function.[52] Second, fighters can be considered not to be "civilians" (benefiting from the protection against attacks unless and for such time as they directly participate in hostilities).[53]

However, this conclusion raises difficult questions in practice. How do government forces determine membership in an armed group while the individual in question does not commit hostile acts? How can membership in the armed group be distinguished from simple affiliation with a party to the conflict for which the group is fighting—in other words, membership in the political, educational or humanitarian wing of a rebel movement? In my view, one of the most convincing avenues is to allow attacks only against a person who either actually directly participates in hostilities or has a function within the armed group to commit acts that constitute direct participation in the hostilities.[54]

c) No Answer Is Provided to the Question by Customary Humanitarian Law

According to the ICRC study, *Customary International Humanitarian Law* (ICRC Customary Law Study), in both international and non-international armed conflicts, "[a]ttacks may only be directed against combatants."[55] The definition of the term "combatant" offered for non-international armed conflicts makes this rule, however, rather circular, if it simply "indicat[es] persons who do not enjoy the protection against attacks accorded to civilians."[56] Other rules of that Study indicate that "[c]ivilians are protected against attack unless and for such time as they take a direct part in hostilities"[57] and civilians are defined as "persons who are not members of the armed forces."[58] The commentary to the rules must however admit that while "State armed forces may be considered combatants . . . practice is not clear as to the situation of members of armed opposition groups,"[59] but rather "ambiguous as to whether . . . [they] are considered members of armed forces or civilians."[60] If they are the latter, an imbalance between such groups and governmental armed forces could be avoided by considering them to take a direct part in hostilities continuously.[61] Customary law is therefore as ambiguous as the treaty provisions on the crucial question whether fighters in non-international armed conflicts may be attacked in the same way as combatants in international armed conflicts.

d) Arguments for and against an Analogous Application of the Rule Applicable in International Armed Conflicts

The general tendency is to bring the law of non-international armed conflicts closer to that of international armed conflicts, which has also the positive side effect of rendering largely moot controversies on whether a given conflict, such as the conflict against Al Qaeda in Afghanistan, is international or non-international and on what law to apply in conflicts of a mixed nature. In the last twenty years, the jurisprudence of international criminal tribunals, the influence of human rights law and even some treaty rules adopted by States have brought the law of non-international armed conflicts closer to the law of international armed conflicts. In the many fields where the treaty rules still differ, this convergence has been rationalized by claiming that under customary international law, the differences between the two categories of conflicts have gradually disappeared. This development has reached its provisional acme with the publication of the ICRC Customary Law Study, which claims, after ten years of research on "State practice" (in the form of official declarations rather than actual behavior), that 136 (and arguably even 141) out of 161 rules of customary humanitarian law—many of which parallel rules of Protocol I, applicable as a treaty to international armed conflicts—apply equally to non-international armed conflicts.[62] Even those who remain skeptical whether State practice has truly eliminated the difference to the extent claimed suggest that questions not answered by the law of non-international armed conflicts must be dealt with by analogy to the law of international armed conflicts, except if the very nature of non-international armed conflicts does not allow for such an analogy (e.g., concerning combatant immunity from prosecution and the concept of occupied territories).[63] There is, in addition, no real difference between the non-international armed conflict between the United States and the Taliban today and the international armed conflict between those same two parties in 2001. To require soldiers in the former conflicts to capture enemies whenever this is feasible (but not in the latter) is unrealistic on the battlefield. In addition, the decision when an enemy may be shot at must be taken by every soldier on the ground in a split second and cannot be left to commanders and courts (as can the decision to intern a person, discussed later). Clear instructions must exist. Whenever possible, the training of soldiers must be the same in view of international and non-international armed conflicts in order to create automatisms that work under the stress of the battle.

On the other hand, strong arguments call into question the appropriateness of applying the same rules as in international armed conflicts. Many non-international armed conflicts are fought against or between groups that are not well structured. It is much more difficult to determine who belongs to an armed group than who belongs to governmental armed forces. Persons join and quit armed groups in an informal way, while members in governmental armed forces are incorporated and formally dismissed. As armed groups are inevitably illegal, they will do their best not to appear as such. Claiming that fighters may be shot at on sight may therefore put many civilians in danger,[64] whether they are sympathizers of the group, are members of the "political wing," belong to the same ethnic group or simply happen to be in the wrong place at the wrong time. In addition, while in international armed conflicts a clear distinction exists between law enforcement by the police against civilians and conduct of hostilities by combatants against combatants, there is no equivalent clear distinction in non-international armed conflicts.

In conclusion, neither the rules nor the context of IHL of non-international armed conflicts provides a clear answer to the question when an enemy fighter may be attacked.

2. On Detention

a) The Traditional Answer of Humanitarian Law of International Armed Conflict

In peacetime as during armed conflict, persons may be detained in view of a trial for a crime or based upon conviction of a crime. What is more specific to armed conflicts is that enemies may also be interned without criminal charge as a preventative security measure. In international armed conflicts this is the essence of prisoner-of-war (POW) status. Prisoners of war may be interned without any further procedure until the end of active hostilities.[65] IHL equally allows for internment of a civilian "if the security of the Detaining Power makes it absolutely necessary"[66] or "for imperative reasons of security";[67] however, it requires an assessment to determine if a civilian poses a threat to security. Thus, Convention IV mandates procedures to be followed for reviewing the internment of civilians, whether they are aliens in the territory of a party to the conflict or interned in occupied territory, designating the type of review body—either an administrative board or court—and providing for appeal and periodic review.[68] Finally, it should be noted that unlawful confinement is a grave breach of Convention IV.[69]

b) The Uncertain Answer of Conventional Humanitarian Law of Non-international Armed Conflicts

Conventional IHL applicable to non-international armed conflict prescribes how persons deprived of liberty for reasons related to the armed conflict must be treated and it prescribes judicial guarantees for those who are prosecuted for offenses relating to the conflict (such as individual non-State actor participation in the conflict, which always constitutes a crime under the domestic law of the State affected by the conflict), but it does not clarify under which circumstances and by which procedures a person may be interned for security reasons. Yet the drafters of Protocol II recognized the possibility of internment taking place in non-international armed conflicts, as demonstrated by the specific reference to internment in Articles 5 and 6.[70]

c) Customary Humanitarian Law

According to the ICRC Study, based upon State practice, which obviously cannot be divided into practice under IHL, and practice under IHRL, customary IHL prohibits the arbitrary deprivation of liberty in both international and non-international armed conflicts.[71] This rule is interpreted through significant reference to IHRL. Applying the two prongs of the principle of legality, the Study states that the basis for internment must be previously established by law and stipulates two procedural requirements: (1) an "obligation to inform a person who is arrested of the reasons for arrest" and (2) an "obligation to provide a person deprived of liberty with an opportunity to challenge the lawfulness of detention," described as the "so-called writ of *habeas corpus*."[72] When trying, as I am attempting to do in this contribution, to determine whether IHL or IHRL regulates a certain issue, a "customary IHL rule" based on IHRL obviously does not provide a useful starting point for determining the *lex specialis*.

d) Apply IHL of International Armed Conflicts by Analogy?

IHL of non-international armed conflicts indicates that internment occurs in non-international armed conflict,[73] but it contains no indication of how it is to be regulated. Such regulation is necessary so that internment can practically take place.

One could therefore apply IHL of international armed conflict to non-international armed conflicts by way of analogy.[74] For members of an armed group with a fighting function captured by international forces in Afghanistan, the closest possible analogy with the regulation of international armed conflicts appears to be with POWs, who may be detained without any legal procedure until the end of active hostilities.[75] The ICRC Customary Law Study indicates the appropriateness of applying by analogy the standards of Convention III to those designated as "combatants" in non-international armed conflict.[76] Most arguments in favor of and against such an analogy are similar to those mentioned above in relation with the admissibility to attack fighters. Some arguments are, however, specific to the detention issue. In favor of POW treatment, it must be mentioned that Article 3 of Convention III encourages parties to non-international armed conflicts "to bring into force by special agreements, all or part of the other provisions of the present Convention." If the parties so agree, they could therefore apply the rules of Convention III to fighters, which do not require any individual procedure to decide upon the internment. As special agreements to the detriment of war victims are void under IHL,[77] application of POW status is therefore not considered as detrimental to fighters. Even without an agreement, a government could obtain the same result, i.e., POW status of fighters, by resuscitating the concept of recognition of the belligerency of an armed group, which concept has fallen into disuse.[78]

Arguments against this analogy are, first, that upon arrest, as at the moment of an attack, it is more difficult to identify fighters than soldiers of armed forces of another State. After an attack, an erroneous decision cannot be corrected, because either the member of international forces who erroneously did not attack is dead or the person who was erroneously attacked is dead. After an arrest, however, the correct classification can be made by a tribunal, which will only have its say if the arrested person is not classified as a POW.[79] Second, while in international armed conflicts POWs must be released and repatriated at the end of active hostilities, that moment in time is more difficult to determine in a non-international armed conflict[80] and repatriation is logically impossible in non-international armed conflicts. Even when the end of active hostilities is determined, no obligation for a government to release rebels at that moment exists in IHL.[81]

It has been suggested elsewhere that even for enemy fighters, the analogy should be made with the regime established for civilians to be interned for imperative security reasons rather than with the regime of POWs.[82] Indeed, the rules applicable to international armed conflict generally apply only to protected-person categories, such as POWs or civilians, while no such categories exist in non-international armed conflict and what counts is each individual's conduct. The precise nature of that conduct can only be established through a procedure. We had to admit that "the practicality of this approach, however, does not make it legally binding."[83]

V. The Substantive Rules of International Human Rights Law

1. On Attacks

Human rights treaties prohibit arbitrary deprivation of life. Most of them do not specify when a killing is arbitrary. Only the ECHR specifies that not to be arbitrary, the killing must be "absolutely necessary:

"a. in defence of any person from unlawful violence;

"b. in order to effect a lawful arrest or to prevent the escape of a person lawfully detained;

"c. in action lawfully taken for the purpose of quelling a riot or insurrection."[84]

In its case law, outside of armed conflicts, the ECtHR has admitted the lawfulness of killing a person whom authorities genuinely thought was about to detonate a bomb, but found the insufficient planning of the operation to violate the right to life.[85] By and large, other human rights bodies take the same approach.[86] The UN Basic Principles on the Use of Force and Firearms by Law Enforcement Officials provide an authoritative interpretation of the principles authorities must respect when using force in order not to infringe the right to life. Those principles limit the use of firearms to cases of self-defense or defense of others against the imminent threat of death or serious injury, of prevention of the perpetration of a particularly serious crime involving grave threat to life, of arrest of a person presenting such a danger and resisting the law enforcement official's authority, or of prevention of his or her escape, and only when less extreme means are insufficient to achieve these objectives.

The intentional lethal use of firearms is only admissible "when strictly unavoidable in order to protect life." In addition, law enforcement officials

> shall . . . give a clear warning of their intent to use firearms, with sufficient time for the warning to be observed, unless to do so would unduly place the law enforcement officials at risk or would create a risk of death or serious harm to other persons, or would be clearly inappropriate or pointless in the circumstances of the incident.[87]

It must however be stressed that the Basic Principles are addressed to officers "who exercise police powers, especially the powers of arrest or detention." Military authorities are included, but only if they exercise police powers,[88] which could be interpreted as meaning, *e contrario*, that the rules do not bind military authorities engaged in the conduct of hostilities.

Theoretically, IHRL is the same in international, in non-international and outside of armed conflicts. The right to life is in addition not subject to derogations, except, under the ECHR, in case of "lawful acts of war."[89] The classic case in which a human rights body has assessed the right to life in the context of an armed conflict is the *Tablada* case. In that case, a group of fighters attacked an army base in Argentina. The Inter-American Commission on Human Rights held that "civilians . . . who attacked the *Tablada* base . . . whether singly or as a member of a group . . . are subject to direct individualized attack *to the same extent as combatants*" and lose the benefit of the proportionality principle and of precautionary measures.[90] It then exclusively applied IHL (of international armed conflicts) to those attackers. Only civilian bystanders and attackers who surrendered were considered to benefit from the right to life. The Commission did not raise the issue whether the fighters should have been arrested rather than killed whenever possible.

In the *Guerrero* case, the Human Rights Committee found Colombia to have arbitrarily deprived persons who were suspected—but even by the subsequent enquiry not proven—to be kidnappers and members of a "guerrilla organization" of their right to life. The police waited for the suspected kidnappers in the house where they had believed the victim of a kidnapping to be held, but which they found empty. When the suspected kidnappers arrived, they were shot without warning, without being given an opportunity to surrender and despite the fact that none of the kidnappers had fired a shot, but simply tried to flee.[91]

The jurisprudence of the ECtHR in cases involving the right to life in the non-international armed conflict in Chechnya includes statements which appear to require that in the planning and execution of even a lawful action against fighters, any risk to life and the use of lethal force must be minimized.[92] These statements were not limited to the protection of the lives of civilians, but the actual victims in the case were civilians. In all other cases in which human rights bodies and the ICJ applied the right to life in armed conflicts not of an international character, the persons killed were either *hors de combat* or not alleged to have been fighters.[93] However, fighters are very often killed, e.g., bombed, while they are not *hors de combat*. Nevertheless, no such case has been brought before an international human rights monitoring body. Some observers have deduced from the absence of any such case law that such killings do not violate the right to life, a case being brought before the Inter-American system by a surviving relative of a FARC member being "unthinkable."[94]

The limited body of case law is thus not really conclusive on the question as to what IHRL requires from government authorities using force against fighters, but there is no clear indication that the principles applicable in peacetime do not apply.

2. On Detention

Human rights provisions regulating deprivation of liberty can be found in a variety of different treaties that stipulate that a person may only be deprived of liberty "on such grounds and in accordance with such procedure as are established by law."[95] All treaties prohibit arbitrary arrest or detention,[96] but only Article 5 of the ECHR specifically and exhaustively enumerates the admissible reasons for depriving a person of his/her liberty. Besides conviction, education of minors, mental illness, drug addiction, vagrancy and immigration control, these include (in Article 5(1)(c)) not only detention on remand, but also, as an alternative, instances "when [the detention] is reasonably considered necessary to prevent his committing an offence . . . ." Under the jurisprudence of the ECtHR, the latter alternative could be seen as implicitly allowing for internment, i.e., administrative detention, to hinder an individual from committing a concrete and specific offence.[97] In that situation, however, the person must also be brought (under Article 5(3)) "promptly before a judge or other officer authorised by law to exercise judicial power and shall be entitled to *trial* within a reasonable time or to release pending *trial*" (emphasis added). Therefore, a majority of writers conclude that article 5(1)(c) covers only detention in the framework of criminal proceedings and therefore does not allow internment (except in a state of emergency).[98] The jurisprudence of the ECtHR is however not clear on this issue and certain *obiter dicta* seem to indicate the contrary.[99]

The ICCPR does not mention specific reasons justifying internment, but requires in Article 9(1) that, even when all other conditions are fulfilled, the internment not be arbitrary. The Human Rights Committee underlines that "[t]he drafting history . . . confirms that 'arbitrariness' is not [simply] to be equated with 'against the law', but must be interpreted more broadly to include elements of inappropriateness, injustice, lack of predictability and due process of law."[100] The arrest and detention must be reasonable and necessary.[101]

Internment of enemy fighters would therefore certainly be admissible even without a trial under the ICCPR, while the jury is still out for the ECHR. Under both instruments, however, two procedures must be complied with for a person to be lawfully deprived of his/her liberty. First, an arrested person must be promptly informed of the reasons for arrest.[102] Second, any person deprived of liberty "shall be entitled to take proceedings before a court, in order that that court may decide without delay on the lawfulness of his detention and order his release if the detention is not lawful."[103]

As such, the right to personal freedom is subject to possible derogations in case of a situation threatening the life of the nation, if such derogation is necessary to face the situation, is proportionate to the threat and is not incompatible with other international obligations of the derogating State (such as, in case of armed conflict, obligations stemming from IHL). Furthermore, the derogation must be officially declared and communicated to the other State parties to the treaty from which a State wishes to derogate. In addition, under the ICCPR, the derogation may not lead to or consist of discrimination on inadmissible grounds. Under the American Convention on Human Rights, judicial guarantees essential for the protection of non-derogable rights may not be subject to derogations. The Inter-American Court of Human Rights has therefore found that the access to *habeas corpus* and *amparo* proceedings are non-derogable rights.[104] Similarly, the Human Rights Committee considers that the right to have any arrest be controlled by a judicial body may never be derogated from because it constitutes a necessary mechanism of enforcement for such non-derogable rights as the prohibition of inhumane and degrading treatment and the right to life.[105] The ECtHR accepted in the past that certain violations of the right to a judicial remedy, provided for in Article 5(4) ECHR, were covered by the right to derogation under Article 15, ECHR.[106] It is however submitted that the Court would not necessarily decide so today, as international practice shown above has since developed toward recognizing the non-derogable nature of *habeas corpus*. As a possible first step in this direction, the Court held that a period of fourteen days before being brought before a judicial authority, together with lack of access to a lawyer and inability to communicate with family and friends, was contrary to the Convention despite a derogation by the State concerned.[107] As for customary IHRL, it is widely claimed that the right to *habeas corpus* is non-derogable.[108]

VI. What Prevails If Both IHL and IHRL Apply?

If both IHL and IHRL apply and provide differing answers in a given situation, the *lex specialis* principle determines which of the two prevails.[109] It must however be stressed that if (for whatever reason) one of the two branches does not apply to certain conduct, no *lex specialis* issue arises. Thus, if the United States is correct in considering that IHRL does not apply extraterritorially or if IHRL does not create obligations for armed groups, as the prevailing opinion goes,[110] their conduct is governed exclusively by IHL.

1. The Determination of the *Lex Specialis*

I have tried elsewhere to explore what the principle "*lex specialis derogat legi generali*" means in general and in particular concerning IHL and IHRL.[111] The principle does not indicate an inherent quality in one branch of law or of one of its rules. Rather, it determines which rule prevails over another in a particular situation.[112] Each case must be analyzed individually.[113]

Several factors must be weighed to determine which rule, in relation to a certain problem, is special. Specialty in the sense of logic implies that the norm that applies to certain facts must give way to the norm that applies to those same facts as well as to an additional fact present in the given situation. Between two applicable rules, the one which has the larger "common contact surface area"[114] with the situation applies. The norm with the scope of application that enters completely into that of the other norm must prevail, otherwise it would never apply.[115] It is the norm with the more precise or narrower material and/or personal scope of application that prevails.[116] Precision requires that the norm addressing explicitly a problem prevails over the one that treats it implicitly, the one providing the advantage of detail over the other's generality,[117] and the more restrictive norm over the one covering the entire problem but in a less exacting manner.[118]

A less formal factor—and equally less objective—that permits determination of which of two rules apply is the conformity of the solution to the systemic objectives of the law.[119] Characterizing this solution as "*lex specialis*" perhaps constitutes misuse of language. The systemic order of international law is a normative postulate founded upon value judgments.[120] In particular when formal standards do not indicate a clear result, this teleological criterion must weigh in, even though it allows for personal preferences.[121]

The principle traditionally deals with antinomies between conventional rules. Whether it also applies to the relationship between two customary rules is less clear. Theoretically, this is not the case, if one adopts a traditional understanding of customary law. The customary rule applicable to a certain problem derives from the practice and *opinio juris* of States in relation to that problem. In relation to the same problem, there cannot be a customary "IHRL" and another customary "IHL" rule. One always focuses on the practice and the *opinio juris* manifested in relation to problems as similar as possible to the one to be resolved. This appears to be the approach of the ICRC, which refers, in its Customary Law Study, to a vast array of practice in human rights, including outside of armed conflicts.[122] In practice, however, when one looks for a customary rule, one often refers to a text, whether a treaty or another instrument codifying customary law or one that instigated the development of a customary rule,[123] or even a doctrinal text. Then, one specific problem could be covered by two contradictory texts, both deduced from State practice.

The choice between these two texts is, in my opinion, governed by the same principles as the choice between two treaty rules. If the State practice clarifying which of the two rules prevails in the given situation is not sufficiently dense, one must discover by the usual methods which of the two rules, derived from the practice analyzed from different perspectives, constitutes the *lex specialis*.

2. On Attacks

First, it must be emphasized that there is a good deal of common ground between IHL and IHRL. In a "battlefield-like" situation, arrest is virtually always impossible without putting the government forces into disproportionate danger. A fighter presents a great threat to life even if that threat consists of attacks against armed forces. The immediacy of that threat might be based not only on what the targeted fighter is expected to do, but also on his or her previous behavior.[124] Therefore, even under IHRL, in such situations, lethal force could be used. On the other hand, the life of a fighter who is *hors de combat* is equally protected by both branches.

It is where the solutions of the two branches actually contradict each other that the applicable rule must be determined under the *lex specialis* principle. The quintessential example of such a contradiction is the Taliban or Al Qaeda leader attending a secret meeting in Kabul. Many interpret IHL as permitting international forces to shoot to kill since he is a fighter, but this is controversial. IHRL would clearly say he must be arrested and a graduated use of force must be employed, but this conclusion is based upon precedents which arose in peacetime and IHRL is always more flexible according to the situation.

In my view, some situations contain more specificities of the situation for which the IHL rule was made and some situations more facts for which human rights were typically made. There is a sliding scale[125] between the lone Taliban leader in Kabul and the Taliban fighter engaged in a nearly conventional battle with international forces in the mountains around Khost. It is impossible to provide a "one size fits all" answer; as shown above, the *lex specialis* principle does not determine priorities between two rules in the abstract, but offers a solution to a concrete case in which competing rules lead to different results. The famous dictum by the ICJ that "[t]he test of what is an arbitrary deprivation of life . . . [must] be determined by the applicable *lex specialis*, namely, the law applicable in armed conflict"[126] should not be misunderstood. It has to be read in the context of the opinion,[127] in which the ICJ had to determine the legality *in abstracto* of the use of a certain weapon.

Such a flexible solution, which makes the actual required behavior depend upon the situation at hand, is dangerous, in particular regarding attacks, where it literally deals with a question of life and death and where it has to be applied by every soldier and leads to irreversible results. It is therefore indispensable to determine factors which make either the IHL of international armed conflicts rule or the IHRL rule prevail.

The existence and extent of control by governmental and international forces over the place[128] where the attack occurs point toward IHRL as *lex specialis*.[129] Even if IHRL obligations under the right to life existed for a given State beyond territory that is under the control of that State, control over the place where the attack occurs is a factor making IHRL prevail over IHL. The latter was made for hostilities against forces on or beyond the front line, i.e., in a place that is not under the control of those who attack them, while law enforcement concerns persons who are under the jurisdiction of those who act. In traditional conflict situations this corresponds to the question of how remote the situation is from the battlefield,[130] although fewer and fewer contemporary conflicts are characterized by front lines and battlefields. What then constitutes sufficient control to warrant IHRL predominating as the *lex specialis*? International forces could not simply argue that the presence of a solitary rebel or even a group of rebels indicates that in fact they are not fully in control of the place and therefore act under IHL as *lex specialis*. The question is rather one of degree. If the international forces could effect an arrest (of a member of the Taliban) without being overly concerned about interference by other Taliban in that operation, then they have sufficient control over the place to make human rights prevail as *lex specialis*.

This criterion of control leaves the solution a little more open in an area that is under firm control of neither side (such as many places in Afghanistan). Even where the strict requirements of necessity of IHRL are not fulfilled (if they are, both branches lead to the same result), the impossibility of arresting the fighter,[131] the danger inherent in an attempt to arrest the fighter[132] and the danger represented by the fighter for government and international forces and civilians as well as the immediacy of this danger[133] may lead to the conclusion that IHL is the *lex specialis* in that situation. These factors are interlinked with the elements of control described above. In addition, where neither party has clear geographical control, in my view, the higher the degree of certainty that the target is actually a fighter, the easier the IHL approach appears as *lex specialis*.[134] Attacks are lawful against persons who are actually fighters, while law enforcement is by definition directed against suspects.

The main weakness of such a flexible approach is its practicability. If the answer depends on the specific situation, how can a soldier know what to apply? This problem can only be solved by precise instructions and orders for every operation and every sortie. In addition, on the international level, guidelines might be developed in discussions among IHL and IHRL experts, law enforcement practitioners and representatives of the military. Logically, (former) fighters should also be involved, in particular if the guidelines equally cover conduct of such groups,[135] to ensure that they can be applied in practice.

3. On Detention

When comparing the rules of IHL of non-international armed conflicts on procedural guarantees for persons arrested with those of IHRL, the former do not exist while, except for the admissible extent of derogations, the latter are clear and well developed by jurisprudence. The latter must therefore prevail. They are more precise and more restrictive. The ICRC Customary Law Study appears to adopt this approach when it interprets the alleged IHL rule prohibiting the arbitrary deprivation of liberty through the lens of IHRL.[136] Unlike a person to be targeted, for whom a flexible approach was advocated above, a detainee is clearly under control of those who detain him or her. It may be added that the result is not so different from that of an application by analogy of the guarantees foreseen by Convention IV for civilians in international armed conflicts, the only difference being that under IHRL a court must decide, while under IHL an administrative body is sufficient.[137] Under IHRL too, however, the court does not necessarily have to be a fully independent and impartial tribunal that could try a person, but it must have a judicial character and it may only take decisions after judicial, adversarial proceedings providing the individual guarantees appropriate to the reasons of the internment in question.

The only exception where IHL must prevail, as it was specifically made for armed conflicts and foresees a rule, exists when either an agreement between the parties or a unilateral recognition of belligerency makes the full regime of POWs applicable. In that case detained fighters have the disadvantage of a lack of access to *habeas corpus* (although there must inevitably exist a procedure to determine whether an arrested person is or is not an enemy fighter benefiting from POW status), but they have the advantage of a detailed regime governing their detention, of immunity against prosecution and of a right to be released at the end of active hostilities. In relation to Afghanistan, the question arises whether the agreements concluded by certain coalition partners such as Canada with the Afghan government in which both parties undertake to "treat detainees in accordance with the standards set out in the Third Geneva Convention"[138] can be considered as a unilateral granting of the protection of Convention III, which would make IHL prevail over the IHRL procedural guarantees. According to the letter of those agreements, this is the case, at least for persons who are actually detained by the Afghan authorities. In reality, however, it would be very astonishing if, through those agreements, the Afghan government waived the right to prosecute those arrested for acts of hostility against their forces, which is part of POW status. Nongovernmental organization reports rather indicate that even the treatment of those persons is far from what Convention III would require.[139] In my view, only full POW status may offer a *lex specialis* compared with the detailed procedural guarantees of IHRL.

The main difficulty with this approach too is whether it is realistic to expect States and non-State actors, interning possibly thousands, to bring all internees before a court without delay during armed conflict. If it is not, such an obligation risks making it extremely difficult to conduct war effectively and, thus, could lead to less compliance with the rules in the long term, e.g., summary executions disguised as battlefield killings.

A second concern derives from the differences between State and non-State actors, which have equal obligations under IHL but not under IHRL. The question of whether a non-State actor may establish a court remains controversial.[140] The requirements that there be a legal basis and procedures established by law for internment raise the same concern. While human rights themselves stipulate at least two procedural requirements, neither they nor IHL applicable to non-international armed conflict provides a specific legal basis for internment. While a State can so provide in its domestic law, how is the non-State actor to establish this basis in law? Could then a non-State actor also derogate from IHRL? Application of IHRL seems to make it impossible for one party to the armed conflict—the non-State actor—to intern legally. Parties to armed conflicts intern persons, hindering them from continuing to bear arms, so as to gain the military advantage. If the non-State actor cannot legally intern persons—recalling that it is a serious violation of IHL to deny quarter[141]—the non-State actor is left with little option but to release the captured enemy fighters. If rules applicable to armed conflict make efficient fighting impossible, they will not be respected, thus undermining any protection the law provides. These may be reasons for not applying the same *lex specialis* reasoning to armed groups even if IHRL were considered to bind non-State armed groups.

VII. Conclusion

In an ideal world, armed forces could apply one set of rules when abroad, they would always know who a person they are confronted with is, they would deal under IHL with enemy fighters, while the Afghan police would deal in full respect of IHRL with everyone else. This ideal world does not exist, and even less so in Afghanistan. It is the very essence of stability operations that they take place in an environment which offers the full spectrum of situations. It is therefore not astonishing but in fact normal that the full spectrum of laws apply: IHL, made for armed conflicts but leaving some questions open, in particular in non-international armed conflicts; IHRL, made for the relations between a State and its citizens, but also applicable to (or at least containing values that must protect) foreigners and people confronted with agents of a State abroad; and the domestic law of the territorial State and of the home State. It is also normal that there is no general answer on how those laws interrelate and which prevails. Everything depends on where on the spectrum a certain encounter with local people is situated. Most often, in addition, the soldier acting in the field, and even the commander responsible for a detention, does not know where on the spectrum he or she is standing. Therefore, the relationship between IHL and IHRL for international forces in Afghanistan depends on many variables, and the identity and weight of those variables are in addition controversial among lawyers. The approach suggested here as to when and whether an Afghan may be attacked and detained like a soldier of the German Wehrmacht in World War II and when he or she must benefit from the guarantees benefiting in peacetime even the most suspect person lurking in a dodgy neighborhood is based upon the fundamental ideas and the typical situations for which the two branches were made. Moreover, it takes into account the practical difficulties of decision making and the risks, consequences and reversibility of mistakes in that decision making, for both the target and the member of the international forces. If the security of the international forces were the overriding consideration, they would not be sent by their governments to such a dangerous place as Afghanistan. Victory does not mainly depend upon their military superiority, but on the impression they leave with the Afghan population, compared with what their enemies have to offer.

Many will consider the very nuanced line suggested in this article, which in addition on some important issues is unable to provide solutions and only lists arguments, as unrealistic. In my view, full-spectrum operations require soldiers at an increasingly lower level to apply, simultaneously, complicated and controversial rules. However, they are not and they should not be left alone. They need the best possible training and clear instructions for every sortie. In addition, international lawyers and practitioners should meet, not to reaffirm the theory or to conclude that the old rules are not adequate for the new situation, but to operationalize the interplay between the existing rules agreed upon by States, including to explain the few issues on which there are genuine divergences of view, the (often rather limited) practical impact of those divergences and the possible solutions.

Notes

1. See *infra* text accompanying note 54.
2. For those requirements in particular, see the decision of the International Criminal Tribunal for the former Yugoslavia in Prosecutor v. Ramush Haradinaj, Idriz Balaj and Lahi Brahimaj, Case No. IT-04-84-T, Trial Chamber Judgment, paras. 37–99 (Apr. 3, 2008).

3. Thus the ICRC position according to Adam Roberts. *See* Adam Roberts, *The Laws of War in the War on Terror*, 32 ISRAEL YEARBOOK OF HUMAN RIGHTS 193 (2002).

4. *See* Convention Relative to the Protection of Civilian Persons in Time of War art. 47, Aug. 12, 1949, 6 U.S.T. 3516, 75 U.N.T.S. 287, *reprinted in* DOCUMENTS ON THE LAWS OF WAR 301 (Adam Roberts & Richard Guelff eds., 3d. ed. 2000) [hereinafter Geneva Convention IV].

5. Convention for the Amelioration of the Condition of Wounded and Sick in Armed Forces in the Field art. 2, Aug. 12, 1949, 6 U.S.T. 3114, 75 U.N.T.S. 31 [hereinafter Geneva Convention I]; Convention for the Amelioration of the Condition of Wounded, Sick and Shipwrecked Members of Armed Forces at Sea art. 2, Aug. 12, 1949, 6 U.S.T. 3217, 75 U.N.T.S. 85 [hereinafter Geneva Convention II]; Convention Relative to the Treatment of Prisoners of War art. 2, Aug. 12, 1949, 6 U.S.T. 3316, 75 U.N.T.S. 135 [hereinafter Geneva Convention III]; Protocol Additional to the Geneva Conventions of 12 August 1949, and Relating to the Protection of Victims of International Armed Conflicts, June 8, 1977, 1125 U.N.T.S. 3 [hereinafter Additional Protocol I]; all *reprinted in* DOCUMENTS ON THE LAWS OF WAR, *supra* note 4, at 197, 222, 244 and 422, respectively; Geneva Convention IV, *supra* note 4.

6. *See* William K. Lietzau, *Combating Terrorism: Law Enforcement or War?*, *in* TERRORISM AND INTERNATIONAL LAW, CHALLENGES AND RESPONSES 80 (Michael Schmitt & Gian Luca Beruto eds., 2002).

7. Loizidou v. Turkey, 1996-VI Eur. Ct. H.R. 2216, 2235–36, para. 56; Cyprus v. Turkey, 2001-IV Eur. Ct. H.R. 1, para. 77. (These and all other decisions of the European Court of Human Rights are available online at http://echr.coe.int/echr/en/hudoc.)

8. *See* Michael J. Dennis, *Application of Human Rights Treaties Extraterritorially in Times of Armed Conflict and Military Occupation*, 99 AMERICAN JOURNAL OF INTERNATIONAL LAW 119, 123–24 (2005).

9. *See* Legal Consequences of the Construction of a Wall in the Occupied Palestinian Territory, Advisory Opinion, 2004 I.C.J. 136, paras. 102, 110 (July 9); Adam Roberts, *Prolonged Military Occupations: The Israeli-Occupied Territories since 1967*, 84 AMERICAN JOURNAL OF INTERNATIONAL LAW 44, 71–72 (1990). The Coalition Provisional Authority Administrator in Iraq, Ambassador L. Paul Bremer, is reported to have stated in a letter to Amnesty International that "the only relevant standard applicable to the Coalition's detention practices is the Fourth Geneva Convention of 1949." *See* AMNESTY INTERNATIONAL, IRAQ: MEMORANDUM ON CONCERNS RELATED TO LEGISLATION INTRODUCED BY THE COALITION PROVISIONAL AUTHORITY (2003), *available at* http://web.amnesty.org/library/Index/ENGMDE141762003?open&of=ENG-IRQ.

10. Legal Consequences of the Construction of a Wall, *supra* note 9, paras. 107–12; Armed Activities on the Territory of the Congo (Dem. Rep. Congo v. Uganda), 2005 I.C.J. 116, paras. 216–17 (Dec. 19). (The decisions of the International Court of Justice are available at http://www.icj-cij.org/docket/index.php?p1=3&p2=4.)

11. U.N. Human Rights Committee, *Concluding Observations of the Human Rights Committee: Israel* para. 10, U.N. Doc. CCPR/C/79/Add.93 (Aug. 18, 1998); U.N. Human Rights Committee, *General Comment 31: The Nature of the General Legal Obligation Imposed on States Parties to the Covenant* para. 10, U.N. Doc. CCPR/C/21/Rev.1/Add.13 (May 26, 2004).

12. *See, e.g.*, UK MINISTRY OF DEFENCE, THE MANUAL OF THE LAW OF ARMED CONFLICT para. 11.19 (2004).

13. See also references in Special Rapporteur, *Report of the Special Rapporteur of the Commission on Human Rights on the Situation of Human Rights in Kuwait under Iraqi Occupation* paras. 50–59, delivered to the U.N. Econ. and Soc. Council, U.N. Doc. E/CN.4/1992/26 (Jan. 16, 1992) (prepared by Walter Kalin).

14. John Cerone, *Human Dignity in the Line of Fire: The Application of International Human Rights Law during Armed Conflict, Occupation, and Peace Operations*, 39 VANDERBILT JOURNAL OF TRANSNATIONAL LAW 1447, 1491–92 (2006).

15. Alejandre v. Cuba, Case 11.589, Inter-Am. C.H.R., Report No. 86/99, OEA/Ser.L/V/II.106 doc. 3 rev. at 586, para. 25 (1999).

16. Bankovic et al. v. Belgium et al., App. No. 52207/99, 2001-XII Eur. Ct. H.R. 333, paras. 70–71.

17. Issa and Others v. Turkey, App. No. 31821/96, 41 Eur. Ct. H.R. Rep. 567, paras. 76–82 (2004).

18. Pad and Others v. Turkey, App. No. 60167/00, Admissibility, paras. 54–55 (Eur. Ct. H.R., June 28, 2007).

19. Nuala Mole, *Issa v. Turkey: Delineating the Extra-territorial Effect of the European Convention on Human Rights*, 1 EUROPEAN HUMAN RIGHTS LAW REVIEW 86–87 (2005).

20. Issa v. Turkey, *supra* note 17, para. 75. In this decision, the Court was drawing on its prior case law regarding Cyprus.

21. Cerone, *supra* note 14, at 1494–1507, frames the discussion in terms of a "range" of applicable rights and in terms of the "level of obligation" binding States acting extraterritorially.

22. Hussein v. 21 States, App. No. 23276/04, 42 Eur. H.R. Rep. SE16 at 3 (Mar. 14, 2006) (Court Decision on Admissibility).

23. *Id.* at 4.

24. Hess v. United Kingdom, 18 YEARBOOK OF THE EUROPEAN CONVENTION ON HUMAN RIGHTS 146, 176 (1975) (Eur. Comm'n on H.R.).

25. Damira Kamchibekova, *State Responsibility for Extraterritorial Human Rights Violations*, 13 BUFFALO HUMAN RIGHTS LAW REVIEW 87, 125 (2007).

26. Hess v. United Kingdom, *supra* note 24, at 176 (emphasis added).

27. A State that is an occupying power has, however, the positive obligation to protect the right to life of persons within its jurisdiction against third parties. The ICJ held that Uganda, as an occupying power in Congo, had an obligation "to protect the inhabitants of the occupied territory against acts of violence, and not to tolerate such violence by any third party." *See* Armed Activities on the Territory of the Congo (Dem. Rep. Congo v. Uganda), 2005 I.C.J. 116, paras. 178–79.

28. On the irrelevance of who arrested a detainee, see Michael Fordham et al., Joint Opinion, In the Matter of the All Party Parliamentary Group on Extraordinary Rendition and in the Matter of the Human Rights Responsibility Arising from the Military Detainee Handovers in Iraq paras. 10 and 15(2) (July 28, 2008), *available at* http://www.extraordinaryrendition.org/index.php?option=com_docman&task=cat_view&gid=30&Itemid=27.

29. Article 15 of the European Convention for the Protection of Human Rights and Fundamental Freedoms, Nov. 4, 1950, 213 U.N.T.S. 222 [hereinafter European Convention], refers to "time of war or other public emergency threatening the life of the nation"; Article 4 of the International Covenant on Civil and Political Rights, Dec. 16, 1966, 999 U.N.T.S. 171 [hereinafter ICCPR], refers to "time of public emergency which threatens the life of the nation and the existence of which is officially proclaimed"; Article 27 of the American Convention on Human Rights, Nov. 22, 1969, 1144 U.N.T.S. 123 [hereinafter American Convention], refers to "time of war, public danger, or other emergency that threatens the independence or security of a State Party."

30. R (on the Application of Al-Jedda) (FC) v. Secretary of State for Defence [2007] UKHL 58 (per Lord Bingham, para. 38), *available at* http://www.publications.parliament.uk/pa/ld200708/ldjudgmt/jd071212/jedda-1.htm) [hereinafter Al-Jedda].

31. *Id.*

32. Nonetheless, it may well be that the illegality of the exercise also means it violates IHRL, as IHRL, contrary to IHL, knows no distinction between *ius ad bellum* and *ius in bello*. *See* William Schabas, Lex Specialis? *Belt and Suspenders? The Parallel Operation of Human Rights Law and the Law of Armed Conflict and the Conundrum of* Jus Ad Bellum, 40 ISRAEL LAW REVIEW 592, 593, 607–10 (2007).

33. Loizidou v. Turkey, 1996-VI Eur. Ct. H.R. 2216, at 2235–36, para. 52 (emphasis added).

34. Al-Jedda, *supra* note 30, paras. 26–39 (per Lord Bingham), 125–29 (per Baroness Hale), 130–35 (per Lord Carswell) and 151 (per Lord Brown). Lord Rodger agrees in principle in *obiter* at paragraph 118. The Law Lords held that Article 5 rights may be "displaced" or "qualified" by UN Security Council Resolution 1546, but insisted that the infringement be limited. Lord Bingham held that they must "ensure that the detainee's rights under article 5 are not infringed to any greater extent than is inherent in such detention." *Id.*, para. 39. Lord Carswell proposed specific "safeguards" to be implemented during such detention "so far as is practicable and consistent with the needs of national security and the safety of other persons." *Id.*, para. 130.

35. *See* Application of the Convention on the Prevention and Punishment of the Crime of Genocide (Bosn. & Herz. v. Serb. & Mont.), 1993 I.C.J. 325, 440–41, paras. 100–102 (Sept. 13) (separate opinion of Judge Lauterpacht).

36. See Behrami v. France and Saramati v. France, 45 Eur. Ct. H.R. 10 (2007). In this case the question of attribution was not clearly distinguished from the above-mentioned question of whether a Security Council resolution overrides the substantive human rights obligations of a State, but in its global reasoning the ECtHR suggested that such resolutions have precisely that effect. *Id.*, para. 149. The two questions were distinguished in the *Al-Jedda* case by the UK House of Lords, which rejected on the facts the claims of the government under the first question but answered the second question affirmatively (Al-Jedda, *supra* note 30, paras. 22–24 (attribution), para. 39 (human rights) (per Lord Bingham); Lord Rodger dissenting on the question of attribution (see particularly para. 99)).

37. U.N. Human Rights Committee, *Consideration of Reports Submitted by States Parties Under Article 40 of the Covenant: Comments by the Government of Germany to the Concluding Observations of the Human Rights Committee*, U.N. Doc. CCPR/CO/80/DEU/Add.1 (Jan. 5, 2005); UN Human Rights Comm., *Concluding Observations of the Human Rights Committee: Poland* para. 3, U.N. Doc. CCPR/CO/82/POL (Dec. 2, 2004). Other State parties have answered questions regarding the actions of their national forces in peacekeeping missions without contending that the ICCPR does not apply beyond their State borders or in that context (Belgium, U.N. Human Rights Committee, *Consideration of Reports Submitted by States Parties under Article 40 of the Covenant* para. 22, U.N. Doc. CCPR/C/SR.1707 (Oct. 27, 1998); Italy, U.N. Human Rights Committee, *Consideration of Reports Submitted by States Parties under Article 40 of the Covenant* para. 22, U.N. Doc. CCPR/C/SR.1680 (Sept. 24, 1998); Canada, U.N. Human Rights Committee, *Consideration of Reports Submitted by States Parties under Article 40 of the Covenant* paras. 29, 32, U.N. Doc. CCPR/C/SR.1738 (Mar. 7, 1999)).

38. *See* Report of the International Law Commission on its Fifty-eighth Session, ch. VII, U.N. GAOR, 61st Sess., Supp. No. 10, U.N. Doc. A/61/10 (2006) (discussing Articles 28 and 29 of the Draft Articles on the Responsibility of International Organizations).

39. Waite and Kennedy v. Germany, 1999-I Eur. Ct. H.R. 393; Bosphorus Hava Yollari Turizm ve Ticaret Anonim Sirketi v. Ireland, 2005-VI Eur. Ct. H.R. para. 154.

40. Additional Protocol I, *supra* note 5, art. 51(3), which reflects customary law, but the exact meaning of which is controversial and presently subject to an ICRC-led process of research and reflection on and clarification of the notion of direct participation in hostilities. *See infra* note 46.

41. JEAN S. PICTET, DEVELOPMENT AND PRINCIPLES OF INTERNATIONAL HUMANITARIAN LAW 75–76 (1985).

42. *See* British War Office, III Manual of Military Law (Law of War on Land) para. 115 (1958).

43. For the divergences of view in the ICRC expert consultations on the notion of direct participation in hostilities, see Direct Participation 2005 Report, *infra* note 46, at 45–46; Louise Doswald-Beck, *The right to life in armed conflict: does international humanitarian law provide all the answers?*, 88 INTERNATIONAL REVIEW OF THE RED CROSS 881, 902 (2006); Vincent-Joël Proulx, *If the Hat Fits, Wear It, If the Turban Fits, Run for Your Life: Reflections on the Indefinite Detention and Targeted Killing of Suspected Terrorists*, 56 HASTINGS LAW JOURNAL 801, 882–83 (2006).

44. Additional Protocol I, *supra* note 5, art. 51(5)(b).

45. *See* Geneva Conventions I–III, *supra* note 5, art. 3; Geneva Convention IV, *supra* note 4, art. 3; Protocol Additional to the Geneva Conventions of 12 August 1949, and Relating to the Protection of Victims of Non-International Armed Conflicts art. 4, June 8, 1977, 1125 U.N.T.S. 609, *reprinted in* DOCUMENTS ON THE LAWS OF WAR, *supra* note 4, at 483 [hereinafter Additional Protocol II].

46. Recently, the ICRC was engaged, in consultation with experts, in a process of research, reflection on and clarification of the notion of "direct participation in hostilities" under IHL. This process has not yet shown definitive results but it clearly demonstrated profound divergences over the question of when enemy fighters may be killed in a non-international armed conflict. *See* Third Meeting on the Notion of Direct Participation in Hostilities under International Humanitarian Law (Oct. 23–25, 2005), http://www.icrc.org/Web/eng/siteeng0.nsf/htmlall/participation-hostilities-ihl-311205/$File/Direct_participation_in_hostilities_2005_eng.pdf [hereinafter Direct Participation 2005 Report]; Second Expert Meeting: Direct Participation in Hostilities under International Humanitarian Law (Oct. 25–26, 2004), http://www.icrc.org/Web/eng/siteeng0.nsf/htmlall/participation-hostilities-ihl-311205/$File/Direct_participation_in_hostilities_2004_eng.pdf; Direct Participation in Hostilities under International Humanitarian Law (Sept. 2003), http://www.icrc.org/Web/eng/siteeng0.nsf/htmlall/participation-hostilities-ihl-311205/$File/Direct%20participation%20in%20hostilities-Sept%202003.pdf. Based upon those discussions, the ICRC is currently preparing an "Interpretative Guidance on the Notion of Direct Participation in Hostilities."

47. University Centre for International Humanitarian Law, *Expert Meeting on the Right to Life in Armed Conflict and Situations of Occupation* 34 (2005), *available at* http://www.adh-geneve.ch/pdfs/3rapport_droit_vie.pdf [hereinafter UCIHL Report].

48. Direct Participation 2005 Report, *supra* note 46, at 64; David Kretzmer, *Targeted Killing of Suspected Terrorists: Extra-Judicial Executions or Legitimate Means of Defence?*, 16 EUROPEAN JOURNAL OF INTERNATIONAL LAW 171, 197–98 (2005).

49. Under Common Article 3, the term "armed forces" includes rebel armed groups. *See* Marco Sassòli, *Terrorism and War*, 4 JOURNAL OF INTERNATIONAL CRIMINAL JUSTICE 959, 977 (2006).

50. COMMENTARY ON THE ADDITIONAL PROTOCOLS OF 8 JUNE 1977 TO THE GENEVA CONVENTIONS OF 12 AUGUST 1949 para. 4789 (Yves Sandoz, Christophe Swinarski & Bruno Zimmermann eds., 1987).

51. Direct Participation 2005 Report, *supra* note 46, at 48–49.

52. Public Committee against Torture in Israel v. Government of Israel et al., HCJ 769/02, Judgment, para. 39 (Dec. 13, 2006), *available at* http://elyon1.court.gov.il/files_eng/02/690/007/a34/02007690.a34.pdf [hereinafter Public Committee against Torture].

53. Direct Participation 2005 Report, *supra* note 46, at 43–44.

54. *Id.* at 64; Kretzmer, *supra* note 48, at 198–99, goes in a similar direction.

55. JEAN-MARIE HENCKAERTS & LOUISE DOSWALD-BECK, I CUSTOMARY INTERNATIONAL HUMANITARIAN LAW 3 (Rule 1) (2005).

56. *Id.*

57. *Id.* at 19 (Rule 6).

58. *Id.* at 17 (Rule 5).

59. *Id.* at 12.

60. *Id.* at 17.

61. *Id.* at 21.

62. *Id.*

63. MARCO SASSÒLI & ANTOINE BOUVIER, HOW DOES LAW PROTECT IN WAR? 251 (2d ed. 2006).

64. Alexander Orakhelashvili, *The Interaction between Human Rights and Humanitarian Law: Fragmentation, Conflict, Parallelism, or Convergence?*, 19 EUROPEAN JOURNAL OF INTERNATIONAL LAW 161, 167 (2008).

65. Geneva Convention III, *supra* note 5, art. 21.

66. Geneva Convention IV, *supra* note 4, art. 42 (for an alien on the territory of a party).

67. *Id.*, art. 78(1) (in occupied territory).

68. *Id.*, arts. 43, 78(2).

69. *Id.*, art. 147. *See also* Statute of the International Criminal Court art. 8(2)(a)(vii), July 17, 1998, 2187 U.N.T.S. 90; Statute of the International Criminal Tribunal for the Prosecution of Persons Responsible for Serious Violations of International Humanitarian Law Committed in the Territory of the former Yugoslavia since 1991 art. 2(g), S.C. Res. 827, U.N. Doc. S/RES/827 (1993).

70. Additional Protocol II, *supra* note 45, arts. 5, 6(5).

71. HENCKAERTS & DOSWALD-BECK, *supra* note 55, at 344–52.

72. *Id.* at 348–51.

73. Additional Protocol II, *supra* note 45, arts. 5, 6.

74. *See* Jelena Pejic, *Procedural Principles and Safeguards for Internment/Administrative Detention in Armed Conflict and Other Situations of Violence*, 87 INTERNATIONAL REVIEW OF THE RED CROSS 375, 377 (2005).

75. For a position rejecting such an analogy, see United Nations Commission on Human Rights, Working Group on Arbitrary Detention, *Situation of Detainees at Guantanamo Bay* para. 24, U.N. Doc. E/CN.4/2006/120 (Feb. 2006).

76. HENCKAERTS & DOSWALD-BECK, *supra* note 55, at 352.

77. Geneva Convention III, *supra* note 5, art. 6.

78. HENCKAERTS & DOSWALD-BECK, *supra* note 55, at 352; LINDSAY MOIR, THE LAW OF INTERNAL ARMED CONFLICT 41 (2002).

79. Article 5 of Geneva Convention III prescribes status determination tribunals only for persons a detaining power wants to *deny* POW status.

80. When are active hostilities against the Taliban over? Only once the last member of the Taliban hidden in a mountain cave is arrested?

81. Article 6(5) of Additional Protocol II simply *encourages* the widest possible amnesty.

82. *See* Marco Sassòli & Laura M. Olson, *The relationship between international humanitarian and human rights law where it matters: admissible killing and internment of fighters in non-international armed conflicts*, 90 INTERNATIONAL REVIEW OF THE RED CROSS 599 (2008).

83. *Id.*

84. European Convention, *supra* note 29, art. 2(2).
85. McCann v. United Kingdom, 324 Eur. Ct. H.R. (ser. A) paras. 200–205 (1995).
86. *See, e.g.*, Las Palmeras Case, 2002 Inter-Am. Ct. H.R. (ser. C) No. 96 (2002).
87. *See* Basic Principles on the Use of Force and Firearms by Law Enforcement Officials ¶¶ 9, 10, U.N. Doc. A/CONF.144/28/Rev.1 at 112 (1990), *available at* http://www.unhchr.ch/html/menu3/b/h_comp43.htm.
88. *Id.*, note. The note clarifies the term "law enforcement officials" by referring to the commentary to Article 1 of the Code of Conduct for Law Enforcement Officials.
89. European Convention, *supra* note 29, art. 5(2). It has been argued that this only refers to international armed conflicts. *See* Doswald-Beck, *supra* note 43, at 883. In any case, no State has ever tried to derogate based on this exception.
90. Abella v. Argentina (Tablada), Case 11.137, Report No. 55/97, Inter-Am. C.H.R., OEA/Ser.L/V/II.95 doc. 7 rev., para. 178 (1997) (emphasis supplied).
91. Camargo on behalf of Guerrero v. Colombia, Hum. Rts. Comm., Comm. No. R.11/45, U.N. Doc. Supp. No. 40 (A37/40) (Mar. 31, 1982) [hereinafter Guerrero case].
92. Isayeva v. Russia, App. No. 57950/00, 41 Eur. Ct. H.R. Rep. paras. 175–76 (2005).
93. For an overview, see NILS MELZER, TARGETED KILLING IN INTERNATIONAL LAW 169–73, 384–92 (2008).
94. UCIHL Report, *supra* note 47, at 36.
95. ICCPR, *supra* note 29, art. 9(1). *See also* European Convention, *supra* note 29, art. 5(1); American Convention, *supra* note 29, art. 7; African Charter on Human and Peoples' Rights art. 6, June 17, 1981, OAU Doc. CAB/LEG/67/3 rev. 5, 21 INTERNATIONAL LEGAL MATERIALS 58 (1982) [hereinafter African Charter].
96. ICCPR, *supra* note 29, art. 9(1); European Convention, *supra* note 29, art. 5; American Convention, *supra* note 29, art. 7(3); African Charter, *supra* note 95, art. 6.
97. *See* Guzzardi v. Italy, 3 Eur. Ct. H.R. Rep. 333, para. 102 (1981).
98. *See* D.J. HARRIS, MICHAEL O'BOYLE & COLIN WARBRICK, LAW OF THE EUROPEAN CONVENTION ON HUMAN RIGHTS 115–21, particularly 117 (1995) (in human rights terms "internment" is more commonly referred to as "preventive detention"); *see also* CLARE OVEY & ROBIN C.A. WHITE, JACOBS AND WHITE: EUROPEAN CONVENTION ON HUMAN RIGHTS 108–10 (3d ed. 2002).
99. Lawless v. Ireland, 3 Eur. Ct. H.R. (ser. A) at 51–53; 1 Eur. H.R. Rep. 15, para. 14 of section entitled "The Law" (1979–80).
100. Mukong v. Cameroon, Comm. No. 458/1991, U.N. Doc. CCPR/C/51/D/458/1991 (1994), *reprinted in* OFFICE OF THE UNITED NATIONS HIGH COMMISSIONER FOR HUMAN RIGHTS, 5 SELECTED DECISIONS OF THE HUMAN RIGHTS COMMITTEE 86 (1994).
101. H. van Alphen v. The Netherlands, Hum. Rts. Comm., Comm. No. 305/1988, U.N. Doc. A/45/40 (vol. II) at 115, para. 5.8 (1990); Spakmo v. Norway, Hum. Rts. Comm., Comm. No. 631/1995, U.N. Doc. A/55/40 (vol. II) at 26, para. 6.3 (1999). *See also* U.N. Human Rights Committee, *General Comment No. 8, Right to liberty and security of persons (Art. 90)*, paras. 1 and 4 (1982).
102. ICCPR, *supra* note 29, art. 9(2); European Convention, *supra* note 29, art. 5(2). *See also* American Convention, *supra* note 29, art. 7(4).
103. ICCPR, *supra* note 29, art. 9(4). *See also* European Convention, *supra* note 29, art. 5(4); American Convention, *supra* note 29, art. 7(6); African Charter, *supra* note 95, art. 7(1)(a).
104. Habeas Corpus in Emergency Situations (arts. 27(2) and 7(6) of the American Convention), Advisory Opinion OC-8/87, January 30, 1987, Inter-Am. C.H.R. (Ser. A) No. 8 (1987).
105. *See* U.N. Human Rights Committee, *General Comment No. 29*, U.N. Doc. CCPR/C/21/Rev.1/Add.11 on Art. 4 ICCPR, para. 16 (2001) [hereinafter General Comment 29].

106. Ireland v. United Kingdom, 25 Eur. Ct. H.R. (ser. A) paras. 202–24 (1978).

107. Aksoy v. Turkey, 1996-VI Eur. Ct. H.R. 2260, paras. 78, 83 and 84.

108. For a list of practice pointing to the non-derogability of *habeas corpus*, see HENCKAERTS & DOSWALD-BECK, *supra* note 55, at 350–51 and accompanying footnotes (including General Comment 29, *supra* note 105, para. 16). *See also* Doug Cassel, *Security Detention under International Human Rights and Humanitarian Law*, 98 JOURNAL OF CRIMINAL LAW & CRIMINOLOGY 811 (2008); Pejic, *supra* note 74, at 387. Although the decision was solely based on the US Constitution, one could also refer to the decision of the US Supreme Court in *Boumediene v. Bush*, 128 S.Ct. 2229 (2008), which indicates that States consider *habeas corpus* to cover even persons characterized as enemy combatants in an armed conflict.

109. Legality of the Threat or Use of Nuclear Weapons, Advisory Opinion, 1996 I.C.J. 226, para. 25 (July 8); Legal Consequences of the Construction of a Wall in the Occupied Palestinian Territory, Advisory Opinion, 2004 I.C.J. 136, para. 106.

110. *See* Nigel S. Rodley, *Can Armed Opposition Groups Violate Human Rights Standards?*, *in* HUMAN RIGHTS IN THE TWENTY-FIRST CENTURY 297 (Kathleen E. Mahoney & Paul Mahoney eds., 1993); U.N. Econ. & Soc. Council, *Report of the Consultative Meeting on the Draft Basic Principles and Guidelines on the Right to a Remedy and Reparations for Victims of Violations of International Human Rights and Humanitarian Law* para. 57, U.N. Doc. E/CN.4/2003/63 (Dec. 27, 2002). For a more progressive view, see ANDREW CLAPHAM, HUMAN RIGHTS OBLIGATIONS OF NON-STATE ACTORS 271–99 (2006).

111. Marco Sassòli, *Le droit international humanitaire, une lex specialis par rapport aux droits humains?*, *in* LES DROITS DE L'HOMME ET LA CONSTITUTION, ETUDES EN L'HONNEUR DU PROFESSEUR GIORGIO MALINVERNI 375–95 (Andreas Auer, Alexandre Flückiger & Michel Hottelier eds., 2007).

112. International Law Commission, *Fragmentation of International Law: Difficulties Arising from the Diversification and Expansion of International Law, Report of the Study Group of the International Law Commission* para. 112, U.N. Doc. A/CN.4/L.682 (Apr. 13, 2006) (*finalized by* Martti Koskenniemi) [hereinafter Fragmentation of International Law]; Heike Krieger, *A Conflict of Norms: The Relationship between Humanitarian Law and Human Rights Law in the ICRC Customary Law Study*, 11 JOURNAL OF CONFLICT & SECURITY LAW 265, 269, 271 (2006); Philip Alston et al., *The Competence of the UN Human Rights Council and its Special Procedures in relation to Armed Conflicts: Extrajudicial Executions in the "War on Terror,"* 19 EUROPEAN JOURNAL OF INTERNATIONAL LAW 183, 192 (2008); Report of the International Law Commission on the Work of its Fifty-Sixth Session para. 304, U.N. GAOR, 59th Sess. Supp. No. 10, U.N. Doc. A/59/10 (2004).

113. Anja Lindroos, *Addressing Norm Conflicts in a Fragmented System: The Doctrine of* Lex Specialis, 74 NORDIC JOURNAL OF INTERNATIONAL LAW 27, 42 (2005).

114. These terms were first used by Mary Ellen Walker, an LL.M. student at the Geneva Academy of International Humanitarian Law and Human Rights in my 2008 IHL class.

115. KARL LARENZ, METHODENLEHRE DER RECHTSWISSENSCHAFT 267–68 (6th ed. 1991).

116. Norberto Bobbio, *Des critères pour résoudre les antinomies*, *in* LES ANTINOMIES EN DROIT: ÉTUDES 244 (Chaïm Perelman ed., 1965).

117. *See, e.g.*, SEYED ALI SADAT-AKHA, METHODS OF RESOLVING CONFLICTS BETWEEN TREATIES 124 (2003).

118. See the ECtHR concerning the relationship between Articles 13 and 5(4) of the ECHR. Brannigan and McBride v. United Kingdom, 258 Eur. Ct. H.R. (ser. A) at 57, para. 76 (1993).

119. Fragmentation of International Law, *supra* note 112, para. 107.

120. Krieger, *supra* note 112, at 280.

121. Bobbio, *supra* note 116, at 240–41. *See also* Wilfred Jenks, *The Conflict of Law-Making Treaties*, 30 BRITISH YEAR BOOK OF INTERNATIONAL LAW 450 (1953).

122. HENCKAERTS & DOSWALD-BECK, *supra* note 55, at 299–383.

123. MARCO SASSÒLI, BEDEUTUNG EINER KODIFIKATION FÜR DAS ALLGEMEINE VÖLKERRECHT—MIT BESONDERER BETRACHTUNG DER REGELN ZUM SCHUTZE DER ZIVILBEVÖLKERUNG VOR DEN AUSWIRKUNGEN VON FEINDSELIGKEITEN (1990).

124. Direct Participation 2005 Report, *supra* note 46, at 52.

125. UCIHL Report, *supra* note 47, at 38; Direct Participation 2005 Report, *supra* note 46, at 51–52.

126. Legality of the Threat or Use of Nuclear Weapons, Advisory Opinion, 1996 I.C.J. 226, *supra* note 109, para. 25.

127. Alston et al., *supra* note 112, at 192–93.

128. If the *person* targeted is under control both IHL and IHRL prohibit summary execution.

129. Doswald-Beck, *supra* note 43, at 897; UCIHL Report, *supra* note 47, at 36; Kretzmer, *supra* note 48, at 203; Cordula Droege, *The Interplay between International Humanitarian Law and International Human Rights Law in Situations of Armed Conflict*, 40 ISRAEL LAW REVIEW 347 (2007).

130. Droege, *supra* note 129, at 347.

131. Public Committee against Torture, *supra* note 52, para. 40; Doswald-Beck, *supra* note 43, at 891.

132. Public Committee against Torture, *supra* note 52, para. 40.

133. Kretzmer, *supra* note 48, at 203.

134. Guerrero case, *supra* note 91, para. 13.1–13.3; Public Committee against Torture, *supra* note 52, para. 40; Orna Ben-Naftali & Keren R. Michaeli, "We Must Not Make a Scarecrow of the Law": A Legal Analysis of the Israeli Policy of Targeted Killings, 36 CORNELL INTERNATIONAL LAW JOURNAL 233, 290 (2003).

135. In relation to armed groups, it is uncertain that the *lex specialis* is the same as for government soldiers. Both parties must be equal as far as the applicable IHL is concerned, but they are not equal as far as IHRL is concerned. Even if the latter is addressed to non-State actors, it can only require from them certain conduct toward persons who are in an area under their control. In addition, a State has the alternative of law enforcement; therefore to plan an operation in such a way so as to maximize the possibility of being able to arrest persons, while the question whether armed groups may legislate to make their enemies' conduct illegal, or whether they may enforce existing legislation, is controversial.

136. *See* HENCKAERTS & DOSWALD-BECK, *supra* note 55, at 344–52.

137. JEAN S. PICTET, COMMENTARY IV ON THE GENEVA CONVENTIONS OF 12 AUGUST 1949, at 260, 369 (1952).

138. *Quoted in* Amnesty International Canada and British Columbia Civil Liberties Association v. Chief of the Defence Staff for the Canadian Forces, Minister of National Defence and Attorney General of Canada, 2008 F.C. 336, para. 175, *available at* http://www.lornewaldman.ca/pdf/aidecision.pdf.

139. AMNESTY INTERNATIONAL, AFGHANISTAN: DETAINEES TRANSFERRED TO TORTURE: ISAF COMPLICITY? (2007).

140. Jonathan Somer, *Jungle justice: passing sentence on the equality of belligerents in non-international armed conflict*, 89 INTERNATIONAL REVIEW OF THE RED CROSS 655 (2007).

141. Statute of the International Criminal Court, *supra* note 69, art. 8(2)(e)(x). *See also* HENCKAERTS & DOSWALD-BECK, *supra* note 55, at 161.

XVIII

Afghanistan Legal Lessons Learned: Army Rule of Law Operations

Eric Talbot Jensen and Amy M. Pomeroy*

In 2002, the White House published the National Security Strategy. Rather than focusing exclusively on military operations, the strategy is comprehensive and recognizes that acts ranging from poverty reduction to disease eradication will contribute to America's national security. However, one of the most crucial components of the National Security Strategy which will impact virtually all other components is the worldwide implementation of the rule of law.[1] In furtherance of the National Security Strategy, National Security Presidential Directive 44 was issued in late 2005 and states that it is US policy to work with other countries toward effective implementation of the rule of law.[2] The directive tasks the Secretaries of State and Defense with coordinating rule of law efforts and with integrating them into military contingency plans. Consequently, by direction of the President, the military has a key role to play in implementing the rule of law and judge advocates (JAs) must be prepared to lead these efforts.

* Lieutenant Colonel Eric Talbot Jensen, Judge Advocate, US Army, and Amy M. Pomeroy, Student, Brigham Young University Law School serving as a Legal Intern, International Law Branch, Office of The Judge Advocate General, US Army. The views expressed in this article are those of the authors and not The Judge Advocate General's Corps, the United States Army or the Department of Defense.

Commanders look to JAs with the expectation that they will be competent and innovative in implementing the unit's rule of law mission.[3] This is clearly demonstrated by the Center for Law and Military Operations' publication of the *Rule of Law Handbook: A Practitioner's Guide for Judge Advocates* (*Rule of Law Handbook*), where a "constantly re-occurring theme" is that "the command naturally turns to the legal expert within the task force to plan, execute, coordinate, and evaluate rule of law efforts."[4]

Over six years of operations in Afghanistan, during which commanders have relied on JAs in their rule of law operations, have created a number of lessons learned; this paper will highlight three:

- Rule of law operations must be totally integrated into all phases and aspects of military operations and the unit mission;
- US Army rule of law efforts must be completely coordinated and synchronized with other rule of law efforts, especially those of the host nation, and must recognize what role the military is organizationally qualified to fill; and
- Military rule of law operations must be effects-based.

Before addressing these lessons learned, it is important to highlight the discussion surrounding the definition of rule of law. There are divergent, and often conflicting, views among academics, US government agencies, US allies and even within the Department of Defense, on what is meant by the rule of law.[5] This definitional ambiguity allows two organizations or individuals to be deeply committed to accomplishing rule of law tasks, yet proceed in diametrically opposed directions.

Additionally, it is important to discuss the obligation that international law creates to conduct rule of law operations. Recent court decisions such as those of the United Kingdom's House of Lords in *Al-Jedda*,[6] the European Court of Human Rights cases from Kosovo[7] and Canada's *Amnesty International v. Canada*[8] have relied on Security Council resolutions to determine the substance and extent of legal obligations imposed on armed forces. The United Nations Security Council has signaled through several resolutions[9] that supporting and promoting rule of law initiatives are not only permissible, but are obligations that participants in armed conflict are required to fulfill. It is incumbent on US forces to be aware of these emerging practices and recognize that these obligations will likely follow any armed conflict, whether brought on by reason of occupation or some other theory. With international law imposing additional obligations to carry out rule of law operations, it is more crucial than ever to catalogue lessons learned, analyze their application to doctrine and ensure that the US military is conducting its rule of law operations appropriately.

I. To Be Effective, Rule of Law Operations Must Be Totally Integrated into All Phases and Aspects of Military Operations and the Unit Mission

In the aftermath of World War II, the US military embarked on a massive rule of law project that continued for years and involved a large pool of military resources. However, as the Cold War heated up, the focus transitioned from rebuilding a devastated Europe to defending a reconstructed Europe from attack. As a result, the focus of military doctrine, training, manning and equipping also adapted to this new environment. While this adaptation was necessary, it drew resources and expertise away from rule of law capabilities. Over the subsequent decades, resources, experience and training remained focused in other areas. The result was that JAs who deployed to Afghanistan felt as though they were working in an emerging area of doctrine without guidance or training.[10]

This was felt not only by JAs, but by the Army as a whole. The lack of doctrine and guidance was a significant lesson learned from early operations and sparked a number of initiatives and actions that have tried to remedy this doctrinal and training gap. These efforts have included a somewhat circular process of (1) analyzing lessons learned from military operations, (2) rewriting doctrine to include principles drawn from these lessons, (3) including this doctrine in mission training and mission rehearsal exercises at combat training centers and then (4) collecting lessons learned from the application of new doctrine in actual military operations which can then be reviewed and fed back into the doctrine review process.

The first step in this process—analysis—led to the recognition that rule of law efforts needed to be reintegrated into Army doctrine. The second step, rewriting doctrine to reflect this recognition, is well illustrated by several publications that emerged after the initial stages of engagement in Iraq and Afghanistan. The most recent Joint Publication 3-0, Doctrine for Joint Operations, divides military operations into three categories: offensive operations, defensive operations and stability operations.[11] Promoting stability operations to the same level as offense and defense is a dramatic change from a Cold War paradigm where defending the Fulda Gap against an invasion by Warsaw Pact forces was the primary focus.

The importance of stability operations is echoed in the 2005 Department of Defense Directive 3000.05, Military Support for Stability, Security, Transition, and Reconstruction (SSTR) Operations, which states:

> Stability operations are a core U.S. military mission that the Department of Defense shall be prepared to conduct and support. They shall be given priority comparable to combat operations and be explicitly addressed and integrated across all [Department

of Defense] activities including doctrine, organization, training, education, exercises, materiel, leadership, personnel, facilities, and planning.[12]

Rule of law operations are an essential subset of stability operations. Declaring stability operations to be a core US military mission has driven an increase in the expenditure of training resources and has changed the planning and execution stages to ensure units can accomplish rule of law missions.

Doctrine has also been rewritten to reflect the roles the military should be prepared to fulfill to further the rule of law. One change in doctrine acknowledges that the military may be called upon to play a supporting governance role. Joint Publication 3-0 discusses the various phases of an operation, the last two of which are "stabilize" and "enable civil authority." To complete these last two phases, "[t]he joint force may be required to perform limited local governance, integrating the efforts of other supporting/contributing multinational, [other government agencies, international government agencies, or nongovernmental agencies (NGOs)], participants until legitimate local entities are functioning. This includes providing or assisting in the provision of basic services to the population."[13] Further, "The joint force will be in a supporting role to the legitimate civil authority in the region throughout the 'enable civil authority' phase."[14]

Current doctrine also recognizes that the military can aid rule of law development by creating security, a prerequisite for the rule of law, and a fundamental military mission throughout all phases of an operation. Depending on the circumstances, "it may be the only real contribution that US forces can make towards implementing the rule of law."[15] Experience has taught that, for a multitude of reasons, there is a direct correlation between the establishment of a safe and secure environment and the ability to accomplish rule of law objectives. Achieving such an environment requires in-depth planning from the very earliest stages of the operation.

Finally, military doctrine has changed to recognize that US forces promote the rule of law when their own actions, across the spectrum of military operations, reinforce the legitimacy of the rule of law even before a stable environment has been created. The *Rule of Law Handbook* accurately states that "[a] command's ability to establish the rule of law within its area of control is dependent in large part on its *own* compliance with legal rules restricting soldiers' (and the command's own) discretion."[16] This idea is echoed in the Center for Army Lessons Learned compilation on counterinsurgency (COIN) operations which states that "[m]ilitary actions [must be] conducted in consonance with specified civil rights, liberties, and objectives."[17] The only way to do that is to ensure that rule of law considerations are an essential part of the unit mission and intertwined with all military operations and training. Every soldier, sailor, airman and Marine must recognize that his or her actions can have a profound effect on the success of the national strategic interest in supporting rule of law operations throughout the world.

To effectively carry out these and other doctrinal changes, the Army has transformed its combat training centers into stability operations training grounds. The National Training Center in California, Joint Readiness Training Center in Louisiana and Joint Multinational Readiness Center in Germany have all incorporated stability operations, including rule of law operations, into their training scenarios. Units routinely conduct "mission rehearsal exercises" at these locations to prepare themselves for the actual events that will take place in an impending deployment to Afghanistan or Iraq. This training not only incorporates the new stability operations doctrine, but also the most recent lessons learned from units currently deployed. With this training, units are better prepared to deploy to Afghanistan and similar environments and support rule of law operations.

The importance of promoting and complying with the rule of law has been clearly stated in almost every "lesson learned" from deployed units. The doctrine is now in place and in the process of continual review based on continuing feedback from current military operations. Furthermore, mechanisms for implementing the doctrine, such as training at the combat maneuver training centers, are also in place. What remains is for the doctrine to be implemented on the ground, ensuring that these legal lessons are truly learned, not lost.

II. US Army Rule of Law Efforts Must Be Completely Coordinated and Synchronized with Other Rule of Law Efforts, Especially Those of the Host Nation, and Must Recognize What Role the Military Is Organizationally Qualified to Fill

Because rule of law efforts are so complex, they are most effective when all contributing groups, especially the host nation, coordinate with one another rather than inadvertently working at cross purposes. The *Rule of Law Handbook* illustrates this point:

> Rule of law operations in Iraq and Afghanistan have repeatedly demonstrated that rule of law practitioners who seek to coordinate efforts, funding, and resources with other agencies and organizations yield the most effective results. . . . [A]s hostilities come to a close other [US Government] agencies . . . will arrive in theater. Regional, state-based economic and security organizations such as the Gulf Cooperative Council or the Organization for Security and Cooperation in Europe . . . may have a presence. The United Nations may, depending upon the operation have a presence, as may nongovernmental agencies with an interest in human rights and justice. Each of these

fail to embrace proposed rule of law operations, not only are the operations doomed to failure, they will not promote the strategic interests of the United States. Conversely, when Afghanis and the Afghan government are a part of a cooperative effort, great progress can be made. One such example of a successful rule of law collaboration with the host nation is the creation of the Provincial Justice Conferences (PJC) program in Afghanistan:

> The Provincial Justice Conferences (PJCs) program attempts to [bring Government of Afghanistan (GoA)] justice officials from Kabul to meet their counterparts in the provinces to discuss the obstacles to delivery of justice services to the province and to identify solutions that can be instituted expediently and in a cost-effective way. Follow-up PJCs are generally scheduled within a period of three to six months to check on progress made on the identified solutions and to discuss outstanding issues. One essential key to a successful PJC has been the invitation and inclusion of all interested [US government (USG)] agencies, the international community, and NGO representatives. Each agency or organization has the benefit of significant, specialized, and diverse experience. With the inclusion of as many subject-matter experts as possible, new ideas may emerge to correct persistent problems.
>
> As of the first quarter of 2007, PJCs and follow-up PJCs [had] been conducted in six provinces in Afghanistan. The first PJCs drew small attendance from among the provincial justice officials, but more recent PJCs have drawn upwards of 150 people from the national, provincial, and district levels, and, in some cases, from neighboring provinces. A typical PJC program consists of several distinct parts. First, all participants are taken on a tour of justice facilities in the provincial capital, to include the prison, police headquarters/detention centers, judges' office, prosecutor's office, courthouse, and defense counsel offices (if any). This feature gives participants a first-hand view of the justice infrastructure and an opportunity to observe justice officials in their own environments. Second, a general session of all participants is convened and hosted by the provincial governor. Brief comments from the governor, justice officials, and USG/international participants are presented. After a communal lunch, hosted by one or more of the USG participants, conferees are divided into groups representing their individual justice interests—police, judges, prosecutors, defense counsel, and prison administrators. These groups discuss specialized problems and their potential solutions. The small groups take notes on their discussions from which a mark plan can be developed. Finally, the small group leaders from either GoA or the provincial government present summaries of their discussions to a final general session at the end of the day.[27]

Organizing a PJC is a difficult and time-consuming process and becomes more so as the organizing rule of law officer attempts to include all interested agencies. However, it is this type of coordination and inclusion that links agency resources with the Afghanis who are attempting to create the rule of law in courtrooms and police stations. This host-nation lead in rule of law programs is vital to their continued vitality and eventual success.

A second lesson is that the military is not the most qualified or appropriate body to conduct many aspects of rule of law operations. Department of Defense Directive 3000.05 recognizes this and states, "[m]any stability operations tasks are best performed by indigenous, foreign, or U.S. civilian professionals."[28] There are simply tasks that the military is not the most qualified to perform. A recent after-action review highlights this point:

> The military possesses an organizational culture that is different from the rest of the interagency. The military skill sets are required in order to establish the rule of law initially, and then other elements of national power are better suited to restore economic and industrial power. Two main points of understanding are (1) civilians are not in the military chain of command and do not accept military leadership and (2) civilians cannot be ordered to do anything. The interagency operates on the unity of effort, while the military prefers unity of command.[29]

Additionally, it would simply be counterproductive for the military to undertake certain tasks, as doing so could create reliance on military action by the host nation and others.

Despite the military's inherently limited ability to implement the rule of law, in the absence of other options, the military may find it necessary to step into a vacuum in order to ensure that certain necessary tasks are accomplished. Department of Defense Directive 3000.05 also recognizes this side of the coin and, after recognizing that many stability operations are ideally left to others, states that, "[n]onetheless, U.S. military forces shall be prepared to perform all tasks necessary to establish or maintain order when civilians cannot do so."[30] While few would likely quibble with this statement, applying it is more difficult, especially determining when the time is right for the military to step up and perform these tasks as opposed to waiting for others. This difficult decision must be made and made competently by commanders and JAs on the ground using their best judgment.

A third lesson is that the rule of law is more effectively implemented when all players act in concert. JAs need to plan for and work within the multinational and interagency environment in order to maximize efficiency, effectiveness and engagement. If the US military doesn't function within the joint, interagency and multinational environment when forwarding rule of law initiatives, it simply does not function effectively. As the *Rule of Law Handbook* accurately states, "[w]hat is agreed upon by almost every individual who has worked in this area is that joint, inter-agency, and multinational coordination is the basic foundation upon which all rule of law efforts must be built."[31] And further:

> Without coordination with other players in the rule of law arena, the efforts of a single contributor in isolation are at best less than optimal and at worst counterproductive to the overall rule of law reform objectives being pursued. Quite simply, coordination and synchronization is to the rule of law effort what fires and maneuver is to the high intensity conflict.[32]

As the Army internalizes this, it will be better able to coordinate with other agencies.

Despite initial and continuing difficulties, there have been instances in which the military has worked successfully with other agencies to create positive results. The following illustration from the *Rule of Law Handbook* is based on lessons learned through after-action reviews. While lengthy, it demonstrates quite clearly the increased likelihood of success for rule of law operations when a broad range of parties are involved.

> Nowhere was the interagency success more evident than the justice sector achievements in the Wardak province known as the Wardak Model Justice Project. In late 2005, the Justice Sector Support Program (JSSP), a contractor of the [Department of State (DOS)] International Narcotics and Law Enforcement Affairs Bureau (INL), began a training program for provincial and district level judges and prosecutors in Maydan Wardak. Almost simultaneously, but without advanced coordination, DOD rule of law and [Civil Affairs (CA)] personnel teamed up to build a justice administration building in Maydan Shar. Using [Commander's Emergency Response Program (CERP)] funds, available to tactical commanders for urgent and humanitarian rebuilding projects in post-conflict Afghanistan and Iraq, the [Combined Forces Command–Afghanistan (CFC-A)] rule of law and CA team obtained the blueprints for a generic administration building from USAID. USAID was using the blueprints to build up to 40 provincial courthouses throughout Afghanistan. Using these blueprints, CFC-A began construction in early 2006 on the justice administration building in Maydan Shar.
>
> Momentum gathered as the people of Maydan Wardak generated more enthusiasm for the improvements being made. The USG agencies began to look more carefully at each other's rule of law activities in Maydan Wardak, and, aided by strong leadership on the Special Committee for the Rule of Law[,] began a concerted coordination effort to build on those successes. Lessons learned were shared among the Special Counselor on the Rule of Law agency representatives, resulting in more efficient delivery of proposed projects.
>
> USAID began construction on a new courthouse, and one of its contractors offered to introduce its new paper-based court administration system in Maydan Shar. CFC-A also provided a justice motor-pool (with maintenance and fuel packages) and sponsored a public awareness campaign to let the citizens of the province know the

> steps being taken to improve the delivery of justice services. At the same time, CFC-A contracted with an Afghan NGO to provide defense counsel services to criminal defendants in Wardak and five other provinces. Ultimately, building on the combined efforts of the other USG agencies, the DOS announced in late 2006 that it would build a new, state-of-the-art prison and national corrections training facility in Maydan Wardak. The result of the ongoing combined efforts of these agencies was the Wardak Model Justice Project, the name reflecting the goal of the agencies involved that the justice system in Maydan Wardak should be rebuilt to serve as a model for the international community and the GoA for such improvements in other provinces.
>
> Interagency cooperation and communications between the agencies involved in Wardak continues in 2007. A group of agency representatives and provincial justice and government officials gathers monthly in Wardak to discuss problems with and future plans for further expansion of the Wardak Model Justice Project. Visibility on this project remains high as the provincial governor continues to chair each monthly meeting. Participants from all USG agencies are invited to these meetings, as well as representatives of the international community and various NGOs. The recently arrived Turkish Provincial Reconstruction Team (PRT) brought a police training team with them, and this program has been incorporated into the Wardak Model Justice Project. Similar efforts are being planned for Nangarhar, Bamyian, and Logar provinces as part of [a] wider DOS strategic plan for implementation of its rule of law program.[33]

While the Wardak Project clearly illustrates the benefits that can be achieved when several agencies each work toward a common end, much of the success achieved in Wardak was more a product of coincidence than of premeditated coordination on the part of the agencies involved. In the vast majority of cases, conscientious, institutionalized coordination will be needed, as illustrated by the following example:

> In early 2006, a Special Counselor on the Rule of Law was appointed by the DOS to coordinate interagency rule of law efforts in Afghanistan, to assure that gaps and overlaps in such efforts were corrected, and to assist in the development of a broader USG rule of law agenda. . . . A committee of representatives from each USG agency involved in rule of law activities was organized and was chaired by the Special Counselor who was later replaced by a senior lawyer who currently holds the title of Rule of Law Coordinator. . . . Regular and frequent rule of law meetings have resulted in much greater coordination of rule of law efforts at the strategic level, the development of strong interpersonal and cooperative relationships, and a greater awareness of each agency's rule of law activities among and between all participants and the rule of law [sic] Coordinator.[34]

If the Provincial Justice Conferences program, the creation of the office of Rule of Law Coordinator and the Wardak Project are indicative of the future of interagency and international coordination, there is much to be optimistic about concerning rule of law operations in Afghanistan. The clear lesson learned is that it is only through complete coordination and inclusion of host-nation components that all the disparate efforts to promote rule of law within Afghanistan can be successful.

III. To Be Effective, Military Rule of Law Operations Must Be Effects-Based

In October 2002 after a year of operations in Afghanistan, Desmond Saunders-Newton and Aaron B. Frank wrote in a National Defense University publication that

> [t]he U.S. military, under the guidance of the Secretary of Defense, is moving toward a new concept of military planning and operations that is agile and adaptable to the conflict at hand. . . . The new concept called effects-based operations encompasses processes, tools, and organizations that focus planning, executing, and assessing military activities for the effects produced rather than merely tallying the number of targets destroyed.[35]

The authors go on to write that what is needed is not a "traditional force-on-force analysis," but "the skillful use of force in conjunction with diplomatic, economic, legal, and other instruments of national power"[36] that are characteristic of effects-based operations.

This effects-based approach has been used effectively in Afghanistan, particularly in rule of law initiatives.[37] Because effects-based operations are "fundamentally about linking end states and objectives to tactical tasks through identifying and producing desired effects to accomplish missions,"[38] it is vital for JAs to focus on the effect desired, rather than on the project that may or may not accomplish this effect. This is reflected in the *Rule of Law Handbook,* which states:

> [*I*]*nstitutional* improvements can be valuable, but rule of law projects should ultimately focus on bringing about particular *effects,* not on the institutions that may exist following the completion of the project. Thus, it is critical to keep in mind what values are represented by the rule of law so that those values, not some intermediate, institutionally focused objectives, drive the rule of law efforts.[39]

To illustrate this point, consider the administrative functioning of a court system. In many areas of Afghanistan, the court system had no administrative structure, such as a docketing and case-tracking system, or method of reporting and documenting case decisions. As JAs recognize the need to institutionalize case administration, they may be tempted to try and recreate a modern court system, complete with computerized databases and transfer and recording capabilities. However, one of the lessons learned from such efforts in Afghanistan is that "it is usually better to favor low-tech solutions, such as manual court reporting and paper filing systems."[40] More modern systems require trained computer personnel to operate and maintain the systems. Even more basic, such systems require continuous access to electricity. While these aspects of running a court system may not be issues in the United States, they are significant constraints in Afghanistan and other similar situations where the US Army operates. Such considerations cause the *Rule of Law Handbook* to conclude, "[w]hen it comes to administrative infrastructure, the clear lesson is that simplicity is key."[41]

The lesson here is that a JA who is not focused on effects may instead focus on creating the best administrative court system possible, using the most modern technologies. However, if the effect desired is a functioning administrative court system that can effectively maintain itself, a concentration on low-tech solutions is much more likely to succeed.

While this is a simplistic example, a similar analysis can be applied to rule of law operations generally. Important initiatives, such as establishing a defense bar, ensuring a trained and independent judiciary, establishing judicial oversight on police activities and maintaining a penal system that complies with fundamental human rights, all benefit from an effects-based approach.

A comprehensive and effective effects-based approach to rule of law operations has several components; the first is the completion of an initial assessment. Such assessments look at the current and prior situations and develop a factual foundation upon which future actions can occur. These assessments are often done in the US Army by civil affairs personnel, but every "Judge Advocate engaged in the rule of law mission must become comfortable with creating and reviewing assessments of foreign nations' legal systems, including courts, private organizations, police, and prisons."[42] Such assessments should include the history and tradition of the local legal system, identification of which persons and organizations have a role in the system, and what capabilities and needs currently exist.[43] A good assessment that is continually updated will provide the foundation for rule of law operations that can focus on and accomplish the desired rule of law effects.

A second component, and one of the most difficult aspects of effect-based operations, is determining measures of effectiveness that will accurately reflect whether the desired effects have been achieved. Metrics, which are quantitative or qualitative systems of measurement, have become an important part of assessing rule of law effectiveness. "Meaningful metrics permit the Judge Advocate . . . to not only measure whether the mission is accomplishing its goals, but to also convey information to superiors and policy makers in a quantifiable manner that is not purely anecdotal."[44] An example of a meaningful metric measuring overall movement toward the rule of law would incorporate individuals' perceptions of whether (or to what degree) the law is superior to individuals, is applied by an impartial and independent body and is applied consistently to all subjects.

In attempting to develop metrics that measure success, it is tempting to revert to focusing on means rather than effects. The *Rule of Law Handbook* reminds us why this urge must be overcome:

> At the sustained deployment stage, merely focusing upon the number of court houses operating, the number of prison cells available, and the number of judges hearing a given number of cases begins to tell an increasingly irrelevant story. Now operations are moving into the higher realm of what constitutes establishment of the rule of law. A tyrannical system despised by its population can have courthouses, cells, and case adjudication statistics and yet the rule of law does not exist. Once a plateau of recovery is reached where the facilities and personnel exist to operate the legal system, then the metrics upon which assessments and planning are built must shift to analyzing the *efficacy* and *legitimacy* of the system.[45]

The veracity of the effects-based approach is echoed in a recent publication from the Center for Army Lessons Learned. Michael McCoy writes that Provincial Reconstruction Teams

> should design measures of effectiveness that delineate the perception of safety, the reduction of security incidences that impact daily life, the capacity of the government to provide basic services and rule of law, and the popular acceptance of legitimate formal and informal organizations and leaders by both the majority of the population and disaffected elements of the population.[46]

Designing metrics that adequately measure the desired effects and provide useful input into the way forward is a difficult task. It is easy to see why Samuel Young, writing concerning V Corps operations, concludes that "[t]he complexity of conducting non-lethal Effects Based Operations in a Joint, Interagency, Intergovernmental, and Multinational (JIIM) environment challenges the mindset, training, and organization of our warfighting formations."[47]

Despite some difficulties, this effects-based approach has been utilized with great success in Afghanistan by members of the 10th Mountain Division whose experiences were recorded in a recent Initial Impressions Report. Prior to deployment, the division developed a comprehensive effects-based plan to guide it during its year in

Afghanistan. Its objectives were to improve security; support the local, provincial and national governments; and improve local and provincial infrastructure.

> Beginning with their campaign plan, operational desired effects were identified as "results/conditions" that[,] when achieved, represent accomplishing stated objectives. Desired effects were clearly articulated for each operational objective that in turn served as guides for developing tactical missions and tasks for subordinate units. Throughout all planning and coordination activities, the staff was disciplined to review stated effects in the campaign plan and then develop activities and tasks to help generate the stated desired effects.
>
> The Division's operations were assessment driven. Daily, weekly, and monthly assessments of the progress of operations helped determine what [Combined Joint Task Force]-76 was doing right and what areas of the plan needed adjustment. These assessments were focused on both measures of performance of tasks and measures of effectiveness in achieving desired effects.[48]

The Initial Impressions Report concludes by stating that "[t]he Division is very comfortable with using an effects-based approach to guide operations" and "[t]he 10th [Mountain] was clearly very successful during their year in Afghanistan."[49]

Though reformulating efforts to focus on effects and finding meaningful metrics to measure these effects may be difficult, it is clear that the effects-based approach to rule of law operations is the most effective. The lesson learned for JAs is that they must adopt and internalize the effects-based approach and become fully engaged in the metrics process of assessment and analysis.

IV. Conclusion

As is aptly illustrated by the Naval War College's dedication of a complete workshop and volume of the "Blue Book" to this topic, there are numerous lessons to be learned from the current military operations in Afghanistan. For the US Army, some of the most significant legal lessons have been in the area of rule of law operations. The Army is still in the process of learning many of these lessons, but some have already been put into practice, benefitting operations in Iraq. As we continue to apply what we have learned by integrating the rule of law into military practice, cooperating with other agencies and measuring the success of our operations by their effects, future rule of law efforts will better serve the US strategic national interest.

Notes

1. The White House, National Security Strategy of the United States 3, 9–10, 17, 19, 22, 28 (Sept. 2002), *available at* http://www.acq.osd.mil/ncbdp/nm/docs/Relevant%20Docs/national_security_strategy.pdf.

2. National Security Presidential Directive/NSPD-44 (2005), *available at* http://www.fas.org/irp/offdocs/nspd/nspd-44.html.

3. Center for Army Lessons Learned, Division Commanders Guide to Information Operation in OIF & OEF Handbook (Dec. 2007), *available at* https://callsearch.leavenworth.army.mil/CALL2Search/isysquery/9e25b547-35fc-469d-8aaf-84ad401c78c1/19/doc/ (available to current DoD employees and their contractors through approved website access).

4. CENTER FOR LAW AND MILITARY OPERATIONS, THE JUDGE ADVOCATE GENERAL'S LEGAL CENTER SCHOOL AND JOINT FORCE JUDGE ADVOCATE, UNITED STATES JOINT FORCES COMMAND, RULE OF LAW HANDBOOK: A PRACTITIONER'S GUIDE FOR JUDGE ADVOCATES i (2007) [hereinafter RULE OF LAW HANDBOOK].

5. *Id.* The UN Security Council's definition is a good starting point and comports with most definitions of the rule of law: (1) The law is supreme, (2) the law is applied by an independent institution (such as a judicial branch) and (3) the law applies equally to all subjects of the law. *See* FEDERAL MINISTRY FOR EUROPEAN AND INTERNATIONAL AFFAIRS (AUSTRIA) & INSTITUTE FOR INTERNATIONAL LAW AND JUSTICE, NEW YORK UNIVERSITY SCHOOL OF LAW, THE U.N. SECURITY COUNCIL AND THE RULE OF LAW: THE ROLE OF THE SECURITY COUNCIL IN STRENGTHENING A RULES-BASED INTERNATIONAL SYSTEM 3–4 (2008).

6. R (Al-Jedda) v. Secretary of State for Defence, [2007] UKHL 58 (House of Lords 2007).

7. Behrami v. France and Saramati v. France, Germany and Norway, apps. nos. 71412/01 and 78166/01, 45 Eur. Ct. H.R. 41 (2007) (Grand Chamber).

8. Amnesty International Canada v. Canada (Attorney General), 2008 FC 336 (2008).

9. S.C. Res. 1806, U.N. Doc. S/RES/1806 (Mar. 20, 2008); S.C. Res. 1662, U.N. Doc. S/RES/1662 (Mar. 23, 2006); S.C. Res. 1746, U.N. Doc. S/RES/1746 (Mar. 23, 2007); S.C. Res. 1802, U.N. Doc. S/RES/1802 (Feb. 25, 2008).

10. Rule of Law Handbook, *supra* note 4, at i.

11. Chairman of the Joint Chiefs of Staff, Joint Publication 3-0, Doctrine for Joint Operations, at V-1 (Sept. 2006, with change 1, Feb. 13, 2008), *available at* http://www.dtic.mil/doctrine/jel/new_pubs/jp3_0.pdf [hereinafter Joint Pub. 3-0].

12. Department of Defense, Directive 3000.05, Military Support for Stability, Security, Transition, and Reconstruction (SSTR) Operations para. 4.1 (Nov. 28, 2005), *available at* http://www.dtic.mil/whs/directives/corres/pdf/300005p.pdf [hereinafter DoD Directive 3000.05]. See also Joint Pub. 3-0, *supra* note 11, at V-1, which defines stability operations as "missions, tasks, and activities [that] seek to maintain or reestablish a safe and secure environment and provide essential governmental services, emergency infrastructure reconstruction, or humanitarian relief."

13. Joint Pub. 3-0, *supra* note 11, at IV-29.

14. *Id.* at IV-30.

15. Rule of Law Handbook, *supra* note 4, at 8.

16. *Id.* at 16.

17. Center for Army Lessons Learned, Southern Afghanistan COIN Operations 24 (2006), *available at* https://callsearch.leavenworth.army.mil/CALL2Search/isysquery/9e25b547-35fc-469d-8aaf-84ad401c78c1/35/doc/ (available to current DoD employees and their contractors through approved website access).

18. RULE OF LAW HANDBOOK, *supra* note 4, at 112.

19. *Id.* at 51 (footnote omitted).

20. M. Ashraf Haidari, *Paris Conference: Aid Effectiveness Key to Addressing Afghanistan's Rebuilding Challenges* (June 12, 2008), EURASIANET, http://www.eurasianet.org/departments/insight/articles/eav061208f.shtml.

21. One of the three focuses of Provincial Reconstruction Teams is to "[i]ncrease provincial stability through international military presence and assist in developing nascent host nation security and rule of law capacity." Michael McCoy, Center for Army Lessons Learned, Provincial Reconstruction Team Playbook (Sept. 2007), *available at* https://callsearch.leavenworth.army.mil/CALL2Search/isysquery/9e25b547-35fc-469d-8aaf-84ad401c78c1/13/doc/ (available to current DoD employees and their contractors through approved website access) [hereinafter PRT Handbook].

22. For example, DoD Directive 3000.05, *supra* note 12, para. 4.4 states:

> Integrated civilian and military efforts are key to successful stability operations. Whether conducting or supporting stability operations, the Department of Defense shall be prepared to work closely with relevant U.S. Departments and Agencies, foreign governments and security forces, global and regional international organizations, U.S. and foreign non-governmental organizations, and private sector individuals and for-profit companies.

23. National Security Presidential Directive/NSPD-44, *supra* note 2, para. 3.

24. *Id.*, para. 4.

25. US Department of State, Office of the Coordinator for Reconstruction and Stabilization, http://www.state.gov/s/crs/ (last visited Feb. 18, 2008).

26. US Department of State, About S/CRS, http://www.state.gov/s/crs/c12936.htm (last visited Feb. 18, 2009).

27. RULE OF LAW HANDBOOK, *supra* note 4, at 56 (footnote omitted).

28. DoD Directive 3000.05, *supra* note 12, para. 4.3.

29. Center for Army Lessons Learned, Leader Challenges – OEF and OIF (Dec. 2005), *available at* https://callsearch.leavenworth.army.mil/CALL2Search/isysquery/9e25b547-35fc-469d-8aaf-84ad401c78c1/33/doc/ (available to current DoD employees and their contractors through approved website access).

30. DoD Directive 3000.05, *supra* note 12, para. 4.3.

31. RULE OF LAW HANDBOOK, *supra* note 4, at ii.

32. *Id.*

33. *Id.* at 54–55 (footnote omitted).

34. *Id.* at 52–53 (footnote omitted).

35. Desmond Saunders-Newton & Aaron B. Frank, *Effects-Based Operations: Building the Analytic Tools*, DEFENSE HORIZONS, Oct. 2002, at 1, http://www.ndu.edu/inss/DefHor/DH19/193-619_DH19.pdf.

36. *Id.* at 2.

37. Center for Army Lessons Learned, A Special Study on Effects-Based Approach to Military Operations (May 2005), *available at* https://callsearch.leavenworth.army.mil/CALL2Search/ isysquery/263df3d8-ca0e-41c9-9d43-0ef4907e39bc/23/doc/ (available to current DoD employees and their contractors through approved website access).

38. *Id.*

39. RULE OF LAW HANDBOOK, *supra* note 4, at 19 (footnote omitted).

40. *Id.* at 75.

41. *Id.*

42. *Id.* at 121.
43. *Id.* at 121–34.
44. *Id.* at 134.
45. *Id.* at 137.
46. PRT Handbook, *supra* note 21.
47. Samuel R. Young, Center for Army Lessons Learned, V Corps as Multi-National Corps – Iraq (June 2007), *available at* https://callsearch.leavenworth.army.mil/CALL2Search/isysquery/263df3d8-ca0e-41c9-9d43-0ef4907e39bc/18/doc/ (available to current DoD employees and their contractors through approved website access).
48. Mike Stark, Initial Impressions Report (IIR) - 10th Mountain Division - Observations of a Modular Force Division Operating as a CJTF in OEF, 1.3 (2007), *available at* https://callsearch.leavenworth.army.mil/call2-search/isysquery/556986ea-00d2-4eb4-a5b6-4c739a45695d/1/doc/ (available to current DoD employees and their contractors through approved website access).
49. *Id.*

PART VI

HUMAN RIGHTS ISSUES

XIX

Is Human Rights Law of Any Relevance to Military Operations in Afghanistan?

Françoise J. Hampson*

I. Introduction

Newspaper reports in Western Europe and the publications of reputable human rights groups, such as Human Rights Watch and Amnesty International, give the impression that innocent villagers are being indiscriminately killed by coalition forces in Afghanistan.[1] News reports also suggest that Afghans complain of the lack of physical security and of very slow progress in the development of physical and social infrastructure. The issue is not, in this context, whether such claims are well founded. The perception of the Afghans and of the human rights groups is that civilians are being killed unnecessarily and, by implication, unlawfully. The forces involved claim to be showing the most rigorous adherence to the requirements of the law of armed conflict.[2] Part of the explanation for the gap in perceptions may be that the Afghans and the human rights groups are thinking in terms of respect for human rights law, in the context of a law and order paradigm, whereas the military forces are thinking exclusively in terms of the law of armed conflict. This raises the question of the relevance of human rights law to the conduct of military operations in Afghanistan, the subject of this article.

Before embarking on an analysis of the principal questions at issue, it is necessary to make a number of preliminary points. The first is that it will be assumed that two, legally significantly different operations are being conducted in Afghanistan.

* Professor, Department of Law & Human Rights Centre, University of Essex, UK.

One is the International Security Assistance Force (ISAF) operation, which has a Security Council mandate and is there to assist the government of Afghanistan.[3] It is said to be dealing with an insurgency, led by the Taliban, and to be governed by the rules applicable in non-international armed conflict. The second is Operation Enduring Freedom, which is said to be a continuation of the conflict which started in 2001 between an ad hoc coalition, working with the Northern Alliance, and the Taliban and Al Qaeda forces. This conflict is said to be international in nature. This characterization of the conflict(s) is not without controversy but will not be further explored here.

The second preliminary point concerns the nature of human rights law. Lawyers with certain armed forces shy away from anything to do with human rights law and, by extension, with human rights more generally, perhaps at least in part owing to fear of the unknown.[4] They claim that it has nothing to do with them and their operations, a claim that, in such broad terms, is patently untrue. This article cannot hope to provide a general introduction to human rights law; for that, readers need to seek elsewhere.[5] It is, nevertheless, necessary to highlight certain features of this body of rules. First, there is a difference between human rights law and human rights. The former refers to legal obligations of States. The focus will be principally on treaty law, which is of course subject to ratification. The main emphasis will be on the international treaties, notably the International Covenant on Civil and Political Rights, with only occasional reference to the regional treaties. It should not be forgotten, however, that there are human rights mechanisms that, ultimately, owe their existence to the UN Charter.[6] All States are subject to their scrutiny. The norms, respect for which they monitor, are either part of customary human rights law or part of Charter law. Human rights more generally refers to values and precepts that may (or should) be the basis of policy decisions, such as the rule of law, democracy, participation, transparency and accountability. Human rights in this sense is part of the "good governance" agenda.

Second, human rights law is civil in character, like any other area of public international law. States found to have violated human rights law may be required to amend their law and to make restitution. The failure to investigate an alleged human rights violation and, where appropriate, to institute domestic criminal proceedings may be a violation of human rights law but the enforcement of that body of law at the regional or international level does not involve criminal proceedings.[7] The individual perpetrator is not the human rights violator. The State which is responsible for the non-investigation will be held responsible under human rights law. This points to a significant difference between human rights law and the law of armed conflict. The former *only* binds the State. Human rights law is not based on the bond of citizenship. The rights are said to be inherent in every human being. This means that they do not need to be earned and are not dependent upon good behavior. Human rights law is about the relationship between those who exercise authority and those subjected to its exercise. It applies to anyone subject to the exercise of such authority or jurisdiction, a concept that will be examined further below.

Third, human rights law contains both positive and negative obligations. Not only is there the negative obligation, for example, not to torture. Only State agents can trigger responsibility for breach of the negative obligation. There is also a positive obligation to protect persons from torture, both at the hands of State agents and third parties. This is generally satisfied by having a properly functioning legal system that penalizes the behavior in question and an effective system of investigation and prosecution that ensures that wrongdoers are punished.[8] In some circumstances, it may require more than that in the way of protection.[9]

The fourth element represents a sweeping generalization. Provided that caveat is not forgotten, the claim may still offer useful insights. Human rights law, at least as enforced by regional human rights courts, is designed principally to be applied after the event. It provides general principles which enable a judge to determine in a precise set of circumstances whether a rule has been violated. It is capable of considerable fine-tuning, particularly with the development over time of fairly consistent case law. What permits such fine-tuning is the use of limitation clauses, which are an intrinsic part of the elaboration of many rights. For example, there is no absolute right of freedom of expression. Rather, the starting point is that such a right exists but it can be subject to restrictions imposed by law and based on one or more generally defined grounds, on condition that the limitation is both necessary and proportionate.[10] In the case of negative obligations, responsibility often appears to be based on the result. One exception is responsibility for unlawful killings, where what the reasonable perpetrator thought would obviously be relevant. In contrast, the law of armed conflict is designed to provide guidance to armed forces at the time decisions are made and actions undertaken. The emphasis in criminal proceedings on what was known at the time should avoid the danger that determinations of responsibility after the event will be based on the twenty-twenty vision of hindsight.[11] The fine-tuning occurs in the mind of the commander, rather than that of the judge.

The fifth issue is that the starting point of human rights law is the protected interest or right. Any limitations or exceptions have to be interpreted restrictively. In the case of the law of armed conflict, the law itself represents a balance. One side of that balance should not be interpreted restrictively in relation to the other. This is a possible explanation for the way in which certain human rights groups, on occasion, appear to interpret the law of armed conflict; they are treating the protection of civilians, for example, as the starting point and any restrictions as an exception.

This article will consider five issues: first, whether human rights law remains applicable when the law of armed conflict is applicable;[12] second, whether human rights obligations apply extraterritorially; third, the impact of the territorial State's human rights obligations for other States assisting it; fourth, the effect of a Security Council mandate on legal obligations that would otherwise be applicable; and, finally, whether human rights notions could offer useful guidance to armed forces, whether or not human rights law is applicable *de jure*.

It is clear that the interplay between human rights law and the law of armed conflict is currently a source of confusion and the subject of debate. There are plausible explanations for how we have come to find ourselves in this muddle. The law of armed conflict, historically, regulated inter-State conflicts and civil wars of such intensity that they resembled inter-State conflicts. In view of the impact of the latter on, for example, trade and ports, third States had to recognize belligerency to protect their rights as neutrals.[13] In 1949, there was the first attempt in treaty law to regulate every type of internal conflict, provided that it constituted an armed conflict and not merely isolated and sporadic acts of violence.[14] Traditionally, such conflicts had been purely the province of domestic law, including constitutional law, criminal law and civil liberties. Domestic law determined the circumstances in which an emergency could be declared. It also dealt with the consequences of such an emergency, including civil liberties safeguards which could not be suspended. In other words, Common Article 3 of the Geneva Conventions[15] made inroads, albeit very minimal ones, in the relationship between the individual and the State.[16] At about the same time, domestic civil liberties rules surfaced on the international plane as human rights law.[17] The shift from domestic to international law owed much to the desire to prevent what was perceived to have contributed to the causes of the Second World War and to the appalling conduct of those exercising governmental authority during the course of the war, in both national and occupied territory. The respect for human rights was seen as a way of ensuring that people did not "have recourse, as a last resort, to rebellion against tyranny and oppression."[18] It was necessary to reinforce domestic provisions, designed to prevent the misuse of authority but which could be subverted, with international guarantees. The regional and international enforcement of human rights law is not an end in itself. It is designed to persuade a State to adopt the necessary measures at the domestic level.

It was recognized that States might well have to deal with emergencies, in which certain rights might be subject to unusual restrictions, but it was made clear that, even in such circumstances, certain guarantees had to be maintained. In other words, the very *raison d'être* for the international spine-stiffening of domestic civil liberties rules was the risk of abuse and misuse of governmental authority in emergencies or periods of conflict. The law sought to prevent the situation from deteriorating to that level but, if it did so, the law sought to ensure that things did not get even worse. From the outset then, one could have predicted overlap between the new inroads made by the law of armed conflict into internal conflicts and the internationalization of domestic constitutional and civil liberties guarantees. Superficially, there may be an obvious solution for those who seek to keep the law of armed conflict and human rights law separate, rather than to seek an accommodation between the two bodies of rules. It would involve eliminating all law of armed conflict rules applicable in non-international armed conflict, other than perhaps those non-international conflicts which resemble international armed conflicts. Human rights law would be the only body of rules regulating affairs within a State, including armed conflict. Quite apart from the problem of eliminating a widely accepted body of rules[19] and the question of the desirability of doing so, it is difficult to see how such a rigid distinction could be made. What would happen to those rules applicable within a State's own territory during international armed conflict?[20] Would States be willing to assist other States dealing with an insurgency, if they were subject to human rights law, without any law of armed conflict–inspired modification?[21]

Where we are at present may appear chaotic and confused but the only solution is to find a way forward, not back. The first step is to seek to clarify the relationship between the two bodies of rules.

II. Whether Human Rights Law Remains Applicable When the Law of Armed Conflict Is Applicable

Before addressing the principal question, it is again necessary to make two preliminary points. First, as any legal system develops, it has to address the question of the boundary between two sets of rules. An obvious example in the context of domestic law is the boundary between contract law and tort. Where a party to a contract discharges his obligation negligently, occasioning loss to the other party, should the claim be brought for breach of contract or for negligence? There is no question of arbitrarily restricting either body of rules. It is a matter of finding a suitable accommodation. The same issue has already arisen and been dealt with in international law. The law of the sea, for example, has had to find a way to accommodate the free passage rights of warships, including submarines, and the need of the coastal State to regulate and protect a range of interests and activities in the territorial sea, contiguous zone and exclusive economic zone.[22] In other words, there is nothing new or unique in the potential overlap of the law of armed conflict and human rights law.

The second point is that the relationship between the two bodies of rules is a general question, rather than one relating to particular rules. It has never been suggested, for example, that one answer could be given for rules of international armed conflict and another for rules of non-international armed conflict. Either the applicability of the law of armed conflict has the effect of "turning off" the applicability of human rights law or it does not. This is a further reason why the solution discussed at the end of the introduction is, in fact, no solution.

Three separate questions need to be distinguished. The first is whether human rights law remains applicable *at all* when the law of armed conflict is applicable. If that is answered in the affirmative, two further, related questions become relevant. First, to what extent is human rights law applicable and, second, how, if at all, are the relevant human rights norms affected by the applicability of the law of armed conflict?

A. Whether Human Rights Law Is Applicable at All

There is overwhelming evidence that human rights law does remain applicable when the law of armed conflict is applicable. This is to be found in treaty law, particularly those treaties dealing with civil and political rights. The derogation clauses[23] provide that certain rights remain applicable even during "war or other public emergency."[24] Such situations clearly include ones in which the law of armed conflict will also be applicable. A large majority of States are bound by one or more of such treaties.[25] State practice confirms this initial impression. As far as political organs are concerned, the General Assembly, the Security Council and the Human Rights Council (and its predecessor, the UN Commission on Human Rights) have passed both subject and situation-specific resolutions in which reference is made to both human rights law and the law of armed conflict.[26] In the case of judicial and quasi-judicial organs, the International Court of Justice (ICJ) stated clearly that human rights law remains applicable in all circumstances, subject only to derogation.[27] The principal human rights treaty monitoring body at the international level, the Human Rights Committee, in its general comment on states of emergency,[28] in its concluding observations on State reports[29] and in determinations in individual cases, has equally made it clear that human rights law is not displaced by the applicability of the law of armed conflict.[30] The most relevant, in this context, of the Special Procedures have also expressed concerns framed in terms of human rights law in situations in which the law of armed conflict was applicable.[31] At the regional level, the Inter-American Commission on Human Rights and the Inter-American Court of Human Rights, the former European Commission of Human Rights and the former and present European Court of Human Rights, and the African

Commission on Human and Peoples' Rights have also applied human rights law in circumstances in which the law of armed conflict was clearly applicable.

The only currently dissenting view is that of two States: Israel and the United States. Israel appears never to have disputed the applicability of the International Covenant on Civil and Political Rights in Israel itself, even though, as a party to actual and/or arguable armed conflicts, it has rights and obligations under the law of armed conflict which have an impact within Israel.[32] Its objection has focused on the applicability of human rights law in occupied territory, which involves both the relationship with the law of armed conflict and the question of the extraterritorial applicability of human rights law.[33] Since the overwhelming weight of evidence suggests that the applicability of the law of armed conflict does not displace that of human rights law, the question then becomes whether Israel and the United States can claim to be persistent objectors. The first difficulty for the United States is that, at the time of its ratification of the International Covenant on Civil and Political Rights, the approach of the Human Rights Committee was already clear. The failure of the United States to enter a reservation or interpretative declaration on this specific question calls into question the persistence of any alleged objection.[34] A similar argument could be made in relation to Israel, which ratified the International Covenant only eight months earlier, on October 3, 1991. First, in assessing such a possible claim, it should be noted that the relevant treaty language is unambiguous. Presumably, the clearer the rule, the more is expected of a would-be persistent objector. Second, it is not clear whether the persistent-objector principle applies to every type of rule of international law. The rule at issue here is about the relationship between the two bodies of rules, rather than a rule of conduct. It is not clear whether that makes a difference. The third difficulty is more fundamental. In the principal ICJ decision addressing the persistent-objector principle, the *Anglo-Norwegian Fisheries Jurisdiction Case*, it was not the persistence of Norway's objections that was decisive but the acceptance of or acquiescence in those objections by the United Kingdom.[35] Whose acceptance of an objection is required under human rights law? In particular, how important is the lack of acceptance by a treaty monitoring body, as opposed to other High Contracting Parties? Human rights treaties are particular, but not unique, in creating "objective" obligations.[36] They are not simply reciprocal inter-State undertakings. Does this imply that States have delegated the power to accept or reject alleged persistent objection to the treaty monitoring body? Even if that is not the case, is the silence of other High Contracting Parties evidence of acceptance, in the face of the opposition of the treaty monitoring body? This is not the only area where the rules of international law have failed to keep pace with the development of new types of international machinery.[37]

It seems clear that human rights law remains applicable even when the law of armed conflict is applicable and it seems doubtful that Israel and the United States can avoid that conclusion by seeking to rely on the persistent-objector principle.

B. To What Extent Is Human Rights Law Applicable When the Law of Armed Conflict Is Applicable?

The General Assembly and the Security Council have not addressed this specific issue. Since their resolutions confirm that both human rights law and the law of armed conflict may be simultaneously applicable but do not explain the *extent* to which the former is applicable, they should probably be interpreted as saying "to the extent that" human rights law is applicable.

The ICJ has been much more specific. In the Advisory Opinion *The Legal Consequences of the Construction of a Wall in the Occupied Palestinian Territory*, the Court stated that human rights law remains applicable subject only to derogation.[38] It then applied its statement in a contentious case, *Armed Activities on the Territory of the Congo*,[39] where it found violations of both the law of armed conflict (Article 51 of Additional Protocol I) and Article 6 of the International Covenant on Civil and Political Rights (prohibition of arbitrary killings) on the basis of the same facts. The facts found were stark and involved a non-derogable right. The case therefore sheds little light on the *extent* to which human rights law was applicable.

On the basis of the ICJ statement in the Advisory Opinion, all non-derogable rights remain applicable in the usual way. It also implies that if a State has not chosen to derogate, the full range of human rights obligations will be applicable. At this point it is necessary to explain briefly what is meant by derogation under human rights law.

Some, but not all, human rights treaties provide a facility for States. In situations of public emergency threatening the life of the nation, they may modify some, but not all, of their human rights obligations but any such modification has to be both necessary and proportionate. States are free not to derogate, even in a situation in which they would be legally entitled to do so. There is a range of reasons why a State might fail to derogate. The first is that lawyers in the relevant government department may simply not think of it. This could either be the product of negligence or incompetence on the part of the relevant governmental authorities or they may not take their international law, or at least their human rights law, obligations sufficiently seriously to conform to the procedural requirements. Another possible explanation could be that the State does not wish to signal the existence of an emergency on its territory. While this is thought to be a common explanation for the unwillingness of States to acknowledge the applicability of Common Article 3 of the Geneva Conventions, this appears less convincing as an explanation for non-derogation. If a State wishes to take measures not normally permitted under human rights law, it is *required* to derogate. It is clear that a public emergency does not *de jure* trigger the modified applicability of human rights law. This is in contrast to the law of armed conflict, which is applicable by virtue of the facts and whether or not the State(s) in question concede(s) its applicability. It is therefore easy to envisage a situation in which a State has not derogated, and in which the full range of human rights obligations are applicable according to the ICJ, but in which the law of armed conflict is applicable.[40] It is not clear whether a State which is assisting a territorial State in dealing with a non-international armed conflict can rely on the derogation of the latter or whether it can derogate in its own right, based on an emergency threatening the life of the nation outside its own territory.

It is up to the human rights body to determine whether the situation represents a public emergency threatening the life of the nation.[41] The body will allow the State a "margin of appreciation" in its characterization of the situation.[42] Under the human rights treaties, the State is required to notify a designated authority that it is invoking its power to derogate.[43] It has to provide an indication of which obligations it is derogating from, what measures it has introduced and an explanation of the need for those measures. Certain provisions, non-derogable rights, cannot be modified in any circumstances. While the list of non-derogable rights varies from treaty to treaty, they all include the prohibition of arbitrary killings, torture[44] and slavery and do not include the provision dealing with detention.[45]

Just because a right is potentially derogable does not mean that the right as a whole can be suspended. As indicated above, any exceptional restriction has to be both necessary and proportionate.[46] Furthermore, certain restrictions are going to be more difficult to justify than others. For example, while it may be possible to justify the creation of a new ground of detention, such as internment or administrative detention, it will be difficult to justify suspension of all form of review of lawfulness of detention (*habeas corpus* and *amparo*).[47]

This brief explanation of derogation helps put in context the statement of the ICJ that human rights law remains fully applicable, subject only to derogation.

In General Comment No. 29, the Human Rights Committee has provided a much fuller analysis of the extent to which human rights law remains applicable during public emergencies.[48] It first clarified the types of situations in which derogation is possible.[49] It emphasized that the limitation clauses enable the Committee to address a range of troubled situations without recourse to derogation.[50] The Committee pointed out that for a situation to be sufficiently grave as to justify derogation will generally mean that the law of armed conflict, in the form of at least Common Article 3, will also be applicable.[51] That reduces the chance of there being a gap, where some human rights guarantees have been withdrawn but law of armed conflict protections are not available.[52] The Committee identifies three basic principles. First, non-derogable rights remain applicable at all times.[53] The second and third principles concern potentially derogable rights. A requirement of human rights law which is *prima facie* derogable may, in effect, be non-derogable if it plays a vital role in preventing violations of a non-derogable right.[54] An obvious example is review of lawfulness of detention, which is said to play a key role in preventing torture and other forms of proscribed ill treatment. It is not that this element of Article 9 of the International Covenant on Civil and Political Rights, dealing with detention, is added to the list of non-derogable rights. That would fly in the face of the express words of the treaty. It is rather that States are likely to find it impossible to justify the necessity of the total extinction of the right, even though they may be able to explain the necessity of changes in its usual modalities. This second principle may apply to specific elements in the context of a wider right. The third principle concerns the essence or core of the wider right itself. The Committee suggested that it would be hard to justify the suspension of the very essence of a right, even if various constituent elements could be modified.[55] Again, an obvious example exists in the field of detention. While, in an emergency, it may be possible to create additional grounds of detention, to modify the modalities of review of lawfulness and to lengthen the period during which a person may be held before being brought before a judicial officer, it would never be possible to justify unacknowledged detention (disappearances).[56] To hold otherwise would be to deprive the detainees of all protection of the law.

When monitoring State reports, the Human Rights Committee has not always made clear, in the Concluding Observations, the precise basis of its analysis. When the Committee raises one issue but not another, it is not clear whether its failure to raise the second is because the alleged violation would, on account of the circumstances, be covered by the operation of a limitation clause or because it would be covered by a derogation or because it did not have the time to consider the issue.[57] All that can be said in general terms is that the practice of the Committee in its Concluding Observations appears to reflect General Comment No. 29. It is also noteworthy that no State has objected to the General Comment, even though three States reacted to General Comment No. 24 on reservations.[58] At the very least, this suggests that the United States, the United Kingdom and France (the three States in question) had no objection to General Comment No. 29.[59]

The Human Rights Committee has dealt fairly regularly with traditional non-international armed conflicts, that is to say an armed conflict between two groups on the territory of one State, where the State itself may be a party to the conflict.[60] It has also dealt with situations of occupation and, less frequently, with States engaged in peace support operations outside national borders.[61] It is less clear how it would deal with the relevance of human rights law to an international armed conflict. The ICJ's statements are in fact contradictory. On the one hand, it has said that human rights law remains applicable in all situations, subject only to derogation, which implies that that body of law is relevant even in relation to the conduct of military operations.[62] On the other hand, the Court has stated,

> As regards the relationship between international humanitarian law and human rights law, there are thus three possible situations: some rights may be exclusively matters of international humanitarian law; others may be exclusively matters of human rights law; yet others may be matters of both these branches of international law.[63]

This implies that there are situations not regulated by human rights law but, given the earlier comment, it is not clear what those might be.

The Inter-American Commission on Human Rights and the Inter-American Court of Human Rights offer a more complicated picture. They apply human rights law, taking account of any derogation, in situations of emergency.[64] In some circumstances, however, they will take account of the law of armed conflict in interpreting human rights law.[65] They do so *proprio motu*. They only make a finding of violation of human rights law, not of the law of armed conflict. What is less clear is whether they take account of the latter in all situations in which it may be relevant. If not, what criteria are they applying? Does it depend on the issue and/or whether there is a relevant and specific rule of the law of armed conflict?[66]

The European Court of Human Rights and the former European Commission of Human Rights have not articulated a view of the relevance of the law of armed conflict, even though they have dealt with situations subject, or arguably subject, to non-international armed conflict, such as Northern Ireland, Southeast Turkey and Chechnya, and even an international armed conflict, the conflict between Turkey and Cyprus. In some cases, the applicant's legal representative raised the relevant law of armed conflict rule, usually to reinforce the human rights law rule. In other words, it is not that the issue has not been raised before the European human rights institutions. To date, it would appear that, in all or virtually all cases of actual or possible non-international armed conflict, the act would have been in breach of both human rights law and the law of armed conflict. In those situations, the European human rights bodies have applied human rights law in the normal way, subject only to derogation where applicable. Most notably, the European Commission of Human Rights failed to apply the law of armed conflict to determine the lawfulness of the detention of prisoners of war in the conflict between Turkey and Cyprus.[67] Turkey had not submitted notice of derogation under which it could have introduced a ground of detention not normally lawful. The detention of prisoners of war was therefore found to be unlawful! One of the ways in which the Court has avoided having to face the issue is as a result of its view of the extraterritorial applicability of human rights law, which will be discussed in the next section.

C. How Are the Relevant Human Rights Norms Affected by the Applicability of the Law of Armed Conflict?

The focus in this subsection will be on the human rights norms dealing with killings and detention. It should be noted that other rights are also relevant, notably those relating to due process, freedom of speech, freedom of assembly and the right to a remedy, particularly when States are assisting another State.[68]

Superficially, there should be no real difficulty in reconciling human rights law and the law of armed conflict for the Human Rights Committee, and for the Inter-American Commission on Human Rights and the Inter-American Court of Human Rights. In both cases, the human rights provision prohibits arbitrary killings.[69] The right is non-derogable.[70] What would be arbitrary in a peacetime context, in which the framework of analysis is a law and order paradigm, is not the same as what would be arbitrary in a law of armed conflict context. It would be straightforward for the human rights monitoring bodies to interpret "arbitrary" as meaning that a killing in conformity with the law of armed conflict was not arbitrary in a conflict context or at least where it occurred as part of a military operation. It should be noted that this would represent a reduction in the current level of protection in non-international armed conflicts, where the framework applied is usually the law and order paradigm.[71]

There is, however, a real difficulty for parties to the European Convention for Human Rights. The provision on the use of potentially lethal force lists exhaustively the only grounds on which State agents may resort to such a use of force.[72] It is based on the law and order paradigm. The derogation provision expressly envisages the possibility of derogation so as to permit "lawful acts of war."[73] In order to invoke the provision, the State would have to derogate. No State has ever derogated from Article 2 of the Convention, whether involved in a non-international armed conflict or international armed conflict and whether the conflict was in national territory or extraterritorial. Since the law of armed conflict is not applicable by virtue of its being invoked but by virtue of the facts, it might be open to the European Court of Human Rights to choose to use the law of armed conflict as a frame of reference.[74] It has not yet chosen to do so in relation to non-international armed conflicts in national territory.[75] It has generally been able to avoid the issue in extraterritorial situations. The Court may have to confront the issue in the inter-State case introduced by Georgia against Russia and the many individual cases brought by Georgians and Russians.

In the case of detention, the International Covenant on Civil and Political Rights and the American Convention on Human Rights again prohibit arbitrary detention.[76] The provisions are potentially derogable.[77] There are elements to the right which may be modified but from which it is unlikely that States will be allowed to depart completely, notably the provision for review of detention.[78] It seems clear that a State may, by derogation, introduce additional exceptional grounds of detention. It is not clear whether a State needs to derogate in order to justify internment or administrative detention.[79] The case law makes it clear that detention has to be lawfully authorized. The law of armed conflict itself provides legal authority for detention under Geneva Conventions III and IV in international armed conflicts. There is no equivalent provision in relation to non-international armed conflicts. Additional Protocol II recognizes that people may be detained and provides guarantees for such detainees but it does not itself authorize detention. This is not surprising, since the underlying assumption is that the fighting is occurring in the territory of one State and the grounds of detention would be expected to be regulated by the domestic law of that State. This is most likely to be a problem where States are involved in an extraterritorial non-international armed conflict. That will be discussed in the following sections.

The situation is different for parties to the European Convention for Human Rights. Again, the Convention does not prohibit arbitrary detention but lists exhaustively the only legitimate grounds of detention.[80] In order to introduce additional grounds, a State is required to derogate. If it does so, it may be able to justify the introduction of internment or administrative detention.[81] The issue of extraterritorial detention will be examined in the next section.

It therefore appears that it may be possible for at least some human rights bodies to accommodate the law of armed conflict but that it may be necessary to derogate to make lawful exceptional grounds of detention. It was also seen that the application of the law of armed conflict would entail the reduction of existing protection in relation to arbitrary killings, at least in non-international armed conflicts. Human rights bodies *can* take account of the law of armed conflict but *should* they do so and, if so, in what circumstances?

When dealing with the inter-relationship between the law of armed conflict and human rights law, the ICJ referred to the former as the *lex specialis*. In some ways, this is unhelpful because *lex specialis* more easily applies to a vertical relationship between two areas of law.[82] When dealing with a commercial tenancy, any special rules regarding such tenancies are the *lex specialis* as compared to general rules on tenancies. In this case, however, two separate legal areas are bumping into one another. The relationship is horizontal, rather than vertical. Nevertheless, it is clear in general terms what the ICJ is saying. Law of armed conflict rules are best suited to conflict situations because they have been designed for that context. What is not clear is what precisely that means in practice. Does it mean that in conflict situations all human rights norms should be interpreted in the light of the law of armed conflict, so that no violation will be found if there is no violation of that body of law? That would be unworkable. There is nothing in the law of armed conflict about the right to marry. The mere fact that suspending the right to marry would not violate the law of armed conflict, which does not address the issue, is hardly sufficient ground for suspending the human rights provision. Another possibility would be that a human rights norm should only be affected by the law of armed conflict where there is a relevant law of armed conflict provision. This would lead to the bizarre result that the law of armed conflict would affect killings and detention but not the right to demonstrate.[83] It has also been suggested that a human rights body should move backward and forward between the two areas of law, depending on the issue.[84] On that basis, the law of armed conflict would deal with grounds of detention and review of detention in international armed conflicts but not in non-international armed conflicts. Since the law of armed conflict does not define "court" or "tribunal," the test to be applied would be a human rights law test. With regard to issues such as the right to summon witnesses, where there is again no provision in the law of armed conflict, reliance would be placed on human rights law. It is submitted that the to-ing and fro-ing between two legal regimes is unworkable in practice. It is rather as though parts of a Mercedes were fitted to a VW Beetle. Human rights law might offer useful *guidance* as to the issues which need to be addressed, but to suggest that human rights law due process guarantees should apply in the normal way would again lead to bizarre results. It would be more workable if a State had derogated from the usual due process guarantees, not by eliminating the guarantees but by modifying them. It is too soon to know how the *lex specialis* rule is going to be applied in practice. A practical way forward will be suggested in the conclusion.

It is clear that to some extent human rights law remains applicable in situations of conflict, particularly non-international armed conflict, but the precise extent of that co-applicability and the manner in which the law of armed conflict impacts upon the interpretation of human rights law is not yet clear.

III. The Extraterritorial Applicability of Human Rights

If human rights law only applies within a State's territory, this has very significant implications for the relationship between that body of law and the law of armed conflict. It would mean that the issue of the overlap between the two would only be relevant in non-international armed conflict and in relation to the State's acts and omissions in its own territory during an international armed conflict. If human rights law applies extraterritorially, the key question becomes to what extent and to what types of activities it is applicable.[85]

The human rights community, in advocating for extraterritorial applicability of human rights law, is concerned with the risk of lack of accountability. It fears that the State would be allowed to do outside national territory what it cannot do within national territory. If this were the only basis on which the argument was constructed, it would be misconceived. The human rights community is forgetting accountability under the law of armed conflict. Its concern might be more specific. While there is theoretical accountability under the law of armed conflict, it can hardly be described as effective. In principle, subject to acceptance of the ICJ's compulsory jurisdiction, a victim State could bring a complaint against a perpetrator State. In fact, the issue of jurisdiction poses a significant barrier. Even when such a case is possible, in practice it is very rare for States to bring alleged violations of the law of armed conflict before the ICJ.[86] It is not clear whether a non-victim State could bring such a case, based on the *erga omnes* character of law of armed conflict obligations.[87] If that is not possible, there are very real difficulties in bringing alleged breaches of the law of armed conflict, whether committed by the territorial State or assisting States, before a court, since the victims are either the civilians in the territorial State or, possibly, members of non-State armed groups. This situation is in marked contrast with human rights law, at least in the case of those States which have accepted a right of individual petition. An individual victim can seek redress, uninhibited by the diplomatic constraints of a State. The obvious solution would be to introduce a right of petition for violations of the law of armed conflict. This will be discussed further in the conclusion.

Lawyers with armed forces should identify precisely to what they take exception. The armed forces should not object to accountability per se. It helps to keep them honest. What they should oppose is *inappropriate* accountability, more accurately accountability based on inappropriate norms. The key question for the military should not be the extraterritorial applicability of human rights law, but ensuring that the solution to the co-applicability of legal regimes is appropriate. If a law and order paradigm were applied to extraterritorial activities, the armed forces would have a well-founded concern, but it would not be the result of extraterritorial applicability. If, on the other hand, the prohibition of arbitrary killings was applied consistently with the law of armed conflict in military operations and according to a law and order paradigm in other areas in the territory, to what can the armed forces legitimately object?

Two States have objected, in principle, to the extraterritorial applicability of human rights law, the United States and Israel.[88] This raises the same issues as their objection to the applicability of human rights law when the law of armed conflict is applicable. In this case, other States may accept some measure of extraterritorial applicability but only in very limited circumstances.

The ICJ's view regarding the extraterritorial applicability of human rights law is clear but it is not clear on what it is based. In the *Wall* Advisory Opinion, the ICJ was dealing with the applicability of human rights law in occupied territory.[89] In *DRC v. Uganda*, the ICJ was dealing with both occupied Ituri and non-occupied territory in the Democratic Republic of the Congo.[90] In both cases, the ICJ assumed the applicability of human rights law. In the contentious case, the ICJ found the same actions to be violations of both Article 51 of Additional Protocol I and Article 6 of the International Covenant on Civil and Political Rights.

The Human Rights Committee has had to deal with obligations in occupied territory but only occasionally with other forms of extraterritorial activities. In occupied territory, it has consistently held the occupying power responsible for ensuring respect of the rights of the occupied population, apparently based on its control of the territory.[91] This position contains both theoretical and practical difficulties. Is the State bound to apply its own obligations or those applicable in the territory occupied? Given that under the law of armed conflict the occupying power is not allowed to change the law of the occupied territory unless necessary for its own security, how is it to provide for those human rights that cannot be delivered by merely executive action?[92] Does the occupying power only have negative obligations, that it is to say that State agents are prohibited themselves from violating human rights law, or is it obliged to protect the population from the risk of violations, including at the hand of third parties? Insofar as the occupying power is in an analogous position in relation to the population as the sovereign, it might not be unreasonable to subject the occupying power to analogous obligations.

In one case, the Human Rights Committee had to deal with the extraterritorial acts of State agents who allegedly cooperated in the infliction of torture, together with agents of the territorial State.[93] Here, there could be no argument as to control of territory. The State agents could, however, be said to have exercised control over the detainee. It was not exclusive control. The Human Rights Committee found the State responsible for a violation. It is not clear whether that was based on the control of the detainee or on the control over the infliction of the alleged violation.

In General Comment 31, the Human Rights Committee addressed the scope of the State's obligation to implement human rights obligations.[94] The focus was on implementation, rather than extraterritoriality. The Committee stated that

> [t]his principle also applies to those within the power or effective control of the forces of a State Party acting outside its territory, regardless of the circumstances in which such power or effective control was obtained, such as forces constituting a national contingent of a State Party assigned to an international peace-keeping or peace-enforcement operation.[95]

This is ambiguous. There are certainly some situations in peace support operations in which individuals are subject to the control of the participating State, such as detention, but that is exceptional. The General Comment, however, suggests that there may be a more generalized responsibility in such situations.

The Inter-American Court of Human Rights has not dealt with a case of extraterritorial applicability. The Inter-American Commission on Human Rights has done so, but only under the American Declaration of the Rights and Duties of Man (American Declaration) and not the American Convention on Human Rights. The former does not contain a jurisdictional limitation clause. The Commission has dealt with the shooting down of an aircraft by the Cuban air force,[96] two cases arising out of the US invasion of Grenada,[97] one involving the US invasion of Panama[98] and currently has cases involving the responsibility of the United States for detentions in Guantanamo Bay.[99]

The European Court of Human Rights is the human rights body which has most often had to address the issue. The English High Court has found that the cases cannot be reconciled.[100] The earlier cases involved non-military issues, such as the issuing of passports.[101] A significant development occurred in the case of *Loizidou v. Turkey*, in which the European Court of Human Rights found that Turkey's occupation of northern Cyprus made it responsible for the full protection of human rights in the territory, including for the acts of Turkish Cypriot officials.[102] In *Ilascu v. Moldova and Russia*, the Court had to address Russia's responsibility for the acts of officials in Transdniestria.[103] The Court found Russia responsible for the unlawful detention of the applicants. While the Court did not use the word occupation, its analysis was strongly reminiscent of the reasoning in *Loizidou*. It is not clear whether the Court is using a law of armed conflict definition of occupation. That confusion resulted in the highest English court, the House of Lords, determining that southern Iraq might be occupied for the purposes of the law of armed conflict but not for the purposes of the applicability of the European Convention for Human Rights.[104] This is clearly an unsatisfactory conclusion.

The language of the European Court of Human Rights suggested that applicants detained extraterritorially would be regarded as "within the jurisdiction" of the detaining State.[105] That was applied in the case of *Öcalan v. Turkey*.[106]

The area of remaining uncertainty concerns situations in which people are killed outside the territory of the State responsible. *Bankovic et al. v. Belgium & 16 members of NATO*[107] suggested that such applicants would not be regarded as "within the jurisdiction" but an *obiter dictum* of the Court in *Issa v. Turkey* implied that a State could be in temporary occupation of territory.[108] More recently, Turkey was found responsible for a killing in the buffer zone in Cyprus.[109] These issues will have to be addressed again in the litigation arising out of the conflict between Georgia and Russia. Other issues which are likely to come before the Court include detention at the hands of the British in Basra in the case of *Al-Jedda*, and killings of persons not in detention in southern Iraq in the case of *Al Skeini*.[110]

The current position leads to apparently arbitrary results. If a person is shot dead at point-blank range, he is presumably within the control of the shooter. What if he is deliberately shot at 50 yards or 500 yards? There is a danger that the approach of the European Court of Human Rights will encourage States to use air power rather than ground-based operations, with foreseeable consequences for civilian casualties. It is submitted that a better approach would be to say that a victim is "within the jurisdiction" if foreseeably affected by an act or omission. This would not be the same as the cause and effect liability of the law of armed conflict. It would leave room for mistakes of fact, weapons malfunctions, the acts of the opposing forces and, above all, it would require that the attacking forces foresaw or should have foreseen the harm to the victim.

It would appear from the case law that a State will have the full range of human rights obligations in occupied territory. It is not clear whether the obligations in question are those of the sovereign or those of the intervening State. It is also uncertain whether the definition of occupation is the same in the law of armed conflict and in human rights law.

It also seems that persons detained extraterritorially will be within the jurisdiction of the detaining State and therefore entitled to have their rights respected. It will be recalled that this issue raises problems when a State is engaged in an extraterritorial non-international armed conflict and that parties to the European Convention for Human Rights would appear to be required to derogate if wishing to detain on a ground not included in the exhaustive enumeration in Article 5 of the Convention. It is not clear to what extent human rights law is applicable extraterritorially in other situations.

IV. The Implication of the Human Rights Obligations of the Territorial State for States Assisting It

When, with or without a UN mandate, a State assists another State dealing with a situation in the territory of the latter, the obligations at issue are not only the extraterritorial obligations of the intervening State. The host State also has obligations and it is not acting outside its national territory. The most likely situation would be a non-international armed conflict in the territorial State, but it could equally involve an international armed conflict.[111] Clearly, all the parties would be bound by their law of armed conflict obligations. It is possible that these could vary, depending on ratification. Such differences would be reduced to the extent to which the treaty rules represent customary law. The issue in this context concerns rather the impact of the territorial State's human rights obligations.

The first possibility is that the armed forces of the intervening States have the status of State agents of the territorial State for the purposes of human rights law. This would appear to be most unlikely, unless the forces came under the command and control of the territorial State. It seems more likely that the territorial State would not have direct responsibility but would only have the responsibility to ensure that the intervening States acted in conformity with its own human rights obligations. In other words, the issue would concern the positive obligation of the territorial State to protect those within its jurisdiction from the risk of violation at the hands of third parties. The obligations in question might not be the same as the human rights obligations of the assisting States.[112] They would presumably be limited to those activities within the mandate of the intervening States. In other words, Afghanistan might be obliged to ensure that adequate steps were taken by the intervening States to protect the right to life of Afghans, but those States would not have any responsibility to deliver education, by virtue of Afghanistan's obligations in that sphere. Where States require assistance, they are unlikely to be in a position to impose terms on the assisting States. It is more likely to be a matter of negotiation. Nevertheless, the obligations of assisting States under general international law would presumably imply that they should not require the territorial State to breach its own obligations.[113]

This clearly has significant implications for the conduct of ISAF States in Afghanistan. The issue of extraterritoriality would cease to be relevant. The question would be the implications of Afghanistan's human rights obligations for ISAF States.[114] The only issue would be the relationship between the law of armed conflict and human rights law. The questions include, first, the circumstances in which ISAF forces can open fire. Does that vary in different areas, with the law and order paradigm being prevalent in the north and west of the country and the law of armed conflict paradigm being applicable at least in some circumstances in other areas? Second, in relation to detention, are the ISAF forces authorized, under Afghan law, to detain in circumstances in which Afghan forces could detain? Has a law been made to that effect? Is the detention regime in Afghan law compatible with the ISAF State's human rights obligations? If the situation is a non-international armed conflict, there is no basis for detention in the law of armed conflict.[115] Detaining powers are entirely dependent on domestic legal provisions. Afghanistan has not derogated under the International Covenant on Civil and Political Rights. Should it do so? Could the ISAF States rely on an Afghan derogation? Does Afghan law adequately protect the rights of detainees, in the light not only of law of armed conflict requirements but also of whatever human rights obligations are applicable? Third, particular difficulties arise relating to the transfer of detainees, whether between ISAF States or between ISAF States and Afghanistan. Under human rights law, the detaining State cannot transfer a detainee to the authorities of another State if there is a real risk of torture, cruel, inhuman or degrading treatment. The right at issue is non-derogable.

The first warning of litigation arose in Canada, where the issue of transfers has been raised.[116] It is not known whether cases are waiting for resolution before domestic courts, the Inter-American Commission on Human Rights, the Human Rights Committee or the European Court of Human Rights. In the course of exercising its general monitoring functions, the Human Rights Committee has usually focused on the responsibility of the intervening State. It did, however, request and receive a report from the United Nations Interim Administration Mission in Kosovo in the context of examining the implementation of the International Covenant on Civil and Political Rights in Serbia.[117] NATO's Kosovo Force (KFOR) concluded a special agreement with the European Committee on the Prevention of Torture, enabling the Committee to exercise its functions in Kosovo.[118]

The responsibility of the territorial State to protect the rights of those within its jurisdiction appears to have implications for States assisting it but the impact of that responsibility is not yet clear.

V. The Implications of a Security Council Mandate

Where an intervening State has a mandate from a recognized authority or where the presence of foreign forces is recognized by a relevant authority, can the mandate make lawful what would otherwise be unlawful?

If the mandate was contained in a Security Council resolution adopted under Chapter VII of the UN Charter and if the mandate *required* conduct in breach of international law, it appears that the resolution would prevail over other legal rules.[119] It is not clear whether that bald judgment needs to be reviewed in the light of the passage of time. In particular, one may question whether the Security Council could require a State to breach a *ius cogens* rule. In practice, Security Council resolutions containing mandates for military forces do not require certain activities; they merely authorize them. As a result of general principles of international law and under the principle of *pacta sunt servanda*, it must surely be the case that States cannot implement an authority to act in a fashion which breaches other international law obligations, unless that is *necessary* to the exercise of the authority. In the case of the ISAF, this is reinforced by a provision in the preamble to Security Council Resolution 1386 of December 20, 2001, which requires "that all Afghan forces must adhere strictly to their obligations under human rights law, including respect for the rights of women, and under international humanitarian law."

This must represent an authority to act subject to the law of armed conflict and human rights law obligations. This does not, of course, define what those obligations are. It does call into question the denial of the extraterritorial applicability of human rights law. Does the mandate subject ISAF States to the full range of human rights obligations involved in the discharge of the mandate or should it be read as referring to human rights law insofar as it is applicable?

In relation to killings, the mandate determines whether there is authority to enter a law of armed conflict context or whether the operation is required to operate in a law and order paradigm. The authority only to use force in self-defense is an example of the latter. Where a force can use "all necessary means," this implies that it may use force other than merely in self-defense. This does not mean that it is the appropriate framework throughout the territory in question or at all times. It is an authority to enter a law of armed conflict framework when and where necessary and not a requirement to do so everywhere and at all times. Participating States will be dependent upon the application of law of armed conflict rules to determine whether they can enter a law of armed conflict framework. Provided that human rights law interprets arbitrary killing in a fashion consistent with the law of armed conflict where that is applicable, and in the "usual" way where it is not, there should be no real difficulties. Rather, if there are difficulties, it is not attributable to the law(s) applicable but to the complexity of the situation on the ground.

Detention is a more complicated matter. As already noted, there is a particular difficulty in relation to the lawful authority to detain under non-international armed conflict rules. The law of armed conflict does not itself provide that authority. Domestic law for detention in conflict situations may be non-existent and/or incompatible with human rights law. It is not clear whether States participating in a peace support operation can rely on domestic authority to detain. A further difficulty for parties to the European Convention for Human Rights is that they can only detain on specific grounds which do not include internment or administrative detention. In order to be able to detain on that ground, they are required to derogate but it is not clear whether they can derogate on account of an emergency in the territory of another State or whether they could benefit from the derogation of the territorial State. It should be noted that Afghanistan has not derogated from its obligations under the International Covenant on Civil and Political Rights. It would be possible for a UN mandate to fill in the gap in a non-international armed conflict. It could provide for authority to detain and specify the grounds on which a person could be detained. In practice, UN mandates simply provide that forces may use "all necessary means" for the fulfilment of the mandate. Detaining persons who threaten security is clearly a means to give effect to the mandate but it is not clear that it is sufficiently specific to constitute a lawful authority to detain. The argument usually used against specificity is that it would require the enumeration of all the other necessary means. It is submitted that this is not the case. There are particular reasons why the authority to detain must be specific—to comply with respect for human rights law, which is required by virtue of the preambular paragraph. That does not mean that other measures need to be enumerated.

Where a mandate gives express authority to take a particular form of action, it would be difficult to challenge the lawfulness of that action under human rights law.[120] It would, however, remain possible to challenge the manner of its execution. If, for example, a mandate gave authority to detain, a challenge as to the lawfulness of the fact of detention would appear bound to fail. A challenge as to its arbitrary application or to the lack of mechanisms of review would not, however, appear to be precluded by the mandate.

To date, the Human Rights Committee has tended to raise the conduct of forces involved in peace support operations with the sending States rather than the territorial State. It has done so in the context of the exercise of its monitoring functions. It has not dealt with an individual complaint arising out of the conduct of such forces. It has, however, had to address a domestic measure of implementation of a Security Council resolution.[121] While the issue is slightly different, this does suggest the approach that would be taken to a case involving the implementation of a mandate in the context of peace support operations.

The Inter-American Commission on Human Rights and the Inter-American Court of Human Rights do not appear to have addressed such an issue. While cases have been submitted under the American Declaration relating to detainees in Guantanamo, it is not known whether similar cases have been submitted in relation to Iraq and Afghanistan. In Europe, the lead has been taken by the European Court of Justice, which deals with questions of European Union (EU) law in relation to EU members.[122] The case before it was similar to the one before the Human Rights Committee, in that it dealt with a national measure of implementation of a Chapter VII Security Council resolution.[123] It found the national measure to breach the human rights obligations of Belgium. Both the Human Rights Committee and the European Court of Justice emphasized that they were not reviewing the Security Council resolution itself but only the national measure. The same argument is presumably applicable to national implementation by the executive, in the form of the security forces of a State, of a Security Council mandate. The European Court of Human Rights has only had to address the issue twice. It avoided the issue by finding that the acts in question (alleged failure to protect the right to life as a result of failing to clear mines when the presence of mines was known to the French forces, and alleged unlawful detention by KFOR) were the responsibility of the UN, rather than of the individual member States complained against.[124] The European Court of Human Rights is likely to get the opportunity to revisit the issue. It remains to be seen whether it will be influenced by the decisions of the Human Rights Committee and the European Court of Justice, which postdate its own admissibility decisions.

It therefore appears likely that human rights bodies will take account of a specific authority to act contained in a mandate, most notably authority to detain. This does not mean that, in the implementation of the mandate, a State will be free to disregard its human rights obligations, particularly when there is express reference to an obligation to act in conformity with such obligations. It is not clear whether the mandate modifies the operation of the normal rules on the scope of the extraterritorial applicability of human rights law and how such bodies will deal with derogation in an extraterritorial context.

VI. How Taking Account of Human Rights Considerations Can Contribute to the Effective Conduct of Military Operations

In this section, the focus is not on human rights *law* but on human rights more generally. Setting aside legal arguments about the applicability of human rights law when the law of armed conflict is applicable and about the extraterritorial applicability of human rights law, would it make sense for the military to take account of human rights considerations?

The objects of the use of military force vary, depending on the nature of the operation. In an international armed conflict, the use of military force is designed to change the status quo so as to permit the resolution of the previous dispute, either as a result of the fighting or as a result of negotiation in the context of the changed situation. Non-international armed conflicts operate in a different context, even if the actual conduct of military operations appears to be similar. The object is to create the space in which a political solution can be made. It is often the case that a successful outcome cannot be achieved by military means alone. Whereas in international armed conflicts it is probably generally assumed that the civilian population supports its own State,[125] in non-international armed conflicts it is an independent constituency. A non-State group needs the civilian population's active or passive support, so as to facilitate its own operations. The State needs its support in order to isolate the non-State group. Where fighters have support from the civilian population, this gives the former a certain legitimacy. Where fighters do not have that support, it is easier to brand the fighters as criminals. Whatever the situation in international armed conflicts, in counterinsurgency (COIN) operations it is very clear that the State needs to act in such a way as to retain or to gain the support of the civilian population, usually referred to as the battle of hearts and minds.[126]

That view is so obvious as to be a platitude, were it not for the fact that States repeatedly play lip service to the notion while acting in a completely contrary fashion. Routinely, States dealing with an insurgency engage in arbitrary round-ups, and unnecessarily abusive and destructive searches. They turn a blind eye to allegations of ill treatment in detention and to alleged unlawful killings. New rules are introduced to deny review of the lawfulness of detention and to replace inconvenient due process guarantees, thereby making convictions much easier. Nowhere is this better illustrated than in Northern Ireland. When the British forces were first deployed, they were greeted as saviors by the Roman Catholic population, who thought the soldiers would protect them from attack by elements in the Protestant population. That view changed as a result of the conduct of the armed forces. The British armed forces behaved significantly less badly than the forces of, for example, Guatemala, El Salvador or Turkey. It is precisely because the British armed forces take the rule of law seriously that much is to be learned from their experience in Northern Ireland. While some positive changes in behavior were probably the result of an internal process, there is no doubt that some were brought about as a result of human rights litigation before the European Commission of Human Rights and the European Court of Human Rights. Either those proceedings speeded up a process that would have occurred anyway, but more slowly, or they were themselves responsible for change. Only when the forces respected restrictive rules of engagement, abandoned internment and introduced an extraordinary range of safeguards against abuse for those detained did the conduct of the armed forces generally cease to be part of the problem.[127] The reaction to the recent bombings in Northern Ireland shows that those engaging in political violence are now seen as merely criminals by the population as a whole.

Over the past forty years, the United States has assumed that its armed forces would be engaged in international armed conflicts. More recently, it has been recognized that they may be frequently involved in COIN operations.[128] The US armed forces have converted the COIN doctrine into practice with amazing speed. Nevertheless, it is not always yielding the results hoped for, particularly in Afghanistan. It is submitted that one of the reasons for that is a flawed implementation of the understandings underlying the COIN doctrine. In order to understand how to conduct COIN operations, forces need to ask themselves what it would feel like to be a civilian in that situation.[129] The priorities and concerns of the civilian population may not be those of the armed forces, but if the hearts and minds of the former need to be won, it is clear which must take precedence. This may mean that armed forces need to operate in ways which are likely to entail more casualties among their own ranks than if they operated in a different way. Those lives are not wasted. On the other hand, if the armed forces fight as they want to, this will entail far more casualties in the long run, including among the armed forces, and will not even achieve the purpose for which the fighting is taking place. Those lives, whether civilian or military, *are* wasted. There is not the space here to outline the ways in which putting yourself in the shoes of a local civilian would impact on military operations.

It is not only in the conduct of military operations that a human rights approach may help avoid problems. It also applies to both the treatment of detainees and their due process guarantees. There is no need to rehearse here the negative impact on the perception of US armed forces and also on those forces themselves of the abandonment of respect for even the prohibition of ill treatment contained in Common Article 3 of the Geneva Conventions. Instead, an illustration will be used from the due process debate. When the original proposal for military commissions attracted fierce criticism, President Bush set up a genuinely bipartisan group to advise him on how the procedures could be improved.[130] Unfortunately, the members had expertise in US constitutional law and civil rights law but not in international human rights law. That meant that their only benchmark was US due process guarantees. When needing to depart from them, they had no other bottom line. Taking the specific issue of the evidence to be used, a human rights lawyer would have said that the starting point is that evidence should be made available in open court and subject to cross-examination. However, in exceptional circumstances, it may be necessary to modify the usual rules. Where, for example, the prosecution is based on the evidence of an undercover policeman, it may be necessary to protect his identity. This does not necessarily mean that he cannot give evidence at all. He may be able to give evidence in the courtroom but behind a screen. Or, if his voice needs to be distorted, he may be able to give evidence from an adjacent room, still permitting cross-examination. Provided that there is a genuine need (as opposed to it being more convenient) to modify the rule and provided that the minimum departure possible has been made from the norm and, if appropriate, other safeguards have been introduced, there may well be no violation of human rights law.[131] Where significant departures are to be made from normal due process guarantees, the State might usefully consider derogating from the relevant human rights law provision. It is not, or not simply, that human rights guarantees are set at a lower threshold than US law. A human rights approach enables the introduction of modifications without the abandonment of all notions of rule of law. The danger with the US approach is that it means normal due process guarantees or nothing.

It is hoped that this all too brief examination of the significance of human rights values will cause the reader to stop and think. A human rights approach is not something to be feared. It may actually enable armed forces to achieve their purposes more effectively and with fewer casualties.

VII. Conclusion

Both human rights law and the law of armed conflict may be applicable at the same time. It remains to be seen how human rights bodies will take account of the relevance of the law of armed conflict. It is submitted that two things need to be avoided. First, finding the right accommodation between the two bodies of rules should not be exclusively a matter for human rights bodies, not least because that would make it subject to the vagaries of particular cases rather than permitting a more coherent way forward to be developed. Second, it should not be approached by academics and governmental players in a top-down fashion, as a matter of legal rules which simply need to be applied. It is submitted that a more effective approach would be to identify situations on the ground that need to be addressed. Each issue should be the subject of a document which would not have any legal status but whose contents could be used as guidelines.[132] They could be refined with the benefit of experience. Each document would address the issue in great detail and would provide alternatives for the different contexts in which the situation can arise.[133] In order to produce these documents, there is a need for a small group composed both of lawyers and of non-lawyers and whose members would have expertise in both human rights law and the law of armed conflict. It goes without saying that there should be members with military experience. Over time, the guidelines could be incorporated into military operations and into the reasoning of human rights bodies. This would increase the chances of them applying the same standards and avoiding conflicts.

It seems clear that human rights law applies extraterritorially in the case of detainees. Human rights bodies and the ICJ are of the view that it also applies to cases of military occupation but it is not clear how human rights bodies understand the concept of occupation, and the application of human rights law is not free of theoretical and practical difficulties. What is wholly unclear is the extent to which and the manner in which it applies in other extraterritorial circumstances, particularly to the conduct of military operations. The impact of the territorial State's human rights obligations on assisting States is also uncertain. While a mandate can provide authority for particular actions, it does not provide blanket authorization for a disregard of human rights law in its implementation. It is unclear to what extent a reference to human rights in the mandate "trumps" the usual limits on the extraterritorial applicability of human rights law. On condition that human rights law is interpreted in the light of relevant rules of the law of armed conflict, armed forces should not fear the extraterritorial applicability of the former. If all the necessary guidelines discussed above could be produced, States might be more willing to concede greater scope to the extraterritorial applicability of human rights law. That would permit the development of a more coherent approach to the question.

A more radical alternative would involve the creation of a right of individual petition in relation to alleged violations of the law of armed conflict, both in international armed conflicts and in non-international armed conflicts. In some circumstances, this would result in two bodies being available to petitioners: a human rights body and a new law of armed conflict body. It would need to be determined whether it would be up to applicants to decide which avenue to pursue or whether they could be required to petition the law of armed conflict body, where the respondent State has accepted its jurisdiction. Demarcation lines would need to be established between the human rights bodies and the new body. Until a right of individual petition exists for violations of the law of armed conflict, individuals can be expected to continue to use human rights bodies to attempt to obtain redress.

It is emphatically not being suggested that the sole explanation for the difficulties of the military operations in Afghanistan are attributable to the failure to take adequate account of human rights law and human rights values. It *is* being suggested, however, that those failures have contributed to the current situation. Provided that human rights law takes proper account of the context and of the relevant rules of the law of armed conflict, human rights law should be seen as a useful tool in the arsenal of a military lawyer, rather than as an alien and terrifying body of rules to be avoided at all cost.

Notes

1. *See, e.g.*, Ben Farmer, *US soldiers "fired indiscriminately at civilians,"* DAILY TELEGRAPH (London), Jan. 8, 2009, *available at* http://www.telegraph.co.uk/news/worldnews/asia/afghanistan/4176874/US-soldiers-fired-indiscriminately-at-civilians.html; Seumas Milne, *The innocent dead in a coward's war*, GUARDIAN (London), Dec. 20, 2001, *available at* http://www.guardian.co.uk/world/2001/dec/20/afghanistan.comment; *US "excessive" in Afghan attack*, BBC NEWS, Apr. 15, 2007, http://news.bbc.co.uk/1/hi/world/south_asia/6556721.stm; HUMAN RIGHTS WATCH, THE HUMAN COST (2007), *available at* http://www.hrw.org/en/node/10984/section/8; HUMAN RIGHTS WATCH, LEGAL ISSUES ARISING FROM THE WAR IN AFGHANISTAN AND RELATED ANTI-TERRORISM EFFORTS (Oct. 2001), http://www.hrw.org/sites/default/files/reports/ihlqna.pdf; AMNESTY INTERNATIONAL, AFGHANISTAN - AMNESTY INTERNATIONAL

REPORT 2007 (2007), *available at* http://www.amnesty.org/en/region/report-2007; AMNESTY INTERNATIONAL, AFGHANISTAN - AMNESTY INTERNATIONAL REPORT 2008 (2008), *available at* http://www.amnesty.org/en/region/afghanistan/report-2008.

2. *See* Brigadier General Carlos Branco, International Security Assistance Force (ISAF) Spokesperson, Opening Statement at News Conference (May 28, 2008), http://www.nato.int/isaf/docu/speech/2008/sp080519a.html; Jaap de Hoop Scheffer, NATO Secretary General, Remarks at the "Security and defence agenda" conference (June 8, 2007), http://www.nato.int/docu/speech/2007/s070608a.html; IRINnews.org, AFGHANISTAN: NGO network raps international forces over civilian deaths (June 20, 2007), http://www.irinnews.org/Report.aspx?ReportId=72838 (*quoting* Major Chris Belchera, US military spokesman at Baghram airfield to the north of Kabul ("We have always respected international law in our military engagements") and Major John Thomas, ISAF spokeman in Kabul ("Sometimes we even call off air strikes to avoid unnecessary harm to noncombatants")).

3. *See* North Atlantic Treaty Organization, NATO's Role in Afghanistan, http://www.nato.int/issues/afghanistan/index.html#mandate (last visited Feb. 23, 2009).

4 Letter from the Chief of Section, Political and Specialized Agencies, of the Permanent Mission of the United States of America to the United Nations Office at Geneva, U.N. Doc. E/CN.4/2003/G/80, at 2–3 (Apr. 22, 2003); Written Statement of the Government of the United States of America at 42–46, Legality of the Threat or Use of Nuclear Weapons (June 20, 1995); *see generally* John Norton Pomeroy et al., *The Competence of the UN Human Rights Council and Its Special Procedures in Relation to Armed Conflicts: Extrajudicial Executions in the "War On Terror,"* 19 EUROPEAN JOURNAL OF INTERNATIONAL LAW 183 (2008).

5. *See generally* BASIC DOCUMENTS ON HUMAN RIGHTS (Ian Brownlie et al. eds., 5th ed. 2006); HENRY J. STEINER & PHILIP ALSTON, INTERNATIONAL HUMAN RIGHTS IN CONTEXT: LAW, POLITICS, MORALS (2d ed. 2000).

6. Roland Schmidt, Introduction into the International Human Rights Regime (Nov. 12, 2008), *available at* http://www.univie.ac.at/bim/php/bim/get.php?id=989.

7. Velásquez-Rodríguez v. Honduras, Judgment of July 29, 1988, Inter-Am. Ct. H.R. (ser. C) No. 4 (1988), paras. 172, 174–75, 177–78, 182.

8. Osman v. United Kingdom, 29 Eur. Ct. H.R. 245 (1998); X and Y v. Netherlands, 91 Eur. Ct. H.R. (ser. A) (1985); Assenov and Others v. Bulgaria, 96 Eur. Ct. H.R. (ser. A) at 3264, para. 102 (1998); Henri Unai Parot v. Spain, Communication No. 6/1990, Committee Against Torture, U.N. Doc. A/50/44 at 62, paras. 10.4 & 6.1 (1995).

9. Osman v. United Kingdom, *supra* note 8, para. 115; *see also* L.C.B. v. United Kingdom, 76 Eur. Ct. H.R. 1390 (1998); A v. United Kingdom, 90 Eur. Ct. H.R. 2692, para. 22 (1998) (stating that Articles 1 and 3 of the European Convention required "States to take measures designed to ensure that individuals within their jurisdiction are not subjected to torture or inhuman or degrading treatment or punishment, including such ill-treatment administered by private individuals"); Report on the Situation of Human Rights in the Republic of Guatemala, Inter-Am. C.H.R., OEA/Ser.L/V/II.53, doc. 21 rev. 2, para. 10 (1981) (declaring that, in the context of violent attacks, "governments must prevent and suppress acts of violence, even forcefully, whether committed by public officials or private individuals, whether their motives are political or otherwise").

10. *See, e.g.*, Lindon, Otchakovsky-Laurens and July v. France, App. Nos. 21279/02 & 36448/02, Eur. Ct. H.R. (2007), *available at* http://cmiskp.echr.coe.int/tkp197/search.asp?skin=hudoc-en (rejecting the applicant's assertion that the domestic law was not "necessary in a democratic Society," the Court held that the question was whether, in the context of the case as a whole, the reasons advanced to justify interference with the right to freedom of expression are "relevant and

sufficient" and "proportionate to the legitimate aim pursued" and that balancing the rights to reputation and free expression, "regardless of the forcefulness of political struggles," it was appropriate to ensure a "minimum degree of moderation and propriety." Given the "virulent content of the impugned passages" and that the statements explicitly named Le Pen and the Front National party, the Court agreed the statements were defamatory. The content of the impugned statements was "such . . . to stir up violence and hatred . . . going beyond . . . tolerable . . . political debate" even against an extremist figure such as Le Pen).

11. The danger of judgments based on hindsight is avoided in the case of individual criminal responsibility where the elements of the crime make it clear that it is necessary to establish what the defendant knew or ought to have known and that determinations are based on what was known *at the time*. It is not clear whether the civil obligations of the State under the law of armed conflict, as opposed to the obligations of the individual under international criminal law, are more onerous.

12. Legality of the Threat or Use of Nuclear Weapons, Advisory Opinion, 1996 I.C.J. 226, paras. 24–25 (July 8); *see also* Legal Consequences of the Construction of a Wall in the Occupied Palestinian Territory, Advisory Opinion, 2004 I.C.J. 136, paras. 102, 105 (July 9); *see* Protocol Additional to the Geneva Conventions of 12 August 1949, and Relating to the Protection of Victims of Non-International Armed Conflicts pmbl. para. 2, June 8, 1977, 1125 U.N.T.S. 609, *reprinted in* DOCUMENTS ON THE LAWS OF WAR 483 (Adam Roberts & Richard Guelff eds., 3d ed. 2000) [hereinafter Additional Protocol II] ("*Recalling* furthermore [in addition to Common Article 3] that international instruments relating to human rights offer a basic protection to the human person"); European Convention for the Protection of Human Rights and Fundamental Freedoms art. 15(1), Nov. 4, 1950, 213 U.N.T.S. 222 [hereinafter European Convention for Human Rights] (providing for derogation "[i]n time of war").

13. *See generally* Section 2: General Rights and Duties of Neutral States, 33 AMERICAN JOURNAL OF INTERNATIONAL LAW SUPPLEMENT 232 (1939); L. H. Woolsey, *Closure of Ports by the Chinese Nationalist Government*, 44 AMERICAN JOURNAL OF INTERNATIONAL LAW 350 (1950).

14. *See* JEAN S. PICTET, COMMENTARY: GENEVA CONVENTION I FOR THE AMELIORATION OF THE CONDITION OF THE WOUNDED AND SICK IN ARMED FORCES IN THE FIELD 37–60 (1952), *available at* http://www.icrc.org/ihl.nsf/COM/365-570006?OpenDocument.

15. Convention for the Amelioration of the Condition of the Wounded and Sick in Armed Forces in the Field art. 3, Aug. 12, 1949, 6 U.S.T. 3114, 75 U.N.T.S. 31; Convention for the Amelioration of the Condition of Wounded, Sick and Shipwrecked Members of Armed Forces at Sea art. 3, Aug. 12, 1949, 6 U.S.T. 3217, 75 U.N.T.S. 85; Convention Relative to the Treatment of Prisoners of War art. 3, Aug. 12, 1949, 6 U.S.T. 3316, 75 U.N.T.S. 135; Convention Relative to the Protection of Civilian Persons in Time of War art. 3, Aug. 12, 1949, 6 U.S.T. 3516, 75 U.N.T.S. 287 [hereinafter Geneva Convention IV]; all *reprinted in* DOCUMENTS ON THE LAWS OF WAR, *supra* note 12, at 197, 222, 244 and 301, respectively.

16. RENÉ PROVOST, INTERNATIONAL HUMAN RIGHTS AND HUMANITARIAN LAW 13–16 (2002).

17. *See* Robert Kolb, *The relationship between international humanitarian law and human rights law: A brief history of the 1948 Universal Declaration of Human Rights and the 1949 Geneva Conventions*, 38 INTERNATIONAL REVIEW OF THE RED CROSS 409 (1998); Universal Declaration of Human Rights, G.A. Res. 217A, at 71, U.N. GAOR, 3d Sess., 1st plen. mtg., U.N. Doc. A/810 (Dec. 12, 1948); European Convention for Human Rights, *supra* note 12.

18. Universal Declaration of Human Rights, *supra* note 17, pmbl.

19. Additional Protocol II, *supra* note 12; Geneva Convention IV, *supra* note 15; Statute of the International Criminal Tribunal for the former Yugoslavia, S.C. Res. 827, U.N. Doc. S/RES/827

(May 25, 1993), extract *reprinted in* DOCUMENTS ON THE LAWS OF WAR, *supra* note 12, at 568; Statute of the International Criminal Tribunal for Rwanda, S.C. Res. 955, U.N. Doc. S/RES/955 (Nov. 8, 1994), extract *reprinted in id.* at 618; Statute of the International Criminal Court, July 17, 1998, 2187 U.N.T.S. 90, extract *reprinted in id.* at 671.

20. *See, e.g.*, Protocol Additional to the Geneva Conventions of 12 August 1949, and Relating to the Protection of Victims of International Armed Conflicts, June 8, 1977, 1125 U.N.T.S. 3, *reprinted in* DOCUMENTS ON THE LAWS OF WAR, *supra* note 12, at 422 (regarding precautions against the effects of attacks and civil defense); Geneva Convention IV, *supra* note 15 (concerning general protection of populations against certain consequences of war and internment of enemy aliens).

21. This was one of the arguments used by the respondent governments in the case of *Bankovic and others v. Belgium and others*, 2001-XII Eur. Ct. H.R. 333. For example, it is unlikely that the United States would be willing to assist other States dealing with an insurgency, if they were subject only to human rights law and not the law of armed conflict, given that it does not even acknowledge the applicability of human rights law during armed conflict. *See* John Cerone, *Jurisdiction and Power: The Intersection of Human Rights Law & the Law of Non-International Armed Conflict in an Extraterritorial Context*, 40 ISRAEL LAW REVIEW 72, 128 n.28 (2007) (In a letter dated Jan. 31, 2006, addressed to the Office of the High Commissioner for Human Rights, the Permanent Representative of the United States of America to the United Nations and Other International Organizations in Geneva wrote, "The United States has made clear its position that it is engaged in a continuing armed conflict against Al Qaida, that the *law of war applies* to the conduct of that war and related detention operations. . . ." (emphasis added). Indeed, the United States justifies its continued detention of the Guantanamo detainees only in reference to the law of armed conflict. In replying to inquiries by UN and related human rights bodies about the legal basis for detaining the individuals at Guantanamo, the United States has consistently asserted that "[t]he law of war allows the United States—and any other countries engaged in combat—to hold enemy combatants without charges or access to counsel for the duration of hostilities." Response of the United States of America dated Oct. 21, 2005 to Inquiry of the UNCHR Special Rapporteurs dated Aug. 8, 2005 Pertaining to Detainees at Guantanamo Bay; *see also* Annex to Second Periodic Report of the United States to the Committee Against Torture, filed on May 6, 2005); *but see* Del Quentin Wilber & Peter Finn, *U.S. Retires "Enemy Combatant," Keeps Broad Right to Detain*, WASHINGTON POST, Mar. 14, 2009, at A6.

22. It was often a matter of negotiating within, rather than between, national delegations. The then-Soviet naval interest had more in common with the US naval interest than either had with the interest in protecting fishing rights in the territorial sea and the exclusive economic zone.

23. European Convention for Human Rights, *supra* note 12, art. 15; International Covenant on Civil and Political Rights art. 4, Dec. 16, 1966, 999 U.N.T.S. 171; American Convention on Human Rights art. 27, Nov. 22, 1969, 1144 U.N.T.S. 123; African Charter on Human and Peoples' Rights, June 27, 1981, OAU Doc. CAB/LEG/67/3 rev. 5, 21 INTERNATIONAL LEGAL MATERIALS 58 (1982) (containing no express derogation clause and held to be non-derogable).

24. U.N. Human Rights Committee, General Comment No. 29, States of Emergency, U.N. Doc. CCPR/C/21/Rev.1/Add.11 (Aug. 31, 2001) [hereinafter General Comment 29]; Abella v. Argentina, Case 11.137, Inter-Am. C.H.R., Report No. 55/97, OEA/Ser.L/V/II.98, doc. 6 rev., para. 160 (1997) ("during situations of internal armed conflict . . . these two branches of international law [human rights law and the law of armed conflict] most converge and reinforce each other").

25. *See, e.g.*, International Covenant on Civil and Political Rights, *supra* note 23 (signatories, 72; parties, 164); American Convention on Human Rights, *supra* note 23 (signatories, 25); European Convention for Human Rights, *supra* note 12, (ratifications/accessions, 47).

26. *See, e.g.*, S.C. Res. 1265, para. 4, U.N. Doc. S/RES/1265 (Sept. 17, 1999); Respect for human rights in armed conflicts, G.A. Res. 3319 (XXIX) (Dec. 14, 1974); S.C. Res. 1296, para. 5, U.N. Doc. S/RES/1296 (Apr. 19, 2000) (noting that "the deliberate targeting of civilian populations or other protected persons and the committing of systematic, flagrant and widespread violations of international humanitarian and human rights law in situations of armed conflict may constitute a threat to international peace and security"); S.C. Res. 237, U.N. Doc. S/RES 237 (June 14, 1967) (stressing that human rights must be respected by all the parties to a conflict); G.A. Res. 2252 (ES-V) (July 4, 1967).

27. Legality of the Threat or Use of Nuclear Weapons, Advisory Opinion, *supra* note 12, para. 25; Legal Consequences of the Construction of a Wall in the Occupied Palestinian Territory, Advisory Opinion, *supra* note 12 paras. 106–13; Armed Activities on the Territory of the Congo (Dem. Rep. Congo v. Uganda), 2005 I.C.J. 116, para. 216 (Dec. 19).

28. General Comment 29, *supra* note 24; *see also* U.N. Commission on Human Rights, *Siracusa Principles on the Limitation and Derogation Provisions in the International Covenant on Civil and Political Rights*, U.N. Doc. E/CN.4/1985/4, Annex (Sept. 28, 1984) [hereinafter Siracusa Principles].

29. Concluding Observations of the Human Rights Committee: United States of America para. 10, U.N. Doc. CCPR/C/USA/CO/3 (Sept. 15, 2006) ("The State party should in particular (a) acknowledge the applicability of the Covenant with respect to individuals under its jurisdiction but outside its territory, as well as its applicability in time of war"); Concluding Observations of the Human Rights Committee: Democratic Republic of the Congo para. 13, U.N. Doc. CCPR/C/COD/CO/3 (Apr. 26, 2006) ("The State party should take all necessary steps to strengthen its capacity to protect civilians in the zones of armed conflict, especially women and children"); *see also* Concluding Observations of the Human Rights Committee: Israel, U.N. Doc. CCPR/CO/78/ISR (Aug. 21, 2003); Concluding Observations of the Human Rights Committee: Sri Lanka, U.N. Doc. CCPR/CO/79/LKA (Dec. 1, 2003); Concluding Observations of the Human Rights Committee: Colombia, U.N. Doc. CCPR/CO/80/COL (May 26, 2004).

30. U.N. Human Rights Committee, General Comment No. 31, Nature of the General Legal Obligation Imposed on States Parties to the Covenant, U.N. Doc. CCPR/C/21/Rev.1/Add.13 para. 11 (May 26, 2004) [hereinafter General Comment 31]; U.N. Human Rights Committee, Concluding Observation of the Human Rights Committee, Israel para. 11, U.N. Doc. CCPR/CO/78/ISR (Aug. 21, 2003).

31. They include the United Nations' Special Rapporteur on Torture and Other Cruel, Inhuman or Degrading Treatment or Punishment; the Special Rapporteur on Extrajudicial, Summary or Arbitrary Executions; and the Special Rapporteur on the Right of Everyone to the Enjoyment of the Highest Attainable Standard of Physical and Mental Health; and the Representative of the Secretary-General on the Human Rights of Internally Displaced Persons; and the Working Groups on Enforced or Involuntary Disappearances and on Arbitrary Detention.

32. See, e.g., sources cited *supra* note 29.

33. U.N. Human Rights Committee, Second Periodic Report: Israel para. 8, U.N. Doc. CCPR/C/ISR/2001/2 (Dec. 4, 2001) ("Israel has consistently maintained that the Covenant does not apply to areas that are not subject to its sovereign territory and jurisdiction. This position is based on the well-established distinction between human rights and humanitarian law under international law").

34. The United States ratified the International Covenant on June 8, 1992. The United States did make a declaration to the effect that the Constitution would remain applicable, even during

emergencies; *see generally* Kristina Ash, *U.S. Reservations to the International Covenant on Civil and Political Rights: Credibility Maximization and Global Influence*, 3 NORTHWESTERN UNIVERSITY JOURNAL OF INTERNATIONAL HUMAN RIGHTS 7, 17 n.56 (2005); Senate Comm. on Foreign Relations, Report on the International Covenant on Civil and Political Rights, S. Exec. Rep. No. 23, at 1, 102d Cong., 2d Sess. (1992), reprinted in 31 INTERNATIONAL LEGAL MATERIALS 645 (1992) (declaring that even in times of emergency, the United States will adhere to its Constitution).

35. Fisheries Case (U.K. v. Norway), 1951 I.C.J. 3 (Dec. 18).

36. France, Norway, Denmark, Sweden, Netherlands v. Turkey, App. Nos. 9940–9944/82, 35 Eur. Comm'n H.R. Dec. & Rep. 143, 169 (1983), finding that

> the general principle of reciprocity in international law and the rule, stated in Article 21, para. 1 of the Vienna Convention on the Law of Treaties, concerning bilateral relations under a multilateral treaty do not apply to the obligations under the European Convention on Human Rights, which are "essentially of an objective character, being designed rather to protect the fundamental rights of individual human beings from infringement by any of the High Contracting Parties than to create subjective and reciprocal rights for the High Contracting Parties themselves" (Austria v. Italy, Yearbook 4, 116, at page 140). The European Court of Human Rights (at para. 239 of its judgment in the Northern Ireland Case) has similarly referred to the "objective obligations" created by the Convention over a network of mutual, bilateral undertakings.

Cyprus v. Turkey, App. No. 8007/77, 13 Eur. Comm'n H.R. Dec. & Rep. 85, 147 (1978) (holding that "[a]n application brought under Article 24 [European Convention for Human Rights] does not of itself envisage any direct rights or obligations between the High Contracting Parties concerned. . . . [T]he special 'objective obligations,' accepted by [the] High Contracting Parties to the Convention, . . . are obligations towards persons within its jurisdiction, not to other High Contracting Parties"). The nature of the rules involved suggests that law of armed conflict treaties may be of a similar character. It is noteworthy, for example, that it appears to be generally accepted that Common Article 3 of the Geneva Conventions, *supra* note 15, binds parties other than High Contracting Parties.

37. U.N. Commission on Human Rights, Sub-Comm. on the Promotion and Protection of Human Rights, *Reservations to human rights treaties, Final working paper submitted by Françoise Hampson*, U.N. Doc. E/CN.4/Sub.2/2004/42 (July 19, 2004); *see also* U.N. Office of the High Commissioner for Human Rights, *Fact Sheet No. 26, The Working Group on Arbitrary Detention*, § VII.A (May 2000), *available at* http://www.unhcr.org/refworld/docid/479477440.html, stating that

> [g]iven the growth of multiple forms of machinery for the protection of human rights, either through resolution (special thematic or country-oriented procedures) or through treaties (machinery set up under conventions, such as the Human Rights Committee established under the International Covenant on Civil and Political Rights, the Committee on the Elimination of Racial Discrimination or the Committee against Torture) . . . it [was] necessary to lay down rules for coordination in order to prevent duplication in the consideration of cases. These rules are in accordance with the principle non bis in idem, under which two bodies may not simultaneously consider a single case involving the same persons, subject-matter and cause of action.

38. Legal Consequences of the Construction of a Wall in the Occupied Palestinian Territory, Advisory Opinion, *supra* note 12.

39. Armed Activities on the Territory of the Congo, *supra* note 27.

40. In the first two cases brought by Cyprus against Turkey, the European Commission of Human Rights determined that, as Turkey had not derogated, the only grounds for detention were those set out in Article 5 of the European Convention for Human Rights; this meant that the detention of prisoners of war was unlawful. In the report of the Commission, two of its members suggested that the law of armed conflict became applicable by virtue of the facts and should have been taken into account with or without derogation. Cyprus v. Turkey, App. Nos. 6780/74 & 6950/75, 2 Eur. Comm'n H.R. 125 (1975). *See also* Khamidov v. Russia, App. No. 72118/01, Eur. Ct. H.R. (Oct. 23, 2006); Isayeva v. Russia, App. No. 57950/00, 41 Eur. H.R. Rep. 38, para. 191 (2005) (Eur. Ct. H.R.); Khashiyev et al. v. Russia, App. Nos. 57942/00 & 57945/00, 42 Eur. H.R. Rep. 20 (2005) (Eur. Ct. H.R.); Isayeva et al. v. Russia, App. Nos. 57947/00, 57948/00 & 57949/00, 41 Eur. H.R. Rep. 39 (2005) (Eur. Ct. H.R.).

41. The Greek Case, App. Nos. 3321/67, 3322/67, 3323/67 & 3344/67, 12 Y.B Eur. Conv. on H.R. 1, 4 (Eur. Comm'n on H.R.); General Comment 29, *supra* note 24, para. 10 (stating that "[a]lthough it is not the function of the Human Rights Committee to review the conduct of a State party under other treaties, in exercising its functions under the Covenant the Committee has the competence to take a State party's other international obligations into account when it considers whether the Covenant allows the State party to derogate from specific provisions of the Covenant").

42. The Greek Case, *supra* note 41; *see also* European Court of Human Rights, Brannigan & McBride v. United Kingdom, App. Nos. 14553/89 & 14554/89, 258 Eur. Ct. H.R. (ser. A) 29, para. 43 (1993) ("[I]t falls to each Contracting State, with its responsibility for 'the life of [its] nation' to determine whether that life is threatened by a 'public emergency' and, if so, how far it is necessary to go in attempting to overcome the emergency"); Ireland v. United Kingdom, App. No. 5310/71, 2 Eur. H.R. Rep. 25 (1980) (Eur. Ct. of H.R.); Rosalyn Higgins, *Derogations under Human Rights Treaties*, 48 BRITISH YEAR BOOK OF INTERNATIONAL LAW 281 (1976–77); JOAN M. FITZPATRICK, HUMAN RIGHTS IN CRISIS (1994).

43. See, e.g., General Comment 29, *supra* note 24, para. 17, noting that

> [i]n paragraph 3 of article 4 [International Covenant on Civil and Political Rights], States parties, when they resort to their power of derogation under article 4, commit themselves to a regime of international notification. A State party availing itself of the right of derogation must immediately inform the other States parties, through the United Nations Secretary-General, of the provisions it has derogated from and of the reasons for such measures.

44. Any reference to torture should be taken as also including cruel, inhuman or degrading treatment or punishment.

45. International Covenant on Civil and Political Rights, *supra* note 23, art. 4(2); European Convention for Human Rights, *supra* note 12, arts. 12(2) & 15(2); American Convention on Human Rights, *supra* note 23, art. 27(2).

46. General Comment 29, *supra* note 24, para. 4 (the principle of proportionality includes elements of severity, duration and scope); *see* Lawless v. Ireland (No. 3), App. No. 332/57, 1 Eur. H.R. Rep. 15, para. 28 (1961) (Eur. Ct. of H.R.) (confirming the determination by the European Commission of Human Rights that Article 15 of the European Convention for Human Rights should be interpreted in the light of its "natural and customary" meaning, the European Court of Human Rights defined "time of public emergency" as "an exceptional situation of crisis or emergency which affects the whole population and constitutes a threat to the organised life of the community of which the State is composed"); The Greek Case, *supra* note 41; Handyside v. United Kingdom, App. No. 5493/72, 1 Eur. H.R. Rep. 737 (1976) (Eur. Ct. of H.R.) (establishing a three-tier test: "reasonableness" (*see, e.g.*, European Convention for Human Rights, *supra* note 11, arts. 5(3) & 6(1)), "necessity" (*see, e.g.*, *id.*, art. 10(2)) and "indispensability"); McCann and

Others v. United Kingdom, App. No. 18984/91, 21 Eur. Ct. H.R. (ser. A) 97, para. 149 (1995), where the Court noted that

> the use of the term "absolutely necessary" in Article [2(2)] indicates that a stricter and more compelling test of necessity must be employed from that normally applicable when determining whether state action is "necessary in a democratic society" under paragraph 2 of Articles 8 to 11 . . . of the Convention. In particular, the force used must be strictly proportionate to the achievement of the aims set out in sub-paragraphs 2(a), (b) and (c) of Article 2.

47. International Covenant on Civil and Political Rights, *supra* note 23, art. 9(4); European Convention for Human Rights, *supra* note 12, art. 5(4); American Convention on Human Rights, *supra* note 23, arts. 25(1) & 27(2); Habeas Corpus in Emergency Situations, Advisory Opinion OC-8/87, 1987 Inter-Am. Ct. H.R. (ser. A) No. 8 (Jan. 30, 1987); Siracusa Principles, *supra* note 28, para. 70(b) (stating "[n]o person shall be detained for an indefinite period of time, whether detained pending judicial investigation or trial or detained without charge . . ."); General Comment 29, *supra* note 24, para. 16 ("In order to protect non-derogable rights, the right to take proceedings before a court to enable the court to decide without delay on the lawfulness of detention, must not be diminished by a State party's decision to derogate from the Covenant"); *see also* A(FC) and Others(FC) v. Secretary of State for the Home Department [2004] UKHL 56, *available at* http://www.unhcr.org/refworld/docid/42ef723c4.html; Boumediene v. Bush, 128 S.Ct. 2229 (2008) (holding that, the procedures laid out in the Detainee Treatment Act are not adequate substitutes for the habeas writ, the Military Commissions Act of 2006 operates as an unconstitutional suspension of that writ. The detainees were not barred from seeking habeas or invoking the Suspension Clause merely because they had been designated as "enemy combatants" or held at Guantanamo Bay, Cuba).

48. General Comment 29, *supra* note 24.

49. *Id.*, para. 2.

50. *Id.*, para. 5.

51. *Id.*, para. 9.

52. *Id. See also* THEODOR MERON, HUMAN RIGHTS AND HUMANITARIAN NORMS AS CUSTOMARY LAW (1989); THEODOR MERON, THE HUMANIZATION OF INTERNATIONAL LAW (2006).

53. General Comment 29, *supra* note 24, para. 7.

54. *Id.*, paras. 7 & 8.

55. *Id.*, para. 13.

56. *Id.*, para. 13(b).

57. *See, e.g.*, Concluding Observations of the Human Rights Committee: United States of America, *supra* note 29 (covering a wide range of issues regarding the International Covenant on Civil and Political Rights in relation to detention during armed conflicts in Iraq, Afghanistan and other overseas locations, the Committee only made a passing reference in paragraph 14 to "alleged cases of suspicious death in custody" although numerous media and human rights organization reports indicate a number of suspicious deaths of those held by the United States in the Bagram Theatre Internment Facility in Iraq (*see, e.g.*, Tim Golden, *In U.S. Report, Brutal Details of 2 Afghan Inmates' Deaths*, NEW YORK TIMES, May 20, 2005, at A1, *available at* http://www.nytimes.com/2005/05/20/international/asia/20abuse.html?ex=1274241600&en=4579c146cb14cfd6&ei=5088)).

58. The United States and the United Kingdom (Report of the Human Rights Committee, U.N. Doc. A/50/40 (Oct. 3, 1995)) and France (Report of the Human Rights Committee, U.N. Doc. A/51/40 (Sept. 16, 1996)).

59. This further weakens any US claim to be a persistent objector.

60. *See, e.g.*, Suarez de Guerrero v. Colombia, Communication No. 45/1979, Human Rights Committee, U.N. Doc. CCPR/C/OP/1, at 112 (Mar. 31, 1982).

61. Concluding Observations of the Human Rights Committee: Israel, U.N. Doc. CCPR/C/79/Add.93 (Aug. 18, 1998); Concluding Observations of the Human Rights Committee: Lebanon, U.N. Doc. CCPR/C/79/Add.78 (Apr. 1, 1977); Concluding Observations of the Human Rights Committee: Syrian Arab Republic, U.N. Doc. CCPR/CO/71/SYR (Apr. 24, 2001); Concluding Observations of the Human Rights Committee: Serbia, U.N. Doc. CCPR/CO/81/SEMO (Aug. 12, 2004).

62. Legal Consequences of the Construction of a Wall in the Occupied Palestinian Territory, Advisory Opinion, *supra* note 12, para. 106–13.

63. *Id.*, para. 106.

64. *See, e.g.,* Judicial Guarantees in States of Emergency, Advisory Opinion OC-9/87, 1987 Inter-Am. Ct. H.R. (ser. A) No. 9 (Oct. 6, 1987); Report on Terrorism and Human Rights, Inter-Am. C.H.R., OEA/Ser.L/V/II.116, doc. 5, rev. 1 corr. (Oct. 22, 2002).

65. *See generally* Abella v. Argentina, *supra* note 24, paras. 160–61; Las Palmeras v. Colombia, Preliminary Objections, Judgment, 2000 Inter-Am. Ct. H.R. (ser. C) No. 67 (Feb. 4, 2000); Bámaca-Velásquez v. Guatemala, 2000 Inter-Am Ct. H.R. (ser. C) No. 70 (Nov. 25, 2000); Coard et al. v. United States, Case 10.951, Inter-Am. C.H.R., Report No. 109/99 (Sept. 29, 1999); Report on the Situation of Human Rights in Colombia, Inter-Am. C.H.R., OEA/Ser.L/V/II.102, doc. 9, rev. 1 (Feb. 26, 1999).

66. *Tablada* Case, Case 11.137, Inter-Am. C.H.R., Report No. 55/97, Argentina, OEA/Ser/L/V/II.97, doc. 38 (Oct. 30, 1997); Abella v. Argentina, *supra* note 24; Avilán v. Colombia, Case 11.142, Inter-Am. C.H.R., Report No. 26/97, OEA/Ser.L/V/II.98, doc. 6 rev. (Apr. 13, 1998); Saavedra v. Peru, Case 10.548, Inter-Am. C.H.R., Report No. 38/97, OEA/Ser.L/V/II.98, doc. 6 rev. (Apr. 13, 1998); Bámaca-Velásquez v. Guatemala, *supra* note 65; Cea et al. v. El Salvador, Case 10.480, Inter-Am. C.H.R., Report No. 1/99, OEA/Ser.L/V/II.95, doc. 7 rev. (Jan. 27, 1999); Ellacuría, S.J., et al. v. El Salvador, Case 10.488, Inter-Am. C.H.R., Report No. 136/99, OEA/Ser.L/V/II.106, doc. 3 (Dec. 22, 1999); Las Palmeras v. Colombia, Merits, Judgment, 2001 Inter-Am. Ct. H.R. (ser. C) No. 90 (Dec. 6, 2001); Monsignor Oscar Arnulfo Romero y Galdámez v. El Salvador, Case 11.481, Inter-Am. C.H.R. Report No. 37/00, OEA/Ser.L/V/II.106, doc. 3 rev. (1999); Riofrío Massacre, Colombia, Case 11.654, Inter-Am. C.H.R., Report No. 62/01, OEA/Ser.L/V/II.111, doc. 20 rev. (Apr. 6, 2001).

67. Cyprus v. Turkey, *supra* note 40.

68. *See infra* Section IV.

69. International Covenant on Civil and Political Rights, *supra* note 23, art. 6; American Convention on Human Rights, *supra* note 23, art. 4.

70. International Covenant on Civil and Political Rights, *supra* note 23, art. 4; American Convention on Human Rights, *supra* note 23, art. 27; General Comment 29, *supra* note 24, para. 7.

71. It should be noted that this would require human rights bodies to be able to determine the often legally difficult and politically contentious question of whether the law of armed conflict was applicable and whether the conflict was an international armed conflict or a non-international armed conflict. They would also, presumably, have to decide whether they could rely on customary rules of the law of armed conflict and to determine what they are. *See* Kenneth Watkin, *Controlling the Use of Force: A Role for Human Rights Norms in Contemporary Armed Conflict*, 98 AMERICAN JOURNAL OF INTERNATIONAL LAW 1 (2004); David Kretzmer, *Targeted Killing of Suspected Terrorists: Extra-Judicial Executions or Legitimate Means of Defence?*, 16 EUROPEAN JOURNAL OF INTERNATIONAL LAW 171 (2005). See also the 2007 Special Issue of the *Israel Law Review* on the parallel applicability of HR and IHL. See especially the contributions by David Kretzmer, Rotem Giladi

and Yuval Shany, *Introduction to the Symposium on International Humanitarian Law and International Human Rights Law*, 40 ISRAEL LAW REVIEW 306 (2007); Cordula Droege, *The Interplay between International Humanitarian Law and International Human Rights Law in Situations of Armed Conflict*, *id.* at 310; and Noam Lubell, *Parallel Application of International Humanitarian Law and International Human Rights Law: An Examination of the Debate*, *id.* at 648.

72. European Convention for Human Rights, *supra* note 12, art. 2.

73. *Id.*, art. 15.

74. Sperduti & Trechsel dissenting in *Cyprus v. Turkey*, *supra* note 40; contrast derogation, which is a facility available to States and therefore optional. If it is not invoked, there is no basis on which the human rights body can do so *proprio motu*.

75. Some of the reasoning of the Court on occasion suggests that, knowingly or otherwise, it has been influenced by law of armed conflict reasoning. *See, e.g.*, Ergi v. Turkey, App. No. 23818/94, 32 Eur. H.R. Rep. 388 (1998) (Eur. Ct. H.R.).

76. General Comment 31, para. 10, *supra* note 30; International Covenant on Civil and Political Rights, *supra* note 23, art. 9; American Convention on Human Rights, *supra* note 23, art. 7.

77. International Covenant on Civil and Political Rights, *supra* note 23, art. 4; American Convention on Human Rights, *supra* note 23, art. 4(1).

78. General Comment 29, *supra* note 24, paras. 7–8, 13 & 16; Advisory Opinion OC-9/87, *supra* note 64; *see also* Advisory Opinion OC-8/87, *supra* note 47.

79. The reservation made by India to Article 9 and the derogation under Article 9 made by the United Kingdom suggest they think that administrative detention or internment requires derogation. U.N. Human Rights Committee, General Comment No. 8 of June 30, 1982, on Right to Liberty and Security of Persons, U.N. Doc. HRI/GEN/1/Rev.1 at 8 (1994), does not make it clear whether administrative detention can be compatible with Article 9.

80. European Convention for Human Rights, *supra* note 12, art. 5.

81. Lawless v. Ireland, *supra* note 46. It is clear from the reasoning of the Court in *Ireland v. United Kingdom*, *supra* note 42, that internment in Northern Ireland would have been unlawful but for the notice of derogation. In *Brogan & Others v. United Kingdom*, App. Nos. 11209/84, 11234/84, 11266/84 & 11386/85, 11 Eur. H.R. Rep. 117 (1988) (Eur. Ct. H.R.), the European Commission of Human Rights found a violation of Article 5 of the Convention on account of the length (rather than the ground) of detention. The United Kingdom then submitted a notice of derogation and, in *Brannigan v. United Kingdom*, *supra* note 42, detention under the same legislation was subsequently found not to violate the Convention, taking account of the derogation. Perhaps the most dramatic example is the Commission decision in *Cyprus v. Turkey*, *supra* note 40, in which the Commission determined that, in the absence of a notice of derogation, detention of prisoners of war during an international armed conflict was a violation of the Convention.

82. *See generally* Nancie Prud'homme, *Lex specialis: Oversimplifying a More Complex and Multifaceted Relationship?*, 40 ISRAEL LAW REVIEW 355 (2007); Françoise Hampson, *Other areas of customary law in relation to the Study*, *in* PERSPECTIVES ON THE ICRC STUDY ON CUSTOMARY INTERNATIONAL HUMANITARIAN LAW 68 (Elizabeth Wilmshurst & Susan Breau eds., 2007).

83. By virtue of the limitation clause, a State might be able to justify the necessity of unusual restrictions on the right to demonstrate during a situation of conflict. Similar considerations would apply to freedom of expression. These would be principally or exclusively relevant in non-international armed conflicts in national territory.

84. Watkin, *supra* note 71.

85. EXTRATERRITORIAL APPLICATION OF HUMAN RIGHTS TREATIES (Fons Coomans & Menno T. Kamminga eds., 2004); Michael J. Dennis, *Application of Human Rights Treaties Extraterritorially in Times of Armed Conflict and Military Occupation*, 99 AMERICAN JOURNAL OF INTERNATIONAL LAW 119 (2005); Michael J. Dennis & Andre M. Surena, *Application of the International Covenant on Civil and Political Rights in Times of Armed Conflict and Military Occupation: The Gap between Legal Theory and State Practice*, 13 EUROPEAN HUMAN RIGHTS LAW REVIEW 714 (2008).

86. Trial of Pakistani Prisoners of War (Pak. v. India), 1973 I.C.J. 328 (Dec. 15); Concerning Military and Paramilitary Activities in and against Nicaragua (Nicar. v. U.S.), 1986 I.C.J. 14 (June 27); Armed Activities on the Territory of the Congo, *supra* note 27; Armed Activities on the Territory of the Congo (New Application: 2002) (Dem. Rep. Congo v. Rwanda), 2006 I.C.J. (Feb. 3); Legality of the Use of Force (Serb. & Mont. v. Belg.), 2004 I.C.J. 720 (Dec. 15).

87. South West Africa (Eth. v. S. Afr.; Liber. v. S. Afr.) Second Phase, 1966 I.C.J. 6 (July 18).

88. Comments by the Government of the United States of America on the Concluding Observations of the Human Rights Committee 2, U.N. Doc. CCPR/C/USA/CO/3/Rev.1/Add.1 (Feb. 12, 2008); Israel has maintained this position consistently before the UN Human Rights Committee in relation to the International Covenant on Civil and Political Rights and before the Committee on Economic, Social and Cultural Rights under the International Covenant on Economic, Social and Cultural Rights. *See also* Dennis, *supra* note 85: his objection is based in part on the interpretation of the phrase "within its [the State's] territory and subject to its jurisdiction" in Article 2 of the International Covenant on Civil and Political Rights, which the Human Rights Committee interprets as containing a disjunctive "and." In other words, the Human Rights Committee interprets "and" as "or."

89. Legal Consequences of the Construction of a Wall in the Occupied Palestinian Territory, Advisory Opinion, *supra* note 12.

90. Armed Activities on the Territory of the Congo, *supra* note 27.

91. General Comment 31, *supra* note 30, para. 10. When examining some State reports, the Human Rights Committee has expressly referred to occupation; in other cases, it has described a form of control that amounts to occupation, e.g., areas in Lebanon over which Israel exercised effective control. See Concluding Observations of the Human Rights Committee: Israel, *supra* note 61, para. 10; contrast Concluding Observations of the Human Rights Committee: Lebanon, *supra* note 61, paras. 4–5, which refers to occupation; alleged violations in Lebanon at the hands of Syrian security forces, discussed in Concluding Observations of the Human Rights Committee: Syrian Arab Republic, *supra* note 61, para. 10; the issue of Moroccan control over Western Sahara has been raised principally in the context of the exercise of the right to self-determination: Concluding Observations of the Human Rights Committee: Morocco para. 9, U.N. Doc. CCPR/C/79/Add.113 (Nov. 1, 1999) and Concluding Observations of the Human Rights Committee: Morocco paras. 8 & 18, U.N. Doc. CCPR/CO/82/MAR (Dec. 1, 2004).

92. Geneva Convention IV, *supra* note 15, art. 64. It should be noted that one of Israel's first acts in the Occupied Territories was to abolish the death penalty, which was, technically, a breach of the law of armed conflict. While the occupying power is in a position of authority, it does not have the claim to legitimacy of the sovereign.

93. Lopez Burgos v. Uruguay, Communication No. 12/52, Human Rights Committee, U.N. GAOR, 36th Sess., Supp. No. 40, at 176, U.N. Doc. A/36/40 (1981); Lopez Burgos v. Uruguay, No. 52/1979, Views of the Human Rights Committee, U.N. Doc. CCPR/C/13/D/52/1979 (July 29, 1981). *See generally* Dominic McGoldrick, *Extraterritorial Application of the International Covenant on Civil and Political Rights*, and Martin Scheinin, *Extraterritorial Effect of the International Covenant on Civil and Political Rights*, both *in* EXTRATERRITORIAL APPLICATION OF HUMAN RIGHTS TREATIES, *supra* note 85, at 41 & 73, respectively.

94. General Comment 31, *supra* note 30, paras. 3 & 10.

95. *Id.*, para. 10.

96. Alejandre et al. v. Cuba, Case 11.589, Inter-Am. C.H.R., Report No. 86/99, OEA/Ser.L/V/11.106, doc. 3 rev. at 586 (1999).

97. Disabled Peoples' International et al. v. United States, Case 9213, Inter-Am. C.H.R. 184, OEA/Ser.L/V/II.71, doc. 9 rev. 1 (1987) (concerning an attack on an asylum in Grenada by US military aircraft during the US invasion of Grenada); Coard et al. v. United States, *supra* note 65 (relating to persons detained by US forces during the intervention in Grenada: the Commission held that the test for "within the jurisdiction" was whether a person is subject to the authority and control of a State).

98. Salas v. United States, Case 10.573, Inter-Am. C.H.R., Report No. 31/93, OEA/Ser.L/V/II.85, doc. 9 rev. (1994).

99. *See* Center for Constitutional Rights, *available at* http://ccrjustice.org/newsroom/press-releases/inter-american-commission-human-rights-extends-precautionary-measures-guant%C3%A1 (last visited May 18, 2009).

100. Al-Skeini & Others v. Secretary of State for Defence, [2004] EWHC 2911 paras. 265 & 267. Al-Skeini & Others v. Secretary of State for Defence [2007] UKHL 26. In particular, the decision in *Bankovic, supra* note 21, has attracted an unusual degree of criticism in academic quarters; *see generally* Rick Lawson, *Life After* Bankovic: *On the Extraterritorial Application of the European Convention on Human Rights, in* EXTRATERRITORIAL APPLICATION OF HUMAN RIGHTS TREATIES, *supra* note 85, at 83.

101. M. v. Germany, App. No. 10307/83, 37 Eur. Comm'n H.R. Dec. & Rep. 113 (1984); Stocké v. Germany, App. No. 11755/85, 199 Eur. Ct. H.R. (ser. A) (1991).

102. Loizidou v. Turkey, 1996-VI Eur. Ct. H.R. 2216.

103. Ilascu v. Moldova & Russia, App. No. 48787/99, 2004 Eur. Ct. H.R. 318 (2004).

104. Separate Opinion of Lord Brown of Eaton-under-Heywood, Al-Skeini & Others v. Secretary of State for Defence, *supra* note 100; Al Skeini & Ors, R (on the application of) v. Secretary of State for Defence, Court of Appeal - Administrative Court, Dec. 14, 2004, [2005] HRLR 3, [2005] 2 W.L.R. 1401, [2004] EWHC 2911 (Admin), [2005] UKHRR 427, [2005] ACD 51.

105. The treaty texts require that the victim of the alleged violation (not the perpetrator) should have been within the (ICCPR: "territory" and) jurisdiction of the respondent State. In *Bankovic v. Belgium, supra* note 21, para. 37, the Court referred to the fact that the respondent governments stated that "[t]he arrest and detention of the applicants outside of the territory of the respondent State in the *Issa* and *Öcalan* cases (*Issa and Others v. Turkey*, (dec.), no. 31821/96, 30 May 2000, unreported and *Öcalan v. Turkey*, (dec.), no. 46221/99, 14 Dec. 2000, unreported) constituted, according to the Governments, a classic exercise of such legal authority or jurisdiction over those persons by military forces on foreign soil."

106. Öcalan v. Turkey (dec.), App. No. 46221/99, Dec. 14, 2000 (unreported).

107. Bankovic v. Belgium, *supra* note 21.

108. Issa & Others v. Turkey, App. No. 31821/96, 41 Eur. Ct. H.R. Rep. 567 (2004).

109. Isaak v. Turkey, App. No. 44587/98, Eur. Ct. H.R. (June 24, 2008). The Court, in its reasoning, made no reference to the fact that the killing occurred in the buffer zone, that is to say outside Turkish territory and outside the territory over which Turkish armed forces are said to exercise control in northern Cyprus. In its admissibility decision, Isaak v. Turkey, App. No. 44587/98, Eur. Ct. H.R. (Sept. 28, 2006), the issue was discussed. The Court appears to have founded its jurisdiction on the fact that Turkish Cypriot policemen had taken an active part in the beating to death of the applicant, thereby bringing him within the jurisdiction of Turkey, *id.* at 21.

110. R (on the application of Al-Jedda) (FC) v. Secretary of State for Defence [2007] UKHL 58 (but it should be noted that he was detained after the passage of UN Security Council Resolution

1546, June 8, 2004, which suggested that the Security Council, at least, thought that Iraq was no longer occupied, legally speaking); Al-Skeini & Others v. Secretary of State for Defence, *supra* note 100; Al Skeini & Ors, R (on the application of) v. Secretary of State for Defence, *supra* note 104.

111. For example, States which assisted Kuwait in expelling the Iraqi occupying forces in 1990/91.

112. In other words, they may have ratified different human rights treaties.

113. This would clearly be the case where the right in question was regarded as having *ius cogens* status.

114. Afghanistan has ratified the International Convention on the Elimination of All Forms of Racial Discrimination; the International Convention on Economic, Social and Cultural Rights; the International Covenant on Civil and Political Rights; the Convention of the Elimination of All Forms of Discrimination Against Women; the Convention against Torture and Other Cruel, Inhuman or Degrading Treatment or Punishment; and the Convention on the Rights of the Child.

115. *See supra* note 79 and accompanying text.

116. Charkaoui v. Canada (Citizenship and Immigration), [2007] 1 S.C.R. 350, 2007 SCC 9.

117. Concluding Observations of the Human Rights Committee: Kosovo (Serbia), U.N. Doc. CCPR/C/UNK/CO/1 (Aug. 14, 2006). It is not clear whether the report was requested and made by the United Nations Interim Administration Mission in Kosovo (UNMIK) in right of Serbia or UNMIK as the authority exercising effective control over the territory. The situation in Kosovo was unlike the majority of peace support operations because the UN *was* the government.

118. EUROPEAN COMMITTEE FOR THE PREVENTION OF TORTURE AND INHUMAN OR DEGRADING TREATMENT OR PUNISHMENT (CPT), 16TH GENERAL REPORT ON THE CPT'S ACTIVITIES 35 (2006), *available at* http://www.cpt.coe.int/EN/annual/rep-16.pdf.

119. U.N. Charter art. 103 ("In the event of a *conflict* between the obligations of the Members of the United Nations under the present Charter and their obligations under any other international agreement, their obligations under the present Charter shall prevail" (emphasis added)); Questions of Interpretation and Application of the 1971 Montreal Convention arising from the Aerial Incident at Lockerbie [Provisional Measures] (Libya v. U.K.), 1992 I.C.J. 3, 15, para. 39 (Apr. 14); Questions of Interpretation and Application of the 1971 Montreal Convention arising from the Aerial Incident at Lockerbie [Provisional Measures] (Libya v. U.S.), 1992 I.C.J. 114, 126, para. 42 (Apr. 14); *see also* W. Michael Reisman, *The Constitutional Crisis in the United Nations*, *in* DEVELOPMENT OF THE ROLE OF THE SECURITY COUNCIL 399, 407 (René-Jean Dupuy ed., 1993).

120. Saramati v. France, Germany & Norway, App. No. 78166/01, Eur. Ct. H.R. (May 2, 2007) (admissibility decision).

121. Sayadi & Vinck v. Belgium, Communication No. 1472/2006, Human Rights Committee, U.N. Doc. CCPR/C/94/D/1472/2006 (Dec. 29, 2008).

122. The European Convention for Human Rights is a Council of Europe treaty and has been ratified by a significantly wider group of States.

123. Kati v. Council and Commission, Joined Cases C-402/05 P and C-415/05 P (Sept. 3, 2008), *available at* http://eur-lex.europa.eu/LexUriServ/LexUriServ.do?uri=OJ:C:2008:285:0002:0003:EN:PDF.

124. Behrami & Behrami v. France, App. No. 71412/01, Eur. Ct. H.R. (May 2, 2007) (admissibility decision); Saramati v. France, Germany & Norway, *supra* note 120. These decisions have been heavily criticized, *inter alia*, for failing to recognize that it is possible for two entities (the United Nations and an individual State) both to bear responsibility. *See, e.g.*, Aurel Sari, *Jurisdiction and International Responsibility in Peace Support Operations: The Behrami and Saramati Cases*, 8 HUMAN RIGHTS LAW REVIEW 151 (2008).

125. This is not always the case. The United States and the United Kingdom hoped that the Iraqi population would support the invasion insofar as it resulted in the overthrow of the regime of Saddam Hussein.

126. *See generally*, MICHAEL MCCLINTOCK, INSTRUMENTS OF STATECRAFT: U.S. GUERRILLA WARFARE, COUNTERINSURGENCY AND COUNTERTERRORISM, 1940–1990 (1992); Michael McClintock, Great Power Counterinsurgency, PowerPoint Presentation at Harvard Kennedy School (2005), *available at* http://www.hks.harvard.edu/cchrp/programareas/conferences/presentations/McClintock,%20Michael.ppt.

127. There remained a problem with certain controversial killings. In some cases, they were controversial because forces opened fire in circumstances thought to be unjustified, often as a result of a material mistake of fact. In other cases, individuals were thought to be victims of a "shoot to kill" policy; that is they were shot rather than being detained. It was also believed that there was collusion between elements in the security forces and certain Protestant paramilitary groups in relation to certain killings.

128. Headquarters, Department of the Army & Headquarters, Marine Corps Combat Development Command, FM 3-24/MCWP 3-33.5, Counterinsurgency (2006), *available at* http://www.usgcoin.org/library/doctrine/COIN-FM3-24.pdf.

129. The author had the great privilege of being invited to participate in a workshop at Fort Leavenworth which examined an early draft of the COIN manual. One of the boxes in the manual gave an illustration from a real situation. If the box had not been entitled El Salvador, it would not have been possible to recognize the situation from the facts given. The perspective was that whatever side the United States supports is, by definition, legitimate and any opponent illegitimate. For operational purposes, it is important to ask how a member of the local population views the question of legitimacy. If the government practices brutal policies of repression, the government may have forfeited its legitimacy in the eyes of the population. That means that the first act of assisting forces should be to require the government forces to "clean up their act" as a precondition for assistance. The fact that the United States supports a particular government has no bearing on whether the conduct of that government is such as to win the hearts and minds of the population nor bearing on the view of the local population as to legitimacy.

130. US Department of Defense, Military Commission Order No. 1 (Revised), Procedures for Trials by Military Commissions of Certain Non–United States Citizens in the War Against Terrorism (Aug. 31, 2005), *available at* http://www.defenselink.mil/news/Sep2005/d20050902order.pdf; *but see* AMNESTY INTERNATIONAL, MILITARY COMMISSIONS FOR "WAR ON TERROR" DETAINEES (2006), *available at* http://www.amnesty.org/en/library/info/AMR51/050/2006.

131. W.M. v. Denmark, App. No. 17392/90, Eur. Comm'n H.R. (Oct. 14, 1992) (admissibility decision).

132. A possible model is the Standard Minimum Rules for the Treatment of Prisoners, adopted by the First United Nations Congress on the Prevention of Crime and the Treatment of Offenders, held at Geneva in 1955, and approved by the Economic and Social Council by its Resolutions 663 C (XXIV) of 31 July 1957 and 2076 (LXII) of 13 May 1977, *available at* http://www.unhchr.ch/html/menu3/b/h_comp34.htm. The topics which would need such guidelines include opening fire, detention (both grounds for and rights relating to, including due process guarantees), treatment in detention, search and seizure, and the relationship with institutions of civil society. A secondary category of topics, where coverage would be useful but possibly not essential, could include the role and responsibilities of private military/security companies.

133. The contexts include inter-State armed conflict, assistance to a government, creation of a government where no effective government exists, occupation, UN-mandated operations, other mandated operations and operations involving UN forces.

XX

Human Rights Obligations, Armed Conflict and Afghanistan: Looking Back Before Looking Ahead

Stephen Pomper*

I. Introduction

On January 22, 2009, President Obama issued three executive orders mandating, among other things, a review of US detention policy, a review of US interrogation policy, and the closure of the Guantanamo Bay detention facility as soon as practicable and, in any case, within a year of the order. With these orders, the President ensured that the US government would revisit a whole range of domestic and international legal positions governing its use of force against al Qaeda and the Taliban, two groups with which it has been engaged in armed conflict since late 2001.

One issue which the new administration may have occasion to consider in the context of the above-mentioned reviews, and as it contemplates further military engagement in Afghanistan, is the question of which body of international law governs the use of force by the United States in extraterritorial armed conflicts—and, in particular, whether the governing international legal regime is the law of armed conflict, human rights law or some combination of the two. In this area, the new

* Attorney-adviser, Office of the Legal Adviser, US Department of State. The views expressed in this essay are given by the author in his personal capacity and do not necessarily represent the positions of the US government or the US Department of State.

administration will be working against a backdrop of a US government position that was vigorously advanced by (though in many respects it did not originate with) the Bush administration to the effect that US human rights obligations do not apply to actions arising in extraterritorial armed conflicts, both because of treaty-based territorial limitations and because of the doctrine of *lex specialis*.

Given the work that lies ahead, it seems a useful moment to pause and revisit some of the key legal and policy arguments advanced by the Bush administration and in some cases its allies or other commentators in this sensitive area. The purpose of this article is not either to advocate or criticize these arguments or to offer a view about whether departure from them is legally available. Instead, it is to lay down a marker on where the prior administration and like-minded participants in the discussion of these issues stood as the transition to a new US administration approached. As discussed in greater detail below, the arguments advanced by this group drew from, among other things, a combination of observations about (1) historical US positions on the territorial limitations of human rights obligations, (2) uncertainty in international case law about the extent to which human rights obligations extend into extraterritorial armed-conflict situations and (3) practical challenges faced by European allies operating within a human rights legal framework in Afghanistan.

II. Overview: General Legal Framework for Military Operations against al Qaeda and the Taliban as of 2008

By way of background, it is useful to review the legal framework in which the United States conducted military operations against al Qaeda and the Taliban in 2008. Between 2001 and 2008, the primary legal basis for the US government's use of force against these groups remained largely the same, while the legal framework for its treatment of detainees changed dramatically (with all three branches of government taking steps to provide additional measures of protection to detainees). The US government's approach to diplomacy concerning these issues changed as well, with an increasing emphasis after 2004 on outreach to European and other close allies to seek common ground on the international legal framework concerning the use of force against transnational terrorists. But despite important legal and policy changes during this period, including the US Supreme Court's 2008 decision in *Boumediene v. Bush*,[1] which recognized the right of Guantanamo detainees to challenge the legality of their detentions in US courts (albeit on constitutional rather than human rights law grounds), the United States maintained its legal position with respect to the non-application of its human rights obligations to extraterritorial armed conflicts.

From 2001 through 2008, the basis for operations rested on the premise that the United States was in an armed conflict with al Qaeda and the Taliban in Afghanistan—a conflict arising out of a series of attacks against the United States, culminating in the attacks of September 11, 2001, to which the United States responded in self-defense as notified to the UN Security Council in October 2001.[2] During the ensuing seven years, US operations were divided between two coalitions. Some US forces fought as part of Operation Enduring Freedom (OEF), a US-led coalition that operated with the consent of the post-Taliban elected government in Afghanistan.[3] Others fought under the auspices of the International Security Assistance Force (ISAF)—a NATO-led coalition that operated both with the consent of the Afghan government and under a UN Security Council mandate.[4] As a result, the legal basis for US operations in Afghanistan might be described as "self-defense plus," with the "plus" being consent of the Afghan government and, in the ISAF case, a UN Security Council mandate. As a matter of domestic law, Congress recognized the US government's right to use force in self-defense in its Authorization to Use Military Force dated September 18, 2001,[5] and the Supreme Court confirmed its right to detain combatants as an incident of its right to use force in its *Hamdi v. Rumsfeld* decision in 2004.[6]

Questions about how to classify the conflict, and what protections detainees should receive, were the source of more pronounced movement in the law. The initial position of the US government at the beginning of the fighting in Afghanistan was to treat the conflicts with both groups as international in character, given that neither was limited to a conflict within the territory of a single State, but to deny detainees captured in the conflicts protections under the Geneva Conventions.[7] With respect to the Taliban, the US government concluded that the conflict was governed by Common Article 2 of the Geneva Conventions[8] because the Taliban qualified as a high contracting party to the Conventions (in light of its governing role in Afghanistan), but that Taliban fighters did not meet the criteria set forth in Article 4 of the Third Geneva Convention. President Bush determined that Taliban detainees accordingly would not benefit from prisoner of war protections. As concerns al Qaeda, the US government concluded that because the group was not a high contracting party to the Geneva Conventions, it was not eligible for any protections under those treaties. In the case of both groups, the US government took the position that Common Article 3[9] was inapplicable, because it governed only conflicts of a non-international character.[10]

In 2006, the landscape shifted when the Supreme Court held in *Hamdan v. Rumsfeld* that the conflict with al Qaeda is of a non-international character and that Common Article 3 accordingly applies as a matter of treaty law.[11] While *Hamdan* did not speak to the legal protections that apply with respect to the

Taliban, the Department of Defense issued, in the same year, a detainee directive that applied Common Article 3 and additional protections as a baseline to all Department of Defense detention operations. These protections were in addition to certain administrative procedures that the Department of Defense created through separate mechanisms to review whether detainees were being properly detained as combatants and, on a periodic basis, whether they posed a threat sufficient to merit continued detention.[12]

In 2008, the Supreme Court determined in *Boumediene v. Bush* that the Combatant Status Review Tribunals created for purposes of Guantanamo status reviews were not an adequate and effective substitute for the ability to seek the writ of *habeas corpus*, and that Guantanamo detainees have a constitutional right to contest the legality of their detentions in a habeas proceeding in US courts.[13] It remained unclear, however, whether the federal courts would extend habeas rights to detention operations at facilities such as Bagram in Afghanistan where the US government exercises control short of the total and indefinite control the Court deemed it to enjoy at Guantanamo.[14]

While the courts were changing the legal landscape, the US government was working to change the diplomatic landscape. Following the 2004 election, the prior administration began to expand its outreach to foreign governments on detention-related issues, responding in part to a recommendation by the 9/11 Commission[15] that the United States should engage its allies to develop a common framework for the treatment and detention of terrorists. A major theme of this outreach effort was to underscore that the international legal framework governing military operations, and in particular detention operations, in extraterritorial non-international armed conflict was underdeveloped. Department of State Legal Adviser John Bellinger argued that among the fundamental issues that the law of armed conflict failed to address were questions about whom a State could hold as enemy belligerents, what sort of status determination procedures detainees should receive, how to determine when the end of conflict had arrived such that detainees must be released, and what sort of "non-refoulement" style protections should apply to the transfer or release of detainees outside a State's territory.[16]

The US government under the prior administration argued that these ungoverned areas in the law of armed conflict presented troubling areas of uncertainty for the US government, its allies and its courts (all of which had reason to be concerned about the conduct of detention operations in the absence of clear legal guidance). But the government nevertheless resisted the position—advanced by human rights advocates, the International Committee of the Red Cross and others—that human rights law did or should present a legal basis for filling them. While the US government agreed that consideration should be given as to how the legal framework governing non-international armed conflict should be expanded, it also maintained that an across-the-board acceptance of the application of human rights principles in conflict was not required by law and was to some extent unrealistic as a matter of policy.[17] The balance of this article describes certain legal and practical arguments that the prior administration (and in some cases its allies) advanced in support of this position.

III. Legal Arguments

This section highlights three of the arguments that the prior administration—or, in one case, the government of Canada—advanced in support of its legal position concerning the territorial limitations of certain human rights obligations. One argument the US government advanced was that both the text and the negotiating history of the International Covenant on Civil and Political Rights[18] (which, as the most comprehensive articulation of relevant human rights obligations to which the United States is party, was the focus of much of the debate in this area) indicated that it was only intended to apply within a State's own territory. Another argument was that even States purporting to apply the law of armed conflict and human rights law conjointly to extraterritorial armed conflicts did not appear to have a clear understanding about how to balance certain fundamental tensions between the two bodies of law. A third relevant argument—advanced in litigation between the Canadian government and Amnesty International—was that certain key decisions by foreign courts and international tribunals reflected a persistent uncertainty about whether and to what extent human rights law should apply in extraterritorial armed conflicts.

A. Text and History

The prior administration's positions with respect to the text and history of the International Covenant on Civil and Political Rights were thoroughly explored in the US government's 2005 report to the UN Human Rights Committee (the body of experts who review treaty reports under the Covenant)[19] and elsewhere.[20] The arguments begin with the text of Article 2, which provides that a State party will apply the Covenant to persons "within its territory and subject to its jurisdiction." While over time commentators, including Thomas Buergenthal,[21] the UN Committee on Human Rights, and some courts developed arguments that Article 2 should be interpreted to mean that obligations under the International Covenant on Civil and Political Rights apply to a State's conduct toward persons who are either in its territory *or* subject to its jurisdiction, the US government continued to take the view that the plainest reading of the text is that both territory and jurisdiction requirements must be met in order for the Covenant to apply.

Moreover, the US government took the position—for example, in its observations to the UN Committee on Human Rights' General Comment 31—that, to the extent it was necessary to look beyond the text of Article 2 to the *travaux préparatoires* to clarify the intent of the framers in drafting the provision, the *travaux* fully supported the US government perspective on the scope of the Covenant.[22] Here, the US government noted that Eleanor Roosevelt and the US team negotiating the Covenant had insisted on the reference to "territory" in Article 2 because they did not believe it would be practicable to apply the guarantees of the Covenant extraterritorially—specifically in situations of occupation.[23] The US delegation encountered resistance from certain other delegations, which tried to amend the operative language that constrained the application of the Covenant to a State's own territory, but the US position prevailed.[24] By way of context, commentators have noted that the post-war environment in which the International Covenant on Civil and Political Rights was framed was one in which much of the international community saw the law of armed conflict and human rights law as coming from different sources and occupying different spheres—with human rights law being derived from enlightenment-era principles about the affirmative rights of individuals vis-à-vis their governments, and the law of armed conflict being a mostly restrictive set of principles reflecting a grand bargain among States about the proper balance of military necessity against humanitarian limits.[25]

The prior administration also noted that, while certain other governments and international bodies had subsequently accepted a broader interpretation of the scope of application of the International Covenant on Civil and Political Rights, the US government's position had been consistent across decades and administrations—and had been advanced not only by Mrs. Roosevelt at the time the Covenant was negotiated but also by State Department Legal Adviser Conrad Harper in the first US report to the United Nations Human Rights Committee in 1995.[26]

B. The Nuclear Weapons/Wall Conundrum

One of the key sources of the position that human rights law and the law of armed conflict apply conjointly in the context of international armed conflict is a 1996 advisory opinion of the International Court of Justice, the so-called *Nuclear Weapons* advisory opinion. In that opinion the ICJ wrote as follows:

> The Court observes that the protection of the International Covenant [on] Civil and Political Rights does not cease in times of war, except by operation of Article 4 of the Covenant whereby certain provisions may be derogated from in a time of national

> emergency. Respect for the right to life is not, however, such a provision. In principle, the right not arbitrarily to be deprived of one's life applies also in hostilities. The test of what is an arbitrary deprivation of life, however, then falls to be determined by the applicable *lex specialis*, namely, the law applicable in armed conflict which is designed to regulate the conduct of hostilities.[27]

Several years later, in its advisory opinion on the *Legal Consequences of the Construction of a Wall in the Occupied Palestinian Territory*, the ICJ reinforced and elaborated on its *Nuclear Weapons* holding as follows:

> More generally, the Court considers that the protection offered by human rights conventions does not cease in case of armed conflict, save through the effect of provisions for derogation of the kind to be found in Article 4 of the International Covenant on Civil and Political Rights. As regards the relationship between international humanitarian law and human rights law, there are thus three possible situations: some rights may be exclusively matters of international humanitarian law; others may be exclusively matters of human rights law; yet others may be matters of both these branches of international law. In order to answer the question put to it, the Court will have to take into consideration both these branches of international law, namely human rights law and, as *lex specialis*, international humanitarian law.[28]

When these two ICJ passages are read together, the key principles that emerge appear to be that (1) human rights law continues to apply in armed conflict; (2) in armed conflict, some rights may be governed by human rights law, some by the law of armed conflict, and some by both; and (3) when a human rights rule is in conflict with a law of armed conflict rule, the law of armed conflict takes precedence as *lex specialis*.[29]

In reflecting on whether tensions between human rights law and the law of armed conflict could be reconciled by applying these or other principles, the prior administration noted that reconciliation might be achieved in some cases, but would be difficult if not impossible in others. One area where it acknowledged that the two bodies might be reconciled concerns the right not to be arbitrarily deprived of one's life, as set forth in Article 6 of the International Covenant on Civil and Political Rights.[30] Here, the US government's analysis tracked that of the ICJ, which discussed the application of Article 6 in armed conflict in the above-quoted language from its *Nuclear Weapons* opinion. The ICJ found that in armed conflict, Article 6 continues to apply, but that a deprivation of life would not be deemed arbitrary for purposes of Article 6 if it occurred in a manner that complied with the law of armed conflict (i.e., in a manner consistent with the principles of proportionality and distinction, and that did not run afoul of any other treaty or customary international law rule). The *Nuclear Weapons* discussion of Article 6 does not make entirely clear whether the law of armed conflict rule displaces the human rights rule (suggesting that in cases where there is a violation the remedy is limited to what is afforded under the law of armed conflict) or whether it more accurately gives content to a human rights rule while the two rules apply simultaneously (suggesting that where there is a violation the individual is accountable under both human rights law and the law of armed conflict). It does, however, make clear that action consistent with the law of armed conflict is not a human rights violation.

But the prior administration also suggested that commentators calling for the joint application of human rights law and the law of armed conflict had failed to give meaningful guidance on how to achieve reconciliation between the two bodies of law where the tension between them is more nuanced—for example, on the issue of whether an individual detained in armed conflict may seek review of detention in court. Here, the Geneva Conventions do not offer procedures by which combatants may challenge the legality of their detentions, either in international or non-international armed conflict. By contrast, Article 9 of the International Covenant on Civil and Political Rights prohibits arbitrary detention and provides a right of review for all prisoners and detainees. A question that accordingly presents itself is whether the absence of a procedure for judicial review of detentions under the Geneva Conventions suggests that the law of armed conflict is not, on this point, the *lex specialis*, leaving human rights law to furnish the relevant rule. In reflecting on this issue, US Legal Adviser John Bellinger asked:

> Would it be practical to expect States detaining tens of thousands of unprivileged combatants in a non-international armed conflict to bring them before a judge without delay? This is not something States must do even for prisoners of war under the Third Geneva Convention. If the answer is that the State should derogate from Article 9 if the exigencies of a civil war so demand, then what contribution has human rights law made to answering questions regarding the procedures owed combatants in non-international armed conflict? [31]

An area of similarly subtle tension between the two bodies of law concerns the principle of "non-refoulement." Under human rights law, the principle of non-refoulement (memorialized in Article 3 of the Convention against Torture and Other Cruel, Inhuman or Degrading Treatment or Punishment[32] and elsewhere) provides a safeguard against the transfer of individuals to situations where they are likely to be tortured. As Legal Adviser Bellinger noted, however, the law of armed conflict provides for no such protection with respect to the transfer of prisoners of war and other detainees at the end of an armed conflict.[33] While in practice the prior administration looked to human rights law to guide its transfer policy with respect to individuals detained in the conflict with al Qaeda (for example, it established a firm policy against transferring Guantanamo detainees to countries where it determined they were more likely than not to be tortured), Bellinger noted the complications that arose as a result, observing that "[t]his policy, central as it is to Western values, has meant that dozens of detainees who cannot be repatriated . . . have remained at Guantanamo for years after we have wished to transfer them."[34]

In a similar vein, the prior administration's pleadings in *Munaf v. Geren* also pointed to certain sovereignty-related complications that may arise through the application of human rights non-refoulement principles in armed conflict—particularly when one State is conducting hostilities against a non-State actor on another State's territory. In *Munaf v. Geren*, the US government argued that the Supreme Court should deny the relief sought by two American citizens held in Iraq, who had requested that the Court enjoin the US government from turning them over to the government of Iraq for prosecution, because of their concerns about post-transfer mistreatment.[35] In ruling for the government, the Court appeared to weigh human rights considerations—noting, among other things, the US government's statement that it had a policy not to transfer individuals in cases where torture would likely result—but also appeared to place greater emphasis on Iraq's legitimate sovereign interest in bringing to justice individuals accused of committing crimes on its territory. The Court wrote that

> because Omar and Munaf [the two prisoners] are being held by United States Armed Forces at the behest of the Iraqi Government pending their prosecution in Iraqi courts . . . release of *any* kind [as opposed to transferring the detainees to Iraqi custody] would interfere with the sovereign authority of Iraq "to punish offenses against its laws committed within its borders."[36]

In this passage, the Court highlighted one of the quandaries that a State may face when it seeks to apply its human rights standards on the territory of another State and accordingly appeared to echo the concern expressed by the US delegation that negotiated the text of Article 2 of the International Covenant on Civil and Political Rights—i.e., that it might not be possible for States to enforce their human rights obligations outside their sovereign territory.

C. Uncertain Litigation Landscape

Another relevant argument—this one successfully advanced by the Canadian government in its litigation with Amnesty International—was that international legal precedent concerning the extraterritorial application of human rights obligations in armed conflict is unsettled, and that to the extent it supports the extraterritorial application of human rights obligations, it does so only in limited cases.[37]

The Canadian government advanced this argument in defending a lawsuit brought by Amnesty International. Amnesty had sued Canada under the Canadian Charter[38] to prevent it from transferring detainees captured in Afghanistan to Afghan custody, because of non-refoulement concerns. Because the question of whether the Canadian Charter applies extraterritorially turns in part on the question of whether Canada's international human rights obligations apply in Afghanistan, the Canadian government's pleadings explored foreign and international case law concerning the extraterritorial application of human rights obligations. In its pleadings, the Canadian government observed that the Grand Chamber of the European Court of Human Rights had ruled in its *Bankovic*[39] opinion of 2001 that the scope of the European Convention on Human Rights[40] is normally confined to the territorial limits of the Convention's contracting States. While *Bankovic* acknowledged that the European Convention on Human Rights applies extraterritorially in certain cases (e.g., where the conduct in question occurs in a State's embassies, consulates, airplanes or vessels, and in cases where a State exercises some or all of the public powers in the territory of another State) the Court ruled that no such additional basis existed in the context of a NATO bombing raid on a Serbian radio station that killed sixteen people.[41]

The Canadian trial court hearing the case acknowledged that several subsequent European Court of Human Rights cases appeared to go considerably further than *Bankovic* on the question of when the European Convention on Human Rights applies extraterritorially (e.g., by finding that the Convention may apply when a contracting State has effective control over a particular person outside its own borders, regardless of whether it controls the territory where that person is being held) but took the position that these cases do not take precedence over the Grand Chamber's decision in *Bankovic*.[42] In ruling for the Canadian government, the court concluded that as a whole the body of jurisprudence relating to the extraterritorial application of human rights law appeared "uncertain,"[43] and that the Charter accordingly did not confer rights on Afghans detained by Canadian forces in Afghanistan.[44]

IV. Practical Issues: Afghanistan

Moving from law to practice, commentators observing ISAF/NATO operations in Afghanistan noted certain practical concerns arising from the application of human rights obligations in extraterritorial armed conflict.

One concern relates to operational constraints that human rights law imposes on combat operations. In May 2008, a European news magazine reported that a European partner in the ISAF coalition had failed to capture a Taliban leader who was believed by NATO commanders to be active in planting roadside bombs and sheltering suicide bombers, and to be responsible for a 2007 attack on a sugar factory that had resulted in almost eighty deaths. When an effort to capture this individual failed, the coalition partner's troops had an opportunity to target him, but had to pull back because they lacked the authorization to do so, permitting him to flee. A senior official from this coalition partner explained to the magazine that "a fugitive like [the escaped Taliban leader] is not an aggressor and should not be shot unless necessary."[45] The magazine additionally reported that this coalition partner considered "[t]he use of lethal force [to be] prohibited unless an attack is taking place or is imminent."[46] The emphasis on using force only in self-defense suggested that either the coalition partner did not believe itself to be engaged in an armed conflict, or that it had nevertheless instructed its troops to act in accordance with a human rights law framework and treat its Afghan operations as a law enforcement exercise. The magazine noted that this coalition partner considered the different approaches by its allies to targeting in Afghanistan as "not being in conformity with international law" and suggested that the difference in legal approaches contributed to "tension and friction" among NATO partners.[47] The magazine's account accordingly suggested that the application of human rights law may impede effective military operations both by limiting the scope of operational flexibility where applied to the exclusion of law of armed conflict principles and by creating coordination issues between coalition partners.

A second concern that has been raised by commentators is that the discrepancy between US and European approaches to detention may be partly responsible for having impaired the ability of NATO/ISAF to conduct effective detention operations. Under a rule that applies to all NATO/ISAF forces (including US components under NATO/ISAF command), forces are generally prohibited from holding detainees for longer than ninety-six hours before transferring them to Afghan authorities.[48] This system avoids legal and other complications that might arise out of medium- or long-term detention, particularly for States that might face challenges under the European Convention on Human Rights, but it has its costs. In 2006, David Bosco, a senior editor at *Foreign Policy* magazine, wrote that, as a result of this system,

> NATO troops have no system in place for regularly interrogating Taliban fighters for intelligence purposes. Whenever possible, they let the Afghan troops they operate with take custody. When that's not possible, they house their prisoners briefly in makeshift facilities while they arrange a transfer to the Afghans. NATO guidelines call for the handover of prisoners within 96 hours, far too brief a time for soldiers to even know whom they're holding. And once prisoners are in Afghan hands, international forces easily lose track of them.[49]

Human rights advocates such as Amnesty International have also criticized the ninety-six-hour rule—from a different angle—arguing that it actually creates human rights concerns, because it requires the transfer of detainees to Afghan authorities notwithstanding what Amnesty has argued to be an unacceptable risk of mistreatment. Indeed, it was concern about NATO/ISAF transfer policies that led Amnesty to bring the above-described lawsuit seeking to enjoin the government of Canada from transferring detainees to Afghan custody pending an improvement in post-transfer human rights safeguards.

V. Conclusion

As discussed, the prior administration took the view that the law of armed conflict did not provide an adequate legal framework for addressing all of the issues that arise in armed conflict with non-State groups, but argued that legal and policy considerations weighed against the notion that gaps in the framework should be filled simply by looking to human rights law. Instead, it emphasized that the international community needed to work together to develop new approaches that would address the gaps while steering clear of the legal and policy pitfalls it associated with the application of human rights law in armed conflict.[50] The new administration will, of course, develop its own views about where the gaps lie and how to address them. In determining whether or how to depart from the path taken by the prior administration, a first step will be to look back at some of the arguments and concerns described in this article and elsewhere that helped to put the US government on its present course.

Notes

1. Boumediene v. Bush, 128 S. Ct. 2229 (2008).
2. Letter from John Negroponte, US Ambassador to the United Nations, to the President of the UN Security Council, U.N. Doc. S/2001/946 (Oct. 7, 2001), *available at* http://avalon.law.yale.edu/sept11/un_006.asp.
3. Christopher Greenwood, Report, International Law Framework for the Treatment of Persons Detained in Afghanistan by Canadian Forces para. 13 (2007), *available at* http://web.ncf.ca/fk624/data/Report%20-%20Greenwood%20(14%20Aug%2007).pdf.
4. *Id.*, para. 9.
5. Pub.L. 107-40, 115 Stat. 224 (2001).
6. Hamdi v. Rumsfeld, 542 U.S. 507 (2004).
7. Convention for the Amelioration of the Condition of the Wounded and Sick in Armed Forces in the Field, Aug. 12, 1949, 6 U.S.T. 3114, 75 U.N.T.S. 31 [Geneva Convention I]; Convention for the Amelioration of the Condition of Wounded, Sick and Shipwrecked Members of Armed Forces at Sea, Aug. 12, 1949, 6 U.S.T. 3217, 75 U.N.T.S. 85 [Geneva Convention II]; Convention Relative to the Treatment of Prisoners of War, Aug. 12, 1949, 6 U.S.T. 3316, 75 U.N.T.S.

135 [Geneva Convention III]; Convention Relative to the Protection of Civilian Persons in Time of War, Aug. 12, 1949, 6 U.S.T. 3516, 75 U.N.T.S. 287 [Geneva Convention IV]; all *reprinted in* DOCUMENTS ON THE LAWS OF WAR (Adam Roberts & Richard Guelff eds., 3d ed. 2000) at 197, 222, 244 and 301, respectively.

8. Geneva Conventions I–IV, art. 2, *supra* note 7, at 198, 222, 244 and 301, respectively.

9. Geneva Conventions I–IV, art. 3, *supra* note 7, at 198, 223, 245 and 302, respectively.

10. Memorandum from George Bush to Vice President et al., Humane Treatment of Al Qaeda and Taliban Detainees (Feb. 7, 2002), *reprinted in* THE TORTURE PAPERS: THE ROAD TO ABU GHRAIB 134 (Karen J. Greenberg & Joshua Dratel eds., 2005), *available at* http://www.gwu.edu/~nsarchiv/NSAEBB/NSAEBB127/02.02.07.pdf.

11. Hamdan v. Rumsfeld, 126 S. Ct. 2749 (2006).

12. For a discussion of these administrative procedures, see Jack Goldsmith & Robert Chesney, *Terrorism and the Convergence of Criminal and Military Detention Models*, 60 STANFORD LAW REVIEW 1079, 1110–11 and 1132 (2008).

13. Boumediene v. Bush, 128 S. Ct. 2229 (2008).

14. In March 2009, the United States District Court for the District of Columbia ruled that certain Bagram detainees who were captured outside Afghanistan enjoyed the same habeas rights as Guantanamo detainees. Al Maqaleh v. Gates, No. 06-1669 (D.D.C. Apr. 2, 2009).

15. The 9/11 Commission Report: Final Report of the National Commission on Terrorist Attacks upon the United States (2004), *available at* http://www.9-11commission.gov/.

16. John B. Bellinger, US State Department Legal Advisor, Oxford Leverhulme Programme Lecture on the Changing Character of War, *available at* http://2001-2009.state.gov/s/l/2007/112723.htm [hereinafter Bellinger Oxford Speech].

17. *Id.*

18. International Covenant on Civil and Political Rights, Dec. 16, 1966, 999 U.N.T.S. 171.

19. Because the United States had two outstanding reports, it consolidated the Second and Third Reports into one report. This single report is referred to as the "Second and Third Periodic Report." U.N. Human Rights Committee, Third Periodic Reports of States Parties Due in 2003: United States of America, U.N. Doc. CCPR/C/USA/3 (Nov. 28, 2005), *available at* http://www.state.gov/g/drl/rls/55504.htm#annex1 [hereinafter Report to the UN].

20. US Observations on Human Rights Committee General Comment 31 (Dec. 27, 2007), *available at* http://2001-2009.state.gov/s/l/2007/112674.htm.

21. Thomas Buergenthal, *To Respect and to Ensure: State Obligations and Permissible Derogations*, *in* THE INTERNATIONAL BILL OF RIGHTS: THE COVENANT ON CIVIL AND POLITICAL RIGHTS 72, 74 (Louis Henkin ed., 1981).

22. *See* US Observations, *supra* note 20.

23. Matthew Waxman, Head of US Delegation, Principal Deputy Director of Policy Planning, US Department of State, Opening Statement (July 17, 2006), *available at* http://geneva.usmission.gov/Press2006/0717Waxman.html.

24. Report to the UN, *supra* note 19.

25. Michelle A. Hansen, *Preventing the Emasculation of Warfare: Halting the Expansion of Human Rights Law into Armed Conflict*, 194 MILITARY LAW REVIEW 1, 2–4 (2008).

26. Summary record of the 53rd Session, 1405th meeting: United States of America, UN Human Rights Committee, U.N. Doc. CCPR/C/SR 1405, paras. 7, 20 (1995).

27. Legality of the Threat or Use of Nuclear Weapons, Advisory Opinion, 1996 I.C.J. 226, 240, para. 25 (July 8).

28. Legal Consequences of the Construction of a Wall in the Occupied Palestinian Territory, Advisory Opinion, 2004 I.C.J. 136, 178, para. 106 (July 9).

29. The ICJ additionally ruled in the *Wall* opinion that the International Covenant on Civil and Political Rights applies extraterritorially, meaning that territorial limitations on human rights obligations are not an available tool for reconciling tensions between the two bodies of law. *Id.*, para. 111.

30. *See* Bellinger Oxford Speech, *supra* note 16 (observing that if human rights obligations applied in armed-conflict situations "[s]ome rights deemed non-derogable by the [International Covenant on Civil and Political Rights], such as the right to life, would be clearly displaced by more specific law of war rules that govern as the *lex specialis*").

31. *Id.*

32. Convention against Torture and Other Cruel, Inhuman or Degrading Treatment or Punishment, G.A. Res. 39/46, annex, 39 U.N. GAOR Supp. (No. 51) at 197, U.N. Doc. A/39/51 (1984).

33. For purposes of international armed conflicts, Article 118 of Geneva Convention III, *supra* note 7, simply states that "[p]risoners of war shall be released and repatriated without delay after the cessation of active hostilities"; as concerns non-international armed conflicts, Common Article 3, *supra* note 9, is entirely silent on repatriation/transfer safeguards.

34. Bellinger Oxford Speech, *supra* note 16.

35. Brief for the Federal Parties, Munaf v. Geren (No. 06-1666) (2008), *available at* http://www.abanet.org/publiced/preview/briefs/pdfs/07-08/07-394_FederalParties.pdf.

36. Munaf v. Geren, 128 S. Ct. 2207 (2008).

37. Respondent's Factum Re: Determination of Two Questions, Pursuant to Rule 107 of the Federal Courts Rules, Regarding the Application of the Canadian Charter of Rights and Freedoms ¶¶ 62–66, Amnesty International Canada v. Chief of the Defence Staff, Court File No. T-324-07 (2008), *available at* http://www.bccla.org/antiterrorissue/factumcrown.pdf.

38. Canadian Charter of Rights and Freedoms, Constitution Act, 1982 (Schedule B to the Canada Act 1982 (U.K.)), *available at* http://laws.justice.gc.ca/en/charter/.

39. Bankovic and Others v. Belgium, 2001-XII Eur. Ct. H.R. 333, 123 ILR 94.

40. Convention for the Protection of Human Rights and Fundamental Freedoms, Nov. 4, 1950, 213 U.N.T.S. 221, *available at* http://conventions.coe.int/Treaty/en/Treaties/Html/005.htm.

41. The *Bankovic* decision states that

> [i]n sum, the case-law of the Court demonstrates that its recognition of the exercise of extra-territorial jurisdiction by a Contracting State is exceptional: it has done so when the respondent State, through the effective control of the relevant territory and its inhabitants abroad as a consequence of military occupation or through the consent, invitation or acquiescence of the Government of that territory, exercises all or some of the public powers normally to be exercised by that Government.

Bankovic, supra note 39, para. 71. In comparing the European Court of Human Rights holding in *Bankovic* to the US government's position that the International Covenant on Civil and Political Rights never applies extraterritorially, it bears mention that unlike Article 2 of the Covenant, the jurisdictional provision of the European Convention on Human Rights does not include a reference to "territory." Article 1 of the Convention provides that "[t]he High Contracting Parties shall secure to everyone within their jurisdiction the rights and freedoms defined in Section I of this Convention."

42. The Canadian court noted in particular the European Court of Human Rights decision in *Issa v. Turkey*—which addressed whether the European Convention on Human Rights governed Turkey's conduct toward a group of shepherds apprehended inside Iraq and advanced the argument that a State may be held accountable for violations of its obligations under the

Convention against "persons who are in the territory of another State but who are found to be under the former State's authority and control." Issa & Others v. Turkey, App. No. 31821/96, 41 Eur. Ct. H.R. Rep. 567 (2004). But the Canadian court agreed with Lord Brown in the UK *al Skeini* case, who stated that the *Bankovic* opinion issued from a higher chamber of the European Court of Human Rights than *Issa* and, to the extent of any discrepancies, appeared to be better law. Amnesty International Canada v. Chief of the Defence Staff (Canada), [2008] F.C. 336, paras. 234–35, *available at* http://www.unhcr.org/refworld/docid/49cb8cff2.html.

43. *Amnesty International Canada*, *supra* note 42, para. 214.

44. While not discussed in *Amnesty*, two other major decisions from the past two years arguably have contributed to the uncertainty surrounding the question of when human rights obligations might be deemed to apply in extraterritorial armed conflict. First, in its *Behrami* and *Saramati* cases, the European Court of Human Rights suggested that provisions of the European Convention on Human Rights do not reach the extraterritorial military activities of member State armed forces if acting as part of a UN mission, because the Court lacks jurisdiction over the United Nations and its operations. Behrami v. France and Saramati v. France, 45 Eur. Ct. H.R. 10 (2007). Second, the UK House of Lords held in its *al Jedda* decision that where a UN Security Council resolution has provided authority for security detention, this effectively trumps the prohibition against detention in Article 5 of the Convention, because Article 103 of the UN Charter provides that in cases where a State's Charter obligations conflict with its other treaty obligations, the Charter prevails. At the same time, however, the House of Lords held that the UK government must ensure that detainee rights under Article 5 are not infringed "to any greater extent than is inherent in such detention." R (on the Application of Al-Jedda) (FC) v. Secretary of State for Defence [2007] UKHL 58, para. 39, *available at* http://www.publications.parliament.uk/pa/ld200708/ldjudgmt/jd071212/jedda-1.htm.

45. Suzanne Koelbl & Alexander Szandar, *Not Licensed to Kill*, SPIEGEL ONLINE INTERNATIONAL (Apr. 19, 2008), http://www.spiegel.de/international/world/0,1518,554033,00.html.

46. *Id.*

47. *Id.*

48. Ashley Deeks, Detention in Afghanistan: The Need for an Integrated Plan (2008), *available at* http://www.csis.org/media/csis/pubs/080213_deeks_afghanistan.pdf.

49. David Bosco, *A Duty NATO Is Dodging in Afghanistan*, WASHINGTON POST, Nov. 5, 2006, at B07.

50. Bellinger Oxford Speech, *supra* note 16.

APPENDIX

CONTRIBUTORS

Contributors

Editor's Note: In order to most accurately portray the events of the conference, the biographical data in this appendix reflects the position in which the authors were serving at the time of the conference, as set forth in the conference brochures and materials.

Commander Alan Cole, Royal Navy, is the international law attorney on the staff of the UK Director of Naval Legal Services. He initially trained at Britannia Royal Naval College before joining his first ship in 1991 and served in a number of positions, including logistics officer of *HMS Splendid*. Since training as a barrister at Gray's Inn and qualifying as a lawyer, he has served as legal adviser to the Commander in Chief Fleet and as an advocate at courts-martial, as well as a period back at sea as logistics officer of a destroyer. As a commander he has served as the senior military legal officer at the UK Permanent Joint Headquarters, responsible for providing advice to the Chief of Joint Operations on all UK joint operations, particularly those in Afghanistan. He has also served in Baghdad on General Petraeus's Reconciliation Team and as legal adviser to the coalition maritime force in Bahrain.

Professor Geoffrey S. Corn joined the faculty of South Texas College of Law in July 2005 as an assistant professor of law. Prior to joining the faculty, Professor Corn served as the Special Assistant for Law of War Matters to the US Army Judge Advocate General, the Army's senior law of war adviser and representative to the Department of Defense Law of War Working Group. Professor Corn spent twenty-one years on active duty in the Army, retiring in the rank of lieutenant colonel. Professor Corn routinely provides expert assistance to military, government and non-governmental agencies. He is a contributor to the legal affairs website Jurist and to the foreign affairs and national security daily World Politics Watch, and also frequently participates in national and international conferences related to national security law issues. He is the faculty adviser to the National Security Law Society at South Texas College of Law. Professor Corn earned his Juris Doctor from George Washington University and his Master of Laws degree from the Army Judge Advocate General's School. He is also a graduate of the Army Command and Staff College.

Professor Yoram Dinstein is Professor Emeritus of International Law at Tel Aviv University (Israel). He is a former President of the University, as well as former

Rector and former Dean of the Faculty of Law. Professor Dinstein served two appointments as the Charles H. Stockton Professor of International Law at the Naval War College. He was also a Humboldt Fellow at the Max Planck Institute for International Law at Heidelberg (Germany), a Meltzer Visiting Professor of International Law at New York University and a Visiting Professor of Law at the University of Toronto. Professor Dinstein is a Member of the Institute of International Law and Vice President of Israel's national branch of the International Law Association and of the Israel United Nations Association. He was also a member of the Executive Council of the American Society of International Law. At present, he is a member of the Council of the San Remo International Institute of Humanitarian Law. He has written extensively on subjects relating to international law, human rights and the law of armed conflict. He is the founder and Editor of the *Israel Yearbook on Human Rights*. He is the author of *War, Aggression and Self-Defence*, now in its fourth edition. Professor Dinstein's latest book is *The Conduct of Hostilities under the Law of International Armed Conflict*.

Professor Charles Garraway is an international law adviser to the British Red Cross. He retired in 2003 after thirty years in the UK Army Legal Services, initially as a criminal prosecutor and then as an adviser on the law of armed conflict and operational law. In that capacity, he represented the Ministry of Defence at numerous international conferences and was part of UK delegations to the First Review Conference for the 1981 Conventional Weapons Convention, the negotiations on the establishment of an International Criminal Court, and the Diplomatic Conference that led to the 1999 Second Protocol to the 1954 Hague Convention on Cultural Property. He was also the senior Army lawyer deployed to the Arabian Gulf during the 1990–91 Gulf conflict. Since retiring, Professor Garraway spent three months in Baghdad working for the Foreign Office on transitional justice issues and six months as a senior research fellow at the British Institute of International and Comparative Law. He was the 2004–05 Charles H. Stockton Professor of International Law at the Naval War College. He is currently a Visiting Professor at King's College, London, a Visiting Fellow in the Department of Human Rights, University of Essex and an Associate Fellow at the Royal Institute of International Affairs (Chatham House) in both its International Law and International Security programs. In 2006, he was elected as a member of the International Humanitarian Fact Finding Commission, established under Article 90 of Additional Protocol I to the Geneva Conventions of 1949.

Professor Ryan Goodman is the Rita E. Hauser Professor of Human Rights and Humanitarian Law and the director of the Human Rights Program at Harvard Law

School. Professor Goodman received his Juris Doctor degree from Yale Law School. He received a Doctor of Philosophy degree in sociology from Yale University. He has worked at the US Department of State, the International Criminal Tribunal for the former Yugoslavia, and non-governmental organizations in India, South Africa, Switzerland, Thailand and the United States. His recent publications have appeared in the *American Journal of International Law*, the *California Law Review*, the *Duke Law Journal*, the *European Journal of International Law*, the *Harvard Law Review*, the *Stanford Law Review* and the *Yale Law Journal*. His publications also include *International Humanitarian Law* (forthcoming 2009, with Derek Jinks & Michael Schmitt) and *International Human Rights in Context* (with Henry Steiner & Philip Alston).

Professor Françoise J. Hampson is Professor of Law, Department of Law and a member of the Human Rights Centre at the University of Essex. Professor Hampson was an independent expert member of the UN Sub-Commission on the Promotion and Protection of Human Rights from 1998 to 2007. She previously taught at the University of Dundee. She has acted as a consultant on humanitarian law to the International Committee of the Red Cross and taught at staff colleges or equivalents in the United Kingdom, United States, Canada and Ghana. She represented Oxfam and Save the Children Fund (United Kingdom) at the Preparatory Committee and first session of the Review Conference for the Certain Conventional Weapons Convention. Professor Hampson has successfully litigated many cases before the European Court of Human Rights in Strasbourg and, in recognition of her contribution to the development of law in this area, was awarded Human Rights Lawyer of the Year jointly with her colleague from the Centre, Professor Kevin Boyle. She has taught, researched and published widely in the fields of armed conflict and international humanitarian law and on the European Convention on Human Rights. She is currently working on international law issues relating to private military/security companies and is a member of the independent panel appointed by the International Court of Justice to examine the conduct of the parties to the conflict in Lebanon in 2006.

Lieutenant Colonel Eric Talbot Jensen, JA, US Army, is currently serving as Chief, International Law Branch, Office of the Judge Advocate General, US Army. Prior assignments include Deputy Staff Judge Advocate for the 1st Cavalry Division and Task Force Baghdad, professor of international and operational law at The Judge Advocate General's Legal Center and School and observer/trainer at the Combat Maneuver Training Center in Hohenfels, Germany. Lieutenant Colonel Jensen has deployed with the US Army to Iraq in support of Operation Iraqi Freedom; to

United Nations Preventive Deployment Force in Skopje, Macedonia; and twice to Bosnia in support of Operation Joint Endeavor/Guard. LTC Jensen is a graduate of Brigham Young University and University of Notre Dame Law School. He holds Master of Laws degrees from The Judge Advocate General's Legal Center and School and Yale Law School. Lieutenant Colonel Jensen has published in a number of law journals and other publications on topics related to international law, the law of war and national security law. Recent publications have appeared in the *Houston Law Review*, *Yale Law Journal* and *Denver Journal of International Law and Policy*.

Professor John F. Murphy is professor of law at Villanova University School of Law. In addition to teaching, Professor Murphy's career includes a year in India on a Ford Foundation Fellowship; private practice in New York City and Washington, DC; and service in the Office of the Assistant Legal Adviser for United Nations Affairs, US Department of State. He was previously on the law faculty at the University of Kansas and has been a visiting professor at Cornell University and Georgetown University. Professor Murphy was the 1980–81 Charles H. Stockton Professor of International Law at the Naval War College. He is the author of numerous articles, comments and reviews on international law and relations, as well as the author or editor of various books and monographs. Most recently, he has authored *The United States and the Rule of Law in International Affairs* (2004). His casebook (with Alan C. Swan), *The Regulation of International Business and Economic Relations* (2d ed.), was awarded a certificate of merit by the American Society of International Law in 1992. Professor Murphy has served as a consultant to the US Departments of State and Justice, the ABA Standing Committee on Law and National Security, and the United Nations Crime Bureau, and has testified before Congress on several occasions. He is currently the American Bar Association's Alternate Observer at the US Mission to the United Nations.

Professor Sean D. Murphy is the Patricia Roberts Harris Research Professor of Law at the George Washington University Law School in Washington, DC. Professor Murphy has a Juris Doctor degree from Columbia University, a Master of Laws degree from Cambridge University and a Doctor of Juridical Science degree from the University of Virginia School of Law. From 1987 to 1995, Professor Murphy served in the Office of the Legal Adviser at the US Department of State, specializing in politico-military matters, international litigation and international environmental law. From July 1995 to July 1998, Professor Murphy served as the Legal Counselor of the US Embassy in The Hague. In that capacity, he represented the US government before the International Court of Justice, the International

Criminal Tribunal for the former Yugoslavia, the Permanent Court of Arbitration, the Hague Conference on Private International Law and served as the US Agent to the Iran-US Claims Tribunal. Since entering academia, Professor Murphy has continued to represent governments and private litigants before international courts and tribunals, most recently Ethiopia and Suriname. Professor Murphy's book entitled *Humanitarian Intervention: The United Nations in an Evolving World Order* won the American Society of International Law 1997 certificate of merit for preeminent contribution to creative scholarship. He has published articles in a variety of national and international law journals, and was awarded the *American Journal of International Law* 1994 Deák Prize for best scholarship by a younger author. His most recent books are *Principles of International Law* and a casebook, *U.S. Foreign Relations and National Security Law* (with Thomas Franck & Michael Glennon). Professor Murphy is a member of the Board of Editors of the *American Journal of International Law* and has served on the Executive Council of the American Society of International Law.

Mr. Stephane Ojeda was appointed Legal Advisor to the Operations at the International Committee of the Red Cross (ICRC) in Geneva in May 2005. In his current capacity, he counsels ICRC field delegations, in particular in the United States, Afghanistan and Iraq, on international law issues relating to detention in the fight against terrorism. He is also in charge of legal support to ICRC operations in Europe and the Balkans. Previously, he served as detention delegate in Ethiopia and Israel, and as a legal advisor in Lebanon, Israel and the Palestinian Territories. Before joining the ICRC in 1999, he worked in Mali for a non-governmental organization implementing development programs. Earlier, he served as an advisor on humanitarian issues in Iraq and France for the French Foreign Ministry. Mr. Ojeda holds a master's degree in international humanitarian action and a master's degree in international law from the University of Aix-Marseille, France.

Mr. W. Hays Parks entered federal service in 1963 as a commissioned officer in the US Marine Corps. Military assignments included service as an infantry officer and senior prosecuting attorney in Vietnam; Marine Corps representative at The Judge Advocate General's School, US Army; congressional liaison officer for the Secretary of the Navy; and as Head, Law of War Branch, Office of the Judge Advocate General of the Navy. Mr. Parks was the Special Assistant to The Judge Advocate General of the Army for Law of War Matters from 1979 to 2003. He has served as a US representative for law of war negotiations in New York, Geneva, The Hague and Vienna. He joined the Office of General Counsel, Department of Defense in August 2003. Mr. Parks occupied the Charles H. Stockton Chair of International

Law at the Naval War College for academic year 1984–85. In 1987 he was a staff member on the presidential commission established to examine alleged security breaches in the US Embassy in Moscow. Mr. Parks has lectured on the law affecting military operations at the National, Army, Air Force and Naval War Colleges; the military staff colleges; and other military schools and units. An adjunct professor of international law at the American University School of Law, he has published articles in a variety of military and legal journals. In 2001 he became the sixth person in the history of the US Special Operations Command to receive that command's top civilian award, the US Special Operations Command Outstanding Civilian Service Medal. In 2006 he was awarded the US Special Operations Command's Major General William F. Garrison Award for his lifetime legal support to US Special Operations Forces.

Mr. Stephen Pomper is an attorney adviser in the Office of the Legal Adviser at the US Department of State. His current portfolio includes matters relating to the law of war and US government counterterrorism operations. In his prior assignment at the Department of State, Mr. Pomper advised the Office of the Coordinator for Counterterrorism on law enforcement issues. Before joining the Department of State in 2002, Mr. Pomper practiced law at Cleary, Gottlieb, Steen, and Hamilton. He is a graduate of Harvard College and Yale Law School.

Professor W. Michael Reisman is the Myres S. McDougal Professor of International Law at the Yale Law School, where he has been on the faculty since 1965. He has been a visiting professor in Tokyo, Hong Kong, Berlin, Basel, Paris and Geneva. He is a Fellow of the World Academy of Art and Science and a former member of its executive council. He is the president of the Arbitration Tribunal of the Bank for International Settlements. He was a member of the Eritrea-Ethiopia Boundary Commission, is a member of the Advisory Committee on International Law of the Department of State, vice chairman of the Policy Sciences Center, Inc., a member of the Board of the Foreign Policy Association and has been elected to the *Institut de Droit International*. He has published widely in the area of international law and has served as arbitrator and counsel in many international cases. Professor Reisman was president of the Inter-American Commission on Human Rights of the Organization of American States, vice president and honorary vice president of the American Society of International Law and editor-in-chief of the *American Journal of International Law*. His most recent books are *Foreign Investment Disputes: Cases, Materials and Commentary* (with Raymond Doak Bishop & James Crawford); *International Law in Contemporary Perspective* (with Mahnoush H. Arsanjani, Siegfried Wiessner & Gayl S. Westerman); *Jurisdiction in International*

Law; and *Law in Brief Encounters*, Chinese Translation, *Shenghuozhongde Weiguan Falu* [Microscopic Laws in Life].

Professor Sir Adam Roberts is a Senior Research Fellow of the Centre for International Studies, Department of Politics and International Relations, University of Oxford; an Emeritus Fellow of Balliol College; and President-elect of the British Academy. He was the Montague Burton Professor of International Relations at Oxford University, 1986 to 2007. From 1968 to 1981, Professor Roberts was Lecturer in International Relations at the London School of Economics and Political Science. From 1981 to 1986 he was the Alastair Buchan Reader in International Relations and Fellow of St Antony's College, Oxford. Professor Roberts was a member of the Council of the Royal Institute of International Affairs (Chatham House), London from 1985 to 1991 and a member of the Council, International Institute for Strategic Studies, London from 2002 to the present. In 1990 he was elected Fellow of the British Academy. In 1997, he was elected Honorary Fellow, London School of Economics and Political Science. In 2002, Professor Roberts was appointed Knight Commander of the Order of St. Michael and St. George (KCMG). Professor Sir Roberts has published several books on the theory and practice of territorial defense and international relations and articles in numerous journals and various newspapers, including the *American Journal of International Law*, *British Year Book of International Law*, *International Affairs*, *International Security*, *Review of International Studies*, *Survival*, *The Times Literary Supplement* and *The World Today*. His most recent book is *The United Nations Security Council and War: The Evolution of Thought and Practice since 1945* (with Vaughan Lowe, Jennifer Welsh & Dominik Zaum).

Professor Marco Sassòli is professor of international law at the University of Geneva (Switzerland) and chairs the boards of the Geneva Academy of International Humanitarian Law and Human Rights and of Geneva Call, a non-governmental organization with the objective to engage armed non-State actors to adhere to humanitarian norms. He is also member of the board of the International Council on Human Rights Policy. From 2001 to 2003, he was a professor of international law at the University of Quebec in Montreal, Canada, where he remains an associate professor. He is also an associate professor at the University of Laval. Professor Sassòli graduated as doctor of laws at the University of Basel (Switzerland) and is member of the Swiss bar. He held a number of positions with the International Committee of the Red Cross from 1985 to 1997, including deputy head of its legal division, head of delegation in Jordan and Syria, and as protection coordinator for the former Yugoslavia. He has also served as executive secretary of the International

Commission of Jurists and as registrar at the Swiss Supreme Court. He has published on international humanitarian law, human rights law, international criminal law, international law and private actors, the sources of international law and on state responsibility. With Antoine Bouvier he authored the second edition of *How Does Law Protect in War?*, which was published by the International Committee of the Red Cross in 2006.

Professor Michael N. Schmitt is the 2007–08 Charles H. Stockton Professor of International Law at the Naval War College. Professor Schmitt was previously Director, Program in Advanced Security Studies at the George C. Marshall European Center for Security Studies in Garmisch-Partenkirchen, Germany, where he returned as Dean of the College of International and Security Studies in August 2008. Before joining the Marshall Center faculty, Professor Schmitt served as a judge advocate in the US Air Force for twenty years. During his military career, he specialized in operational and international law and was senior legal adviser to multiple Air Force units, including units conducting combat operations over northern Iraq. Formerly on the faculties of the US Air Force Academy and US Naval War College, he also has been a visiting scholar at Yale Law School and lectures regularly at the International Institute of Humanitarian Law and the NATO School. The author of many scholarly articles on law and military affairs and contributing editor for multiple volumes of the Naval War College's International Law Studies ("Blue Book") series, his works have been published in Belgium, Chile, Germany, Israel, Italy, Norway, Peru, Sweden and Switzerland. Professor Schmitt serves on the editorial boards of the *International Review of the Red Cross* and *Yearbook of International Humanitarian Law*, the Executive Committee of the American Society of International Law's Lieber Society, the Steering Committee for Harvard University's International Humanitarian Law Research Initiative and as Professorial Fellow at the University of Surrey's International Law Centre.

Professor Gary D. Solis is the 2006–08 Scholar in Residence at the Law Library of the Library of Congress. He is an adjunct professor of law at Georgetown University Law Center, where he teaches the law of armed conflict. He teaches the law of war in San Remo, Italy as well. He is a retired US Marine with twenty-six years of active duty, including tours in Vietnam as an armor officer. He holds a Juris Doctor degree from the University of California at Davis, a Master of Laws degree in criminal law from George Washington University and a Doctor of Philosophy degree in the law of war from the London School of Economics and Political Science. He taught in the London School of Economics Law Department for three years and then moved to the United States Military Academy in 1996. He received the 2006

Apgar Award, given to West Point's outstanding professor. He retired from West Point in 2006. His books are *Marines and Military Law in Vietnam* and *Son Thang: An American War Crime.* He is writing a law of war textbook for Cambridge University Press.

Professor David Turns is Senior Lecturer in Laws of War at the Defence Academy of the United Kingdom (Cranfield University). Prior to assuming his current position, he was a lecturer in law at the University of Liverpool (1994–2007). In 2002 he spent six months in Vienna as a visiting professor at the *Institut für Völkerrecht und Internationale Beziehungen, Universität Wien.* He specializes in public international law, with particular emphasis on international humanitarian law and international criminal law. He is an invited member of the International Humanitarian Law Discussion Group at the British Institute of International and Comparative Law, London, and a contributor to the group's *Perspectives on the ICRC Study on Customary International Humanitarian Law.* Professor Turns has published on several public international law topics in a variety of journals in the United Kingdom and other countries, including Australia, Austria, Germany and the United States. His latest publications are "The 'War on Terror' Through British and International Humanitarian Eyes: Comparative Perspectives on Selected Legal Issues" in the *New York City Law Review*; "Weapons in the ICRC Study on Customary International Humanitarian Law," which appears in the *Journal of Conflict & Security Law*; and "The Treatment of Detainees and the 'Global War on Terror'" in the *Israel Yearbook on Human Rights.*

Brigadier-General Kenneth Watkin, Canadian Forces, is the Judge Advocate General of the Canadian Forces. During his twenty-five years as a military legal officer, Brigadier-General Watkin has served as the Deputy Judge Advocate General/Operations, Special Assistant to the Judge Advocate General and the Assistant Judge Advocate General/Atlantic Region. He has also been the director of offices dealing with human rights and information law, operational law, claims and civil litigation, and training. His operational law experience has included service as a legal adviser to the Canadian Navy, adviser to Canadian commanders in Bosnia, and as the Deputy Judge Advocate General/Operations at the time of the terrorist attacks on September 11, 2001 and during a significant portion of the subsequent deployments in connection with the "Campaign Against Terrorism." He was the legal adviser to a 1993 Canadian military/civilian board of inquiry that investigated the activities of the Canadian Airborne Regiment Battle Group in Somalia. From 1995 until 2005, he was counsel in respect to various investigations and inquiries arising from the 1994 genocide in Rwanda. Brigadier-General Watkin is a widely published author on a variety of operational law topics, including the law of armed conflict, discipline and human rights.

Professor Matthew C. Waxman is associate professor of law at Columbia Law School, where he specializes in international law and national security law. He previously served at the US Department of State, as Principal Deputy Director of Policy Planning (2005–7). His prior government appointments include Deputy Assistant Secretary of Defense for Detainee Affairs, Director for Contingency Planning and International Justice at the National Security Council, and special assistant to National Security Adviser Condoleezza Rice. He is a graduate of Yale College and Yale Law School, and studied international relations as a Fulbright Scholar in the United Kingdom. After law school, he served as law clerk to Supreme Court Justice David H. Souter and US Court of Appeals Judge Joel M. Flaum. He is a member and International Affairs Fellow of the Council on Foreign Relations and a member of the Hoover Institution Task Force on National Security and Law. His publications include *The Dynamics of Coercion: American Foreign Policy and the Limits of Military Might* (with Daniel Byman).

Index

A

D

E

F

G

H

I

J

K

L

M

N

O

S

T

U

V

W

Y

Z

www.ingramcontent.com/pod-product-compliance
Lightning Source LLC
Chambersburg PA
CBHW080554030726
47589CB00003B/125
* 9 7 8 1 7 8 2 6 6 2 3 7 2 *